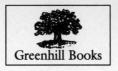

HUNS, VANDALS AND THE FALL OF THE ROMAN EMPIRE

G. Nattress, del.

Chromo-Lith^d by C. F. Kell, Furnival S^t, Holborn E.

CHAPEL OF S. PETER CHRYSOLOGUS, RAVENNA.

HUNS, VANDALS AND THE FALL OF THE ROMAN EMPIRE

THOMAS HODGKIN

With a New Introduction
by Tim Newark

GREENHILL BOOKS, LONDON
STACKPOLE BOOKS, PENNSYLVANIA

Greenhill Books

This edition of *Huns, Vandals and the Fall of the Roman Empire*
first published 1996 by
Greenhill Books, Lionel Leventhal Limited,
Park House, 1 Russell Gardens, London NW11 9NN
and
Stackpole Books, 5067 Ritter Road, Mechanicsburg, PA 17055, USA

British Library Cataloguing in Publication Data
Hodgkin, Thomas, 1831-1913
Huns, Vandals and the fall of the Roman Empire. – New ed.
1. Huns   2. Vandals   3. Rome – History – 284-476
4. Europe – History – 392-814
I. Title   II. Italy and her invaders
936.3'02

ISBN 1-85367-242-4

Library of Congress Cataloging-in-Publication Data
Hodgkin, Thomas, 1831-1913
[Italy and her invaders.   V. 2]
Huns, Vandals, and the fall of the Roman empire / by
Thomas Hodgkin: new introduction by Tim Newark.
688p. 22cm.
Originally published: Italy and her invaders, v. 2,
The Hunnish and Vandal invasion. Oxford: Clarendon Press, 1880.
Includes index.
ISBN 1-85367-242-4 (HC)
1. Rome – History – Germanic Invasions, 3rd-6th centuries.
2. Italy – History – To 476.   3. Italy – History – 476-774.
4. Germanic peoples – Italy – History.   I. Title.
DG312.H6   1996
937'.09 – dc20
95-52075
CIP

Publishing History
Huns, Vandals and the Fall of the Roman Empire was first published as
Italy and her Invaders, Volume II: The Hunnish and Vandal Invasion
(first edition 1880, second edition 1892, Oxford). *Italy and her Invaders*
comprised eight volumes in total. The second edition of Volume II is
reproduced here, with a new Introduction by Tim Newark.

Printed and bound in Great Britain
by Bookcraft (Bath) Limited, Midsomer Norton

CONTENTS

CHAPTER II.

ATTILA AND THE COURT OF CONSTANTINOPLE.

Contents.

BOOK II.

THE VANDAL INVASION AND THE HERULIAN MUTINY.

CHAPTER I.

EXTINCTION OF THE HUNNISH EMPIRE AND THE THEODOSIAN DYNASTY.

CHAPTER II.

THE VANDALS, FROM GERMANY TO ROME.

CHAPTER III.

THE LETTERS AND POEMS OF APOLLINARIS SIDONIUS.

Contents.

CHAPTER IV.

AVITUS, THE CLIENT OF THE VISIGOTHS.

CHAPTER V.

SUPREMACY OF RICIMER. MAJORIAN.

CHAPTER VI.

SUPREMACY OF RICIMER (*continued*). SEVERUS II, THE LUCANIAN.
ANTHEMIUS, THE CLIENT OF BYZANTIUM.

CHAPTER VII.

OLYBRIUS, THE CLIENT OF THE VANDAL. GLYCERIUS, THE CLIENT OF THE BURGUNDIAN. JULIUS NEPOS, THE CLIENT OF BYZANTIUM. ROMULUS AUGUSTULUS, SON OF ORESTES.

CHAPTER VIII.

ODOVACAR, THE SOLDIER OF FORTUNE.

CHAPTER IX.

CAUSES OF THE FALL OF THE WESTERN EMPIRE.

A. D.   PAGE

4. *Panem et Circenses*, or the Pauperisation of the
    Roman Proletariat .   .   .   565–576

In her earlier ages Rome cruelly oppressed her poorer
    citizens 566

In her later ages she foolishly pampered them . 567

The grain distributions: their economic absurdity . 568

Market price of corn. Price fixed by legislation of
    Gracchus 569

Grain given instead of being sold . . 570

Legislation of Aurelian (270) . . 571

Legislation of the Valentinians as to the *Panis
    Gradilis* . . . 572–575

5. Destruction of the Middle Class by the Fiscal Op-
    pression of the *Curiales* . . . 576–596

Origin of the Municipia . . . 577

Their Golden Age (B.C. 30—A.D. 220) . . 579

Their Decline and Fall under the legislation of Dio-
    cletian and Constantine . . . 581

The office of *Curialis* from a dignity becomes a burden 583

Legislation preventing the *Curialis* from escaping his
    Curial obligations . . . 585–591

Slight compensating privileges of the *Curialis* 592–595

Fate of the municipalities in the East . . 595

Their revival in the West . . . 596

6. Barbarous Finance 597–606

Roman ignorance of principles of finance . . 597

Conjectural estimates of Imperial Revenue . . 598

Heads of taxation 599

The Land-Tax. The Indictions . . 600

Mischievous system of farming the Taxes . . 601

Pressure of Debt at exorbitant Interest . . 602

Speculation on the probable effect of a National Debt
    upon the duration of the Empire . 604

7. Causes, or Symptoms, of Decay . . 606–610

The power of the Emperors not in itself destructive . 606

But the interference of the Household was uniformly
    disastrous 607

Demoralisation of the Army . . . 608

Decline in Population, a symptom rather than a cause
    of ruin 610

Must England fall as Rome fell ? . . 611

LIST OF ILLUSTRATIONS

INTRODUCTION.

Why the Roman Empire collapsed is one of the great political and cultural questions of all time. If a superpower as sophisticated and rich and extensive as this could disintegrate, bringing with it a long period of chaos and retardation, what hope is there for our civilisation? In this book, Thomas Hodgkin gives us at least nine reasons for the end of the Roman Empire, and being an Englishman writing in the late nineteenth century he ends by wondering whether Britain will fall as Rome fell. A hundred years later, at the end of the twentieth century, the British Empire has indeed come to an end and more recently we have witnessed the break-up of the mighty Soviet Communist empire. It is not unreasonable to wonder whether that other great continental superpower, the United States of America – itself a confederation of states of varying racial mix with one great land border exposed to greatly poorer people – is also on the verge of decline and disintegration. Thomas Hodgkin's conclusion is as relevant today as it was when he first wrote it, but first let us look at the man and his monumental literary achievement.

Thomas Hodgkin was born in 1831 in Tottenham, north London, into a middle-class Protestant family belonging to the Religious Society of Friends. At the age of five he began learning Latin. His Quaker faith barred him from attending either Oxford or Cambridge universities, but he found a place at University College London, famous for its tolerance and progressive teaching. There, he studied classical history with the intention of becoming a lawyer, but an epileptic fit shook his confidence and he went instead into banking. As a young man, his career and raising a family kept him busy and in 1859 he moved to Newcastle to join a newly opened bank. By now, his mind was beginning to wander back to his studies, and trips with his friends to Hadrian's Wall presented him with the imagery of an empire in decline. Finally, in his late thirties he visited Italy with his wife and was bewitched: 'I can understand now,' he wrote, 'why Kings and Emperors in the Middle Ages flung away whole realms of dim transalpine regions to secure one bright duchy or county on the sunny side of the Great Wall.'[1]

Originally, his intention was to write a 'good, handy history' of Italy, but his classical training led him to concentrate on the history of its birth out of the collapse of the Roman Empire. With research trips to the British Museum in London and the Bodleian Library in Oxford as well as his travels abroad, Hodgkin began amassing notes based on the primary texts of Latin and Greek chroniclers. Putting one day aside a week, usually a Friday, he sat in his conservatory, ignoring the noise of his children, and wrote his eight-volume history of *Italy and her Invaders*, from the fourth century to A.D. 814, almost 4000 pages. The project took him nearly twenty years and was published between 1880 and 1899. It was generally well received by contemporary critics, being praised for its readability and scholarship, 'likely to make history popular by true and honest methods', but 'his habit of bringing in constant analogies and illustrations from modern times and even from the passing events of the day, was irritating to some'.[2] And yet it is this realisation of the relevance of these distant events to our own times that makes the book such vivid history.

Hodgkin's research for the material reprinted in this book was originally intended to be the first volume in his series entitled *The Death of Rome*, but on publication it became the second volume following a history of the Visigoths. The only other work on ancient history to compare with Hodgkin's achievement is, of course, Edward Gibbon's *The History of the Decline and Fall of the Roman Empire*, published a hundred years earlier. Hodgkin was unconvinced by Gibbon's theory that Christianity was a fundamental cause of Rome's fall, pointing to the continued survival of the Byzantine Empire as evidence against this argument. That said, as a member of an unorthodox sect himself he had little time for the persecutions of either Emperors or Popes, but his nonconformity is perhaps best expressed by his great empathy for the Germanic barbarians. He criticises Gibbon for playing down the achievement of these Germanic lords in transforming a decaying empire into a series of vigorous kingdoms. Such a view of the Germanic barbarians as a morally superior race plucking the light of civilisation away from a decadent Rome was an image embraced by many historians in the late nineteenth century, especially German historians, who saw the Anglo-Saxon-Teutonic race as the great reformer of Western history, sweeping away

Latin corruption. 'We have only one thing to regret,' wrote Houston Stewart Chamberlain, 'that the Teuton did not destroy with more thoroughness, wherever his victorious arm penetrated.'[3] Ultimately, this idealising of the barbarian would have its most grotesque expression in Adolf Hitler who declared in 1933: 'Yes, we are barbarians! We want to be barbarians! It is an honourable title. We shall rejuvenate the world!'[4] But Hodgkin's appreciation of the Germanic barbarians was not at all racially motivated. It was inspired by the common sense of an outsider who makes judgments on the evidence before him and it is with this spirit that he guides us through the texts of the period. For example, when discussing the origin of the Huns he gives us both sides of the argument, advising only as a judge before a jury on the weight of proof.

Through the works of Procopius, Priscus, Jordanes, and other Greek and Latin chroniclers, Hodgkin draws together a vivid portrait of the fifth century and the collapse of the Western Roman Empire. At the beginning of each chapter, he describes his principal sources and evaluates them. In one witty passage, Hodgkin parodies some of the poorer chroniclers of his time, writing a history of the mid Victorian period in their frustrating style, summarising the most important events and yet lavishing gossipy detail on the beauty of an emperor's wife. Most usefully, when the occasion demands, Hodgkin quotes entire passages from the works of writers such as Jordanes and Sidonius who cannot be bettered when describing the campaigns of Attila or life in barbarian Gaul. He also draws on contemporary archaeological discoveries and sometimes has himself visited the sites in question.

When it comes to explaining the end of the Western Roman Empire, Hodgkin proceeds in characteristic analytical style, outlining all the main causes in a final chapter. The overall message is simple and clear: 'the Roman Empire rather died of internal decline than was slain by the sword of an enemy.' He uses this truth to draw a parallel with the United States, pointing to the institution of slavery in the Confederacy as a fatal weakening point in its battle with the North, just as it undermined the vigour of the Roman Empire. More pertinent to us, however, at the end of the twentieth century, is Hodgkin's criticism of the great central-isation of the imperial state, whose hand-outs of free food and other prizes, linked with intolerable taxes, destroyed the entrepreneurial class and created a society of sycophants and pressure-groups depending wholly on the patronage of one man and his court. Although placing his faith in democracy and a gener-ally improving condition for all members of society, he nevertheless maintains that the search for political popularity can get out of hand and lead to a situation in which 'British or American despots ... will guide mighty empires to ruin, amidst the acclamations of flatterers ...', or, as he also puts it, describing the impoverishing largesse of emperors, 'Communism thus robed in the purple is an excellent destroyer of Commonwealths' – something Russia knows only too well. It is therefore not the barbarians we have to fear, but our own governments' response to internal pressures. Such a concern is already at the heart of political debate in the European and American super-states at the end of this century. Let us hope it is resolved with the lessons of history in mind, or a

Hodgkin of the next century will sit in his conservatory once more describing the fall of the West.

Tim Newark
1996

NOTES

1. Bullough, D. A., *Italy and Her Invaders*, Nottingham, 1968, p. 11. The best analysis of Hodgkin as historian.
2. Creighton, L., *Life and Letters of Thomas Hodgkin*, London, 1917, p. 109. Best source for Hodgkin's background.
3. Chamberlain, H. S., *The Foundations of the Nineteenth Century*, London, 1910, Vol. 1, p. 495.
4. Rauschning, H., *Hitler Speaks*, London, 1939, p. 87.

Books by Tim Newark include *Medieval Warfare, The Barbarians, Celtic Warriors, Medieval Warlords,* **and** *Women Warlords.*

CORRIGENDA

(Supplied by Mr. G. M^cN. Rushforth).

Page 55, note 2. In favour of the identification of Παταβίων with Pettau, and against the identification, here suggested, with Passau, Mommsen in C. I. L. iii. p. 510 collects the following evidence. Poetovio is called Patavio in the Antonine Itinerary, p. 129. At this time it was included in Noricum, as is shown by Ammianus Marc. 14. 11. 19, 'Petobio urbs in Norico,' and the Jerusalem Itinerary (A. D. 333). Batava Castra was on the Raetian side of the Aenus (Inn), which was the boundary between Raetia and Noricum (Tacitus, Hist. 3. 5), and the Notitia Dignitatum therefore places the 'tribunus cohortis novae Batavorum Batavis' under Raetia. See C. I. L. iii. p. 690.

P. 107, note 1. The 'Bellonoti' are probably the same as the 'Ballonoti' mentioned by Valerius Flaccus (Arg. 6. 160) in connection with the Sarmatians and Moesians as a 'gens Scythica.' See De Vit, Onomasticon.

P. 247, l. 12 from bottom, 'the fortieth of his episcopate.' Rather, the fortieth since his ordination. The words of Possidius are (cap. 31), 'vixit annis LXXVI, in clericatu autem vel episcopatu annis ferme XL.' Augustine was ordained in 391. He did not become a Bishop till 395.

P. 255, note 1. For 'Note F' read 'Note G, p. 503.'

P. 298, l. 1. For 'It is' read 'Is it,' with ? at end of the sentence.

P. 386, note 1. The fact that the Equester Ordo still existed at this time in the City of Rome is proved by Cod. Theod. vi. 36 (of 364), re-enacted by Cod. Just. xii. 32, 'De Equestri Dignitate,' which begins, 'Equites Romani quos secundi gradus in Urbe omnium optinere volumus dignitatem.' If they are meant by Sidonius, the reference to their participation in the Judicia is an anachronism, as the Quaestiones Perpetuae had long ceased to exist.

P. 394, l. 8 from top, 'at the worst a charge of luxury.' It must be remembered however that 'luxuria' has a distinctly worse connotation than 'luxury,' and may well imply moral depravity. Instances of this use of the word will be found in the Dictionaries. Here it is enough to refer to Suetonius, Caligula 25 : 'luxuriae ac lasciviae perditae.' This of course does not affect the vagueness of the charge.

P. 406, marginal note, for 45 read 458.

P. 510, l. 5 from top, 'naturalised barbarians,' οἰκείων βαρβάρων of Joannes Antiochenus (note 2). Rather 'barbarians who belonged to him,' i.e. his barbarian followers; or 'who belonged to him by race,' i.e. those who were barbarians like himself.

P. 586, note 1. The Collegia of Centonarii were Fire-brigades. The firemen were called *centonarii*, from the *centones* or coverings made of rags, which were steeped in water and used for extinguishing fires or protecting neighbouring buildings. Marquardt, Privatleben, ii. 585.

Huns, Vandals
and the Fall
of the
Roman Empire

BOOK I

THE HUNNISH INVASION

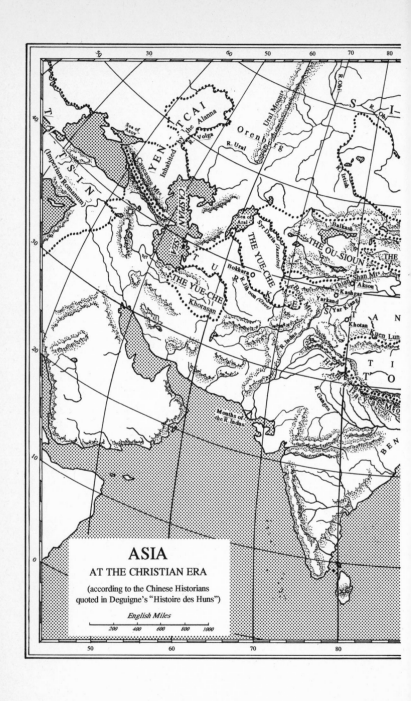

ASIA

AT THE CHRISTIAN ERA

(according to the Chinese Historians
quoted in Deguigne's "Histoire des Huns")

English Miles

200   400   600   800   1000

BOOK I.

THE HUNNISH INVASION.

CHAPTER I.

EARLY HISTORY OF THE HUNS.

Authorities.

Guide:—

THIS chapter is for the most part a mere compilation from a previous compiler. Our chief guide is M. Deguignes, 'de l'Académie Royale des Inscriptions et Belles-Lettres, Censeur Royal, Interprète du Roi pour les Langues Orientales, et Membre de la Société Royale de Londres,' who published at Paris (1756–8) a 'Histoire Générale des Huns, des Turcs, des Mongols, et des autres Tartares Occidentaux, avant et depuis Jésus-Christ jusqu'à présent' (4 vols. small 4to; the first volume being divided into two parts). Only the second part of the first volume (and not the whole of that) is occupied with the history of the Huns properly so called. The fortunes of the different branches of the Turkish and Mongol races fill up the remainder of the work, which might in fact be called 'The History of the Northern Turanians,' though that term was not known to ethnology when Deguignes wrote.

During the period for which we follow his guidance he draws his materials entirely from Chinese historians, whose names are scrupulously quoted. The chief appear to be KAM-MO, LIE-TAI-KI-SOU, HAN-CHOU, and SSU-KI. As he was one of the first Chinese scholars of his day, and as his work has stood its ground for more than a century as an authority on the history of Central Asia, it is reasonable to presume that no gross inaccuracies have been discovered in his manner of using his Chinese authorities.

It was stated in the first edition of this work that 'it would be prudent to hold the theory as to the origin of the Huns as not much more than a possible hypothesis.' Perhaps we ought now to go further than this and to discard that theory altogether. Mr. Howorth, than whom no English scholar, perhaps no European scholar, is more qualified to express an opinion on points of Turanian ethnology, pronounces decidedly against it in a paper contributed to the Journal of the Anthropological Institute (vol. v. 396–474). But upon the whole, remembering the length of time during which it was accepted with unquestioning faith, and considering that the Huns, who were undeniably an Asiatic people, may probably enough have passed through some of the experiences here recorded of the Hiong-nu, even if they were not the people bearing that name, I have thought it best to let this chapter stand nearly as it was first written, referring the reader to the note at the end of the chapter for a brief summary of Mr. Howorth's arguments against the theory of Deguignes.

The article above referred to is incorporated with a 'Translation of the Han Annals' by Mr. A. Wylie. This, as far as Chinese history is concerned, goes over very much the same ground which has been already traversed by Deguignes. I have compared the two accounts and have sometimes altered the spelling of a name on Mr. Wylie's authority.

> 'THERE is a race on Scythia's verge extreme
> Eastward, beyond the Tanais' chilly stream.
> The Northern Bear looks on no uglier crew:
> Base is their garb, their bodies foul to view;
> Their souls are ne'er subdued to sturdy toil
> Or Ceres' arts : their sustenance is spoil.
> With horrid wounds they gash their brutal brows,
> And o'er their murdered parents bind their vows.
> Not e'en the Centaur-offspring of the Cloud
> Were horsed more firmly than this savage crowd.
> Brisk, lithe, in loose array they first come on,
> Fly, turn, attack the foe who deems them gone.'
>
> CLAUDIAN, In Rufinum, i. 323–331.

Such is the account which the courtier-poet of Rome gave of the Huns half a century before the name of

Attila became a terror to the nations. In the fifth chapter of the first book [1] we witnessed the effect which the appearance of these wild Tartar hordes produced upon the Gothic warriors. The swarthy faces, without either beard or whisker, the twinkling black eyes, the squat figures, the perfect understanding which seemed to exist between the riders and their little steeds, were there described in the words of the Gothic bishop, Jordanes, and we heard what he had to say concerning their ' *execranda origo*,' descended, as he believed them to be, from Gothic sorceresses and from evil spirits.

The German professor of to-day emerges from his library to gaze at the descendants and representatives of the Huns, and liking them as little as his primeval kinsmen did, brands them with a term of deeper condemnation than Jordanes's epithets of ' witch-born ' or ' fiend-begotten '—the terrible name, *Turanian* [2]. *The Huns were Turanians.*

For by thus defining their ethnological position he cuts them off from all connection with the great Aryan stem whose branches have overspread Europe, America, and Australia, Persia, and India ; he equally destroys their claim to share in any of the glory of the Semitic races through whose instrumentality Judaism, Christianity, and Mohammedanism were given to the world ; and he shuts them up with a multitude of dull barba-

---

[1] Vol. i. p. 244.

[2] It is true that this term, Turanian, seems to be going somewhat out of fashion in ethnological circles, and that it is confessedly a merely conventional designation. But either it or some other similar name will apparently be always required to denote those races in Europe and Asia which are neither Aryan nor Semitic, and which speak what are called ' agglutinative languages.'

rians, mighty in destruction, powerless in construction, who have done nothing for the cause of civilisation or human progress, and who, even where they have adopted some of the varnish of modern customs, have remained essentially and incurably barbarous to the present day [1].

376.

Now this Turanian (or, to speak popularly and with less accuracy, Tartar) race which burst upon the affrighted Goths in the reign of the Emperor Valens, being a people of unlettered nomads, neither cared to give, nor probably could give to the European nations whom they terrified, any information as to their history in the remote past. Some traditions of a mythical kind as to the origin of their race they probably possessed, and had they established themselves

---

[1] This statement will be admitted to be generally true of all the Turanian tribes. There are however two honourable exceptions, the Finn and the Magyar. The Tartar sovereigns of India and China conformed to the civilised tastes of their subjects, but cannot claim the merit of having originated them. The following is a sketch of the chief historic races bearing the Turanian characteristics :—

TURANIANS.
(Northern Division.)

Tungusic family.
The Mantchoos, the last Tartar conquerors of China.

Mongolic.
(1) The great Tartar conquerors of the Middle Ages, Chingis-Khan (Jengis-Khan) A.D. 1225, and Timour Beg (Tamerlane) A.D. 1369.
(2) The Mogul Dynasty in India, Baber A.D. 1530 to last Mogul Emperor A.D. 1857.

Turkic
Huns (in Europe), A.D. 370 to 468.
Seljukian Turks, A.D. 985 to 1294.
Ottoman Turks A.D. 1301 to ?

Finnic.
Finns.   Bulgarians.   Magyars or Hungarians.

The Southern Division, comprising races in Thibet and the two Indian peninsulas, we may omit as too distant kinsmen of the Huns, our present subject.

in Europe permanently, these might, like the Scandinavian sagas, have floated down into a literary age and been so preserved. But the Huns vanished out of Europe almost as suddenly as they came, leaving no trace behind of their history, their language, or their religion. But for one somewhat disputed source of information, all is dark concerning them. That source is the History of China. If the Huns be the *Hiong-nu*, whose ravages are recorded in that history, then we have a minute account of their doings for centuries before the Christian era, and we know, in fact, far more about them than about the inhabitants of Gaul or Britain before the time of Julius Cæsar : if they are not, our ignorance is complete.

Proposed identification of the Huns with the Hiong-nu of Chinese history.

A learned and laborious Frenchman, M. Deguignes, in the middle of last century, conceived the idea that the Huns might be thus identified, and with infinite pains he wrote out their history from Chinese sources, and exhibited it in its connection with that of the various Tartar conquerors who, since their day, have poured down upon the civilised kingdoms of Europe and Asia, and wasted them.

This theory worked out by Deguignes.

As before hinted, this identification has been questioned, and it must be admitted that mere similarity of name is dangerous ground to build upon in the history of barbarous races. But as the hypothesis though looked upon with much less favour than it received a century ago, does not seem to be yet absolutely disproved, we may be permitted to spend some pages on the history of the Hiong-nu, in the possibility that we are thus contemplating the formation of that volcano which hurled forth Attila.

From the description which physical geographers

give of Central Asia, it would surely be one of the most striking features of our globe, in the sight of any visitor who might be approaching us from another sphere. Eastwards from longitude 73° it rises, we are told, to the almost incredible average height of 8000 feet, bearing the character of a vast insulated upland, and, its extent and average elevation being taken into account, it may be said to form on the whole the most considerable projection on the surface of our planet [1].

From this mighty upraised altar great rivers flow down in all directions, the Obi, Yenisei, and Lena through Siberia into the Arctic Sea, the Amour and the two great rivers of China, the Hoang-ho and Yang-tsi-kiang, into the Pacific; the Irawaddy, Brahmahpootra, Ganges, Indus, into the Indian Ocean; the Oxus and Jaxartes into the sea of Aral. Rivers of its own it has none (or only one, the Yar-kiang), having apparently no deep valleys: the small streams which it does possess find their way to some insignificant inland lake, and are lost there.

Four great mountain chains, limiting or traversing it, run from west to east. The mountains of Altai mark it off from Siberia on the north. The Thian Shan, or Mountains of Heaven, pass across the middle of it at about the 42nd parallel of latitude. The Kuen-Lun fence off what is now Chinese Tartary from Thibet. The Himalayas bound the great plateau to the south.

No mountain chain of any importance appears to intersect the country from north to south till we reach

---

[1] Prichard, Researches into the Physical History of Mankind, iv. 288 (quoting Ritter).

the Bolor Mountains (longitude 73°), which are its western boundary, and which form a kind of step down into the lower, but still lofty plateau (4000 feet high) of Eastern Turkestan.

The dominions of the Hiong-nu at the time of their greatest supremacy reached over the whole of the northern and central sections of this plateau—from Mount Altai, that is, to the Kuen-Lun. And westwards, their rule extended beyond the Bolor Mountains down into Turkestan, down lower still to the old sea-bed between Lake Aral and the Caspian, nay, even across the Ural Mountains to the Volga. In its more contracted state, their empire still touched the Irtish (long. 80°) on the west; but it seems to have receded to the Thian-Shan Mountains on the south; and the proper home of the race—if nomads can be said to have a home—was that district between China and Siberia bounded on the east by the Inshan Mountains (long. 115°), which is marked in modern maps Mongolia. Very roughly estimated, it is probably about as large as Germany and Austria put together. Across the centre of it stretches the great sandy desert of Gobi or Shamo.

Extent of the dominions of the Hiong-nu.

Here, then, if we may trust our French guide, the nation of the Huns was roaming before the date usually assigned to the Call of Abraham. In winter they crowded down upon the Northern frontier of China, which lies in the latitude of Madrid; in summer they drove their cattle northwards, across the great desert of Gobi, and took refuge from the heat in the cool valleys under the mountains which lie to the south of Lake Baikal, and which are in the same latitude as London.

Relation
of the
Hiong-nu
to the early
dynasties
of China.

Under the first two historic dynasties of China (the *Hia*, B.C. 2207–1767, and the *Shang*, 1767–1122), the Huns—if it be indeed the same race—are spoken of under the name of Chan-yong (barbarians of the mountains) and Tchong-yo. Their country was called Kuei-fang, ' the country of spirits,' so denominated by the same unchanging nation which at this day calls us Europeans ' foreign devils.'

About one hundred years before the building of Solomon's Temple, the *Chow* dynasty ascended the Chinese throne, and slumbered there for nearly nine centuries, till the year 258 B.C. These were the Carolingians of China, monarchs nominally supreme, but really overshadowed and overawed by their great feudatories; in their personal character debauched and cruel—in short, conspicuous offenders against the golden-mean maxims of morality so dear to the Chinese heart. This cycle of anarchy (it would probably have lasted but a century in Europe) was the harvest-time of the northern barbarians, who are now spoken of as *Hien-yun*. The three northern provinces of the Chinese Empire, Shen-se, Shan-se, and Pe-tche-li (which comprise an area about equivalent to the whole of Great Britain) seem to have been in a state of perpetual border-warfare with these savage enemies, who after each inroad retired laden with booty to the northern portion of their own territory. Their fleet ponies and trackless wildernesses rendered hopeless any attempt on the part of regular troops to pursue or to avenge.

At length, about the middle of the third century B.C., the long-smouldering light of the Chow dynasty went out, and the Tsin dynasty succeeded. Ching-wang,

otherwise Che-Hwang-te [1], the greatest monarch of this
new house, the Napoleon of China, united her warring
provinces into one compact empire, took the title of
Hwang-te (universal Emperor) instead of *Wang* (King),
which had been borne by all previous monarchs, drove
back the *Hiong-nu* (for such is now the name of the
barbarians) to their deserts, and finally, about the time
of the Second Punic War, completed the Great Wall
of China (portions of which had been already built
by two provincial sovereigns) in order to protect the
northern frontier from their incursions.   Thus then (if
only the theory of Deguignes be true) this great work,
1500 miles long, the name of which has been familiar to
all of us from our childhood, was really built to guard
the civilisation of Eastern Asia from the inroads of
the ancestors of Attila, and might as fairly be called the
Huns' Wall as Hadrian's barrier across the Northumbrian
isthmus is called by many the Picts' Wall.

China,
builds the
Great Wall
to keep out
the Hiong-
nu.

Che-Hwang-te in the course of his great career
found himself frequently thwarted by the traditions,
the etiquette, the state-maxims of the literati, who
seem to have been even then a powerful class in China.
To recur to a former simile, the Napoleonic idea could
not be made to accord with the Bourbon tradition.
Violently breaking with the Past of his country, he
ordered, it is said, that all the books of history which
could be found should be destroyed, sparing however
those on medicine, agriculture, astrology, and other
branches of science [2].

His alleged
destruction
of Chinese
historical
books.

---

[1] Deguignes calls him Chi-hoam-ti; but I have endeavoured, though
at the risk of some inconsistency, to keep the English spelling of
these Chinese names.   The names of the Hiong-nu princes I have not
dared to alter from Deguignes.

[2] The very name of Che-Hwang-te (The Beginning Emperor) was

This strange story may be the invention of national vanity, unable to trace up the written history of China beyond the third century B.C. In this case, all that has been hitherto said as to the early history of China and the Hiong-nu must be relegated to dreamland, for an oral transmission of the events of sixteen centuries may be set aside as an impossibility.

On the other hand, if the story be true, and if Che-Hwang-te was in the main successful in his onslaught on the works of the earlier historians, it does not follow that Chinese history must necessarily begin with him. For if the Chinese were by this time a literary nation, which the story seems to imply, no mere destruction of books would avail to wipe out from the fully-formed historical consciousness the general outlines of their past national life. Had every roll of manuscript perished out of the world at the time of the Peloponnesian war, the Greeks of that period would still have been able to reconstruct, with sufficient distinctness, by an act of memory, both the mythical and the historical record of previous ages which they had read from their childhood. Considering the apparently early development of the literary character in this enigmatic nation with which we are dealing, one is inclined to conjecture that this is the true view of the subject, and that there is at least some historic value in the Chinese annals previous to the third century B.C.

Titles among the Hiong-nu. The Tanjou and his officers. From this time onwards, at any rate, the chronicle seems to be complete, and full, to the reader's exhaustion, of the doings of the robber-nation, the Hiong-nu.

meant to set forth this claim of his to be the beginning of Chinese greatness.

These latter had now 'taken to themselves a king after
the manner of the nations.' He was called the *Tan-jou*,
which we are told is a contraction of the formidable
title *Tcem-li-ko-to-tan-jou* (mighty son of Heaven [1]).
The Tan-jou's queen was always called Yen-chi. All
the great commands of the state were filled up in
duplicate, one officer for the Right and one for the
Left. Characteristically enough, as showing how their
faces were ever set towards the fertile and opulent
South, the Left with them meant the east and the
Right the west. The Left was, as we are informed
that it is still with their Tartar nephews at Constantinople, the post of honour; and thus Hien-wang
(which signifies 'wise-king') being the highest grade
of office under royalty, the 'Hien-wang of the Left,' or
Viceroy of the East, was the next greatest person to
the Tan-jou, and the office was generally held by the
heir-apparent of that monarch.

In their prosperous days the sovereigns of the
Hiong-nu trampled upon the civilised and literary pride
of the Chinese Emperors with the greater pride of the
uncouth barbarian. On tablets, the exact size of which
had been prescribed by generations of Masters of the
Ceremonies, the Chinese monarch thus wrote with the
vermilion pencil, 'The Emperor respectfully begs the
Great Tan-jou of the Hiong-nu, &c.' To which, on
much larger tablets, the Tan-jou replied, 'The Great
Tan-jou of the Hiong-nu, born of the Heavens and the
Earth, established by the Sun and Moon, respectfully
begs the Emperor of China, &c.'

Frequently an invading Tan-jou would ask for the

*Diplomatic
incivilities
between
the Hiong-
nu and the
Chinese.*

---

[1] Tan-jou = mighty; ko-to = son; Tcem-li = Heaven. Wylie calls
the shorter name Shen-yu, and the longer Chang-le-kwa-too Shen-yu.

hand of a Chinese princess as the price of his return to
his own land, and the Court, not unwilling to plant by
the side of the robber-king a representative of its own
interests, would comply with the request. National
vanity however will not allow the Chinese historians to
confess that one of the princesses of the blood-royal
was really given in marriage to a barbarian, and they
accordingly relate that a custom prevailed of adopting
for the occasion a female slave into the family of the
Emperor, giving her the title of Kum-tcheou, or
Princess of the Blood, and then sending her off to be
the bride of the Tan-jou.   An improbable story doubtless ; but what is certain is that the transition from the
highly civilised luxurious life of a Chinese palace to the
squalor of the Tan-jou's home would be keenly felt by
the sufferer, whatever her station in life might be, and
perhaps even more by the domestic than by the mistress.
Here is the melancholy outpouring in verse of one of
these victims of policy, sent indeed not to a king of
the Hiong-nu but to a prince of the neighbouring
nation, the Ou-sioun, whose mode of life was indistin-
guishable from theirs :—

> ' Me to a husband have my kindred tied,
>   And in a far-off land have bid me bide;
> A wretched tent is now my palace-hall,
>   And a rough paling is its only wall.
> Raw flesh must now my hunger satisfy,
>   And curdled milk, my thirst : nought else have I.
> Oh native land! I still must think of thee,
>   And my heart's wound bleeds ever inwardly.
> Why am I not a happy bird of air
>   To thee, dear home, that I might straight repair ? '

The Hiong-nu were ignorant of the art of writing,
but the Chinese historians, with a candour which we

should scarcely have expected, admit that when they
had verbally pledged themselves to a treaty they
generally showed strict good faith in the observance
of it. The children were early trained in the use of
missile weapons. It is said that they were first taught
to ride on the wild scampering moorland sheep, and to
shoot with their little bows at birds and mice. As boys
they hunted hares and foxes, as young men they
assumed the weapons of war. They were not deemed
full-grown men till they had slain a foe. When they
reached old age they fell into poverty and contempt,
all the good things being reserved for the active
warriors of the nation. Flight was, as hinted in the
verses of Claudian, a great part of their strategy. Like
the Parthians, they would discharge a cloud of arrows
at the pursuing foe, and even if their rapid return
failed to throw his ranks into confusion, they easily
vanished into the terrible solitudes of those trackless
deserts whither for many generations their harassed
neighbours feared to pursue them.

Of the two chief residences of the Tan-jous, one
appears to have been situated in the north of their
dominions, under the continuation of the Altai mountain-range, and near the place which, as the capital of
later Tartar chieftains, was known as Karakorum; the
other near the Inshan mountains on the eastern frontier,
where a large manufactory of bows and arrows was
established.

At the first moon of each year there was a general
assembly of all the officers of the kingdom and army at
the Tan-jou's court, and a solemn sacrifice was then
offered up. They met again in the fifth month, and
sacrificed to the Heavens, the Earth, and the Spirits of

their ancestors. At another assembly held in the
autumn they numbered the people and their flocks,
thus taking stock, and striking a balance of the profit
or loss of the summer's operations in the way of
plunder.

Every morning the Tan-jou issued from his tent on
the left hand of the camp to pay his devotions to the
Sun, and in the evening he offered similar adoration to
the Moon, presumably during that part of the month
only when she was visible. Such was the simple and
primitive nature-worship of this tribe. We are informed that one of the other tribes of Central Asia
stuck a naked sabre hilt-downwards into the earth, and
then gathered round to adore it.

The great aim of the Hiong-nu in war was to take as
many prisoners as possible. They reduced them, of
course, to a state of slavery, and employed them to
tend their flocks and herds, that they themselves might
be left more free to practise the one art of the barbarian—war. If one of their number fell in battle, the
comrade who succeeded in carrying off his dead body
(as in the Homeric combats) to a place of safety, might
claim his inheritance. In the later days of the Hiong-
nu empire, when we might have expected that their
contact with the Chinese would have exerted some
civilising influence upon them, we find the Tanjou
Hou-han-sie confirming an oath by drinking blood from
the skull of a hostile chief who had been slain by one
of his ancestors 130 years before.

Such was the general character of the relations between the Hiong-nu and their southern neighbours.
A few striking features of the history of the two
nations, selected from a mass of monotonous details,

B.C. 40.

will sufficiently explain the movement which eventually launched the Hunnish nation, not upon Pekin, but upon Rome.

In China the Tsin dynasty, founded by the book-destroying Che-Hwang-te, was of short duration, like that of the Buonapartes, to which it has been already compared. *Tsin Dynasty in China, B.C. 258–207.*

In the year 207 B.C. another period of anarchy was ended by Kaou-te, who, gathering up again all China under his rule, founded the celebrated *Han* dynasty, which flourished till 220 A.D., or, roughly speaking, from the days of Hannibal to those of Caracalla. *Han Dynasty, B.C. 207–A.D. 220.*

Contemporaneously with Kaou-te in China, the terrible Mé-té-Tanjou [1] reigned over the Hiong-nu. His father, his step-mother, his half-brother, all atoned to him with their lives for an abortive attempt to exclude him from the succession. Yet, fierce as he had shown himself against his own flesh and blood, he appeared to submit with patience to the accumulated insults of the Sien-pi, a nation perhaps of Tungusic origin on the east of his dominions. Me-té had in his stable a horse of fabulous speed and endurance, which could travel, it was said, 150 miles in one day. The Sien-pi [2] sent to ask for this horse; he gave it up to them. Emboldened by this act of submission, they demanded one of his wives; she was sent to their king's tent. Then came a requisition for some waste lands, on a disputed frontier between the two nations, and at last the pent-up rage of Me-té burst forth, 'Whatever touched my own honour or profit I have given up for the sake of peace, but of the land of my people I will not surrender *Mé-té-Tanjou, B.C. 209–174.*

---

[1] Wylie calls him Maou-tun Shen-yu.
[2] Or the Tung-hoo (Wylie).

to you a foot's-breadth.' And he smote the people of
the Sien-pi with a great destruction, and pursued them

B.C.
209-174.

till they took refuge in the mountains of Mantchooria,
where they remained a crippled and enfeebled remnant,
but ever brooding over their wrongs, till, after the
lapse of nearly three centuries, they sallied forth to
enjoy their long-delayed vengeance.

Me-té's
wars with
China.

Towards China, Me-té assumed an attitude of permanent hostility. He fixed his court at Ta-tum-fou, or
Tai-tong, just south of the Great Wall, and pushed
forward his Hien-wang of the Left as far as Changkow,
and him of the Right to Yen-gan, both apparently from
100 to 200 miles within the Chinese frontier.

The Emperor Kaou-te levied an army of 320,000
men and marched against him, but was out-manœuvred,
and shut up in a fortress near Ta-tum-fou, where for
seven days his army was left without provisions. By
the favour of the Tanjou's wife he escaped from this
perilous position; but those seven days of semi-starva-
tion were long remembered by the sleek Chinese troops.
Peace of some sort was patched up between the two
powers, but after the death of Kaou-te an audacious
Hien-wang of the Right pushed his inroads so far that
his barbarian hordes came almost within sight of Sin-
gan-fou (in the province of Shen-si), which was then
the capital of the empire. The Chinese Court complained, and the Tanjou sent his too zealous Viceroy of
the West on a tour of conquest through Central Asia.
Thibet, all that we now call Eastern and Western
Turkestan, and part of Siberia, were made subject to
Me-té's domination, and it is even said that the conquering Hiong-nu reached on this occasion as far as
the Volga itself. With a great show of courtesy, the

Tanjou sent an embassy to inform the Chinese Emperor
of these conquests, by which he had become the greatest
potentate in Asia ; and hereupon, after a copious ex- B.C.
change of compliments, the Emperor, we are informed, 209–174.
concluded to accord to him a renewal of the treaty of
peace. As it is clear that at this time China was
almost helpless in the hands of her barbarian foe, the
Tanjou's humble supplications for peace, and the
gracious concession of it by the Emperor, were probably
recorded by the literati of that day, the contemporaries
of Hannibal, with about as much accuracy as may be
evinced by some Chinese historian, upon whom in our
own day may have devolved the duty of chronicling
the destruction of the Summer Palace, and the treaty A.D. 1860.
graciously conceded to El-gin and Mon-to-ban.

From the death of Me-té-Tanjou, which occurred B.C. Endless
174, we have, for the space of 260 years, a history of wars
and negoti-
the wars of China and the Huns, almost as detailed and ations
between
circumstantial as the records of Roman conquest during China and
the Hiong-
the same period. Happily for the reader there is no nu.
necessity to reproduce these details here. The same B.C. 174–
A.D. 93.
kind of events repeat themselves with monotonous
regularity. ' The Tanjou sought for peace from the
Chinese Emperor. A wife was sent to him, and presents
were exchanged. The Hiong-nu at once recommenced
their inroads and ravaged a great belt of country in the
three provinces of Shen-se, Shan-se, and Petche-li. The
Emperor sent three armies, amounting to 200,000 men,
into the country of the Hiong-nu. Two of the generals
obtained great successes, the third lost all his men in a
march through the desert. He ought to have returned
to China, and there submitted to degradation from all
his posts of honour, and afterwards committed suicide.

But he preferred to take refuge at the Court of the Tanjou, where the information which he gave as to the movements of the troops and the strength of the frontier-cities proved extremely injurious to the interests of China.   The Tanjou now supplicated for peace ; rich presents were exchanged, and various complimentary speeches were made, but both parties understood that there was no reality in the peace thus arranged.   A Chinese princess was sent as a wife for the heir-apparent, the Hien-wang of the Left.   The Hiong-nu recommenced their invasions of the three provinces of Shen-se, Shan-se, and Petche-li,' and so on as before.

The barbarian power declines.

There was however during all this period a pretty steady decline of the power of the barbarians, and an equally steady increase in that of their civilised neighbours.   Especially noteworthy in this respect was the long reign of the great Emperor *Woo-te*, which lasted from B.C. 140–86, or, shall we say, from the time of Cato the Censor to that of Cicero.   This monarch Woo-te, whose victorious arms extended to Pegu, Siam, and Bengal, and who was a zealous patron of the morality of Confucius, was contemporary with seven successive Tanjous, and, but that his prosperity did not desert him at the end of his reign, he might, not inaptly, be called the Louis XIV of China.

Long and prosperous reign of the Chinese Emperor Woo-te.

The lives of three of his servants may be briefly noticed here for the sake of the light which they throw on the history of the Hiong-nu.

B.C. 138-126. Mission of Chang-kiao.

Chang-kiao [1] was instructed by his master to establish communications with the Yue-ché, a Tartar people whom the Hiong-nu had driven from the east to the west of Central Asia, and who had now established

---

[1] Or Chang-keen (Wylie).

themselves in great force between the Oxus and Jaxartes, and even within the confines of the present Persian kingdom. Chang-kiao was made prisoner by the Hiong-nu while seeking to pass through their country in disguise. After ten years of captivity he escaped, reached the country of the Yue-ché (the modern Khorasan), remained there some time, storing up a large amount of valuable political information, and returned by way of Thibet, but even so was unable to escape from the Hiong-nu. His second captivity however was of short duration. Under cover of the troubles of a disputed succession, he again made his escape, and after an absence of twelve years, returned to his master's court.

Li-kwang-li, one of the bravest of the Chinese officers, was for sixty years perpetually giving and receiving hard blows in the wars with the northern barbarians. They themselves so highly esteemed the skill and rapidity of his movements that they called him 'the Winged General.' Once, it is said, at the head of 100 horsemen, he put a large body of their cavalry to flight. Yet even he, after a defeat, had to endure the systematic ingratitude of his countrymen, and after counterfeiting death on the field of battle, was on the point of receiving it at the hands of the executioner. He was permitted, however, to redeem his life by the payment of a large sum of money, but was degraded from all his dignities. But in the very next year the Emperor found himself compelled to restore him to the chief military command, so pressing was the danger from the northern invaders.

In the decline of life, this veteran soldier had the misfortune to see the honour of his family tarnished by

Marginal notes: B.C. 144–85. Hard fate of the veteran Li-kwang-li.

B.C. 99.

the treason of his grandson Li-ling, one of the many Chinese generals who after defeat fled to the Court of the Tanjou, and sold their knowledge of the strategic combinations of their countrymen for honours and offices in the barbarian court.

About nine years later, the brave old general, who must now have been fully eighty years of age, again headed a grand attack upon the Hiong-nu. He met at first with complete success, and pushed the foe before him to the mountain-barrier at the extreme north of their dominions. The forced marches, however, across the terrible desert of Gobi had too much weakened his troops. The Tanjou brought 50,000 fresh men into the field, dug in the night a deep ditch in the rear of the Chinese forces, and thus added to the disorder and panic of their flight after the defeat of the morrow[1].

Li-kwang-li was compelled to surrender at discretion, and taken prisoner to the Court of the Tanjou, who treated him with such marked favour (partly, perhaps, on account of his relationship to the already exiled

[1] The historians, consulted by Mr. Wylie, put a somewhat different colour on this campaign of Li-kwang-li. According to them, Li-kwang-li, in the midst of a victorious expedition against the Hiong-nu, received a message, brought him by his servant Hoo-A-foo, to the effect that his wife and family had all been sentenced to death on account of Li-ling's defection. (This defection had happened nine years before, but was perhaps only now bearing fruit manifestly in Li-ling's command of the Hiong-nu troops.) Hereupon Li-kwang-li, determined to do a desperate deed and either conquer Fate or die, planned his march across the great desert. The Chief Historian of the Chinese army warned his comrades that the General was fighting wildly and staking his all on a single throw. He therefore advised them to seize Li-kwang-li, who however was beforehand with his critic, and cut off the Chief Historian's head. According to these writers the trench was cut by the Hiong-nu in front of the Chinese troops and the attack was made in their rear.

Li-ling) that all the barbarian officers became jealous of his predominating influence [1]. Superstition was enlisted on the side of envy; in a dangerous illness of the Queen-mother, the soothsayers declared that the gods of the Hiong-nu were offended because they received no more human sacrifices as of yore, but prisoners of war were now preserved alive, and even received into favour. Li-kwang-li was seized and sacrificed; a terrible succession of snow-storms followed, which destroyed a vast number of cattle, and prevented the seeds from germinating in the earth. Then they changed their minds and said that they had mistaken the will of the gods; but the fine old warrior, after his sixty years of battle, was beyond the reach of their repentance.

Woo-soo [2] was sent by the Emperor Woo-te upon one of those endless embassies for the arrangement of 'a lasting and honourable peace,' which vary with their monotony of fraud the monotony of bloodshed. In the course of the discussions on this subject, he addressed himself to one of the Chinese fugitives, who had been promoted to a subordinate kingship in Western Siberia, and reproached him so bitterly for his treason and want of patriotism, that the Tanjou, disregarding the sanctity of an ambassador's person, seized him and cast him into a ditch. There he lived for several days, exposed to all the rigour of the climate, and feeding only upon snow and the offal of the camp. The barbarians conceived that there must be something divine in the

B.C. 100.

The Ambassador Woo-soo ill-treated by the barbarians.

---

[1] One of the chief calumniators of Li-kwang-li, and he who eventually succeeded in getting him offered up as a sacrifice, was Wei-leuh, who had himself many years before deserted from the Chinese service, and who was bitterly jealous of the favour shown to the new-comer (Wylie).

[2] Soo-woo (Wylie).

nature of a man who could endure such hardships,
but they chose a singular means of testifying their admiration. They carried him off to the inhospitable
shores of Lake Baikal, in the east of Siberia, where he
dragged out life for nineteen years, his food being mice
and the bitter fruits of the desert. Some of his countrymen, deserters, tried to reconcile him to his lot, and to
persuade him to accept, as they had done, the bounty
of the barbarian. 'No,' said he, 'I will remain true
to my country, whatever tortures her enemies may in-
flict upon me. A minister owes to his king the same
affectionate duty which a child does to his parent.'
And when he heard of the death of his master, the
great Woo-te, he turned his face to the beloved South,
looked towards China, and burst into tears. The remorse
which the Tanjou felt for the death of Li-kwang-li
turned out beneficially for Woo-soo, who, after his
weary captivity, was at length restored to his country.

The Hiong-
nu position
turned by
Chinese
alliances in
Central
Asia.
In the early days of the conquering Tanjous, Thibet
appears to have felt their influence, and the whole of
Eastern Turkestan (or what Deguignes calls 'Little
Bukharia') seems to have been in complete dependence
upon them. Even then, however, for some reason
which is not explained, but which is probably connected with the physical geography of the country,
their invasions of China were always made on the
north, never on the west frontier. If they thus missed
an opportunity of taking their enemy in flank, he, when
his turn of superiority came, showed more skilful
strategy ; and the great triumph of the reign of
Woo-te was the series of conquests and alliances by
which he turned the south-west flank of the Hiong-nu
position.

Any one who now looks at the map of Asia will see a long thin slice of territory stretching forth at the north-western angle of China (from the Hoang-ho to Su-chow, long. 98°). This is ground won from the barbarians, and made strong by the Chinese monarchs for the defence of the Empire. It is, in fact, an arm stretched forth into the desert, by which China seems to say, 'Not this way, barbarians of the North! fight, if you will fight, fairly, face to face ; but you shall not come round to my left side, and there deal me stealthily an assassin's blow.'

After the conquest of this territory came the secret mission of Chang-kiao through Thibet, to the country between the Oxus and Jaxartes, and this produced immense results. Where the stealthy emissary had gone, victorious armies followed. Khotan, Yarkand, Kashgar accepted the alliance, or became the subjects of the Chinese Emperor. The Ou-sioun, a powerful people, kindred with but hostile to the Hiong-nu, and dwelling to the south of Lake Balkhash, were encouraged to lean on China for protection against the common intervening foe : and a Chinese governor was permanently established at Aksou, under the steeps of the Thian Shan (about 78° long. and 42° lat.).

In the year 71 B.C. a great army amounting, it is said, to 200,000 men, was sent against the Hiong-nu under the command of seven generals. Notwithstanding the mismanagement and cowardice of some of the generals, this expedition seems, more than anything else, to have broken the power of the Hiong-nu.

It was not without some protest from the timid conservatism of the Chinese ministers that this energetic policy was pursued. When Siven-ti, the great-grand-

B.C. 66.
A Chinese Cabinet-Council.

son of Woo-te, was meditating an expedition, half-
hostile, half-friendly, to the country of the Ouigours
(near Turfan, long, 89°) he was met by the outspoken
remonstrances of a wise old counsellor named Goei-
siang.   This sage appears not to have been perplexed
by any of those difficulties as to the triumph of injustice and the downfall of the good which have
troubled the sages and seers of other nations.

B.C. 66.
Wars
Classified.
'There are five sorts of wars,' said he. 'The first, for
the suppression of civil tumult.   This is a war of
Justice, and it is sure to be successful.   The second, in
which you oppose a foreign invader, is a war of Necessity, and is generally crowned with victory.   In the
third kind of war, one of Rage and Fury, in which men
take up arms about mere trifles, one is often beaten.
To invade the lands of others for the sake of spoil is
the fourth species of war, that of Avarice, and in this
success is not to be expected.   But when a monarch
fights only in order to acquire glory, to render his
family illustrious and become a terror to his neighbours, that is a war of Ambition and Pride, the results
of which are uniformly disastrous.   These five points
are so many maxims founded on the dealings of Heaven.
At present the Hiong-nu desire peace, while our own
internal condition is far from satisfactory.   It is no
rare occurrence to see a son murder his father, a younger
brother the elder, a wife her husband.   Twenty-two
crimes of this kind have occurred in the course of the
past year.   We ought to apply a remedy to these social
disorders instead of carrying war into the country of
our neighbours.'

Rapid de-
cline of the
power of
Notwithstanding these excellent remarks, the policy
of war and annexation prevailed.   The Ouigours be-

came tributary, and the Hiong-nu felt the predominant influence of China all round their southern and western frontiers. The barbarians saw that their Empire was the Hiong-nu. departing from them, and fell into confusion and anarchy. In the year 58 B.C. five Tanjous were warring B.C. 58. against one another. Hou-han-sie, apparently the rightful heir, at length emerged from the contest, sole Tanjou ; but, almost immediately after, had to enter upon a new and fiercer contest with two fresh competitors, one of them his own brother. The upshot of the whole business was, that he humbly presented himself at the court of the Chinese Emperor, promised subjection and tribute, and received from this hereditary enemy assistance which at length enabled him to reign without a rival [1].

In a feeble and crippled state, the Hiong-nu Empire B.C. 58–
A.D. 93.

[1] On the death of Hou-han-sie, B.C. 31, a generous rivalry took place between his children, which should *not* succeed him. Besides other wives he had married two sisters, daughters of his Prime Minister. The elder sister, chief in rank, had the younger children, and this led to a discussion whether the dignity of the mother or the age of the children ought to be most regarded. Eventually all the four sons in question succeeded, first the two elder by the inferior wife, and then the two younger by the chief consort. Their regal names were as follows, and as they are a fair type of their class, the reader will perceive the reason for so often speaking of the Tanjou by his title and not quoting his name.

1. Feou-tchou-loui-jo-ti (Jo-ti=the Greek Philopator).
2. Seou-hiai-jo-ti.
3. Tche-ya-jo-ti.
4. Ou-tchou-lieou-jo-ti.

In course of time two more sons of Hou-han-sie succeeded to the throne,

5. Ou-loui-jo-ti and
6. Hou-tou-ulh-chi-tao-jo-ti.

It is perhaps an unworthy Aryan prejudice which finds a certain amount of uncouthness in these Turanian names.

lasted on for a century and a half from this time, but never again as the equal foe, generally as the vassal, occasionally as the revolted subject of the Court of China.

A.D. 46.
Separation between Northern and Southern Hiong-nu.
About the middle of the first century after Christ, the nation became finally divided into two hostile sections—a northern and a southern. Doubtless the dwellers in the immediate neighbourhood of China became more dependent on the good things which accompany civilisation than the wild nomads of the north-west; and then the physical barrier of the great desert of Gobi would probably intensify and perpetuate the moral division. From this time forwards the Tanjou of the south becomes one of the most eager enemies of the northern kingdom, ever besieging the ear of the Chinese Emperor with cries for its demolition.

Vengeance of the Sien-pi.
At the same time a new enemy pressed upon them from the east. The neighbouring tribe of the Sien-pi whom the great Tanjou Meté had cooped up in the mountains of what is now called Mantchuria, after brooding for three centuries over their wrongs, now found the longed-for opportunity of vengeance. After forty years of more or less constant warfare with this triple league of foes, symptoms of dissolution began to show themselves in the northern kingdom. Vast hordes of the Hiong-nu, in one case amounting to a quarter of a million of fighting men, went over bodily to the Chinese. A terrible famine, the work of some locust-like insect, then wasted the country. A combined invasion of the Chinese and the southern Hiong-nu on a large scale took place in the year 89. The Chinese general, Teou-hien, put the Tanjou to flight, and having

A.D. 89.

advanced 1000 miles into his kingdom, left upon one
of the mountain ranges an inscription composed by the
historiographer who accompanied the expedition, recording the success of his arms. In two years however
even this effort was surpassed : the Chinese troops
reached the Irtish, the western frontier of the dominions
of the Hiong-nu, the Tanjou had again to take shelter
in some Siberian desert, and his mother was taken
prisoner.

Teou-hien, though victorious, recommended his im- Fall of the Hiong-nu Empire.
perial master to spare his fallen foes. But on his death
sterner counsels prevailed. A new Tanjou who had A.D. 93.
been raised to the throne was driven into revolt, a
revolt hopeless from the first. He himself fell into the
hands of the Chinese forces, and was beheaded. The
Sien-pi poured into the defenceless country like a
torrent. Great multitudes of the Hiong-nu consented
to pass under their yoke and bear their name, the rest
fled westwards across the Irtish, settling by the Ural
River and near the modern Russian Government of
Orenbourg. Thus did the great barbarian empire,
which for 2000 years had been measuring its forces
against the civilisation of China, fall, with apparently
irretrievable ruin.

All this occurred in the reign of Domitian. It was Hunnish invasion three centuries after these events.
not till nearly three centuries later that the Huns,
during the reign of Valens, crossed the Sea of Azof or
the stream of the Volga, and fell upon the affrighted A.D. 376.
and disgusted Gothic subjects of King Hermanric. This
long interval of quiescence and of obscurity is the weak
place in the identification of the Hiong-nu and the
Huns. It is impossible not to feel that many changes
might have occurred during that time, and that mere

similarity of name is a slight clue by which to traverse so vast a distance.

Doubtful benefit to China from its victories over the Hiong-nu. The Chinese historians necessarily give during this interval far scantier information than previously as to the affairs of Central Asia. The expulsion of the northern Hiong-nu appears to have been a 'victory of Pyrrhus' for the Chinese Empire. The southern Hiong-nu and the Sien-pi, under various barbarous names, formed settlements within its limits and erected dynasties which disputed the throne of China itself with its native princes. In such a state of things the historians of that country had but little inducement or opportunity to record the revolutions of Western Asia. We are enabled however, dimly and at long intervals, to trace the continued existence of a Hiong-nu people along the line of the Volga and the northern shores of the Caspian.

Chinese description of a great civilized state on the West frontier of Asia.
Deguignes, vol. I, pt. ii, p. lxxviii. To the west of them, but separated by one fierce Tartar people, the Chinese historians placed the great kingdom of Ta-Tsin. Their description of this kingdom is so curious that a few of its leading features may be here inserted. 'It is a country of large extent with many dependent kingdoms. The walls are built of stone; inns are placed along the lines of road. All sorts of trees and plants are found there. The inhabitants are given to agriculture, and even understand how to keep silkworms. They cut their hair and wear very fine clothes. They have all sorts of chariots with white coverings: in war they have drums, flags, and tents. The capital is thirty-four miles in circumference; it contains five palaces by the waterside, supported on pillars. Every day the king goes to one or other of these palaces to administer justice. Before his

chariot walks an officer holding an open bag in which
are placed the petitions of all who present themselves,
which are examined by the king when he enters the
palace. Thirty-six generals of the army form a Council
of State to deliberate on the affairs of the Empire. The
king does not always hold his office for life; they generally endeavour to choose a wise man, but should any
extraordinary calamity occur, for instance any great
whirlwind or inundation, they change their ruler, and
he who is thus deposed appears to descend into private
life without a sigh.

'Gold, silver, precious stones, rich and beautifully
embroidered vestments abound in this country. They
have both gold and silver money : ten pieces of the
latter are equivalent to one of the former. They trade
both with the Parthians and Indians. They have often
endeavoured to enter into direct commercial relations
with China, but have always been prevented by the
Parthians. Recently' [in the year corresponding to
A.D. 166] 'the king of the Ta-Tsin named Gan-tun succeeded in sending ambassadors, who were followed by
merchants, to China by way of India. The inhabitants
of Ta-Tsin are tall and well-made like the Chinese,
whence their name' [Ta = Great : Tsin = China or the
Chinese]. This last sentence will probably have disclosed to the reader the real name of the country in
question. Only the Romans of that day could be considered worthy of being called by a Chinese historian
'Great as the Chinese.' He has been reading a description of *Imperium Romanum* by a Chinese pen, and the
king, Gan-tun, is the Emperor Marcus (Aurelius)
Antoninus.

The question will naturally be asked, ' Why, if these

Hiong-nu, marauders as they were by nature, had wandered so near to the confines of this alluring kingdom of Ta-Tsin, did they allow three centuries to elapse before they commenced their invasions of that empire?' Dimly and vaguely, through the faint twilight of their history, we may conjecture the following reasons for their quiescence : there may have been a hundred others which are to us undiscoverable.

Why did the Huns linger for three hundred years before invading Europe?

First, their eyes were still turned eastwards ; their expeditions still sometimes reached as far as Khamil (long. 95° E.), and for generations they seem to have cherished the hope of once more ravaging the valley of the Hoang-ho. At length their old enemies, the Sien-pi, under the dynasty of the Topas, built up, in the old country of the Hiong-nu, a sufficiently solid empire to check all eastward incursions on their part. But,

They might still hope to revenge themselves on China.

A.D. 261–376.

Secondly, between their new home and western civilization a strong barrier was presented by the fierce nation of the Alani, Turanian nomads like themselves, who, under the name of Alanna, are spoken of by the Chinese historians as occupying the country of Yen-Tcai, the extensive district which is bounded by the Volga on the north, the Caucasus on the south, the Sea of Azof and the Don on the west, and the Caspian and Volga on the east. These are the people who for so many generations adored a naked sabre stuck into the earth as their only divinity. They were at length, after contests the duration and severity of which are hidden from us, overcome by those neighbours of theirs whom we may now without fear of contradiction venture to call the Huns. Some, the Alani of the Don, became amalgamated with the armies of the

The Alani were between them and Europe.

conqueror, others fled westwards and bore a part, recognised in history, in the subversion of the Roman Empire, though it did not fall to their lot to found any enduring kingdom within its borders.

Hopes of Chinese spoil on the east, the reality of Alan resistance on the west, were doubtless two reasons for the long sojourn of the Hiong-nu eastwards of the Volga. A third, which it is sufficient merely to indicate, is the prestige, slowly and with difficulty impaired, of the Roman Empire, of that 'Ta-Tsin' which 'Gantun' and his immediate predecessors had ruled so wisely and made so strong. *Prestige of the Roman Empire.*

A fourth is the utterly broken and dispirited state of the Hiong-nu themselves. After their flight from their old home in Central Asia, they seem to have ceased to elect Tanjous; the unity of the nation was gone, the degree of organisation, the semblance of a polity which they had before possessed, probably vanished. Removed from the civilizing influences of contact with China they doubtless sank lower and lower into mere squalid savagery, becoming a loosely united bundle of roving hordes, until at length increase of numbers brought with it confidence, the remembrance of past supremacy stirred up shame at their present abject condition, the success of their conflict with the Alans assured them of victory, and turning their backs definitively on the East, they crossed the Cimmerian Bosporus—whether guided by a demon-stag or not we need not inquire—to work, both directly and indirectly, more ruin and greater changes in the fair kingdoms of Ta-Tsin than their mightiest Tanjous had ever done in the often-wasted provinces of the real China. *Dispirited condition of the Hiong-nu.*

This chapter was commenced by Claudian's poetical

description of the Huns ; at its close let us listen to the historian Ammianus Marcellinus, a soldier, and more strictly a contemporary, describing in what guise they showed themselves when first 1500 years ago, they burst upon Europe.

' The nation of the Huns, little known to ancient records, but spreading from the marshes of Azof to the Icy Sea, surpasses all other barbarians in wildness of life. In the first days of infancy, deep incisions are made in the cheeks of their boys, in order that, when the time comes for whiskers to grow there, the sprouting hairs may be kept back by the furrowed scars : and hence they grow to maturity and to old age beardless as eunuchs. They all, however, have strong and well-knit limbs and fine necks. Yet they are of portentous ugliness and so crook-backed that you would take them for some sort of two-footed beasts, or for the roughly-chipped stakes which one sees used for the railings of a bridge. And though they do just bear the likeness of men (of a very ugly pattern), they are so little advanced in civilization that they make no use of fire, nor of any kind of relish, in the preparation of their food, but feed upon the roots which they find in the fields, and the half-raw flesh of any sort of animal. I say half-raw, because they give it a kind of cooking by placing it between their own thighs and the backs of their horses. They never seek the shelter of houses, which they look upon as little better than tombs, and will only enter upon the direst necessity : nor would one be able to find among them even a cottage of wattled rushes : but wandering at large over mountain and through forest, they are trained to bear from their infancy all the extremes of cold, of hunger, and of thirst.

'They are clad in linen raiment, or in the skins of
field-mice sewn together, and the same suit serves them
for use in-doors and out. However dingy the colour
of it may become, the tunic which has once been hung
round their necks is never laid aside nor changed till
through long decay the rags of it will no longer hold
together. Their heads are covered with bent caps,
their hairy legs with the skins of goats ; their shoes,
never having been fashioned on a last, are so clumsy
that they cannot walk comfortably.

' On this account they are not well adapted to pedestrian encounters ; but then on the other hand they are
almost welded to their horses, which are hardy, though
of ugly shape, and on which they sometimes ride
women's fashion. On horseback every man of that
nation lives night and day ; on horseback he buys and
sells ; on horseback he takes his meat and drink, and
when night comes he leans forward upon the narrow
neck of his horse and there falls into a deep sleep, or
wanders into the varied phantasies of dreams.

'When a discussion arises upon any matter of importance they come on horseback to the place of meeting.
No kingly sternness overawes their deliberations, but
being upon the whole well-contented with the disorderly
guidance of their chiefs, they do not scruple to interrupt
the debates with anything that comes into their heads.

'When attacked, they will sometimes engage in regular
battle. Then, going into the fight in order of columns,
they fill the air with varied and discordant cries. More
often, however, they fight in no regular order of battle,
but being extremely swift and sudden in their movements, they disperse, and then rapidly come together
again in loose array, spread havoc over vast plains, and

flying over the rampart, they pillage the camp of their
enemy almost before he has become aware of their approach.   It must be owned that they are the nimblest
of warriors ; the missile weapons which they use at a
distance being pointed with sharpened bones admirably
fastened to the shaft : when in close combat, they fight
without regard to their own safety, and while their enemy
is intent upon parrying the thrusts of their swords, they
throw a net over him and so entangle his limbs that he
loses all power of walking or riding.

'Not one among them cultivates the ground, or ever
touches a plough-handle.   All wander abroad without
fixed abodes, without home, or law, or settled customs,
like perpetual fugitives, with their waggons for their
only habitations, in which their wives weave their foul
garments, and bring forth children, and rear them up to
the age of puberty [1].   If you ask them, not one can tell
you what is his place of origin ; he was conceived in one
place, born in another, educated perhaps in some yet
more distant one.   They are great truce-breakers, fickle,
always ready to be swayed by the first breath of a new
desire, abandoning themselves without restraint to the
most ungovernable rage.

'Finally, like animals devoid of reason, they are
utterly ignorant of what is seemly and what is not;
they are tricksters with words, and full of dark sayings ;
they are never moved by either religious or superstitious
awe ; they burn with unquenchable thirst for gold, and
they are so changeable and so easily moved to wrath,
that many times in the day they will quarrel with their
comrades on no provocation, and be reconciled having
received no satisfaction.'

[1] The squalid prototype of the gorgeous Harem of the Ottomans.

NOTE A. On the Identification of the Hiong-nu with the Huns.

I quote from Mr. Howorth's 'Introduction to the Translation of the Annals of the Han Dynasty' (by Mr. Wylie), contributed to the Journal of the Anthropological Institute (iii. 398), the following criticism of the theory adopted in my first edition.

'De Guignes, than whom no one has done more for the elucidation of the ethnology of Asia in ancient times, propounded the doctrine that the European Huns were descended from the Hiong-nu of the Chinese writers, and he consequently in his history of the Huns worked out in some detail the account of the Hiong-nu, so far as it could be collected from the narratives of Matuanlin and the other epitomisers of the Chinese annals. Minute ethnology was then in its infancy. The distinctions between Mongols, Turks, Ugrians, &c., &c. were hardly recognised because hardly known. Since the days of De Guignes the subject has received immense illustration from various quarters, and now no European scholar of any repute—save perhaps Dr. Latham—connects the Huns with the Hiong-nu. The Huns, as I have elsewhere argued, were a race of Ugrians, led by a caste of another race now represented by some of the Lesghian tribes of the Caucasus. The Hiong-nu were not Ugrians. It was Klaproth who first proved that the Hiong-nu were Turks, and his conclusions were endorsed by the very competent authority of Abel Remusat, and since by other scholars.' The argument thus divides itself into two parts.

I. *Proof that the Huns were Ugrians.*

This rests on the existence of some 'Lesghian' tribes in the Eastern Caucasus who bear names which appear to be corrupted from 'Hun' and 'Avar.' Among these tribes, names closely corresponding with those of Attila and his family are still, it is said, in common use. The dialect of the 'Andi,' whom Howorth takes to be the representatives of the Huns, 'approximates very closely to the Ugrian or Finnic dialects proper, while the Avar has many idiosyncrasies related to the Samoyedic class of Siberian languages.'

II. *Proof that the Hiong-nu were a Turkic tribe.*

This rests chiefly on the Turkic character of the vocabulary of the Thiu-Khiu, a fragment of the dispersed Hiong-nu who, in the fifth century, settled in the Altai mountains. Fifteen or sixteen words in use among the Thiu-Khiu, including those for house, meat, horse, wolf, black, white, old, camp, and warrior, are shown to be identical with or closely analogous to words in the Turkish or Mongol languages. Hence it is argued, the Hiong-nu must have been closely related to the Turks.

The question is one which must be decided by experts in ethnology. To me, knowing scarcely anything of that science, there seem one or two weak links in the chain of argument ; but then, on the other hand, we must not forget that the equation

$$\text{Hun} = \text{Hiong-nu}$$

rests on nothing more than one, perhaps accidental, similarity of names. It is difficult not to be attracted by the theory of Deguignes, because of the almost ludicrous similarity between the treatment of the Chinese Emperors by the Tanjous and that of the Roman Emperors by Attila and his progenitors. But of course there is nothing in this similarity which can weigh against any well-settled conclusion of ethnological science.

CHAPTER II.

ATTILA AND THE COURT OF CONSTANTINOPLE.

Authorities.

Sources :—

PRISCUS, born at Panium, a town of Thrace, probably about the beginning of the fifth century. He wrote (in Greek) a history in eight books, 'Of Byzantium and the occurrences connected with Attila,' which apparently narrated the events between 433 and 474. He is commonly spoken of as 'the Rhetorician,' or 'the Sophist,' and his pure, elegant, and lively style agrees with the supposition that he was by profession a man of letters. He was admitted to the intimate friendship of Maximin, one of the generals of Theodosius II, whom he accompanied on his celebrated embassy to Attila, and also on a visit to Syria. It is probable that both he and his friend Maximin were Pagans. Only fragments of his work remain, but one of these, of considerable length, describing Attila and his court and the reception of the Roman ambassadors, is the most interesting piece of contemporary history which the fifth century has bequeathed to us.

Guides [1] *:—*

Deguignes, Histoire des Huns, Liv. iv, § 1 Les Huns Occidentaux (a most convenient summary of all the passages in Greek and Latin authors bearing on the history of Attila). The same may be said of

Mascou, History of the Ancient Germans (translated from the German 1738), Book ix.

[1] This enumeration of guides applies to all the remaining chapters of the Second Book.

Amédée Thierry's Histoire d'Attila (2 vols.) is a well-constructed narrative, with which the relation of the embassy of Priscus is skilfully interwoven.

'Attila, King of the Huns,' by the Hon. and Rev. W. Herbert (London, 1838), is an Epic Poem in twelve books on the career of Attila from his defeat on the Catalaunian Plains (451) till his death (454). The most useful part of the book to a historical student is the second half of it, 'Attila and his Predecessors, an Historical Treatise.' Here all the materials for writing the life of Attila are collected with great industry, but there is no sufficient separation between the precious and the vile. The contemporary Priscus, who drank wine with Attila, appears to be quoted with no more deference than is paid to Hungarian and Italian romancers.

The Huns do not at once come in contact with Rome. For half a century after the irruption of the Huns into Dacia, they exercise but little direct influence on the course of Roman history. Occasionally they made a predatory inroad into the Empire, as, for instance, in the year 395, when, at the instigation, it was said, of the Prefect Rufinus, they moved southwards from Caucasus upon Armenia, and pressed on through Cappadocia and Cilicia[1], until

> 'The pleasant fields of Syria waste were laid,
> And hostile chargers trampled down the glade
> Of soft Orontes, to her children's dance
> And song more used than War's dread dissonance[2].'

Uldis. And thirteen years later, under the guidance of a chief named *Uldis*[3], they crossed the Danube and penetrated far into Bulgaria. When the Prefect of Thrace sought humbly for peace, Uldis proudly pointed to the sun and said, 'All that *he* shines upon I can conquer if I will.'

---

[1] See I. 654.

[2] Claudian, In Rufinum, ii. 32–35.

[3] Perhaps the same person as Uldin, Stilicho's Hunnish auxiliary in the campaign against Radagaisus (405).

But in the midst of his boastings his power was undermined : the imperial emissaries were at work among
his troops, contrasting the hard life of a Hunnish
marauder with the ease and the dignity of a stipendiary
of Rome. So large a part of his army yielded to these
suggestions that Uldis was obliged to fly, and escaped
but with life to the Dacian shore.

409.

Upon the whole, during this period, while their
enemies the Visigoths and other Teutonic tribes were
still hovering about the Danube and the eastern ranges
of the Alps, the attitude of the Huns seems to have
been more often friendly than hostile to the Romans,
in whose armies we saw them serving when Honorius
decreed the overthrow of Stilicho, and when Aetius
came too late to the succour of Joannes against Placidia.

Huns as
Roman
auxiliaries.

And, mere barbarians as they remained to the end of
their history, it is easy to see that this half-century of
intercourse with Rome had taught them some few of the
needs and enjoyments of civilized life. The whole
character of Attila's court and camp was sensual, but
the sensuality was by many degrees less squalid and
less disgusting than that of the men who first crossed
the Sea of Azof, and whose habits were described by
Ammianus.

They
become
slightly
less savage.

Doubtless it was the interposition of the Teutonic
nations which, during this half-century, prevented the
Huns from coming to close quarters with the Roman
power. After the Visigoths, the Vandals, and the Suevi
had settled in Spain, the Alans in Gaul, the Burgundians
in that province which yet bears their name, the Huns,
having only the Danube and the Alps between them
and the Empire, began to make the two Augusti, but
especially him of Constantinople, feel their heavy hand.

In 432 we find a certain *Roua* or *Rugula* reigning
over the Huns, and receiving from Theodosius II an

annual payment, which might be called either subsidy
or tribute, of 350 pounds weight of gold (£14,000 sterling). Finding that the Romans had dared to make
alliances with some barbarous tribes, dwellers by the
Danube, whom he claimed as his subjects, Roua in great
wrath declared that all *his* treaties with Rome should
be at once made null and void unless the Emperor renounced his alliance with these nations. Another question of a more personal nature also arose now, if it had
not arisen before, and was the subject of ceaseless negotiation for the next seventeen years. Many deserters
had fled from the harsh yoke of Roua, and taken shelter
on Roman territory. The demand was made, and was
pressed home with every circumstance of insult upon
the trembling Theodosius, 'Restore to me my fugitives.'
Imagine such a request having been hinted, ever so
courteously, to any Roman magistrate who in the old
days sat upon the curule chair, with his lictors and
fasces round him. Had it not been better for the omnipotent Mistress of the Nations to have died rather than
live on to endure such degradation ?

But Theodosius II, who was a meek man and an excellent illuminator of manuscripts, if not a born king of
men, was preparing to send an embassy to mitigate the
wrath of Roua, when tidings arrived that he was dead,

and that the kingdom of the Huns had devolved upon
his two nephews, sons of his brother Mundzuk, men in
the vigour of early manhood, named *Attila* and *Bleda*.

It was in the year 433 that the two brothers ascended
the throne. Bleda is to us the mere shadow of a name,
but it is far otherwise with Attila.

It is almost needless to say that no coin, or picture, or bust remains to bring before us the lineaments of the terrible savage. Yet he seems almost to live again in the pages of Jordanes and Priscus. We see him short of stature, with the small, bead-like eyes, and snub nose and swarthy skin of his Tartar ancestors, yet with a haughty step, and a fierce way of darting his glances hither and thither, as though he felt himself lord of all, and were perpetually asking of the by-standers, ' Who is he that shall deliver you out of my hand ? ' He had a broad and well-formed chest and a large head, a scanty beard, like most of the Tartar race, and his hair was early sprinkled with white. Attila's appearance

Few men that ever lived have had such a power of inspiring fear in the minds both of their subjects and their enemies as this Turanian chieftain. Enthusiasm, loyalty, gratitude, these were not the motives by which he swayed mankind, but the amount of abject, slavish fear which this little swarthy Kalmuck succeeded in instilling into millions of human hearts is not to be easily matched in the history of our race. and character.

Whether he had much military talent may be doubted, since the only great battle in which he figured was a complete defeat. The impression left upon us by what history records of him is that of a gigantic bully, holding in his hands powers unequalled in the world for ravage and spoliation, by the mere threat of loosing which he extorts from trembling Caesars every concession which his insatiable avarice, or his almost superhuman pride, requires, and by the same terror compelling Ostrogoths and Gepidae, and other Germanic races far nobler than his own, to assist in drawing his triumphal chariot. But of true constructive genius, of any notion of the right way to found an enduring empire, of the statesmanship of Ataulfus, or even of Alaric, he shows not a trace. To drink out of vessels of gold and silver, to put his foot upon the neck of his enemies, to be the terror of the world, these seem to be his only delights as a ruler of men.

Extent of Attila's Empire.

Some doubt has recently been thrown on the received accounts of the wide extent of Attila's power. So much of our information, it is said, is derived from Gothic sources, and a proud nation like the Goths had so obvious an interest in magnifying the might of the monarch by whom they themselves had been humbled, that we are bound to make considerable deductions from their statements, and may perhaps reduce the dominions of the world-wide conqueror to an extent not quite equal to that of the modern Austrian Empire [1]. But it may fairly be urged on the other hand that the Greek historian Priscus confirms, or even amplifies the statements of the Goth. According to him, when the ambassadors from the Eastern and Western Empires were met in trembling conference, consulting how they might possibly obtain a reasonable answer from the haughty barbarian, the Romans said, ' His head is turned by his successes. No ruler of Scythia or of any other country has ever achieved so much in so short a time as he has. He rules over the islands in the ocean ' (by which we must probably understand the Scandinavian islands and peninsulas [2]) ; ' he has made the whole of Scythia his

P. 199 (Bonn edition).

---

[1] This view is urged by Dr. Latham in his article ' Hunni' in Smith's Dictionary of Greek and Roman Geography.

[2] It is perhaps deserving of consideration whether, if this northward impetus of Attila's subjects and allies really carried them to the Baltic and far into Denmark, it may not have something to do with

own ; he has put the Roman Empire to tribute, and he
thinks of renewing his attacks upon Persia. The road
to that eastern kingdom is not untrodden by the Huns ;
already they have marched fifteen days' journey from a
certain lake [the Sea of Azof the Romans thought, but
more probably the Caspian], and have ravaged Media.'

Add to this apparently trustworthy statement of
Priscus the firm belief of Deguignes [1] that he has found
traces in the historians of China of a confederacy between Attila and the rulers of that country, and we
have reasons for not lightly abandoning the old belief
in the wide extent of the Empire of Attila. The prince
who felt China on his left, who threatened Persepolis,
Byzantium, Ravenna in front, who ruled Denmark and
its islands in his rear, and who ultimately appeared in
arms on the soil of Champagne on his right, was no
minor monarch, and had his empire been as deep as it
was wide-spread, he might worthily have taken rank
with Cyrus and Alexander.

At the same time it is well to remember that over far
the larger part of this territory, Attila's can have been
only an over-lordship, Teutonic, Slavonic, and Tartar
chieftains of every name bearing rule under him. His
own personal government, if government it can be called,
may very likely have been confined nearly within the
limits of the modern Hungary and Transylvania.

the migrations of the English into Britain between the years 430
and 450. What they had before done against the 'Littus Saxonicum'
had been apparently mere piracy and robbery. Now the whole nation
migrates, a proceeding to which we can easily imagine them to have
been stirred by the Teuton's loathing dread of the Mongol. And
thus Attila may have been the unconscious founder of the English as
well as of the Venetian dominion.

[1] Vol. I. part ii. pp. 298–301.

For nineteen years, from 434 to 453, the sullen might of Attila lay like a thunder-cloud over Europe. During that time the Eastern and Western Courts were so closely united, as well by the bonds of relationship as by the overwhelming sense of their common danger, that it is not possible to disentangle their histories. Let us give a glance at the chief personages in the two Courts.

Character of Theodosius II.

425.

The younger Theodosius, son of Arcadius, and Emperor of the East, was in the twenty-fifth year of his age when we met with him, leading his people from the Hippodrome to the Basilica, to return thanks for the victory of his generals at Ravenna, which replaced his kinsfolk of the West on the Imperial throne. The fatuous dullness of his father and uncle no longer repels us in this member of the Theodosian family; he has some other employment than hunting; he illuminates sacred manuscripts with such skill as to earn the title of the Calligrapher; and he does not rush from blind confidence in his ministers to equally blind suspicion, with the instability which was so conspicuous in Arcadius and Honorius. Still, he is not a true King; he possesses no real momentum in the affairs of the state : as a rule, every important measure is decided upon by his sister Pulcheria, who is two years older than himself, who governs the East—as her aunt Placidia governs the West—respectably, but without genius, powerless to stem the quick-rushing torrent of barbarian ravage and change, but not conspicuously adding to the calamities of Rome by vices of her own [1].

---

[1] It should be said that the historian Eunapius (Excerpt 70) gives a terrible picture of the evils which afflicted the state 'under the

Theodosius himself, all through these years of political trouble and anxiety, is much engrossed in the controversy concerning the union of the divine and human natures in Christ; but he does not win from it the same ecclesiastical renown which the Council of Constantinople brought to his more celebrated namesake and grandfather. At the Council of Ephesus he appears (through his ministers) to favour the heresy of Nestorius; at the close of his reign he leans towards the opposite heresy of Dioscorus and Eutyches, which is, immediately after his death, condemned by the great Council of Chalcedon. At no time does he conspicuously defend the narrow *via media* of Orthodoxy.

His theological position.

It is strange that the marriages of the Emperors of this family, which were daring and unconventional, did not remove from the race that effete and worn-out character which attaches to its later scions. The mother of Theodosius II was a Frankish princess, beautiful and impetuous, who bore the name of Eudoxia. His wife, the equally beautiful but portionless daughter of an Athenian rhetorician, brought up in the worship of the Olympian gods, was known in childhood by the name of Athenais, which, on her conversion to Christianity, she exchanged for that of Eudocia. She was twenty-seven when her marriage with Theodosius, who was seven years her junior, raised her to the Imperial throne; but her influence seems never to have outweighed that of her sister-in-law Pulcheria, and after

The Empress Eudocia.

421.

Empress Pulcheria' (ἐπὶ Πουλχερίας τῆς Βασιλίσσης). But he does not appear to attribute them to her personal agency, and the root-evil of all, the sale of public offices and the frightful corruption of the ministers of state, is spoken of in precisely similar terms a generation earlier, in the days of Arcadius and the eunuch Eutropius.

twenty-three years of married life, at the mature age of fifty, she incurred a suspicion of unfaithfulness to her husband, and was banished to Jerusalem, where she died in 460, after an exile of sixteen years.

Eudoxia wife of Valentinian III.

The only child of this marriage, with whom history has to concern itself, is a daughter, a *third* Eudoxia (for that name and Eudocia seem to be interchangeable), who, as we have seen, was betrothed in her babyhood,

437.

and in the sixteenth year of her age married, to Valentinian III, son of her father's aunt, but her own contemporary, with whom we have already made acquaintance as Emperor of the West, reigning, but not governing, under the tutelage of his mother Placidia.

The Princess Honoria.

After one more granddaughter of the great Theodosius has been named, the sketch of the two Imperial groups in the East and West will be complete. Besides her son Valentinian III, Placidia had a daughter

Born 418.

Honoria, whose name was, for nearly twenty years, a by-word and a horror in the two Courts of Ravenna and Constantinople. Inheriting the coarse and sensual temperament of her father Constantius, and, like him, probably chafing at the restraints imposed on all the

434.

family of the 'sacred' Emperors, she was detected in a low intrigue with one of the chamberlains of the palace. Her mother sent her to Constantinople, where, for the next sixteen years of her life, she was kept more or less closely guarded, at the court of her cousin Theodosius. The foolish girl, who was but in the seventeenth year of her age, filled with wild resentment against her family and her native land, hating the calm and sorrowful face of her mother, hating the severe dignity of Pulcheria, the psalmodies, the

weaving, the visitations of the poor, in which she
and her sisters passed their lives [1], looked away to the
gloomy North for vengeance, and called upon the
squalid Hun to be her deliverer. She contrived to *Honoria*
sends her
send a ring to Attila, who had become King of the *ring to*
Attila.
Huns in the year preceding her disgrace, and begged
to be considered as his wife, or rather, probably, as
one of his wives, for the Huns, unlike the Goths, were
polygamists. It was the wild act of a girl of sixteen,
perhaps half-crazy with passion. We hear nothing of
Attila's reply, nothing of any renewed applications
on Honoria's part for his assistance. Probably her
apartments in the palace at Constantinople were thenceforward too strictly guarded to allow of her repeating
the message. But Attila treasured the ring, and in
after-days pulled through that tiny circlet long threads
of diplomacy and a bloody skein of war.

Immediately upon Attila's accession, an embassy from *Treaty of*
Margus be-
Theodosius waited upon him and Bleda, in order to *tween Ro-*
mans and
settle the various questions which had been raised *Huns.*
between the Emperor and their deceased uncle Roua.
The ambassadors met the kings at Margus, a town
which stood at the point where the Morava, now the
chief river of Servia, empties itself into the Danube.

---

[1] Sozomen, who was a contemporary historian, writes thus concerning Pulcheria and her sisters Arcadia and Marina: 'They all
pursue the same mode of life, are sedulous in their attendance in the
house of prayer, and evince great charity towards strangers and the
poor. These sisters generally take their meals and walks together,
and pass their days and their nights together in singing the praises
of God. Like other exemplary women, they employ themselves in
weaving and in similar occupations, avoiding idleness as unworthy of
the life of virginity to which they have devoted themselves' (book ix,
chap. 4).

433.

Not only the Hunnish kings, but all their retinue, remained seated on horseback, and, that the dignity of Rome might not suffer in their persons, the ambassadors did the same.   Yet, though etiquette might be maintained, Plinthas and Epigenes, the Roman envoys, did not win any very brilliant diplomatic triumph for their master.   The *honorarium,* or stipend, or by whatever name the Romans chose to style that yearly payment which Attila, with ever-increasing frankness, called by its true designation, tribute, was raised from £14,000 to £28,000; the fugitive Huns and Romans were to be surrendered, or a fine of £8 per head paid for each who was not forthcoming; there were to be free markets at which the Romans and Huns should meet on equal terms, and any barbarian tribe upon which Attila might choose to levy war, was to be excluded from the alliance of Rome.   In compliance with this treaty, two children of the royal blood of the Huns were surrendered by the Roman officers, and crucified on Roman territory by the orders of Attila. Their only crime was flight.

Eight years of peace.

The next eight years are a blank in the Roman annals, as far as the Huns are concerned.   It was at this time probably that Attila made those extensive conquests northwards and eastwards to which reference has already been made, that he pushed his dominion to the shores of the German Ocean, and sent his armies fifteen days' march from the Caspian into Media[1].

---

[1] This may have been an earlier invasion.   Priscus uses very vague language concerning it, and attributes it to 'Basik and Cursik, men belonging to the royal family of Scythia [the Huns] who commanded a great multitude of followers, and afterwards entered into alliance with Rome' (p. 200, ed. Bonn).

According to some accounts, he also, during the same interval, marched into the country watered by the Rhone, and fought the Burgundians. However this may be, in 441 the curtain again lifts, and the first scene of conflict is that same Servian town of Margus on the Morava, where we last saw Attila doubling the Roman tribute and discussing terms of peace with Plinthas and Epigenes. The bishop of this place had crossed the Danube on a marauding expedition, and robbed one of the royal treasure-houses of the Huns of the wealth deposited therein. Naturally this imitation of their own predatory tactics excited the fierce wrath of the barbarians. At the time of one of the great markets by the banks of the Danube, which were arranged for by the last treaty, the Huns made a savage attack on the unsuspecting Romans. To the expostulations of the Imperial Court but one reply was returned : 'Give us up our refugees, and with our refugees the marauding bishop of Margus.' It began to be discussed among Prefects and Chamberlains whether it might not be better to give up this one rash bishop, that the whole nation should not perish. The rumour reached the ears of the reverend prelate, who determined to be beforehand with Fate. Stealing across to the camp of the barbarians, he undertook to put them in possession of the city of Margus if the kings of the Huns would hold him harmless. Clasping his right hand, they swore to confer upon him all sorts of benefits if he would fulfil this promise. Then, having planted the barbarian host in a well-selected ambuscade on the northern shore of the Danube, he returned into the city, unsuspected by his fellow-citizens, and at a given signal opened the gates to his new allies. They rushed in and sacked the place, and one of the chief border cities of Moesia was thus lost to the Empire.

441.

An incident like this seems worth recording, since it marks the rapidly changing manners and positions of men during this century of barbarian invasion. Of course the occupant of the see of Margus was no fair specimen of his order, either in his first marauding expedition, or in his subsequent treachery: but when we look back over two centuries, from the time we have now reached to the days of Cyprian, or over one century to the courtly theologian-disputants who hurried to the numberless councils of Constantius, and compare them with this mitred combatant, we feel that we have already passed from Ancient History into the Middle Ages: we might imagine ourselves standing before the warrior bishop of Beauvais, or one of the robber-bishops of the Rhine.

The Vases of Sirmium.

Out of the invasion, for which the fall of Margus gave the signal, another ecclesiastical complication, this time not with the Eastern but the Western Empire, took its rise. The town of Sirmium on the Save, situated in what is now the Austrian province of Sclavonia, though it has left no modern representative of its former glories, was once one of the most important cities of Pannonia. The bishop of Sirmium, seeing his city invested by the Hunnish army, gathered together the chalices and patens and other sacred vessels of his church, all of gold, and apparently of considerable value, and contrived to send them secretly to one Constantius, a Gaul, who was at that time officiating as Attila's secretary. The object of the trust hereby created was to liberate the bishop if he should survive the capture of the city, or if he should die, then to ransom as many as possible of the citizens. The city was taken, and what became of the bishop we know not; but Constantius, ignoring the trust reposed in him, went off to Rome on private business, and there pawned the golden chalices for a large sum of money to a silversmith, named Silvanus[1]. Meanwhile his masters, Attila and Bleda, who probably did not like this journey to Rome on urgent private affairs, came to the conclusion that their secretary was playing the traitor, and soon after Constantius's return, he was crucified. Some time afterwards, the story of the embezzlement of the golden chalices came to the ears of Attila, and filled him with wrath. 'Had my secretary,' said he, 'not deposited these chalices at Rome, they would have come into *my* possession on the death of the swindler. Silvanus therefore has really stolen my property, and unless the Emperor of the West can restore the chalices, I insist that he shall surrender Silvanus to my vengeance.' How the affair, which dragged on for many years, at length terminated we know not, but we shall meet hereafter with an embassy from Valentinian III commissioned to treat on this important subject.

Three years after these events Bleda died, and Attila became sole ruler of the Huns. Historians have accepted, perhaps too readily, a version of the story which attributes to the great Hun the guilt of fratricide, not in passion, but with premeditation and

442.

445.
Death of
Bleda.

---

[1] This Silvanus held some official position, but what, it is difficult to say. He was 'President of the Board of Silver at Rome.' This may mean either that he was a *Praepositus Argentariorum*, or *Primicerius Scrinii ab Argento*, probably the latter. (See Notitia Dignitatum, Occidens, cap. x.)

cunning. With all his vices, treachery and secret assassination scarcely seem consonant with the rest of his character [1].

447.
Attila lays
waste the
Empire up
to the walls
of Constan-
tinople. In the year 447, Attila led his barbarian warriors on the most formidable of all his expeditions against the Eastern Empire. No detailed account of it has been preserved, but it is evident that no inroad of so destructive a kind had pierced the provinces between the Adriatic and the Aegean since Alaric met Stilicho in the Peloponnesus. The Huns pushed southwards as far as Thermopylae, and eastwards to the shore of the Dardanelles, where, at Gallipoli, they inflicted a disastrous defeat on the Roman troops [2]. The walls of Constantinople, on this occasion as on so many subsequent ones, saved the very existence of the Empire. But though the tide of barbarian invasion rolled back into its old bed when there was nothing more left to ravage in the open country, a panic fear seized the rulers of the state, who submitted with abject eagerness to every demand which their Master, for such they now considered him, might please to make upon them. Anatolius, a man of high rank who had held the office, still regarded with some of its old veneration, of Roman Consul, was sent to Attila's camp to negotiate

---

[1] Marcellinus and Jordanes, the chief authorities for the story of the fratricide, were separated by an interval of nearly a century from the event. On the other hand Priscus, the contemporary and guest of the king, speaks of Bleda's death (τὴν τοῦ Βλήδα τελευτήν) casually and calmly, and does not hint at any tragedy connected with it. But it is true that only fragments of his history remain.

[2] It need hardly be observed that, in the language of the historians of the time, the inhabitants of Thrace, of Syria, and of Egypt are still as uniformly spoken of under the name of Romans as those who were born and died by the banks of the Tiber.

terms of peace. The yearly tribute, which had been
doubled at Attila's succession, was now tripled, and
stood at £84,000, and at the same time £240,000 in
gold were handed over as a settlement of past arrears.
In order to raise this sum, all the usual fiscal expedients
of a weak, yet tyrannical government were resorted to.
To have the reputation of wealth was the surest pass-
port to misery. Each senator was assessed upon a
certain sum, often greatly in excess of his real fortune;
but the amount which stood opposite to his name had
to be provided, whether he possessed it or not. Blows
and insults enforced the demands of the officers of the
Imperial Exchequer, and the upshot of the whole was
that in some cases the family jewels of ladies of high
rank, or the articles of household furniture of men
who had passed all their lives in affluence, were exposed for sale in the market-place; while in other yet
more desperate cases, the unhappy Roman noble escaped
by the aid of a cord, or by the slower process of self-
starvation, into a land whither even the ministers of
Theodosius could not follow him. And all this time
the misery of the situation was aggravated by the
thought that while the defence of the country was
neglected, and, in consequence, these frightfully heavy
subsidies had to be paid to her invaders, 'the country's
wealth and the royal treasures were being applied, not
to their proper uses, but to ridiculous shows, tawdry
pageants, and all the pleasures and all the extrava-
gances of sensuality, such as no sensible man would
have wasted money upon, even had the state been in
the height of prosperity. Far less ought these men
to have thus acted, who had so far neglected the
military art that not only the Huns, but all the other

447.
Extortions
practised
to raise
the tribute.

barbarous tribes round had bound the Roman State to
the payment of tribute [1].'

447.
Attila's op-
pressive
embassies.

The ruler of the Huns marked well the abject terror
of the Byzantine Court, and traded upon it with the
low cunning of a savage. Scarcely had the treaty of
Anatolius been concluded, when Attila sent ambassadors
to Theodosius, demanding, in the usual formula, 'the
surrender of the fugitives.' The Roman Emperor could
only reply, ' We have surrendered all who were in our
power ; ' but in order to secure powerful friends in the
Hunnish encampment, he not only treated the ambassadors with splendid hospitality, but loaded them with
rich presents on their departure. Again, and again,
and again, four times in the space of a twelvemonth,
did Attila repeat this process, selecting always for his
ambassador some needy favourite whom he had a desire
to enrich, and inventing such ridiculous pretexts for his
embassies that all could see his real motive in sending
them. This plan of pacific invasion began to tire out
the patience of the meek Emperor and his ministers.
His sister Pulcheria no longer now exercised a predominant influence in the affairs of state. Theological
discussions seem to have divided the Imperial pair.
She adhered to that side which was eventually, at the
Council of Chalcedon, decreed to be the side of or-

Ascend-
ancy of
Chrysa-
phius.

thodoxy ; while the rival, and now reigning influence
at court was that of the eunuch Chrysaphius, godson
and partisan of Eutyches, the fanatic asserter of the
absolute oneness of the nature of Christ even during
the time of his Incarnation. Judging by the acts of
Chrysaphius, we may safely conclude that any opinion
of his on such a question was as valuable as the opinion

[1] Priscus, p. 142 (Bonn edition, 1829).

of an Australian savage concerning the philosophy of Plato.

In the year 448, yet another embassy arrived at Constantinople, more famous and more fateful than any which had preceded it. Let us observe well the names of the two chief ambassadors, for these are men who either by themselves or by their offspring will make a deep and ineffaceable mark on the history of their time. *Edecon* is introduced to us as a 'Scythian,' that is, a Hun[1], 'who had accomplished mighty deeds in war.' He was evidently also one of the most intimate coun- sellors of Attila. No small degree of jealousy existed between him and his colleague *Orestes*. This man, as we might have inferred from his name, was not of barbarian extraction. He was of 'Roman' descent (a term which is of course consistent with any provincial nationality within the limits of the Roman Empire), and 'he dwelt in that part of Pannonia which borders on the Save,' that is to say, within the limits of the modern Austrian province of Sclavonia. He was at this time a regular subject of Attila, his country, which was included in the Western Emperor's share of Illyri- cum, having recently been ceded by Aetius to the Huns. He married the daughter of a certain Count Romulus, who dwelt at Patavio in Noricum, the place which is now called Passau[2], and which marks the junction of

448.
Embassy of Edecon and Orestes.

Orestes father of Augus- tulus.

---

[1] As before remarked, the term Scythian, as used by the Greek historians, is of no ethnological value whatever. In classical times it meant probably sometimes Sclavonic tribes, sometimes a race with Thracian affinities. Zosimus uses it regularly of the Goths, and now, in Priscus, it is the accepted equivalent for the Huns. Probably it was not intended to mean more than 'the barbarians (of whatever race) living north of the Danube and the Euxine.'

[2] This seems the most probable equivalent of 'Patavio, a city of

the mountain-nourished Inn with the more placid Danube. From this marriage was born to Orestes, probably about ten years after the date at which we have now arrived, a son who was named after his maternal grandfather Romulus, and upon whom history has fastened the unkind nickname of Augustulus. The other ambassador, Edecon, was probably already the father of a son whom he had named Odovacar (Odoacer). These two ambassadors, on arriving at the Imperial Court, presented the letters of their lord, in which, as usual, he expressed his high displeasure at the conduct of the Romans with reference to the refugees. War, immediate war, was threatened unless these were surrendered. Further, there must be no attempt on the part of the Romans to cultivate the district which would in later times have been called the March of the Danube. This was a belt of territory about 100 miles[1] wide on the southern side of the great stream, which Attila claimed to have annexed by right of conquest after his recent campaign. If this condition were not observed, war. The position of the great market for

448.

Edecon father of Odovacar.

Attila's demands.

Noricum' (Priscus, 185, 22). We know that its ancient name was 'Batava Castra,' from the Ninth Batavian Cohort being stationed there, and that in the ninth century (or earlier) it was called Pattavia, whence the modern Passau (see Böcking's Notitia, 784). Poetovio, the modern Pettau, in Styria, would have seemed more likely to be the place, except that it was not in Noricum but in Pannonia.

[1] Its width was 'five days' journey for a well-trained pedestrian' (εὐζώνῳ ἀνδρί). This certainly would not mean less than twenty miles a day. It was to reach from Pannonia (now Attila's by treaty with Aetius) on the West to Novae, now Sistova, in Bulgaria on the East. Eastward of Novae probably commenced the territory of the imperfectly subdued Acatziri. The dimension of the March from West to East would be about 300 miles.

the interchange of Roman and Hunnish commodities
must be shifted. It had been fixed at Margus, on the
Danube; now it was to be at Naissus, the modern
Nisch, 150 miles up the Morava, in Servia. And, lastly,
ambassadors were to be sent to Attila, to talk over the
points in dispute; and these were to be no men of
second-rate position in the state, but men who had sat
in the curule chair of the consuls, and the most eminent
even among them. If these high dignitaries were
afraid to undertake so long and wild a journey, he, the
great king, would condescend to come as far as Sardica
to meet them. Such was the imperious mandate of
Attila, uttered by the lips of Edecon, and translated by
the interpreter Vigilas to him, who was saluted by the
names, once so mighty, Imperator and Augustus.
Edecon then went to the house of Chrysaphius to confer
with that minister as to the subject of his embassy.
On his way he said to the interpreter, Vigilas, ' How
beautiful is the Emperor's palace, how richly adorned
with all precious things, and how happy must be the
lives of the lords of such magnificence.' Vigilas repeated the remark to Chrysaphius, and with the words
a wicked thought entered the mind of the Monophysite
eunuch. He said to Edecon, ' You, too, might sit
under gilded ceilings [1] of your own, and be lord of vast
wealth, if you would leave the party of the Huns and
take up ours.'

Edecon. ' I could not do that, being another man's
servant, without my lord's consent.'

448.

Conversation between Chrysaphius and Edecon.

---

[1] Compare Horace,   ' Non ebur neque *aureum*
                          Mea renidet in domo *lacunar*,'
and his favourite phrase ' *laqueata tecta.*'

448.

Chrysaphius. 'Have you free access to your lord's person?'

Edecon. 'Yes. I am one of the nobles selected for the purpose of keeping watch in arms over his person. We serve for so many days and then are relieved.'

Chrysaphius. 'If you will promise secrecy, I can tell you something very greatly to your advantage. Come to dine with me, without Orestes and your other colleagues, and we can talk the matter over at our leisure.'

Assassination plot hatched.

So a secret meeting was arranged at the house of the eunuch, and there in the presence and by the assistance of Vigilas, evidently a Byzantine *dragoman* of the worst type, a vile plot was hatched. Chrysaphius first swore that what he had to say should in no case injure Edecon. Edecon swore a counter oath that he would not reveal, even if he could not accomplish, the designs of the minister; and then Chrysaphius at length uttered the fatal secret. 'If when you return to Scythia you will slay Attila and then come to us, you shall have a happy life here and vast wealth.'

Edecon. 'I promise to do so. But I shall want some small sum of money to be paid me in advance, say about fifty pounds of gold [£2000], in order to ensure the co-operation of the common soldiers under my command.'

Chrysaphius. 'There will be no difficulty about that. You shall have the money at once.'

Edecon. 'No, I will not take it at once, for Attila will ask me on my return, as he asks all his ambassadors, how much the mission has been worth to me; and I could not deceive him because all my colleagues will know what weight of gold I am carrying back.

You must let me return to report the answer of your master as to the refugees, and Vigilas must come with me to receive the rejoinder of mine. Then, through Vigilas, I will send you word how the rest of the gold (beyond the ordinary gratuity to an ambassador) had better be sent to me.'

448.

This plan met with the full approval of the eunuch, who, as soon as he had dismissed his guest, hurried away to the palace to inform Theodosius of the new prospect of an early termination of Attila's embassies. The Imperial Calligrapher, the Illuminator of Sacred Manuscripts, at once accepted the proposal, and calling in Martialius, the *Magister Officiorum*, and chief of what we should call ' the Secret Service Department,' consulted with him what shape the return embassy to Attila should now assume. Of a truth many things were changed, and not altogether for the better, since the Consul Fabricius handed over to Pyrrhus the traitor, who proposed to purchase the favour of Rome by administering poison to his master.

The plot communicated to Theodosius.

In order to cloak the atrocious scheme thus concocted, the Emperor and his minister decided to send to the coast of Attila a sham embassy, in whose train the intending murderers might travel unsuspected, regardless, of course, of the danger to which they exposed the innocent envoy, who in the event of the plot being discovered was likely to plead in vain the sanctity of an ambassador's person. The man selected for this post was Maximin, an officer of high, but not the highest, rank, and of illustrious lineage, but whose name had not figured in the Consular Fasti. He invited Priscus ' the sophist,' or, as we should say, professor of rhetoric and man of letters, to accompany him, and it is to the

To be carried into effect by a sham embassy

on which Maximin is sent.

diary[1] of the embassy kept by Priscus, and afterwards
interwoven by him into his history, that we are indebted for almost all trustworthy details of the Court
and Camp of Attila. He assures us emphatically, and
the whole course of the history tends to confirm his
statement, that the murder-secret was not confided
either to him or to his patron, but that the ostensible
object of their mission was to them the real one. As
both Maximin and Priscus seem still to have adhered
to the worship of the Olympian divinities, we are
driven, however reluctantly, to the conclusion that by
this time the traitors, the time-servers, and the hypocrites had ranged themselves on the side of successful
Christianity, and that when the Emperor wanted a man
of indisputably high character and sterling honesty to
mask by his innocence a dark and nefarious design, his
thoughts naturally turned to the few remaining Pagan
statesmen, who probably held at his court a position
not unlike that of the Roman Catholics under Queen
Elizabeth or the Huguenots under Louis XIII.

The message which was entrusted to Maximin was
couched in a less servile tone than the recent replies of
Theodosius. As if they already saw the knife of the
assassin piercing the heart of the great Hun, the
Emperor and the eunuch began to express their weariness of Attila's perpetual reclamations. 'You ought
not to overleap the obligations of treaties and invade
the Roman territory. As for fugitives, besides those
already surrendered, I now return you seventeen, and I

448.

Maximin
and Priscus
Pagans.

Stout
answer
sent to the
Hun.

---

[1] Many of the details which Priscus gives as to the movements of
the ambassadors are so unnecessarily minute as to suggest the conclusion that they were jotted down from day to day and almost from
hour to hour while the embassy was still proceeding.

really have no more.' So ran the letter. Verbally
Maximin was instructed to say that Attila must not
expect ambassadors of any higher rank than him who
now spoke to be sent to him, since this had not been
the usage with his own ancestors or any of the other
northern rulers, but the custom had hitherto been to
send any chance person, soldier or letter-carrier, whose
services were available. And as for the king's proposition to come and meet an ambassador of consular rank
at Sardica, he himself had made that impossible by his
sack of that very town. Such was the contemptuous
reply of the Byzantine to the Hunnish court as it was
intended to have been delivered ; but not such was the
actual message which reached the ears of Attila ; for,
as we shall see, like good wine it mellowed considerably
on the journey.

The first fortnight of travel seems to have been
pleasant and uneventful enough. During all this time
the Roman and barbarian ambassadors were passing
through the comparatively tranquil and prosperous
province of Thrace. At the end of it they reached
Sardica, about 350 miles from Constantinople, and the
first city of 'Dacia Mediterranea.' This was the place
at which almost exactly a century before (343) the
celebrated council had been held which enunciated again
the Nicene Creed, and gave to the See of Rome the
right of deciding whether a bishop had been lawfully
deposed. Other matters, however, than theological
wrangles had of late forced themselves on the attention
of the unhappy inhabitants of Sardica. As we have
just heard from the lips of Theodosius, the town had
been terribly pillaged and laid waste by Attila. The
destruction, however, was not complete. There were

448.

Constanti-
nople to
Sardica.

448.

still houses and some inhabitants from whom it was possible for the ambassadors to buy sheep and oxen. These they killed and roasted; and having prepared a goodly repast, they thought it would be but courteous to ask Edecon and the barbarians attending him to **Brawl at the banquet.** partake with them. As they sat long over the meal, conversation turned upon the greatness and majesty of their respective masters. The Huns, of course, magnified the might of Attila; the Romans tried to extol their great Augustus. At this point of the conversation, Vigilas, with an indiscretion which can only be accounted for by supposing that he had plied the wine-cup too freely, said, 'I cannot think it right to compare gods and men together. Attila, after all, is but a man, while Theodosius I look upon as a god.' At these words the Huns started up with flushed cheeks and angry eyes; and the pleasant diplomatic banquet was on the point of ending in bloodshed. Priscus and Maximin however succeeded in silencing their noisy colleague, guided the conversation into safer channels, and by their civility mollified the wrath of the Huns. That there might be no chance of any rancorous feeling remaining in their minds, Maximin, when the banquet was over, made handsome presents, both to Edecon and Orestes, of silken raiment and 'Indian jewels[1].'

Dark words of Orestes. The bestowal of these presents led to another curious outburst of angry feeling. Orestes sat out all his companions, and when they were gone came up to Maximin and thanked him heartily for his presents. 'You,' said he, 'are a wise man, of a most excellent disposition. You are not like those insolent courtiers at Byzantium, who gave presents and invitations to

---

[1] Were these diamonds, or pearls?

Edecon but none to me.' 'When? where? how?' gasped out the puzzled ambassador; but Orestes, vouchsafing no more particular statement of his griev- 448. ances, stalked moodily out of the room.

Next day, on the journey, Maximin and Priscus re- Social position of the Hun and the Roman. ported this strange conversation to Vigilas. He, of course, knew well enough to what it referred, but did not choose to explain. He only said, 'Orestes has no business to be offended. He is but a secretary, a mere squire of Attila : Edecon is of course differently treated. He is a great warrior and a Hun by birth, and far superior in position to the other.' Already then, in the estimation of a Byzantine dragoman, to be 'a Hun by birth' was a higher position than that of a well-born Roman provincial. Vigilas afterwards repeated this conversation to Edecon and had much difficulty, so he told his companions, in soothing the barbarian's resentment against the pretensions of Orestes to be put on an equality with him.

A further hundred miles of travel brought the am- Sardica to Naissus. bassadors to Naissus (now Nisch, on the confines of Servia), and here they found such traces of the ravage of the Hun as his Turkish kinsman has often in later days left behind him in the same regions. A city utterly empty of inhabitants, in the churches a few sick folk too weak to fly, every place down to the river's bank full of human bones and skulls : that is how the Turanian leaves his mark. 'But we found,' says Priscus, with simplicity, 'a clean spot a little above the river, and there we rested for the night.'

Near to this city, which had become a tomb, lay the Fugitives surrendered. Imperial 'army of Illyricum,' under the command of the General-in-chief, Agintheus. Five out of the

seventeen fugitives, whom Theodosius had promised to
surrender to Attila, were there, imagining themselves

448.   safe under the shelter of the eagles.   But the Emperor's
orders were clear.   The Roman General had to give up
the five suppliants to the Roman ambassador for him to
hand over to the Hunnish king.   Agintheus spoke
kindly[1] to them ; but as they knew, in all probability,
that they were going to a death of torture, kind words
from the ghost of the old Roman war-wolf were not
much to the purpose.

Attila's
hunting.   At length the ambassadors reached the shores of the
Danube.   The roads leading down to the river were
crowded with Huns; and ferrymen were plying across
the stream in their uncouth boats, each made of a single
tree roughly hollowed out.   They were thus without
delay transported to the northern bank of the river ;
but if they had supposed that all this stir was made in
expectation of their own arrival they were soon un-
deceived.   The barbarian king had announced that he
meant to cross over into the Romans' land to hunt, and
the expectation of his coming had caused this stir
among his subjects.   Like the Percy's ' Hunting of the
Cheviot,' Attila's hunting meant war, war over the
endless grievance of the unsurrendered refugees.   It
was in fact the barbarian's device to accomplish what
the modern strategist calls ' Mobilisation.'

Insolence
of the Bar-
barians.   On the second day after crossing the Danube, the
Roman party came in sight of the numerous tents of
Attila, and were about to pitch their own on a hill-top
near.   But this the Huns around them would by no
means permit : ' they must come down and pitch their
tents in the plain : it would be quite improper for the

[1] φιλοφρονησάμενος.

Roman ambassador to occupy the hill while Attila was below in the valley.' When this difficulty was settled, the Romans, as it was still early afternoon, expected doubtless an audience that day with Attila. Instead of this, however, several of the Hunnish nobility came, together with Edecon and Orestes, to their tent, and demanded to know the tenour of their message to the king. Naturally the ambassadors replied that their commission was for Attila alone, and they would disclose it to no other person. At that reply, Scotta, one of the Hunnish magnates, burst out with a passionate question, 'Do you take us for busybodies, who came here out of our own prying curiosity? Attila sent us, and we must have your answer.' The ambassadors firmly declined, pleading the invariable usage of their profession. Whereupon the Huns galloped away, and soon returned, ominous exception, without Edecon. 'Your commission,' said they, 'to our king is so and so; such concessions about refugees, such messages about future ambassadors. Deny that this is the purport of your instructions if you can. If you have nothing to add to this, return at once to your own country.' In vain did the Romans try to maintain the proper official reserve and refuse to say whether this was indeed a true summary of their instructions or not. Their faces doubtless showed that the arrow had hit the mark : the barbarians' version of their commission was correct in the smallest particulars, and to all further protestations of the Romans the Huns had but one reply continually repeated, 'Begone directly.'

Maximin and Priscus were bewildered, as well they might be, by this strange innovation on the customs of diplomacy. Vigilas, who knew that for his part, the

448.

darker part of the enterprise, access to the court of
Attila and some days' sojourn there were essential,
bitterly complained of his colleagues' truthfulness.
'They might have vamped up some other matter, and
declared that the Huns had not revealed the whole of
the commission. It would have been better to be detected eventually in a falsehood, than to return without
even seeing Attila.'

Little did the false interpreter guess upon what a
volcano he himself was standing. The true cause of
Attila's strange demeanour was that Edecon had revealed the plot. Either he had only feigned compliance
from the first—the more probable supposition—or else
that wild conversation at Sardica and the tidings which
Vigilas himself had brought him, of the rage and
jealousy of Orestes, had satisfied him that the risk was
too great to run, with such an unwise person as the interpreter for confederate, and with such an angry rival
as the secretary for spy on his movements. And therefore, at the very first opportunity when he found
himself alone with Attila, he rehearsed to him the
whole plan for his intended assassination, and at the
same time furnished him with the particulars of the
intended Roman reply, which Edecon had, no doubt,
received from Chrysaphius.

It was night when the party of the ambassadors
received their peremptory orders to depart. With
heavy hearts they were watching their attendants
loading the beasts of burden, when they received
another message, giving them an ungracious permission
to remain where they were till daybreak. A present
of an ox for roasting, and some fish, salted, no doubt, as
it came from the Euxine, attested the surly hospitality

448.

The plot
revealed
by Edecon
to Attila.

Priscus
makes
friends
with
Scotta.

of Attila.   Next morning, they thought, 'Surely some
act of kindness and gentleness will now be shown to us
by the barbarian.'   But no : there came only the same
harsh command, 'Begone, if you have no other commission to unfold.'   Hereupon Priscus, seeing the deep
dejection of his patron, resolved to try what prayers
and promises could accomplish with one of Attila's
ministers.   His chief minister, Onégesh, who was well-
known by the Romans, and on the whole favourably inclined towards them, was absent ; but Scotta, the
brother of Onégesh, was in the Hunnish camp, and to
him Priscus betook himself, using another interpreter
than Vigilas.   He enlarged on the advantages to the
two nations, but still more to the house of Onégesh,
which would result from the peaceful outcome of the
negotiations, on the presents which were in store for
Onégesh at Constantinople, and on those which Maximin
would immediately bestow on Scotta.   And finally, he
wound up with a diplomatic appeal to the vanity of the
Hun.   'I have heard,' said he, 'that Attila pays great
deference to the advice of Scotta, but I shall never
believe it if you cannot accomplish so small a matter as
to obtain for us this interview.'   'Doubt not that I can
do it,' he answered : 'my influence with the king is
just as great as my brother's.'   And with that he
mounted his horse and galloped off to the king's tent.
The faithful Priscus returned to his master, who was
lying on the grass with Vigilas, while again the packing
of the horses was going forward.   As soon as they
heard of the slight hope which had arisen, and of the
influence which Priscus had brought to bear on the
mind of Attila, they sprang to their feet, and while
warmly commending the sophist for his happy inspira-

448.

tion, began to discuss what they should say to the king,
and how the presents of Theodosius and of Maximin
himself should be offered for his acceptance.

448.

An inter-
view
granted.

Soon Scotta returned and escorted them to the royal
tent. 'When we obtained admittance,' says Priscus,
'we found the monarch seated on a wooden stool[1]. We
stood a little way off from the throne, but Maximin
went forward, and after making obeisance to the barbarian, and handing him the emperor's letter, said, "Our
Sovereign prays for the safety of thyself and all around
thee." Attila answered, " May the Romans receive
exactly what they desire for me." Then, turning sharp
round to Vigilas, " Shameless beast ! " he said, " How
have you dared to come to me, knowing, as you do right
well, the terms of peace which I settled with you and
Anatolius ; and how I then said that no more ambassadors were to come to me till all the fugitives were
given up." When Vigilas replied that the Romans no
longer had with them any refugees of Scythian origin,
since we had surrendered all that were with us, Attila
grew still more furious, and shouted out with a loud
voice every opprobrious epithet that he could think of ;
" I would impale you," he roared out, " and leave you as
food for vultures, if it were not for your sacred character
of envoy, which I would not seem to outrage, fitting as
the punishment would be for your impudence and your
reckless falsehoods. As for Scythian refugees, there are
still many among the Romans." And here he bade his
secretaries read out their names, inscribed on a roll of
paper. When they had rehearsed them all, he bid
Vigilas depart without delay. With him was to go
Eslas the Hun, commissioned to order the Romans to

[1] δίφρος. Perhaps something like the *sella curulis* of the Romans.

restore all the fugitives who had gone over to them
from the days of Carpilio, son of Aetius, who was sent
as a hostage to his court, and had escaped. "For," 448.
continued Attila, "I will never endure that my own
servants should come forth and meet me in battle, all
useless though they may be to help those with whom
they have taken refuge, and who entrust to them the
guardianship of their own land. For what city, or
what fortress has any of these men been able to defend
when I have determined on its capture?"'

After this outburst the king condescended to accept Presents accepted.
the presents which Maximin had brought, and then he
repeated his commands as to the future conduct of the
negotiations. Having satisfied himself, probably, in the
course of this interview that Maximin was an honest
man, and guiltless of any complicity in the design
against his life, he felt that he could safely indulge in
the pleasures which such an embassy brought to him—
gifts for himself, gifts for his dependents, and the grati-
fication of trampling on the pride of Rome by exhibiting
the Imperial ambassadors as frightened suppliants for
his favour. All, therefore, except Vigilas, received
orders to repair to his palace in the interior, and there
to wait for the written reply which he would send to
Theodosius.

Vigilas, on the other hand, whose presence doubtless Vigilas remanded to Constantinople.
suggested, even to the brave Hun, uncomfortable
thoughts of midnight alarms and the assassin's dagger,
was ordered to return at once to Constantinople with
the routine message and menace concerning the refugees.
Eslas went with him as a spy on his movements:
Edecon visited him immediately after the interview in
the royal tent, to assure him that he was still true to

448.

the plot, and to press him to bring back the promised gold. At the same time, with considerable ingenuity, Attila issued a proclamation, ' forbidding Vigilas to purchase any Roman captive or barbarian slave, or horses, or anything else but necessary food until the differences between the Romans and Huns should be arranged.' The effect of this proclamation was to deprive Vigilas of any plausible pretext for bringing back any large amount of gold from Constantinople. If, notwithstanding this prohibition, he still brought gold with him, that gold could only be the blood-money of Attila.

Maximin and Priscus in the heart of Hunland.

There is no need to trace the return of the base and blundering Vigilas to Constantinople, whither he went still entirely unwitting that Attila had sapped below his mine. We follow honest Maximin and his friend as they journey northwards into the recesses of Hungary. For a certain distance they travelled in the train of the Barbarian ; then they received orders to turn off into another road. Attila was about to visit a certain village, and there add to his numerous harem another wife, the daughter of one Escam [1]; and apparently he did not choose that the courtly Byzantines should look on the rude wedding festivities of a Hunnish polygamist. The ambassadors had to cross three large rivers in the course of their journey. The names of these rivers are not easy to recognise, but they may possibly be repre-

---

[1] Some authors understand that the new bride's name was Escam, and that she was herself Attila's daughter. But the Greek does not absolutely require this interpretation, and if it had been correct, such an incestuous union would probably have called forth stronger comment on the part of Priscus. His words are—ἐν ᾗ γαμεῖν θυγατέρα Ἐσκὰμ ἐβούλετο, πλείστας μὲν ἔχων γαμετάς, ἀγόμενος δὲ καὶ ταύτην κατὰ νόμον τὸν Σκυθικόν.

sented by the Drave, the Temes, and the Theiss. They
crossed them, as before, in tree-trunk boats ; while, for
the smaller streams and the marshes, they availed
themselves of the convenient rafts which the Huns
always carried about with them on their waggons in all
their journeys through that often inundated country.
They were kindly entertained in the Hunnish villages,
and received such provisions as the inhabitants had to
offer ; no wheat, indeed, but millet, for food, and for
drink *medus* and *camus*, two beverages which seem to
correspond to our mead and beer.

One night, after a long day's march, they pitched
their tent beside a lake which offered them the advantage of good and sweet water. 'Suddenly,' said
Priscus, 'there arose a great storm of wind, accompanied by thunderings and frequent flashes of light-
ning and torrents of rain. Our tent was blown down,
and all our travelling furniture was rolled over and
over into the waters of the lake. Terrified by this
accident and by the din of the storm which filled all the
air, we left the spot and soon wandered away from each
other, everyone taking what he supposed to be the
right road. At length, by different paths, we all
reached the neighbouring village, and turned in to the
huts for shelter. Then, with loud outcry, we began in-
quiring into our losses. Roused by our clamour, the
Scythians started up, kindled the long reeds which
serve them for candles, and which threw a good light
upon the scene, and then asked us what on earth we
wanted that we were making such an uproar. The
barbarians who were with us explained how we had
been thrown into confusion by the storm, whereupon
they kindly called us into their houses, and by lighting

448.

The storm
by the
lake.

a very great number of torches did something to warm us.

'The chieftainess of the village, who was one of the wives of Bleda [Attila' brother], sent us a supply of food, of which we gladly partook. Next morning, at daybreak, we set about searching for our camp furniture, and were fortunate enough to find it all, some in the place where we pitched our tents, some on the shore, and some in the lake itself, from which we succeeded in fishing it up. The whole of that day we spent in the village, drying our things, for the storm had now ceased and the sun was shining brightly. After attending to our beasts, we visited the queen, saluted her respectfully, and repaid her for her hospitality with presents. These were three silver bowls, some red skins, Indian pepper [1], dates, and other articles of food, which the barbarians prize as foreign to their climate. Then we wished her health and happiness in return for her hospitality to us, and so we departed.'

Meeting
of Eastern
and
Western
Ambassa-
dors.

At length, after seven days' journey, they reached a village, where they were ordered to stop. Their road here joined that by which the royal bridegroom would be approaching, and they were not to presume to proceed till Attila should have gone before them. In the little village where they were thus detained they met some unexpected companions. Primutus [2], the Roman governor of Noricum, Count Romulus of Passau, the father-in-law of Orestes, and Romanus, a general of legionaries, with probably a long train of attendants,

---

[1] It will be remembered that both these two kinds of goods, red skins and pepper, figured forty years before this in the ransom which Alaric exacted from Rome.

[2] Possibly a mistake for Promotus.

were already testing, perhaps somewhat severely, the resources and accommodation of the Hunnish village. They, too, had come on an embassy : they represented the Emperor of the West, and it is needless to say that the subject which they had come to discuss was that interminable one, the sacred vases of Sirmium. The father of Orestes, and Constantius the Roman secretary of Attila, journeyed, in an unofficial capacity, with the ambassadors. It was certainly a striking scene : the ambassadors from Ravenna and Constantinople, the representatives of the dignity of the two Imperial courts, the functionaries who between them could set forth the whole majesty that might still survive in the title *Senatus Populus Que Romanus*, meeting in a dingy little village in Hungary, and waiting with abject sub- mission till a snub-nosed Kalmuck should ride past and contemptuously toss them a permission to follow in his train. It is difficult to resist the conclusion that Attila, who had a genius for scenic effect in the enhancement of his glory, not unlike that which our century has witnessed in the Napoleons, had purposely arranged this confluence of the two embassies, and partly for this cause had invited Maximin to follow him into Hungary.

After crossing a few more rivers, the united embassies came in sight of the village in which was situated the palace of Attila. Students have discussed whether this Hunnish capital is represented by the modern city of Pesth, by Tokay, or by some other less-known name ; but we may dismiss with absolute indifference the inquiry in what particular part of a dreary and treeless plain a barbarian king reared his log-huts, of which probably, twenty years after his death, not a vestige remained.

448.

As Attila entered the village he was met by a procession of maidens in single file wearing linen veils, thin
and white, and so long that under each veil, held up as
it was by the hands of the women on either side of the
path, seven maidens or more were able to walk. There
were many of these sets of girls, each set wearing one
veil ; and as they walked they sang national songs in
honour of the king. The last house which he reached
before his own was that of his favourite and chief
minister Onégesh [1], and as he passed it the wife of the
owner came forth with a multitude of attendants bearing food and wine—'the highest honour,' says Priscus,
'which one Scythian can pay to another'—saluted
him, and begged him to partake of the repast which
she had provided as a token of her loyalty. The king,
wishing to gratify the wife of his most trusted counsellor, partook accordingly, without dismounting from his
horse, his attendants holding high before him the silver
table on which the banquet was spread. Having eaten
and drunk he rode on to his palace.

This edifice, the finest in all the country round, stood
on a little hill, and seemed to dominate the whole
settlement. Yet it was in truth, as has been already

---

[1] Priscus calls him Onegesius, and Thierry remarks, 'Onégèse dont
le nom grec indiquait l'origine,' vol. i. p. 98. But everything seems
to show that Onegesius was a pure Hun. His brother's name was
Scotta. The dialogue at Sardica, in which Vigilas compared the
positions of Edecon the Hun and Orestes the Roman provincial, shows
how impossible it would have been for any but a full-blooded barbarian to attain to the rank which Onegesius held. And the name of
Oebar*sius*, Attila's paternal uncle, recorded by Priscus (p. 208, ed.
Bonn), shows his habit of Grecising the names of undoubted Huns.
We may therefore conclude that Onegesius is the similarly Grecised
form of some such name as Onégesh, by which it seems better to call
him in order to mark his barbarian origin.

said, only a log-hut of large dimensions. Externally it
seems that it was built of half-trunks of trees, round
side outwards, and within, it was lined with smoothly-
planed planks. Round the enclosure in which the
dwellings of the king and his wives were placed ran a
wooden palisading, for ornament, not defence ; and the
top of the palace was fashioned into the appearance of
battlements. Next to the king's house in position, and
only second to it in size, rose the dwelling of Onégesh.
The only stone building in the place was a bath, which
Onégesh had built at a little distance from his palisading. The stone for this building had been brought
from quarries in the Roman province of Pannonia ;
and in fact all the timber used in the settlement had
been imported likewise, for in the vast and dreary plain
where the nomad nation had pitched its camp, not a
tree was growing, not a stone underlay it. With the
building of the bath of Onégesh a grim jest was connected. The architect, a Roman provincial, who had
been carried captive from Sirmium, hoped that his ingenuity would at least be rewarded by the boon of
freedom, if no other architect's commission was paid
him. But no such thoughts suggested themselves to
the mind of Onégesh. When he had completed his
task, the architect was rewarded by being turned into
bath-man, and had to wait upon his master and his
master's guests whensoever they had a mind for the
pleasures of the *sudatorium* and the *tepidarium*. Thus,
as Priscus remarks, with a hint, no doubt, at the personal uncleanliness of the Huns, the unhappy man of
science 'had prepared for himself unconsciously a worse
lot than that of ordinary servitude among the
Scythians.'

448.

The house
of the
Prime
Minister.

Onégesh himself, who was absent when Priscus sought an interview with his brother Scotta, had now returned to his master's court. He had been engaged in quelling the last remains of independence among the Acatziri, a people possibly of Slavonic origin, who dwelt on the Lower Danube. The Byzantine ministers had endeavoured to parry Attila's attack by stirring up some of the petty chieftains of this nation against him. But, with their usual tendency to blunder, they had sent their most costly and honourable presents to the wrong man, and consequently Curidach, the real head of the confederacy, having received only the second gift, called in the aid of Attila to avenge the insult and beat down the power of his associated kings. The Hun was nothing loth, and soon succeeded in quelling all opposition. He then invited Curidach to come and celebrate their joint triumph at his court; but that chieftain, suspecting that his benefactor's kindness was of the same nature as the promised boon of Polyphemus to Ulysses, 'I will eat Outis last [1],' courteously declined. 'It is hard,' he said, 'for a man to come into the presence of a god; and if it be not possible to look fixedly even at the orb of the sun, how shall Curidach gaze undistressed upon the greatest of gods?' The compliment served for the time, but Attila understood what it was worth, and at a convenient season sent his Grand Vizier, Onégesh, to dethrone Curidach and to proclaim the eldest son of Attila king of the Acatziri in his stead. From this expedition the Prime Minister had now just returned successful and in high favour with his master.

The ambassadors were hospitably entertained by the

448.
Onégesh's
campaign
against the
Acatziri.

[1] Odyssey, ix. 369.

wife and family of Onégesh. He himself had to wait
upon the king to report the success of his mission, and
the only drawback which had befallen his party, an
accident namely to the young prince, who had slipped
off his horse and fractured some of the bones of his
right hand. At nightfall Maximin pitched his tents
a little way off the enclosure of the royal dwellings,
and next morning he sent Priscus early to the house
of Onégesh with servants bearing presents both from
himself and from Theodosius. The zealous rhetorician
was actually up before the barbarian. The house was
still close barred and there was no sign of any one
stirring.

448.

While Priscus was waiting, and walking up and
down before the palisading which surrounded the house
of Onégesh, a man, with the dress and general appearance of a Hun, came up and saluted him with a well-
pronounced Greek χαῖρε ('How d'ye do?'). A Hun
speaking Greek was an anomaly which aroused all the
attention of the Sophist, for, as he says, 'though it is
true that this people, who are a kind of conglomerate
of nations, do sometimes affect the speech of the Goths,
or even that of the Italians, in addition to their own
barbarous language, they never learn Greek, except
indeed they be inhabitants of Thrace or Dalmatia, who
have been carried captive into the Hunnish territory.
And these captives or their offspring may be easily
known by their ragged garments and scabby heads,
and all the other tokens of their having changed their
condition for the worse. But this man seemed like a
flourishing Scythian, handsomely dressed, and having
his hair neatly clipped all round his head. So, returning his salutation, I asked him who he was, and

The Greek
who had
turned
Hun.

from what part of the world he had come into that barbarian land to adopt the Scythian life. "What has put it into your head to ask me such a question as that?" said he. "Your Greek accent," answered I. Then he laughed and said, "'Tis true I am of Greek parentage, and I came for purposes of trade to Viminacium, a city of Moesia, on the Danube" [about sixty miles below Belgrade]. "There I abode for a long time, and married a very wealthy wife. But on the capture of the city by the Huns I was stripped of all my fortune, and assigned as a slave to this very Onégesh before whose door you are standing. That is the custom of the Huns: after Attila has had his share, the chiefs of the nation are allowed to take their pick of the wealthiest captives, and so Onégesh chose me. Afterwards, having distinguished myself in some actions with the Romans and the Acatziri, I surrendered to my master all the spoils which I had taken in war, and thus, according to the law of the Scythians, I obtained my freedom. I married a barbarian wife, by whom I have children: I am admitted as a guest to the table of Onégesh, and I consider my present mode of life decidedly preferable to my past. For when war is over, the people of this country live like gentlemen, enjoying themselves to the full, and free from worry of any kind. But the people in Romanland are easily worsted in war, because they place their hopes of safety on others rather than themselves. Their tyrants will not allow them the use of arms, and the condition of those who are armed is even more dangerous, from the utter worthlessness of their generals, who have no notion of the art of War. Then, too, Peace has its injuries not less severe than War. Think

of all the cruelties practised by the collectors of the
revenue, the infamy of informers, and the gross in-
equalities in the administration of the laws.   If a rich   448.
man offends, he can always manage to escape punishment; but a poor man, who does not know how to
arrange matters, has to undergo the full penalty, unless
indeed he be dead before judgment is pronounced, which
is not unlikely, considering the intolerable length to
which lawsuits are protracted.   But what I call the
most shameful thing of all is that you have to pay
money in order to obtain your legal rights.   For a man
who has been injured cannot even get a hearing from
the court without first paying large fees to the judge
and the officials who serve him." '

In reply to this angry outburst, Priscus entered into Priscus's
a long and sophistical disquisition on the advantages of for the
Empire.
division of labour, the necessity that judges and bailiffs,
like men of other occupations, should live by their
calling, and so on.   It is easy to see that Priscus felt
himself to be talking as sagely as Socrates, upon whose
style his reply is evidently modelled; but that reply
has the fault so common with rhetoricians and diplomatists, of being quite up in the air, and having no
relation to the real facts of the case.   His conclusion
is the most interesting part of the speech : ' " As for the
freedom which you now enjoy, you may thank Fortune
for that and not your master, who sent you to war,
where you were likely to have been killed by the enemy
on account of your inexperience.   But the Romans
treat even their slaves better than this.   True, they
correct them, but only for their good as parents or
schoolmasters correct children, in order that they may
cease to do evil and behave as is suitable for persons

in their station.   The Roman master is not allowed, as the Hun is, to punish his slave so as to cause his death.   Besides, we have abundant legal provisions in favour of freedom, and this gift may be bestowed not only by men who are in the midst of life, but also by those who are on the point of death.   Such persons are allowed to dispose of their property as they please, and any directions of a dying man concerning the enfranchisement of his slaves are binding on his heirs." Thus I reasoned with him.   He burst into tears, and said, "The laws are beautiful, and the polity of the Romans is excellent; but the rulers are not like-minded with the men of old, and are pulling down the state into ruin."'

The interview with Onégesh.

By the time that this conversation was ended, the household of Onégesh had awoke, and the door was unbarred.   Priscus obtained an interview with the minister and delivered the presents, which were graciously received.   It is needless to transcribe the memoranda, almost tediously minute, which Priscus has kept of his various conversations.   The general drift of them was, on the Roman side, to press for an interview with the king of the Huns, and to urge Onégesh to undertake in person the return embassy, and win for himself eternal glory and much wealth by bringing his candid and impartial mind to bear upon the points in dispute, and settling them in favour of the Romans.   Onégesh indignantly repudiated the idea that any arguments of the Romans could ever induce him to betray his master, to forget his Scythian life, his wives, and his children, or to cease to consider servitude with Attila preferable to wealth among the Romans.   He could be far more useful to them, he said, by remaining at

Attila's court and mollifying his resentment against
their nation, than by coming to Byzantium and nego-
tiating a treaty which his master might very probably   448.
disavow. On the other hand, he pressed them repeatedly with the question, ' What man of consular dignity
will the Emperor send as ambassador ? ' The fact that
Maximin, a man who had never filled the office of
consul, should have been selected as envoy, evidently
rankled in the mind of the barbarian king, sensitive,
as all upstarts are, about his dignity. And at length,
Attila having named three, Nomus, Anatolius, and
Senator, any one of whom would be, in the language
of modern diplomacy, a *persona grata* at his court,
declared that he would receive no one else. The envoys
replied that to insist so strongly on the selection of
these three men would bring them into suspicion at
the Imperial Court; a charming piece of inconsistency
in the men who were constantly petitioning that Onégesh
and no one else might undertake the return embassy.
Attila answered moodily, ' If the Romans will not do as
I choose, I shall settle the points in dispute by war.'

While diplomacy was thus spinning her tedious web, Queen
Kreka's
the ambassadors saw some sights in the barbarian camp palace.
which deserved to be recorded by the careful pen of
the professor of rhetoric. One day he had an audience
of the Queen Kreka, the chief in dignity of the wives
of Attila, and mother of three of his sons. Her palace
was built of well-sawn and smoothly-planed planks,
' resting on the ends of logs [1].' Arches at certain
intervals, springing from the ground and rising to a
pretty considerable height, broke the flat surface of

---

[1] The meaning of this clause is not very clear.

448.

the wall[1]. Here Kreka was to be found, lying on a soft couch, and with the floor around her covered with smooth felts to walk upon. Carpets were evidently still an unwonted luxury in Hun-land. There was no trace of the Oriental seclusion of women in the palace of Kreka. A large number of men-servants stood in a circle round her, while her maids sat on the floor in front, and were busied in dying linen of various colours, intending afterwards to work it up into ornamental costumes of the barbarian fashion.

The King himself.

When Priscus had offered his gifts and emerged from the queen's dwelling, he heard a stir and a clamour, and saw a crowd of men hurrying to the door of Attila's palace. These were the signs that the king was coming forth, and the rhetorician obtained a good place to watch his exit. With a stately strut Attila came forth, looking this way and that. Then he stood with his favourite Onégesh in front of the palace, while all the multitude of his people who had disputes one with another came forward and submitted them to him for his decision. Having thus in true Oriental fashion administered justice 'in the gate,' he returned into the interior of his palace in order to give audience to some barbarian ambassadors who had just arrived at his court.

The Ambassadors of East and West compare notes.

Scarcely was this scene ended when Priscus fell in with the ambassadors of the Western Empire, with whom he naturally began to compare notes. 'Are you dismissed,' said they, 'or pressed to remain?' 'The very thing,' he answered, 'that I myself want to know;

---

[1] This seems to be the purport of the sentence: οἱ δὲ κύκλοι ἐκ τοῦ ἐδάφους ἀρχόμενοι ἐς ὕψος ἀνέβαινον μετρίως. But what part arches can have played in an architecture dealing only with planks and logs it is not easy to see.

and that keeps me all day hanging about near the palisading of Onégesh. Pray has Attila vouchsafed a gentle answer to your petition?' 'No; nothing will turn him from his purpose. He declares he will either have Silvanus or the sacred vessels, or else will make war.' Priscus then expressed his wonder at the folly of the barbarian; and Romulus, who was an old and experienced diplomatist, answered, 'His extraordinary good fortune and unbounded power have quite turned his head: so that he will listen to no argument which does not fall in with his own caprices. For no former ruler of Scythia or of any other land has ever achieved so much in so short a time as this man, who has made himself master of the islands in the ocean, and besides ruling all Scythia has forced even the Romans to pay him tribute.' Then Romulus proceeded to tell the story of Attila's intended Persian campaign, to which reference has already been made. The Byzantine ambassadors expressed their earnest desire that he would turn his arms against Persia and leave Theodosius alone; but Constantiolus, a Pannonian in the retinue of Romulus, replied that he feared if Attila did attack and overcome, as he assuredly would, the monarch of that country, 'he would become our lord and master instead of our friend. At present,' said he, 'Attila condescends to take gold from the Romans and call it *pay* for his titular office of General in the Roman armies. But should he subdue the Parthians, and Medes, and Persians, he would not endure to have the Roman Empire cutting in like a wedge between one part and another of his dominions, but would openly treat the two Emperors as mere lacqueys, and would lay upon them such commands as they would

448.

find absolutely intolerable. Already he has been heard to remark, testily, "The generals of Theodosius are but his servants, while my generals are as good as emperors of Rome." He believes also that there will be before long some notable increase of his power; and that the gods have signified this by revealing to him the sword of Mars, a sacred relic much venerated by the Huns, for many years hidden from their eyes, but quite lately re-discovered by the trail of the blood of an ox which had wounded its hoof against it, as it was sticking upright in the long grass [1].'

Such was the conversation between the representatives of Ravenna and Constantinople, amid the log-huts of the Hungarian plain. Later on in the same day they all received an invitation to be present at a banquet of the great conqueror.

'Punctually at three o'clock we, together with the ambassadors of the Western Romans, went to the dinner and stood on the threshold of Attila's palace. According to the custom of the country, the cup-bearers brought us a bowl of wine, that we might drink and pray for the good-luck of our host before sitting down. Having tasted the bowl, we were escorted to our seats. Chairs were ranged for the guests all round the walls. In the centre Attila reclined on a couch, and behind him a flight of steps led up to his bed, which, hidden by curtains of white linen and variegated stuffs tastefully arranged, looked like the nuptial bed, as the Greeks and Romans prepare it for a newly-wedded couple.

'The seat of honour on the right hand of Attila's

---

[1] Compare the worship of a naked sabre fixed hilt-downwards in the earth, as practised by the Alans (see p. 30).

couch, was occupied by Onégesh. We did not receive
even the second place, that on his left, but saw Berich,
a Hun of noble birth, placed above us there. Opposite 448.
Order of
prece-
dence.
to Onégesh, on a double chair [1], sat two of the sons of
Attila. His eldest son sat on the king's couch, not
near to him, however, but on the very edge of it, and
all through the banquet he kept his eyes fixed on the
ground in silent awe of his father.

'When we were all seated the cup-bearer came in The toasts.
and handed to Attila his ivy-wood drinking-cup, filled
with wine. Remaining seated, the king saluted the
one nearest to him in rank. The slave standing behind
that person's chair advanced into the centre of the hall,
received the cup from the hand of Attila's cup-bearer,
and brought it to the guest, whom etiquette required
to rise from his seat and continue standing till he had
drained the cup and the slave had returned it into
the hands of Attila's cup-bearer.' This process of salutation and drinking was gone through with each guest
and in the intervals of every course. The length of the
solemnity, and perhaps the tediousness of it, seem
greatly to have impressed the mind of Priscus, who
describes it in much detail. After the banqueters had
all been 'saluted' by Attila, the servants began to
bring in the provisions, which were set upon little
tables, one for every three or four guests, so that each
could help himself without going outside the row of
seats. 'For all the rest of the barbarians,' says Priscus,
'and for us, a costly banquet had been prepared, which
was served on silver dishes; but Attila, on his wooden
plate, had nothing else save meat. In all his other
equipments he showed the same simple tastes. The

[1] Δίφρος.

other banqueters had drinking cups of gold and silver handed to them, but his was of wood. His clothes were quite plain, distinguished by their cleanness only from those of any common man : and neither the sword which was hung up beside him, nor the clasps of his shoes (shaped in the barbarian fashion), nor the bridle of his horse, was adorned, as is the case with other Scythians, with gold or jewels, or anything else that is costly.

'When evening came on, torches were lighted, and two barbarians coming in, stood opposite to Attila and chanted verses in praise of his victories and his prowess in war. The banqueters, looking off from the festal board, gazed earnestly on the minstrels. Some gave themselves to the mere delight of the song; others, remembering past conflicts, were stirred as with the fury of battle; while the old men were melted into tears by the thought that their bodies were grown weak through time, and their hot hearts were compelled into repose.' After tears laughter, and after the tragedy a farce. A mad Hun next came in, who by his senseless babble made all the guests laugh heartily. Then entered a Moorish dwarf named Zercon, hump-backed, club-footed, with a nose like a monkey's. Almost the only anecdote[1] that is preserved to us about Bleda, Attila's brother, records the inextinguishable mirth which this strange creature used to awaken in him, how he had him always by his side at the battle and in the banquet, and how when at last the unlucky dwarf tried to make his escape

448.

Minstrelsy.

Bleda's fool.

---

[1] This anecdote is preserved by Suidas. The commentator Valesius thinks he took it from a portion of the history of Priscus now lost to us : but there are some slight divergences in the story which seem to point to a different conclusion.

together with some other fugitives, Bleda disregarded all
the others, and devoted his whole energies to the recapture of the pigmy. Then when he was caught and
brought into the royal presence, Bleda burst into another
storm of merriment at seeing the queer little creature
in the dignity of chains. He questioned him about the
cause of his flight : the dwarf replied that he knew he
had done wrong, but there was some excuse for him
because he could get no wife in Hun-land. More de-
licious laughter followed, and Bleda straightway provided him with a wife in the person of a Hunnish
damsel of noble birth who had been maid of honour
to his queen, but had fallen into disgrace and been
banished from her presence. After Bleda's death,
Attila, who could not abide the dwarf, sent him as
a present to Aetius. He had now come back again,
apparently to beg to have his wife restored to him, a
prayer which Attila was not inclined to grant.

This strange being came into the banquet-hall, and
by his grotesque appearance, his odd garb, his stutter-
ing voice, and his wild promiscuous jumble of words,
Latin, Hunnish, Gothic, hurled forth pell-mell in un-
utterable confusion, set every table in a roar. Only
Attila laughed not ; not a line in his rigid countenance
changed till his youngest son Ernak came, laughing like
everybody else, and sat down beside him. He did not
shrink away like his elder brother and sit on the edge
of the couch. His bright, happy eyes looked up into
the face of his father, who gently pinched his cheek and
looked back upon him with a mild and softened gaze.
Priscus expressed aloud his wonder that the youngest
son should be so obviously preferred to his elder
brethren : whereupon one of the barbarians who sat

448.

near him, and who understood Latin, whispered to him confidentially that it had been foretold to Attila by the prophets that the falling fortunes of his house should by this son be restored.

448.

Affair of
the family
of Sulla.

The drinking-bout was protracted far on into the night, and the ambassadors left long before it was over. At daybreak next morning they again sought an interview with Onégesh, and petitioned that without further loss of time they might receive Attila's answer and return to their master. Onégesh set his secretaries, Roman captives, to work at the composition of the letter of reply. Then they preferred another request, for the liberation of the widow and children of a certain Sulla, a citizen of Ratiaria [1], who had apparently been killed at the same time when they were taken captive and their home destroyed. Onégesh entirely refused to hear of their gratuitous liberation, but at length, when the ambassadors begged him to reflect on their former prosperity, and to pity their present misfortunes, he laid the matter before Attila, and obtained a reluctant consent to send the children back as a present to Theodosius. As to the widow the Hun remained inexorable: the price of her freedom was fixed at £500. Such abject entreaties to a squalid barbarian for the liberation of the family of a Roman bearing the name of him

> 'Whose chariot rolled on Fortune's wheel,
> Trumphant Sulla,'

seem to intensify the force of Byron's magnificent apostrophe— [2]

---

[1] Now Arzar Palanka on the Danube.
[2] Childe Harold, iv. 84.

> 'Couldest thou divine
> To what would one day dwindle that which made
> Thee more than mortal, or that so supine
> By else than Romans Rome could e'er be laid ;
> She who was named Eternal, and arrayed
> Her warriors but to conquer, she who veiled
> Earth with her haughty shadow, and displayed,
> Till the o'ercanopied horizon failed,
> Her rushing wings—oh ! she who was Almighty hailed ? '

448.

Another visit to Attila's chief wife [1] beguiled the tedium of the ambassadors' sojourn in the royal village. ' She received us,' says Priscus, 'both with honeyed words and with an elaborate repast. And each of the company wishing to do us honour in Scythian fashion, arose and presented us with a full cup of wine ; and when we had drank it they put their arms round us and kissed us, and then received it back from our hands.'

A final supper with Attila himself followed. The monarch seems to have had an increasing appreciation of the worth and honesty of Maximin : and now that the 'shameless beast,' Vigilas, was gone, and Attila no longer had the unpleasant sensation as of the near presence of a venomous reptile, which was always suggested by his false smile and cringing salutation, the companionship of the Roman ambassadors agreeably diversified the monotony of the barbarian carousals. This time the relative who shared his royal divan was not one of his sons but Oébarsh, his uncle. Attila treated the ambassadors during this meal with great politeness, but at the same time frequently reminded them of a grievance which for the moment absorbed all his

Last banquet with Attila.

---

[1] Here called Recan : apparently the same name as the Kreka of whom we have already heard (p. 81).

thoughts, to the exclusion of the Hunnish refugees and the vases of Sirmium. Aetius, who was continually sending presents to the Hunnish monarch or receiving them from him, had consigned to him, perhaps in exchange for the Moorish dwarf, a Latin secretary, named Constantius. This secretary, the second of that name who had entered Attila's service, was eager, like all the adventurers who hovered on the confines between barbarism and civilization, to consolidate his position by marrying one of the ' enormously wealthy[1]' heiresses who were to be found among the Romans. Such an one seemed to be within his grasp when he was sent a few years before as an embassy to Constantinople, and when he succeeded in smoothing some of the negotiations between Theodosius and the Hun. The Emperor, a facile promiser, undertook to bestow upon the secretary the hand of the daughter of Saturninus, a man of high lineage and fortune, who held the office of *Comes Domesticorum*. Shortly after, however, Eudocia the Empress revenged herself on Saturninus for having, in obedience to her husband's commands, put two favourite ecclesiastics of hers to death, by sending him to join them. The fortunes of the house of Saturninus declined, and a powerful general, Zeno, bestowed the daughter of the fallen minister in marriage on one of his creatures named Rufus[2]. The disappointed secretary, Constantius, who had doubtless boasted not a

448.

The fortune-hunting Secretary.

---

[1] ζαπλούτων.

[2] This intrigue is well illustrated by a curious Title in the Theodosian Code (Lib. iii. Tit. 6): 'Si Provinciae Rector, vel ad eum pertinentes sponsalia dederint.' It is directed against the abuse of their power by provincial governors, who terrified the parents or guardians of wealthy heiresses into betrothing them to the governor's sons or dependents.

little of the 'enormously wealthy' bride that was to be assigned to him, besieged the ear of Attila with his clamours, and even promised him money if he would still obtain for him one of the longed-for heiresses. All through this banquet therefore Attila urged the fortune-hunter's claims upon Maximin, saying repeatedly, 'Constantius must not be disappointed. It is not right for kings to tell lies [1].'

448.

Three days after this banquet the ambassadors from the Eastern Court, after receiving presents which Priscus acknowledges to have been 'suitable,' were at length dismissed under the escort of Berich, the Hunnish nobleman who had sat above them at their first repast in Attila's presence. It is singular that we hear nothing as to the success or failure of the Embassy of the West.

The return journey of Maximin and Priscus was not marked by any striking adventures. They saw a Scythian refugee, who had crossed the Danube and returned into his own country as a spy, subjected to the cruel punishment of impalement, common among these Turanian nations. And two Scythian slaves who had murdered their masters were put to death by crucifixion, a mode of execution which the Christian Empire, from religious rather than humane sentiment, had by this time abandoned. But the only other incidents of their journey were caused by the testy and capricious humour of their companion Berich, who seemed bent on picking a quarrel with them. His ill-temper was chiefly shewn by his violent resumption of the horse which, at Attila's command, he had presented to Maxi-

Return journey of the ambassadors.

Sulkiness of their Hunnish colleague.

---

[1] Compare the words of Aspar to the Emperor Leo I, some twenty years after this time: 'Emperor, he who is clothed with this purple robe should not be a deceiver.'

448.

min. Indeed all the Hunnish nobility had been ordered to make tender of their horses to the ambassador; but he had shewn the wise moderation of his character by accepting only a few. Among these few however was Berich's; and considering the centaur-like union which had for generations existed between the Huns and their steeds, we may conjecture that it was the pain of daily beholding his favourite horse bestridden by an unwarlike stranger which caused the irritability of the Hunnish nobleman.

Vigilas
arrested,

Vigilas had started from Constantinople before the return of the ambassadors, and met them on their road. They communicated to him the final answer of the barbarian, and he continued his route. As soon as he reached the camp of Attila, a detachment of Huns, who had been watching for his arrival, made him their prisoner, and took from him the £2000 which he was bringing, as he supposed, to Edecon as the price of blood. They carried him at once before the king, who enquired why he travelled with so much money about him. 'To provide for my own wants and those of my attendants,' said Vigilas, 'lest by any mischance my embassy should lack its proper splendour. Also for the redemption of captives, since many persons in the Roman territory have begged me to purchase the liberation of their kinsfolk.' 'Evil beast!' said Attila, 'thou in truth shalt not blind Justice by all thy quibbles, and no pretext shall be strong enough to enable thee to escape punishment. Thou hast provided far more money than could possibly be wanted for the purchase of beasts of burden and for the redemption of captives, which last I expressly forbade thee to undertake when thou camest hither with Maximin.'

With these words he signalled to his attendants to seize the son of Vigilas, who had for the first time accompanied his father on this journey. 'Next moment,' said Attila, 'hew him down with the sword, unless his father will say to whom and for what purpose he has brought this money into my territory.' Vigilas burst into passionate lamentations, begged the executioner to slay him instead of his son, and when he saw that all was of no avail, confessed the whole plot, told how Chrysaphius had originated it, how Edecon had accepted it, how Theodosius had sanctioned it, and then once more earnestly entreated Attila to put *him* to death and to spare his son. The king, who from his previous information knew that Vigilas had now disclosed the whole truth, coldly replied that for the present he should be loaded with chains and await, in close confinement, the return of his son who must start at once for Constantinople to obtain another sum of £2000[1], which, with that already taken from him, should constitute their joint ransom.

448. and compelled to confess.

Leaving Vigilas in this dangerous predicament, let us now see what kind of messages Theodosius had to listen to from the King of the Huns. Maximin seems to have been instructed to dwell principally on the Emperor's breach of promise to Constantius. 'No one,' Attila argued, 'could have dared to betroth the daughter of Saturninus to another than Constantius without the Emperor's consent. For either he who had presumed to do such a deed would have suffered condign punishment, or else the affairs of the Emperor were in such a

Attila's message to Theodosius.

---

[1] Mr. Herbert (Attila, p. 417) inadvertently raises this ransom to the enormous figure of £20,000, by calling it 500 lbs. of gold. The words of Priscus are clear, πεντήκοντα λίτρας χρυσοῦ.

448.

state that he could not manage his own servants, against whom therefore, if he desired it, Attila would be ready to grant him the advantage of his alliance.' The taunt, which must surely have proceeded from the lips of Berich, not of Maximin, struck home ; and Theodosius showed his anger by confiscating the fortune of the ' enormously wealthy' young lady whose matrimonial affairs had caused him so much annoyance. This act was of course followed by a loud outcry from her husband Rufus and his patron Zeno, whose position towards his Imperial master was in fact pretty accurately described by the sneers of Attila. Zeno chose however to attribute the whole incident to the machinations of Chrysaphius, and began to clamour for the eunuch's life.

449.
A still more insulting message brought by Orestes.

Such was the position of affairs at Constantinople when the two special ambassadors of Attila, Orestes and Eslas, arrived. Their message was yet harder to digest than that which had preceded it. When they appeared in the Imperial presence, Orestes wore, suspended round his neck, the purse (or rather the large bag) in which the blood-money had been packed. Turning first to Theodosius and then to the Eunuch, he asked each of them : 'Dost thou recognise this bag ?' Then Eslas, the Hun, took up his parable, and said roundly [1], ' Theodosius is the son of a well-born father. Attila too from his father Mundzuk has inherited the condition of noble birth, which *he* has preserved. Not so Theodosius, who fell from the estate of an *ingenuus* and became Attila's slave, when he submitted to pay him tribute. He has now conspired against the life of a better man than himself, and one whom Fortune has made his master. This is a foul deed, worthy only of a caitiff slave, and

[1] ἀπὸ στόματος.

his only way of clearing himself from the guilt which
he has thus contracted is to surrender the Eunuch to
punishment.'

449.

How this harangue, every word of which had been
composed by Attila himself, was received by Theodosius,
as he sat surrounded by his courtiers, we know not.
The general expectation of the Court was that it would
go hard with Chrysaphius, whose punishment was thus
simultaneously demanded by the two men whom the
Emperor most feared, Zeno his general, and Attila his torment. But 'threatened men live long,' and the Eunuch
seems to have been not unpopular with the other
courtiers, who exerted themselves zealously for his deliverance.

Anatolius and Nomus were selected as the new ambassadors to the Hunnish Court. Both had been named
by Attila [1] as persons of sufficiently exalted rank to visit
him, such as he would be willing to welcome. Anatolius,
who had been the chief figure of the embassy of 447,
was a man of high military rank, in fact, general of the
household troops [2]. Nomus, a patrician as well as his
colleague, was in the civil service as Master of the
Offices, renowned not only for his wealth, but for his
willingness to spend it lavishly, and moreover kindly
disposed towards Chrysaphius. They were commissioned to employ money freely, to deprecate Attila's
resentment against the Eunuch, and to assure Constantius that he should yet have a wealthy Roman bride,
though the law would not permit the Emperor to give
him the daughter of Saturninus, as she was married to
another man from whom she did not desire to be

Embassy of Anatolius and Nomus.

---

[1] See p. 81.

[2] ἄρχων τελῶν τῶν ἀμφὶ βασιλέα=Magister Militum praesentalis.

divorced. The trifling circumstance of the confiscation of her property appears not to have been mentioned in the instructions of the ambassadors.

449.

Success
of the
Embassy.

This embassy was completely successful. Attila came as far as the river Drave [1], in order to testify his respect for the persons of the envoys, and to spare them the fatigue of too long a journey. At first his speech was full of arrogance and wrath, but when he saw the beautiful things which the ambassadors had brought for him, the presents of Theodosius, the presents of Chrysaphius, the presents of the lavish Nomus, the child-nature in the heart of the barbarian asserted itself, his eyes gleamed with pleasure, and he suffered himself to be mollified by their gentle words. Peace was concluded pretty nearly on the old terms : in fact, he seems even to have surrendered his claim to the belt of territory, five days' journey wide, south of the Danube. He promised to worry the Emperor no more about any refugees whom he might have received in past times; ' only,' he said, ' Theodosius must receive no more of these men in future.' Vigilas was liberated, his son having brought the £2000 of ransom ; and the demand for the head of Chrysaphius seems to have been quietly withdrawn [2]. Of his own accord, in order to mark his special esteem for Anatolius and Nomus, he liberated many captives without ransom ; and he made them presents of several horses (whether belonging to himself or to his courtiers we are not informed), and of the

[1] A conjectural translation of Δρέγκων.

[2] Thierry (Attila, i. 126) says, in describing this interview, ' Il délivra Vigilas, . . . mais il exigea la tête de Chrysaphius. Sur ce point il fut inflexible.' I do not find any evidence in Priscus in support of this statement; and the fact that Attila received, apparently, the eunuch's presents, seems to render it very improbable.

skins of wild beasts, 'such as the royal family among the Scythians wear by way of ornament.' For once, diplomacy really prevented war.

449.

The important question of satisfying the noble long- An heiress ings of Constantius for a wealthy bride was soon solved. found for Attila's He returned with the ambassadors to Constantinople, secretary. and was there mated to a lady of very high birth and large fortune, the widow of a certain Armatius, who had died when on service against some of the fierce tribes of Libya, and the daughter-in-law of Plinthas (Consul 419), who had headed the first Embassy to Attila in the year 433. Thus the last point in dispute between the son of Mundzuk and the son of Arcadius was disposed of.

In the following year (450) Theodosius II died in the 450. 50th year of his age and the 43rd of his reign. His Death of Theodosius death was the result of an accident in hunting, his II. horse having run away, swerved aside into a stream and thrown him off. He was carried home to his palace in a litter, but he had received a fatal injury to the spine, and died on the following night (July 28, 450). He left no male offspring, and his sister Pulcheria ascended Accession of Marcian. the throne, which she shared with a brave and honest soldier, Marcian, whom, for the good of the state, she consented to call her husband.

The immediate results of this change were, the calling Chrysa- phius put together of the Council of Chalcedon (451), at which the to death. orthodox Roman view of the union of the two natures in Christ was finally adopted; the execution of Chry- saphius, whether as maladministrator, as Eutychian heretic, or as private foe to the new Augusta, we are not informed; and, lastly, the assumption of an altered and more manly tone in reply to the intolerable preten-

EUROPE
IN THE YEAR 451

Roman Miles
100 200 300 400

sions of Attila. When that monarch claimed his arrears of tribute, the new Emperor sent as ambassador to his court, Apollonius, the brother of that Rufus who had married the 'enormously wealthy' bride, for whose fortune Constantius had languished. Apollonius crossed the Danube, but when Attila learned that he had not brought the tribute, which—to use the words of the Hun—'had been promised to him by better and more king-like men[1] than the present ambassador,' he refused to grant him an audience. Attila said expressly that he acted thus in order to show his contempt for the envoy, whom, nevertheless, he ordered, on pain of death if he refused, to hand over the presents which the Emperor had sent. 'Not so,' said Apollonius, who spoke with a boldness worthy of old Rome, and in a tone which was now strange to Scythian ears. 'The Huns may kill me if they like, and then my presents will be spoils of war (if they choose to call murder warfare). Or they may receive me as ambassador, and then I willingly offer my gifts. But if not admitted to an audience, I do not part with these presents while I live.' The boldness of the ambassador prevailed. He returned with his gifts and his message alike undelivered, but Attila saw that he had now at length men to deal with at Constantinople, and that the policy of braggadocio would avail no longer. He did not care for a campaign in the often-harried plains of Moesia, but looked out for some richer if not easier prey. And thus, with a dignity which we had ceased to hope for in any Emperor of Byzantium, the long negotiations terminate, and we close the chapter of the doings of Attila in the East.

45°.
Brave
words of
Apollonius.

---

[1] Auatolius and Nomus.

CHAPTER III.

ATTILA IN GAUL.

Authorities.

Sources :—

AT the outset we derive a little further information as to Attila's embassies from PRISCUS, but our chief source is again JORDANES. He gives, of course, always the Gothic version of the events which he describes; but the chapters relating to the invasion of Gaul and the battle of Châlons, rise to a far higher level of literary merit than the rest of the history, and seem to have something of the vividness and picturesqueness of contemporary narration.

APOLLINARIS SIDONIUS, the Gaulish nobleman, wit and bishop, whose relation to the politics of the time will be hereafter portrayed, writes about the events of this year in his usual declamatory style. He lived 430–488, and was therefore twenty-one years old at the time of Attila's invasion of Gaul. I quote from Grégoire and Collombet's edition of his works in three vols. : Lyons 1836.

GREGORY of Tours, who wrote his History of the Franks about 590, supplies some meagre details about Attila's invasion.

The Bollandist ACTA SANCTORUM, in the lives of St. Geneviève, St. Lupus, and St. Anianus, give further details of a more or less legendary character. A student who should possess sufficient patience and discrimination to winnow the wheat from the chaff in the vast mass of ecclesiastical literature collected by the Bollandists, would bestow a great service on the history of the Middle Ages.

The Panegyric of Aetius, attributed to a Spanish poet named

Merobaudes, and edited by Niebuhr, contains some interesting hints as to the life of Aetius previous to the year 446 (the date of the poem), but in its extremely fragmentary state it is difficult to extract much solid historical material from it. The imitation of Claudian's style is obvious.

A story of very doubtful authority [1] represents the monarch of the Huns as sending, shortly before the death of Theodosius II, a Gothic messenger to each of the two Roman Emperors, with this insulting mandate, 'Attila, thy master and mine, bids thee to prepare a palace for his reception.' Whether any such message was actually sent or not, the story indicates not inaptly the attitude which the great Hun maintained for the ten years between 440 and 450, hovering like a hawk over the fluttered dove-cots of Byzantium and Ravenna, and enjoying the terrors of the Eastern and the Western Augustus alternately.

Attila turns his menaces towards the Western Empire.

Now that the palace by the Bosporus was occupied by an inmate whose beak and claw looked more like those of the old Roman eagle than any that had been seen there for the last half-century, the Barbarian began to turn his thoughts more definitely to the hapless pigeon of the West. He needed to be at no loss for pretexts in making war on Rome. Whether the great grievance of the communion-plate of Sirmium was still unredressed we cannot say, for History, after wearying us with the details of this paltry affair, forgets to tell us how it ended, whether the vases were surrendered to the service of the king or the silversmith

---

[1] The story rests only on the authority of the Alexandrian Chronicle and John Malalas. The former was composed during the reign of Heraclius, about 630; the date of the latter historian is uncertain, not earlier, however, than 600, and not later than 900.

to his rage, or whether the latter was deemed to be 'a
bona-fide holder of the goods for valuable consideration,' and his title respected accordingly.

But the grievances of the Princess Honoria undoubt- Champion-
edly still remained, possibly even were increased by the ship of
Honoria.
death of the easy-tempered Theodosius and the accession to the Byzantine throne of that severe model of
feminine virtues, the Augusta Pulcheria, who was now
fifty-one years of age, while her cousin was but thirty-
two, a juniority which was in itself almost treason
against a female sovereign. It is possible that the
unhappy princess was removed at this time from the
Eastern to the Western court, for we find Attila sending   4:0.
one of his usual insulting embassies to Valentinian III,
'to say that Honoria, whom he had betrothed to himself, must suffer no harm, and that he would avenge her
cause if she were not also allowed to wield the imperial
sceptre.' The Western Emperor replied, 'that Honoria
could not enter into the married state with him, having
been already given to a husband' (to whom, when, or
under what circumstances, we are not informed); and
they met the audacious claim set up on behalf of the
princess by an equally audacious misstatement of their
own customs, daring to assert in the face of the still-
existing royalty of Placidia and Pulcheria, 'that Honoria
ought not to receive the sceptre, since the succession to
the throne among the Romans was vested not in
females, but in males.' Both parties probably felt that
the claim was an unreal one : the Hun was determined
on war, and would have it, whether he redeemed the
ring of Honoria or no. One more embassy takes place,
in which Attila prefers the modest claim to one half of
the Western Empire, 'as the betrothed husband of

Honoria, who had received this portion from her father, and was wrongfully kept out of it by her brother's covetousness.' This request is of course refused. Then Honoria too, like the vases of Sirmium, fades out of history ; whether she ever saw the fierce face of her affianced, when he wasted Italy in her name, nay even whether she was present at the death-bed of her mother Placidia, who expired at Rome in the same year as Theodosius (450), and there received and conferred a mutual forgiveness, we know not.

Two more pretexts for war must Attila accumulate, or at least two more alliances must he conclude, and then all would be ready for his great westward movement.

One was with a Frankish prince. A certain king of the Franks, whose name is not recorded, had just died, and there was strife between his sons as to the succession to his rude royalty. The younger son was the candidate whom the Romans favoured. He had been to Rome (probably some years before) on an embassy from his father. He had gazed there, doubtless, on the still undiminished glories of the Palatine and the Forum and the great Flavian Amphitheatre, and while he gazed, the observant eye of the rhetorician Priscus, who happened to be at Rome, had likewise gazed on him. A young warrior, with not even the first down of manhood on cheek or lip, but with a cloud of yellow hair descending thickly upon his shoulders, such is the appearance of the first Frankish king whom we meet with in history. Whether he was Meroveus himself [1], the half-

---

[1] Meroveus is the so-called grandson of Pharamond and grandfather of Clovis; but no names of the Frankish kings before Childeric, father of Clovis, are now accepted as thoroughly historical.

mythical ancestor of the Merovingian dynasty, may be
doubted, and cannot now be ascertained ; but that long
tawny *chevelure* identifies him with the race who
reigned in France for 250 years, till the hair of the last
fainéant king fell beneath the scissors of Pepin.

450.

The all-powerful Aetius regarded this young Frankish
chief with favour. He loaded him with presents, conferred upon him the title of his adopted son, and sent
him back to his father as the bearer of a treaty of
friendship and alliance. It may have been this title of
adopted son of the great Aetius which suggested ambitious thoughts to the mind of the young prince. At
any rate, on the death of his father, he, though the
younger son, with Roman help, made good his claim to
the succession to the kingdom. His elder brother fled
to the court of Attila, who undertook to recover for him
his lost inheritance.

The other alliance of Attila was with Gaiseric, king
of the Vandals. This monarch, whose career we shall
have to trace in the following book, was now undisputed
master of the whole Roman province of Africa, had
ravaged Sicily, and was making the name of Carthage,
his capital city, as terrible to Italian hearts as ever it
had been in the days of Hannibal. There can be little
doubt that if the Hunnish hordes by land, and the Vandal
pirates by sea, had simultaneously attacked the Western
Empire, they must have achieved a complete and crushing success. But for some reason or other, perhaps
because neither nation wished to share so rich a booty

Alliance
with
Gaiseric.

The silence of Gregory of Tours as to some of these earlier kings and
the hesitating way in which he speaks of others seem almost conclu-
sive against the pretension of the medieval genealogists to trace their
names and pedigree. (See Sismondi, Hist. des Français, i. 177.)

with a rival, this united action was not taken; and
though the Hunnish king received large sums of money
by way of subsidy from the Vandal, it may be doubted
whether he did not lose far more than he gained by an
alliance which made him accessory after the fact to a
cruel and impolitic outrage. For Theodoric, king of the
Visigoths, who was at this time far the most powerful
ruler in the Gaulish provinces, had bestowed his
daughter in marriage on Hunneric, the son of Gaiseric.
Gaiseric chose to suspect, apparently on very trifling
grounds, that the new bride had attempted to poison
him; and with a cruelty which seems to have been
characteristic of the Vandal nature, he cut off the nose
and ears of the Visigothic princess, and in this condition
sent her back to the palace of Theodoric, a living and
daily remembrancer of the vengeance due to the Vandal,
and therefore an argument against any co-operation with
Attila, who was that Vandal's friend.

One more, not ally, but summons to war must be
mentioned, which may perhaps have assisted powerfully
in turning the hosts of Attila towards Gaul rather than
towards Italy. The iniquities of judges and the exactions of tax-gatherers, which were so loudly complained
of by the barbarianised Roman in the camp of Attila,
had in Gaul stirred up the peasants to a tumultuary
war not unlike that which the mediaeval knights termed
a *Jacquerie*. The name given to the peasant warriors
with whom we are now concerned was Bagaudae[1]; and

---

[1] The authorities quoted by Ducange (Glossarium, s.v. Bagaudae)
imply that the name was of Celtic origin and meant 'robbers' or
'native oppressors.' He suggests a derivation from Bagat, which, he
says, is the Welsh for a mob of men, and the Breton for a flock or
herd. The monastery of Fossat, four miles from Paris, was called in

their insurrection, a striking proof of the hollowness of the fabric of Roman prosperity, had smouldered for more than a century and a half, ever since the days of Diocletian. A man, of whom we would gladly know more than the few lines which the chroniclers bestow on him, was the link between these marauders within the Empire and the great Barbarian without. In the year 448, as we learn from the Pseudo-Prosper, ' Eudoxius, a doctor by profession, a man of evil, though cultivated intellect, being mixed up with the movements of the Bagaudae at that time, fled to the Huns[1].' It is probable enough that we have here to do with a mere selfish adventurer such as float ever upon the surface of revolutionary change: yet before condemning the man of ' evil though highly-cultured intellect,' who

450.

the time of Charles le Chauve, Castrum Bagaudarum. Salvian (De Gubernatione Dei, v. 6) draws a striking picture of the judicial and fiscal iniquities which had driven men into the ranks of the Bacaudae (as he spells the word), ' De Bacaudis nunc mihi sermo est: qui per malos judices et cruentos spoliati, afflicti, necati, postquam jus Romanae libertatis amiserant, etiam honorem Romani nominis perdiderunt. Et imputatur his infelicitas sua? Imputamus his nomen calamitatis suae? Imputamus nomen, quod ipsi fecimus? Et vocamus rebelles? Vocamus perditos, quos esse compulimus criminosos? Quibus enim aliis rebus Bacaudae facti sunt, nisi iniquitatibus nostris, nisi improbitatibus judicum, nisi eorum proscriptionibus, et rapinis, qui exactionis publicae nomen in questus proprii emolumenta verterunt et indictiones tributarias praedas suas esse fecerunt.' Compare also the following interesting notices in ' Tiro's ' Chronicle: 435, ' Gallia ulterior Tibatonem principem rebellionis secuta, a Romanâ societate discessit, a quo tracto initio omnia paene Galliarum servitia in Bagaudam conspiravere.' 437, ' Capto Tibatone et caeteris seditionis partim principibus vinctis, partim necatis, Bagaudarum commotio conquiescit.'

[1] ' Eudoxius arte medicus, pravi sed exercitati ingenii, in Bagauda id temporis mota delatus, ad Chunnos confugit' (Chronicle of ' Tiro,' 448).

flashes thus for a moment upon the page of history, we would gladly have known whether he too may not have been in his day an apostle of ' the Enthusiasm of Humanity,' whether the miseries which Eudoxius' ' *arte medicus*' saw among the pillaged peasants of Gaul were not the original cause of his being condemned as a ' Bagauda ' by delicately-living senators and prefects, and forced to appeal against the injustices of civilization at the bar of its terrible antagonist.

450.

451.
The army
of Attila
moves
westwards.

At length, in the spring of 451, the preparations of Attila were completed, and the huge host began to roll on its way towards the Rhine. This army, like those which modern science has created, and under which modern industry groans, was truly described as a nation rather than an army ; and though the estimates of the chroniclers, which vary from half a million to seven hundred thousand men, cannot be accepted as literally accurate, we shall not err in believing that the vast multitude who looked to the tent of Attila for orders were practically innumerable. Sidonius describes how the quiet life of the Roman provincial senator was suddenly disturbed by the roar of a mighty multitude, when barbarism seemed to be pouring over the plains of Gaul all the inhabitants of the North. If his enumeration of the invading tribes, which no doubt partakes of some of the vagueness of his style of poetry, be

The na-
tionalities
which com-
posed it.

at all correct, the Geloni from the shores of the Volga, the Neuri and Bastarnae from the Ukraine, the Sciri, whom we are in doubt whether to place near Riga on the Baltic or Odessa on the Euxine, were serving in that army. The ethnological affinities of these obscure tribes are very doubtful. Some of them may have been of Sclavonic origin. The Teutonic family was represented by the Rugii from Pomerania, the Bructeri from the Weser; one half of the Frankish people from ' the turbid Neckar;' the Thuringians (Toringi) from Bavaria, and the Burgundians—these too only a portion of the tribe who had lingered in their old homes by the Vistula. The bone and marrow of the army were of course the Huns themselves, and the two powerful Teutonic tribes, enemies to the Hun in the past and to be his enemies in the future, but for the present his faithful allies and counsellors, the Gepidae and the Ostrogoths. Thus if we go back to the old story of the Gothic migration from ' the island of Sweden,' we have the crews of two of the ships being led on to attack their fellows in the other vessel, the Ostrogoths and the ' torpid' Gepidae marching right across Europe at the bidding of a leader whose forefathers came from Siberia, to overwhelm their Visigothic brethren, who are dwelling by the Garonne[1]. The Ostrogoths, who possibly occupied a territory in the north of Hungary, were commanded by three brothers, sprung from the great Amal lineage, Walamir and Theudemir and Widemir;

451.

[1] The lines of Apollinaris Sidonius which enumerate the nations at Attila's disposal are these—

'Subito cum rupta tumultu
Barbaries totas in te transfuderat arctos,
Gallia; pugnacem Rugum comitante Gelono
Gepida trux sequitur; Scyrum Burgundio cogit,
Chunus, Bellonotus, Neurus, Basterna, Toringus,
Bructerus, ulvosâ quem vel Nicer abluit undâ
Prorumpit Francus.'—(Panegyric of Avitus, 319–325.)

It is singular that he makes no mention of the Ostrogoths. 'Bellonotus' seems to be the name of some tribe not yet identified. The Geloni are probably only inserted because their name fits in nicely into a hexameter and has a classical ring about it, as having been used by Horace.

'nobler,' as the patriotic Jordanes observes, 'than the king whose orders they obeyed.' The Gepidae, whose land probably bordered on the northern confines of the Ostrogothic settlement, were led to battle by Arderic, bravest and most famous of all the subject-princes, and him on whose wise and loyal counsels Attila chiefly relied.

451.

While this vast medley of nations are hewing down the trees of the Thüringer Wald, in order to fashion their rude boats and rafts for the passage of the Rhine [1], let us glance for a moment at the tribes, scarcely less various and not so coherent, which, on the Gaulish side of the river, are awaiting their dreaded impact.

Tribes inhabiting Gaul.

Near the mouths of the Rhine, the Scheldt, and the Somme, that is to say, in the modern countries of Belgium and Picardy, clustered the great confederacy of the Salian Franks. Their Ripuarian brethren held the upper reaches of the Great River, and it is to these probably that Sidonius refers when he places them by the turbid Neckar, and describes them as furnishing a contingent to the army of Attila. All the Franks were still heathen, the fiercest of the Teutonic settlers in Gaul, and they bore an ill repute for unfaithfulness to their plighted word and even to their oaths. Small sign as yet was there that to them would one day fall the hegemony of the Gallic nations. In the opposite corner of the country, between the Loire, the Garonne, and the Bay of Biscay, the Visigoths had erected a monarchy, the most civilized and compact

Franks.

Visigoths.

---

[1] So Sidonius—

'Cecidit cito secta bipenni
Hercynia in lintres, et Rhenum texuit alno.'

(Panegyric of Avitus 325-6.)

of all the barbarian kingdoms, and the one which
seemed to have the fairest promise of a long and
triumphant life. By the peace which their king Walia   451.
concluded with Honorius (416) after the restoration of
Placidia, they had obtained legal possession of the
district called Aquitania Secunda, together with the
territory round Toulouse, all of which allotment went
by the name of Septimania[1] or Gothia. For ten years
(419-429) there had been firm peace between Visigoths
and Romans ; then, for ten years more (429-439), fierce
and almost continued war, Theodoric, king of the
Visigoths, endeavouring to take Arles and Narbonne ;
Aetius and his subordinate Litorius striving to take the
Gothic capital of Toulouse, and all but succeeding.
And in these wars Aetius had availed himself of his
long-standing friendship with the Huns to enlist them
as auxiliaries against the warriors of Theodoric, dangerous allies who plundered friends and enemies, and
carried back doubtless to their dreary encampment in
Hungary vivid remembrance of the sunny vineyards of
Languedoc and Guienne. For the last twelve years
(439-451) there had been peace, but scarcely friendship,
between the Courts of Ravenna and Toulouse.

North of the Visigoths, the Celtic population of Armorican
Brittany, known by the name of the Armoricans, had confederacy,
risen in arms against their Roman rulers, and had with
some degree of success maintained their independence.
From this time, perhaps, we ought to date that isolation
of Brittany from the politics of the rest of France,
which has not entirely disappeared even at the present

---

[1] From the seven chief cities comprised therein, which were—
taking them from south to north—Toulouse (the Visigothic capital),
Agen, Bordeaux, Perigueux, Angoulême, Saintes, and Poitiers.

day. But the terrible invader from the East welded even the stubborn Breton into temporary cohesion with his neighbours, and in the pages of Jordanes we find the 'Armoritiani' fighting side by side with the Roman legions against Attila.

The same list includes a yet more familiar name, 'Saxones.' How came our fathers thither; they, whose homes were in the long sandy levels of Holstein? As has been already pointed out, the national migration of the Angles and Saxons to our own island had already commenced, perhaps in part determined by the impulse northward of Attila's own subjects. Possibly like the Northmen, their successors, the Saxons may have invaded both sides of the English Channel at once, and may on this occasion have been standing in arms to defend against their old foe some newly-won possessions in Normandy or Picardy.

In the south-east of Gaul, the Burgundians had after many wars and some reverses established themselves (443) with the consent of the Romans in the district then called Sapaudia and now Savoy. Their territory was somewhat more extensive than the province which was the cradle of the present royal house of Italy, since it stretched northwards beyond the lake of Neufchatel, and southwards as far as Grenoble. Here the Burgundian immigrants, under their king, Gundiok, were busy settling themselves in their new possession, cultivating the lands which they had divided by lot, each one receiving[1] half the estate of a Roman host or *hospes*,

451.

Saxons.

Burgundians.

---

[1] A later division was effected, which gave the Burgundian two-thirds of the arable land; but the primary apportionment seems to have been in equal shares (see Binding's Burgundisch-Romanische Königreich, i. p. 28).

(for under such gentle names the spoliation was veiled,)
when the news came that the terrible Hun had crossed
the Rhine, and that all hosts and guests in Gaul must
unite for its defence.

The Alans, who had wandered thus far westwards
from the country between the Volga and the Don,
had received (440) the district round Valence for a
possession from the Romans, on much the same terms
probably as those by which the Burgundians held
Savoy[1]. Of all the barbarian tribes now quartered
in Gaul they were the nearest allied to the Huns, and
Sangiban, their king, was strongly suspected of having
some secret and treacherous understanding with Attila[2].

This chaos of barbarian tribes occupied perhaps one
half of Gaul. Wherever Chaos was not, wherever some
remains of the old imperial Cosmos were still left un-
submerged, there was Romania. We may conjecture

---

[1] 'Tiro' says (440), 'Deserta Valentinae urbis rura Alanis, quibus
Sambida praeerat partienda traduntur' [ab Aetio]. (442) 'Alani,
quibus terrae Galliae ulterioris cum incolis dividendae a Patritio
Aetio traditae fuerant, resistentes armis subigunt, et expulsis dominis
terrae, possessionem vi adipiscuntur.'

[2] Jordanes (cap. 36) thus enumerates the nations who fought
against Attila : 'Hic enim adfuere auxiliares Franci, Sarmatae,
Armoritiani, Litiani, Burgundiones, Saxones, Riparioli, Ibriones
aliaequae nonnullae Celticae vel (=et) Germanicae nationes.' The
Sarmatae may perhaps stand for the Alani (or the Taifalae whom
Thierry speaks of as settled at Poitiers). The Litiani are identified
both by Böcking (Notitia, p. 1057) and by Thierry (Hist. d'Attila, i.
169) with the Laeti, military colonists from among various Teutonic
nations, many of whom had been settled in Gaul since the time of
Diocletian. The Riparioli are probably the Ripuarian Franks. The
Ibriones are declared by Thierry to be 'un petit peuple des Alpes,
les Brenes ou Brennes, qu'Aetius avait ralliés pendant son voyage et
amenés en Gaule ;' but he does not quote his authority for this identification.

that by this time very little of Roman domination remained in the Belgic Gaul. The eastern portions of Gallia Lugdunensis and Gallia Aquitanica, especially the city of Lyons and the mountains of Auvergne, seem to have been fervently loyal to the Emperor. Gallia Narbonensis with its capitals of Arles and Narbonne, but excepting Toulouse and its surrounding country, had successfully beaten back the Visigothic invader, and was almost more Roman than Rome itself.

451.

Would the Romans and Barbarians in Gaul coalesce against the Huns?

But the question of transcendent importance for Gaul, and indirectly for the whole future of Western Europe, was—'Would Chaos and Cosmos blend for a little space to resist the vaster and wilder Chaos which was roaring for them both, fierce from its Pannonian home? Especially could Aetius and Theodoric, so lately at death-grips for the possession of one another's capitals—Aetius who had all but lost Arles, Theodoric who had all but lost Toulouse, unite heartily enough and promptly enough to beat back Attila?'

Attila's embassies to the Roman and Visigothic courts.

This was the doubt, and Attila thought he saw in it an opportunity to divide his foes. 'A subtle man, and one who fought by artifice before he waged his wars[1],' he sent ambassadors to Valentinian, representing his intended invasion as only a continuation of the old joint campaigns of Roman and Hun against the Visigoth. To Theodoric he sent other messengers, exhorting him to break off his unnatural alliance with Rome, and to remember the cruel wars which so lately had been kindled against his people by the lieutenants of the Augustus.

Happily there was a little too much statesmanship

[1] 'Homo subtilis antequam bella gereret, arte pugnabat' (Jordanes, cap. 36).

both at Ravenna and Toulouse to allow of the success of so transparent an artifice. Valentinian's ambassadors to Theodoric addressed the Visigothic nation (if we may believe their panegyrist Jordanes) in some such words as these :

451.
Valentinian's embassy to Theodoric.

'It will comport with your usual wisdom, oh bravest of the nations, to confederate with us against the tyrant of the universe, who longs to fasten the chains of slavery on the whole world, who does not seek for any reasonable excuses for battle, but thinks that whatsoever crimes he may commit are lawful because he is the doer of them. He measures the frontiers of his dominions by what? By the space that his arms can ravage. He gluts his pride by license, he spurns the ordinances of earth and of heaven, and shows himself the enemy of our common nature[1]. Surely he deserves your hatred who proves himself the spiteful foe of all. Recollect, I pray you, (what assuredly he does not forget) blood has once flowed between you, and with whatever wiles he may now cover his thirst for vengeance, it is there, and it is terrible. To say nothing of our grievances, can you any longer tolerate with patience the pride of this savage ? Mighty as you are in arms, think of your own griefs' [and here, doubtless, words were used which would recall to the mind of Theodoric the cruel outrages inflicted on his daughter by Attila's Vandal ally], 'and join your hands with ours. Help the Republic which has given you one of her fairest provinces for a possession. If you would know how necessary the alliance of each of us is to the other, penetrate the council-chamber of the foe, and see how he labours to divide us.'

[1] 'Hostem se exhibet naturae cunctorum.'

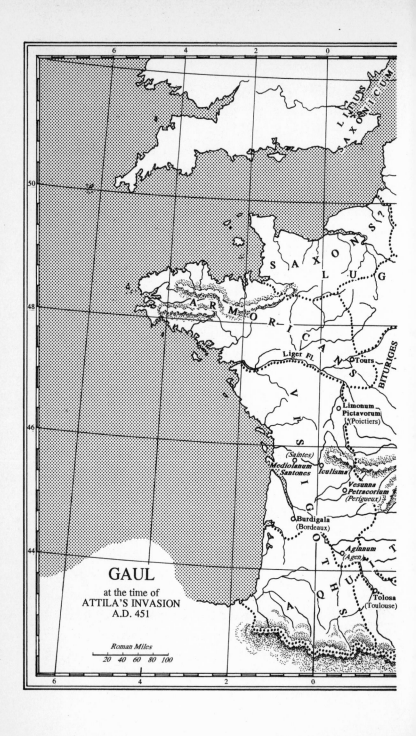

GAUL

at the time of
ATTILA'S INVASION
A.D. 451

Roman Miles

20 40 60 80 100

Theodoric was probably already meditating the Roman alliance, but these words are said to have decided him, and he replied, 'Romans, you have your will. Attila is your foe; you have made him ours also. Wheresoever the sound of his ravages shall call us, thither will we follow him; and all-inflated as he is with his victories over so many proud nations, yet the Goths too know how to do battle with the proud. Strong in the goodness of my cause, I deem no war laborious. No evil omen daunts me when the majesty of the Emperor of Rome smiles upon me.'

There is something hollow and unreal, doubtless, in these orations. In point of fact the Goths showed no alacrity in the defence of Roman Gaul till the storm of war rolled up to their own borders, and even then, according to one account [1], required a special messenger to rouse them from their unreadiness. But the foundation for an alliance between Roman and Visigoth was laid, and it saved Gaul.

Attila, foiled in his diplomacy, swept with his vast host across the Rhine, and began the congenial work of destruction. City after city of the Belgic Gaul (which comprised all France north-east of the Seine) fell before him. What help he may have received from the Bagaudae, or rendered to the young Frankish chieftain, his ally, we know not. We only hear that one city after another was broken up (*effracta*) by his savage hordes; but no simple human voice comes out of the Chaos to tell us what common men and women suffered in that breaking up of the great deep. The ecclesiastics, intent on the glorification of their own favourite saint or chapel, tell us a little of what was done, or was

[1] Sidonius, Panegyric of Avitus, 329–351.

not done in the way of miraculous interposition on
behalf of particular places, and even for their childish
legends, of uncertain date, and bearing elements of
fiction on the face of them, we have to be grateful,
so complete is the silence of authentic history as to the
earlier events of the invasion.

The bishop of Tongres in Belgium, Servatius by
name, implored God, amidst fastings and watchings and
constant showers of tears, that he would never permit
'the unbelieving and ever-unworthy nation of the
Huns' to enter Gaul [1]. Feeling sure in his spirit that
this prayer was not granted, he sought the tomb of
the Apostle Peter at Rome, and there, after three days'
fasting, pressed his suit. The Apostle appeared to him
in a vision and told him that according to the councils
of the Most High, the Huns must certainly enter Gaul
and ravage it for a time. But so much was conceded
to Servatius, that he should not see the misery which
was coming on his flock. He was therefore to return
at once to his home, choose out his grave-clothes, and
set his house in order, and then should he 'migrate
from this body.' He returned accordingly, set all things
in order for his burial, and told his flock that they
should see his face no more. 'But they following him
with great wailing and many tears, humbly prayed
him—"Leave us not, oh holy father; forget us not,
oh good shepherd!" Then, as they could not prevail
upon him to stay, they received his blessing, kissed
him, and departed. He went to the city of Utrecht,
where he was seized with a mild fever, and his soul
departed from his body. His corpse was brought back
to Tongres, and buried by the city wall.' Such was

451.

Vision of
the Bishop
of Tongres.

---

[1] Gregory of Tours, ii. 5.

the end of Servatius. Of the fate of his flock we have no further particulars.

'On the very eve of the blessed Easter, the Huns, coming forth out of Pannonia and laying waste everything on their march, arrived at Metz. They gave up the city to the flames, and slew the people with the edge of the sword, killing the priests themselves before the sacrosanct altar of the Lord. And in all that city no place remained unburnt except the oratory of the blessed Stephen, protomartyr and Levite.' Gregory of Tours [1] then proceeds to describe at unnecessary length a vision in which some one saw the blessed Levite, Stephen, interceding for this oratory with the Apostles Peter and Paul, and obtaining a promise that it should remain unharmed, 'that the nations might see that he availed somewhat with the Lord.'

From Lorraine into Champagne rolled on the devastating flood. St. Nicasius, bishop of Rheims, was hewn down before the altar of his church, while his lips were uttering the words of the Psalm, 'My soul cleaveth unto the dust, quicken thou me according to thy word.' Thus he attained the crown of martyrdom, though it has been truly remarked [2] that the bishops and priests who fell beneath the swords of the Huns perished, not strictly as confessors of a religion, but as chief citizens of their dioceses, and as guardians of sacred treasure. Attila was a plunderer, but not a persecutor. He made war on civilization and on human nature, not on religion, for he did not understand it enough to hate it.

The inhabitants of a little town [3] upon a clayey island in the Seine, near its junction with the Marne,

---

[1] ii. 5, 6.   [2] By Thierry and Herbert.

[3] πολίχνη, Zosimus, Julian.

were in such dread of its invasion by the Huns that
they had made up their minds to flee, when a young
girl of the neighbouring village of Nanterre, named
Genovefa, succeeded in communicating to the wives
of the inhabitants her own calm and heaven-born confidence that the place would not be assailed. The men
disbelieved her mission, called her a false prophetess,
would gladly have stoned her, or drowned her in the
river. But the influence of the women, aided by the
remembrance of the undoubted holiness of a neighbouring saint, Germanus of Auxerre, who had in former
days taken the part of Genovefa, saved her from insult,
and her counsels from rejection. The inhabitants remained; the prayers of the women, or the insignificance
of the place, saved it from the presence of the enemy.
Could the squalid Pannonian hordes have overleapt
fourteen centuries of time as well as the few miles of
space which intervened, how their eyes would have
sparkled, and their hearts well-nigh stopped beating
with the ecstasy of rapine, for the town which was
then scarcely worth attacking is now known by the
name of Paris. Justly, if the story be true, are Sainte
Geneviève and Saint Germain among the names still
held in highest honour by the beautiful city on the Seine.

In the after-growth of mediaeval ecclesiastical chronicles it may well be supposed that Attila's destroying
hand is made responsible for even more ruin than it
actually caused. Thus, 'Maistre Jacques de Guise,'
writing his history of Hainault in the fourteenth
century, informs his readers that 'they must know that
no town, fortress, or city, however strong it might be,
could resist this people, so cruel was it and malevolent.
. . . . Moreover, by this tyrant Attille were destroyed

451.

Mediaeval tales of Attila's destructions.

nearly all the cities of Gaul and Germany[1]. Firstly, Reims, Cambray, Treveres (Trèves), Mectz (Metz), Arras, Tongres, Tournay, Therouenne, Coulongne (Cologne), Amiens, Beauvais, Paris, and so many towns, cities, and fortresses that whoso should wish to put them all in writing he would too much weary the readers[2]. . . . .

'Item, by him were destroyed in Germany, Maience, a very noble city, Warmose (Worms), Argentore (Strasburg), Nymaie (?), Langres and Nerbonne (?). In this year, as saith Sigebert, were martirised the eleven thousand virgins in the city of Coulongne[3].'

This extract does not, of course, possess any shadow of historical authority. It is certainly wrong as to Narbonne and Nismes (if that be the city intended by Nymaie), and it is probably wrong as to Paris. But, with these exceptions, the cities named are all either in or upon the confines of Gallia Belgica, the chief scene of Attila's ravages, and the list is not an improbable one, though we can well believe that, as every defaced tomb and mutilated statue in an English church claims to have been maltreated by ' Cromwell's soldiers,' so no monkish chronicler who had a reasonable opportunity of bringing ' Attille ' and his malevolent Huns near to the shrine of his favourite saint would be likely to forego the terrible fascination.

---

[1] 'Et est a scavoir que nulle ville / forteresse : ou cite tant forte ꝗlle fust ne resistoit a ce peuple / tant estoit cruel et maliuolent.

' Dessouz celluy tirant Attille furēt destruictes presque toutes les citez de Gaulle et de Germanie,' ii. 18.

[2] 'Et tant de villes citez et forteresses / que qui les vouldroit toutes mectre en escript / il pourroit trop ennuyer les lisants.' Ib. 19.

[3] 'En celluy an / comme dit Sigibert / furēt martirisez les xi mil vierges en la cité de Coulongne.'

When Belgic Gaul was ravaged to his heart's content, the Hun turned his footsteps towards Aquitaine,
which contained the settlements of the Visigoths, and 451.
where, as he well knew, his hardest task awaited him. Attila
marches to
The Loire, flowing first northwards, then westwards, the Loire.
protects, by its broad sickle of waters, this portion of
Gaul, and the Loire itself is commanded at its most
northerly point by that city which, known in Caesar's Defence of
Orleans.
day as Genabum, had taken the name Aureliani from
the great Emperor, the conqueror of Zenobia, and is
now called Orleans. Three times has Aureliani played
an eminent part in the history of Gaul. There broke
out the great insurrection of B. C. 52 against the victorious Caesar ; there Attila's host, in A. D. 451, received
their first repulse ; and there in 1429, the maid of
Domremy, by forcing the Duke of Bedford to raise the
siege, wrested from the English Plantagenets their last
chance of ruling in France.

The hero of Orleans, in this defence of her walls, was St. Anianus.
the Bishop, Anianus. He had visited Aetius at Arles,
and strongly impressed upon the mind of that general
the necessity of relieving Orleans before the 24th of
June at the very latest. Then returning to the city he
cheered his flock with words of pious hope. The battering-rams of Attila thundered against the walls, and
the hearts of the people began to fail them. To Anianus
himself the promised help seemed to linger. He knew
not, and we cannot with certainty state the true cause
of the delay which is related to us only by one doubtful
authority [1]. Aetius, it is said, emerged from the Alpine

---

[1] Apollinaris Sidonius, Panegyric of Avitus, 328–356. As the
whole object of this poem is to pour laudation on the head of Avitus,
it is not unreasonable to suppose that the backwardness of the Visi-

451.

passes with only a slender and ill-officered train of soldiers, and then found that the Goths, instead of moving eastward to join him, were thinking of awaiting the attack of the dreaded foe in their own territory behind the Loire. In this unforeseen perplexity, Aetius availed himself of the services of Avitus, a Roman noble of Auvergne, and a *persona grata* at the court of Theodoric. His visit to the Gothic king proved successful.

' He aroused their wrath, making it subservient to the purposes of Rome [1], and marched in the midst of the skin-clothed warriors to the sound of the trumpets of Romulus.'

Meanwhile the consternation within the city of Orleans went on increasing, as the citizens saw their walls crumbling into ruin beneath the blows of the battering-rams of Attila. One day, when they were fervently praying in the church, ' Anianus said, " Look forth from the ramparts and see if God's mercy yet succours us." They gazed forth from the wall, but beheld no man. He said, " Pray in faith : the Lord will liberate you to-day." They went on praying ; again he bade them mount the walls, and again they saw no help approaching. He said to them the third time, " If ye pray in faith, the Lord will speedily be at hand to help you." Then they with weeping and loud lamentation implored the mercy of the Lord. When their prayer was ended, a third time, at the command

goths has been exaggerated or even invented in order to enhance his glory. He may have simply borne to the camp of Theodoric a message from Aetius arranging the time and place of meeting for the two armies.

[1] ' Famulas in proelia concitat iras.'

of that old man, they mounted the wall, and looking
forth they saw from afar, as it were, a cloud rising out
of the ground. When they brought him word of it   451.
he said, "It is the help of God." In the meanwhile,
as the walls were now trembling under the stroke of
the rams, and were already on the point of falling into
ruin, lo! Aetius and Theodoric, the king of the Goths,
and Thorismund, his son, come running up to the city,
turn the ranks of the enemy, cast him out, and drive
him far away[1].' It was apparently on the very day
fixed between the bishop and the general (the 24th of
June) that this relief came.

Foiled in his attempt to take Orleans and to turn the   Retreat
line of the Loire, Attila, with his unwieldy host, began   towards the Rhine.
to retreat towards the Rhine. It is the weakness of
those marauding warriors of whom he may be considered the type, that their recoil must be as rapid as
their onset. A ruined and devastated country cannot
be compelled to furnish the subsistence for lack of
which it is itself perishing. Everywhere along the line
of march are thousands of bitter wrongs waiting for revenge. And the marauders themselves to whom pillage,
not patriotism or discipline, has been the one inspiring
motive, and the common bond of union, when the hope

---

[1] This is the account of the siege of Orleans given by Gregory of
Tours about a century and a half after the event. (ii. 7.) The story
given in the life of St. Anianus in the Acta Sanctorum differs in
some particulars from this. Nothing is said of the three visits to the
walls or the far-off cloud of dust; but the prayers of the saint bring
a four-days' storm of rain, which greatly hinders the works of the
besiegers. They have, however, made a practicable breach and are
actually within the city, when the relieving army appears. Gregory's
word 'ejiciunt' (cast them out of the city) gives some probability to
this part of the narrative.

of further pillage fails, are each secretly revolving the same thought, how to leave the ravaged country as soon as possible with their plunder undiminished.

451.

Attila
reaches
Troyes.

Bishop
Lupus.

Doubtless Aetius and Theodoric were hovering on Attila's rear, neglecting no opportunity of casual vengeance on the stragglers from the host, and endeavouring to force him to battle at every point where, from the nature of the country, he would be compelled to fight at a disadvantage. But we hear no details of his retreat till he reached the city of Troyes, 114 Roman miles from Orleans[1]. The Bishop of Troyes was the venerable Lupus, a man who was by this time nearly 70 years of age, and who, in common with St. Germanus, had greatly distinguished himself by his opposition to the Pelagian heresy, which he had combated in Britain as well as in Gaul. Troyes was an open city, undefended by walls or arsenals, and the immense swarm of the Huns and their allies who came clamouring round it were hungering for spoil and chafed with disappointment at their failure before Orleans[2]. Lupus, as we are told in the Acta Sanctorum, betook himself to his only weapon, prayer, and thereby successfully defended

[1] The distances and the stations on the Roman road between Metz and Orleans are quoted by Thierry (Hist. d'Attila, i. 162). He makes five halting-places between Orleans and Troyes (Aureliani and Tricasses).

[2] It is only by conjecture that the following incident is assigned to the time of Attila's retreat. The words of the Acta Sanctorum would be consistent with the interpretation that the Huns were still moving on into Gaul. But the expression 'Rheni etiam fluenta visurum,' looks as if Attila's face was now set Rhinewards. The first Life given by the Bollandists is evidently of far greater value than the second: in fact, this latter is worthless. It is curious to observe that it contains the cant phrase 'flagellum Dei,' which is absent from the other record.

his city from the assaults of the enemy. The ecclesiastical biographer seems to be purposely enigmatic and
obscure, but there are touches in the story which look
like truth. It appears that Attila, who may have been
partly swayed by the remembrance that the allies were
close upon his track, and that a night of pillage would
have been a bad preparation of his troops for the
coming battle, was also impressed—'fierce wild beast
as he was[1]'—by something which seemed not altogether
of this earth in the face and demeanour of Lupus, something unlike the servile and sordid diplomatists of
Byzantium who had hitherto been his chief exemplars
of Christianity. In granting the bishop's prayer for the
immunity of his city from pillage, he made one stipulation, that, 'for the safety of himself and his own army
the holy man should go with them and see the streams
of the Rhine, after which he promised that he would
dismiss him in peace. And so it was; as soon as they
arrived at the river he offered him a free passage back,
did not hinder his return, sent guides to show him the
way; and even earnestly besought, by the mouth of
the interpreter Hunagaisus, that the bishop would
pray for him.'

This Hunagaisus is undoubtedly the same minister
with whom we have made acquaintance in the Hunnish
camp under the name of Onegesius or Onégesh, and the
introduction of his name here in a biography probably
composed about the middle of the sixth century, affords
some guarantee that we are on the track of a genuine
tradition. If so, the thought that a Gaulish theologian
was present in the camp of Attila during the scenes

[1] 'At ille feralis Attila et immitis' (Bollandist Acta Sanctorum,
July 29).

451.

which are next to follow, gives a fresh interest to the picture, some of the details of which he may himself have described.

Battle of
the Mau-
riac Plain,
commonly
called the
Battle of
Châlons.

For in the interval between Attila's arrival before Troyes, and his dismissal of Lupus on the banks of the Rhine, occurred that great clash of armed nations which decided the question whether the West of Europe was to belong to Turanian or to Aryan nationalities. Posterity has chosen to call it the battle of Châlons, but there is good reason to think that it was fought fifty miles distant from Châlons-sur-Marne, and that it would be more correctly named the battle of Troyes, or, to speak with complete accuracy, the battle of *Mery-sur-Seine*[1].

By what preceding arts of strategy the campaign was marked, whether Attila willingly offered battle or was so sorely harassed in his retreat that he was unable to decline it, we know not, except that we read of a skirmish between the Franks and Gepidae on the night preceding the general engagement[2]. It was probably in the early days of July[3] that the two great armies at length came together. What followed shall be told in the (freely rendered) words of Jordanes himself, who throws all his heart into the narration, rightly feeling that this death-grapple with the enemies of Rome was in some sense the mightiest deed that his kinsmen had achieved, and sympathising, notwithstand-

[1] In contemporary language 'the battle of the Mauriac Plain.'

[2] See Jordanes, cap. 41, quoted below.

[3] I venture here to dissent from a conclusion arrived at in the Fasti Romani (i. 642). Clinton, on the authority of Isidore of Seville, fixes the date of the battle after Sept. 27th. This seems contrary to the whole tenour of the history and to the order of events described in Idatius, from whom Isidore has copied.

ing his own Ostrogothic descent, with Theodoric the
Visigothic antagonist of Attila, rather than with
Walamir his Ostrogothic feudatory [1].

After enumerating in the passage already quoted [2]
the various nationalities which fought under the banner
of Aetius, he continues, 'All come together therefore
into the Catalaunian, which are also called the Maurician plains, 100 Gallic *leugae* in length and 70 in
breadth. Now the *leuga* is equivalent to one Roman
mile and a half. So then that district of the world becomes the parade ground of innumerable nationalities.
Both the armies which there meet are of the mightiest;
nothing is done by underhand machinations, but everything by fair and open fight. What worthy reason
could be assigned for the deaths of so many thousands?
What hatred had crept into so many breasts and bidden
them take up arms against one another? It is surely
proved that the race of man live but for the sake of
Kings; since the mad onset of one man's mind could
cause the slaughter of so many nations, and in a
moment, by the caprice of one arrogant king, the fruit
of nature's toil through so many centuries could be
destroyed.

'Chapter 37.

'But before relating the actual order of the fight, it
seems necessary to explain some of the preliminary
movements of the war, because famous as the battle

451.

*Prelimi-
nary move-
ments.*

----

[1] Mommsen (p. xxxvi of the Introduction to his Jordanes), while
highly praising this part of the history, thinks it is probably taken
over straight from Priscus. But how then account for the Gothic
colour of the narrative? Cassiodorus seems to me a more likely
source.

[2] See note on p. 111.

was, it was no less manifold and complicated. For Sangiban, king of the Alans, foreboding future disaster, had promised to surrender himself to Attila, and to bring into obedience to him the city of Orleans where he was then quartered. When Theodoric and Aetius had knowledge of this, they built great mounds against the city and destroyed it before the coming of Attila[1]. Upon Sangiban himself they set a close watch, and stationed him with his own proper tribe in the very midst of their auxiliaries. Attila meanwhile, struck by this occurrence, distrusting his own powers, fearing to engage in the conflict, and secretly considering the expediency of flight, which was more grievous to him than death itself, resolved to enquire as to the future from the augurs. These men, according to their wont, first pored over the bowels of some sheep, then pondered the direction of the veins in some scraped bones, and at last gave forth their augury, "Ill fortune to the Huns." They qualified it however with this crumb of comfort, "that the chief leader on the opposite side should fall in the midst of victory, and so mar the triumph of his followers." To Attila the death of Aetius [whom he supposed to be intended by the words "the chief leader of the enemy"] seemed to be worth purchasing even by the defeat of his army, yet being naturally rendered anxious by such an answer, and being a man of much address in warlike matters, he determined, with some fear and trembling, to join battle about the ninth[2]

(margin notes: 451. Auguries.)

---

[1] If the text is not corrupt here, Jordanes must have received some very distorted account of the events of the siege of Orleans.

[2] This note of time suits July better than October. Even for July, the interval between three o'clock and sunset seems full short for such a battle 'multiplex et immane.'

hour of the day [3 p.m.], so that if his affairs turned out ill, impending night might come to his aid. . . . .

451.

'Chapter 38.

'Now this was the configuration of the field of battle[1]. It rose [on one side] into a decided undulation which might be called a hill; and as both parties wished to get the not inconsiderable advantage of the ground which this eminence conferred, the Huns took possession of the right-hand portion of it with their troops; the Romans and Visigoths of the left with their auxiliaries[2].' Leaving for a while the fight for the possession of this ridge [let us describe the order of the main battle]. On the right wing stood Theodoric with the Visigoths, on the left Aetius with the Romans. In the middle they placed Sangiban, the leader of the Alans,—a piece of military caution to enclose him, of whose disposition they were none too confident, in a mass of loyal soldiers. For the man in the way of whose flight you have interposed a sufficient obstacle, easily accepts the necessity of fighting.

'The line of the Huns was drawn up on a different principle, for in their centre stood Attila with all his bravest warriors. In this arrangement the king consulted his own personal safety, hoping that by taking his place in the very heart and strength of his own people he at least should be delivered from the impending danger. Upon the wings of his army hovered

Skirmish.

Roman line of battle.

Hunnish line of battle.

---

[1] 'Erat autem positio loci declivi tumore, in modum collis excrescens.'

[2] Perhaps Jordanes means that the right wing of the Hunnish army and the left wing of the confederates both endeavoured to occupy this ground. 'Dextram partem Hunni cum suis, sinistram Romani et Vesegothae cum auxiliariis occuparunt.'

the many nations and tribes whom he had subjected to
his dominion. Preeminent among these was the host of
the Ostrogoths, led by the three brothers, Walamir,
Theodemir, and Widemir, men of nobler birth than the
king himself whom they then obeyed, since the mighty
line of the Amals was represented by them. There too,
at the head of the countless warriors of the Gepidae,
was their king Ardaric, that man of valour and of fame
who for his extraordinary fidelity towards Attila was
admitted into his inmost counsels. For Attila, who had
well weighed his sagacious character, loved him and
Walamir the Ostrogoth, above all his other subject
princes; Walamir, the safe keeper of a secret, the
pleasant in speech, the ignorant of guile, and Ardaric,
who, as we have said, was illustrious both by his loyalty
and his wise advice. To these two nations Attila believed, not undeservedly, that he might safely entrust
the battle against their Visigothic kindred. As for all
the rest, the ruck of kings—if I may call them so—and
the leaders of diverse nationalities, these, like subaltern
officers, watched each nod of Attila ; and, when a look
of his eye summoned them, in fear and trembling they
would gather round him waiting in submissive silence
to receive his commands, or at any rate ' (*i.e.* if their
subservience was less abject) ' they would carry out
whatever he ordered[1]. But Attila alone, king of all
the kings, was over all in command, and had the care
of all upon his shoulders.

[1] ' Reliqua autem, si dici fas est, turba regum, diversarumque
nationum ductores, ac si satellites, nutibus Attilae attendebant, et
ubi oculo annuisset, absque aliquâ murmuratione cum timore et
tremore unusquisque adstabat, aut certe quod jussus fuerat exseque-
batur.'

' As I before said, the fight began with a struggle for the possession of some rising ground. Attila directed his troops to occupy the summit of the hill, but he was anticipated by Thorismund and Aetius, who [from the other side] struggled up to the highest point, and then, having the advantage of the hill in their favour, easily threw into confusion the advancing Huns.

451.

' Chapter 39.

' Then Attila, seeing his army somewhat disturbed by this skirmish, thought the time a suitable one for confirming their courage by an address.

Attila's speech to his troops.

' SPEECH OF ATTILA.

' " After your victories over so many nations, after a whole world subdued, if ye only stand fast this day, I should have deemed it a fond thing to whet your spirits with words, as though ye were yet ignorant of your business. Let a new general or an inexperienced army try that method. It were beneath my dignity to utter, and beyond your obligation to listen to, any of the commonplaces of war. For what other occupation are you practised in, if not in fighting? And to the strong man what is sweeter, than with his own right hand to seek for his revenge? It is one of the greatest boons which nature gives us to glut our souls with vengeance. Let us therefore go forward with cheerfulness to attack the enemy, since they who strike the blow have ever the boldest hearts. You who are united under my sway— I tell you to despise these jarring nationalities, leagued together for the momentary purpose of self-defence by an alliance which is in itself an index of their terror.

451.

Lo! ere they have yet felt our onset, they are carried to and fro by their fear; they look out for the rising ground, they are exciting themselves over the occupation of every little hillock, and bewailing too late their own rashness; they are clamouring for ramparts in these open plains[1]. Known to you right well are the flimsy arms and weak frames of the Roman soldiers; I will not say at the first wound, at the first speck of dust on their armour they lose heart. While they are solemnly forming their battle array and locking their shields together into the *testudo*, do you rush into the conflict with that surpassing courage which it is your wont to show, and, despising the Roman line, charge at the Alans, press heavily on the Visigoths. It is there that we must look for speedy victory, for they are the key of the position. Cut the sinews and the limbs will be at once relaxed; nor can the body stand if you have taken away its bones.

'"O ye Huns, raise your hearts battle-high and let your wonted fury swell your veins. Now put forth all your cunning; now use all your arms. Let him who is wounded seek still for at least one enemy's death; let him who is unhurt revel in the slaughter of the foe. Him who is fated to conquer, no dart will touch; him who is doomed to die, fate will find in the midst of slothful peace. And, last of all, why should Fortune have set her mark upon the Huns as conquerors of so many nations, unless she was preparing them for the delights of this battle too? Who

---

[1] 'Et serâ poenitudine in campis munitiones efflagitant.' An incidental argument against the theory that the so-called 'Camp of Attila' (which would be precisely 'in campis munitio') was occupied by his troops.

opened the way across the pool of Maeotis[1], for so
many centuries an impenetrable secret from our ancestors ? Who made armed men bow before them while
they were still unarmed ? Yonder motley host will
never endure to look upon the faces of the Huns.   The
event cannot mock my hopes; this, this is the field
of victory which so many previous successes have
avouched us of.   I shall be the first to hurl my weapon
against the enemy, and if any one can linger inactive
when Attila fights, he is a thing without a soul, and
ought to be buried out of hand[2]."

45I.

'Their hearts were warmed at these words, and all
rushed headlong into the fray.

'Chapter 40.

'The position of their affairs was not without its
suggestions of fear, but the presence of their king removed all tendency to delay even from the most
hesitating.

'Hand to hand the two armies were soon engaged.
It was a battle,—ruthless, manifold, immense, obstinate,
—such as antiquity in all its stories of similar encounters has nought parallel to, such as, if a man failed
to see, no other marvel that he might behold in the
course of his life would compensate for the omission[3].
For if we may believe the report of our elders, a brook
which was gliding down between low banks through the
aforesaid plain, receiving the blood which gushed from

The Battle
com-
menced.

---

[1] The sea of Azof.

[2] 'Si quis potuerit Attila pugnante otio ferre, sepultus est.'

[3] A free translation of 'ut nihil esset quod in vitâ suâ conspicere
potuisset egregius qui hujus miraculi privaretur aspectu.' *Egregius*
is evidently the neuter comparative.

thousands of wounds, was, not by showers of rain, but by that ghastly intermingling, swollen from a brook 451. into a torrent. And those whom parching thirst, the consequence of their wounds, drove to its banks, found that murder was mixed with the dráught. A miserable fate for them who drank of the gore which their own wounds poured forth.

Death of Theodoric.

'Here the King Theodoric, while he was galloping backwards and forwards, cheering on his army, was thrown from his horse, and being trampled under the feet of his own party, thus ended his life in a ripe old age. Others however assert that he was smitten by a javelin from the hand of Andages, of the nation of the Ostrogoths who were then following the lead of Attila. This was the event which Attila's sooth-sayers had foretold to him in their divinations, though he understood them to speak of Aetius.

Visigothic onset before which Attila gives way.

'Then the Visigoths, splitting off from the Alans, rushed upon the squadrons of the Huns, and had well-nigh slaughtered Attila himself, but he prudently fled, and straightway enclosed himself and his followers within the defences of his camp, upon which he had placed the waggons by way of rampart. It seemed a frail bulwark to be sure, still they clung to it as their last chance of life; and yet these were the men whose desperate onset a little while ago stone walls could not stand against. Meanwhile Thorismund, the son of King Theodoric, the same who had taken part with Aetius in the occupation of the hill, and in driving down the enemy from that higher ground, lost his way in the blind night, and thinking that he was rejoining his own men on their line of march, came unawares upon the waggons of the enemy. Here, while he was

fighting bravely, his horse was killed under him by a
wound in the head. He fell to the ground, but was
rescued by the care of his people, and persuaded to
desist from the unequal encounter. Aetius in the same
way was separated from his host in the confusion of
the night, and went wandering through the midst of
the enemy[1], trembling lest some untoward event should
have occurred to the Goths, and ever asking the way,
till at length he arrived at the camp of his allies, and
passed the remainder of the night under the shelter of
their shields.

451.

'Next morning when day dawned, and the allied
generals beheld the vast plains covered with corpses,
but saw that the Huns did not venture to sally forth,
they concluded that the victory was theirs. They knew
perfectly well that it could have been no common
slaughter which had compelled Attila to fly in confusion
from the battle-field; and yet he did not act like one
in abject prostration, but clashed his arms, sounded his
trumpets, and continually threatened a fresh attack.
As a lion, close pressed by the hunters, ramps up and
down before the entrance to his cave, and neither dares
to make a spring, nor yet ceases to frighten all the
neighbourhood with his roarings, so did that most warlike king, though hemmed in, trouble his conquerors.
The Goths and Romans accordingly called a council of
war and deliberated what was to be done with their
worsted foe. As he had no store of provisions, and
as he had so posted his archers within the boundaries
of his camp as to rain a shower of missiles on an
advancing assailant, they decided not to attempt a

Morning after the fight.

---

[1] Having from his youth been accustomed to intercourse with the
Huns, he probably spoke their language like a native.

storm, but to weary him out by a blockade. It is
said however that seeing the desperate condition of
his affairs, the aforesaid King, high-minded still in the
supreme crisis of his fate, had constructed a funeral
pyre of horses' saddles, determined, if the enemy should
break into his camp, to hurl himself headlong into
the flames, that none should boast himself and say,
"I have wounded Attila," nor that the lord of so
many nations should fall alive into the hands of his
enemies.

451.

'Chapter 41.

Burial of
Theodoric.

'During the delays of this blockade the Visigoths
were looking for their old king, and marvelling at his
absence from the scene of victory. After a long search
they found him, as is wont to be the case with brave
men, lying there where the bodies were thickest; and
singing their songs in his honour, they bore away his
corpse from the gaze of the enemy. Then should you
have seen the Gothic companies lifting up their un-
tuned voices in a wild strain of lamentation, and, while
the battle still raged around them, giving all heed to
the exact observance of the rites of burial. Tears were
shed, but they were the tears which are rightly paid to
brave men dead. The death had been on our [the
Gothic] side, but the Hun himself bore witness that
it had been a glorious one, and even Attila's pride
might bow when he saw the corpse of such a king
borne out to burial with all his kingly ornaments
about him [1].

[1] A conjectural expansion of 'Nostra mors erat, sed Hunno teste
gloriosa, unde hostium putaretur inclinata fore superbia, quando tanti
regis efferre cadaver cum suis insignibus inspiciebant.'

'The Goths, while still paying the last honours to Theodoric, by the clash of their weapons hailed the majesty of a new king, and the brave and glorious Thorismund, decked with that title, followed the funeral of his dearly-loved father as became a son. Then, when that was finished, grief for the loss which he had sustained, and the impulse of his own fiery valour, urged him to avenge the death of his father upon the Hunnish host. First, however, he consulted Aetius the patrician, as the senior general and a man of ripened experience, what step he would advise to be next taken. He, fearing lest if the Huns were destroyed root and branch, the Roman Empire might be still more hardly pressed by the Goths, earnestly tendered this advice, "that he should return to his own capital and grasp the kingdom which his father had left; lest otherwise his brothers should seize on his father's treasures, and so make the realm of the Visigoths their own, whereupon he would have to commence a laborious campaign, and one in which victory would be a wretched business, since it would be over his own flesh and blood."

451. Elevation of Thorismund.

'Thorismund received this advice as the best thing for his own interest, without perceiving the duplicity which lurked beneath it, and leaving the Huns, he returned to his own district in Gaul. So does human frailty, if it becomes entangled in suspicion, often lose irretrievably the opportunity of achieving great results [1].

Return of Thorismund to Toulouse.

'In this most famous battle, which was fought between the bravest nations in the world, it is reported

Numbers of the slain.

---

[1] 'And thus the native hue of resolution
    Is sicklied o'er with the pale cast of thought.'

that 162,000 [1] men were slain on both sides, not including 15,000 of Gepidae and Franks, who, falling foul of one another the night before the battle, perished by mutually inflicted wounds, the Franks fighting on the side of the Romans, the Gepidae on that of the Huns.

451.

Unexpected deliverance of Attila.

'When Attila learned the departure of the Goths, the event was so unexpected [2] that he surmised it to be a stratagem of the enemy, and kept his troops within the camp for some time longer. But when he found that the absence of the enemy was followed by a long time of silence, his mind again rose with the hope of victory, future joys unfolded themselves before him, and the courage of this mighty king returned again to its old level. Meanwhile Thorismund, who had been clothed with the regal majesty on the Catalaunian plains on the very place where his father had fallen, entered Toulouse, and here, notwithstanding that his brothers had a strong party among the chiefs, he so prudently managed the commencement of his reign, that no dispute was raised as to the succession.'

Why was the victory not followed up?

So far Jordanes. The battle then was lost but not won : lost as far as Attila's invasion of Gaul was concerned, but not won for the Roman Empire by the destruction of its most dreaded foe. In reading the story of Attila's escape from Aetius, one is naturally reminded of Alaric's escape from Stilicho, forty-eight years before, and of the imputations then thrown out [3]

---

[1] Idatius puts the number of slain at 300,000. Of course all estimates of the slain on such a battle-field are of the vaguest and most untrustworthy kind.

[2] Doubtful translation.

[3] By Orosius, vii. 37, 'Taceo de Alarico cum Gothis suis saepe victo, saepe concluso, semperque dimisso.'

as to the connivance of the Roman general. And the same remark which was made then may be to some extent applicable now. With troops of such uncertain temper, and, in this case, with such imperfect cohesion as the greater part of the Roman auxiliaries showed, it might be dangerous to animate the vast host of Attila with the irresistible courage of despair. In all ages, from Sphacteria to Saratoga, and from Saratoga to Sedan, the final operation of compelling the surrender of a beaten army, the landing, so to speak, of the fisherman's prize, has been an operation requiring some nicety of generalship and a pretty high degree of confidence in the discipline of the victorious troops. Even the clash of arms and the blast of trumpets in the camp of the Huns—the lashing of the lion's tail, and the deep thunder of his roar—may have struck some terror into the hearts of his hunters. But after all, Jordanes is probably not very wide of the mark when he imputes both to Aetius and to Thorismund a want of whole-heartedness in securing the fruits of victory.

451.

Aetius had not, most probably, such accurately wrought-out views of the balance of power as the historian imputes to him, nor such an over-mastering dread of Gothic bravery as their countryman supposed. But, in the very outset of his career, his life had been passed alternately in the Hunnish camp and the Roman palace; he had been 'mingled among the heathen and learned their works.' He had used the help of his barbarian friends in the marshes of Ravenna and under the walls of Toulouse. Reasons of sentiment as well as of policy may have made him reluctant to aid in obliterating the very name of the Huns from the earth.

Reasons which influenced Aetius.

And above all, as the events of the next few years showed, he himself was safe only so long as he was indispensable. There was a dark and rotten-hearted Augustus skulking in the palace at Ravenna, who endured the ascendancy of Aetius only because he trembled at the name of Attila.

Reasons which influenced Thorismund.

On the Gothic side there were also good reasons for not pushing the victory too far. It scarcely needed the whisper of the Roman general to remind Thorismund how uncertain was his succession to the royalty of his father. The kingly office among the Visigoths became, in days subsequent to these, a purely elective dignity. If at this time some notion of hereditary right, or at least of hereditary preference, hovered round the family of the dead king, it was by no means clear that one son alone must succeed, nor that son the eldest. All was still vague and indeterminate in reference to these barbaric sovereignties. In point of fact Thorismund, though he now succeeded to the throne, was, only two years later, deprived of crown and life by his brother Theodoric II, who, after a peaceful and prosperous reign, succumbed in like fashion to the fratricidal hand of his successor Euric. Every motive therefore of individual ambition and far-seeing patriotism concurred in recommending to Thorismund and his chiefs a speedy return to Toulouse, that the same army which brought the tidings of the death of Theodoric might also announce the election of his successor.

451.

453.

466.

Recent discovery of the grave of a Gothic chief near the site of the battle.

This is all that history can say with unhesitating voice concerning the death of the Visigothic king and the accession of his son on the Mauriac plain. Archaeology, however, offers a contribution to our knowledge, which, if not raised beyond the reach of all contradiction, is at least curious and interesting. In 1842, a labourer digging for gravel near the little village of Pouan, on the south bank of the Aube, and about ten miles from Mery-sur-Seine, found at a depth of nearly a yard below the surface 'some human bones, two rusted blades, and several jewels and golden ornaments of considerable weight.' Examined more in detail, the most interesting objects in this find appeared to be

451.

I. A two-edged sword, 2 feet 8 inches long, and 3 inches broad. The point is protected by a little oblong hoop of iron, to prevent it from penetrating into the scabbard, which was probably of wood, and which of course has disappeared.

II. A cutlass, about 22 inches long, and 1½ inch broad. Both of these two weapons have the hilts richly adorned with gold, and at the top a sort of lattice-work of gold and purple glass.

III. A golden necklace, serpent-shaped, weighing three ounces.

IV. A golden armlet, five ounces in weight, with the ends left open, so as to give it elasticity in fitting it on to the forearm.

V. Two golden clasps (*fibulae*) with the same lattice-work of gold and purple glass which is found on the hilts of the swords.

VI. A golden signet-ring, an ounce-and-a-half in weight, with the word HEVA in Roman capitals on the flat surface.

Some gold buckles and other ornaments, one of which has an inlay of garnets instead of purple glass, complete the treasure-trove, which, having been eventually purchased by the Emperor Napoleon III, was presented by him to the museum of the city of Troyes.

The question arises, ' Can we form any probable conjecture whose grave is this in which we find a skeleton surrounded with articles of adornment, worth even now perhaps £100 in intrinsic value, and pointing by the style of their workmanship towards the fifth or sixth century, as the time of their fashioning, and towards a Gothic or Frankish artificer as their maker.

M. Peigné Delacourt, to whom we are indebted for these details [1], answers unhesitatingly, ' We can. It is probably the tomb of Theodoric I, king of the Visigoths.' But how reconcile such a theory with the narrative of Jordanes? To accomplish this, M. Delacourt imagines a few unrecorded details, which of course no one is bound to accept, but which certainly seem to bring us a little nearer to that tremendous battle-field, dim with the haze of fourteen centuries. ' When the servants of Theodoric,' so his imagined story runs, ' found that their king was wounded to death, they dragged him a little aside from the " vast and manifold and ruthless conflict." They dug a shallow trench in the gravelly soil, and there they laid the bruised and trampled body of the snowy-bearded warrior. His golden-hilted sword was still by his side, his cutlass hung from the baldric, the purple robe of his royalty was fastened over his shoulders by the golden *fibula*. Round his neck was the golden torque, his forearm was clasped by the unclosed bracelet, on his finger was the ring of gold bear-

---

[1] See ' Recherches sur le lieu de la Bataille d'Attila en 451 par Peigné-Delacourt, Membre correspondant de la Socéité Imperiale des Antiquaires de France,' &c., Paris, 1860, with Supplement published at Troyes, 1866. This monograph is sumptuously illustrated with chromo-lithographic pictures of the find itself and of other ornaments found in France and Spain, which, in the author's opinion, point to a similarity of date or origin.

ing the mysterious name Heva, perhaps a remembrance
of his dead wife, perhaps [1] a symbol of his kingship.
All these things were buried with him. The only
object of his henchmen was to find a temporary resting-
place for their lord. When the tide of battle should
have rolled away from that spot, they would come again
and disinter him and carry him southwards, to be laid
with proper pomp in Gothic Toulouse by the Garonne.
Such was their thought, but Fortune, in making void
their counsel, worked a strange reprisal for the barbarity
practised in the burial of Alaric.   As *his* tomb was dug
by the unwilling hands of captives, whose instant death
insured their secrecy, so the few faithful friends of
Theodoric were all slain in the terrible turmoil of war
which raged round the spot where he had fallen, and
thus his grave remained unmarked for 1391 years. The
battle was won, and the cry was raised, "Where is the
body of the king?" They found it at last, says Jordanes, after a long search, lying under a heap of dead.
Who knows if they really did find it ? In those hot
July days it might not be an easy task to identify a body
gashed with wounds and lying under a pile of slain.
Thorismund's interest was obviously to get his father's
funeral and his own elevation to the sovereignty accomplished as speedily as possible. Perhaps he did not
insist too punctiliously on the recovery of the right
corpse out of all that vast slaughter-house, the one
strangely missing body out of all those acres upon acres
of dead Romans, Goths, and Huns.'

----

[1] Heva *may* possibly mean 'wife' or 'house.' But it seems more
probable that it is a proper name. The termination *a* is frequent in
Gothic names; more so, however, we must admit in those of men
than of women.

451.

And so, M. Delacourt suggests, the body round which the Visigothic warriors circled, singing their wild chorus of lamentation, may have been not that of Theodoric at all. He all the while lay in that shallow trench in the gravel-bed at Pouan, not to be disturbed there till Jacques Bonhomme, in blouse and sabots, came with his pick-axe in 1842 to break the repose of centuries. The story is well imagined, and certainly cannot be pronounced impossible. What militates most against it is that Jordanes says that the body was borne out to burial *with its ornaments* [1]. In its favour is a certain peculiar silence of his concerning the actual interment of the corpse. He may have felt that it was improbable that the Goths should have left their beloved chieftain lying there in alien territory, in the cold Catalaunian plains, and yet no tradition authorised him to say that they took him back to the sepulchre of his predecessors at Toulouse, a course which Thorismund may have had sufficient reasons for emphatically prohibiting.

Finally, whether this body and these ornaments be Theodoric's, or belong to one of the 'turba regum,' who swarmed around the car of Attila ; in either case their discovery, coupled as it appears to be with that of numerous other human remains in the not distant village of Martroy, seems to add great probability to the theory that here and not at Châlons (two days' march to the northward) was fought the great battle which decided that Europe was to belong to the German and the Roman, not to the Tartar race.

---

[1] 'Cum suis insignibus.'

NOTE B. ON THE SITE OF THE SO-CALLED BATTLE OF
CHÂLONS.

As such recent historians as Aschbach (Geschichte der Visi-
gothen) and Thierry (Histoire d'Attila) place the site of the
great battle at Châlons-sur-Marne, it may be well to show how
little there is to support this view in the earliest authorities.

The place which we now call Châlons was probably under the
Romans named Duro-Catalaunum. It was the chief place of
the Catalauni, a tribe who dwelt next to the Suessiones. As in
so many other parts of Gaul, the old tribal name has finally
prevailed, and Duro-Catalaunum has become Châlons, as Lutetia
Parisiorum is Paris, Augusta Suessionum, Soissons, and so on.
In Roman miles (ten of which are about equal to nine English),
and by the Roman roads, Châlons was 170 miles distant from
Metz, and 51 from Troyes. Fanum Minervae, now La Cheppe,
where the so-called 'Camp of Attila' is to be found, is about
ten miles to the north-east of Châlons 'as the crow flies,' but
owing to the interposition of the river Vêle, seems to have been
55 miles by road (which went northwards to Rheims, and then
returned on the other bank of the river to Châlons. This camp
is square, of Roman origin, and was therefore certainly not
constructed by Attila even if he encamped inside it.

We may now consider the words of the original authorities.

Jordanes says, 'They come together therefore at the Catalaunian plains, which are also called the *Maurician* plains, 100
Gaulish leagues in length and 70 in breadth.' ('Convenitur
itaque in campos Catalaunicos qui et Mauricii nominantur c
leugas ut Galli vocant in longum tenentes et lxx in latum.')
These measurements would cover the whole space between 48°

and 50° N. latitude, and 3° and 5° E. longitude, or a district at least equal to the old French province of Champagne.

Gregory of Tours says (ii. 7), ' Aetius and Theodore put Attila to flight [from Orleans], and he, going to the *Mauriac* plain, arrays his troops for battle.' ('Attilam fugant qui Mauriacum campum adiens se praecingit ad bellum.') Here we have no mention of the Catalaunian, but only of the Mauriac plain.

Idatius (28th year of Theodosius II) puts the battle ' in the Catalaunian plains not far from the city of Metz which the Huns had broken up' ('in campis Catalaunicis haud longè de civitate quam effregerant Mertis '). This statement is evidently quite wide of the mark, and shows that the Gallician bishop had such vague notions of the geography of north-eastern Gaul that we cannot safely accept his guidance.

The *continuer of Prosper* gives the most precise details : ' The battle was fought at the fifth milestone from Troyes, at a place called Maurica in Champagne.' ('Pugnatum est in quinto milliario de Trecas, loco nuncupato Mauricâ in Campaniâ.')

Now when we look (1) at the exceedingly wide range which, as we see from Jordanes, was given to the term Campi Catalaunici ; (2) at the persistent reference to the Campus *Mauriacus* or some similar name as the field of battle ; (3) at the fact that there is still existing a place called Mery-sur-Seine, which may fairly be supposed to represent the ancient Mauriacum ; (4) at the situation of this place, not indeed at the fifth milestone from Troyes, apparently about twenty miles distant from it, but situated in a plain which may very probably have been called the Campus Mauriacensis, and may have extended to the fifth milestone from Troyes ; (5) at the great strategical import- ance of Troyes, placed at the centre of a perfect cobweb of roads, in the Roman time as well as now, and commanding apparently the passage of at least one important river ; considering all these facts and comparing them with the authorities, we must, as it appears to me, accept the conclusion that the battle was fought near to Mery-sur-Seine, but upon widely extended lines, and that it may easily have rolled over into what were properly called the Catalaunian plains (the Catalauni being the next tribe to the Tricasses), though it cannot have extended as far as the modern Châlons-sur-Marne, which was two days' march from the field of battle.

It will be observed that this argument represents the conclusion to which we are brought by a simple consideration of the language of the chroniclers, and is wholly independent of the interesting discoveries described in the Mémoire of M. Peigné Delacourt to which reference is made in the text.

[Von Wietersheim takes the same view as to the site of the battle.]

CHAPTER IV.

ATTILA IN ITALY.

Authorities.

451. A chapter in JORDANES and a paragraph in the HISTORIA MISCELLA, with one curious anecdote from SUIDAS the well-known lexicographer (of uncertain date), are all the materials that we possess for the history of this immeasurably important campaign, except the brief memoranda of the Annalists.

Attila's return to Pannonia. IN the summer of 451, Attila, with his beaten army, recrossed the Rhine, and dismissed the courageous Lupus with a safe-conduct back to Troyes, bidding his chief minister and interpreter Onégesh intercede with the holy man that he might receive the benefit of his prayers.

All that autumn and winter we may imagine him dwelling, moody and sore of heart, within his wooden stockade upon the plains of Hungary, receiving the homage of his nobles as he drank to them out of his goblet of ivy-wood, scowling while all around were laughing at the gabble and the jests of Zercon, or passing his fingers through the dark locks of Ernak, while he whispered to himself, 'This boy shall build up the house of Attila.'

With spring, the spring of 452, came back the long-

ing for 'the joys of strife [1],' and the determination to
wipe out the shame of the Mauriac plains on some fresh
battle-field.　But this time he would not try conclusions
with the hardy Visigoth.　Aetius, Valentinian, Italy,
should bear the sole weight of his revenge [2].　He
marched, probably through the passes of the Julian
Alps and down the valley of the Frigidus, by the route
already trodden by Theodosius and Alaric, and stood,
perhaps before the spring had ripened into summer,
before the walls of Aquileia.

This town was then, both as a fortress and a commercial emporium, second to none in Northern Italy.　It
was situated at the northernmost point of the Gulf of
Hadria, about twenty miles north-west of Trieste, and
the place where it once stood is now in the Austrian
dominions, just over the border which separates them
from the kingdom of Italy.　In the year 181 B.C. a
Roman colony had been sent to this far corner of Italy
to serve as an outpost against some intrusive tribes,
called by the vague name of Gauls, who were pressing
into the Adriatic shores over the passes of the Carnic
Alps, those Alps which are so familiar to the sojourners
in Venice as 'blue Friuli's mountains.'　The colonists
built their town about four miles from the sea by the

[margin note: 452. Italian campaign of 452.]

[margin note: Situation and importance of Aquileia.]

---

[1] 'Certaminis gaudia' (Jordanes, xxxix).

[2] Possibly there had intervened some slackening of the alliance or
even actual dissensions between Ravenna and Toulouse.　Jordanes
says that Attila watched his opportunity in the departure of the
Visigoths, and seeing, what he had often hoped for, his enemies
divided into two parts, with a feeling of security moved forward his
array for the destruction of the Romans.　('Attila vero nacta occa-
sione de secessu Vesegotharum et, quod saepe optaverat, cernens
hostium solutionem per partes, mox jam securus ad oppressionem
Romanorum movit procinctum.')

banks of the river Aquilo [1] (the River of the North Wind) from whence it probably derived its name. Possessing a good harbour, with which it was connected by a navigable river, Aquileia gradually became the chief entrepôt for the commerce between Italy and what are now the Illyrian provinces of Austria. Under the Emperors, and especially after Trajan's conquest of Dacia, these provinces, rich in mineral and agricultural wealth, and enjoying long intervals of settled government, attained to a high degree of prosperity, and had the glory of seeing many Illyrian brows bound with the Imperial diadem. Naturally Aquileia rose in importance with the countries whose broker she was. She sent the wine, the oil, the costly woven fabrics of the Mediterranean provinces over the Julian and Carnic Alps into Pannonia and Noricum, and she received in return their cattle, their hides, amber from the shores of the Baltic [2], and long files of slaves taken in the border wars which were being perpetually waged with the Germanic and Slavonic tribes beyond the Danube and the Carpathians. The third century after the Christian era was probably the most flourishing period of her commercial greatness, some of the springs of which must have been dried up by the troubles with the barbarians after the loss of the province of Dacia. Still, as far as can be ascertained from the language of contemporary authors, she was, at the time at which we have now arrived, entitled to contest

[1] Otherwise called the Natiso, now the Isonzo.

[2] Mommsen thinks that the traffic in amber between Germany and Italy may be traced back as far as the times of the Roman kings. A silver coin of the Etrurian town, Populonia, of very early date, has been found, he says, 'on the old amber-route in the district of Posen' (Hist. of Rome, book i, chap. 13).

with Milan and Ravenna the distinction of being the most important city of Northern Italy. Ecclesiastical had followed commercial supremacy, and the Bishop of Aquileia ruled as Metropolitan over the provinces of Western Illyricum and Venetia, so that, between the years 350 and 450, Silistria on the lower Danube and Verona in the heart of Lombardy, both (though not both at the same time) owned his spiritual sway [1]. In a military point of view the city held a yet higher place. The strength which she derived from the river, the sea, perhaps the intervening marshes, had been increased by the elaborate fortifications of successive emperors. The savage Maximin (dethroned by the Senate in 238) had in vain attempted to take it, and had eventually been murdered under its walls by his mutinous soldiers. Equally vain had been the efforts of the army of Julian more than a century later, though they built huge wooden towers and floated them on rafts down the stream past the walls of the city. The inhabitants set the towers on fire, and were continuing a vigorous resistance when the news which arrived of the death of Constantius II, in whose cause they were fighting, released them from the necessity of further defence, and justified them in opening their

452.

---

[1] Probably the ecclesiastical limits would so far agree with the political, that the portion of Illyricum which was assigned to the Eastern sceptre at the accession of Theodosius ceased before long to be within the obedience of the See of Aquileia. On the other hand Verona and the whole of Western Venetia were (possibly as some indemnification for this loss) transferred from the metropolitan jurisdiction of Milan to that of Aquileia, at the death of St. Ambrose or shortly after that event. Such at least is the conclusion of Count Maffei (Verona Illustrata, book x), who has carefully examined both the political and ecclesiastical relations of Aquileia with the Venetian province.

gates to Julian, now sole and lawful Emperor. Rightly
therefore might Aquileia have claimed to herself the
proud title of a virgin fortress [1] ; ' and we can now
understand why it was that Aetius, who apparently
regarded the defence of all the rest of Northern Italy
as hopeless, left troops—we know not how many, nor
for how long a siege prepared—to hold the great
fortress by the Natiso against the enemy.

Attila's
siege of
Aquileia.

The Roman soldiers of the garrison were of unusually
good quality and high courage, and under their guidance the town made so long and stubborn a defence
that Attila's soldiers began to weary of their work.
Ominous murmurs began to be heard in the camp, and
it seemed as if Aquileia was about to add another
and more terrible name to the list of her unsuccessful
assailants. But just then, while Attila was pacing
round her walls, moodily deliberating with himself
whether to go or stay, the flapping of wings and
the cry of birds overhead arrested his attention. He
looked up, and saw the white storks [2] which had built
their nests in the roofs of the city, rising high in the
air, and inviting their callow young to follow them,
evidently with the intention of leaving the beleaguered
town, and contrary to their usual habits, betaking
themselves to the open country. The mother-wit of
the Hunnish chieftain caught at the expressive augury.
'Lo, there!' he cried to his grumbling soldiers. ' See
those birds, whose instinct tells them of futurity ; they

---

[1] The sudden attack by which Theodosius wrested it from Maximus
(388) was so completely a surprise that the city can hardly be deemed
to have lost its character of impregnability thereby (see vol. i. p. 467).

[2] 'Animadvertit candidas aves, id est ciconias, quae in fastigio
domorum nidificant de civitate foetus suos trahere' (Jordanes, xlii).

452.

are leaving the city which they know will perish, the
fortress which they know will fall. It is no mere
chance, no vague uncertainty which guides their movements. They are changed from all their natural love
of home and human kind by their knowledge of the
coming terror.' The wild hearts of the Huns were
stirred by the speech of their king, and took courage
from the fresh voice of Nature on their side[1]. They
again pushed up their engines to the walls, they plied
the slings and catapults with renewed energy, and, as
it were in an instant, they found themselves masters
of the town.

In proportion to the stubbornness of the defence was
the severity of the punishment meted out to Aquileia.
The Roman soldiers were, no doubt, all slain. Attila
was not a man to encumber himself with prisoners.
The town was absolutely given up to the rage, the
lust, and the greed of the Tartar horde who had so
long chafed around its walls. The only incident of
the capture which enables us to grasp more definitely
these commonplaces of barbaric conquest, is the story [2]
of a noble lady, named Digna, eminent for beauty and
virtue, whose house was situated upon the walls of
the city. Close to her house was a high tower, overlooking the glassy waters ('*vitreis fluentis*') of the
Natiso. When she saw that the city was taken, in
order to save her honour from the scornful outrages
of those filthiest of foes ('*sordidissimis hostibus*'), she
ascended the tower, and having covered her head in
the old Roman fashion, plunged into the stream below.

*margin: 452.*

margin: The punish-ment of Aquileia.

---

[1] It is important to remember the tradition that they had been
guided into Europe by a hind, a somewhat similar kind of augury.

[2] Told in the Historia Miscella, book xiv.

452.

When the barbarians could plunder no more, they probably used fire, for the very buildings of Aquileia perished, so that, as Jordanes tells us, in his time, a century later than the siege, scarcely the vestiges of it yet remained. A few houses may have been left standing, and others must have slowly gathered round them, for the Patriarch of Aquileia retained all through the middle ages considerable remains of his old ecclesiastical jurisdiction, and a large and somewhat stately cathedral was reared there in the eleventh century. But the City of the North Wind never really recovered from the blow. Her star had fallen from the firmament, and from this time she almost disappears from history. At the present day two or three mean-looking little villages cower amid the vast enclosure, which is chiefly filled with maize-fields and cherry-trees, while the high-pitched roof of the Duomo, with its tall detached campanile, dominates the plain.

Destruction of cities of Venetia.

The terrible invaders, made more wrathful and more terrible by the resistance of Aquileia, streamed on through the trembling cities of Venetia. Each earlier stage in the itinerary shows a town blotted out by their truly Tartar genius for destruction. At the distance of thirty-one miles from Aquileia stood Concordia. the flourishing colony of Julia Concordia, so named, probably, in commemoration of the universal peace which, 480 years before, Augustus had established in the world. Concordia was treated as Aquileia, and only an insignificant little village now remains to show where it once stood[1]. At another interval of thirty-

[1] In the Academy of Sept. 3rd, 1881, there is a notice by F. Barnabei of the very interesting excavations by S. Bertolini in Concordia and its neighbourhood. Especially noteworthy must have

one miles stood Altinum, with its white villas cluster-
ing round the curves of its lagunes, and rivalling
Baiae in its luxurious charms. Altinum was effaced
as Concordia and as Aquileia. Yet another march of
thirty-two miles brought the squalid invaders to
Patavium, proud of its imagined Trojan origin, and,
with better reason, proud of having given birth to
Livy. Patavium, too, was levelled with the ground.
True it has not, like its sister towns, remained in the
nothingness to which Attila reduced it. It is now

'Many doméd Padua proud,'

but all its great buildings date from the middle
ages. Only a few broken friezes and a few inscriptions in its museum exist as memorials of the classical
Patavium.

As the Huns marched further away from Aquileia,
and the remembrance of their detention under its
ramparts became less vivid, they were less eager to
spend their strength in mere blind rage of demolition.
Vicenza, Verona, Brescia, Bergamo, all opened their
gates at their approach, for the terror which the fate of
Aquileia had inspired was on every heart. In these
towns, and in Milan and Pavia (Ticinum), which followed
their example, the Huns enjoyed doubtless to the full
their wild revel of lust and spoliation, but they left the

452.
Altinum.
Patavium.

Attila in
the upper
valley of
the Po.

been the great sarcophagi with their heavy lids, grouped on both sides
of the Roman road which led to Aquileia and the East. 'In some
places we see slabs that have been completely wrenched from their
sarcophagi by means of levers; and in imagination we witness the
desolating invasion of the ruthless Huns, who cared not one jot for
the pains and penalties with which he who should desecrate the tombs
was threatened, but broke them open in every direction in order to
rifle the valuables which had been buried with the corpse.'

buildings unharmed, and they carried captive the inhabitants instead of murdering them [1].

At Milan a characteristic incident, which rests on
fair if not contemporaneous evidence, is said to have
occurred. The Hunnish king took up his quarters at
the Imperial Palace, the stately edifice in which Constantine signed the edict for the legalization of Christianity, the same edifice in which, eighty years later,
Theodosius expired, sick at heart for the ruin which he
saw impending over the Empire. Besides other works
of painting and sculpture with which the palace was
no doubt liberally adorned, Attila beheld a picture
representing 'The Triumph of Rome over the Barbarians.' Here were the two Augusti of the East and
West seated on their golden thrones, and here in the
front of the picture were the figures of the vanquished
Scythians, some slain, others crouching in abject submission before the feet of the Emperors. Even so may
the King of Prussia have looked, in the long galleries
of Versailles, upon the glowing battle-pieces in which
the genius of Lebrun and of Vernet commemorates the
prowess of France and the humiliations of Germany.
Attila took the insult as aimed at his own ancestors,
though it is almost certain that the 'Scythians' whom
any painter at Milan delineated would be Goths rather

---

[1] This distinction between the cities of Eastern Venetia and their
Western neighbours, which is quite evident to any one at the present
day who is in quest of Roman remains, is very clearly brought out by
the Historia Miscella (Book xiv) which is here our best authority.
'Concordiam, Altinum sive (=et) Patavium vicinas Aquilejae civi-
tates, illius instar demoliens solo coaequavit. Exinde per universas
Venetiarum urbes, hoc est Vincentiam, Veronam, Brixiam, Pergamum,
seu (=et) reliquas, nullo resistente, Hunni bacchabantur, Mediolanum
Ticinumque pari sorte diripiunt, *ab igne tamen abstinentes et ferro.*

than Huns. With that grim humour which flashed
forth now and again upon the sullen background of his
character, he called for an artist whom he commissioned
to paint, perhaps on the opposite wall, a rival picture.
In this, king Attila sat on his throne, and the two
Emperors bowed low before him. One still bore upon
his shoulders a large miller's sack filled with pieces of
gold, the other was already pouring out the contents of
a similar sack at his feet. This reference to the tributary obligations which Attila had forced upon both
Rome and Constantinople harmonises with the language
of Priscus, and seems to invest the story with a
semblance of probability. Would that amidst the
subsequent changes of fortune which have befallen
the fair city of Milan, notwithstanding the despair of
the Ostrogoths and the rage of Barbarossa, that picture
might have survived to tell us what the great Hun
looked like in his pride, the artistic Theodosius and the
sensual Valentinian in their humiliation [1].

The valley of the Po was now wasted to the heart's
content of the invaders. Should they cross the Apennines and blot out Rome as they had blotted out
Aquileia from among the cities of the world? This
was the great question that was being debated in the
Hunnish camp, and strange to say, the voices were not

margin note: 452.

[1] This story is preserved for us in the work—half dictionary, half
encyclopaedia—of Suidas. Unfortunately his own date is so uncertain, and so many additions have been made to the original work,
that it is quite impossible to say from external evidence whether this
anecdote was committed to writing in the 5th century or at a much
later period. Suidas relates it twice, once under the heading Κόρυκος
and once under Μεδιόλανον. The former word, which signifies 'a
sack' is of very infrequent occurrence, and it has been suggested
that this is probably the cause of the preservation of the story.

all for war. Already Italy began to strike that strange awe into the hearts of her northern conquerors which so often in later ages has been her best defence. The remembrance of Alaric, cut off by a mysterious death immediately after his capture of Rome, was present in the mind of Attila, and was frequently insisted upon by his counsellors, who seem to have had a foreboding that only while he lived would they be great and prosperous.

452.

Roman embassy to the Hunnish camp.

While this discussion was going forward in the barbarian camp, all voices were hushed, and the attention of all was aroused, by the news of the arrival of an embassy from Rome. What had been going on in that city it is not easy to ascertain. The Emperor seems to have been dwelling there, not at Ravenna. Aetius shows a strange lack of courage or of resource, and we find it difficult to recognise in him the victor of the Mauriac plains. He appears to have been even meditating flight from Italy, and to have thought of persuading Valentinian to share his exile[1]. But counsels a shade less timorous prevailed. Some one suggested that possibly even the Hun might be satiated with havoc, and that an embassy might assist to mitigate the remainder of his resentment. Accordingly ambassadors were sent in the once mighty name of 'the Emperor and the Senate and People of Rome' to crave for peace, and these were the men who were now ushered into the camp of Attila.

---

[1] This hint as to the feebleness of Aetius is to be found in Prosper of Aquitaine—'Nihil duce nostro Aetio secundum prioris belli opera prospiciente; ita ut ne clusuris quidem Alpium quibus hostes prohiberi potuerant, uteretur; hoc solum spei suis superesse existimans, si ab omni Italiâ cum Imperatore discederet.'

The envoys had been well chosen to satisfy that punctilious pride which insisted that only men of the highest dignity among the Romans should be sent to treat with the Lord of Scythia and Germany [1]. Avienus, who had, two years before, worn the robes of consul, was one of the ambassadors. Trigetius, who had wielded the power of a prefect, and who, seventeen years before, had been despatched upon a similar mission to Gaiseric the Vandal, was another. But it was not upon these men, but upon their greater colleague that the eyes of all the barbarian warriors and statesmen were fixed. Leo, Bishop of Rome, had come on behalf of his flock, to sue for peace from the idolater.

452. The Roman ambassadors.

The two men who had thus at last met by the banks of the Mincio are certainly the grandest figures whom the fifth century can show to us, at any rate since Alaric vanished from the scene. Attila we by this time know well enough : adequately to describe Pope Leo I, we should have to travel too far into the region of ecclesiastical history. Chosen pope in the year 440, he was now about half way through his long pontificate, one of the few which have nearly rivalled the twenty-five years traditionally assigned to St. Peter [2]. A firm

Character of Pope Leo I.

[1] We know, from a letter of the Ostrogothic king Theodoric, that the grandfather of his Secretary Cassiodorus was sent on an embassy to Attila and obtained peace for Rome. (Cassiodori Variarum, i. 4.) Some historians have perplexed themselves by trying to reconcile that account with this of the embassy of Leo and his two colleagues. But it seems much more probable that the embassy of the grandfather of Cassiodorus was an earlier one, perhaps one of the many relating to the vases of Sirmium. He was accompanied by Carpilio, son of Aetius, who, as we learn from Priscus (p. 179, Bonn edition), had passed many years as a hostage at Attila's court.

[2] 'Non videbis annos Petri,' the exhortation which is said to be addressed to each Pope on his accession, and which no Pope till

disciplinarian, not to say a persecutor, he had caused the Priscillianists of Spain and the Manichees of Rome to feel his heavy hand. A powerful rather than subtle theologian, he had asserted the claims of Christian common sense as against the endless refinements of Oriental speculation concerning the nature of the Son of God. Like an able Roman general, he had traced in his letters on the Eutychian Controversy the lines of the fortress in which the defenders of the Catholic verity were thenceforward to entrench themselves, and from which they were to repel the assaults of Monophysites on the one hand, and of Nestorians on the other. These lines had been enthusiastically accepted by the great Council of Chalcedon (held in the year of Attila's Gaulish campaign), and remain from that day to this the authoritative utterance of the Church concerning the mysterious union of the Godhead and the Manhood in the person of Jesus Christ.

And all these gifts of will, of intellect, and of soul, were employed by Leo with undeviating constancy, with untired energy, in furthering his great aim, the exaltation of the dignity of the Popedom, the conversion of the admitted primacy of the bishops of Rome into an absolute and world-wide spiritual monarchy. Whatever our opinions may be as to the influence of this spiritual monarchy on the happiness of the world, or its congruity with the character of the Teacher in whose words it professed to root itself, we cannot withhold a tribute of admiration from the high temper of this Roman bishop, who in the ever-deepening degradation of his country still despaired not, but had

Pius IX lived to falsify. The Pontificate of Leo I lasted only twenty-one years.

the courage and endurance to work for a far-distant future, who, when the Roman was becoming the common drudge and footstool of all nations, still remembered the proud words, ' *Tu regere imperio populos, Romane, memento !* ' and under the very shadow of Attila and Gaiseric prepared for the city of Romulus a new and spiritual dominion, vaster and more enduring than any which had been won for her by Julius or by Hadrian.

452.

Such were the two men who stood face to face in the summer of 452 upon the plains of Lombardy. The barbarian king had all material power in his hand, and he was working but for a twelve-month. The Pontiff had no power but in the world of intellect, and his fabric was to last fourteen centuries. They met, as has been said, by the banks of the Mincio. Jordanes tells us that it was 'where the river is crossed by many wayfarers coming and going.' Some writers think that these words point to the ground now occupied by the celebrated fortress of Peschiera, close to the point where the Mincio issues from the Lake of Garda [1]. Others place the interview at Governolo, a little village hard by the junction of the Mincio and the Po [2]. If the latter theory be true, and it seems to fit well with the route which would probably be taken by Attila, the meeting took place in Virgil's country, and almost in sight of the very farm where Tityrus and Meliboeus chatted at evening under the beech tree.

Interview by the Mincio.

[1] This is the opinion of Maffei (Verona Illustrata, ii. 377, ed. 1825).

[2] This is the opinion of Muratori (Annali d'Italia, iii. 154) and has also in its favour the authority of Andrea Dandolo (Doge of Venice, 1343–1354), whatever that authority may be worth (And. Danduli Chronicon, book v, cap. 5, § 6).

Leo's success as an ambassador was complete. Attila laid aside all the fierceness of his anger and promised

452.
Complete
success of
Leo's em-
bassy.

to return across the Danube, and to live thenceforward at peace with the Romans. But, in his usual style, in the midst of reconciliation he left a loophole for future wrath, for 'he insisted still on this point above all, that Honoria, the sister of the Emperor, and the daughter of the Augusta Placidia, should be sent to him with the portion of the royal wealth which was her due ; and he threatened that unless this was done he would lay upon Italy a far heavier punishment than any which it had yet borne.'

Legendary
amplifica-
tions.

But, for the present, at any rate, the tide of devastation was turned, and few events more powerfully impressed the imagination of that new and blended world which was now standing at the threshold of the dying Empire than this retreat of Attila, the dreaded king of kings, before the unarmed successor of St. Peter. Later ages have encrusted the history with legends of their own. The great picture in the Vatican, which represents the abject terror of the Huns in beholding St. Peter and St. Paul in the air championing the faithful city, gives that version of the story which has received eternal currency from the mint-mark impressed by the genius of Raphael. As mythology has added to the wonder, so criticism has sought of later days to detract from it. The troops of Marcian, the Eastern Emperor, are said to have been in motion. Aetius, according to one account, had at length bestirred himself and cut off many of the Huns. But on carefully examining the best authorities we find the old impression strengthened, that neither miracle, nor pious fraud, nor military expediency determined the retreat of Attila. He was already predisposed to moderation by the counsels of his ministers. The awe of Rome was upon him and upon them, and he was forced incessantly to ponder the question, 'What if I conquer like Alaric, to die like him?' Upon these doubts and ponderings of his supervened the stately presence of Leo, a man of holy life, firm will, dauntless courage—that, be sure, Attila perceived in the first moments of their interview—and, besides this, holding an office honoured and venerated through all the civilized world. The Barbarian yielded to his spell as he had yielded to that of Lupus of Troyes, and, according to a tradition which, it must be admitted, is not very well authenticated, he jocularly excused his unaccustomed gentleness by saying that 'he knew how to conquer men, but the lion and the wolf (Leo and Lupus) had learned how to conquer him.'

The renown and the gratitude which Leo I earned by this interposition placed the Papal Chair many steps higher in the estimation both of Rome and of the world[1]. In the dark days which were coming, the senate and people of Rome were not likely to forget that when the successor of Caesar had been proved useless, the successor of Peter had been a very present help. And thus it is no paradox to say that indirectly the king of the Huns contributed, more perhaps than any other historical personage, towards the creation of that mighty factor in the politics of mediaeval Italy, the Pope-King of Rome.

His share in the creation of another important actor on the same stage, the Republic of Venice, has yet to be noticed. The tradition which asserts that it and

452.

Effect on the authority of the Papacy.

Attila the true founder of Venice

[1] Urbis et Orbis.

its neighbour cities in the Lagunes were peopled by fugitives from the Hunnish invasion of 452, is so constant, and in itself so probable, that we seem bound to accept it as substantially true, though contemporary, or nearly contemporary evidence to the fact is utterly wanting.

The thought of 'the glorious city in the sea' so dazzles our imaginations when we turn our thoughts towards Venice, that we must take a little pains to free ourselves from the spell, and reproduce the aspect of the desolate islands and far-stretching wastes of sand and sea, to which the fear of Attila drove the delicately-nurtured Roman provincials for a habitation. And as in describing the Hiongnu at their first appearance in history we had to refer to Physical Geography for an account of that vast Asian upland which was their home, so now that we are about to part with the Huns for ever, we must hear what the same science has to tell us of that very different region (the north-eastern corner of Italy) in which they, who came but to destroy, unwittingly built up an empire.

Streams pouring into the north-west corner of the Adriatic.

If we examine on the map the well-known and deep recess of the Adriatic Sea, we shall at once be struck by one marked difference between its eastern and its northern shores. For three hundred miles down the Dalmatian coast not one large river, scarcely a considerable stream, descends from the too closely towering Dinaric mountains to the sea. If we turn now to the north-western angle which formed the shore of the Roman province of Venetia, we find the coast-line broken by at least seven streams, two of which are great rivers. Let us enumerate them. Past the desolate site of Aquileia flows forth that *Isonzo*, once

called the river of the North Wind, with which we
have already made acquaintance. It rises in an all but
waterless range of mountains on the edge of Carniola [1],
and flows, milk-white with its Alpine deposits, through
the little Austrian county of Goritzia. *Tagliamento*
and *Livenza* rise in 'blue Friuli's mountains,' and just
before they reach the sea encircle the town of Concordia, with which we have also made acquaintance as
the second Italian city which Attila destroyed. Rising
among the mysterious Dolomites, and flowing through
Cadore and Titian's country, then past Belluno and
Treviso, comes a longer and more important river, the
Piave. The shorter but lovely stream of the *Brenta*,
rising within a few miles of Trient, and just missing
the same Dolomite ancestry, washes with her green and
rapid waters the walls of Bassano, full of memories of
Ezzelin's tyrannies, and of a whole family of Venetian
painters, and then, running within sight of Padua,
empties her waters into the sea a few miles south of
Venice [2]. *Adige* comes next, dear to the heart of the
pedestrian traveller in South Tyrol, who has through
many a mile of his pilgrimage towards Italy been
cheered by the loquacious companionship of its waters,
who has seen its tributary, the Eisach, swirling round
the porphyry cliffs of Botzen, and the united stream
rushing under the old battlemented bridge at Verona.
Last and greatest of all, the *Po*, the Eridanus of the
poets, rising under the shadow of Monte Viso, flowing

---

[1] See a striking description of the upper valley of the Isonzo in
'The Dolomite Mountains,' by Gilbert and Churchill, p. 233.

[2] The mouth of the Brenta was formerly just opposite to the
island of Rialto. The Venetian canal-makers took the river round
to Brondolo.

nearly 300 miles through the rich plain of Lombardy, and receiving in its course countless affluents from the southern gorges of the Alps and the northern face of the Apennines, empties its wealth of waters into the Adriatic about a dozen miles from the all but united mouths of the Brenta and the Adige. The Delta of this abundant, but comparatively sluggish river, projecting into the Adriatic Sea, makes a marked alteration in the Italian coast-line, and causes some surprise that such a Delta should not yet have received its Alexandria; that Venice to the north, and Ravenna to the south should have risen into greatness, while scarcely a village marks the exit of the Po.

These seven streams, whose mouths are crowded into less than eighty miles of coast, drain an area which, reckoning from Monte Viso to the Terglou Alps (the source of the Isonzo), must be 450 miles in length, and may average 200 miles in breadth, and this area is bordered on one side by the highest mountains in Europe, snow-covered, glacier-strewn, wrinkled and twisted into a thousand valleys and narrow defiles, each of which sends down its river or its rivulet to swell the great outpour.

For our present purpose, and as a worker out of Venetian history, Po, notwithstanding the far greater volume of his waters, is of less importance than the six other smaller streams that we named before him. He, carrying down the fine alluvial soil of Lombardy, goes

Formation of the lidi and the lagune.

on lazily adding foot by foot to the depth of his Delta, and mile by mile to its extent. They, swiftly hurrying over their shorter course from mountain to sea, scatter indeed many fragments, detached from their native rocks, over the first meadows which they meet with in the plain, but carry some also far out to sea, and then, behind the bulwark which they thus have made, deposit the finer alluvial particles with which they too are laden. Thus we get the two characteristic features of this ever-changing coastline, the *lido* and the *laguna*. The *lido*, founded upon the masses of rock, is a long, thin slip of *terra firma* which forms a sort of advanced guard of the land. The *laguna*, occupying the interval between the lido and the true shore, is a wide expanse of waters generally very few feet in depth, with a bottom of fine sand, and with a few channels of deeper water, the representatives of the forming rivers, winding intricately among them. In such a configuration of land and water the state of the tide makes a striking difference in the scene. And unlike the rest of the Mediterranean, the Adriatic does possess a tide, small it is true in comparison with the great tides of ocean, (for the whole difference between high and low water at the flood is not more than six feet, and the average flow is said not to amount to more than two feet six inches), but even this flux is sufficient to produce large tracts of sea which the reflux converts into square miles of oozy sand [1].

Here, between sea and land, upon this detritus of the rivers, settled the Detritus of Humanity. The Gothic and the Lombard invasions contributed probably their share of fugitives, but fear of the Hunnish world-waster (whose very name, according to some, was derived from

[1] No reader of Ruskin's ' Stones of Venice ' will need to be reminded of that magnificent chapter, ' The Throne,' at the commencement of the Second Volume, in which the influence of this Adriatic tide on the history and architecture of Venice, and the whole connection between the physical configuration and political development of the city, are worked out with inimitable clearness and force.

452.

Allocation
of the
refugees
among the
villages by
the la-
gunes.

one of the mighty rivers of Russia[1]) was the great
'degrading' influence that carried down the fragments
of Roman civilization and strewed them over the
desolate lagunes of the Adriatic.

The inhabitants of Aquileia, or at least the feeble
remnant that escaped the sword of Attila, took refuge
at Grado. Concordia migrated to Caprularia (now
Caorle). The inhabitants of Altinum, abandoning their
ruined villas, founded their new habitations upon seven
islands at the mouth of the Piave, which, according to
tradition, they named from the seven gates of their old
city—Torcellus, Maiurbius, Boreana, Ammiana, Con-
stantiacum, and Anianum. The representatives of some
of these names, Torcello, Mazzorbo, Burano, are familiar
sounds to the Venetian at the present day. From
Padua came the largest stream of emigrants. They
left the tomb of their mythical ancestor, Antenor, and
built their humble dwellings upon the islands of Rivus
Altus and Methamaucus, better known to us as Rialto
and Malamocco. This Paduan settlement was one
day to be known to the world by the name of Venice.
But let us not suppose that the future Queen of the
Adriatic sprang into existence at a single bound like
Constantinople or Alexandria. For 250 years, that is
to say for eight generations, the refugees on the islands
of the Adriatic prolonged an obscure and squalid
existence,—fishing, salt-manufacturing, damming out
the waves with wattled vine-branches, driving piles
into the sand-banks [2]; and thus gradually extending

---

[1] Etzel (=Attila) is said to have been the Tartar name of the Volga.

[2] See the well-known letter of Cassiodorus, Praetorian Prefect
under the successors of Theodoric the Ostrogoth: written probably
about 537 (Variarum, xii. 24).

the area of their villages. Still these were but fishing villages, loosely confederated together, loosely governed, poor and insignificant; so that the anonymous geographer of Ravenna, writing in the seventh century, can only say of them : 'In the country of Venetia there are some few islands which are inhabited by men[1].' This seems to have been their condition, though perhaps gradually growing in commercial importance, until at the beginning of the eighth century the concentration of political authority in the hands of the first doge, and the recognition of the Rialto cluster of islands as the capital of the confederacy, started the Republic on a career of success and victory, in which for seven centuries she met no lasting check.

But this lies far beyond the limits of our present subject. It must be again said that we have not to think of 'the pleasant place of all festivity,' but of a few huts among the sand-banks, inhabited by Roman provincials, who mournfully recall their charred and ruined habitations by the Brenta and the Piave. The sea alone does not constitute their safety. If that were all, the pirate ships of the Vandal Gaiseric might repeat upon their poor dwellings all the terror of Attila. But it is in their amphibious life, in that strange blending of land and sea which is exhibited by the lagunes, that their safety lies. Only experienced pilots can guide a vessel of any considerable draft through the mazy channels of deep water which intersect these lagunes ; and should they seem to be in imminent peril from the approach of an enemy, they will defend themselves, not like the Dutch by cutting

452.

Cause of the safety of Venice.

[1] 'In patria vero Venetiae sunt aliquantae insulae quae hominibus habitantur' (v. 25).

the dykes which barricade them from the ocean, but
by pulling up the poles which even those pilots need
to indicate their pathway through the waters.

452.

Contrast
between
Venice
and her
founder.

There, then, engaged in their humble beaver-like
labours, we leave for the present the Venetian refugees
from the rage of Attila.   But even while protesting, it
is impossible not to let into our minds some thought
of what those desolate fishing villages will one day
become.   The dim religious light, half-revealing the
slowly-gathered glories of St. Mark's ; the Ducal Palace
—that history in stone ; the Rialto, with its babble of
many languages ; the Piazza, with its flocks of fearless
pigeons ; the Brazen Horses ; the Winged Lion ; the
Bucentaur; all that the artists of Venice did to make
her beautiful, her ambassadors to make her wise, her
secret tribunals to make her terrible ; memories of
these things must come thronging upon the mind at
the mere mention of her spell-like name.   Now, with
these pictures glowing vividly before you, wrench the
mind away with sudden effort to the dreary plains of
Pannonia.   Think of the moody Tartar, sitting in his
log-hut, surrounded by his barbarous guests, of Zercon
gabbling his uncouth mixture of Hunnish and Latin, of
the bath-man of Onégesh, and the wool-work of Kreka,
and the reed-candles in the village of Bleda's widow ;
and say if cause and effect were ever more strangely
mated in history than the rude and brutal might of
Attila with the stately and gorgeous and subtle Republic of Venice.

One more consideration is suggested to us by that
which was the noblest part of the work of Venice, the
struggle which she maintained for centuries, really on
behalf of all Europe, against the Turk.   Attila's power

was soon to pass away, but in the ages that were to come, another Turanian race was to arise, as brutal as the Huns, but with their fierceness sharp-pointed and hardened into a far more fearful weapon of offence by the fanaticism of Islam. These descendants of the kinsfolk of Attila were the Ottomans, and but for the barrier which, like their own *murazzi* against the waves, the Venetians interposed against the Ottomans, it is scarcely too much to say that half Europe would have undergone the misery of subjection to the organised anarchy of the Turkish Pachas. The Tartar Attila, when he gave up Aquileia and her neighbour cities to the tender mercies of his myrmidons, little thought that he was but the instrument in an unseen Hand for hammering out the shield which should one day defend Europe from Tartar robbers such as he was. The Turanian poison secreted the future antidote to itself, and the name of that antidote was Venice.

452.

Our narrative returns for a little space to the Pannonian home of Attila. Before the winter of 452 he had probably marched back thither with all his army. Jordanes tells us that he soon repented of his inactivity, as if it were a crime, and sent one of his usual blustering messages to Marcian, threatening to lay waste the provinces of the East unless the money promised by Theodosius were immediately paid. Notwithstanding this message, however, he really had his eyes fixed on Gaul, and burned to avenge his former defeat upon the Visigoths. The Alans, that kindred tribe now encamped on the southern bank of the Loire, seemed again to hold out some hope of facilitating his invasion. King Thorismund, however, detected the subtle schemes of Attila with equal subtlety, moved

Alleged Gaulish campaign of Attila.
453.

speedily towards the country of the Alans, whom he
either crushed or conciliated, then met the Hunnish

453.

king in arms once more upon the Catalaunian plains,
and again compelled him to fly defeated to his own
land. 'So did the famous Attila, the lord of many
victories, in seeking to overturn the glory of his
conqueror, and to wipe out the memory of his own
disgrace, bring on himself double disaster, and return
inglorious home.'

Dis-
believed
by his-
torians.

By the unanimous consent of historians, this second
defeat of Attila by the Visigoths is banished from the
historical domain. The silence of all contemporary
chroniclers, the strange coincidence as to the site of the
battle, the obvious interest of the patriotic Goth to
give his countrymen one victory over the Hun, of
which neither Roman nor Frank could share the credit :
these are the arguments upon which the negative
judgment of historians is based, and they are perhaps
sufficient for their purpose. It may be remarked,
however, that the events assigned by the chroniclers
to the year 453 do not seem absolutely to preclude the
possibility of a Gaulish campaign, and that it is somewhat unsafe to argue against positive testimony from
the mere silence even of far more exhaustive narrators
than the annalists of the fifth century.

For the next scene, however, we have far more
trustworthy authority, for here the words of Jordanes
—'ut Priscus refert'—assure us that we have again,
though at second-hand, the safe guidance of our old
friend the Byzantine ambassador.

Marriage
with Ildico,

It was in the year 453, the year that followed his
Italian campaign, that Attila took to himself, in
addition to all his other wives (and, as we have seen,

his harem was an extensive one), the very beautiful damsel, Ildico. At the wedding-feast he relaxed his usual saturnine demeanour, drank copiously, and gave way to abundant merriment. Then when the guests were departed, he mounted the flight of steps that led up to his couch, placed high in the banqueting hall [1], and there lay down to sleep the heavy sleep of a reveller. He had long been subject to fits of violent bleeding at the nose, and this night he was attacked by one of them. But lying as he was upon his back in his deep and drunken slumber, the blood could not find its usual exit, but passed down his throat and choked him. The day dawned, the sun rose high in the heavens, the afternoon was far spent, and no sign was made from the nuptial chamber of the king. Then at length his servants, suspecting something wrong, after uttering loud shouts, battered in the door and entered. They found him lying dead, with no sign of a wound upon his body, the blood streaming from his mouth, and Ildico, with downcast face, silently weeping behind her veil. Such a death would, of course, excite some suspicion—suspicion which one of the Eastern chroniclers [2] expanded into certainty—of the guilt of Ildico, who was probably regarded as the Jael by whose hand this new and more terrible Sisera had fallen. It is more probable, however, that the cause assigned by Jordanes, apparently on the authority of Priscus, is

453.

and death
of Attila.

---

[1] See Priscus' description quoted in the second chapter.

[2] Marcellinus says 'Attila, king of the Huns, despoiler of the provinces of Europe, is [at the instigation of Aetius] stabbed in the night by the hand and dagger of a woman. Some, however, relate that he lost his life by a hemorrhage' ('sanguinis rejectione').

the true one, and that the mighty king died, as he says, a drunkard's death.

453. Marcian's dream.

It seems to be a well-attested fact, and is a curious incidental evidence of the weight with which the thought of Attila lay upon the minds even of brave men, that on the same night in which he died, the stout-hearted Emperor of the East, Marcian, who had gone to sleep anxious and distressed at the prospect of a Hunnish invasion, had a dream in which he saw the bow of Attila broken. When he awoke he accepted the omen that the Huns, whose chief weapon was the bow, were to be no longer formidable to the Empire.

Attila's obsequies.

In proportion to the hope of other nations was the grief of Attila's own people when they found that their hero was taken from them. According to their savage custom they gashed their faces with deep wounds [1], in order that so great a warrior might be honoured by the flowing, not of womanish tears, but of manly blood. Then in the middle of the vast Hungarian plain they erected a lofty tent with silken curtains, under which the corpse of the great chieftain was laid. A chosen band of horsemen careered round and round the tent, like the performers in the Circensian games of the Romans, and as they went through their mazy evolutions they chanted a wild strain, rehearsing the high descent and great deeds of the departed. What the form of these Hunnish songs may have been, it is impossible to conjecture; but the thoughts, or at least some of the chief thoughts, have been preserved to us by Jordanes, and may perhaps, without unfitness, be

[1] Compare the lines of Claudian quoted at the beginning of the second book.

clothed in metre, for in truth his prose here becomes almost metrical.

453.

THE DIRGE OF ATTILA.

Mightiest of the Royal Huns[1],
  Son of Mundzuk, Attila!
Leader of Earth's bravest ones,
  Son of Mundzuk, Attila!
Power was thine, unknown before.
German-Land and Scythia bore,
Both, thy yoke. Thy terror flew
Either Roman Empery through.
O'er their smoking towns we bore thee,
Till, to save the rest, before thee,
Humbly both the Caesars prayed.
Thy wrath was soothed, and sheathed thy blade.
Slave-like[2] at thy feet they laid
Tribute, as their master bade,
  The son of Mundzuk, Attila.

At the height of human power
  Stood the chieftain, Attila,
All had prospered till that hour
  That was wrought by Attila.
Thou diedst not by the foeman's brand,
Thou felt'st no dark assassin's hand.
All thy landsmen, far and wide,
Were safe from fear on every side.

[1] As this translation is somewhat paraphrastic the original is sub-joined. 'Praecipuus Hunnorum Rex Attila, patre genitus Mundzucco, fortissimarum gentium dominus, qui inauditâ ante se potentiâ solus Scythica et Germanica regna possedit, necnon utraque Romani orbis Imperia captis civitatibus terruit, et ne praedae reliquae subderentur, placatus precibus, annuum vectigal accepit. Cumque haec omnia proventu felicitatis egerit, non vulnere hostium, non fraude suorum, sed gente incolumi, inter gaudia laetus, sine sensu doloris occubuit. Quis ergo hunc dicat exitum, quem nullus aestimat vindicandum.'

[2] This thought is taken from Attila's message to Theodosius by Orestes, quoted in the Second Chapter.

In the midst of thy delight,
    'Mid the joys of Wine and Night
    Painless, thou hast taken flight
    From thy brethren, Attila !

453.

Shouldest thou thus have ended life,
    With no pledge of future strife ?
    Thou art dead : in vain we seek
    Foe on whom revenge to wreak
    For thy life-blood, Attila !

The Interment.

When the wild dirge was ended, the great funeral-feast, which they call the *Strava* [1], was prepared, and the same warriors who but a few days before had been emptying great goblets of wine in honour of the marriage of Attila, now with the same outward semblance of jollity, celebrated his death. Even while the feast was proceeding, the dead body was being secretly consigned to the earth. It was enclosed in three coffins; the first of gold, the second of silver, the third of iron, to typify the wealth with which he had enriched his kingdom, and the weapons wherewith he had won it. Arms won from valiant foes, quivers studded with gems, and many another royal trinket, were buried with him. Then, as in the case of Alaric, in order to elude the avarice of future generations and keep the place of his burial secret for ever, the workmen, probably captives, who had been engaged in the task of his sepulture, were immediately put to death.

As far as we know, the grave of Attila keeps its

---

[1] There is some doubt whether the word *Strava* does not mean the heap of arms and trophies of war which was sometimes raised over the body of a dead warrior; but here the emphasis laid on the obscurity of the burial-place seems to negative that interpretation. Ducange (Glossarium Mediae et Infimae Latinitatis) seems on other grounds to prefer the banquet-interpretation.

secret to this day.　But his deeds had made an in-
delible mark on the imagination of three races of men
—the Latin peoples, the Germans, and the Scandi-
navians ; and in the ages of darkness which were to
follow, a new and strangely-altered Attila, if we should
not rather say three Attilas, rose as it were from his
mysterious Pannonian tomb, gathered around themselves all kinds of weird traditions, and hovered ghost-
like before the fascinated eyes of the Middle Ages.
To trace the growth of this Attila-legend, however
interesting the work might be as an illustration of the
myth-creating faculty of half-civilized nations, is no
part of my present purpose.　Moreover, the task has
been so well performed by M. Amedée Thierry in the
last section of his *Histoire d'Attila*, that little remains
for any later inquirer but simply to copy from him.
It will be sufficient therefore to note as briefly as
possible the chief characteristics of the different versions
of the legend.

1. The traditions of the Latin races, preserved and
elaborated by ecclesiastics, naturally concerned themselves with the religious, or rather irreligious, aspect
of his character.　To them he is, therefore, the great
Persecutor of the Fifth Century, the murderer of the
eleven thousand virgins of Cologne, but above all, he
is the *Flagellum Dei*, the scourge of God, divinely
permitted to set forth on his devastating career for the
punishment of a world that was lying in wickedness.
This title, 'Flagellum Dei,' occurs with most wearisome
frequency in the mediaeval stories about Attila ; and
wheresoever we meet with it, we have a sure indication
that we are off the ground of contemporaneous and
authentic history, and have entered the cloud-land of

ecclesiastical mythology. Later and wilder develop-
ments in this direction, attributed to him the title of
' grandson of Nimrod, nurtured in Engedi, by the grace
of God King of Huns, Goths, Danes, and Medes, the
terror of the world.' There may have been a tendency,
as Mr. Herbert thinks, to identify him with the Anti-
Christ of the Scriptures, but this is not proved, and is
scarcely in accordance with the theological idea of
Anti-Christ, who is generally placed in the future or in
the present rather than in the past.

Teutonic
Traditions.

The Niebe-
lungen
Lied.

2. Very unlike the semi-Satanic Attila of ecclesiastical legend is the Teuton's representative of the
same personage, the Etzel of the Niebelungen Lied.
In the five or six centuries which elapsed between the
fall of the Hunnish monarchy and the writing down of
this poem, the German seems to have forgotten almost
everything about his mighty lord and foe, except that
he dwelt by the Danube, that there was glorious
feasting in his palace, and that he had relations both
in peace and war with the Burgundians and the
Franks. Hence, in the Niebelungen Lied all that is
distinctive in Attila's character disappears. He marries
the Burgundian princess Kriemhilde, the widow of
Siegfried, and at her request invites her kindred, the
Niebelungs, to visit him in Hunland. There, good-
nature and hospitality are his chief characteristics ; he
would fain spend all day in hunting and all night at
the banquet ; he is emphatically the commonplace
personage of the story. True, it is in his hall that the
terrible fight is waged for a long summer day between
the Niebelungs and the Huns, till the floor is slippery
with the blood of slaughtered heroes. But this is not
his doing, but the doing of his wife, that terrible figure,

the Clytemnestra or the Electra of the German tragedy,
'reaping the due of hoarded vengeance' for the murder
of her girlhood's husband Siegfried. Her revenge and
Hagen's hardness, and the knightly loyalty of Rudiger
only serve to throw the genially vapid king of the
Huns yet further into the background. This round
and rubicund figure, all benevolence and hospitality, is
assuredly not the thunder-brooding, sallow, silent
Attila of history.

3. The Scandinavian Atli, the husband of Gudruna, *Scandinavian Traditions.*
is a much better copy of the original. He himself is
the cause of the death of the Niblung heroes, he plots
and diplomatises and kills in order to recover the
buried treasure of Sigurd, just as the real Attila moved *Saga of the Niblungs.*
heaven and earth for the recovery of Honoria's dowry
or the chalices of Sirmium. Above all, the final scene
in which he with a certain grand calmness discusses,
with the wife who has murdered him, the reason of her
crime and appeals to her generosity to grant him a
noble funeral, is not at all unlike what Attila might
have said to Ildico, if the suspicion of the Byzantine
courtiers had been correct, that he had met his death at
her hand.

That the King of the Huns should be mentioned at
all, far more that he should play so large a part in the
national epic of the far-distant Iceland, is a strange
fact, and suggests two interesting explanations. First:
the statement of the Western ambassadors to Priscus
that Attila had penetrated even to the isles of the
Ocean may have been more nearly true than one is
disposed, at first, to think possible, and he may have
really annexed Norway and Sweden (the 'island of
Scanzia,' as Jordanes calls it) to his dominions.

Second : throughout the early Middle Ages there was probably an extensive reciprocal influence between the literatures of the countries of Western Europe, especially a borrowing of plots and scenery and characters by the minstrels of various nations from one another, and it may have been thus that the fiction of the King of the Huns and his murdered guests travelled from the Danube to the North Sea. It seems a paradox, yet it is probably true that the thought of Austria had more chance of blending with the thought of Iceland in the days of the Skald and the Minnesingers than in the days of the Railroad and the Telegraph.

Hungarian imaginations about Attila, quite valueless for History. Another line of inventions rather than of traditions must be referred to, only to reject them as containing no valuable element for the historian or the archaeologist. The Magyars, a race of Turanian origin, and bound by certain ties of kindred to the Huns, entered Europe at the close of the 9th century, and established themselves in that country which has since been known as Hungary. As they slowly put off the habits of a mere band of marauders, as they became civilised and Christian, and as they thus awoke to historical consciousness, like a man sprung from the people who has risen to riches and honour, they looked about them for a pedigree. Such a pedigree was found for them by their ecclesiastics in an imagined descent from Attila, 'Flagellum Dei.' Little of course did they then foresee that their own noble deeds would furnish them with a far prouder escutcheon than any that even a genuine affinity to the great Marauder could bestow upon them. So, from the 11th to the 15th century a series of Magyar chroniclers, Simon Keza, Thurocz, Nicolaus Olahus, and others, made it their task to glorify the nation of the Hungarians by writing out the great deeds of Attila. There is no sufficient evidence that they were recording that which had been truly handed down, however vaguely, from their ancestors. On the contrary, there is everything to show that they were, as they supposed, embellishing, and certainly expanding the literary history of Attila by imaginations of their own. Inventions of this kind are valuable neither as fact nor as legend. They no more truly illustrate the history of Attila than the Book of Mormon illustrates the history of the Jews; and they probably reflect no more light on the genuine traditions of the Asiatic and heathen Magyars than is thrown by the 'Mort d'Arthur' on the thoughts of British minds in the days of Cassivelaunus and Boadicea. All this invented history should be sternly disregarded by the student who wishes to keep before his mind's eye the true lineaments of the great Hunnish warrior.

We return for a moment, in conclusion, to the true historic Attila, whose portrait, as painted by Priscus and Jordanes, has been placed, it may be with too great fulness of detail, before the reader. It is impossible not to be struck by a certain resemblance both in his character and in his career to those of the latest world-conqueror, Napoleon. Sometimes the very words used to describe the one seem as if they glanced off and hit the other. Thus a recent German historian [1] in an eloquent passage, contrasting the Hun and his great Roman antagonist, Aetius, says—

'Conspicuous above the crowd, the two claimants to the lordship of the world stood over against one another.

Resemblance between Attila and Napoleon.

---

[1] Professor Binding, Geschichte des Burgundisch-Romanischen Königreichs, p. 44.

Attila in his wild dream of building up a universal empire in the space of one generation : opposite to him the General of that Power which, in the course of a thousand years, had extended its dominions over three Continents, and was not disposed to relinquish them without a struggle. But in truth, the idea of a world-empire of the Huns had passed out of the sphere of practical politics even before the battle on the Catalaunian plains. Far and wide Attila enslaved the nations, but the more the mass of his subjects grew and grew, the more certain they were, in time, to burst the fetters which the hand of one single warrior, however mighty, had bound around them. With Attila's death at latest his empire must fall in ruins, whether he won or lost on the battle-field by Troyes. But the Roman would still stand, so long as its generals had the will and the power to hold it together.'

Do we not seem to hear in these words a description of Napoleon's position, sublime but precarious, when he was at the zenith of his glory? As the Hun led Scythia and Germany against Gaul, so the Corsican led Gaul and Germany against Scythia in the fatal campaign of 1812. The Kings of Saxony and Bavaria were his Ardaric and Walamir; Moscow his Orleans; Leipsic his 'Campus Mauriacensis.' He won his Honoria from an 'Emperor of the Romans,' prouder and of longer lineage than Valentinian. Like Attila, he destroyed far more than he could rebuild; his empire, like Attila's, lasted less than two decades of years; but, unlike Attila, he outlived his own prosperity. Of course, even greater than any such resemblance are the differences between the uncultured intellect of the Tartar chieftain, and the highly-de-

veloped brain of the great Italian-Frenchman who
played with battalions as with chessmen, who thought
out the new Paris, who desired ' to go down to posterity
with his code in his hand.' But in their insatiable
pride, in the arrogance which beat down the holders of
ancient thrones and trampled them like the dust beneath
their feet, in their wide-stretching schemes of empire,
in the haste which forbade their conquests to endure, in
the wonderful ascendancy over men which made the
squalid Hun the instrument of the one, and the Jacobin
of the other, and above all, in the terror which the
mere sound of their names brought to fair cities and
widely-scattered races of men,—in all these points no
one so well as Napoleon explains to us the character
and career of Attila.

NOTE C. On the Date of the Foundation of Venice.

THE assertion in the text, that the story of Venice having been founded by fugitives at the time of Attila's invasion rests on mere tradition, may surprise some readers. Others, with the popular histories of Venice in their hands, may think that an earlier date ought to have been assigned to that event. Daru (Histoire de Venise, i. 27), after asserting that the invasions of *Alaric* sent some fugitives across the Lagunes (a very probable hypothesis, though one entirely unsupported by proof), goes on to state that twenty-four houses on the Rialto having been destroyed by fire, a church to St. James was dedicated there in the year 421. 'La ville de Padoue y envoya des magistrats annuels, avec le titre de Consuls. On trouve dans un vieux manuscrit le plus ancien monument de l'histoire de Venise; c'est un décret du sénat de Padoue, sous la date de 421, qui ordonne la construction d'une ville à Rialte, pour y rassembler, en une seule communauté, les habitants répandus sur les îles environnantes, afin qu'ils puissent y tenir une flotte armée, parcourir la mer avec plus de sûreté, et se défendre avec plus d'avantage dans leur asyle. Tels furent les commencements de la superbe Venise.'

This seems circumstantial enough, and has been copied in good faith by the writers of popular manuals who have to deal with the early history of Venice, though they are evidently puzzled by finding the foundation of the city thus assigned to the year 421, thirty-one years, as they well know, before the invasion of Attila, which they have also to represent to their readers as the main cause of the settlement of Venice.

The fact is, and it cannot be stated too clearly in order to relieve this useful class of writers from an unnecessary dilemma, that the whole story of the foundation of the city or the building of the Church of St. James in 421, is a mere fable (the result of ignorance rather than of dishonesty), and that the alleged

'Decree of the Senate of Padua,' is as valuable a contribution to history as the forgeries of Ireland or Chatterton, but no more so.

I. The earliest historian of Venice is *Andrea Dandolo*, who was born in 1307, was Doge from 1343 to 1354, and was the immediate predecessor of Marino Faliero. His history (Chronicon Venetum, in the twelfth volume of Muratori) is very uncritical, but in his account of the events of the fifth century he builds a good deal on Jordanes and the Historia Miscella, though also to some extent on the Hungarian Romancers (historians they cannot be called) who wrote about Attila. He appears to be under the impression that Attila began to reign over the Huns about 415, since he places his accession before the election of Pope Zosimus in 417 ; and he describes [1] a battle which took place between him and Macrinus, 'Tetrarch of Pannonia, Dalmatia, Macedonia, Phrygia, and Pamphylia,' in which 40,000 Huns were slain, but Macrinus also fell, and the Roman army was routed. The title attributed to Macrinus is sufficient to show that Dandolo is here working with absolutely unhistorical materials.

He then proceeds in the next part to relate how the chiefs and people of the cities of Venetia, exhausted by the incursions of the Barbarians, decided to construct certain maritime cities of refuge. 'First of all, Gallianus de Fontana, Simeon de Glauconibus, and Antonius Calvus de Limianis, Consuls of Patavium (Padua), not unmindful of the past invasion, went to the maritime regions, and there near the mouth of the river Realtis, having found an island suitable for their purposes, laid the foundations of the city of Rivoaltus on the 25th March in the year of our Lord 421.' The fire (issuing from the house of a Greek shipmaster named Eutinopus), by which twenty-four mansions were consumed, and the building of a church dedicated to St. James are then recorded. This is the first and best authority for the statement quoted above from Daru, and it is hardly necessary to say that it has not the slightest claim to be regarded as authentic history. The three Consuls of Padua, with such names as ' de Fontana,' 'de Glauconibus,' and 'de Limianis,' in the early part of the fifth century, are alone quite enough to condemn it.

---

[1] Book v, chap. 1, part 9.

But Dandolo, though he was quite at fault as to the date of the commencement of Attila's reign, knew, with something like accuracy, the date of the fall of Aquileia, which he puts about 454. He knew very little however as to the circumstances of that disaster. We have the story of the storks, of course, and of the matron Digna, who threw herself headlong into the Natiso. But he says that after 9000 of Attila's men and 2000 of the citizens of Aquileia had been slain, the latter, ' being no longer able to resist so great a multitude, put statues as sentinels on the walls, and thus, by distracting Attila's attention, almost all escaped to Grado.' Soon after, however, Attila let fly his hawk, which settled on the hand of one of the statues. The boldness of the bird and the immobility of the man revealed the trick to Attila, and in his anger he rased the city to the ground. (Book v, chap. 5.) Attila then presses on to Concordia, whose inhabitants fly to Caprulae (Caorle), to Altino (whose inhabitants colonise Torcello and the five neighbouring islands, and name them after the six gates of their city), and lastly to Padua (which Dandolo here calls by its modern name and not Patavium). ' The king of the city of Padua sent his queen with his sons, their wives and little ones, and all his treasure to Rialto and Malamocco. Attila attacked the city, was first defeated, then he gained a victory and destroyed Padua.' Again we have here a narrative which is absolutely unhistorical, and which, even as an invention, must have belonged to a period long subsequent to the fifth century.

II. *Andrea Nogier,* a Venetian noble, who lived about 1500, is the reputed author of a History of Venice, which is printed in the twenty-third volume of Muratori. It would be an insult to Dandolo to put Nogier's work for a moment in comparison with his. Muratori truly says that it is full of fables and anachronisms in the early part, and that the man who can read it through must have plenty of spare time on his hands. It is only worth noticing here as showing the growth of the legend about the foundation in 421 and its utter historic worthlessness.

Attila, according to this account, was the grandson of a King of Hungary named Osdrubald. His invasion of Italy is placed in the years 420–428. His sieges of Aquileia, Concordia, Altino, and Pafagonia (Padua) are described at great length, and with no regard to truth. The name of the King of Padua is Janus, his Queen is ' Andriana ovvero Vitaliana.' The siege of Padua is said to have lasted seven years. In the second year of Attila's invasion, i.e. 421, ' on the 15th of March, which was a Saturday, it was determined by the Nobles and Tribunes of the kingdom of Padua, to build a city on the island of Rivoalto. And three Consuls were set over this work whose names were Julius Falier, Thomas Candianus, and Cosmas Paulus.' By some mistake the author represents the design to build the city as formed on the 15th of March, though the first stone is laid three days earlier, on the 12th of March 421, ' in which year[1], month, and day the arrangement of the heavens was by the Divine will and ordering of such favourable aspect as verily to promise that the aforesaid city should be noble and powerful, as is seen at this day[2].'

Then follows a good deal more atrociously disjointed history, in which for instance Totila the Ostrogoth[3] (who really reigned from 541 to 552) is represented as invading Italy and persecuting the Christians in 440. Soon after, the mendacious scribe, who must surely be laughing at his readers, says, ' From 442 to 648 the History of Venice is lost, and none of it can be written.' There need not have been any blank spaces in a history written on such principles.

III. *Marino Sanuto* (in the twenty-second volume of Muratori), who flourished towards the end of the fifteenth century, and was still alive in the year 1522, admits that there are various opinions about the time of the *principio* of Venice, one author putting ' it in the year 456 [453], so indicating the time in which, at the death of Attila, reigned Pope Leo I, Marcian, Gaiseric, Meroveus, and Valentinian Junior.'

' But the truth is that in the year 421, as I have said, on the 25th of March, Friday, " e ascendendo, come nell' Astrologica figura appare, gradi 25 di Cancro," was laid the first stone, as many writers tell, of the Church of S. Jacopo di Rivoalto. On which day, as Holy Scripture testifies, our first father Adam was formed at the beginning of the Creation of the World.

---

[1] Millesimo (?).   [2] Muratori, xxiii, 925-932.

[3] Totila and Attila seem to have been generally confounded by the Italians of the Middle Ages. Dante (Inferno, xiii, 149) makes Attila instead of Totila the destroyer of Florence. And the Ottimo Commento, in its note on that passage, says, ' Some say that Attila and Totila were two different persons, and others that they were the same.'

On the same day was the Annunciation of the Angel Gabriel to the blessed Virgin Mary, and the Son of God was conceived in her womb. And on the same day, according to some theologians, Jesus Christ, our Redeemer, was crucified by the Hebrews on Mount Calvary. So this day is a very memorable one. "Sicchè è giorno molto memorabile [1]."' An astrological diagram is appended, to shew the aspect of the heavens at that day and hour. It is of course a great matter, from this point of view, to get for the foundation of the city a day which corresponds according to the days of the week as well as according to those of the year with the supposed day of the crucifixion. (Not however an ecclesiastical Good Friday which, according to 'L'Art de vérifier les dates,' fell in 421 a week later, on the 1st April.)

IV. It is scarcely necessary to quote the passage in which *Marco Antonio Sabellico*, another great Venetian historian (who died in 1504), gives his opinion concerning 'la vera origine Veneta.' He is slightly heterodox about the year, which according to him is 422, but he is quite certain about the day. 'Almost all agree in this that on the 25th of March began the origin of this city.' And then he proceeds, like Sanuto (who perhaps copied from him), to enumerate the wonderful events which according to Scripture and tradition happened on this most auspicious day.

For all the statements which have been quoted from these four historians, it is abundantly clear that there is not the slightest true historical foundation. They are mere fancies of mediaeval Venetian patriotism, which may be revered or smiled at according to the mood of the reader, but which, having no relation to fact, should be carted away out of the domain of History with the least possible delay.

Whether the mistake under which the early Venetian historians evidently laboured as to the accession of Attila, and which led them to antedate his operations against Italy by nearly thirty years, or the astrological and ecclesiastical back-reckonings which led them up to the 25th of March, 421, as a very choice day on which their city should have been built, were the original cause of the error, it is not likely that we can now ascertain. Perhaps the historical error and the chronological conceit grew together and each strengthened the other.

[1] Muratori, xxii, 405–408.

The student however will expect, before the subject is dismissed, to hear something of that which Daru calls ' the most ancient monument of the history of Venice, the decree of the Senate of Padua under the date of 421, which orders the construction of a city at Rialto.' Daru quotes this document. It begins, ' Anno a nativitate Christi ccccxxi in ultimo anno papae Innocentii primi . . . Aponencis, regno Pataviencium feliciter et copiose florenti, regentibus rempublicam Galiano de Fontana, Simeone de Glausonibus, et Antonio Calvo dominis consulibus . . . decretum est . . . aedificari urbem circa Rivoaltum,' &c.; and he concludes, ' Nam Gothorum multitudinem et instantiam verebantur et recordabantur quod anno Christi ccccxiii [sic] ipsi Gothi cum rege eorum Alarico venerant in Italiam, et ipsam provinciam igne et ferro vastatam reliquerant et ad urbem processerunt eam spoliantes.'

According to Daru ' Le bibliographe ajoute " Reliquum legere non potui." ' It was really not worth while his reading so far. Every scholar must at once perceive that this document, the so-called ' most ancient monument of the history of Venice,' is an absurd and clumsy fabrication. The misdating of Alaric's invasion by at least three years is a comparatively trifling error. The use of the date ' Anno Christi,' in the year 421, a century before Dionysius Exiguus, and the ridiculously unclassical names of the three consuls of Padua, at once stamp the document as a forgery, and give one a very low idea of the attainments of the historian who could be imposed upon by it[1].

The real ' most ancient monument of the history of Venice ' is the celebrated letter of Cassiodorus to the Venetians in the early part of the sixth century. This letter proves that already among the Venetian islands, though very likely not precisely at the Rialto, there was collected such a population of fishermen, salt-manufacturers, and hardy mariners as those whom we find thriving there when in 697 the first Doge is elected and the continuous history of Venice commences.

[1] Endeavouring to follow up at Venice the reference which Daru gives as to this MS., I was unable to discover where it is at present. The Camaldulensian convent in whose library it was placed is, as I understood, dispersed. But I was informed that the Tomaselli collection, of which this MS. formed part, consisted chiefly of ' copie di copie di copie,' and was of extremely slight archaeological value.

BOOK II

*THE VANDAL INVASION AND THE HERULIAN
MUTINY*

BOOK II.

THE VANDAL INVASION AND THE HERULIAN MUTINY.

CHAPTER I.

EXTINCTION OF THE HUNNISH EMPIRE AND THE THEODOSIAN DYNASTY.

Authorities.

Sources :—

FOR the disruption of the Hunnish Empire, JORDANES. For the deaths of Aetius and Valentinian, PROSPER, whose original chronicle ends with a long and eloquent paragraph at the year 455.

The *Continuer of Prosper* (Codex Havniensis) is an important authority on the deaths of Aetius and Valentinian III.

With the termination of Prosper's chronicle we are introduced to a new set of Annalists.

VICTOR TUNNUNENSIS flourished in the sixth century. He was bishop of a place in the province of Africa, the exact situation of which is not known. He wrote a chronicle (edited by Roncalli), continuing that of Prosper down to the first year of Justin II (565). He can only be looked upon as a second-rate authority for fifth-century matters, but, writing from the neighbourhood of Carthage, he may have sometimes preserved the local traditions as to the acts of the Vandal conquerors.

ANONYMUS CUSPINIANI is the uncouth designation of a mysterious MS. (also edited by Roncalli), which is our most valuable authority for the last quarter-century of the Western Empire. The MS. of this chronicle is in the Imperial Library at Vienna. It was first published by a certain Joseph Cuspinianus, a scholar of the Renaissance (who died in 1529), and hence the name by which it is technically known. It begins with a mere list of names of Consuls, very fragmentary, and of no great value. With the year 378, the point where St. Jerome's Chronicle ends, 'the Anonymous of Cuspinian' becomes more valuable. He begins to insert much fuller notices of passing events, and is exceedingly precise in mentioning the day of the month on which each event occurred. It would not probably be too much to assert that at least half of the dates recorded by historians who write of the accessions and depositions of the Roman Emperors in the fifth century, are due to the Anonymus Cuspiniani. His information becomes perceptibly fuller and richer as the historical interest approaches Ravenna. From this and various other reasons it is conjectured that we have here an official record compiled at Ravenna, possibly by some Minister of the Imperial Court, or else part of the lost history of Bishop Maximian [1]; and some of the scholars of Germany have gone so far as to endeavour to reconstruct from it the original 'Ravennatische Fasten.' But putting aside all minute conjectures as to its origin and preservation, there can be no doubt that we have here an exceedingly valuable and nearly, or quite, contemporary record of the events between 455 and 493. There is an unfortunate chasm in the chronicle between 403 and 455 [2].

Besides the above-mentioned sources we derive some details from APOLLINARIS SIDONIUS and PROCOPIUS, who will be described more fully in future chapters.

WITH dramatic suddenness the stage after the death of Attila is cleared of all the chief actors, and fresh

[1] See vol. i. p. 915.

[2] [Anonymus Cuspiniani is now reprinted by Mommsen under the title 'Fasti Vindobonenses Priores' in the 'Chronica Minora Saec. iv. v. vi. vii.,' which form the 9th volume of 'Monumenta Germaniae Historica.' Mommsen objects with some reason to the term 'Fasti Ravennates' proposed by Waitz and proposes to call the lost document instead 'Consularia Italica.' These frequent changes of name are very bewildering to a student.]

performers come upon the scene, some of whom occupy
it for the following twenty years. Before tracing
the character and following the fortunes of the Vandal   454.
invaders of Rome, let us briefly notice these changes.

The death of Attila was followed by a dissolution Dissen-
of his empire, as complete and more ruinous than that tween the
which befell the Macedonian monarchy on the death Attila.
of Alexander. The numerous progeny of his ill-assorted
harem were not disposed to recognise any one of their
number as supreme lord. Neither Ellak, the eldest
son, who had sat uneasily on the edge of his chair
in the paternal presence, nor Ernak, the youngest,
his father's darling, and he upon whom the hopes of
Attila had most confidently rested, could obtain this
preeminence. There were besides, Emnedzar, Uzindur,
Dinzio, and one knows not how many more uncouthly-
named brethren ; in fact, as Jordanes says, 'these
living memorials of the lustful disposition of Attila
made a little nation themselves. All were filled with
a blind desire to rule, and so between them they upset
their father's kingdom. It is not the first time that
a superabundance of heirs has proved more fatal to
a dynasty than an absolute deficiency of them.'

To end the quarrel, it was decided that this tribe Attempted
of sons should partition between them the inheritance causes
of their father. But the great fabric which had been among the
upheld by the sullen might of Attila was no longer ates.
a mere aggregation of nomad clans, such as the Hunnish
nation had once been. If it had still been in this
rudimentary condition, it might perhaps have borne
division easily. But now it contained whole nations
of more finely fibred brain than the Huns, astute
statemen-kings like Ardaric, sons of the gods like the

three Amal brothers who led the Ostrogoths to battle.
These men and their followers had been awed into
subservient alliance with the great Hun. They had
elected to plunder with him rather than to be plundered
by him, and they had perhaps found their account
in doing so.   But not for that were they going to
be partitioned like slaves among these loutish lads,
the sons of Attila's concubines, men not one of whom
possessed a tithe of their father's genius, and who,
when they had thus broken up his empire into fragments, would be singly but petty princelings, each
of far less importance than many of their own vassals.
Should the noble nation of the Ostrogoths lose the
unity which it had possessed for centuries, and be
allotted part to Ellak and part to Ernak ?   Should the
Gepidae be distributed like agricultural slaves, so
many to Emnedzar, and so many to Uzindur ?   That
was not Germania's understanding of the nature of
her alliance with Scythia, as it would not have been
the King of Saxony's or the King of Bavaria's understanding of the tie which bound them to Napoleon.
Ardaric, king of the Gepidae, lately the chosen confidant of Attila, now stepped forth to denounce this
scheme of partition, and to uphold Teutonic independence against Attila's successors.   The battle was
joined near the river Nedao [1], a stream in Pannonia
which modern geographers have not identified, but
which was probably situated in that part of Hungary
which is west of the Danube.   'There,' says Jordanes [2],
whose Gothic heart seems to beat faster beneath his

454.

Battle of
the Nedao.

---

[1] This and not Netad, is according to Mommsen the reading of the
best MSS. of Jordanes.

[2] De Rebus Geticis, cap. L.

churchman's frock whenever he has a bloody battle to describe,—' There did all the various nations whom Attila had kept under his dominion meet and look one another in the face. Kingdoms and peoples are divided against one another, and out of one body divers limbs are made, no longer governed by one impulse, but animated by mutual rage, having lost their presiding head. Such were those most mighty nations which had never found their peers in the world if they had not been sundered the one from the other, and gashed one another with mutual wounds. I trow it was a marvellous sight to look upon. There should you have seen the Goth fighting with his pike, the Gepid raging with his sword, the Rugian breaking the darts of the enemy at the cost of his own wounds; the Sueve pressing on with nimble foot ; the Hun covering his advance with a cloud of arrows ; the Alan drawing up his heavy-armed troops ; the Herul his lighter companies, in battle array.' We are not distinctly told what was the share of the Ostrogoths in this great encounter, and we may reasonably doubt whether all the German tribes were arranged on one side and all the Tartars on the other with such precision as a modern ethnologist would have used in an ideal battle of the nationalities. But the result is not doubtful. After many desperate charges, Victory, which they scarcely hoped for, sat upon the standards of the Gepidae. Thirty thousand of the Huns and their confederates lay dead upon the field, among them Ellak, Attila's firstborn, ' by such a glorious death that it would have done his father's heart good to witness it.' The rest of his nation fled away across the Dacian plains, and over the Carpathian mountains to those

Disruption of Attila's Empire.

wide steppes of Southern Russia, in which at the commencement of our history we saw the three Gothic nations taking up their abode. Ernak, Attila's darling, ruled tranquilly under Roman protection in the district between the lower Danube and the Black Sea, which we now call the Dobrudscha, and which was then ' the lesser Scythia.' Others of his family maintained a precarious footing higher up the stream, in Dacia Ripensis, on the confines of Servia and Bulgaria. Others made a virtue of necessity, and entering '.Romania,' frankly avowed themselves subjects and servants of the Eastern Caesar, towards whom they had lately shown themselves such contumelious foes. There is nothing in the after-history of these fragments of the nation with which any one need concern himself. The Hunnish empire is from this time forward mere drift-wood on its way to inevitable oblivion.

Settlement of Teutonic nations in Hun-land.

What is more interesting for us, as affecting the fortunes of the dwellers in Italy during the succeeding century, is the allotment of the dominions of Attila among the Teutonic tribes who had cast off the Hunnish yoke. Dacia, that part of Hungary which lies east and north of the Danube, and which had been the heart of Attila's domains, fell to the lot of the Gepidae, under the wise and victorious Ardaric. Pannonia, that is the western portion of Hungary, with Sclavonia, and parts of Croatia, Styria and Lower Austria, was ruled over by the three Amal-descended kings of the Ostrogoths. What barbarous tribe took possession of Noricum in the general anarchy does not appear to be clearly stated, but there is some reason to think that part of it at least was occupied by the Heruli, and that the south-eastern portion, Carinthia

and Carniola, received those Sclavonic settlers (coming
originally in the triumphant train of Attila) whom,
to increase the perplexity of the politicians of Vienna,   454.
it still retains.

The death of Attila and the disruption of his empire   Aetius no
removed the counterpoise which alone had for many   longer
necessary
years enabled the Western Emperor to bear the weight   to Valentinian.
of the services of Aetius.   It is true that quite recently
vows of mutual friendship had been publicly exchanged
and sealed with the rites of religion between these
two men, the nominal and the real rulers of Italy.
It is true that a solemn compact had been entered into
for the marriage of the son of Aetius[1] with the
daughter of Valentinian, and thus, as the Emperor
had no son, a safe path seemed to be indicated in the
future, by which the ambition of the general might
be gratified, yet the claims of the Theodosian line not
sacrificed.   All this might be, but nothing could avail
against the persuasion which had rapidly insinuated
itself into the Emperor's mind that the minister, so
useful and so burdensome, was now no longer needed.
Just as Honorius forty-six years before had planned
the ruin of Stilicho, so now did the nephew of Honorius
plot the murder of the only Roman general who was
worthy to rival Stilicho's renown.   The part which
was then played by Olympius was now played by
the Eunuch Heraclius.   Whether, as some chroniclers
say, the Eunuch filled his master's mind with suspicions as to the revolutionary designs of Aetius, or
whether, as others, the Emperor first resolved on the

---

[1] Probably Gaudentius, so named after his paternal grandfather.
But there was at least one other son, Carpilio, who had been sent as
a hostage to the Huns (see p. 69, and compare p. 157, n. 1).

murder of his general, and secured the grand chamberlain's assistance, does not greatly signify. As planet

454.

attracts planet and is itself attracted by it, so villain
works on villain, and is worked upon by him, when
a great crime, profitable to both, presents itself as
possible.

Murder of
Aetius.

The Emperor enticed Aetius into his palace without
an escort. Possibly the pretext was some further
conversation as to the marriage treaty between their
children. Possibly when the general had entered the
presence-chamber, his master announced that he must
consider this contract as at an end, for we are told
that Aetius was urging with uncourtly warmth the
pretensions of his son, when he was suddenly stabbed
by the Emperor himself. The swords of the by-
standers finished the work with unnecessary circumstances of cruelty, and the chief friends of the murdered
minister having been on one pretence or other allured
singly into the palace, were all slain in like manner.
Among them was his most intimate friend, Boethius,
the Praetorian Prefect, and the grandfather, probably,
of the celebrated author of the 'Consolations of Philosophy.'

In narrating this event, the Count Marcellinus
(writing about a century after it had occurred) rises
above his usual level as a mere chronicler, and remarks, 'With Aetius fell the whole Hesperian realm,
nor has it hitherto been able to raise itself up again.'
We seem, in the faded chronicle, to read almost the
very words of Shakespeare—

> ' O, what a fall was there, my countrymen!
> Then I, and you, and all of us fell down,
> Whilst bloody treason flourished over us.'

Another historian [1] tells us that immediately after
the murder, 'a certain Roman uttered an epigram,
which made no small reputation for its author. The   454.
Emperor asked him if in his opinion the death of
Aetius was a good deed to have accomplished. Whereupon he replied, "Whether it was a good deed, most
noble Emperor, or something quite other than a good
deed, I am scarcely able to say. One thing, however,
I do know, that you have chopped off your right hand
with your left."'

A contemporary author, the Gaulish poet Apollinaris
Sidonius, in some verses written a year or two after
the event, alludes in passing to the time when

> 'The Thing, scarce Man, Placidia's fatuous son
> Butchered Aetius [2].'

So that this deed at least had not to wait for a late
posterity to be judged according to its desert.

It was probably towards the end of 454 that the
murder of Aetius was perpetrated, and the scene of
the crime was Rome, which for ten years previously
seems to have been the chief residence of the Emperor,
though Ravenna was occasionally visited by him.

In the middle of the succeeding March the Emperor   455.
rode out of the city one day to the Campus Martius.   Valenti-
He halted by two laurel bushes in a pleasant avenue, nian assas-
and there, surrounded by his court and his guards,   sinated.
was intently watching the games of the athletes [3].

---

[1] Procopius (De Bello Vandalico, i. 4).

[2] 'Aetium Placidus mactavit semivir amens' (Panegyric of Avitus,
359).

[3] This seems to be the meaning of the very elliptical words of
Prosper, 'egressum extra Urbem principem et ludo gestationis in-
tentum.' Marcellinus, Cassiodorus, and others add 'in Campo Martio.'

Suddenly two soldiers of barbarian origin, named Optila and Traustila, rushed upon him and stabbed him[1]. The Eunuch Heraclius, the confidant who had planned the death of Aetius, was also slain. No other blood seems to have been shed, and apparently it must be taken as an evidence how low the Emperor had fallen in the esteem of his subjects, that in all that courtly retinue, and in all that surrounding army, not a hand stirred to avenge his death. The murderers were well known as henchmen of Aetius, who, moved partly by resentment at his fate, and partly, no doubt, by chagrin at the interruption of their own career of promotion, had for months been dogging the steps of the heedless Emperor with this black design in their hearts.

Valentinian III left no son, and thus the Imperial line of Theodosius became extinct, after it had held the Eastern throne seventy-four years (379–453)[2], and the Western sixty-one (394–455). The choice of the people and army fell on Petronius Maximus, an elderly

---

The Augustan MS. of Prosper supplies 'ad duas Lauros,' a little detail which is also contained in the Paschal Chronicle. Holder-Egger (Neues Archiv. i. 270) argues that we have here a blundering attempt to mix up two inconsistent versions of the story: the Campus Martius having been on the West of the city, within the walls, and the 'Duae Laurus' having been (as he shews from the Liber Pontificalis) at the third milestone from the city, to the South-East of it, on the Via Labicana. But surely there might very easily be two places in the environs of Rome bearing the name of 'the Two Laurels,' so that there is no necessary conflict of evidence.

[1] We get the names of the assassins from Marcellinus, whom Jordanes (De Regnorum Successione, 334) follows. Codex Havniensis calls them Accila the armour-bearer ('bucillarius') of Aetius, and Trasila, son-in-law of Aetius.

[2] Pulcheria died in the year 453, aged 54.

senator, who assumed the purple with every prospect of a wise and perhaps even a successful reign.

The new Emperor was apparently related to Probus, the eminent Roman, whose two sons were made consuls in the same year (395) amid the high-flown panegyrics of Claudian. He is said to have been also grandson of that usurping Emperor Maximus, who was taken prisoner by the soldiers of Theodosius at the third milestone from Aquileia. But his own career as a member of the civil hierarchy had been so much more than merely respectable, that it seems impossible to deny to him the possession of some ability, and even of some reputation for virtue, as Roman virtue went in those days. At the age [1] of nineteen he was admitted into the Imperial Council as tribune and notary; then Count of the Sacred Largesses, and then Prefect of Rome, all before he had attained his twenty-fifth year. When he was holding this last office, the Emperor Honorius, at the request of the senate and people, erected a statue to his honour in the great Forum of Trajan. Consul at the age of thirty-eight, Prefect of Italy from the age of forty-four to forty-six, again Consul at forty-eight, and again Prefect, he had attained at fifty the crowning dignity of the Patriciate. This was evidently a man whom both prince and people had delighted to honour, and from whom, now that he had reached his sixtieth year, a reign of calm and statesmanlike wisdom, and such prosperity as those evil days would admit of, might not unreasonably have been hoped for.

How different was the result, and how far he was

455. Elevation and previous career of Maximus.

[1] These facts are collected by Tillemont, Hist. des Empereurs, v. 257.

from attaining, much more from bestowing, happiness during the seventy days, or thereabout, that he wore the Imperial Purple, we learn from a letter addressed, some time after his death, by one [1] who was himself well acquainted with the inner life of courts, to Serranus, a faithful friend, who still ventured to proclaim his attachment to an unpopular and fallen patron.

' I received your letter,' says Sidonius, ' dedicated to the praises of your patron the Emperor Petronius Maximus. I think, however, that either affection or a determination to support a foregone conclusion has carried you away from the strict truth when you call him most happy (*felicissimus*) because he passed through the highest offices of the state and died an emperor. I can never agree with the opinion that those men should be called happy who cling to the steep and slippery summits of the State. For words cannot describe how many miseries are hourly endured in the lives of men who, like Sulla, claim to be called Felix because they have clambered over the limits of law and right assigned to the rest of their fellow-citizens. They think that supreme power must be supreme happiness, and do not perceive that they have, by the very act of grasping dominion, sold themselves to the most wearisome of all servitudes : for, as kings lord it over their fellow-men, so the anxiety to retain power lords it over kings.

' To pass by the proofs of this that might be drawn from the lives of preceding and succeeding emperors, your friend Maximus alone shall prove my maxims [2].

[1] Apollinaris Sidonius, Ep. ii. 13.
[2] ' Solus peculiaris iste tuus *Maximus maximo* nobis ad ista documento poterit esse.' Sidonius is an inveterate punster.

He, though he had climbed up with stout heart into
the high places of Prefect, Patrician, Consul, and had,
with unsatisfied ambition, claimed a second turn at
some of these offices, nevertheless when he arrived,
still vigorous, at the top of the Imperial precipice,
felt his head swim with dizziness under the diadem,
and could no more endure to be master of all than
he had before endured to be under a master. Then
think of the popularity, the authority, the permanence
of his former manner of life, and compare them with
the origin, the tempestuous course, the close of his
two months'[1] sovereignty, and you will find that the
least happy portion of his life was that in which he
was styled *Beatissimus.*

'So it came to pass that he who had attracted
universal admiration by his well-spread table, his
courtly manners, his wealth, his equipages, his library,
his consular dignity, his patrimonial inheritance, his
following of clients,—he who had arranged the various
pursuits of his life so accurately that each hour marked
on the water-clock[2] brought its own allotted employment—this same man, when he had been hailed as
Augustus, and with that vain show of majesty had
been shut up, a virtual prisoner, within the palace
walls, lamented before twilight came the fulfilment
of his ambitious hopes. Now a host of cares forbade
him to indulge in his former measure of repose; he
had suddenly to break off all his old rules of life, and
perceived when it was too late that the business of
an emperor and the ease of a senator could not go
together. Moreover, the worry of the present did not

---

[1] 'Paulo amplius quam bimestris principatus.'
[2] Clepsydra.

455.

blind him to the calamities which were to come, for he who had trodden the round of all his other courtly dignities with tranquil step, now found himself the powerless ruler of a turbulent court, surrounded by tumults of the legionaries, tumults of the populace, tumults of the barbarian mercenaries[1] ; and the forebodings thus engendered were but too surely justified when the end came—an end quick, bitter, and unlooked-for, the last perfidious stroke of Fortune, which had long fawned upon the man, and now suddenly turned and stung him to death as with a scorpion's tail. A man of letters, who by his talents well deserved the rank which he bore of *quaestor*, I mean Fulgentius, used to tell me that he had often heard Maximus say, when cursing the burden of empire, and regretting his old freedom from cares, ' Ah, happy Damocles! it was only for one banquet's space that you had to endure the necessity of reigning.'

Sidonius then tells in his most elaborate style the story of Damocles feasting sumptuously under the suspended sword-blade, and concludes, ' Wherefore, Sir Brother, I cannot say whether those who are on their way to Sovereign Power may be considered happy; but it is clear that those who have arrived at it are miserable.'

Let the reader store up in his mind this picture of a sorely worried Emperor vainly striving to maintain his authority amid the clamours of mutinous legionaries full of fight everywhere but on the battlefield, of Roman demagogues haranguing about Regulus and Romulus, and of German *foederati* insatiable in their claims for donative and land. For this picture,

---

[1] ' Foederati.'

or something like it, will probably suit equally well
for each of the eight other weary-browed men who
have yet to wear the diadem and be saluted with the
name of Augustus.

As for the Emperor Maximus, his mingled harshness
and feebleness, both misplaced, soon earned for him
the execration of his subjects. They saw with astonishment the murderers Optila and Traustila not only
not punished, but received into the circle of the
Emperor's friends. This might be only the result
of a fear of embroiling himself with the Barbarians,
but it was only natural that it should be attributed
to a guilty participation in their counsels. Then, after
a disgracefully short interval, all Rome heard with
indignation that the Empress Eudoxia had been commanded to cease her mourning for Valentinian, whom,
notwithstanding his many infidelities, she fondly loved,
and to become the wife of the sexagenarian Emperor.
At the same time he compelled her to bestow the hand
of one of her daughters on his son, the Caesar Pal-
ladius. The widowed Empress[1], who was now in the
34th year of her age, was one of the loveliest women
of her time. The motive of Maximus may have been
passion, but the double marriage looks rather like
policy, like a determination on the part of the fire-new
Emperor to consolidate his dynasty by welding it with
all that yet remained on earth of the great name of
Theodosius.

Maximus takes the murderers of Valentinian into favour,

and forces his widow to marry him.

If this was the object of Maximus, he signally failed,
and the precautions which he took to ensure his safety
accelerated his ruin. Eudoxia, the daughter, the niece,

Eudoxia appeals to the Vandal:

---

[1] Εὐπρεπεστάτῃ γυναικὶ Εὐδοξίᾳ, Theophanis Chronographia, p. 93 (ed.
Paris, 1655).

and the wife of emperors, writhed under the shame of her alliance with the elderly official. As a still mourning widow she resented her forced union with the man whom some deemed an accomplice in her husband's murder. Her aunt Pulcheria was dead, and she feared that it was vain to hope for succour from Byzantium. In her rage and despair, she imitated the fatal example of Honoria, and called on the Barbarian for aid. Not the Hun, but the Vandal was the champion whose aid she invoked. Her emissary reached Carthage in safety. Gaiseric, only too thankful for a good pretext for invading Rome, eagerly promised his aid. He fitted out his piratical fleet, and soon from mouth to mouth in Rome flitted the awful tidings, 'The Vandals are coming.' Many of the nobles fled. The Emperor, torn from his sweet clepsydra-round of duties and pleasures, and depressed by the scorn of the beautiful Avenger, whose love he could not win, devised no plan for defence, but sat trembling and helpless in his palace, and when informed of the flight of the nobility could think of no more statesmanlike expedient than to publish a proclamation, 'The Emperor grants to all, who desire it, liberty to depart from the city.' The fact was that he was meditating flight himself. Better the immediate abandonment of Empire than to sit any longer under that ever-impending sword of Damocles. But then the smouldering indignation of all classes against the man whom they deemed the author of the coming misery, burst forth. The soldiers mutinied, the rabble rose in insurrection, the servants of the Imperial Palace, faithful probably to the old Theodosian traditions, prevented the meditated escape. Soon the tragedy, which near sixty

455.

years before had been perpetrated at Constantinople (after the fall of Rufinus), was repeated in Rome. The Imperial domestics tore their new master limb from limb, and after dragging the ghastly fragments through the city, scattered them into the Tiber, so that not even the rites of burial might be granted by any one to Petronius Maximus [1].

This event happened on the 31st of May [2], less than three months after the new Emperor's accession. The sails of Gaiseric's fleet are already upon the Tyrrhene sea, and before three days are ended the third great Barbarian Actor, the Vandal nation, will appear upon the stage of Italy. But, before they come, we must turn back the pages of history for awhile, and trace the successive steps of the migration which had led them from the forests of Pomerania to the burning shores of Africa.

[1] According to Jordanes, a Roman soldier named Ursus dealt the fatal blow. A passage in Apollinaris Sidonius (Panegyric of Avitus, 442) seems to attribute to the Burgundians some share in the tragedy:

'Infidoque tibi [Romae] Burgundio ductu
Extorquet trepidas mactandi principis [sc. Maximi] iras.'

Binding (p. 49) thinks that the Burgundians had just made a foray into Italy. But the passage seems too obscure for interpretation.

[2] Not Midsummer Day, as inadvertently stated in the first edition. Anonymus Cuspiniani puts it on the 12th of June.

NOTE D. On the Character of Petronius Maximus.

THE account of the character and actions of this Emperor, given in the text, is drawn almost exclusively from the writings of his contemporaries—Apollinaris Sidonius (430–488) and Prosper of Aquitaine (about 400–460). In some respects it is less unfavourable than that which is usually given and which is derived from later authorities.

The chief difference is in the degree of culpability which has to be assigned to him for the death of his predecessor. Some suspicion undoubtedly rested upon him in the minds of his contemporaries, but I have endeavoured not to treat this suspicion as more of a certainty than it actually was. The obvious, patent cause of Valentinian's murder was the two barbarians' desire to revenge the death of Aetius ; and, to a certain extent, the whole people and army of Rome, by witnessing it unmoved, made the crime their own. It was the extraordinary conduct of Maximus *after* the murder, in admitting the assassins to his most intimate counsels, which naturally raised a suspicion that he was their accomplice, but this suspicion does not appear ever to have reached the stage of proof. The following words of Prosper no doubt express all that the immediate contemporaries of the two emperors knew about the chief actors in the tragedy.

'As soon as this parricide' (the murder of Valentinian by the friends of Aetius) 'had been perpetrated, Maximus, a man who had twice filled the office of consul, and was of patrician rank, assumed the imperial dignity. It had been supposed that he would be in all ways serviceable to the imperilled commonwealth, but he very soon showed what disposition he was of, since he not only did not punish the murderers of Valentinian, but even received them into the circle of his friends, and moreover, forbidding the widowed Empress to mourn the loss of her lord, within a very few days he constrained her to contract a marriage with himself.'

This scandal of his precipitate marriage with the widow of his predecessor, and the ruin which resulted from it for Rome, made evidently a deep impression on the minds of contemporary and succeeding annalists, especially in the Eastern Empire, and disposed them to put the harshest construction on all his previous actions. It is curious to note how the suspicion which is but faintly marked in the pages of Prosper, and is not even alluded to in those of Sidonius, deepens and hardens in the later historians.

The Spanish ecclesiastic, *Idatius* (fl. about 400–470), says that 'Maximus was racked by a disturbing fear of great commotions. Through desire of reigning he had contributed by his wicked advice to the deaths of the persons slain by Valentinian, and even to that of Valentinian himself.'

Marcellinus, a Count of the Eastern Empire (whose chronicle ends at 558), says, 'Valentinian the Prince, by the stratagem of Maximus the Patrician, by whose deceit Aetius also perished, was mangled in the Campus Martius by Optila and Traustila.'

But the anti-Maximian prejudice reaches its height in *Procopius* (fl. about 500–560) who has unfortunately made the largest contribution to the history of this Emperor with the smallest claim to be regarded as a trustworthy authority. In the long and disagreeable romance with which he favours us, Valentinian is represented as winning the ring of Maximus from him at play, entrapping his wife to the palace by means of this ring, and then seducing her. The dishonour of his wife fills the mind of Maximus with thoughts of vengeance, in order to accomplish which he first of all induces Valentinian to assassinate Aetius, and then, 'without any trouble, he killed the Emperor and took the sovereignty.' He marries Eudoxia, and incautiously tells her one night that it was for love of her that he killed her late husband. As soon as day dawns she sends the fatal message to Gaiseric, knowing that she will receive no help from Byzantium.

It is not worth while to point out the internal improbabilities of this story, the jumble of different motives which it ascribes to the chief actors, the disparity of years between Valentinian the seducer and his victim (who was mother of a grown-up son and wife to the elderly Maximus), and other points which might be remarked upon. The history into which it is inserted is thoroughly inaccurate in a chronological point of view (for instance, it represents the fall of Aquileia as succeeding the death of Aetius), and Procopius, even in reference to the events of his own time, is notoriously apt to let his history degenerate into a mere 'chronique scandaleuse,' inserting apparently many an unauthentic piece of gossip, simply because it is unsavoury. Gibbon truly remarks that 'Procopius is a fabulous writer for the events which precede his own memory.' Whatever judgment we may be disposed to pass on the alleged share of Maximus in the murder of his predecessor—and I am disposed to ask for a verdict of 'Not Proven'—at least let the fables of Procopius no longer pass current as History.

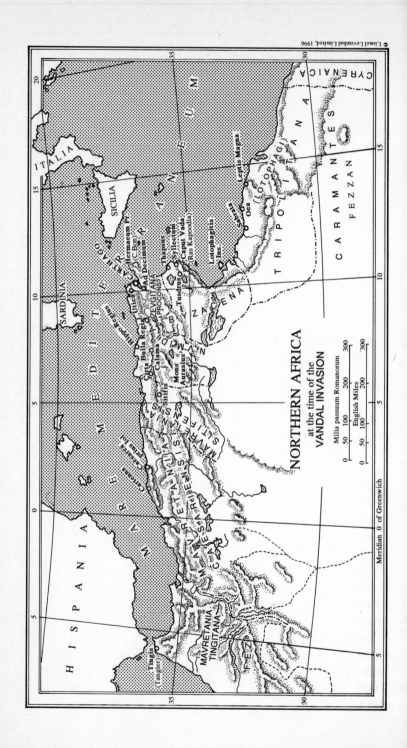

NORTHERN AFRICA
at the time of the
VANDAL INVASION

Milia passuum Romanorum
0   50   100   200   300

English Miles
0   50   100   200   300

Meridian 0 of Greenwich

CHAPTER II.

THE VANDALS FROM GERMANY TO ROME.

Authorities.

Sources :—

FOR the events which happened during the Vandals' stay in Spain IDATIUS is our best authority.

For the Vandal Conquest, PROCOPIUS. This Historian, Secretary, and Commissariat Officer to Belisarius is well known as the chief authority for the events of the reign of Justinian. He flourished from about 500 to 560, and wrote, besides other histories, two books, *De Bello Vandalico*. The Vandalic war, which it is his main object to describe, is of course that in which Belisarius overthrew the Vandal Kingdom (533–534). But he devotes seven chapters of the First Book (thirty-six pages in the Bonn edition) to a description of the foundation of that Kingdom by Gaiseric and the chief events of his life.

Although Procopius is an authority of the first class for the events of which he was himself an eye-witness, he is somewhat slip-shod and inaccurate as to those events concerning which he had to gather his information from others. Hence his chronology is often erroneous : and when he is separated by a considerable distance of time from his subject, it seems clear that he cannot always have used the best material which contemporary historians might have afforded him. He has also an extreme love of historical gossip, and generally leans to the ill-natured view of a man's character. But the reader will see by the references how large a part of our knowledge of the Vandal settlement in Africa is derived from this source, only partially trustworthy as we must admit it to be.

VICTOR VITENSIS, an African bishop, who was driven into banishment for the faith by Huneric, son of Gaiseric, wrote about 486 a History of the Persecution of the African Province in five books.   He is therefore an all but contemporary authority even for the early part of the Vandal settlement.

He used to be cited as Victor *Uticensis*.   It is now admitted that *Vitensis* is the correct form.   Vita appears to have been a city in the Byzacene province, but its exact position is unknown.

The Life of St. Augustine by POSSIDIUS, Bishop of Calama, his disciple and friend, gives us some particulars as to the siege of Hippo and the death of the great African Father.

Another authority which the student will sometimes find quoted is VICTOR CARTENNENSIS, but this name raises a curious question of literary good faith.   It is admitted that there was a Victor, bishop of Cartenna in Mauretania, who lived at the time of the Vandal invasion and engaged in controversy with the Arians.   Some theological works of his are preserved, but they contain nothing of importance for history.   In 1836, however, a French author named Marcus published an ' Histoire des Vandales,' containing numerous and important quotations from Victor Cartennensis concerning the political institutions of the Vandals. These quotations profess to be made from a work published at Madrid (1653) called ' Mientras' Schediasmata Antiqua.'   The curious part of the story is that no other scholar has yet been able to find a copy of these ' Schediasmata,' though the libraries of Paris, Madrid, Rome, Naples, Florence, London, Oxford, Berlin, Vienna, Göttingen, and Munich have all been searched for the precious volume.   Was it then a literary forgery on the part of Marcus ?   That natural suggestion is to some extent rebutted by a statement of Professor Waitz (Deutsche Verfassungsgeschichte, I. 231, n. 3 : third edition) that he met Marcus at Dijon, who seems to have satisfied him that he had veritably handled the apocryphal Mientras.   Professor Hübner (in a paper published in the proceedings of the Royal Prussian Academy for 1861) suggests that the work consulted by Marcus was really a MS. now extant at Madrid, called ' Schediasmata Latina de rebus diversis,' written by a certain Tomas Tamayo de Vargas, and this suggestion is adopted by Wattenbach (Deutschlands Geschichtsquellen, II. 396).   But why Marcus should have said Mientras when he meant de Vargas is not very clear.   Nor does the sug-

gestion really help the authority of the so-called Victor Cartennensis, for de Vargas, though personally honest, appears to have
been the disciple and unwitting accomplice of the Jesuit
Geronimo de la Higuera, who beguiled the tedium of the last
years of the seventeenth century by forgeries, on a most extensive scale, of the missing works of chroniclers of the fifth, sixth,
and seventh centuries.   There is thus a double chance of fraud.
Marcus the Frenchman may be laughing at us by citing a non-
existent ' Schediasmata,' or Higuera the Spaniard may have
foisted on de Vargas a spurious Victor.   In this state of things
the student will for the present do wisely to accept no assertion
as to Vandal polity which is made on the authority of ' Victor
Cartennensis.'

Guides :—

The best guide to the history of the Vandals is *Dr. Felix
Papencordt's* ' Geschichte der Vandalischen Herrschaft in Afrika '
(Berlin, 1837)—an admirable specimen of a German monograph
of the best type.   This book received the prize of the 'Académie
Royale des Inscriptions et Belles Lettres' in August, 1836.
Cardinal Wiseman, in his ' Recollections of the last Four Popes'
(pp. 148–9), gives an interesting sketch of this 'most promising
young German scholar, cut off before he had time to fulfil the
expectations of his friends.'... ' His acquaintance with mediaeval
history,' says the Cardinal, ' was amazing : he remembered the
dates of the most insignificant events, and would make excursions
into the desolate border tracts in the mountains between Rome
and Naples to visit the theatre of the most puny action between
pugnacious barons in Central Italy.'   In my copy of Roncalli's
' Chronica ' I find the autograph ' Papencordt,' with the note
' 2 Scudi Rom, 8 August, 1836.'

Dahn's ' Könige der Germanen ' (part 1), and ' Urgeschichte
der Germanischen und Romanischen Völker ' (vol. 1), will also
be found very useful by the student.

IN the Germania of Tacitus, the best contribution The Van-
made by any Roman writer to the science of ethnology, tioned by
the author says (cap. ii.):   Tacitus,

' My own opinion is that the Germans are the
aboriginal inhabitants of their country, with the least

possible admixture of any foreign element.   For in old times all national migrations were made by sea rather than by land, and the inhospitable ocean which washes the shores of Germany has been seldom visited by ships from our world.   Besides, putting the perils of a tempestuous sea out of the question, who would leave behind him the pleasant shores of Asia, Africa, or Italy, and set sail for Germany, with its ugly landscape, its rigorous climate, its barren soil ; who, I mean, except a native of that land, returning thither ?

' In ancient songs, the sole kind of annals possessed by this people, they celebrate the name of a certain Tuisco, an earth-born deity, and his son Mannus, as the original founders of their race.   To Mannus they assign three sons, after whom are named three tribes, the *Ingaevones*, who live nearest to the ocean, the *Hermiones* in the middle of the country, the *Istaevones* who occupy the remainder.   Some, however, presuming on the antiquity of their tribes, affirm that the aforesaid god had many other sons, from whom many gentile appellations are derived, *e. g.* Marsi, Gambrivii, Suevi, *Vandalii*.   These, they say, are the real and ancient names, that of Germans is a modern one, first given in fear by the vanquished Gauls to the warriors who crossed the Rhine to invade them, and afterwards proudly assumed by the conquerors.'

This interesting passage, besides showing us the *Deutsch* nationality in its earliest stage, then as now called German by the foreigner but not in its own home ; besides giving us the name of the primeval *Mann*, who corresponds to the Adam of the Hebrews, and suggesting some other interesting ethnological speculations ; brings before us the Vandals as already a powerful and long-descended tribe in the days of Tacitus, that is at the close of the first century of our era.

The slightly earlier author, Pliny, in the geographical and by part of his Historia Naturalis [1], mentions the Vind*i*li as Pliny. one of the five great Germanic races, and the Burgundians as one of their sub-branches. There can be no doubt that these are the same people as the historic Vandals, who are indeed always called Band*i*li or Band*e*li by the Greek historians.

The Vandals were nearly allied in blood to the Affinities Goths. 'The greatest names of this confraternity of Vandals. nations,' says Procopius, 'are Goth and Vandal and Visigoth and Gepid. They all have fair skins and yellow hair; they are tall of stature, and goodly to look upon. They all possess the same laws, the same faith, Arian Christianity; and the same language, the Gothic. To me they appear all to have formed part of one nation in old time, and afterwards to have been distinguished from each other by the names of their leaders.' The general description therefore which has Their character. been already given of the Visigoths will apply to the Vandals; but by combining the testimonies of various chroniclers, we may find some traits of character which belonged specially to the Vandal race. Thus, their disposition seems to have been wanting in some of the grander features of the Gothic. They were perhaps more subtle-witted [2], but they were even more greedy of gain. They were confessedly less brave in war [3],

---

[1] Book iv. cap. 14 : 'Vindili, quorum pars Burgundiones, Varini, Carini, Guttones.'

[2] Ἀγχίνους is Procopius' description of Gaiseric (i. 4).

[3] Orosius (vii. 38), rather spitefully, says of Stilicho that he was 'descended from the *unwarlike* (imbellis), avaricious, perfidious, and

and they were more cruel after victory. On the other hand, they were conspicuous even among the chaste Teutonic warriors for their chastity, and both in Spain and Africa their moral standard was, and for some time continued to be, far above that of the uncleanly-living Roman provincials.

Early history of the Vandals.

The home of the Vandals, when we first meet with them in history, appears to correspond with the central and eastern part of Prussia, but a loose aggregation of restless tribes must not be too definitely assigned to any precise district on the map [1]. While they were settled here they fought under their two leaders, Ambri and Assi, a memorable battle with their neighbours, the Langobardi. The legends concerning this battle, which resulted in the complete defeat of the Vandals, are reserved for the Lombard portion of this history [2]. As the Roman Empire grew weaker, the Vandals pressed southward, and eventually they gave their name (*Vandalici Montes*) to the Riesen Gebirge (Giant Mountains) between Silesia and Bohemia.

Marco-mannic War. 167–175 and 177–181.

The southward movement of the barbarians, of which this Vandal migration formed part, brought on that great struggle known as the Marcomannic War,

---

crafty nation of the Vandals.' Salvian (vii. 7) says that 'God, by handing over the Spanish nation to the Vandals for punishment, showed in a double degree his hatred of the sins of the flesh, since the Spaniards were conspicuous for their immorality and the Vandals for their chastity, while on the other hand the latter were the weakest of all the barbarian tribes.' Their rapid decline in martial vigour after the death of Gaiseric points to the same quality in their character.

[1] Jordanes (De Rebus Geticis, iv) speaks of the Vandals at this period of their history as pressed upon by the victories of the Goths during their settlement by the Baltic.

[2] See Paulus Diaconus : Hist. Langobard, i. 7, 10.

in which the German tribes on the Middle Danube strove, almost successfully, to pierce the gap between Pannonia and Dacia, and to establish themselves permanently within the limits of the Empire. In the heroic contest which Marcus Aurelius, the philosopher-Emperor, waged against these barbarians, a contest which well-nigh over-taxed both his energies and those of the Empire, he seems to have had at first the Vandals for his foes [1]; but, at the conclusion of the war, we find the Asdingi, whom we know to have been a Vandal tribe, making their peace with Rome, and receiving from the Emperor settlements in Dacia [2]. When, upon the death of Marcus, his son Commodus made his unsatisfactory peace with the Marcomanni, the Vandals were one of the tribes taken under Roman protection, against whom the Marcomanni were forbidden to declare war.

167–181.

A generation later, the Emperor Caracalla, in one of his boastful letters to the Senate, prided himself on the fact that whereas the Vandals and Marcomanni had previously been friendly to one another, he had succeeded in setting them at variance [3]. If we look at that curious specimen of map-making, the *Tabula Peutingeriana* (which is thought to have been originally executed in the time of Caracalla's father Severus [4]),

Caracalla.
215.

---

[1] This is inferred from the language of Capitolinus, ' Pannonias ergo et Marcomannis, Sarmatis, *Wandalis* simul etiam Quadis extinctis, servitio liberavit' (Vita M. Ant. Phil. xvii).

[2] Dion Cassius, lxxi. 12. His account of the movements of the Vandals under their leaders Räus and Raptus is very obscure, but the result is that indicated above.

[3] ἐμεγαλοφρόνει δὲ ἐπὶ τῷ τοὺς Βανδίλους καὶ τοὺς Μαρκομάνους φίλους ὄντας ἀλλήλοις, συγκεκρουκέναι (Dion Cass. lxxvii. 20).

[4] Or perhaps his cousin Severus Alexander. See Mannert's Intro-

we shall see a striking comment on these words : for
there, immediately on the other side of the broad
limitary stream of the Danube, we see in straggling
letters the name VANDVLI, and a little beyond, but
almost intermingled therewith, the name MARCOMANNI.
Such close juxtaposition was very likely to breed
hostility between two barbarous tribes.

Aurelian.
271.

More than half a century passes : and the Emperor
Aurelian, the great restorer of the Roman power in the
Danubian lands, gains a signal victory over the Vandals.
We know nothing concerning the battle ; we only hear
of the negotiations which followed it.   The Vandals
sent ambassadors to sue for peace.   After hearing their
lengthy harangues, on the following day Aurelian
mustered his army and asked for its advice whether he
should accept or reject the terms of the barbarians.
With one consent the army shouted for peace, which
was accordingly granted, the Kings of the Vandals and
several of their chief nobles, readily giving their sons
as hostages for its due observance.   The mass of the
Vandal host returned to their Dacian home, the Emperor granting them sufficient provisions to last them
till they reached the Danube.   Notwithstanding this
concession, 500 men, straggling from the main body of
the returning host, committed cruel devastations on the
plains of Moesia.   For this breach of the treaty all the
marauders who could be caught were put to death by
their King [1].

duction to the Tabula Peutingeriana (p. 15).   The insertion of Constantinople in the Tabula is believed to be the work of a mediaeval
copyist (p. 18).

[1] See Dexippus (Excerpt 2, de Bellis Scythicis, p. 19, ed. Bonn) and
Priscus (Excerpt 11, p. 126, ibid.).

A select portion of the Vandal host remained in the Imperial camp. One of the conditions of the peace was that they should supply 2000 horsemen as *foederati* to the Roman army; and this stipulation seems to have been faithfully observed, for the army list of the Roman Empire at the commencement of the fifth century shows us 'the Eighth Wing of the Vandals serving in Egypt[1].' It was probably in this way that in the next century Stilicho, a man of Vandalic extraction, entered the service of that Empire which he afterwards ruled.

Vandal
auxiliaries
in Roman
army.

A few years later a fragment of the Vandal nation, which seems to have wandered to the Rhine in company with a troop of Burgundians, was by adroit tactics defeated by the Emperor Probus. Many were slaughtered, but some were taken prisoners; Igil, the Vandal leader, being one of the latter class. These prisoners were all sent to the island of Britain, where, in some obscure insurrection against the Emperor, they did good service to their recent conqueror[2].

Probus.
277.
Settlement
of Vandals
in Britain.

---

[1] 'Sub dispositione viri spectabilis comitis rei militaris per Aegyptum:—
    Ala Octava Vand*i*lorum Neae.'

Notitia Imperii, Oriens, cap. xxv.

The situation of Nea is not known. The number of the *Ala* is stated by Joannes Lydus (De Magistratibus, i. 46) to have been 600 men. It was always composed of cavalry.

[2] "Οσους δὲ ζῶντας οἵός τε γέγονεν ἐλεῖν, εἰς Βρεττανίαν παρέπεμψεν· οἳ τὴν νῆσον οἰκήσαντες ἐπαναστάντος μετὰ ταῦτά τινος γεγόνασι βασιλεῖ χρήσιμοι (Zosimus, i. 68. Cf. Vopiscus: Vita Probi, xviii). The statement sometimes attributed to Camden, that there was a fortress near Cambridge, on the Gogmagog Hills, built by these Vandal captives and named after them Vandlebury, is not made in that form by Camden, and does not really rest on his authority, but on that of Gervase of Tilbury, from whom he quotes it; nor does it seem to be more than a piece of fantastic etymology. The words of Gervase ' the Vandals, who made a camp here when they ravaged part of Britain and cruelly

Near the end of the reign of Constantine there came a crisis in the fortunes of the Vandal nation.   They were then dwelling in Moravia and the north-west of Hungary, having the Marcomanni of Bohemia as their western neighbours, and the Danube for their frontier to the south.   Geberich, king of the Goths, whose territory bordered upon theirs to the east, determined to get him glory upon the Vandals, and sent a challenge to their king, Visumar.   The two armies met by the Hungarian river Maros [1], and fought through a long day doubtfully.   At length the Goths prevailed, and Visumar, with a great part of his host, lay dead upon the

field.   The scanty remnant of the nation entreated Constantine to permit them to enter the limits of the Empire, and settle as his subjects in the province of Pannonia.   The position was not unlike that in which the Visigoths themselves were placed forty years later when they sought the Moesian shore of the Danube, flying from the terrible Huns.   The permission was granted, and for nearly seventy years the Vandals were obedient subjects of the Roman Emperors [2].   During this time it is likely that they made some advances in civilization ; they probably often served in the Roman army, and learnt something of the legionary's discipline.

---

massacred the Christians,' show the thoroughly unhistorical character of his information, which, moreover, has nothing to do with the exiles under Probus (see Camden's Britannia by Gough, ii. 213, ed. 1806).

[1] That is, supposing the name given by Jordanes, *Marisia*, to be correct.   The *Marus*, now March, a river of Moravia, which flows into the Danube above Presburg, would suit the rest of his geographical description better.

[2] [Vandali] ' Pannoniam sibi a principe Constantino petiere, ibique, per LX annos plus minus sedibus locatis, imperatorum decretis ut incolae famularunt' (Jordanes de Reb. Get. c. 22).

It was without doubt during the same period that they embraced Christianity under that Arian form which Ulfilas was teaching to their Gothic neighbours and conquerors. At a later date, when they were invading Spain, we are told that they carried the Bible with them and consulted it as an oracle [1]. It was of course the translation of Ulfilas which thus became the Urim and the Thummim of the Vandal.

At length, in the year 406 [2], the Vandals, or a portion of the confederacy which went by that name, left their Pannonian settlements, and linking their destinies with those of the Turanian tribe of Alans and with their High-German kinsmen the Suevi, they marched north-westwards for the Rhine, intent on the plunder of Belgic Gaul. There is no need to accept the suggestion [3] that 'Stilicho invited them.' After the fall of that statesman, everything that had gone wrong in the Empire for the last twenty years was conveniently debited to his account. But no invitation was needed to set any Germanic tribe in motion towards the

337–406.

406. The Vandals enter Gaul.

[1] Salvian, vii. 11. This appears to be the meaning, but the good Presbyter is rhetorically obscure. 'Nam cum armis nos atque auxiliis superbiremus, a parte hostium nobis liber divinae legis occurrit. Ad hanc enim praecipue opem timor et perturbatio tunc Wandalica confugit, ut seriem nobis eloquii coelestis opponeret et adversum venientes aemulos suos sacri voluminis scripta quasi ipsa quodammodo divinitatis ora reseraret.'

[2] See vol. i. p. 739 (note) for the chronology of this important event.

[3] Made by 'Tiro' and by Orosius (Hist. vii. 38), and apparently echoed by St. Jerome (Epist. ad Ageruchiam): 'Non vitio principum sed scelere semibarbari accidit proditoris.' Papencordt suggests that Stilicho may, with perfect loyalty to the Empire, have invited the Vandals into Gaul, intending to use them as a counterpoise to the Franks.

Empire in the year of the Nativity 406. The fountains of the great deep were broken up. Radagaisus

406–409.

and Alaric, with their mighty nation-armies, had crossed
the Alps and poured down into Italy. One, indeed,
had failed, and the other had only partially succeeded,
but both had shown plainly to all 'Varbaricum' that
'Romania' was now at its last gasp, and would have
enough to do to defend itself in Italy, without any hope
of permanently maintaining its hold on its rich outlying
provinces, such as Gaul and Spain. The Teuton adventurer was swept across the Roman boundary by a
current as strong as that which drew the Spanish
adventurer across the Atlantic in the days of Cortez
and Pizarro.

Battle
with the
Franks.

Of the struggles of the Vandals with the Franks we
have only dim rumours. We hear, however, of a great
battle, in which 20,000 Vandals were slain, their king
Godigisclus, himself of the royal lineage of the Asdings,
being among the number of the dead[1]. It is said,
indeed, that only the timely arrival of their allies, the
Alans, saved them from utter destruction ; but, however this may be, they crossed the Rhine frontier, and
after three years of war and probably of wild ravage of
the cities of Gaul, drawn southwards by the impulse
which ever attracted the barbarian to the sunnier
climate, and powerfully helped by the dissensions
among the Romans themselves, which had arisen out of
the sudden elevation of the upstart British soldier
Constantine[2], they stood, after three years' time, at the
foot of the Pyrenees and thundered at the gates of

[1] We get our fullest information as to this battle from Gregory of
Tours, quoting from Renatus Profuturus Frigeridus (Hist. Franc. ii. 9).
[2] See vol. i. pp. 741–745.

Spain [1]. The kinsmen of Honorius, Verenianus and Didymus, who had loyally struggled to guard this ram-part against usurpers and barbarians, had been, rather more than a year before, treacherously slain by Con-stantine, and thus but a feeble resistance, or no resist-ance at all, was opposed to the fierce tide of Vandals, Alans, Suevi, which swept through the Pyrenean passes and ravaged the Hither and Farther Spain without mercy.

28 Sept.–13 Oct. 409. They enter Spain.

Of the twenty years which followed, some mention has already been made in describing the career of Ataulfus. It may be remembered that in 414, five years after the Vandals had entered Spain, the Visi-gothic chieftain followed them thither. There he and his successors carried on a long and bloody struggle with their fellow-Teutons, during part of which time the Goths professed to fight as champions of Rome, and for the remainder on their own account. The provinces, lately fertile and flourishing, were so harried by friend and foe that the Vandal soldiery were fain to buy wheat at thirty-six shillings a pint, and a mother slew and ate her own children.

Struggles with other invaders.

At length the barbarians and the representatives of the Empire concluded some sort of peace or truce, of which a hint is given us by the declamation of Orosius [2], and a somewhat more detailed but still per-plexing account in the pages of Procopius. 'Then,' says he, ' Honorius made an agreement with Godigis-clus [3], on condition that they [the Vandals] should settle

Truce between the Van-dals and the Empire.

[1] The leader of the united host was Guntheric or Gunderic, King of the Vandals. For the chronology see vol. i. p. 824, n. 2.

[2] See i. 837.

[3] If Gregory is right this name is an error for that of Guntheric, son of Godigisclus.

there, not for the devastation of the country. And
whereas the Romans have a law that if men do not
keep their property in their own hands, and an
interval of time elapses which amounts to thirty years,
then they have no longer the right to proceed against
those who have dispossessed them, but their recourse to
the Courts is barred by prescription. The Emperor
passed a law that the time during which the Vandals
should sojourn in the Roman Empire should by no
means be reckoned towards this thirty-years prescription.' Difficult as it is to see how such a law would
work out in the actual experience of Roman or Vandal
land-holders, it well illustrates the attitude of Imperial
statesmen and jurists towards all the barbarian intruders. Every peace made with them was considered
to be really only a truce. However securely the Visigoth might seem to reign at Toulouse, the Ostrogoth
at Ravenna, or the Vandal at the New or the Old Carthage, the Roman Augustus and his counsellors looked
upon their dominion as only a parenthesis, an unfortunate parenthesis, in the age-long life of the great Republic,
and in their own counsels admitted no derogation thereby
to the imprescriptible rights of the sovereign Empire[1].

Geographi-
cal distri-
bution of
the con-
querors of
Spain.

The settlement of the barbarian nations in Spain
seems to have been on this wise. The Suevi were in
the North-west of the peninsula, the Visigoths in the
North-east, the Alans in Portugal, while the Vandals
occupied two widely-sundered allotments. One tribe
which seems to have borne the same name as the royal
clan, that of *Asdingi*[2] was settled close to the Suevi in

---

[1] See Dahn (Könige der Germanen, i. 145, n. 4), whose view, I think,
nearly coincides with that here expressed.

[2] Though this, as Papencordt remarks (p. 17), is nowhere expressly

Gallicia; the other and probably the larger tribe, that of the *Silingi*, took up its quarters in Baetica, the modern Andalusia [1].

In the year 416 Constantius, then the accepted suitor of Placidia, by some cunning stratagem captured a king of the Vandals named Fredibal, and sent him as a captive to Honorius [2], before whose chariot he may possibly have walked in chains when the phantom-Emperor in the following year celebrated his triumph at Rome.　But on the whole it was the hand of Wallia the Visigoth that fell most heavily on the Vandals and their allies.　In 418 the Silingian Vandals in Baetica were absolutely 'extinguished' by the Goths, and the Alans were so terribly cut to pieces by the same people, that the few survivors willingly merged their nationality in that of the Gallician Vandals, whose king is said to have assumed thenceforward the title 'King of the Vandals and Alans [3].'

Defeats of the Vandals.

stated, but is a very probable conjecture of Mascou's from Dio Cassius, lxxi. 12.

[1] The derivation of Andalusia from the Vandals must now be considered more than doubtful.　Papencordt (p. 16, n. 1) quotes Casiri as his authority for the assertion that the true form of the name is Handalusia, the Arabic equivalent for Hesperia, and that it was originally given by the Moors to the whole country of Spain.

[2] As we hear nothing of Fredibal's relationship to Guntheric or Gaiseric he was probably King of the Silingian Vandals.　It seems to me more probable that Constantius was Fredibal's captor than Wallia, though the entry in Idatius is not clear.　It is as follows:—

'(Anno Honorii) xxii.

'Constantius Placidiam accepit uxorem.

'Fredibalum regem gentis Wandalorum sine ullo certamine ingeniose captum ad Imperatorem Honorium destinat.

'xxiii.　Wallia rex Gothorum, Romani nominis causâ, intra Hispanias caedes magnas efficit barbarorum.'

[3] Idatius s. a. xxiv Honorii.　'Wandali Silingi in Baetica per Wal-

In 419 war broke out between this latter, newly-
united people and their neighbours the Suevi. Guntheric apparently gained a victory over the Suevic king
Hermanric, and drove him and his followers into the
fastnesses of the Asturias [1], where they were subjected
to a strict blockade. In the following year, however,
under pressure from Asterius, the Roman governor of
Spain, Guntheric broke up this mountain-siege, left
Suevi and Romans alike to work their will in the North
of Spain, and marched across the Peninsula to Baetica.
There the Asdingian Vandals settled themselves in the
fair land lately occupied by their Silingian brethren
(some remnants of which nation may possibly have
joined them), and there gazing Eastward and Westward
over the waters of the Mediterranean and the Atlantic,
they began to dream of maritime greatness.

*War with
the Suevi.
419.*

420.

*Campaign
of Castinus
in Baetica.
422.*

In the closing years of Honorius, the Court of
Ravenna, moved by some strange impulse of spasmodic
energy, made an attempt to recover Baetica from the
Vandals. Castinus, Master of the Soldiery (the same
officer who in the following year set up the Arch-notary
Joannes as Emperor in derogation of the claims of the
son of Placidia), set sail with a large body of troops,
and, having effected a junction with the Goths, invaded

liam regem omnes extincti. Alani qui Wandalis et Suevis potenta-
bantur, adeo caesi sunt a Gothis ut extincto Atace rege ipsorum, pauci,
qui superfuerant, abolito regni nomine de Gunderici regis Wandalorum,
qui in Galloecia resederat, se patrocinio subjugarent.'

[1] 'Inter Gundericum Wandalorum et Hermericum Suevorum reges
certamine orte. Suevi *in Nervasis montibus* obsidentur a Wandalis '
(Idatius). There can be little doubt that some of the mountains of
Asturias are here referred to. Dahn (Könige der Germanen, vi. 547)
quotes Masdeu as suggesting the mountains of St. Maria de Arvas
between Leon and Oviedo, which agree well enough with the geographical requirements of the history.

Baetica. But there were jealousies and divided counsels at the Imperial head-quarters. We have seen how Bonifacius, the second in command, although, by the admission of all men, one of the bravest soldiers of the day, unable to bear the petty jealousy and insulting arrogance of his incapable superior, hastily travelled from Ravenna to Porto, and thence set sail for Africa, which province he afterwards held for Placidia and her children against his rival's puppet-Emperor Joannes[1]. Still, notwithstanding this defection, the Imperial arms in Spain seemed likely to be victorious. The Vandals were besieged, apparently in one of the cities of Baetica, and suffered such severe privations that they were on the point of surrender. Castinus, however, 'that inept commander[2],' rashly engaged in battle with men made desperate by famine, was deceived by his Gothic allies, sustained a signal defeat, and fled in disorder to Tarragona[3].

At length, after the Vandals had sojourned nearly twenty years in Spain, came the day when Count Bonifacius, ill-requited for his loyalty to Placidia and her children, slandered, outlawed, and driven to the brink of destruction, sent that fatal Embassy, fatal for himself and for his country, by which he invited the barbarians into Africa. The Vandals had already, without this invitation, shown that they were not disposed to accept the frontiers of Baetica as the fate-fixed limit of their dominion. In 425, after sacking Cartha-

---

[1] See vol. i. pp. 872, 889, and 890.

[2] 'Inepto et injurioso imperio' (Prosper).

[3] The account of this expedition against the Vandals, chiefly important on account of its bearing on the after-history of Bonifacius, is given us by Idatius and Prosper.

gena and Seville, and roaming for plunder over the whole Tarraconensian province, they had laid waste the Balearic Isles—which came perhaps at this time permanently under their rule—and had invaded Maure- tania, but apparently without then gaining any foothold south of the Pillars of Hercules[1]. The messengers of Bonifacius found Guntheric and his bastard brother Gaiseric at the head of the Vandal state. They proposed[2] (it is said) that the conquests to be effected in Africa should be considered as made on joint account, and should eventually be divided into three parts, one for each of the barbarian kings, and one for the Roman Count. The proposal was accepted, and the Vandals began to prepare ships and men for the great expedi- tion. But before the enterprise was set in hand, Guntheric died. A century after the event, a rumour[3] obtained credence that he, like Bleda, the brother of Attila, was slain by the partner of his throne. But the contemporary chronicler Idatius, writing as he does in Spain, gives no hint of any such an imputation, but in some mysterious manner connects the death of the Vandal king with an act of sacrilege at Seville. 'Gun- deric, king of the Wandals, having taken Hispalis [Seville], when, in his impious elation, he had stretched

Death of King Gun- theric.

---

[1] 'Wandali Balearicas insulas depraedantur: deinde Carthagine Spartariâ [Spartaria is an epithet of Carthago Nova] et Hispali eversâ et Hispaniis depraedatis, Mauritaniam invadunt.' Idatius, s. a. 425.

[2] This story of the tripartite division rests only on the authority of Procopius, which is not first-rate for this period.

[3] This rumour is mentioned by Procopius, who, however, discredits it and says that the Vandals would not admit its truth. Procopius adds, 'I have myself heard from men of this nation that Gontharis was taken prisoner in Spain by the Germans and crucified by them.'

forth his hand against the church of that city, speedily perished, being by the judgment of God attacked by a demon.' A fever (Spain's natural revenge upon her northern invaders), followed by raging madness and death, is perhaps the historical equivalent of this rhetorical statement.

428

But, whatever the cause of the death of Guntheric, the result was that the chief power in the Vandal state, and the sole conduct of the African invasion, were thereby vested in the hands of his bastard brother. For fifty years that brother was, except during the short meteoric career of Attila, the foremost figure in Europe, and we pause therefore for a moment to collect such light as the faint tapers of the chronicles afford us on the character and aspect of *Gaiseric* [1].

Gaiseric (Genseric) sole King of the Vandals.

---

[1] His name is commonly written Genseric; but there can be little doubt that the great Vandal's real name was *Gaiseric*, and that is the form which I have therefore preferred to use.

Idatius (5th century) calls him	Gaisericus.
Prosper of Aquitaine (5th century) and Victor Vitensis (5th century)	Geisericus.
At the end of Prosper's Chronicle he is called Genseric. This is probably an alteration by a later hand.	
Jordanes and Procopius (6th century) . .	Gizerichus.
Chronicon 'Cuspiniani' (end of 5th century) .	Gesericus.
Malchus and Cassiodorus (early part of 6th century)	Ginsericus.
Marcellinus (6th century), Victor Tunnunensis (6th century), and Historia Miscella (8th century?).	Gensericus.

The incorrect form which has been accepted by History seems to have been that which was current at Byzantium.

It will perhaps be objected that we have coins bearing Genseric's name spelt in the usual manner. But Julius Friedländer, the chief authority on the subject of Vandal Numismatics, shows strong reasons

428.
Character
of Gaiseric.

Till he arose, his nation, though willing enough to join in the great plundering expeditions of the North, can scarcely be said to have prevailed in any encounter with an enemy. Defeated long ago by Geberich in Moravia, defeated more recently by the Franks on the borders of the Rhine, generally worsted in Spain by the Visigoths, the nation seemed upon the whole to be gradually losing ground, and justifying the general impression of 'Varbaricum,' that the Vandals were less warlike than their neighbours. During the long lifetime of Gaiseric this imputation at any rate was never made against them. His nimble mind[1] and his unshaken courage proved to be the steel point needed to give penetrating power to the Vandal impact. He was cruel, not a doubt of it; his savage deeds look ghastly by the side of the knightly career of Alaric or Ataulfus. He was greedy of gain, but none of the northern invaders was greatly superior to him in this respect. But he had that power of estimating his own resources and the resources of his foe, that faculty of inventing useful political combinations, that transcendent ability in adapting his means to his chosen ends, which denote the successful man of business in the market-place of Empire. In his strong, remorseless common-sense, in the awe-struck tone with which, a century after his death, people still spoke of him as the cleverest

for reducing the three so-called copper coins of Genseric to one, and for believing that this one is not Vandal at all but Byzantine of the 8th or 9th century, with the inscription, not 'Genser. Augus.' but 'Mense Augus.' He concludes emphatically 'We know of no coins of this king.' (Die Münzen der Vandalen, p. 18.) Friedländer, apparently approving the spelling Gaiserich, derives the name from Gais 'a javelin' and Reiks 'a king' (p. 6).

[1] 'Αγχίνοια (Procopius, Bell. Vand. i. 4).

of all men [1], there is something which reminds us of his fellow-Teuton (we might almost say his fellow-Prussian), who, like him, besieged and took the chief city of the Latin races. If Attila was the Napoleon of the fifth century, we may perhaps look upon Gaiseric as its Bismarck.

428.

Yet the outward presentment of the Vandal king was by no means like that of the stalwart Prussian colonel of cuirassiers. 'A man of moderate stature,' says Jordanes, 'and limping in his gait, owing to a fall from his horse.' He goes on to say that this man, 'most renowned in the world by his slaughter of the Romans, was deep in mind, sparing of speech, a despiser of luxury, tempestuous in his wrath, greedy of gain, full of far-reaching schemes for harassing the nations, ever ready to sow the seeds of contention, and to play upon the animosities of mankind.'

His outward appearance.

Another Byzantine rhetorician [2], speaking of the change which came over the Vandal nation after the death of their mightiest king, says, 'they fell into every kind of effeminacy and had no longer the same vigour in action, nor kept together their former reserves, which Gaiseric [3] always held in readiness for every expedition, so that he was quicker in striking than any one else in making up his mind to strike.'

The resources wielded by this iron will and remorseless heart were pertinaciously directed to two great objects, the humiliation of the Roman Empire and the extirpation of the Catholic faith. His hatred towards

Gaiseric's creed.

---

[1] Γιζέριχος τά τε πολέμια ὡς ἄριστα ἐξήσκητο καὶ δεινότατος ἦν ἀνθοώπων ἁπάντων (Procopius, Bell. Vand. i. 3).

[2] Malchus (Excerpt 5, p. 240, ed. Bonn).

[3] Γινζερίχος.

the professors of the orthodox creed was, according to the Spanish Bishop, Idatius, attributed by some persons to the fact that he was himself an apostate from their ranks [1]. If this story be true (it will be seen that Idatius himself does not vouch for its accuracy), it may be owing to the fact that the Vandal prince as the son of some Gaulish or Spanish concubine of Godigisclus was brought up in his mother's form of faith which, on attaining manhood, he abjured in favour of the Arian creed of his martial forefathers [2].

428.

Such was the man, who, in the month of May, 428 [3], mustered all the families of his nation and of the Alans on the northern shore of the Straits of Gibraltar in obedience to the call of Bonifacius. But before he set sail on his new enterprise, he struck one parting blow at an old enemy. Hearing that Hermigarius [4], King of the Suevi, was devasting some of the provinces near to his line of march, he turned back with a troop of his followers, pursued the pursuing marauder, and came up with him near the city of Merida. Many of the Suevi were slain; Hermigarius fled from the field, mounted on a steed which as he trusted should carry him swifter than the east wind, but was whelmed in the rapid waters of the Gaudiana [5]. He died almost in sight of

428.
A parting
thrust at
the Suevi.

---

[1] Chronicon (s. a. 428) 'Gaisericus succedit in regno: qui, ut aliquorum relatio habet, effectus apostata de fide Catholicâ in Arianam dictus est transisse perfidiam.'

[2] This explanation is suggested by Papencordt (p. 63).

[3] The date chosen by Tillemont. Pagi, followed by Gibbon and Clinton, prefers 429. See Note E on Vandal Chronology.

[4] Not the same as Hermanric who, having been mentioned by Idatius under the year 419, is again met with in 430 and 433, and whose death is recorded in 438.

[5] This story is told, but not very clearly, by Idatius.

the towers of Merida, and the churchmen of that city
saw in his fall a divine judgment for an insult which
he had offered to their saintly patroness Eulalia, one of
the child-martyrs in the persecution of Diocletian [1].

428.

The Suevi thus punished, Gaiseric again addressed
himself to the invasion of Africa. Before embarking,
in order doubtless to facilitate the orderly transport of
the assembled multitude, the king had all the males of
his nation numbered, 'from the feeble old men to the
babe born yesterday,' and found that they amounted to
80,000 persons. Such a number, representing at the
utmost 50,000 fighting men, encumbered with women,
children, and dotards, should not have been formidable
to the once well-garrisoned and well-stored provinces
of Africa [2]. But the line to be defended was a long
one, there was discord in the camp of the defenders,
and although twelve legions of Infantry and nineteen
'vexillations' of Cavalry were nominally assigned to
the defence of Africa, in the attenuated state of the
Imperial army in the fifth century, that force, even if
it were all enlisted on the side of loyalty, probably composed a less powerful army than two legions in the

Numbering of the people.

Number of the Imperial troops in Africa.

---

[1] St. Eulalia's is one of the most beautiful faces in the procession of
virgin-martyrs represented on the north wall of S. Apollinare Nuovo
at Ravenna. She is said to have miraculously prevented Theodoric II
from sacking her native city in 456 (Idatius s. a.).

[2] Victor Vitensis expressly mentions that some erroneously supposed
that 80,000 was the number of the fighting men. However, I think
we must understand, in accordance with the strict interpretation of
Victor's words ('Quia reperti sunt senes, juvenes, parvuli, servi vel
domini octoginta millia numerari') that females were excluded from the
reckoning, in order to get anything like an approximation to the
50,000 soldiers mentioned by Procopius (καίτοι οὐ μᾶλλον ἢ ἐς μυριάδας
πέντε τὸ τῶν Βανδίλων τε καὶ Ἀλανῶν πλῆθος ἔν γε τῷ πρὶν χρόνῳ ἐλέγετο
εἶναι: Proc. de B. V. i. 5).

days of Caesar the Dictator[1]. It should be stated, however, that there were certain limitary garrisons, probably composed in great part of barbarian *foederati*, whose warriors, from the analogy of the troops who defended the frontier walls of Britain and Germany, may well have amounted to a very considerable number[2].

Survey of Roman Africa.

Let us briefly survey the political and social condition of the vast territory for which Gaiseric and his Vandals have set sail, determined to reap from it a harvest of plunder, and possibly hoping to erect in it an enduring empire. The whole coast line from the Pillars of Hercules to the borders of the Cyrenaic Pentapolis was under Diocletian divided into seven provinces.

1 Mauretania Tingitana.

2 　Do. 　Caesariensis.

3 　Do. 　Sitifensis.

---

[1] At the time of the Notitia (Occ. vii. compared with v.) we find stationed 'intra Africam'—

> Three Legiones Palatinae,
>> Armigeri propugnatores seniores
>> Armigeri propugnatores juniores
>> Cimbriani.
> One Auxilium Palatinum,
>> Celtae juniores.
> One Legio Pseudo-Comitatensis of uncertain name.
> Seven Legiones Comitatenses,
>> Secundani Italiciani
>> Primani
>> Secundani
>> Tertiani
>> Constantiaci
>> Tertio Augustani
>> Fortenses,

and (as above stated) nineteen 'vexillations' of Cavalry.

[2] From the Notitia Dignitatum (Occ. xxiii, xxix, and xxx, ed. Böcking) we learn that there were sixteen limitary garrisons in Proconsular Africa, eight in Mauretania Caesariensis, and fourteen in Tripolitana.

4 Numidia.

5 Africa Proconsularis or Zeugitana.

6 Byzacena.

7 Tripolitana.

428.

(1) With the westernmost province, that of which Tangiers was the capital and which corresponds with the modern kingdom of Fez, we have now no concern. At the time of Diocletian's reconstitution of the Empire it was separated from the other African provinces, and assigned to the diocese of Spain and the prefecture of the Gauls[1]. The reason for this arrangement doubtless was [2] that the province comprised nothing but a strip of Atlantic coast-line reaching from Tangiers to Sallee, separated by more than 200 miles of roadless desert from the next province on the east, and therefore, as accessible only by sea, most naturally connected with the great and civilized country on the northern side of the Straits of Gibraltar. Probably, then, from all that is about to be said touching the Vandal conquests in Africa, Tingitana may be safely excluded. We may infer that, in so far as it had any government at all and was not abandoned to mere Moorish barbarism, it still formed a part of the Roman Empire. *Tingitana.*

(2 & 3) The two next provinces, *Mauretania Caesar-iensis* and *Sitifensis* once belonged to the kingdom of Bocchus (who in the great Civil War took the side of Caesar against the Senate), and for more than seventy years after his death were governed by his descendants, but under Caligula they were formally annexed to the Empire, the general employed in suppressing the revolt, which was occasioned by this change, being the same *Caesarien-sis and Sitifensis.* A.D. 40.

---

[1] See vol. i. p. 619.

[2] As pointed out by Mommsen (Römische Geschichte, v. 636).

Suetonius Paulinus who, twenty years later, was to lead his legions against the black-robed Furies of Anglesea, and to pierce the dense masses of Britons that swarmed round the indignant Boadicea.

These two provinces, which occupied about three-quarters of the modern territory of Algiers, had shared very imperfectly, if at all, in the civilising influence of Carthage, and though there were in them probably large breadths of cornland between the mountains and the sea, there were not many towns besides the great commercial city of Caesarea, once the capital of the Mauretanian kings. No doubt these provinces formed a part, but neither the most highly prized nor the most hardly won part of the new heritage of the Vandals [1].

Tripolitana.

(7) The same description would probably suit the easternmost province, which from its three chief cities [2] derived that name of *Tripolitana* by which it is still known. Fourteen 'limitary' bodies of Imperial troops attested the difficulty with which the long and straggling frontier was guarded from the invasions of the Garamantes and the other nomadic tribes of Fezzan, who, from the ambush of their oases, poured fitfully across the desert to attack the cities of the sea-borne stranger. A strange and mysterious region it is: almost unknown in history except for the fact that it gave the Emperor Severus to Rome; but one of which

---

[1] See Mommsen (u. s. vol. ii. p. 321 of the English translation), 'Caesarea' (formerly called Iol) 'remained a considerable commercial town; but in the province the fixed settlement was restricted to the northern mountain-range, and it was only in the eastern portion that larger inland towns were to be found. Even the fertile valley of the most considerable river of this province, the Shelif, shows weak urban development.'

[2] Leptis Magna, Oea and Sabrata.

we may possibly hear more, if ever the pressure of
population or the means of subsistence should force the
Italian or some other nation on the opposite shore of
the Mediterranean to see what harvests may be reaped
in the land of the Lotus-eaters of the Odyssey.

(4, 5 & 6) The three provinces which have not yet been
described, *Numidia, Proconsularis* or *Zeugitana,* and
Byzacena, formed the very heart and centre of the Roman
dominion in Africa.   On this subject I cannot do better
than quote the words of the great German scholar[1] who
has written, with a fulness which no future historian is
likely to surpass, the history of the Imperial provinces.
' Roman civilisation entered upon the heritage partly
of the city of Carthage, partly of the kings of Numidia,
and if it here attained considerable results, it should
never be forgotten that it, properly speaking, merely
wrote its name and inscribed its language on what was
already there.   Besides the towns, which were demon-
strably founded by Carthage or Numidia, both states
guided the Berber tribes, which had some inclination to
agriculture, towards fixed settlements.   Even in the
time of Herodotus the Libyans westward of the bay of
Gabes were no longer nomads, but peacefully cultivated
the soil ; and the Numidian rulers carried civilisation
and agriculture still further into the interior.   Nature,
too, was here more favourable to husbandry than in the
western part of North Africa ; the middle depression
between the northern and the southern range is indeed
here not quite absent, but the salt lakes and the steppe
proper are less extensive than in the two Mauretanias.
The military arrangements were chiefly designed to

Numidia, Proconsularis, Byzacena.

[1] Mommsen, book viii. cap. 13 (Prov. of Roman Empire, vol. ii.
p. 316, English translation).

plant the troops in front of the mighty Aurasian
mountain-block, the Saint-Gotthard of the southern
frontier-range, and to check the irruption of the non-
subject tribes from the latter into the pacified territory
of Africa and Numidia. . . . Of the details of the warfare [against these tribes of the desert] we learn little ;
it must have been permanent, and must have consisted
in the constant repelling of the border-tribes, as well as
in not less constant pillaging raids into their territory.'

Economic
condition
of these
provinces.

The plains between the Aurasian mountains and the
sea, well-irrigated and rich in grain, in oil, and in wine,
so far back as in the days of Agathocles, had probably
increased in fruitfulness during at least the earlier
centuries of the Empire.   Carthage herself, indeed, lay
in ruins for the greater part of the two centuries which
intervened between the Third Punic War and the
dictatorship of Julius Caesar[1] ; but there seems no
reason to suppose that even during this interval the
smaller cities (such as Utica and Hippo, which had
sided with Rome against Carthage), or the bright villas
which dotted the plain, and attested the long influence
of the Carthaginians, were abandoned to desolation.   At
any rate, when the new Roman Carthage arose in all
her luxury and pride, the three provinces nearest her,
or so much of them as was embraced between the
mountains and the sea, basked in the sunshine of her
prosperity.   An unfavourable element in the condition
of the African provinces was probably the vast estates
belonging to the Imperial exchequer.   Enormous confiscations were practised in the days of Nero, and that

[1] The prosperity of the colony sent to Carthage by Caius Gracchus
(B.C. 122) was of short duration.

the process had not ceased in the days of Honorius is
evident from the fact that a special Count was appointed to administer 'the patrimony of Gildo [1],'
whose rebellion was suppressed by Stilicho in the year
398 [2]. These *latifundia*, cultivated by slaves and
administered too often by corrupt and oppressive
functionaries, were probably a blot upon the general
prosperity of the province. And no doubt, here as
elsewhere throughout the Empire, the process of the
degradation of the cultivator into a serf, and the
cruel impoverishment of the middle classes by ruinous
taxation had been going on throughout the fourth
century. Still, from the pages of Salvian and Augustine we may safely infer that there was, at any rate
relatively, a large amount of wealth, and culture, and
prosperity in the three most important African provinces, up to the day when the first footprint of the
Vandal was seen on the Numidian sands.

It would be an interesting enquiry, had we sufficient
evidence on which to form a judgment, how far the
civilisation which prevailed in Africa in the fifth
century of our era was Aryan, and how far still Semitic
in its character. The language of the Phoenician
settlers who first founded cities and established markets
on the Libyan shore, the language in which Hiram
spoke to Solomon and Jezebel to Ahab, was still spoken
from Tangier to Tripoli at the time of the Christian era,
and was even used in the days of Tiberius by the
colonies which prided themselves on their derivation

Was there still a Semitic element in the civilisation of Carthage?

---

[1] In the Notitia (Occ. xii.) we find—

    'Sub dispositione viri illustris comitis privatarum

    . . . Comes Gildoniaci patrimonii.'

[2] See vol. i. pp. 665–670.

from Rome[1]. Gradually, however, Punic gave way to
Latin, first in official then in social life. At the end of
the fourth century the relative position of the two
languages seems to have resembled that of English and
Welsh in our own day in the Principality. Latin was
the language of the wealthy and fashionable, but a
priest who was unacquainted with Punic was in
danger, at least in the country districts, of becoming
isolated from his congregation. Just in the same way,
too, as the representatives of the earlier race in our own
land call themselves not Welsh but Cymry, so the true
old national name, that name which recalled to a
Hebrew the contemporaries of his forefather Abraham,
the name of *Canaanites* was still naturally applied to
themselves by the Punic contemporaries of St. Augustine[2].

Latin Fathers of the African Church. But upon the whole there can be no doubt that
during the five centuries of the Empire the Latin
language and literature had been striking deeper and
deeper roots in the African world. It is one of the
common-places of Church history that in the early ages
of Christianity the chief of the Latin-speaking champions of her cause were African provincials. Tertullian,
Cyprian, Arnobius, Lactantius, all men of African birth,

[1] I am here depending on the authority of Mommsen (Prov. of
Roman Empire, ii. 327), 'Perhaps already under Caesar, certainly
under Augustus and Tiberius the towns of the Roman province and of
the Mauretanian kingdom employed in official use the Phoenician
language.... But this limited recognition of the Phoenician language
did not long subsist. There is no proof of the official use of Phoenician after Tiberius, and it can hardly have survived the first dynasty.'

[2] 'Interrogati rustici nostri quid sint, punicè respondentes, "Canani,
corrupta una littera quid aliud respondent quam Cananaei ?"' Augus-
tini Expositio Apostolica ad Romanos (quoted by Papencordt).

were conspicuous as Christian apologists in the third and fourth centuries, and the catalogue ends with the name of the greatest of all, Augustine of Hippo. The first translation of the Bible into Latin, the so-called ' Itala,' is generally supposed to have been due in great part to the labours of African ecclesiastics; and—a less enviable distinction—the first great schism, Novatianism undoubtedly originated in the Church of Carthage.

A century after the Vandal invasion of Africa it was still the opinion of the men of letters at Constantinople that the Roman provincials, in that continent, spoke Latin more fluently than the citizens of Rome itself [1]. It is very likely true that there was an affected prettiness, a want of spontaneity and naturalness about this Carthaginian Latin [2]; still, the fact that Roman rhetoric was so extensively and successfully taught in the African provinces—a fact which receives abundant confirmation from the 'Confessions' of St. Augustine— throws an important light on the progress of Roman civilisation in that region.

Such then, in brief outline, was the state of the African provinces in the fifth century after Christ ; and their prosperity—for after making every necessary

Prosperity and greatness of Imperial Carthage.

[1] So says Joannes Lydus (De Magist. iii. 73), Λίβυν ἐπιζητῶν [διδά-σκαλον τῆς 'Ιταλίδος φωνῆς] αὐτοὺς γὰρ ἔφασκεν ἐγνωκέναι στωμυλωτέρως παρὰ τοὺς 'Ιταλοὺς διαλέγεσθαι. The generous Prefect Phocas, though really able to speak Latin perfectly, professed to want an African master of the language in order to assist the destitute Speciosus.

[2] Mommsen says (l. c. p. 342), ' But the black spot of the African literary character is just its scholasticism. . . . The language swarmed partly with scholastic reminiscences, partly with unclassical or newly-coined words and phrases. There is a lack of both the graceful charm of the Greek and of the dignity of the Roman. Significantly we do not meet in the whole field of Africano-Latin authorship a single poet who deserves to be so much as named.'

deduction we must still believe them to have been
prosperous—was all summed up and symbolised in the
glory and magnificence of their capital, the 'happy
Carthage[1]' of her Roman lords. We have already
seen[2] the picture drawn by the stern Salvian of the
seductive immorality of the great African city, but even
through all his denunciations there runs a reluctant
acknowledgment of her surpassing beauty. Topo-
graphers dispute, and will perhaps long dispute, as to
the exact limits of the old Phoenician city, but there
cannot be much doubt as to the general position of its
Roman successor, and the main features of the landscape around it are still unchanged. There Carthago
lay upon her superb isthmus looking forth upon her
lake and her sea, even the sea land-locked and with the
two-horned mountain of the Hot Springs[3] rising to the
south of it. Below, was her harbour the celebrated
Cothon, once blocked up by the mole constructed by
Scipio during the last fatal siege, but now probably again
opened to the commerce of the world. Northwards, the
long sad street of tombs stretched up to the Hill of
Camart. In the city itself, besides the baths, the forum,
the amphitheatre, and all the other accustomed splendours of a Roman city, were five temples bearing witness
by the names of their tutelary gods to that antique civilisation of the sons of Canaan which Rome might crush
but could not obliterate. These were the temples dedicated under the Empire to Aesculapius, to Saturn, to
Juno, to Hercules, and to Mercury, but which had once
borne the means of Ashmon, of Moloch, of Ashtaroth, of

---

[1] 'Felix Kartago' is a frequent legend on the Imperial coins.
[2] Vol. i. p. 931.
[3] Aquae Calidae, now Hammam Elenf.

Melkarth, and of Baal-Ammon. Some of these, it is true, may have been destroyed in the outbreak of Christian zeal which marked the close of the fourth century in Africa ; but the temple of Juno Coelestis at any rate still remained, for it was consecrated in 425 by Aurelius, Bishop of Carthage, as a temple of the newer faith which had come forth from Palestine to claim all the shores of the Mediterranean for its heritage.

On an eminence within the city rose the stately Byrsa, the Acropolis of Carthage, bounded by a wall two miles in circumference [1]. Here, according to the legend transmitted by the Greeks, was the scene of Dido's famous purchase from the natives of ' a hide of land' which she interpreted to mean so much land as could be encompassed by a bull's hide [2] cut into strips. Modern philologists, struck with the obvious absurdity of supposing that Dido and her Phoenicians would resort to the Greek language for the name of their new city, have preferred to connect Byrsa with Bozra, a name well known to us from the Hebrew Scriptures as descriptive of the mountain fortress of the Edomites [3].

The Byrsa of Carthage.

---

[1] So says Orosius, who, on account of his friendship for St. Augustine, is probably a good witness at any rate as to the Carthage of the fifth century. ' Arx, cui Byrsae nomen erat, paulo amplius quam duo millia passuum tenebat. Ex unâ parte murus communis erat urbis et Byrsae imminens mari, quod mare Stagnum vocant quoniam objectu protentae linguae tranquillatur' (Hist. iv. 22). I must confess that there seems to me considerable force in the arguments of Dr. Davis (Carthage and her Remains, chap. xvii.) against the identification of the Byrsa with the hill of St. Louis, though the site which he contends for will not altogether suit the above passage in Orosius.

[2] Βύρσα = a hide.

[3] But בָּצְרָה Botsrah requires some gentle violence to press it into Bursa. I cannot help thinking that the old Greek derivation may be nearer the truth than modern scholars admit. Gesenius postulates the

Here, at any rate, appear to have been situated the chief buildings not only of Punic Carthage, but of its Roman successor : here was the Temple of Ashmon, or Aesculapius, and here in all probability the lordly *Praetorium*, once inhabited by the great Proconsul of Africa, but soon to receive the retinue of the Vandal king.

Relative position of the Proconsul and the Count of Africa.

I have said that the Proconsul of Africa once dwelt in the Praetorium of Carthage, and this was certainly his abode in the first century of the Christian era, but at the time which we have now reached, he may have been thrust out of his palace, or if still dwelling there, he may have been reduced almost to insignificance by the overshadowing might of his military rival, the Count. The position of the Proconsul was a somewhat peculiar one. The whole diocese of Africa, including all its six provinces, bounded by Tingitana on the West, and Cyrenaica in the East, was, as we have already seen, part of the Prefecture of Italy. According to analogy it should have been all subject to its own Vicarius, who should have been responsible for the whole to the Praefectus Praetorio Italiae. In fact, however, at the time of the Diocletianic reorganisation of the Empire, only five provinces (the two Mauretanias, Numidia, Byzacena, and Tripolitana) were placed under the Vicarius Africae, while the Proconsul of Zeugitana (otherwise called the Proconsul of Africa, as his, though the smallest, was by far the richest and most important of all

existence of an unused root בָּרַשׁ (barash), ' to cut ' (especially to cut into slices, see בְּרוֹשׁ). If the legend about Dido's bargain was, as seems probable, home-grown, Byrsa may have been derived from a kindred root to this. The similarity with the Greek βύρσα was, of course, a mere coincidence.

¹ Vol. i. p. 619.

the Provinces) was retained under the immediate order of the Praetorian Prefect of Italy. If, as seems highly probable, the Vicarius as well as the Proconsul had his residence at Carthage[1], there was already some material provided for jealousies and heart-burnings between the civil governors of the Diocese. But, from what we know of the cause of affairs throughout the fourth and fifth centuries, and especially from the glimpses vouchsafed to us of the history of Roman Africa during that time, we may safely say that the Proconsul, venerable as was the name of his office and great as his theoretical authority, was ever losing more of the substance of power, and that his losses were the gains of the military ruler of the Diocese, the far-feared Count of Africa[2].

[1] This is made probable, but is not actually proved by the language of Salvian (De Gubern. Dei, vii. 16) which is, in itself, an interesting description of the condition of Carthage on the eve of the Vandal invasion.

'I speak of Carthage, once the mightiest enemy of Rome, and now like another Rome in the world of Africa. She alone is sufficient for my purpose as an example and a witness, since she contained within herself all the resources whereby throughout the whole world the good order of the commonwealth is established or maintained. For there are all the appliances of the offices of State, the schools of the liberal arts, the lecture-rooms of the philosophers, in short, all the institutions for training students either in literature or in morals. There, too, are the military forces and the authorities in command of the army, the honour of the proconsul, that daily judge and ruler, proconsul, indeed, in name but a very consul in power ('illic honor proconsularis, illic judex cotidianus et rector, quantum ad nomen quidem proconsul, sed quantum ad potentiam consul'); there, finally, are all the distributors of wealth, the rulers, so to speak, of every street and square, who, with every imaginable variety of rank and name, govern all the regions of the city and all the members of the nation.'

[2] The official staff of the *Proconsul Africae* is described in the 17th chapter of the Notitia Occidentis: that of the *Vicarius Africae* in the 19th, and that of the *Comes Africae* in the 23rd chapter. Papencordt

This was the office which, in the middle of the reign of Honorius had been held by Heraclian, and which was now held by Bonifacius.

From this sketch of Roman Africa we return to trace the fortunes of its Vandal invaders. We have seen that in the month of May, and probably in the year 428, Gaiseric, with the whole body of his countrymen (the males alone of whom numbered 80,000 souls), set sail in the ships of Bonifacius for the coast of Africa. Of the details of their first conquests we know nothing [1]. All that we can say is that in the early part of 430, only three cities remained which had not been sacked by the barbarians, but these three were the strongly-fortified towns of Hippo, Cirta [2], and the capital of the province, Carthage. We know not when Cirta fell.

A peculiar interest attaches to the Vandals' siege of Hippo, which was commenced about the end of the month of May, 430. This town, situated on the sea-coast about 180 miles west of Carthage, and represented by the modern French-Arabic city of Bona, was, as every

---

(p. 29) considers that all three dignitaries, Vicarius, Proconsul, and Comes resided at Carthage.

[1] Papencordt (p. 69) points out that we have in the Theodosian Code (xii. 6. 33) an ordinance entrusting the care of the magazines of provisions in the Proconsular and Byzacene provinces to the *Curiales*. This ordinance being dated from Ravenna, 15 Feb., 430, looks as if at that time the Imperial Court did not consider these two provinces in danger from Gaiseric's movements. Perhaps it was framed in some interval of truce obtained by the mediation of Bonifacius.

[2] There can be little doubt that this is the place meant by Possidius, the biographer of St. Augustine, when he says, 'Vix tres superstites videbat ex innumerabilibus ecclesiis, hoc est Carthaginensem, Hipponensem et Circensem.' Possidius, it is true, speaks of churches, but we may conclude that if the Vandals had ruined all the other churches, they had also taken the towns.

one knows, the abode of the great bishop and father, Augustine. There he was busily employed, adding a Confutation of Julian of Eclana, the Pelagian heretic, to the vast library of books [1] which already owned him as author, when the news came of the Vandal invasion. He heard of the burnings, the massacres, the torn-up fruit-trees, the churches levelled to the ground, which everywhere marked the progress of the barbarian hosts through the orderly and quiet province, the beautiful land which from every side seemed smiling upon the stranger [2]. Bishop after bishop asked his counsel whether they should stay in their sees or fly to one of the few remaining strongholds. His first advice was, 'Remain with your flocks and share their miseries.' 'What,' said one, 'is the use of our remaining, simply to see the men slain, the women ravished, the churches burned, and then to be put to the rack ourselves to make us disclose the hiding-place of treasures which we have not?' They pleaded the words of Christ, 'When they persecute you in one city, flee into another,' and Augustine, reflecting on the examples of Cyprian and Athanasius, who had for a time quitted their bishoprics, with some hesitation, and with some limitations, admitted the plea. So it came to pass that Possidius, Bishop of Calama, to whose pen we are indebted for this account of the last days of his master, with many other bishops from all the country round, were shut up in Hippo, sitting at the feet of the great doctor of the

430.

[1] ' Two hundred and thirty-two books, besides innumerable epistles, an exposition of the Psalter and the Gospels and popular *tractates*, called *Homilies* by the Greeks, the number of which it is impossible to ascertain' (Victor Vitensis, i. 3).

[2] Victor Vitensis, i. 1.

African Church, and listening to ' that river of eloquence which had once flowed forth abundantly over all the meadows of the Church, but was now almost dried up with fear, to that fountain sweeter than honey which was being turned into the bitterness of wormwood [1]. So the good bishops sat, ' often talking together over these calamities, and reflecting on the tremendous judgments of God daily exhibited before us, saying, ' Righteous art thou, O Lord, and thy judgment is just,' mingling our tears, our groans, and our sighs, and praying the Father of Mercies and the God of all Consolation that he would see meet to deliver us from this tribulation [2].'

Count Bonifacius.

But, shut up in the same town of Hippo, was one man more sad at heart and more weary of life than Augustine himself, the author of all this misery, and the betrayer of his trust, Bonifacius Count of Africa. It has been already told [3] how, by the intervention of his friends, his character was cleared at Rome, and he returned to his old loyalty to Placidia. Too late, however, for the desolated province. ' When with the most earnest entreaties and a thousand promises he besought his late allies to depart from Africa, they would not listen to his words, but thought he was making fools of them [4].' A battle followed, in which he was defeated, and in consequence we find him now within the walls of the old capital of the Numidian kings (Hippo Regius) directing the defence of the beleaguered city, and listening to the tragic stories told by each fresh fugitive, of the ruin wrought in his

430.

[1] Victor Vitensis, i. 3. [2] Possidius, cap. 28, 29.
[3] Vol. i. p. 878. [4] Procopius, De Bell. Vand. i. 3.

province by his own invited guests. He had repented,

> ' Ay, as the libertine repents who cannot
> Make done undone, when thro' his dying sense
> Shrills "lost through thee [1]." '

It is strange to reflect that this, the most miserable
man in all Africa, whose treason had brought such
innumerable woes upon his people, was the same man
who had sighed after a monastic life, and had scarcely
been persuaded to continue to discharge the duties of
a husband and a general. A conscience, this, which
was always above or below the average common-sense
morality of ordinary men.

The generalship of Bonifacius, or the prayers of
Augustine, or the natural unskilfulness of the northern
barbarians in the siege of walled cities, enabled Hippo
to make a successful defence. For fourteen months
the Vandals blockaded the town, from May 430 till July
431. In the third month of the siege, the great Bishop
of Hippo died, in the seventy-sixth year of his age
and the fortieth of his episcopate. He had often
uttered the maxim [2] that even the aged and experienced
Christian ought not to depart out of the world except
in a state of profound penitence for all sins committed
after baptism ; and acting on his own principle, he had
the penitential Psalms of David copied for him by his
friends, and gazed constantly at the wall to which the
sheets thus inscribed were affixed. For ten days before
his death he ordered that, except when the doctor
visited him, or his meals had to be brought to his bedside, no one should enter his chamber, in order that all
his waking thoughts might be given to prayer. So,

*Death of
St. Augus-
tine.*

*August 28,
430 (Pros-
per).*

---

[1] Tennyson, Harold, iii. 1.   [2] Possidius, cap. 31.

amid the sorrows of the siege, in silence and contrition, passed away the spirit which, more mightily than any other since the age of the Apostles ended, has moulded the thoughts of the European nations concerning the dealings of the Almighty with mankind.

431.

Siege of Hippo raised.

In the fourteenth month of the siege the Vandals, pressed by famine, broke up from before the walls of Hippo. Soon after, Bonifacius, being joined by large reinforcements from Rome and Byzantium (the latter under the command of the veteran Aspar), tried conclusions once more with Gaiseric in the open field [1]. The Romans were again defeated. Aspar returned to Byzantium and Bonifacius to Rome, where (as has been before related) he received his death-wound from Aetius [2].

435. Treaty between Valentinian and Gaiseric.

Three years passed. It became clear to the Imperial Court that the Vandals would never be forced to relinquish their prize. It had also become clear to the mind of Gaiseric that it would be wise to consolidate his conquests, that Carthage would not easily be wrested in fair fighting from a watchful foe, and that it was time for his people to desist from mere marauding ravages and to settle down as lords of the soil in such part of Africa as the Emperor might be forced to surrender. Accordingly, on the 11th February [3], 435, peace was concluded between the Emperor and the Vandal, the chief conditions being apparently that the latter was to leave unmolested the city of Carthage, and that part of the Proconsular Province which lay

[1] Papencordt (p. 69) quotes 431 for the date of this battle. I have assigned it to 432 (vol. i. p. 878). I do not think we can fix the date with certainty.

[2] See vol. i. p. 879.

[3] Not 30th January, as inadvertently stated in the first edition.

immediately around it; was to pay a yearly tribute, and to send his son Huneric to Rome as a hostage for his fidelity. On the other hand, Gaiseric's rule over the part of Africa which he had already conquered, and which probably included the remainder of the Proconsular Province, Byzacena and Numidia, was recognised under the formula probably in frequent use on similar occasions that 'this portion of the Empire was given to the Vandals to dwell in[1].' The treaty was signed at Hippo, which city appears to have fallen into the hands of the Vandals, and to have been burned by them[2]. Probably it may have been rebuilt, re-occupied by an Imperial garrison, and now handed over to Gaiseric, but as to these vicissitudes in its history we cannot speak with certainty[3].

Procopius greatly praises the forethought and moderation which Gaiseric showed in concluding this peace. He says that he had reflected on the possibility that Rome and Byzantium might again combine their forces against him, and that another time he might not be able to resist their united strength, that he was sobered rather than puffed up by the good fortune which he had already experienced, and remembered

435.

Gaiseric's reasons for concluding the treaty.

---

[1] 'Pax facta cum Vandalis, datâ eis ad habitandum per Trigetium Africae portione. III Idus Februarii, Hippone,' Prosper. s. a. 435. Trigetius, the negotiator of this peace, was afterwards Prefect and one of the ambassadors sent in 452 with Pope Leo to the camp of Attila (see p. 157). Papencordt (p. 344) proposes to read 'per Trigennium' for 'per Trigetium,' and to make the Imperial concession ostensibly limited to a period of thirty years, but this does not seem probable.

[2] 'Licet post ejus [Augustini] obitum urbs Hipponensis incolis destituta ab hostibus fuerit concremata.' Possidius, Vita S. Aug. 28. I am indebted to Papencordt for this quotation.

[3] The statement in the first edition (ii. 252) as to the surrender of Hippo to the Vandals under the treaty of 435 is too positive.

how often the gods delight to trip up human prosperity. No doubt this was the attitude which the Vandal wished to assume, but considering how easily the tribute might be left unpaid, the hostage enabled to escape, the promise broken, and on the other hand of what immense importance to the establishment of the Vandal rule was the recognition of its legitimacy even for a few years by the only source of legitimate authority in the Western Empire, we shall not find much difficulty in believing that the moderate and sober-minded barbarian got the best of the bargain.

439.
Capture of
Carthage.
In point of fact, the promise to desist from further attacks on the Proconsular Province held good for rather less than five years. We have already had occasion briefly to notice [1] those vain and futile battlings to and fro in Southern Gaul between the Romans at Narbonne and the Visigoths at Toulouse, which preceded by about twelve years the far wiser confederacy of both nations against the terrible Attila. While all the energies of Rome, and all the intellect of Aetius, who was the brain of Rome, were concentrated on the next move in this purposeless struggle, suddenly, without warning, Gaiseric, (says Prosper) 'of whose friendship no doubt was entertained, attacked Carthage, under cover of peace, and converted all its wealth to his own use, extorting it from the citizens by various kinds of torments [2].' This happened on the 19th October, 439. We may conjecture that the

[1] p. 109.

[2] 'Aetio rebus, quae in Galliis componebantur, intento, Geisericus, de cujus amicitiâ nihil metuebatur, xiv Kal. Novembris Carthaginem dolo pacis invadit, omnesque opes ejus, excruciatis diverso tormentorum genere civibus, in jus suum vertit.' Marcellinus puts the date four days later, on the 23rd of October.

hostage Huneric had been before this upon some pretext or other recalled from Italy.

Now at length the great prize was won, and the
Vandals were undoubted masters of Africa. Their
chief, who for ten years or more had been leading
them from victory to victory, seems now for the first
time to have assumed the full title of king[1]. His
true statesmanlike instinct is shown by the fact that
as soon as he touched the coast, or at least as soon as
the docks and harbours of Hippo and Carthage were
in his power, he, the leader of a tribe of inland barbarians, who had been indebted to the friendly offices
of Bonifacius for the transport of his people across the
Straits of Gibraltar, turned all his energies to ship-
building, and soon possessed incomparably the most
formidable naval power in the Mediterranean. The
remaining thirty-seven years of his life, especially the
later ones, were made merry by perpetual piratical expeditions against Italy, against Sicily, against Illyria,
against the Peloponnesus, against the rich and defenceless islands of the Aegean[2]. There was a joyous

439.
Gaiseric's
rule in Car-
thage.

[1] Victor Vitensis ascribes the capture of Rome (455) to the fifteenth
year of Gaiseric's reign, and says that he continued in his kingship
thirty-seven years and three months, evidently reckoning this reign,
which ended in Jan. 477, from the date of the capture of Carthage.
Prosper and Procopius also date his reign from the same event.
What title, then, did he now assume? In the decrees quoted by
Victor Vitensis he styles himself ' King of the Vandals and Alans ;' but
this looks as if he may also have styled himself ' King of Carthage' or
' King of Africa.' Theophanes (s. a. 449) says that he called himself
' King of the land and the sea,' but he is a late writer.

[2] Gaiseric even rounded the pillars of Hercules and attacked the
coasts of Gallicia in Spain. ' Wandali navibus Turonio (?) in litore
Gallaeciae repenté advecti, familias capiunt plurimorum' (Idatius, s. a.
445).

impartiality in these expeditions, an absence of any special malice against the victims of them, a frank renunciation of all attempts to find a pretext for making them, which is thoroughly characteristic of their author. Once when his armament was lying in the harbour of Carthage, all ready for sailing, and when the brigand-king had come limping down from the palace which had been dwelt in for centuries by the Proconsuls of Africa, as soon as he set his foot on board, the pilot asked for orders to what land he should steer. The object of the expedition was the only point which the king had not yet troubled himself to determine. 'For the dwellings of the men with whom God is angry,' he said, and left the decision of that question to the winds and the waves. This was the true counterpart of the stories about 'the scourge of God,' with which Legend has falsely invested the history of Attila[1].

The Carthaginian Nemesis. So it came to pass that again after nearly six centuries of quiet submission to the rule of Rome, the name of Carthage became terrible to the dwellers by

---

[1] In the Novellae Valentiniani III. (Tit. ix. ed. Haenel) under the date 440, occurs the following interesting reference to the piratical excursions of Gaiseric: 'Geisericus hostis imperii nostri non parvam classem de Karthaginensi portu nuntiatus est eduxisse, *cujus repentinus excursus et fortuita depraedatio cunctis est litoribus formidanda.*' The object of the decree which was entitled 'De reddito jure armorum' was to convey to 'our most loving Roman people' the Imperial permission and command to use arms and band themselves together for the defence of the threatened coasts. Valentinian at the same time states that 'the army of our father, the unconquered Theodosius (II), is drawing nigh,' that 'we believe the most excellent man, our Patrician Aetius, to be at hand with a great power,' and that 'the most illustrious master of the soldiery, Sigisvuld, ceases not to array both *milites* and *foederati* for the defence both of the cities and the coasts.'

the Tiber. The poets of the period described Gaiseric's invasions of Italy as a fourth Punic War [1], and it was scarcely a license of poetry so to speak of them. We are reminded of the mediaeval superstitions about Vampire-spirits inhabiting the bodies of the dead and sucking the blood of the living, when we find this Teutonic people entering the long-buried corpse of the Punic nationality, and striking, from its heart, deadlier blows at Rome than ever were delivered by Hamilcar or Hannibal. We know not on what scale God writes his lessons for the nations, and we fear to push too far the paradox expressed in the old proverb, ' The fathers have eaten sour grapes, and the children's teeth are set on edge.' But, remembering the ignoble jealousy, the cruelty born of fear, with which the Romans prepared for and consummated the 'deletion' of their fallen enemy, in the Third Punic War, we cannot but feel that there is something like a judgment of the Eternal Righteousness in the conspicuous part assigned to the city and harbour of Carthage in harassing and embittering the dying days of Rome.

During the years immediately following the fall of Carthage, Sicily appears to- have been the main object of the Vandal expeditions. Gaiseric was, in the year 440, moving up and down through the island, cruelly wasting her fruitful valleys, when the tidings brought to him that Sebastian, a brave man and son-in-law to Bonifacius, had landed in Africa, caused him to return to Carthage. Sebastian,

440.

The Vandals in Sicily.

---

[1] Thus Sidonius—

'Heu facinus! in bella iterum *quartosque labores*
Perfida Eliseae crudescunt classica Byrsae.'

(Panegyric of Avitus, 444–5.)

however, as we shall hereafter see, came not as an enemy but as a suppliant, and Gaiseric, we may presume, returned to his career of spoliation. Next year an expedition fitted out by the Eastern Emperor under the command of Areobindus and two other generals, came to dispute the sovereignty of the Western seas with the Vandal king. But as was so often the case with these laboriously prepared Byzantine armaments, the generals wrangled and procrastinated ; the favourable moment— if there were one—for striking was lost, and the expedition failed to accomplish anything for the reconquest of Africa, and did much to increase the miseries of the unhappy Sicilians [1].

441.

Treaty between Gaiseric and Valentinian.

In the next year (442) the army was recalled to defend the Eastern Empire from one of Attila's inroads, and Valentinian, feeling it hopeless to continue the contest single-handed, concluded another treaty with Gaiseric by which possibly Sicily or some portion of it was surrendered [2], and Africa was divided by certain fixed limits between the Emperor and the Vandal [3]. Unfortunately these ' fixed limits ' have not been mentioned by the historians, and it must remain doubtful how much of Mauretania on the west and Tripolitana on the east may still have owed a precarious allegiance to the Roman Empire.

Fate of Sicily.

But the fate of Sicily is less doubtful. It is clear that either at this time or some years later, it became a recognised part of the Vandal dominions, and so remained till there was no longer a Western Emperor

---

[1] Prosper, s. a. 441. The disputes of the generals may fairly be inferred from what Prosper tells us of their long delays.

[2] This is not expressly stated by Prosper.

[3] ' Cum Geiserico autem ab Augusto Valentiniano pax confirmata, et certis spatiis Africa inter utrumque divisa est ' (Prosper).

to claim it. Then probably in the year 477, the greater
part of it was ceded by Gaiseric to Odovacar, the
barbarian ruler of Italy, on condition of his paying
an annual tribute. But already, as we see, the great
island is falling into that condition of partial detachment from the great peninsula, which generally marked
its history under its Greek lords, and which was so
frequently again to prevail in the Middle Ages, and
even down to the days of our fathers [1].

As for Gaiseric, though peace was formally concluded between him and Valentinian, we need not
suppose that the buccaneering exploits of the Vandal
king were ended. Pretexts were doubtless still found
for the visits paid with each returning spring to some
'nation with whom God was angry,' and if serious
war was not being waged, life was still made exciting
by light-hearted piracy.

The few details which are preserved as to the
internal administration of Gaiseric, and his manner
of parcelling out the conquered territory among his
followers, are of great value, as affording one of the
earliest illustrations of that great land-settlement of
the victorious Teutons which was one day to form
the basis of the Feudal System.

'He arranged,' says Procopius [2], 'the Vandals and
Alans into regiments [3], over whom he set no fewer
than eighty colonels, whom he called Chiliarchs (cap-
tains of thousands), so creating the belief that his
forces amounted to 80,000 men. Nevertheless the
number of the Vandals and Alans was said in the

---

[1] See Note F. Vandal Dominion over the Islands of the Mediterranean.
[2] De Bello Vandalico, i. 5. (I have transposed the order of the two
paragraphs.) [3] Λόχοι.

previous time (in the time before the invasion) not to amount to more than 50,000 ; but the natural increase of the population, together with their practice of admitting other barbarians into their confederation, had enormously added to their numbers. The names, however, of the Alans, and of every other barbarous tribe in the confederacy except the Moors, were all merged in the one designation of Vandals.

Land-settlement after the conquest.

'Among the provincials of Africa, if he saw any man flourishing in reputation and wealth, he gave him, with his lands and other possessions, to his sons Huneric and Genzo, as servile property[1]. From the other Africans he took away the largest and best part of their lands, and distributed them among the nation of the Vandals ; and from that time these lands are called the Vandal Allotments (*Sortes Vandalorum*) unto this day. The former possessors of these lands were for the most part left poor and free—at liberty, that is, to take themselves off whither they would. Now all these estates which Gaiseric had bestowed upon his sons and the other Vandals were, according to his orders, free from the payment of all taxes. But all the land which seemed to him to be of poorer quality, he left in the hands of the former owners, so burdened however with taxes and public charges that nothing beyond a bare subsistence could be reaped by the nominal possessors. Many of these tried to flee, but were arrested and put to death ; for sundry grievous crimes were laid to their charge, the greatest of all, according to his estimate, being the attempted concealment of treasure. Thus did the African provincials fall into every kind of misery.'

[1] Ἐν ἀνδραπόδων μοίρᾳ.

We are able to supplement the information as to the land settlement given by Procopius by an important sentence from Victor Vitensis [1]. 'He' [Gaiseric] thus disposed of the several provinces : reserving to himself the Byzacene and Abaritan provinces, Getulia and a part of Numidia, he portioned out the Zeugitana or Proconsular province to his army by the tie of inheritance [2].' The Proconsular province, as has been said, was that corner of the coast line in the middle of which Carthage was situated, the smallest of all the provinces, being only about a hundred miles wide by fifty long, but doubtless also by far the richest. Numidia bordered it on the west, the Byzacene province [3] on the south. No such province as Abaritana was known to the Imperial geographers : but it was probably a small district in the Proconsular province.[4]

The historical student who considers the account thus given by Procopius and Victor of the Vandal land-settlement will see that we have here the germs of the same state of society which prevailed in France under the Karolingian monarchs and out of the inevitable decay of which arose the Feudal System.

1. We have first a vast Royal Domain (*dominicum*) the land of 'Dominus noster, Gaisericus.' If we take the expression of Victor literally, this domain included

Domain land.

---

[1] de Pers. Vand. i. 4.

[2] 'Disponens quoque singulas quasque provincias, sibi Byzacenam, Abaritanam atque Getuliam et partem Numidiae reservavit, exercitui vero Zeugitanam vel Proconsularem funiculo hereditatis divisit.' Ibid. i. 4.

[3] Or Byzacium.

[4] This is Papencordt's suggestion (p. 181). He says that the way in which Abara is mentioned in the list of African churches shows that it was near to Carthage.

nearly the whole of the two great provinces of Numidia
and Byzacena, as well as some part of Proconsularis.
Probably, however, we may interpret it by the light of
Procopius' explanations, and infer that Gaiseric chose
for himself and his sons all the valuable estates in these
provinces [1] leaving the poorer soils in the hands of the
old cultivators. The immense domain so chosen was
cultivated of course entirely by slaves, and Gaiseric
chose especially those who have been the richest and
most influential proprietors, appropriating them and
their slaves to service on his domain land. The insolence of the barbarian was gratified by thus reducing
the proudest, wealthiest, and most refined of the provincials to the condition of menials absolutely dependent
on his will. But in course of time no doubt superior
education and the old habits of command would assert
themselves. These aristocratic slaves would become
intendants, stewards, managers of their fellow-slaves.
If the experiment had been continued for a sufficient
length of time (which it was not in the case of the
Vandals) these highly-educated slaves would have become supple courtiers, and would have perhaps proved
a formidable counterpoise to the descendants of Vandal
chiefs, who once looked upon Gaiseric himself as scarcely
more than first among his peers. In fact, very soon
after the settlement (in 442) there was an actual conspiracy among the nobility against what they considered
the overgrown power and pride of their king : but the
plot was detected and the conspirators atoned for their
share in it by a death of torture. The suspicions and

---

[1] This process is, I believe, called in Australia ' picking out the eyes '
of a district.   Dahn's explanation of Victor (Könige der Germanen, i.
205) substantially agrees with the above.

jealousies engendered by this conspiracy were very detrimental to the Vandal state [1].

2. The Vandal Allotments (*Sortes Vandalorum*) denote the next class of lands, those which are divided among the warriors of the conquering nation. Divided, surely, by lot [2], in a manner which suited well the ardent love of games of hazard inherent in these Teutonic nations, and in accordance with a custom widely diffused among them, as is testified by the occurrence of the same word, *sors*, among the Visigoths in Spain, among the Burgundians on the banks of the Lake of Geneva, and among the Ripuarian Franks of the Rhine. The estates were hereditary—this we learn from Victor's express testimony [3]—but though hereditary they doubtless carried with them some obligation of service in that 'army' to which they were originally 'portioned out.' Except for this implied obligation of military service they were free from all taxes. These *Sortes Vandalorum* were, as before said, chiefly to be found in the rich Proconsular province, where they must have clustered thickly, perhaps overflowing a little into

Allotments of the soldiers, or Sortes Vandalorum.

---

[1] 'In Geisericum apud suos de successu rerum superbientem quidam optimates ipsius conspiraverunt : sed molitione detectâ, multis ab eo suppliciis excruciati atque exstincti sunt. Cumque idem audendum etiam aliis videretur, multis regis suspicio exitio fuit, ut hac sui curâ plus virium perderet, quam si bello superaretur.' Prosper s. a. 442.

[2] Hallam seems to doubt whether the partition really took place by lot, and would make *sors* simply the equivalent of the Greek κλῆρος (Supplemental Notes, p. 71). But Binding, who has examined the subject very carefully, pronounces decidedly in favour of the meaning which is etymologically the obvious one, viz. that the *sors* implied 'sortilegy,' an 'allotment,' a casting of lots (Geschichte des Burgundisch-Romanischen Königreichs, 18).

[3] 'funiculo hereditatis divisit.'

the neighbouring Numidia[1].   Here doubtless the power
of the old Vandal nobility was greatest, and the spirit
of Vandal nationality the strongest.   Here, if it had
been written in the book of Fate that an enduring
German kingdom of North Africa should be founded,
would the speech of the Vandals have struck the
deepest root, and the songs of Vandal minstrels as to
the bye-gone ages spent in the forest of the Elbe and
the Danube would have been the longest preserved.

Lands left to the provincials.   3. There remain the poor, the unimproved, the
outlying lands, abandoned half-contemptuously to the
Roman provincials, who tilled, and crouched, and paid
where their fathers fought, and ruled, and robbed.
Would this kind of holding in the course of centuries
have sunk down into the 'base-tenure' whence our
copyholds sprang, or would it have slowly risen into
what our ancestors called *free-socage*?   In other words,
would these down-trodden provincials have developed
into villeins or freeholders?   That is an interesting
question, the answer to which is drowned by the trumpets of Belisarius.   But, nevertheless, it is worth while
noticing that we have here in Africa, half way through
the fifth century after Christ, a division of the nation
into two distinct classes, a burdened, tax-paying, toiling
commonalty, and a lordly, untaxed, warrior class above
them—that same division which in France lasted on to
the days of our grandfathers, and was shattered by the
oath of the Tiers Etat in the Tennis-Court of Versailles.

Enslaved provincials.   But it is not to be supposed that a majority of the
subject population were left, even in this degraded
state, to enjoy the blessings of freedom.   The vast
estates of the king, his sons, and the Vandal warriors,

[1] Gaisericus sibi *partem* Numidiae reservavit.   Victor Vit. l. c.

required vast tribes of slaves to cultivate them, and to
slavery accordingly, as has before been said, the bulk
of the provincial population were reduced. A story
which is told us by Procopius [1], and which has something in the ring of it that reminds one of the far-
distant legendary moralities of Herodotus, brings this
wholesale enslavement of the people clearly before us.
'The Byzantine general Aspar, as was before said, brought
help to the Roman Provincials of Africa, but was defeated by the barbarians. After the battle, Gaiseric
ordered all the captives to be mustered in the court-
yard of his palace that he might allot them masters
suitable to their several conditions. There then they
were collected in the open air, and as the noonday
sun '—the fierce sun of Libya—' beat hotly on their
heads, most of them sat down. But one among them,
who was named Marcian, carelessly composed himself
to sleep ; and while he lay there an eagle, so they say,
with outspread wings, hovered over him, now rising,
now falling, but always contriving to shelter him, and
him only, from the sun by the shadow of her wings.
From the window of an upper chamber Gaiseric watched
this occurrence, and being a quick-witted man, at once
perceived that there was in it something of the nature
of an omen. So he sent for the man, and asked him
who he was, and whence he came. He replied that he
was a confidential servant, or *domesticus*, as the Romans
call it, of Aspar. On hearing this, and reflecting what
the bird had done '—the typical Eagle of Rome—' and
comparing it with the influence which Aspar possessed
at the court of Byzantium, Gaiseric saw clearly that
the captive before him would attain to some high career.

432.

---

[1] De Bello Vandalico, i. 4.

To kill him, however, did not appear to be at all the right thing to do : for that would only show that the omen had no significance, since certainly the bird would never have taken the trouble to overshadow, as future Emperor, a man who was just on the point of dying. And besides, he had no just cause for putting him to death. Nor could he do it if he was really destined to wear the purple, since what God has resolved upon, Man will never be able to hinder. He therefore bound him by an oath that if he was restored to freedom he would never bear arms against the Vandals. Thus was Marcian liberated, and came to Byzantium, where, not long afterwards, upon the death of Theodosius II, he was made Emperor.' He is the same Marcian with whom we have already made acquaintance as the husband of Pulcheria, the courageous defender of the Empire against Attila, the prince who saw in his dreams the broken bow, on the night when the mighty Hun expired. ' And, though (says Procopius) in all other respects he made an excellent ruler, he never seemed to take any thought for the province of Africa,' mindful as he was of his vow not to bear arms against the Vandals.

The land-settlement, the outlines of which are thus preserved to us, was probably completed soon after the capture of Carthage in 439. We have seen that by the peace of 442 some fragments of African dominion, probably in Tripolitana and Mauretania were still left to the Empire, but after the death of Valentinian III (455) the Vandal dominion spread unchallenged over these as well as over all the islands of the Western Mediterranean [1].

---

[1] After enumerating (in the extract previously quoted) the Byzacene and Abaritan provinces, Getulia, a part of Numidia and Zeugitana,

As to the administration of government in this wide territory, there are not wanting indications that here, as in so many other portions of the Empire, much was still left in the hands of the trained Roman officials. Doubtless the lawless will of the Vandal king could make itself felt wherever it pleased. Doubtless, subject to that omnipotent will, the great nobles, each in his own circle, could exercise unchecked dominion. Still there remained an infinite number of details of daily government in a community which, though half ruined was still civilised, and these details the German conquerors had neither intellect nor patience to arrange. They remained therefore in the hands of the Roman bureaucracy, and hence it is that we still, even under the Vandal kings, meet with a Proconsul of Carthage [1], a *Primarius Provinciae* [2], and a *Praepositus Regni* [3], though to attempt now to settle the exact functions of these governors would be a hopeless task.

Some parts of the Roman machine of government still preserved.

With all the barbarous violence and contempt of the rights of the subject population which characterised the Vandal conquest, it deserves one praise : it was not financially oppressive. While the Imperial government, with phrases of law and right for ever on its lips, was practically sucking the life-blood out of the people by its Indictions and its Superindictions, its *Angaria* and its *Chrysargyron*, Gaiseric, though

Absence of financial oppression.

Victor Vitensis proceeds (i. 4) : ' Valentiniano adhuc Imperatore, reliquas licet jam exterminatas Provincias defendente. Post cujus mortem, totius Africae ambitum obtinuit, necnon et insulas maximas, Sardiniam, Siciliam, Corsicam, Ebusam, Majoricam, Minoricam vel alias multas superbiâ sibi consuetâ defendit.'

[1] Victor Vitensis, v. 4.
[2] Vita S. Fulgentii, cap. 14.
[3] Victor Vitensis, ii. 5. (I owe these references to Papencordt.)

helping himself and his soldiers to all the fairest lands in the province, did leave to the poor provincial liberty to live on the sterile soil which he contemptuously abandoned to him. Procopius expressly assures us that when the Emperor Justinian regained Africa it was no longer possible to discover in the public archives the amount of taxes which ought to be paid by each property, since Gaiseric, in the beginning of his reign, had thrown up the whole system and destroyed the registers [1].

At first sight this seems contradictory to the same author's statement previously quoted, that the lands abandoned to the Romans were 'so burdened with taxes and public charges that nothing beyond a bare subsistence could be reaped by the nominal possessors.' On reflection, however, we may perhaps come to the conclusion that in that passage Procopius is speaking chiefly of the great Roman land-owners, whom it was evidently part of the Vandal policy to worry out of existence. The mass of cultivators and the little burgesses in the towns, who were known under the Empire as *Curiales,* were, it seems, practically untaxed. The grievous discontent which arose in the province when this operation was reversed by the Roman re-conquest, and when the people found that in their liberator they had gained a relentless task-master, is a striking testimony to the general lightness of the financial yoke of the Vandal kings.

Whence comes the stigma of 'Vandalism?'   In all that has yet been said concerning the career of this people, little has appeared to justify that charge of senseless and brutal destructiveness with which the word 'vandalism' makes us familiar. We have heard

[1] De Bello Vandalico, ii. 8.

of the pillage of towns—that, of course, is one of the commonplaces of barbaric conquest; of populations reduced to slavery—but the slave-dealer followed also in the track of the Roman armies; even of the fruit-trees being rooted up—but that was consistent with the cruel logic of war, being done in order to prevent the inhabitants from deserting the towns and prolonging a guerilla campaign in the country on such support as they could derive from the produce of the orchards. We have yet, however, to see the Vandal in his most repulsive aspect, that of a religious persecutor; and when we have beheld him in this capacity, the kernel of truth and the large envelope of passionate exaggeration which both together make up the common idea of 'vandalism' will be more clearly perceived and more easily separated from one another.

The Vandals, like almost every other Teutonic nation, Arianism had shared in that great process of religious change Vandals. of the of which the bishop Ulfilas was the most conspicuous instrument. Little as their deeds savoured of Christianity, they were, by profession, Christians, holding, as a matter of course, the Arian creed of their great apostle.

They came then with all the rancour of the Arian- Previous Catholic feud, which had now endured for more than a religious century, bitter in their hearts. And they came into a Africa. feuds of parties in province which was, beyond all the other provinces of the Roman Empire, undermined by hot volcanic fires of theological passion and bigotry. There is much in the religious controversies of Africa in the fourth and fifth centuries which reminds us of the bloody disputes between Episcopalian, Presbyterian, and Independent at the time of our own 'Great Rebellion.' Even the very names of men, not of one party only, have a

Puritan sound about them: 'What-God-wills,' 'Thanks-to-God,' 'Given-by-God[1],' and so forth, recall the 'Praise-God Barebones' and his piously named confederates of those stormy days. In Africa, over and above the ordinary religious dissensions of the fourth and fifth centuries, there was a special strife, the

Donatists. Donatist, which had arisen out of the cowardly conduct of some bishops and presbyters during the persecution

303-313. of the Church by Diocletian and his successors. A hundred and twenty years had elapsed since that time, and it might have been thought that purely personal questions, such as whether this bishop had under terror of death delivered up the sacred books to the Imperial officers, or whether that presbyter had with too great eagerness grasped the crown of martyrdom, might have been now allowed to slumber in oblivion. But sects and churches have long memories, and the Donatists, the Cameronians of Africa, were still as earnest in discussing the election of the so-called 'traditor[2]' Caecilian to the see of Carthage, as if that event had happened yesterday instead of four generations ago. Round the Donatists, and in more or less close connection with them, were grouped the wild,

Circumcelliones. fanatical Circumcelliones, savage boors, whose zeal, where it was not assumed as a cloak for rapine and lust, must have been hovering on the verge of insanity, who carried fire and sword through the villages of Africa, and whose war-cry, 'Praise be to God[3],' was

---

[1] Quod-vult-Deus, Deo-gratias, A-deo-datus.

[2] The name given to those who in time of persecution surrendered their Bibles to be burnt by the executioner.

[3] 'Deo Laudes.' The battle-shout of the Catholic party was 'Deo Gratias.'

heard in those villages with greater terror than the
roar of the Numidian lion. The portrait of all these
fanatics, being drawn only by their antagonists, must
be received with much caution, but after making every
conceivable allowance for exaggeration, we cannot
avoid the conclusion that in this instance Christian
common sense was represented by the party which
successfully maintained its title to the envied designation, Catholic. But, Donatists and Catholics having
both appealed to the state, and judgment having gone
in favour of the latter, they, not unnaturally, according
to the ideas of that age, but most unwisely according
to our manner of thinking, brought down the iron
hand of Imperial despotism with all its weight upon
their foes.

It happens that the greater part of the laws against
the Donatists[1] which are preserved to us belong to
the reign of Honorius and the first twenty years of
the fifth century, and we are thus able to see clearly
mirrored in the Roman statute-book the theological
animosities and the petty persecutions which preceded
the advent of the Vandals into Africa[2]. The power of

*Legisla-
tion of
Honorius
against
the African
heretics.*

---

[1] In many of the edicts the Donatists are coupled with the Manicheans, who asserted the combined agency of two eternal principles,
Good and Evil, in the Creation. Thus one of the most special and
technical of sectarian squabbles was coupled with the oldest, the
strongest, and the most alluring form of unfaith.

[2] See especially Book xvi of the Theodosian Code, Tit. v, Laws 37
to 54. By Law No. 54 the scale of fines was fixed thus :—A man who
had filled one of the highest offices of state, Proconsul, Vicarius, or
Comes, 'if found in the Donatist flock,' was to pay 200 lbs. weight of
gold (about £8000) ; a Senator 100 lbs. weight (about £4000) ; one
who had held the Pagan dignity of Sacerdos, the same sum ; one of
the leading ten men in a corporation (Decemprimi Curiales), 50 lbs. of
silver (about £133 sterling); a Common-Council-Man (Decurion), 10

buying, selling, and bequeathing property was denied
to the Donatists, 'whom the patience of our Clemency
has preserved until now, but who ought to be branded
with perpetual infamy, and shut out from all honourable assemblies, and from every place of public resort.'
Their churches were to be taken from them and given
to the Catholics. They were to pay fines, varying,
according to their condition in life, from £25 to £8000
sterling (those wild boors, the Circumcelliones, were to
pay £25 a head); and these fines were to be repeated
as often as the offender renewed his communion with
the Donatist Church. The slaves and the semi-servile
agricultural labourers were 'to be prevented from
audacious acts of this kind by the severest punishment;' 'to be recalled from their evil religion by more
frequent blows'—if blows still proved ineffectual, to
lose the third part of their accumulated savings (*pe-
culium*). We have here, it is true, not a ruthless or
bloodthirsty persecution, but we have a great deal of
injustice of a very galling kind, perpetrated under the
name of religion, just the kind of quiet, crushing,
monotonous intolerance by which the Hapsburgs ex-
tirpated the Protestantism of Styria, and the English
Parliament strove to extirpate the Papistry of Ireland.
There can be no doubt that the Catholics had thus
earned a rich legacy of hatred and revenge, which was
punctually paid to them when the Vandals, heretics
like the Donatists, entered Africa[1].

lbs. of silver, a little more than £25 sterling. After one of the officials
of higher rank had paid the fine five times, 'if he be not then by his
losses recalled from the error of his ways, let him be referred to our
Clemency, that we may pass some more severe sentence concerning the
capital which belongs to him, and concerning his rank in life.'

[1] We might naturally expect to find the Donatists, though ortho-

We will now hear a little of what Victor Vitensis has to tell us of the Vandal persecutions in the reign of Gaiseric. His style is declamatory and he is full of prejudices, both national and ecclesiastical, but he is all but a contemporary—writing, as he does, 'in the six-tieth year after that cruel and savage nation reached the boundaries of our miserable Africa,'—and he gives us that life and colour which we ask for in vain from the meagre and cautious annalists.

Victor Vitensis on the Vandal persecutions of the Catholics.

'The wicked rage of the Vandals was especially directed against the churches and basilicas, the cemeteries and the monasteries, and they made bigger bonfires of the houses of prayer than of whole cities and towns. If by chance they found the door of the holy house fast closed, it was who should soonest force an entrance by thumping it down with his right hand; so that one might truly say, "They break down the carved work thereof at once with axes and hammers. They have cast fire into Thy sanctuary; they have defiled by casting down the dwelling-place of Thy name to the ground." Ah, how many illustrious bishops and noble priests were put to death by them with divers kinds of torments in the endeavour to compel them to reveal what treasures they had of gold or silver, belonging to themselves or to their churches. If, under the pressure of the torture, they easily revealed their possessions, the persecutors plied them with yet more cruel torments, declaring that part only had been surrendered, not the whole; and the more they gave up the more they were supposed to

De Persecutione Vandalorum, i. 1.

i. 2.

dox, taking sides with the Arians against their Catholic persecutors: but Papencordt (pp. 284–286) shows some ground for believing that this was not the case either before or after the Vandal Conquest.

be keeping back. Some had their mouths forced open
with stakes and crammed with noisome filth. Some
were tortured by having strings tightly twisted round
the forehead or leg-bone [1]. Some had bladders filled with
sea-water, with vinegar, with the dregs of the olive-
presses, with the garbage of fishes, and other foul and
cruel things laid upon their lips. The weakness of
womanhood, the dignity of noble birth, the reverence
due to the priesthood—none of these considerations softened those cruel hearts; nay, rather, where they saw
that any were held in high honour, there was their
mad rage more grievously felt. I cannot describe how
many priests and illustrious functionaries had heavy
loads piled upon them, as if they were camels or
other beasts of burden, nor how with iron goads
they urged them on their way, till some fell down
under their burdens and miserably gave up the ghost.
Hoary hairs enwrapping the venerable head like
whitest wool won for the bearer no pity from those
savage guests. Innocent little children were snatched
by the barbarian from the maternal embrace and
dashed to the ground. Well might our captive Zion
sing " The enemy said that he would burn my borders
and slay my infants and dash my little ones to the
earth." In some large and stately buildings [probably
churches], where the ministry of fire had proved insufficient to destroy them, the barbarians showed their
contempt of the edifice by levelling its fair walls
with the ground; so that now those beautiful old
cities have quite lost their former appearance, and many
whole towns are now occupied by a scanty remnant

i. 3.

---

[1] ' Nonnullos in frontibus et tibiis, nervis remugientibus torquendo
cruciabant.' (Translation doubtful.)

of their former inhabitants, or even left altogether desolate.

'Yea, and even to-day, if any buildings remain, they are continually laying them waste, as, for instance, the Temple of Memory, that worthy appendage to the Theatre of Carthage, and the street called the Street of Heaven [1], both of which they have destroyed from top to bottom. Then too, the large basilica, where the bones of the blessed martyrs Perpetua and Felicitas are laid, the church of Celerina, and others which they have not destroyed, they have, with the license of tyrants, enslaved to their own religious rights. Did they see any strongholds which they were unable to carry by the rush of their barbarian fury, they collected vast multitudes around the walls and slew them with the bloody sword, leaving their carcases to putrefy under the ramparts, that they might slay with the stench those whom their arms were powerless to assail.'

This last sentence may serve as an example of the style in which the indictment against the Vandals has been framed. It is evident that they committed all the excesses which might be expected from a horde of triumphant barbarians, greedy beyond measure of gold, and utterly reckless of human life, but it is also evident that the very blunders of their savage warfare have been made to appear as parts of a diabolical machinery of cruelty by the ecclesiastical pamphleteer [2]. *Untrustworthy character of this account.*

When we come to the details of the Vandal perse-

---

[1] 'Via Coelestis.'

[2] Gibbon sensibly remarks, 'I cannot believe that it was a usual stratagem to slaughter great numbers of their prisoners before the walls of a besieged city, for the sole purpose of infecting the air and producing a pestilence, of which they themselves must have been the first victims.' (Vol. iv. p. 182, ed. Smith.)

cution of the Catholics under Gaiseric (for we have no present concern with that which happened in the next

generation), we find further reason to suppose that there has been some exaggeration in the passages already quoted. Two bishops, Papinianus and Mansuetus, seem to have been burnt, but there is something in the language of the historian here which leads us to conjecture that this was the work of cruel pillagers

rather than a solemn state-sanctioned martyrdom. The Bishop of Carthage, 'What-God-wills[1],' and a great multitude of his clergy, were put on board unsound ships and sent out to sea, but they were favoured with a prosperous wind, and arrived in Campania, safe in body, though stripped of all their possessions. The churches of Cathage were claimed for the Arian worship, among them two stately and noble edifices outside the walls, which commemorated respectively the martyrdom and burial[2] of St. Cyprian. 'But who,' says the good Victor, 'can bear to remember without tears that Gaiseric ordered us to bear the bodies of our dead, without the solemnity of hymns, in silence to the grave?' When this silent-burial grievance of the African Catholics assumes so prominent a place in the catalogue of their woes, we may perhaps conclude that the religious persecution, considered apart from the mere rapine of the barbarians, was not extremely severe.

A deputation of bishops and leading men of the

---

[1] Quod-vult-Deus.

[2] The latter church was called *Mappalia*, 'the Huts,' showing the humble origin from whence it had sprung. It is interesting to meet again this word Mappalia, which Sallust mentions as the name of the long, hull-shaped dwellings of the Numidian rustics in the time of Jugurtha.

provinces which the Vandals had divided among themselves, waited upon the King, when he had gone down,
as his custom was, to the coast of Numidia [1], perhaps
to inhale such freshness as might be found in the sea-
breezes. They pleaded with him to restore to the
Orthodox some places in which they might worship
God. 'What? Are you here still?' he bade his interpreter [2] say to the bishops. 'I decreed the banishment
of your whole name and race : and yet you dare to ask
for such things.' And so great was his anger that he
would fain have drowned them all at once in the Mediterranean at his feet, had not his counsellors after long
entreaty persuaded him to abandon his purpose. They
departed and continued their service of God in such
lowly dwellings as they could obtain, not unlike probably to those in which Paul had discoursed till break
of day, and the elders of Ephesus had fed the flock of
God. For some years, we infer from the language of
the historian, this unobtrusive worship of the Catholics
was permitted, if not expressly sanctioned. Then came Victor Vit.
denunciations and calumnies, especially against those i. 7.
priests who officiated 'in the regions which paid tribute
to the Palace.' If one of these, in his sermons to his
flock, happened to mention the name of Pharaoh, or
Nebuchadnezzar, or Holofernes, or any similar tyrant—
and we may conjecture that these references were rather
more frequent than were absolutely needful to explain
the Lessons for the day—he was accused of speaking
against the person of the King, and banishment was
his immediate sentence. For this cause a whole batch

---

[1] 'To the place which is commonly called Lugula.' I cannot find
any trace of this name.

[2] 'Internuntium.'

of bishops (among whom we find 'He-has-God,[1]' Bishop of Teudala) was banished at once, and the Holofernes of their denunciation would not allow the consecration of any successors to their sees. At length, on the urgent entreaty of Valentinian, he permitted the Orthodox Church of Carthage to ordain for itself a bishop, the gentle and charitable 'Thanks-to-God,[2]' who for three years governed the Metropolitan See with general approval. On his death there was another long interval of widowhood for the Churches, till at last, about the year 475, towards the very end of the reign of Gaiseric, on the intercession of Zeno, Emperor of the East, the surviving bishops were permitted to return from the widely-scattered seats of their long banishment.

i. 8.

454–457.

Other oppressions of the Catholic congregations.

Besides the exile, and in some cases the enslavement of the bishops, other oppressions were practised upon the Orthodox. The demand made in the time of Diocletian for the surrender of sacred books and vessels was repeated. The officer of the barbarians, a man with the Roman name of Proculus, who was sent to enforce this demand, finding his authority resisted, laid violent hands on all the treasures of the sacristies that he could find, and adding contumely to rapine, caused the beautiful altar-cloths which were already used in the Churches to be cut up into shirts and drawers for his followers. The sacrilege was remembered, and was deemed to have been divinely punished when, not long after, Proculus died of cancer in the tongue. In a town called Regia a battle took place between Catholics and Arians for the possession of the Church, which reminds us of the last fatal fray in St. Mark's Chapel at Florence at the time of the downfall of Savonarola. It was

Vict. Vit. i. 12.

i. 13.

---

[1] 'Habet-Deum.'   [2] 'Deo-gratias.'

Easter-time : the Catholics were celebrating the festival, and the Arians finding the doors of the Church closed against them, under the guidance of a Presbyter named Andiot[1], got together a band of armed men and proceeded to hammer at the doors, to mount the roofs of the neighbouring houses, to shoot their arrows through the windows of the Church. The people within the Church loudly chanted the defiant Alleluia; especially one *Lector*, who was sitting in the pulpit, made his voice heard above the tumult. An arrow which was shot through the window transfixed his throat, still quivering with the holy hymn ; the roll from which he was singing dropped at his feet, and the *Lector* fell down dead. In rushed the assailant Arians and slew around the altar nearly all the survivors from the previous fight, the older men being especially selected as victims of their wrath.

We have seen how it fared with churches and churchmen at the hands of the Vandals; let us now see how individual laymen were dealt with. Sebastian, the before-mentioned son-in-law of Bonifacius, a keen-witted counsellor and brave warrior, had shared the ill-fortune of his kinsman, and after the fatal conflict between him and Aetius, had been driven forth from Ravenna and wandered over the face of the earth. First Constantinople and then the Visigothic court had been his asylum, and he had won Barcelona from the Empire for Theodoric. At last in 440[2] he quarrelled with the Visigoths also and sought refuge in Africa. Gaiseric, who had feared him as a foe, welcomed him as a suppliant, and would gladly have promoted him to

The king's behaviour to Sebastian.
Vict. Vit. i. 6.

---

[1] Or Adduit. Is this a Teutonic name ?

[2] Prosper gives this date : Idatius 445.

great honour. But he was a Catholic, and for that reason formidable to the Arian king who could not reckon upon him with certainty while he belonged to the rival Church. One day, in the presence of his courtiers and Arian bishops, Gaiseric said to Sebastian, 'I know that your faith is firmly pledged to me and mine, but it would make our friendship more lasting, if here, in the presence of these holy men, you would profess yourself a follower of the same religion which is dear to me and to my people.' Sebastian answered, 'I beseech you, oh king, order that a loaf of the finest and whitest flour be now brought hither.' The king, wondering what could be his meaning, gave the order : the bread was brought, and Sebastian said, 'Oh king ! to prepare this white bread and make it fit for the royal table, the wheat had to be separated from the chaff, the flour to be carefully bolted from the bran, the mill-stone, water, and fire had each to do their work upon it before it attained this 'spotless purity. Even so have I been from my youth up separated from all heretical contagion, the Church has made me hers by the water of baptism, and the fire of the Holy Spirit has purified me. Now if by crumbling up this bread into little pieces and baking it afresh you can increase its whiteness, then I will take up with another faith and become an Arian as you desire me. But if not I remain a Catholic.' The king saw that he had the worst of the argument for that time, 'but afterwards he tried a different sort of logic and put that brave man to death.'

The same command 'to pass over to the sect of the Arians' was given to four men of Spanish birth, Arcadius, Probus, Paschasius, and Eutychius, who had

served Gaiseric with fidelity and stood high among his
counsellors. Their persistent refusal was punished by
exile, tortures, and eventually by martyrdom. A young
lad named Paulillus, brother of Paschasius and Eutychius, whose beauty and talents had gained him a high
place in the royal household, was for the same reason
cruelly flogged and then sent into vile bondage. The
crown of martyrdom was not awarded him, that the
king might be spared the disgrace of being vanquished
by a boy of such tender years [1].

Eventually the order was given that none but Arians
should be tolerated about the Court and person of the
king. A certain Armogast, who must have been a
Teuton by his name, and who seems to have been
a Count [2] by office, refused to conform to the Courtly
religion. The persecutors tried to change his resolution
with the rack and the cord, but the cords, we are
assured, broke like spider's webs when the saint looked
towards heaven. They hung him head downward by
one foot from the ceiling, and he slept as sweetly as if
he had been on a feather bed. His master, Theodoric,
the king's son, wished to slay him out of hand, but was
wisely warned by his Arian chaplain, 'If you kill him
with the sword, the Romans will preach him up as a
martyr.' The former Count was therefore sent into
the fields to dig ditches and to keep sheep. There
he soon died, but not before he had disclosed to a
faithful disciple the approaching day of his death, and
the place destined for his burial, a place apparently
obscure and sordid, but where the obedient disciple,

Persecu-
tion of
Armogast.
Vict. Vit.
i. 14.

---

[1] Prosper s. a. 437.

[2] Victor's expression, 'Comes bonae confessionis de hâc vitâ migra-
vit,' I think implies this.

when he came to dig, found a sarcophagus of the most splendid marble prepared for the reception of the saint's body.

The Come-
dian-Con-
fessor.

Vict. Vit.
i. 15.

An example of firm adherence to the faith was found where it would scarcely have been looked for, among the comic actors who performed before the new barbaric Court. A certain 'arch-mime,' named Masculanus, had been long pressed by the king, with flatteries and promises, to join the religion of the dominant caste. As he ever stood firm, Gaiseric gave public orders for his execution, but, with his usual hard craftiness, being determined not to present the Catholic Church with a single martyr more for her veneration, he gave the following secret commands to the executioner. 'If he flinches at the sight of the sword and denies his faith then kill him all the more [1], for then he cannot be considered a martyr. But if he remains firm, sheathe your sword again and let him go free.' Perhaps the acting of the executioner, perplexed by such intricate orders, failed to deceive the practised eye of the arch-comedian. At any rate he stood ' firm as a pillar on the solid rock of Christ,' and saved both life and truth. 'And thus,' says the historian, 'if that envious enemy refused to allow us a martyr, he could not prevent our having a confessor [2], and a glorious one.'

Vict. Vit.
i. 16.

In a similar manner a certain Saturus, steward over the house of Huneric, the king's son, who had made himself conspicuous in many discussions with the Arians, was ordered to change his religion. Riches

---

[1] ' Magis eum occideret.'

[2] A Christian who lived in the Imperial persecutions remained true to his faith, but from any cause escaped the extreme penalty of death, was generally called a ' confessor.'

and honours were promised him in the event of his compliance ; tortures for himself, poverty for his children, another and apparently a hated husband for his wife, were to be the punishments of his refusal. That wife joined her entreaties to those of the persecutors, begging him not to subject her to the yoke of a base and unworthy hnsband, 'while the husband Saturus, of whom I have so often boasted, still lives.' 'Thou speakest as one of the foolish women speaketh,' replied the African Job. ' If thou truly lovedst thy husband, thou wouldst not seek to entice him to his second death, I am ready to give up wife and children, and house, and lands, and slaves [1], that I may continue to be a disciple of Christ.' The cruel and unjust sentence was executed. 'Saturus was spoiled of all his substance, was worn down with punishment, was sent away into beggary. His wife was given to a camel-driver. He was forbidden to return to the Court ; they took every thing from him, but they could not take away the white robe of his baptism.'

Firmness of Saturus.

The reader has now before him the chief evidence against the Vandals as religious persecutors during the first generation after their conquest of Africa. He may reasonably ask why there should be set before him, with so much detail, facts which have no direct bearing on the History of Italy. The answer is that our information as to the social aspects of the struggle between Romans and Barbarians in Italy itself during the fifth century is so miserably meagre, we might almost say

The African persecutions illustrate the relations of Catholics and Arians throughout the Empire.

---

[1] As Papencordt remarks, this clause in the sentence pronounced on Saturus is important, as showing that the Provincials who were attached in a servile capacity to the royal household had slaves of their own.

so absolutely non-existent, that we must be content to supply the deficiency to the best of our power from what we know of the mutual relations of conquerors and conquered, of Arians and Orthodox, in other provinces of the Empire, especially in Africa and Gaul. And this peculiar attitude of the Teutonic nations towards their Catholic subjects in the dawn of the Middle Ages, tending as it did to sever for a time the connection of the Orthodox Clergy with the State, and to throw them back into somewhat of their old position as men of the people, and sympathisers with the people, is so important with reference to the subsequent growth and development of the Spiritual Power, that it cannot be said we are wasting time in considering it a little more closely.

Character of the persecution.

Reviewing then the indictment which has been framed by Victor Vitensis against the persecutor Gaiseric, we come to the following conclusions :—

Churches demolished.

1. It is clear that the Churches were as a rule either handed over to the Arians for their worship, or else destroyed. And it is this wanton demolition and desecration of ecclesiastical buildings which more than anything else has caused the name of Vandalism to be synonymous in later days with senseless destructiveness.

Bishops banished.

2. The bishops were for the most part banished, and their flocks were forbidden to elect successors to them. The Vandal king, himself surrounded by Arian bishops, knew, better probably than Decius or Diocletian, how sore a blow, according to the prevailing theories of ecclesiastical organization, he was thus dealing at the very existence of the Church. But under the influence of occasional solicitations from Rome and from Byzantium, he wavered more than once in the execution of this

stern policy ; and even had he been always constant to
it, one cannot easily see how the mere mandate of the
king could have permanently and universally prevented
the consecration of at least some bishops, and the transmission of the episcopal prerogatives, throughout the
whole province of Africa.

3. Individual Catholics were not as a rule persecuted
on account of their faith.   Occasionally the headstrong
arrogance of the king or his sons was roused into fury
by the discovery that the officers of their household, or
the menials who ministered to their amusement, would
not yield servile obedience to their nod in all things,
but claimed a right in matters appertaining to God to
act according to the dictates of their own consciences.
But even in these cases, from mere motives of expediency, Gaiseric was intensely anxious to avoid making
new martyrs for the Catholic Church.   And as to the
great mass of the people, the down-trodden slaves who
tilled the vast domain lands of the crown, or the hungry
coloni who eked out a scanty subsistence on the edge of
the desert, or even the traders and artisans of Hippo
and of Carthage, Gaiseric was too much of a statesman
to attempt to convert them wholesale, by persecution,
to Arianism, and probably too little of a theologian to
care greatly whether truth, or what he deemed to be
error, was being supplied as food to the souls of all that
base-born crew.   In the heart of the Teuton invader
there perhaps lurked the thought that the confession of
Nicaea was good enough for slaves, and that it was well
for the free-born warrior of the north to keep his own
bolder speculations to himself.   The willingness to persecute was clearly in the hearts of these Vandals.   They
did not in the slightest degree recognise the right of the

Individual
laymen not
generally
molested.

individual conscience to decide for itself how best to express its loyalty to the Great Maker. But they had some dim perception what it was worth while for the ruler to attempt, and what he had better leave to itself. And, above all, their action in the Church, as in the State, was rude, fitful, and ill-sustained. The quiet, grinding oppression which the Roman Caesars practised upon the Donatist and the Arian, bore to the spasmodic outbreaks of Vandal bigotry the same relation which the pressure of a hydraulic ram bears to the random strokes of a child's hammer [1].

Gaiseric receives Eudoxia's message.

Such then was the state of the Vandal kingdom, when, in the year 455, twenty-seven years after the passage of the Barbarians into Africa, and sixteen after their conquest of Carthage, the cry of the widowed Eudoxia for help reached the court of Gaiseric [2]. Little stimulus did the great Buccaneer need to urge him to the spoil of the capital of the world. It was clear that 'the city with which God was angry' this time was Rome, and the pilot had not to ask his master twice for sailing orders. It was in the early days of June when the sentinels at Ostia saw the Vandal fleet in the offing. The helpless consternation which prevailed at Rome has been already described,—no attempt to man the walls, not even courage enough to parley with the enemy, only a blind universal *sauve qui peut* which the Emperor himself would fain have joined in, had he not been arrested by the indignant people, and torn limb

---

[1] It is to be remarked, however, that Huneric, son of Gaiseric, copied exactly the Imperial decrees against heresy, and launched them against the Catholics. (See Papencordt, 196.) But his reign was short, and on his death the persecution was much relaxed.

[2] See p. 204.

from limb by the Imperial domestics, a sacrifice to the
Manes of Valentinian.

On the third day [1] after the death of Maximus,
Gaiseric, with his yellow-haired Vandal giants, appeared
before the gates of the defenceless city.　Utterly defenceless, as far as the weapons of the flesh were concerned ;
but the majestic Bishop Leo, followed probably by a train
of venerable ecclesiastics, met him outside the gates of
the city, eager to discover whether the same spiritual weapons which he had wielded so well three years before
against the mighty Hun by the banks of the Mincio
would avail now by the banks of the Tiber against the
yet more dreaded Vandal.　The Pope's success was not
complete, yet it was something.　Gaiseric's sole object
was booty, not power now, nor revenge, only that simple
and intelligible motive which led Pizarro and his adventurers to the capital of the Incas, and which made their
eyes gleam when they gazed upon Atahualpa's room of
gold.　This being Gaiseric's one desire, he could well
afford to concede to the Pope that there should be no putting to death, no burning of public or private buildings,
and he also granted, what it must have been harder for
a Vandal to yield, that no torture should be applied to
compel a discovery of hidden treasure.　Having framed
this secular Concordat with the occupant of the chair of
St. Peter, the Vandal king passed in, and rode slowly
through the unresisting city.　For fourteen days—that
interval at least was distinctly fixed on the memories of
the Romans, and every chronicler reports it as the same,
whatever their variations on other points—for fourteen

*455.
The Van-
dals at the
gates of
Rome.*

*Interces-
sion of
Pope Leo.*

----

[1] So says Victor Tunnunensis, not our best authority.　This would
be the 15th of June, according to Anon. Cuspiniani, 3rd of June
according to Prosper, 25th of May according to 'Incerti Chronicon.'

days the city was subjected to 'a leisurely and unhindered[1]' examination and extraction of its wealth. The gold, the silver, and the copper were carried away from the Imperial Palace, and stored with business-like thoroughness in the Vandal galleys. The churches were probably despoiled of their ornaments and plate. The Temple of Jupiter Capitolinus was pillaged, and half of its roof was stripped off, 'which was made of the finest copper, with a thick coating of gold over it, magnificent and wonderful.' Why only half should have been taken we know not ; such moderation is surprising and almost painful to behold. Possibly the Barbarians commenced the laborious process in the belief that they were stripping off solid gold, and desisted from it when they found that their reward would be only copper gilt. Statues too, good store of them, were carried off and loaded upon one of Gaiseric's vessels. Most unhappily, this one ship, out of all the fleet, foundered on the return voyage. The marble limbs of many a Nymph and Faun, of many a dweller on Olympus, and many a deified dweller on the Palatine, must have been lying for these fourteen centuries, fathoms deep in the Sicilian or Carthaginian waters. If the engineers of the electric cable in spinning their marvellous web from continent to continent should come across the sunken cargo of that Vandal trireme, may it be in our own day, and may we see that harvest from the deep !

But on the whole it is clear from the accounts of all the chroniclers that Gaiseric's pillage of Rome, though insulting and impoverishing to the last degree, was in no sense destructive to the Queen of cities. Whatever

---

[1] 'Per quatuordecim dies *secura et libera* scrutatione omnibus opibus suis Roma vacuata est ' (Prosper).

he may have done in Africa, in Rome he waged no war
on architecture, being far too well employed in storing
away gold and silver and precious stones, and all manner   455.
of costly merchandise in those insatiable hulks which
were riding at anchor in the Tiber.   Therefore, when
you stand in the Forum of Rome or look upon the grass-
grown hill which was once the glorious Palatine, blame
if you like the Ostrogoth, the Byzantine, the Lombard,
blame above all, the Norman, and the Roman Baron of
the Middle Ages, for the heart-breaking ruin that you
see there, but leave the Vandal uncensured, for, notwithstanding the stigma conveyed in the word ' vandalism,' he is not guilty here [1].

Among the spoils which were carried in safety from   Vessels
Rome to Carthage were, we are told, the sacred vessels   of the
Temple
of the Jewish Temple with the sculptured effigies of   carried off.
which, on the Arch of Titus, we are all familiar.   No
contemporary historian refers to them, and we might
have been disposed to reject the story of their capture
as a romance of later writers, but that in the next century we find Procopius, the friend and companion of
Belisarius, distinctly asserting that on the fall of the
Vandal monarchy, these vessels with countless other
treasures, golden saddles, golden carriages for the ladies
of the court, hundreds of thousands of talents of silver,
and all kinds of ornaments inlaid with precious stones,
were found in the palace of Gelimer, great grandson of
Gaiseric.   All the rest of the glittering spoil was taken   534.
to Byzantium, and having given lustre to the triumph

---

[1] Evagrius, the ecclesiastical historian, accuses Gaiseric of setting
fire to the city, but he lived more than a hundred years after the capture, and his testimony may be disregarded, the contemporary authorities so clearly speaking of pillage, not fire.

of Belisarius, was there retained; but the vessels which had been consecrated to the service of Jehovah were carried back to Jerusalem, and placed in the Christian churches there, a Jew, who saw them among the spoil, having pointed out to a friend of the Emperor's that their presence (like that of the Ark in the towns of the Philistines) had brought capture and desolation first on Rome and then on Rome's Vandal conquerors.

Captivity of Eudoxia and her daughters.

But the fortunes of the sacred vessels of the Jewish worship have carried us eighty years away from our present moorings. We return to Gaiseric and his treasure-laden fleet. He took back with him to Carthage Eudoxia, the widow of two Emperors and the daughter of a third. It was probably a greater kindness to take her as a captive to Carthage than to leave her face to face with the exasperated people of Rome, upon whom her blind desire for revenge on Maximus had brought so much misery. In the captive train also were her two daughters, Eudocia and Placidia, and (strange companion of their adversity) the son of Aetius, Gaudentius, who had once aspired to the hand of one of them. But the match upon which Aetius had set his heart so earnestly was not to be brought about by their common captivity. Gaiseric gave the elder princess, Eudocia, in marriage to his son Huneric, being the second princess of the house of Theodosius who was wedded to a Teutonic prince. One would like to believe that the young Vandal, while a hostage in Rome, had won the heart of the daughter of the Emperor; but as he must certainly have returned before the surprise of Carthage (439) this cannot be. His future wife was but a babe in arms when he was loitering in the palace of her father. The other princess, Placidia, with her mother, after seven

years detention at Carthage, where they were treated
with all honour and courtesy, was sent to Constantinople,
on the earnest entreaty of the Emperor Leo.   She married the Roman Senator Olybrius, whose name we shall
meet with among the last Emperors of Rome.

462.

Besides the Empress and her daughters, the Vandal
host carried a great multitude of Roman citizens back
with them into captivity.   It was like one of the great
transportations of unwilling multitudes which we read
of in the Jewish Scriptures as practised by a Shal-
maneser or a Nebuchadnezzar.   The skilful craftsman,
the strong labourer, the young and handsome cup-
bearer, the experienced house-steward, were all swept
away, all ruthlessly sundered from one another,
husbands from wives, and parents from children, and
distributed as bondslaves through Morocco, Algiers,
and Tunis [1].   It is a strange thought, how many drops
of pure Roman blood may now be flowing through
the veins of the half-civilized inhabitants of Northern
Africa.   A Kabyle robber from Mount Atlas, with
cotton *burnous*, such as I remember to have seen
in captivity on the Isle St. Honorat, near Cannes,
spreading his carpet, turning his face towards the
setting sun, and jabbering out his long and rapid
prayer from the Koran, may be a truer descendant
of the Fabii and the Camilli than any living inhabitant
of the Eternal City.

Other Roman captives.

The sufferings of the unhappy captives from Rome
were to some extent, but it could only be to a small
extent, alleviated by the charity of the saintly Bishop
of Carthage, ' *Deo-Gratias.*'   He sold all the gold and

Charity of Deo-Gratias.

---

[1] 'They took many thousands of captives, according as each by their
age or their skill (arte) pleased them,' are the words of Prosper.

silver vessels of his church in order to ransom such
captives as he could, and as much as possible to

455.

prevent the disruption of the family ties of those
whom he could not ransom. There were no proper
warehouses for receiving all this vast human live-stock
which the freebooters had brought back with them.
He placed two large basilicas at their disposal; he
fitted them up with beds and straw; he even took
upon himself the heavy charge of the daily commissariat. Sea-sickness, pining for home, the sad and
awful change from the luxury of the Roman villa to
the miseries of a Vandal slave-ship, had prostrated
many of the captives with disease. He turned his
church into an infirmary : notwithstanding his advanced age and his tottering limbs, day and night he
went the round of the beds of his patients, following
the doctors like a careful nurse, making himself
acquainted with the state of each, seeing that each
received the food and medicine which was suited
to his condition. Often, while he was thus moving
through the wards of his basilica-hospital, intent on
his work of mercy, must the words ' *Deo Gratias* '
have risen to the feeble lips of the sufferers, who,
perhaps, scarcely knew themselves whether they were
expressing gratitude to Heaven or to Heaven's fitly-
named representative on earth. Before his charitable work was complete, his life, which had been
threatened more than once by the violence of the
Arian party, who were jealous even of his goodness,
came to a peaceful close ; and when they heard that
he was taken from them, the captive citizens of Rome
felt as if they were a second time delivered into the
hands of the Barbarians. He was buried secretly in

an unusual place, to guard his body from the pious irreverence of relic-hunters, who would have dismembered the venerable corpse in their eagerness to obtain wonder-working memorials of so great a saint.

And so we leave the many thousands of Roman captives to the unrecorded sorrows of their house of bondage.

NOTE E. Chronology of the Vandal Kings.

There are some difficulties besetting the subject of the Chronology of the Vandal dominion in Africa, and though no question of importance turns upon them, and I have no reason to dissent (except in one particular where I follow Tillemont) from the ordinary chronology as given in Gibbon's 'Decline and Fall,' it may be worth while to point out what these difficulties are, and on what foundation the received chronology rests.

The first point, the only one that can now be considered a matter of controversy, is the date of the *Passage of the Vandals into Africa*. As to this it may be well to quote the entry of Prosper in full.

"Hierio et Ardabure Coss [=427].

"Bonifacio, cujus potentia gloriaque in Africâ augebatur, bellum ad arbitrium Felicis, quia ad Italiam venire abnuerat, publico nomine illatum est, ducibus Mavortio et Galbione et Sinoce, cujus proditione Mavortius et Galbio, cum Bonifacium obsiderent interempti sunt : moxque ipse a Bonifacio dolo detectus occisus est. Exinde gentibus, quae uti navibus nesciebant, dum a concertantibus in auxilium vocantur, mare pervium factum est, bellique contra Bonifacium coepti in Sigisvultum Comitem cura translata est.

"Gens Vandalorum ab Hispaniis ad Africam transiit."

Felice et Tauro Coss [=428].

Then follow the events of this year which do not relate to Africa.

The author of the Chronicon Imperiale, or the so-called ' *Tiro*,' says ' VIII Theodosii II post mortem Honorii[=431], Wandali in Africam transfretantes, ingentem, laceratâ omni provinciâ, Romanis cladem dedere.' (This is evidently wrong, as Augustine's death during the siege of Hippo by the Vandals is quite clearly fixed to 430.)

Idatius writes 'V Theodosii II post mortem Honorii, Gaisericus rex de Baeticae provinciae litore cum Wandalis omnibus eorumque familiis mense Majo ad Mauretaniam et Africam relictis transit Hispaniis.'

Clinton truly remarks that, according to Idatius' chronology, the fifth year of Theodosius II after the death of Honorius would be 429, since he gives Honorius' reign a year more than its due, and thus puts his death in 424 instead of 423.

Still, as a matter of fact, the fifth year of Theodosius II after his uncle's death would be not 429 but 428; and it is clear that some of Idatius' dates require correction. Take, for instance, the papal accessions. Celestine I's accession is four years too late, 426 instead of 422; that of Sixtus III two years, 434 instead of 432; that of Leo I one year, 441 instead of 440. Evidently there is a tendency at this part of Idatius' Chronicon to bring down his dates too low, and this may be in part owing to his having made the reign of Honorius too long by one year (Tillemont makes this remark. 'Idace ne le met néanmoins qu'en 429, mais ce serait s'éloigner beaucoup de S. Prosper. Et peut-être cela ne vient-il que de ce qu'il a mis la mort d'Honoré un an trop tard, *ce qui brouille beaucoup sa suite*').

Cassiodorus here, as elsewhere, for the most part, does little more than transcribe Prosper.

Marcellinus has no entry on the subject.

Victor Tunnunensis does not begin till 444.

Isidore, in his ' Historia Wandalorum,' has under 'Era quadringentesima sexagesima septima' [the 467th year of the Spanish Era corresponding with A. D. 429]. ' Gesericus frater Gunderico succedit in regno annis quadraginta. Qui ex Catholico effectus Apostata in Arianam primus fertur transisse perfidiam. Hic de Baeticae provinciae litore cum Vandalis omnibus eorumque familiis ad Mauritaniam et Africam relictis transit Hispaniis.

Isidore appears here to be transcribing Idatius, and therefore adopts his chronology. Isidore's own Vandal chronology, as we shall see further on, is an inconceivable muddle of errors.

The *Chronicon Paschale* (seu Alexandrinum) has the entry ' 11th year of the 20th Indiction [428] Consulship of Felix and Taurus. Under these Consuls the Vandals entered Africa.'

This date, 428, I believe to be the true date of the Vandal invasion of Africa. Herein, I follow Tillemont, and differ from Pagi, Gibbon, and Clinton, who put it in 429.

My reasons for this view are—

(1) The Paschal Chronicle, which seems to be accurate in its dates at this point, is the only one, except Prosper, which mentions the *names of the Consuls* under whom the event occurred. Any one who studies the principle on which these lists are composed, will see how extremely easy it is for an event to be dated a year too high or too low, when only the *number* of the regnal year is given. Much less is the chance of error when the date is linked with the names of the Consuls.

(2) It is generally admitted that Prosper's apparent date (427) is too early, since the war waged by the Court of Ravenna against Bonifacius, which was the cause of the invitation, only began in that year, and there is some reason to respect the statement of Idatius that the Vandals crossed in May.

I am not sure, however, that Prosper is really an adverse authority to the date 428. It will be seen that he describes under 427 at some length the war against Bonifacius, and then at the end of this entry, and immediately before 'Felice et Tauro Coss,' says 'Gens Vandalorum ab Hispaniis ad Africam transiit.' He perhaps, therefore, means to describe under 427 rather the events which led up to the crossing of the Mediterranean than the crossing itself.

The over-running of at least four African provinces, and the capture of all their cities but three, are events quite sufficient to fill up the two years between 428 and the siege of Hippo.

The next event of importance in Vandal chronology is the *Taking of Carthage*. This is fixed by the consenting voice of Prosper, Idatius, Cassiodorus (who must be looked upon as only an echo of Prosper), Marcellinus, and the Paschal Chronicle to the year 439 (Consulship of Theodosius and Festus). 'Tiro,' who assigns it to 444, may be safely pronounced inaccurate. Idatius and Marcellinus agree that the capture was in the month of October, Idatius placing it on the 19th and Marcellinus on the 23rd of that month. The Paschal Chronicle also places it μηνὶ Ὑπερβερεταίῳ, which corresponds with October.

Prosper says that Carthage was taken by the Vandals 'Anno postquam Romana esse coeperat DLXXXV' (alias DLXXXIII). The Vatican MS. of Prosper says 'Cartago capitur a Vandalis anno postquam Romana esse coeperat quingentesimo octogesimo quarto.' As the year of the Roman capture of Carthage was B. C. 146, these dates correspond to 439, 437, and 438 respectively.

Still, as before said, there can be no doubt that the true date is near the end of October, 439.

The Death of Gaiseric took place on or about the 25th January, 477. We get this date from Victor Vitensis (I. 17), who says (reckoning from the capture of Carthage), 'Duravit in regno annis triginta septem mensibus tribus': and who is confirmed by the appendix to Prosper (Augustan MS. in Roncalli's Chronica I. 702). 'Post consulatum' (this, as Clinton remarks, must be corrected to 'Consulatu') 'Theodosii XVII et Festi, Geisericus Wandalorum Rex Carthaginem ingressus est die xiv Kalendarum Novembrium [= 19 October, 439 ; the date given by Idatius]. 'Qui regnavit eandem Africam civitatem annis xxxvii, mensibus iii, diebus vi.'

Gaiseric therefore died 25 January, 477.

Reigns of Gaiseric's successors. From the same appendix to Prosper (Roncalli I. 702) we get our most accurate chronology of these reigns.

'Post hunc regnavit Hunerix, filius ejus annis vii, mensibus x, diebus xviii.'

> Accession of HUNERIC, 25 Jan. 477.
> Death of   „   13 Dec. 484.

'Post eum regnavit Guntamundus Gentunis ejusdem Hunerici Regis fratris filius annos xi, menses ix, dies xi.'

> Accession of GUNTHAMUND, 13 Dec. 484.
> Death of   „   24 Sep. 496.

'Post quem regnavit Trasamundus Gentunis filius annos xxvi, menses viii, dies iv.'

> Accession of THRASAMUND, 24 Sep. 496.
> Death of   „   28 May, 523.

'Post quem regnavit Hildrix filius Hunerici annos viii, dies viii.'

> Accession of HILDERIC, 28 May, 523.
> Dethronement of „   5 June, 531.

'Quo regnante assumptâ tyrannide Geilamer regnum ejus invadit in quo sedit annos iii, menses iii.'

> Accession of GELIMER, 5 June, 531.
> End of reign of   „   5 Sep. 534.

But this brings down the dethronement of Gelimer a year too low, as we know that the expedition of Belisarius against Carthage sailed in June, 533, and had accomplished all its work, including the captivity of Gelimer himself, by March, 534. We find also that we have one year too many, from the summation made by Prosper's continuer himself. ' Fiunt ergo ab exordio Regis Geiserici usque ad exitum Wandalorum anni xciii, menses x, dies xi.'

But the numbers above given add up to 94 years, 10 months, and 16 days. We therefore reduce the reign of Gelimer to ii years and iii months (agreeing herein with the tenour of the narrative of Procopius), and thus the end of the reign of Gelimer is brought to 5th September, 533: almost the exact date of Belisarius' landing in Africa. According to the view of an Imperialist chronicler the Vandal domination in Africa would end *de jure* as soon as Justinian's army entered the province.

Upon the whole it must be admitted that this chronology has been preserved with great accuracy, and it accords with the general course of the history.

Very different is the judgment which must be passed upon the only system of Vandal chronology, which has any pretension to compete with that of Prosper and his continuer [1], namely, that of Isidore of Seville. This Spanish bishop (who lived from about 560 to 636) in his ' Historia Wandalorum,' which is compiled chiefly from Idatius and Victor Tunnunensis, gives us a series of dates, which is apparently very complete, but which must be the result of some bewildered back-reckoning of events, and is entirely and hopelessly inaccurate. His dates are given according to the Spanish Era or Era of Augustus, which corresponds with 38 B.C. ; but translating them into dates of the Christian Era they are as follows :—

Irruption of the Vandals and allied nations into Gaul	A.D. 366[2] should be 406.	
Their entry into Spain	408 „ 409.	
Division of Spain between Vandals, Alans, and Suevi	411	

[1] Not the author who is technically known as 'Continuator Prosperi' in the Copenhagen MS. edited by Hille.

[2] ' Era quadringentesima quarta,' but the omission of 'quadragesima' is probably due to a transcriber's error.

Reign of Gunderic	18 years		
Accession of Gaiseric . . .	429		
(who reigned 40 years [1]).			
Accession of Huneric . . .	463	should be	477
(who reigned 7 years and 5 months).			
Accession of Gunthamund . .	476	,,	484
(who reigned 12 years).			
Accession of Thrasamund . . .	488	,,	496
(who reigned 27 years and 4 months).			
Accession of Hilderic . . .	515	,,	523
(who reigned 7 years and 3 months).			
Accession of Gelimer . . .	522	,,	531
Fall of the Vandal monarchy . .	525	,,	534

'Africa was recovered by Belisarius in the 97th year of the entry of the Vandals.' This agrees sufficiently well with Isodore's reckoning (525−429=96). 'The kingdom of the Vandals had lasted 113 years from King Gunderic to the death (interitum) of Gelimer.' According to Isidore's reckoning this interval was 114 years (525−411=114), and moreover it was not terminated by the death of Gelimer, but by his defeat and captivity. It will be seen that the dates of Huneric's and Gunthamund's accessions do not correspond with the periods allotted for the reign of their predecessors. And the whole chronology is so hopelessly at variance with history that the expedition of Belisarius against Carthage is brought to the year 524–5, *two years before the accession of Justinian to the Empire.* It is clear that Isidore did not understand the rudiments of the subject about which he professed to inform his readers, and that his scheme of chronology is absolutely worthless.

Of the other chroniclers, *Marcellinus Comes* does not mention the accessions of the Vandal kings, but is of course acquainted with the true date of the completion of the conquest of Africa (534). He puts it, however, in the 96th year after the capture of Carthage by the Vandals. According to his own dates it should have been the 95th year.

Victor Tunnunensis is utterly wrong in his earlier Vandal chronology, but struggles into accuracy for the later period. He has evidently been the chief author of confusion to Isidore.

[1] The lengths of the Vandal reigns are those given by Isidore himself, though inconsistent with his chronology.

He puts the death of Gaiseric ' Anno Regni xl' in the year 464 instead of 477.

This mistake, which vitiates all this part of his chronology, perhaps arises from a confusion between the accession of Gaiseric (which *may* have happened in 424) and the capture of Carthage in 439. But, even so, it is only in round numbers that Gaiseric can be said to have reigned at Carthage for 40 years.

The reign of Huneric is said by Victor to have lasted 7 years and 5 months (7 years, 5 months, and 18 days, according to Prosper's continuer), but to have ended in 479, though his accession is placed in 464. By this arithmetical blunder 8 years of the redundant 13, arising from the ante-dating of the death of Gaiseric, are silently cancelled and Huneric's death is made only five years too early.

Gunthamund comes to the throne in 479, reigns 12 years (instead of 11 years, 9 months, and 11 days), and dies in 497. The whole of the redundant years are now cancelled, and Thrasamund actually comes to the throne a year too late (497 instead of 496).

Thrasamund reigns 27 years and 4 months (instead of 26 years, 8 months, and 4 days), and dies in 523, the correct year.

Hilderic comes to the throne in 523, and reigns 7 years and 3 months (instead of 8 years and 8 days). This would probably bring his deposition to 530, but Victor agrees with Prosper's continuer in fixing it for 531. The fall of Gelimer is assigned to the year of Belisarius' landing in Africa, 533.

Probably these inaccuracies of the ecclesiastical chroniclers and their desperate attempts to remedy them by a suspension of the laws of arithmetic, are due to the fury of the Vandal persecution, which had caused the registers of the churches to fall into hopeless confusion.

CHAPTER III.

THE LETTERS AND POEMS OF APOLLINARIS SIDONIUS.

Authorities.

Sources:—

APOLLINARIS SIDONIUS: edited and translated by Grégoire and Collombet (3 vols., Lyons and Paris, 1836). The notes are full, but both in them and the translation the editors have a disagreeable habit of evading the real difficulties of their author.

A somewhat more scholarly edition, but without notes, has recently been put forth by C. Baret (Paris, 1878).

The edition by Christian Luetjohann, which forms the eighth volume of 'Auctores Antiquissimi' in the 'Monumenta Germaniae Historica' (1887), must now be considered as superseding all others, at least as far as the text is concerned.

Guides:—

Dr. Fertig's 'Apollinaris Sidonius und seine Zeit' (Würzburg and Passau, 1845, 6 and 8) is an interesting and helpful sketch. 'Saint Sidoine Apollinaire et son Siècle' (2 vols.) by Abbé Chaix (Clermont-Ferrand, 1866) has some useful information, especially as to ecclesiastical affairs, and is pervaded by a healthy local patriotism, but is too diffuse. The use which Guizot makes of the works of Sidonius in his 'Histoire de la Civilisation en France,' is known to every student.

EIGHT Emperors, and a space of twenty-one years, 455-476. separate the capture of Rome by Gaiseric from the familiar date of the fall of the Empire of the West,

It is worth while to do more than enumerate the mere names of these shadowy Emperors, of whom only one, Majorian, has anything of the dignity of manhood, and who might all, with that one exception, share the title of the last of them, Augustulus, 'The Little Emperor'. Is not Avitus as Severus, and Glycerius as Nepos? May we not take for granted all this history of monotonous feebleness, these sham elections and involuntary abdications, this burlesque of the awful tragedy of the earlier Caesars, and planting ourselves at once in the year 476, learn amid what accompaniments the twelve centuries of Roman dominion expired?

Reasons for not leaving the story of the last twenty-one years of the Empire untold. Such is naturally one's first thought, but it may well be modified on further reflection. If physiologists have found the study of the humblest forms of life useful, as illustrating the connection between the animal and vegetable worlds, and if some of them have descended into the lowest zones of organic existence in the hope of bringing up from thence some further light on the great problem of Life itself, it may well be, in like manner, that from the study of these, the lowest types of an Emperor which Rome has to set before us, we may learn something as to that inextinguishable *idea of the Caesar* which not all the storms of the Middle Ages were able utterly to destroy. We shall observe how, even in his deepest degradation, there was something which marked off the Roman Imperator from the Barbarian King. Above all, we shall see how reluctantly even the world of the Northern Invaders parted from the idea of Caesarian rule; how willingly they would have kept the pageant Augustus in his place, if he had been simply able to sit upright in his world-too-wide throne; how, notwithstanding all the rude blows of Goth, and Hun, and Vandal, the Roman Empire rather died of internal decline than was slain by the sword of an enemy.

Unfortunately the materials out of which we have to reconstruct the history of this quarter of a century are singularly meagre and unsatisfactory. Had the genius of a Tacitus, or even the clear, calm intellect of a Sallust, thrown its light over this troublous time, much more had it been possible for a De Tocqueville to have analysed the causes, and a Carlyle to have painted the scenes of this revolution, we might have learned from it many a lesson, useful even in our own day to those who labour to preserve an aged empire from falling. But what can we do when the only really trustworthy authorities for the events of the time are the Annalists, that is to say, some six or seven men, who having the whole history of the world from Belus and Nimrod downwards to relate, can spare only a line or two, at the outside a paragraph of moderate length, for the occurrences of the most eventful years in their own lives. The history of modern Europe, if told by Annalists of this type, would run into some such mould as this —

'A.D. 1851. The Queen reigning in England, and Louis Bonaparte being President of the French Republic, there was opened in a certain park near to London, a great market-place for all the wares of the world. That was the Palace of Crystal. The Queen of England gave birth to a son, who was named Arthur. Bishops, in obedience to the see of the Holy Peter, had been sent to England. Whom the adherents of the other Church, which is called the Protestant Church, being unwilling to receive, passed a law forbidding any man to say "God speed" unto them, or to salute them by the names of their dioceses. That was called the Ecclesiastical Titles Act. In Paris, the President of the Republic bade many persons to be shot.

'A.D. 1852. The Republic of France was changed into an Empire, Louis Buonaparte being declared Emperor. He was nephew of the Emperor Napoleon.

'A.D. 1853. The Emperor of Russia sent a proud man, named Menschikoff, as an ambassador, to the Sultan of the Ottomans. There was much dissension between the Emperors of Russia and France touching a certain silver star in the sanctuary at Bethlehem.

'A.D. 1854. It was fought most bloodily between the nation of the Russians on the one side, and those of France, England, and Turkey on the other, in the peninsula which is called the Chersonesus Taurica.

'A.D. 1855. After much slaughter the August City (Sebastopolis) in the Chersonesus Taurica was taken by the armies of France and England, whom the island of Sardinia had also joined.

'A.D. 1856. Peace was made in Paris between the nations which were at war. That was called the Peace of Paris. The treaty was signed by all the ambassadors, using a feather which had been plucked from the wings of a certain eagle. Now the eagle is the emblem of power in France and in Russia, but not in England, for in England the lion is the National emblem. That feather had a silver handle fastened to it, beautiful and costly, and it was given to the wife of the Emperor Napoleon. She was a very beautiful woman, and was named Eugenia.'

No one who has read the chronicles of Idatius, of

Prosper, and of Marcellinus will consider this an unfair specimen of their mode of writing annals. After all, the most important events are there, and we are grateful to the patient scribes who have preserved even so much for us from the sea of oblivion which was rising high around them, but from such scanty chronicles as these it is impossible to deduce with certainty the true proportions of those events or their exact relation to one another. We can excuse the brevity of the Annalists, but it is much harder to excuse their occasional prolixity. When we find one of the best of them (Marcellinus) devoting only four lines to the capture of Rome by Alaric, and fifty-four to an idle legend about the discovery at Emesa of the head of John the Baptist, it is difficult not to grumble at the want of appreciation of the relative importance of things which must have existed in the mind of the writer, though he was no monkish recluse but a layman and a governor of a Province.

Mingled meagreness and prolixity of the Annalists.

It is perhaps not surprising that in Italy itself there should have been this utter absence of the instinct which leads men to record the events which are going on around them for the benefit of posterity. When History was making itself at such breathless speed and in such terrible fashion, the leisure, the inclination, the presence of mind, necessary for writing History, might well be wanting. He who would under happier auspices have filled up the interval between the bath and the tennis court by reclining on the couch in the winter portico of his villa, and there languidly dictating to his slave the true story of the abdication of Avitus or the death of Anthemius, was himself now a slave keeping sheep in the wilderness under the hot Numidian sun, or

Why History was not written in the fifth century.

shrinking under the blows of one of the rough soldiers of Gaiseric.

We find it much more difficult to understand why the learned and leisurely Provincials of Greece, whose country for more than a century (396–517) escaped the horrors of hostile invasion [1], and who had the grandest literary traditions in the world to inspire them, should have left the story of the downfall of Rome unwritten. But so it was. Zosimus, seeing and foreseeing the inevitable decay, commenced the lamentable history, but none of his compatriots (if we except the slight references of Procopius) seems to have had the spirit or the inclination to finish it.

Intellect of the age wasted on theological squabbles. The fact seems to be that at this time all that was left of literary instinct and historiographic power in the world had concentrated itself on theological, we cannot call it religious, controversy. And what tons of worthless material the ecclesiastical historians and controversialists of the time have left us! Blind, most of them [2], to the meaning of the mighty drama which was being enacted on the stage of the world, without faith enough in a living God to believe that he could evolve a fairer and better order out of all the chaos round them, anticipating perhaps, the best among them, the speedy return of Christ and the end of the world, they have left us scarcely a hint as to the inner history of the vast revolution which settled the Teuton in the lands of the Latin; while they force upon us details, endless and wearisome, as to the squabbles of self-seeking monks

---

[1] Except in so far as the plundering raids of Gaiseric might be termed invasions.

[2] I except from this condemnation Salvian, the author of the treatise 'De Gubernatione Dei.'

and prelates over the decrees of the Council of Chalcedon. They describe to us how with stealthy step
Timothy the Weasel crept into the Patriarchate of
Alexandria; his brawls, his banishments, and his death.
They are anxious to inform us that Peter the Stam-
merer succeeded Timothy the Weasel in the Egyptian
see, and that Peter the Fuller, his contemporary at
Antioch, obtained his episcopate by bloodshed, and signalised it by adding four words to a hymn [1]. Who
really cares now for the vulgar bickerings which the
ecclesiastical historians relate to us with such exasper-
ating minuteness? The Weasels, the Fullers, and the
Stammerers, are all deep in mummy-dust. To the non-
Christian the subject of their controversies is imaginary;
to the Christian the pretensions of these men of violence
and blood to settle anything concerning the nature of
the spotless Son of Man are a blasphemy.

To sum up then; from the Annalists we get some
grains of fine gold, from the Literati of Greece we get
nothing, from the Ecclesiastical Historians we get chiefly
rubbish, concerning the history of these eventful years.
One man alone, he whose name stands at the head of
this chapter, gives us that more detailed information
concerning the thoughts, characters, persons of the
actors in the great drama which can make the dry
bones of the chronologers live. This is Caius Sollius
Apollinaris Sidonius, man of letters, Imperial functionary,
country-gentleman and bishop, who, notwithstanding
much manifest weakness of character, and a sort of
epigrammatic dulness of style, is still the most interesting literary figure of the fifth century.

Sidonius our chief authority for the inner life of this period.

[1] He added, 'Who wast crucified for us' to the 'Holy! Holy!
Holy!'

Sidonius was born at Lyons about the year 430. His father, grandfather, and great-grandfather had each held the high office of Praetorian Prefect in Gaul. Upon the whole they had been faithful to the line of Theodosius, though one of them, the grandfather, had derived his office from the usurper Constantine. Such high honours, enjoyed for three generations without any serious reverses, would alone have carried the family of Apollinaris high among the noble houses of Gaul at a time when the hierarchy of office, reaching from the Emperor to the Notary, was incomparably the most important factor in the social system of the provinces. But besides this official position, the wealth, the culture, and the respectable, if not heroic, character of most of the near ancestors of Sidonius placed him at the outset of life on a vantage-ground, from which, whatever he had of literary ability could soon make itself recognised. A man thus situated, born near the centre of the national affairs, and surrounded from his cradle with influential and hereditary friends, knows nothing of that difficulty of 'emerging' which is so forcibly described in the well-known lines of a Roman poet [1].

His birth and ancestors.

His education.

Sidonius received at Lyons as good an education probably as a young Roman noble of the fifth century could have met with anywhere in the Empire. It was an education however in words rather than things. Men had ceased to believe in the Olympian gods; so the schoolmasters taught their scholars the name of every Nymph and every Muse. All earnest thought about the nature of the world and the mind of man ran in Christian channels; so they taught elaborately the

---

[1] 'Haud facile emergunt quorum virtutibus obstat
Res angusta domi.' Juvenal, iii. 164–5.

speculations of every Greek philosopher from Thales to Chrysippus. The sword of the barbarian was carrying everything before it in the world of politics ; so they went on teaching all the arts of rhetoric by which brilliant orators had won honour for themselves or exile for their adversaries from the sovereign multitude in the cities of free Greece. But though it is easy for us to see how little the teaching of these schools can have done in helping the student to face any of the real difficulties of his after-life, we must, on the other hand, do justice to the vast amount of intellectual activity which still remained in the Empire and which this teaching both denoted and fostered. Sometimes we think of the hundred years between Theodosius and Theodoric as wholly filled with rapine and bloodshed. Sometimes we carry back into the fifth century the thick darkness which hung over the intellectual life of Merovingian France or Lombard Italy. In both these estimates we are mistaken. A careful perusal of the three volumes of the Letters and Poems of Sidonius reveals to us the fact that in Gaul at any rate the air still teemed with intellectual life, that authors were still writing, amanuenses transcribing, friends complimenting or criticising, and all the cares and pleasures of literature filling the minds of large classes of men just as though no Empires were sinking and no strange nationalities were suddenly rising around them. We need not believe, upon the authority of the highly-wrought panegyrics of Sidonius, that he had a score of friends all more eloquent than Cicero, more subtle than Plato, and diviner poets than Homer or Virgil ; but the interesting fact for us is that such forgotten philosophers and poets did exist in that age, and that their works, produced in lavish abundance, seem to have had no lack of eager students.

Impulse
towards
rhetoric
from the
oration of
Nicetius.

The impulse towards rhetoric, which was conspicuous in every part of the career of Sidonius, may very likely have been communicated by an oratorical display which he witnessed, in early adolescence, at Arles the Roman capital of Gaul. There, at the commencement of the year 449, the general Asturius was to assume the office of Consul. A crowd of Roman dignitaries assembled to witness the ceremony. In the centre, on a curule chair, sat Apollinaris, Praetorian Prefect of Gaul, and by his side stood his son, the young Sidonius. As one after another of the great persons of the State, *consulares*, *praesides*, masters of horse, and masters of foot, tribunes, bishops, notaries, advanced to kiss the purple robe of the representative of the Emperor, each one doubtless spared a less formal salutation for the bright, highly-cultured lad who was watching the scene with eager interest, and with a mind keenly conscious, as it ever was, of the great difference between those who have rank and position and those who have them not. The new Consul was proclaimed, the slave, who was always forthcoming on these occasions, received the buffet from his hand which bestowed freedom [1], the largesse (*sportula*) and the ivory tablets, upon which the names of the two new magistrates had been inscribed, were distributed to the people. Then stood forth Flavius Nicetius, and in brilliant, well-chosen words, pronounced the customary panegyric on the virtues and capacities of Consul

---

[1] This curious custom, which seems to have been peculiar to the last ages of the Empire, is mentioned by Claudian (De Quarto Consulatu Honorii, 615, and In Eutropium, i. 310), also by Sidonius himself (Panegyric of Anthemius, 545).

Asturius. The pompous periods, the applause which followed, the compliments paid and received by the smooth-tongued orator, produced a profound impression on the boyish imagination of Sidonius, and we may perhaps conjecture that he secretly resolved that he too would one day be a Prefect like his father, an orator like Nicetius, and a Consul like Asturius. The first two of his aspirations were realised.

'The rest the gods dispersed in empty air.'

Sidonius was probably about twenty-one years of age when the blast of Attila's invasion swept over Belgic Gaul. Sheltered behind the walls of Lyons he felt, in all likelihood, not even the outskirts of the storm. But he may have conversed with Lupus, Anianus, and others of the chief actors in the defence of Gaul, and no doubt his imagination was powerfully impressed by all that he saw and heard of that 'horde of many-nationed spoilers' who, according to the lines which have been already quoted from him [1], hewed down the trees of the Thuringer Wald to bridge with their rafts the bosom of the Rhine. There was even a possibility that Sidonius might have been the historian of that eventful campaign. His friend Prosper, successor of Anianus in the see of Orleans, urged him to undertake the task. He began to write, apparently in prose, and occupied himself with the origin of the barbarians who composed the host of Attila. But his genius was all for epigram or pompous panegyric. Plain historical narrative wearied him, and moreover the duties of his episcopate (for the work was commenced in the later period of his life) seemed to call him to other occupations. Even the

Attila's invasion. 451.

[1] See pp. 107 and 108.

fragment which he wrote has perished, and we regret its loss, for though he was not well-fitted by nature or education to be the historian of such a war, he would assuredly have preserved for us some interesting details with reference to that year of terror.

Marriage of Sidonius.

About the time of the Hunnish invasion, or soon after, Sidonius married. His wife, Papianilla, was the daughter of the most powerful citizen of Auvergne, of that Avitus whom we have already met at the court of Theodoric, cementing the alliance between the Romans and the Visigoths against Attila, and whom we are shortly to meet again in a more exalted station. Sidonius was related by descent to the family of Avitus, and this new tie linked him very closely to the mountainous land of the Arverni (the modern Auvergne) with which henceforward his life became more nearly associated than with his own foggy city of Lyons. His marriage also brought him more decisively forward on the broad stage of Imperial politics, and during the years which intervene between 455 and 469 we shall have frequently to rely on his letters and poems for our sole information as to the events which occurred at the court of the Western Emperors.

He retires to Avitacum.

In the year 469 he finally retired from public life and from the court of the Caesars, and took up his abode at the charming villa of Avitacum in Auvergne, part of his wife's dowry, a place of which he has given us, evidently in imitation of the younger Pliny, a description which, though prolix and too much laboured, is not devoid of interest. In this description, notwithstanding one or two minor discrepancies, which may be easily accounted for by the changes in the configuration of land and water wrought during the course of fourteen centuries, we can still recognise the characteristic features of the shores of the Lac d'Aydat. This little lake, which is about twelve miles to the south-west of Clermont-Ferrand, lies near the junction of the two great volcanic ranges of the Monts Dôme and the Monts Dore. From two summits of the former range (the Puy de la Vache and the Puy de Lassolas) descended, in that far distant age when the volcanoes of Auvergne were still glowing against the midnight sky, a great stream of molten lava, which has left a wilderness of rock five miles long and in some places a mile wide, sprawling over the once fruitful valley. This stony cataract, with its significant Celtic name, La Cheyre [1], though ugly and desolate itself, has been the cause of beauty to the landscape, for the little stream of Pontava coming down from some other mountains on the west, and finding its course impeded by this barrier of lava, has formed the lovely little lake of Aydat, at the south-western corner of which (if this identification be correct) once stood the villa of Sidonius. There is, of course, no trace of that stately dwelling now. A few humble cottages cluster round the little Romanesque Church, which dates from the twelfth century, and has three round buttress-towers on each side, built apparently only for strength not for ornament. Inside the church, high up on the north wall of the chancel, is a long flat stone coffer built into the wall, and bearing on its front the words

HIC S̄T̄ [SUNT] DVO IÑOCENTES ⊕ ET S. SIDONIVS.

There is a mystery about 'the two Innocents,' nor is it probable that this is the actual burying-place of the poet-bishop, but it may very probably contain some

---

[1] Crégut refers this name to the Celtic word Car = Stone.

relic of the saint, to whom in fact the church appears to be dedicated. There is a deep well in an adjoining house said to be of Roman excavation, and a few strokes of the pickaxe in the soil of the little village street bring to light pieces of undoubtedly Roman cement, an evidence probably of a once existing pavement.

But leaving these faint archaeological traces of a past which almost eludes our research, it is pleasant to climb the most easterly of the two hills between which Aydat nestles, and there with the unchanged, or but slightly changed, face of Nature before us, to read the description of his villa given by the Gallo-Roman nobleman. He writes to his friend Domitius, and says [1] :—

' We are now at Avitacum : that is the name of this property, which having come to me in right of my wife, is even sweeter than a paternal inheritance. A mountain on the west, steep though not rocky [2], sends forth lower hills, as if from a double focus, which are about four acres apart. But while the ground broadens out sufficiently to afford a fitting vestibule for the house, the sides of the hills hold straight on their course through the valley up to the margin of the villa, which has two fronts, one to the north and the other to the south [3].' Sidonius then goes on to describe with much detail the bath-house, the fish-pond, the women's apartment (*triclinium matronale*), the pillared portico over-

---

[1] Epist. ii. 2.

[2] 'Quanquam terrenus, arduus tamen.'

[3] ' Sed donec domicilio competens vestibuli campus aperitur, mediam vallem rectis tractibus prosequuntur latera clivorum usque in marginem villae, quae in Boream Austrumque conversis frontibus tenditur.' This obscure sentence is one of the difficulties in the identification of Avitacum. But the real difficulty is in the Latin of Sidonius rather than in the configuration of the country round Aydat.

looking the lake, the winter-parlour (*hiemale triclinium*), the little dining-room (*coenatiuncula*), and the summer-parlour (*diversorium aestivum*), looking towards the north. 'This room,' he says, 'lets in the daylight, but not the sun, a narrow closet being interposed' (apparently between it and the south face) ' where the drowsy grooms of the chamber sit nodding, though they may not lie down to sleep [1]. How pleasant it is here to let the chirp of the cicalas beat upon one's ear at noon, the croak of the frogs in the twilight, the swans and geese calling upon their mates at night, the cocks crowing in the small hours of the morning, the crows with their augural voice, three times repeated, saluting the ruddy face of rising Aurora, and at daybreak Philomela trilling among the fruit-trees, or Progne (the swallow) twittering upon the palings. To this concert you may join the pastoral Muse, goddess of the seven-holed reed, for oftentimes in their nightly rivalry of song the sleepless Tityri of our mountains make their notes heard in the meadows above the tinkling bells of their flocks. And yet, believe me, all this strife of varied sounds only plunges one into the deeper slumber.

' Below us lies the lake, winding down towards the east, and sometimes when the winds ruffle it, it moistens the stones of the villa, whose foundations are laid in its sandy shores. Its right bank is abrupt, winding and wooded, its left open, grassy, and level. By nautical measurement it is seventeen furlongs in length. A stream enters it which has foamed over the rugged rocks that seek to bar its passage, but which has a short period of tranquillity before it mingles with the

---

[1] A guess at the meaning of 'interjecto consistorio perangusto, ubi somnolentiae dormitandi potius quam dormiendi locus est.'

lake. Its exit is through hidden subterranean channels, which afford a passage to the water, but not to the fish, and these latter, forced back into the lake's slothful tranquillity, grow fat in their prison, and daily swell out a greater extent of pink flesh under their gleaming bellies. Sometimes from the villa we see the fisherman launching forth into the deep, spreading out his nets with their corks floating on the water, or arranging his hook-armed cords at certain well-marked intervals, in order that the greedy trout in their nightly prowlings through the waters may fall into the snares which are laid for their cannibal tastes. For surely it is a fitting stratagem that fish should be tempted by fish to rush upon their own destruction. Sometimes, when the winds have fallen, the surface of the fickle deep is cloven by a whole fleet of pleasure-boats. In the middle of the lake is a little island, where, upon a natural heap of stones, rises a goal often worn by the blades of the rowers' oars in their nautical contests. For this is the point round which they must steer when they would imitate the Sicilian boat-races of our Trojan ancestors, and many a comic shipwreck takes place here as one boat dashes into another.'

Such, greatly abbreviated and freely translated (for it is hardly possible to translate Sidonius literally), is the description, the not unpleasing description, of the home of a great Gaulish noble under the Empire [1].

---

[1] It will be seen that I have adopted the theory that the Avitacum of Sidonius is the modern Aydat. The only other site whose claims are worth considering is the lake of Chambon, about twenty-five miles south-west of Clermont, and immediately under the range of Mont Dore. Having only seen Lac d'Aydat and not Lac Chambon, I have no right to express any opinion of my own as to the respective claims of the two sites, but certainly the arguments of Abbé Crégut in his

After a year or two of seclusion Sidonius re-entered public life in a new capacity. He was elected Bishop of the chief city of the Arverni (now called Clermont-Ferrand), and he continued in the same see for the remaining eighteen years of his life[1]. This election seems to have been a voluntary tribute of respect on the part of his fellow-citizens to an unstained private character, and to the memory of an official career which, if not signalised by any brilliant services to the State, had at least not been abused to sordid and ignoble ends. His position in the literature of the age was both a recommendation and a stumbling-block. It was an honour for a rural diocese in the mountains to have as its president a man who had recited amid the applause of the multitude the panegyrics of three Emperors, whose statue in brass stood between the Greek and the Latin Libraries in the Forum of Trajan, whose letters were humbly prayed for and treasured up as invaluable literary possessions by all the rhetoricians and philosophers of Gaul. Yet, on the other hand, his very panegyrics were crammed full of the conceits of Pagan mythology; his Epithalamia, though morally pure, turned, according to the fashion in such compositions, on the voluptuous splendours of the dwelling of Venus.

Sidonius elected Bishop of Arverni 471 or 472.

Essay on Avitacum (Clermont-Ferrand, 1890), seem to me very convincing on behalf of Aydat. The similarity of name (the earlier form of Aydat is Aydac) and the persistent local *cultus* of St. Sidonius are both of them arguments of weight, but the strongest point is, in my judgment, the character of the exit of the river from the lake. Owing to the nature of the wild jumble of rocks (la Cheyre) which form the eastern end of the lake, the Pontava does escape from it ' per colla subterranea,' a feature of the landscape which we are told is entirely wanting at Chambon.

[1] His wife Papianilla was still alive at the time of his elevation to the episcopate.

on the charms of the bride, surpassing those of all the
heroines of classical antiquity, and on the success of
Cupid in piercing with his arrows the bridegroom's
heart. This was not exactly the kind of composition
which it was considered safe or decorous for a Christian
Bishop to indulge in, so soon after the great struggle between the new and the old faiths, and while the religion
of the Olympian gods, though prostrate and wounded
to the death, still, by a few convulsive spasms, showed
signs of a vitality not yet wholly extinct. Sidonius
felt the incongruity as strongly as any one, and as,
unlike the Cardinal de Retz[1], he was determined to
bring his private life into conformity with the sacred
character which he had assumed, he broke off abruptly
and finally from the service of the Muses. He could
not indeed bring himself to suppress poems which were
in his view so charming as his Panegyrics and Epithalamia, but he wrote no more verses of this description.
Invocations to the Holy Spirit take the place of invocations to Apollo, and the names of the Martyrs meet us

---

[1] These are De Retz's words with reference to his appointment as
Coadjutor-Archbishop of Paris : 'I was not ignorant of the necessity
there is for a Bishop to live regularly . . . . But at the same time I
found that it was not in my power to live in that manner, and that all
the reasons which conscience or honour could suggest to me against
an irregular life would prove but insignificant and weak. After six
days' deliberation, I chose to act ill, designedly, which as to God is
beyond comparison the most criminal, but which is without doubt the
wisest as to the world. The reason is, that when you act in that
manner you always take some previous measures that will cover part
of the ill action, and that you avoid besides the most dangerous sort
of ridicule that persons of our profession can be exposed to, which is
the mixing preposterously sin with devotion. . . . . However, I had
fully resolved to discharge exactly all the outward duties of my profession, and to take as much care of other people's souls as I took
little of my own ' (Memoirs, book ii).

instead of those of the Argonauts. The result is not a happy one, and to a taste formed by the Christian hymnology of subsequent ages, the later poems of Sidonius are rather less attractive than his earlier ones.

Sidonius appears to have made an excellent Bishop, according to the notions of his day, which scarcely ex- His success as a Bishop. pected every prelate to rise to the saintliness of a Polycarp, but would not have tolerated his sinking to the infamy of a Borgia. He applied himself with earnestness to the study of the Scriptures, in which he had probably not been well instructed as a child. He steered through the theological controversies of a difficult time with an unimpeached reputation for orthodoxy. His experience as a Roman official helped him to govern his diocese with the right apportionment of firmness and suavity. His unfailing good-nature joined to a certain ingredient in his character, which can only be described as fussiness, made him the willing counsellor and confidant of his people even in their business difficulties, in the law-suit, and the family quarrel. Above all, his hearty sympathies with the Romanised population of Gaul, and his antipathies, national and religious, to their Arian and barbarian conquerors, made him willing to risk life and fortune, and even his dearly-loved social position, on behalf of the liberties of Auvergne. During the years while the struggle between the Arverni and the Visigoths was going on, the courtier and the rhetorician were lost in the patriot, and his life rose into real grandeur. At the close of the struggle (475) Sidonius had to feel the full weight of the displeasure of the Visigothic king, Euric, who was now undisputed master of Auvergne. He was banished from his diocese, and His banishment. kept, probably for about a year, in captivity in the

fortress of Livia, not far from Carcassonne [1]. His confinement was not of the most rigorous description ; he
was allowed to employ himself, if he wished, in literary
labour, and his quarters for the night seem to have been
appointed him in a private dwelling-house. But his days
were occupied with harassing duties, and both study
and sleep were driven away from his evening hours
by the clamours of two Gothic hags, whose window
looked upon the court-yard of his lodging, and whose
life was passed in one perpetual round of scolding,
intoxication and gluttony. The fastidious Roman noble,
forced into hourly companionship with these scenes of
barbarian vulgarity, passed his nights in sighing for the
seclusion of his mountainous Auvergne, for the baths,
the lake, and the fish-ponds, the airy summer apartment, and the chorus of rural voices of his own beloved
Avitacum.

His return
from exile

At length, by the mediation of his friend Leo, a
Roman, a lover of literature [2], and the chief minister at

---

[1] His biographers seem generally to treat this as an ordinary imprisonment, but there are some indications that Sidonius was entrusted
with some difficult and disagreeable commission at Livia, no doubt
with the intention of taking him away from his faithful Arverni.
Compare especially Ep. ix. 3, ' Nam *per officii imaginem vel, quod est
verius, necessitatem* solo patrio exactus, hic relegor variis quaquaver-
sum fragoribus, quia patior hic incommoda peregrini, illic damna
proscripti.'

[2] Partly as an act of friendship, and partly by way of ransom,
Sidonius translated for Leo the life of Apollonius of Tyana, the
Paracelsus-Cagliostro of the first century, whose marvellous career was
by some of the opponents of Christianity claimed as a counterpoise to
the Gospel-history of Jesus. Sidonius does not seem to be aware of
this polemical use of the biography : at least, he speaks of Apollonius
in terms of unqualified praise, and pays court to Leo by drawing a
very strange parallel between the philosopher and the minister.

the court of Euric, he was restored to his home and diocese ; and the remaining years of his life were passed in comparative tranquillity, but probably with an impaired fortune, and certainly with an ever-present pang of humiliation at the enforced subjection of his high-spirited Arverni to the degrading yoke of the barbarians. He had probably not reached his sixtieth year when (about 489) [1] he was carried off by a fever. He died with Christian calmness and hope. When he felt his end approaching he desired his attendants to carry him to the church where he had been wont to officiate, and lay him before the altar. A multitude of men, women, and children crowded into the church after his bearers, and filled it with their passionate lamentations. 'Why art thou deserting us,' they cried, 'O good shepherd ? Who will take care of us, thy orphans, when thou art gone ? Who will feed us with the salt of the true wisdom ? Who will guide us into the fear of the Lord as thou hast done.' He gently rebuked their want of faith, and said, 'Fear not, my people. My brother Aprunculus still lives, and he will be your Bishop.' Then with a prayer to his Creator he yielded up his life. His dying words were verified by the election of Aprunculus (a fugitive for the sake of the Catholic faith from the wrath of the Burgundian king) to fill the vacant see [2].

---

[1] This is Tillemont's date, but it is possibly too late. Mommsen (in the Introduction prefixed to Sidonius' letters in the 'Monumenta,' p. xlix) argues strongly for 479, but this seems hardly to leave time enough for that part of his life which followed his imprisonment at Livia. And several of the expressions used by Sidonius seem to point to a more advanced period of life than his fiftieth year.

[2] The particulars of the death of Sidonius are given us by Gregory of Tours, ii. 23.

The end of Sidonius was in harmony with the dignified thoughtfulness which had marked his whole epis-
Conflict of
the Bishop
and the
Poet in the
character
of Sidonius. copal life.   He played his part as a Christian Bishop
well; and yet, without imputing to him any shade of
conscious insincerity or hypocrisy, it is difficult when
reading his letters and pre-eminently his letters to his
brother Bishops, to resist the conviction that he was,
in a certain sense, playing a part throughout; that he
was essentially an author or a courtier, and only
accidentally a divine.   That strong bias of the mind
towards the Invisible which impelled St. Augustine,
through all his immoralities, through all his years of
Manicheanism, to ponder continually on the relation of
his soul to the God of the Universe; that keen intellectual interest in the Scriptures which drew St. Jerome
into Palestine, and supported him through all the heroic
toil of his translations and his commentaries; these
are qualities which it would be absurd to mention in
connection with the character of Sidonius.   But though
his taste probably preferred the mythology of Greece,
his reason accepted the doctrines of Christianity.   The
career of secular office was closed to him by the hard
circumstances of those stormy times.   The Church
offered him a safe and honourable retreat from war
and revolution.   The voices of his fellow-citizens called
him to a post of dignity in that Church; and he therefore accepted the retreat and the dignity, and made his
life harmonise fairly well with his new vocation.   If
some sprays of the poet's laurel were still seen under
the mitre of the bishop, if his thoughts were sometimes
running on Helicon and Parnassus when he was celebrating the Divine mysteries in the basilica of Arverni,
at least he kept his secret well, and made his actions

congruous to his character as a shepherd of the Christian flock.

He was by the general voice of his people recognised Canonised. as a saint after his death, and the Church of Clermont still, upon the 21st of August, the day of his death, celebrates the festival of Saint Sidonius. The only reason for any hesitation about canonising him would appear to be that he had never claimed any power of working miracles, that he was not, as a biographer [1] says, 'one of those great thaumaturgic pontiffs whose glory was made common property, and whose virtues were immortalised by the generous instincts of Gaul;' but the entire absence of all pretentions of this kind will not be accounted a demerit by the present age. In his attitude towards men of other faiths than his own, he showed a tolerance of spirit more like the eighteenth century than the fifth. He could not but deplore and condemn the fury of the Arian persecutors, but he speaks with some kindliness of the Jews. 'Gozolas is the bearer of these letters of mine, a Jew by nation, and a man for whose person I should feel a cordial regard if he did not belong to a sect which I despise [2].' And again, 'This letter commends a Jew to your notice. Not that I am pleased with the error in which that nation is involved, and which leads them to perdition, but because it becomes us not to call any one of them sure of damnation [3] while he yet lives, for there is still a hope that he may turn and be forgiven [4].' This is the language of an orthodox Catholic, but certainly not of a man who is by nature a persecutor.

Of the literary style of Sidonius it is difficult to speak

---

[1] Abbé Chaix, ii. 401.

[2] Ep. iii. 4.

[3] 'Ex asse damnabilem.'

[4] Ep. vi. 11.

with fairness.   His obscurity, his long and uncouth
words, often clumsily coined from the Greek, his con-
stantly-recurring epigrams, which, when examined,
generally turn out to have as much point in them
as the clever things which a man utters in his dreams,
his preposterous and monotonous adulation of his cor-
respondents, evidently dictated by the desire to receive
their adulation in return, his frigid conceits, his childish
display of classical learning, which after all was neither
deep nor thorough [1],—all these qualities make much
study of the works of this author emphatically a weariness to the flesh.   But it is doubtful how far he is to
be blamed individually, and how far his age is responsible for the faults of his style.   Latin poetry had fallen
during the fourth century into the hands of elegant
triflers, of the composers of triple and quintuple
acrostics [2], and the manufacturers of vapid centoes [3].
Claudian had snatched the Latian lyre out of the hands
of these feeble poetasters, and made it give forth some
manlier harmonies; but even Claudian, with his courtier-
like exaggerations, and his creaking mythological machinery, was not a very safe guide to follow.   Suffice it
to say, without attempting further to apportion the
blame of a most miserable style between the author and
his age, that in his poems, Sidonius bears the same re-

---

[1] Sidonius is guilty of such false quantities as Euripīdes, phĭloso-
phus, and diastĕma (διάστημα).   He puts Babylon on the Tigris and
the rocks of the Symplegades hard by Corinth.

[2] Like Optatian's Panegyrics on Constantine, things distracting even
to look at.

[3] Like Faltonia Proba's, telling, after a fashion, the story of the Fall
and Redemption of Man in a poem of some 650 lines entirely drawn
from the Aeneid of Virgil, and laboriously twisted from their original
meaning.

lation to Claudian that Claudian bears to Virgil, and that in his letters he is as far from attaining the purity of style of the younger Pliny as the latter is from rivalling the easy grace of Cicero. It remains to reproduce from the pages of Sidonius some of his most striking pictures of social life among the Romans and Barbarians.

1. ROMAN LIFE. *The Church Festival, and the Game at Tennis* [1].

'Sidonius wishes health to his friend Eriphius.

'You wish me to send you the verses which I made to please that most respectable man your father-in-law. I will do so; but as, in order to understand this trifle, you wish to know the scene and the cause of its composition, you must not complain if the preface is more long-winded than the work itself.

'We had assembled at the Sepulchre of St. Justus [at Lyons]; there was a procession before dawn, to celebrate the yearly festival of the saint, and a great multitude had assembled, larger than the basilica could hold, though it was surrounded with spacious arcades. When the office of Vigils was ended (chanted by monks and clergy in alternate choruses) we parted from one another, but did not go far, that we might be in readiness for *Tierce*, when the priests should return to celebrate it. The crowd in the church, the many lights, and the closeness of the weather (for it was summer, though just passing into autumn) had made us feel as

---

[1] Ep. v. 17. This letter is quoted by Guizot (Hist. de la Civilisation en France, Leçon iii). He is probably in error in treating it as a scene in the life of a *Bishop* of the fifth century, for everything seems to show that the letter was written several years before Sidonius' elevation to the episcopate.

if we were being stewed, and we longed for the fresh air.
So when the various ranks of citizens dispersed, we who
belonged to the first families of Lyons, decided to make
our rendezvous at the tomb of Syagrius, which was
scarce a bowshot from the church. Here some reclined
under the shade of a trellis-work covered with the leaves
and clusters of a vine ; others, of whom I was one, sat
on the green sward, which was fragrant with flowers.
The conversation was full of light fun and banter ; and
what was best of all, there was no talk about great
people or the incidence of taxation, not a word to compromise anybody, not a person whom anybody else
thought of compromising. Any one who could tell a
good story, and adorn it with proper sentiments, was
listened to most eagerly. But really there was such
general merriment that it was not easy to hear any
story distinctly to the end. At length we got tired of
idleness, and discussed what we should do. The young
men voted for tennis, the elder ones for the tables [back-
gammon]. I was prime champion of the ball, of which,
as you know, I am as fond as of my books. On the
other side, my brother[1] Domnicius, a man full of wit
and courtesy, shook the counters about in the tables, and
thus, as with a sound of a trumpet, summoned his party
to the dice-box. I played for a long time with a troop
of students till my limbs, which had grown numb, were
made supple again by the healthful exercise. Then the
illustrious Philimatius, as Virgil says[2],

> ' He too adventuring to the task
>   That matches younger years,'

---

[1] Apparently, this is a title of courtesy. Domnicius was not probably the actual brother of Sidonius.

[2] Aeneid v. 499 (Conington's translation).

boldly joined the group of tennis-players. He had once played the game well, but that was when his years were fewer. Poor man! he was often forced from the place where he was stationed, by the mid-current of eager players; then, when he had to keep the middle of the ground, he could neither ward off nor dodge the quickly-flying ball. Moreover he often met with a catastrophe and fell flat on the ground, from which he raised himself slowly and laboriously. So that the upshot of the matter was that he was the first to retire from the rush of the game, which he did with deep sighs and a fearful stitch in his side. Very soon I left off too, out of kindness to him, that he might not be mortified at so soon showing signs of distress. So, when we were seated again, the sweat running down his face obliged him to ask for a basin of water. It was brought him, and with it a thick cloth which, cleaned from yesterday's dirt, happened to be hanging on a pulley behind the door of the porter's lodge. While he was slowly drying his cheeks he said, "How I should like you to dictate four lines of poetry on the cloth which does me this service." "It shall be done," said I. "But so as to bring in my name in the metre?" "What you ask for is possible." "Dictate them, then." To which I answered, smiling, "You know the Muses will not like it if there are any by-standers when I commune with their holy band." He said, very politely, but with that jocosely passionate manner of his, "Take care, Mr. Sollius, that you don't much more exasperate Apollo if you ask for secret interviews with his young ladies." Imagine the applause which greeted this sally, as sudden as it was happily conceived. Then, without more delay, I called to my side his amanuensis, who was standing near with his tablets in hand, and dictated the following epigram :

'Oh Towel! in the early morn, when the bath has made him
    glow,
Or when with heated brow he comes at noontide from the
    chase,
Into thy thirsty reservoirs let the big sweat-drops flow,
When Philimatius shall wipe on thee his handsome face.'

'Scarcely had our friend Epiphanius read over what had been written, when word was brought us that the time was come for the bishop to leave his private apartment, and we all rose up. Pray pardon the verses which you asked for. Farewell.'

2. ROMAN LIFE. *The Country-house*[1].

'Sidonius wishes health to his friend Donidius.

'You ask me why, though I set out for Nismes some time ago, I have not yet returned home. I will tell you the agreeable cause of my delay, since I know that the things which please me please you too.

'The fact is that I have been spending some days in a very pleasant country with two most delightful men, my hereditary friend Tonantius Ferreolus, and my cousin Apollinaris. Their estates adjoin one another and their houses are not far apart, a long walk but a short ride. The hills which rise behind are covered with vineyards and oliveyards. The view from each house is equally charming; the one looks upon woods, and the other over a wide expanse of plain. So much for the dwellings ; now for the hospitality shown to us there.

'As soon as they found out that I was on my return

----

[1] Ep. ii. 9.

journey, they stationed skilful scouts to watch not only
the high-road but every little track and sheep-walk into
which I could possibly turn aside, that I might not by
any chance escape from their friendly snares. When I
had fallen into their hands, not very reluctantly I must
confess, they at once administered to me a solemn oath
not to entertain one thought of continuing my journey
till seven days were over. Then, every morning a
friendly strife arose between my hosts whose kitchen
should first have the honour of preparing my repast,
a strife which I could not adjust by a precisely equal
alternation of my visits, although I was bound to one
house by friendship and to the other by relationship,
because Ferreolus, as a man who had held the office of
Prefect, derived from his age and dignity a claim beyond
that of mere friendship to take precedence in entertain-
ing me. So we were hurried from pleasure to pleasure.
Scarce had we entered the vestibule of either house when
lo! on one side the pairs of tennis-players stood up to
oppose one another in the ring[1]; on the other, amid
the shouts of the dicers, was heard the frequent rattle of
the boxes and the boards. Here too were books in
plenty; you might fancy you were looking at the
breast-high book-shelves of the grammarians, or the
wedge-shaped cases of the Athenaeum, or the well-filled
cupboards of the book-sellers[2]. I observed however
that if one found a manuscript beside the chair of one
of the ladies of the house, it was sure to be on a religious

[1] 'Et ecce huc sphaeristarum contra stantium paria inter rotatiles
catastropharum gyros duplicabantur.' Perhaps some future researches
into the tennis of the Romans may elucidate these mysterious words.

[2] The three words used in this sentence, *plutei*, *cunei*, and *armaria*,
were all technical terms in Roman libraries.

subject, while those which lay by the seats of the fathers
of the family were full of the loftiest strains of Latin
eloquence.   In making this distinction, I do not forget
that there are some writings of equal literary excellence
in both branches, that Augustine may be paired off
against Varro, and Prudentius against Horace.   Among
these books Origen, 'the Adamantine,' translated into
Latin by Turranius Rufinus, was frequently perused by
readers holding our faith.   I cannot understand why
some of our Arch-divines should stigmatise him as a
dangerous and heterodox author.

'While we were engaged, according to our various
inclinations, in studies of this nature, punctually as the
water-clock [1] marked 5 [11 a.m.], there would come into
the room a messenger from the chief cook to warn us
that the time for refreshment had arrived.   At dinner
we made a full and rapid meal, after the manner of
senators, whose custom it is to set forth a large banquet
with few dishes, though variety is produced by sometimes cooking the meat dry and sometimes with gravy.
While we were drinking we had merry stories told,
which at once amused and instructed us.   To be brief,
the style of the repast was decorous, handsome, and
abundant.

'Then rising from table, if we were at Voroangus
(the estate of Apollinaris) we walked back to the inn
where was our baggage, and there took our *siesta* [2]); if
at Prusianum (the name of the other property) we had

---

[1] Clepsydra.

[2] It may be observed that the very word 'siesta' (at the sixth
hour) marks the permanence of Roman customs in the lands bordering
on the Mediterranean.   As the 'prandium' was at the fifth hour, the
repose would naturally be at the sixth.

to turn Tonantius and his brothers—nobles as they were, and our equals in age—out of their couches, as we could not easily carry our sleeping-apparatus about with us.

'When we had shaken off our noontide torpor, we rode on horseback for a little while to sharpen our appetites for supper. Both of my hosts had baths in their houses, but neither of them happened to be in working order. However, when my attendants and the crowd of their fellow-revellers, whose brains were too often under the influence of the hospitable wine-cup, had made a short pause in their potations, they would hurriedly dig a trench near to the fountain or the river. Into this they tossed a heap of burnt stones, and over it they would weave a hemisphere of hazel-twigs. Upon this framework were stretched sheets of coarse Cilician canvas, which at once shut out the light, and beat back the steam rising from the hot flints sprinkled with water. Here we often passed hours in pleasant and witty talk, while our limbs, wrapped in the fizzing steam, gave forth a wholesome sweat. When we had spent as long as we chose in this rude *sudatorium*, we plunged into the heated waters to wash away the perspiration; and, having so worked off all tendency to indigestion, we then braced our bodies with the cold waters of the well, the fountain, or the river. For I should have mentioned that midway between the two houses flows the river Vuardo[1], red with its tawny gravel, except when the melting snow makes pale its waters, gliding tranquilly over its pebbly bed, and well-stocked with delicate fish.

'I would also describe the luxurious suppers which

---

[1] The Gard of the celebrated 'Pont du Gard.'

we used to sit down to, if my talkative vein, which knows no check from modesty, were not summarily stopped by the end of my paper.   And yet it would be pleasant to tell over again their delights if I did not blush to carry my scrawl over to the back of the sheet. But now, as we are really in act to depart, and as you, with Christ's help, are going to be good enough to pay us an immediate visit, it will be easier to talk over our friends' suppers when you and I are taking our own ; only let the end of this week of feasting restore to me as soon as possible my vanished appetite, since no refinements of cookery can so effectually soothe an overcharged stomach as the remedy of abstinence. Farewell.'

3. ROMAN LIFE.   *The new Basilica*[1].

The Bishop Patiens, an earnest and liberal-handed man, raised in his city of Lyons a magnificent church, which was dedicated to the popular Gallic saint, Justus.   Sidonius and two other poets, the most eminent of their age and nation, were requested to write three inscriptions which were to be engraven on tablets at the west end of the building.   The church itself, after witnessing some interesting passages of mediaeval history, was destroyed in the religious wars of the sixteenth century ; and these lines written by Sidonius, and by him transcribed at the request of a youthful admirer, alone remain to testify of its departed glories.   The chief reason for quoting them is the proof which they afford that the use of mosaics on the walls and of golden decorations on the ceiling was not

[1] Ep. ii. 10.

confined, as we may have been inclined to suppose, to those places where Byzantine taste was predominant. Many touches in the following description would suit some of the still surviving churches of Ravenna. The Atrium or oblong porch in front of the church, the triple doorway from the Atrium into the nave, and from the outside of the building into the Atrium, the 'forest of columns' within, and the slabs of marble in the windows, are all also characteristic of the ecclesiastical architecture of Constantine and his successors[1].

Sidonius uses the metre called hendecasyllabic

$$- - \; | - \cup \cup \; | - \cup \; | - \cup \; | - \cup$$

to which he was very partial, and which has been employed in the following translation :

'Stranger ! come and admire this temple's beauty,
Know, 'twas reared by the zeal of Bishop Patient.
Here put up the request that earns an answer:
Here shall all of thy heart's desires be granted.
See how shines from afar the lofty building
Which, square-set, nor to left nor right deflected,
Looks straight on to the equinoctial sunrise.

Inly gleams there a light: the golden ceiling
Glows so fair that the sunbeams love to wander
Slowly over the sun-like burnished metal.
Marbles varied in hue, with slabs resplendent,
Line the vault and the floor, and frame the windows[2].

---

[1] All these points occur in the description of Constantine's 'Church of the Saviour' at Jerusalem, and Justinian's Church of St. Sophia at Constantinople, given in Smith's Dictionary of Christian Antiquities, art. Church.

[2]   'Distinctum vario nitore marmor
            Percurrit cameram, solum, *fenestras*.'
'The windows (of St. Sophia) are filled with slabs of marble, pierced with square openings filled with thick pieces of cast glass' (Smith's Dict. of Christ. Antt. l. c.).

And, in glass on the walls, the green of spring-tide
Bounds the blue of the lake with winding margent[1].

Here a portico, three-arched, fronts the gazer,
Reared on pillars from Aquitanian quarries.
There its counterpart stands, an inner portal,
At the Atrium's end, three-arched and stately;
While within, and around the floor of worship
Rise the stems of a slender marble forest.

Fair it rises, between the Road and River;
Here it echoes the horseman's clanging footfall
And the shout of the slave who guides the chariot.
There, the chorus of bending, hauling bargemen,
As they pace by the turgid Arar's waters
Send to heaven the joyful Alleluia!

Sing thus! Wayfarers sing by land or water,
Sing at sight of the house which all may enter,
Where all learn of the road that leads to safety.'

4. ROMAN LIFE. *The family setting out for the country*[2].

Evodius had asked Sidonius to furnish him with
twelve verses to be engraved on the inside of a large
shell-shaped silver basin which he was about to present
to Ragnahild the Visigothic queen. Sidonius replies
as follows:—

' Sidonius wishes health to his friend Evodius.

[1]   ' Ac sub versicoloribus figuris
                Vernans herbida crusta sapphiratos
                Flectit per prasinum vitrum lapillos.'
As the meaning of these lines is not very clear, I have ventured to
interpolate a memory of Ravenna. In the vaulted roof above the
tomb of Galla Placidia, one sees a bright mosaic picture of two stags
drinking, and the pool between them is blue, lined with emerald-
green grass ('sapphirati lapilii' surrounded with 'prasinum vitrum').
   [2] Ep. iv. 8.

' When the messenger brought me your letter, inform-
ing me that you were about soon to visit Toulouse at
the command of the king, we too were leaving the town
for a place in the country some way off. From early
morning I had been detained by one cause or another,
and the arrival of your letter only just gave me an
excuse to shake off the crowd of attendants and try to
satisfy your request while I was either walking or
riding. At the very break of day my family had gone
forward, meaning to pitch the tent when they had
accomplished eighteen miles of the journey. The spot
which they would then reach was one which many
reasons combined to make desirable for the purpose of
a halt ; a cool spring in a shady grove, a level lawn
with plenty of grass, a river just before our eyes well
stocked with fish, and a favourite haunt of water-birds ;
and besides all this, close to the river's bank stood the
new house of an old friend, so immensely kind that
neither by accepting nor by refusing can you ever get
to the end of his civilities.

' Hither then my people had gone before me and here
I stopped for your sake, that I might send your slave
back by the shortest way from the chief town in the
district. By this time it was four hours and more after
sunrise ; already the sun which was now high in the
heavens had sucked up the night-dews with his increasing rays ; we were growing hot and thirsty, and in the
deep serenity of the day a cloud of dust raised by our
horses' feet was our only protection against the heat.
Then the length of the road stretching out before us
over the green and sea-like plain made us groan when
we thought how long it would be before we should get
our dinner. All these things, my dear Sir, I have

mentioned to you that you may understand how adverse the circumstances of my body, my mind, and my
time were to the fulfilment of your commission.'

Sidonius then gives the verses, twelve in number,
which were to be engraved in twelve grooves, reaching
from the centre to the circumference of Queen Ragnahild's silver basin.   The heat and the remoteness of the
prospect of dinner must have been unfavourable to his
courtship of the Muse, for the verses are vapid, and
there is scarcely a thought in them which would survive translation[1].

5. ROMAN LIFE.   *The Fortune-hunter*[2].

In the early days of the Episcopate of Sidonius a
certain Amantius asked him for letters of introduction
to Marseilles.   With his usual good-nature Sidonius
gave him a letter to Graecus, Bishop of that city, describing him as a poor but honest man, who transacted
what we should call a commission-business in the purchase of cargoes arriving at the seaports of Gaul.   He

---

[1] These are the verses in the original—

'Pistigero quae concha vehit Tritone Cytheren
   Hac sibi collata cedere non dubitet.
Poscimus, inclina paulisper culmen herile,
   Et munus parvum, magna patrona, cape:
Evodiumque libens non aspernare clientem,
   Quem faciens grandem tu quoque major eris.
Sic tibi cui rex est genitor, socer atque maritus,
   Natus rex quoque sit cum patre postque patrem.
Felices lymphae, clausae quae luce metalli,
   Ora tamen dominae lucidiora fovent!
Nam cum dignatur regina hinc tingere vultus,
   Candor in argentum mittitur e facie.'

[2] Ep. vii. 2.

had been lately appointed a Reader in the Church—a
post which was not incompatible with his transactions
in business—and this gave him an additional claim on
the good offices of the two Bishops[1]. The letter concluded with the expression of a hope that Amantius
might meet with splendid success as a merchant, and
might not regret exchanging the cold springs of Auvergne for the fountain of wealth flowing at Marseilles[2].

Not long after, Sidonius discovered that he had been
imposed upon by a swindler, that the modest young
man who desired an introduction to Marseilles was in
fact too well known at Marseilles already, and that the
honest broker was an impudent and mendacious fortune-
hunter. Having occasion to write again to Graecus,
who had asked him for ' one of his long and amusing
letters,' he thought that he could not do better than
send him the history of Amantius, though the Bishop
of Marseilles must have been already in good part
acquainted with it, and the Bishop of Arverni must
have been conscious that the part which he had played
did not reflect great credit on his shrewdness. After a
complimentary preface, the letter proceeds thus :

' His native country is Auvergne ; his parents are
persons in a somewhat humble position in life, but free
and unencumbered with debt ; their duties have been in
connection with the service of the Church rather than
of the State. The father is a man of extreme frugality,
more intent on saving up money for his children than
on pleasing them. This lad accordingly left his home

---

[1] As a *lector* he was entitled to receive ' *literae formatae* ' from the
Bishop, a certificate which was given to no one who was not in some
sense *clericus*.

[2] Ep. vi. 8.

and came to your city with a very slender equipment
in all respects. Notwithstanding this hindrance to his
ambitious projects he made a fairly successful start
among you. Saint Eustachius, your predecessor, welcomed him with deeds and words of kindness, and put
him in the way of quickly obtaining comfortable quarters. He at once began to cultivate assiduously the
acquaintance of his neighbours, and his civilities were
well received. He adapted himself with great tact to
their different ages, showing deference to the old,
making himself useful to his coëvals, and always exhibiting a modesty and sobriety in his moral conduct
which are as praiseworthy as they are rare in young
men. At length, by well-timed and frequent calls, he
became known to and familiar with the leading personages of your city, and finally even with the Count
himself. Thus the assiduous court which he paid to
greatness was rewarded with ever-increasing success ;
worthy men vied in helping him with their advice and
good wishes; he received presents from the wealthy,
favours of one kind or another from all, and thus his
fortune and his hopes advanced "by leaps and
bounds[1]."

'It happened by chance that near the inn where he
was lodging there dwelt a lady of some fortune and
high character, whose daughter had passed the years of
childhood, yet had scarcely reached the marriageable
age. He showed himself very kind to this girl, and
made, as her youth allowed him to do, trifling presents
to her of toys and trash that would divert a girl, and
thus, at a very trifling expense, obtained a firm hold on
her affections. Years passed on ; she became old enough

---

[1] 'Raptim saltuatimque.'

to be a bride. To make a long story short, you have
on the one side a young man, alone, poorly off, a
stranger, a son who had skulked away from home not
only without the consent, but even without the knowledge of his father; on the other, a girl not inferior to
him in birth, and superior to him in fortune; and this
fellow, through the introduction of the Bishop because
he was a Reader, by favour of the Count because he
had danced attendance in his hall, without any investi-
gation as to his circumstances by the mother-in-law
because his person was not displeasing to her daughter,
woos and wins and marries that young lady. The
marriage articles are signed, and in them some beggarly
little plot of ground which he happened to possess near
our borough is set forth with truly comic pomposity.
When the solemn swindle was accomplished, the poor
beloved one carried off his wealthy spouse, after diligently hunting up all the possessions of his late father-
in-law, and converting them into money, besides adding
to them a handsome gratuity drawn from the easy
generosity of his credulous mother-in-law, and then,
unrivalled humbug that he was, he beat a retreat to his
own native place.

'Some time after he had gone, the girl's mother discovered the fraud, and had to mourn over the dwindling
proportions of the estates comprised in her daughter's
settlement, at the very time when she should have been
rejoicing over the augmented number of her grand-
children. She wanted to institute a suit for recovery
of her money, on the ground that he had fraudulently
overstated his property; and it was in fact in order to
soothe her wrath that our new Hippolytus[1] set forth for

---

[1] Referring to the affair of Hippolytus and his step-mother Phaedra.

Marseilles, when he first brought you my letter of introduction.

'Now, then, you have the whole story of this excel-
lent young man, a story, I think, worthy of the
Milesian Fables or an Attic comedy. It remains for
you to show yourself a worthy successor of Bishop
Eustachius by discharging the duties of patronage to
the dear youth whom he took under his protection.
You asked me for a lengthy letter, and therefore if it is
rather wordy than eloquent you must not take it amiss.
Condescend to keep me in your remembrance, my lord
Pope[1].'

What was the issue of the quarrel between the ama-
tory Amantius and his mother-in-law we are not
informed, but as he acted twice after this as letter-
carrier[2] between Sidonius and Graecus, we may conjecture that the affair of the settlement took some time to
arrange.

6. ROMAN LIFE. *The Master murdered by his Slaves*[3].

'Sidonius wishes health to his friend Lupus.

'I have just heard of the murder of the orator Lam-
pridius, whose death, even if it had been in the course
of nature, would have filled me with sorrow on account
of our ancient friendship. Long ago he used, by way
of joke, to call me Phoebus, and I gave him the name
of the Odrysian bard [Orpheus]. Once, when I was
going to visit him at Bordeaux, I sent forward to him

---

[1] *Papa* was the common form of address used towards all Bishops
at this time.

[2] *Nugi-gerulus* is the curious term used by Sidonius.

[3] Ep. viii. 11 (much abridged in translation).

a poem, like a soldier's billet, claiming his hospitality for Apollo.'

Then follows the poem in hendecasyllabics. Phoebus directs his favourite Muse, Thalia, to go before him to Bordeaux, to knock at the door of one Orpheus whom she will find there, charming all nature by his minstrelsy, and to tell him that Phoebus has left his home, that already his oars are splashing in the rapid Garonne, that he will soon be at the house of his friend. The remembrance of these long-past, merry days draws from Sidonius a sentence in prose, which comes nearer to poetry than anything else written by him. ' O necessitas abjecta nascendi, vivendi misera, dura moriendi[1]!' He proceeds—

'See whither the fickle wheel of Fortune leads us. I confess I loved the man, though in his character there were mingled some traits unworthy of his real virtues. He was of a hasty temper, easily moved to anger by slight offences, and there was a taint of cruelty in his nature, though I used to seek to extenuate it by calling it severity. . . .

'The worst and most fatal fault which he committed was in resorting to astrologers in order to learn what the end of his life should be. They were natives of some of the cities of Africa, men whose dispositions were as burning as their sun. They concurred in naming to him the year, the month, and the day which, in their jargon, would be "climacteric" for him; and when they had cast his nativity they predicted for him a bloody fate, because all the planets which had risen prosperously upon his birth set in sinister aspects and

---

[1] Oh humiliating necessity of birth, sad necessity of living, hard necessity of dying !

with lurid fires. However false and deceptive the pre-
dictions of these mathematicians as a rule may be, in
the case of our friend they were strictly correct both as
to the time and manner of his death. For having been
held down in his own house, and strangled by his own
slaves, he died by the same death as Lentulus, Jugurtha, Sejanus, and even Scipio of Numantia. The least
melancholy part of the business is that the parricidal
deed was discovered as soon as morning dawned. For
no one could be so dull as not to see the signs of foul
play on first inspection of the corpse. The livid skin,
the starting eyes, the yet lingering traces of anger and
pain in the face told their own tale. The earth too
was wet with his blood, because after the deed was done
the villains had laid him face downwards on the pavement to make it seem as if he had died of hæmorrhage.
The chief agent in the crime was taken, tortured, and
confessed his guilt. Would that I could say that our
friend was altogether undeserving of his fate. But he
who thus pries into forbidden mysteries, deviates from
the safe rule of the Catholic faith, and while he is using
unlawful arts must not complain if he is answered by
some great calamity.'

7. ROMAN LIFE. *The Oppressive Governor*[1].

' Sidonius wishes health to his friend Pannychius.

'If you have not already heard that Seronatus is
returning from Toulouse, let this letter inform you of
the fact. Already Evanthius[2] is on his way to Clau-
setia, and is forcing people to clear away the rubbish

---

[1] Ep. v. 13.
[2] Some subordinate official under Seronatus.

from the works that have been let out on contract, and
to remove the fallen leaves from his path[1].   Poor man!
if there is an uneven surface anywhere, he himself,
with trembling hand, brings earth to fill up the
trenches, going before the beast whom he is escorting
from the valley of Tarmis, like the little mussels who
pioneer the mighty body of the whale through the
shallow places and rocky channels of the sea.

‘Seronatus, however, as quick to wrath as he is unwieldy in bulk, like a dragon just rolled forth from his
cave, comes towards us from the district of Gabala,
whose inhabitants he leaves half dead with fright.
This population, scattered into the country from their
towns, he is now exhausting with unheard-of imposts[2];
now entangling them in the winding meshes of false
accusations, and scarcely permitting the labourers at
length to return home, when they have paid him a
year’s tribute in advance.   The sure and certain sign
of his approaching advent is the gangs of unhappy
prisoners who are dragged in chains to meet him.
Their anguish is his joy, their hunger is his food, and
he seems to think it an especially fine thing to degrade
before he punishes them, making the men grow their
hair long, and the women cut theirs.   If any here and
there meet with a chance pardon, it will be due to a
bribe, or to his flattered vanity, but never to compas-
sion.

‘But to set forth all the proceedings of such a beast
would exhaust the rhetoric of a Cicero and the poetry
of a Virgil.   Therefore, since it is said that this pest is
approaching us, (whose ravages may God guard us
from!) do you forestall the disease by the counsels of

[1] Translation doubtful.   [2] ‘Indictionibus.’

prudence; compromise your lawsuits if you have any; get security for your arrears of tribute; do not let the wicked man have any opportunity of hurting the good, or of laying them under an obligation. In fine, do you wish to hear what I think of Seronatus? Others fear his fines and his punishments: to me the so-called benefits of the robber seem even more to be dreaded.'

We do not know what was the subsequent history of this oppressive governor, nor how long the crushed provincials had to endure his yoke. In another letter [1] Sidonius speaks of him as 'the Catiline of our age, fawning on the barbarians, trampling on the Romans, joking in Church, preaching at the banquet, passing sentence in bed, sleeping on the judgment-seat; every day crowding the woods with fugitives, the villas with barbarians, the altars with criminals, the prisons with clergymen; insulting prefects, and conniving at the frauds of revenue-officers, treading under foot the laws of Theodosius, and exalting those of Theodoric' [the Visigoth], 'every day bringing forth old accusations and new exactions.' And he states in conclusion that if Anthemius, the then reigning Emperor, affords them no assistance against the tyranny of Seronatus, 'the nobility of Auvergne have resolved to sacrifice either their country or their hair,' that is, to retire either into exile or into monasteries.

8. ROMAN LIFE. *The Country Magnate* [2].

'Sidonius wishes health to his friend Industrius.

'I have just been visiting the Right Honourable Vectius [3], and have studied his actions at my leisure, and

---

[1] Ep. ii. 1.   [2] Ep. iv. 9.   [3] 'Vectio illustri viro.'

from close quarters. I think the result of my investigations is worth recording. In the first place I will mention what I consider the highest praise of all ; the house and its master both exist in an atmosphere of unsullied purity. His slaves are useful ; his rural [1] labourers well-mannered, courteous, friendly, obedient, and contented with their patron. His table is as ready to welcome the guest as the retainer ; his civility is great, and yet greater his sobriety.

'Another and less important matter is that he of whom I speak is inferior to none in the arts of breaking horses, training dogs, and managing falcons. There is the utmost neatness in his raiment, elegance in his girdles, and splendour in his accoutrements. His walk is dignified, his disposition serious : the former well maintains his private dignity, the latter is set upon preserving public faith. He is equally removed from spoiling indulgence and from bloody punishments, and there is a certain austerity in his character, which is stern without being gloomy [2]. Moreover he is a diligent reader of the sacred volumes, with which he often refreshes his mind while in the act of taking food for the body. He frequently peruses the Psalms, and yet more frequently chants them, and thus, in a novel fashion, acts the monk, not under the habit of a recluse, but under the uniform of a general [3]. He abstains from game, though he consents to hunt, and thus, with a delicate and unobtrusive religiousness, he

---

[1] *Rustici.* These are evidently the *coloni*, free-born, yet dependent on their *patronus*, the precursors of the villeins 'adscripti glebae' of later centuries.

[2] 'Quae non sit tetra sed tetrica,' an untranslateable pun.

[3] 'Non sub palliolo sed sub paludamento.'

uses the processes of the chase but denies himself its produce.

' One only daughter was left to him on her mother's death as the solace of his widowerhood, and her he cherishes with the tenderness of a grandfather, the assiduity of a mother, and the kindness of a father. As to his relations towards his household, when he is giving orders he " forbeareth threatening ;" when he receives their advice he does not spurn it from him as valueless ; when he discovers a fault he is not too persistent in tracing it ; and thus he rules the state and condition of those who are subject to him, more as a judge than as a master ; you would think that he rather administered his house as a trust than owned it as an absolute possession.

' When I perceived all this industry and moderation in such a man, I thought it would be for the common good that the knowledge of it should be thoroughly and widely spread abroad. To follow such a life, and not merely to don a particular [monastic] habit, whereby the present age is often grievously imposed upon, would be a useful incitement for all the men of our profession ' [the clerical]. ' For—let me say it without offending my own order—when a private individual shows such excellent qualities as these, I admire a priest-like layman more than a priest himself. Farewell.'

9. ROMAN LIFE. *The Juvenile Sexagenarian*[1].

[This letter is addressed to the subject of the preceding one.]

' Sidonius wishes health to his friend Vectius.

[1] Ep. iv. 13.

'Lately, at the request of the Hon.[1] Germanicus, I inspected the church of Cantilla.

'He himself is certainly one of the most noteworthy men of the district, for although he has already put sixty years behind him, every day, in dress and manners, he becomes, I will not say more like a young man, but actually more boyish. His robe is closely girt around him, his buskin tight-laced, his hair is cut so as to make it look like a wheel, his beard is cropped close to the chin by pincers which pierce to the bottom of each fold of his skin. Moreover, by the blessing of Providence, his limbs are still strongly knit, his sight is perfect, he has a firm and rapid gait, in his gums there is an untouched array of milk-white teeth. With no weakness in his stomach, no tendency to inflammation in his veins, no perturbation of his heart, no distress in breathing, no stiffness in his loins, no congestion of his liver, no flabbiness in his hand, no bending of his spine, but endowed with all the health of youth, he claims nothing that belongs to age but reverence.

'In consideration of all these peculiar benefits which he has received from God, I beg you, as his friend and neighbour, and one whose example justly exerts a great influence over him, to persuade him not to trust too much in these uncertain possessions, nor to cherish an overweening confidence in his own immunity from disease; but rather to make a decided profession of religion, and so become strong in the might of renewed innocence. Let him thus, while old in years, be new in merit; and since there is scarcely any one who is devoid of hidden faults, let him openly show his penitence and give satisfaction for those wrong things

---

[1] 'Spectabilis viri.'

which he has committed in secret. For a man in his
position, the father of a priest and the son of a bishop,
unless he lead a holy life himself, is like a briar,
rough, prickly and unlovely in the midst of roses,
from which it has sprung, and which it has itself
produced.'

10. ROMAN LIFE. *Teachers and Pupils, Masters and Slaves* [1].

' Sidonius wishes health to his friends Simplicius
and Apollinaris.

'Good God [2]! how do the emotions of our minds
resemble a sea strewn with shipwrecks, the tempests
which sweep over them being the evil tidings which
messengers sometimes bring to us. A little while ago
I was, together with your son [3], Simplicius! revelling
in the delicate wit of the Hecyra of Terence. I sat
beside the young student forgetting my clerical profession in the delight which the human nature of the play
afforded me. In order that I might help him to follow
the flow of the comic verses more easily, I kept before
me a story with a similar plot, the Epitrepontes of
Menander. We read at the same pace, we praised our
authors, we laughed over their jokes, and, according to

---

[1] Ep. iv. 12.

[2] ' Deus bone ! ' Sidonius is very fond of this exclamation. If it
was especially affected by the Christians of Gaul, it may help to explain the frequency of the French ' Bon Dieu ! '

[3] This is how I understand the expression ' ego filiusque communis.'
We know from one of Sidonius' letters (v. 4) that the sons of Simplicius studied as pupils with him. He complains that on account of his
too great kindness to them at first, they did not treat him with proper
respect.

our respective tastes, he was captivated by the reading, and I by his intelligence.

'Suddenly there stood by my side a slave of my household, pulling a very long face. "What is the matter?" said I. "I have just seen," said he, "at the gate the reader [1] Constans, returning from my lords Simplicius and Apollinaris; he says that he delivered your letters to them, but has lost the replies which were entrusted to his care." When I heard this the calm, bright sky of my gladness was overspread with a cloud of sorrow, and so much was my bile stirred by the untoward intelligence thus brought me, that for many days I inexorably forbade that most stupid Mercury to venture into my presence. For I should have been vexed if he had lost any ordinary letters entrusted to him by anybody, but how much more, yours, which, so long as my mind retains its vigour, will always be deemed least common and most desirable.

'However, after my anger had gradually abated with the lapse of time, I enquired of him whether he had brought me any verbal message from you. Trembling and prostrate before me, stammering and half-blind with the consciousness of his offence, he answered that all those thoughts of yours, by which I had hoped to be charmed and instructed, were committed to those unlucky letters which had disappeared on the way.

'Go back therefore, dear friends, to your tablets [2], unfold your parchments and write over again what you wrote before. For I cannot bear with equanimity

---

[1] The slave who was called *Lector* was apparently also the letter-carrier.

[2] *Pugillares*, the little wax-covered tablets, meant to hold in the hand, upon which hasty memoranda were inscribed.

this unlucky failure of my hopes unless I know that you are assured that your written speech has never reached me. Fare you well.'

11. ROMAN LIFE. *Husbands and Wives, Parents and Children* [1].

' Sidonius wishes health to his wife Papianilla.

' The quaestor Licinianus, who has just arrived from Ravenna, as soon as he had crossed the Alps and touched the soil of Gaul, sent letters forward to announce his arrival, stating that he was the bearer of an imperial ordinance, bestowing the honour of the Patriciate on your brother and mine Ecdicius [2], whose titles will rejoice you as much as mine. This honour comes very early if you consider his age, though very late if you look to his merits. For he has long ago paid the price for his new dignity, not with gold but with steel, and though a private individual, has enriched the treasury, not with money, but with trophies of war.

' This debt, however, under which your brother, by his noble labours, laid the Emperor Anthemius, has now been honourably discharged by his successor Julius Nepos, a man whose character, no less than the success of his arms, entitles us to hail him as Supreme Augustus. The promptitude of the act makes it all the more praiseworthy, for one Emperor has at once done what the other a hundred times promised to do. Henceforward, therefore, our best men may with joyful certainty spend their strength in the service of the

---

[1] Ep. v. 16. This letter was written in 475. Sidonius was probably at Lyons; his wife at Auvergne.

[2] Ecdicius had done good service in defending Auvergne against the Visigoths.

Commonwealth, knowing that even if the Emperor dies, the Imperial Dignity will faithfully perform every promise by which their devotion has been quickened.

'Meanwhile you, if I rightly read your affectionate heart, will derive, even in these gloomy times, great solace from these tidings, and will not be diverted from sharing in our common joy even by the terrors of the siege which is going on so near you. For I know right well that not even my honours, which you legally share, will bring you so much gladness as this intelligence; since though you are a good wife you are also the best of sisters. Wherefore I have made haste to inform you in this congratulatory letter, of the augmented dignity which, through the favour of Christ our God [1], has been bestowed upon your line, and thus I have at the same time satisfied your anxiety and your brother's modesty, to which, and not to any want of affection on his part, you must attribute his silence respecting this promotion.

'For myself, great as is my rejoicing at the added honours of your family for which you have hitherto sighed impatiently, I rejoice even more at the harmony which reigns between Ecdicius and me. And I pray that this harmony may continue as the heritage of our children, for whom I put up this prayer in common, that even as we two have, by God's favour, added the Patrician dignity to the Praefectorial rank which we inherited from our fathers, so they may yet further enhance it by the office of Consul [2].

'Roscia [3], our common charge, salutes you. Favoured

[1] 'Propitio Deo Christo.'

[2] This gradation of ranks, Familia Praefectoria, Patritia, Consularis, is worth noticing.   [3] His daughter.

above most other grand-children, she is fondled in the kindest embraces of her grandmother and aunts, while at the same time she is being strictly trained, and thereby her tender age is not rendered infirm while her mind is healthily informed [1].　Farewell.'

12.　ROMAN LIFE.　*Debtor and Creditor.　The Courtier turned devout* [2].

'Sidonius wishes health to his friend Turnus.

'Well indeed with your name, and with your present business, harmonises that passage of the Mantuan poet—

> 'Turnus! what never god would dare
> To promise to his suppliant's prayer,
> Lo, here, the lapse of time has brought
> E'en to your hands, unasked, unsought [3].'

Long ago, if you remember, your [late] father Turpio, a man of tribunician rank, obtained a loan of money from an officer of the palace named Maximus.　He deposited no security either in plate or in mortgage on land; but as appears by the written instrument prepared at the time, he covenanted to pay twelve [4] per cent. to the lender, by which interest, as the loan has lasted for ten years, the debt is more than doubled. But your father fell sick, and was at the point of death : in his feeble state of health the law came down

---

[1] 'Tenerum non infirmatur aevum sed informatur ingenium.'

[2] Ep. iv. 24.　It will be seen that Sidonius plays upon the name of his correspondent, which recalls the antagonist of Aeneas.

[3] Aeneid ix. 6, 7 (Conington's translation).

[4] 'Cauta centesima est foeneratori.'　Interest, by the Romans, was reckoned monthly; and this expression, therefore, means one per cent. per month, or twelve per annum.

upon him harshly to compel him to refund the debt : he could not bear the annoyance caused by the Collectors [1], and therefore, as I was about to travel to Toulouse, he, being now past hope of recovery, wrote asking me to obtain from the creditor, at least, some moderate delay. I gladly acceded to his request, as Maximus was not only an acquaintance of mine, but bound to me by old ties of hospitality. I therefore willingly went out of my way to my friend's villa, though it was situated several miles from the highroad. As soon as I arrived he himself came to meet me. When I had known him in times past he was erect in his bearing, quick in his gait, with cheery voice and open countenance. Now how greatly was he changed from his old self! His dress, his step, his bashfulness, his colour, his speech, all had a religious cast : besides, his hair was short, his beard flowing : the furniture of his room consisted of three-legged stools, curtains of goat's hair [2] canvas hung before his doors : his couch had no feathers, his table no ornament; ven his hospitality, though kind, was frugal, and there was pulse rather than meat upon his board. Certainly, if any delicacies were admitted, they were not by way of indulgence to himself, but to his guests. When he rose from table I privily enquired of his attendants what manner of life was this that he was leading, a monk's, a clergyman's, or a penitent's. They said that he was filling the office of priest which had been lately laid upon him by the goodwill of his fellow-citizens, notwithstanding his protests.

 ‘ When day returned, while our slaves and followers

---

[1] ‘ Exsecutorum ;’ as we should say, ‘ the sheriff's officers.’

[2] ‘ Cilicium,’ the kind of fabric that St. Paul used to manufacture.

were occupied in catching our beasts of burden, I
asked for an opportunity for a secret conversation with
our host. He afforded it : I gave him an unexpected
embrace, and congratulated him on his new dignity :
then with my congratulations I blended entreaties. I
set forth the petition of my friend Turpio, I urged his
necessitous condition, I deplored the extremities to
which he was reduced, extremities which seemed all
the harder to his sorrowing friends because the chain
of usury was tightening, while the hold of the body
upon the soul was loosening. Then I begged him
to remember his new profession and our old friendship,
to moderate, at least, by a short respite the barbarous
insistance of the bailiffs barking round the sick man's
bed ; if he died, to give his heirs one year in which to
indulge their grief without molestation ; but if, as I
hoped, Turpio should recover his former health, to
allow him to restore his exhausted energies by a period
of repose.

‘ I was still pleading, when suddenly the kind-hearted
man burst into a flood of tears, caused not by the
delay in recovering his debt, but by the peril of his
debtor. Then suppressing his sobs, “ God forbid,” said
he, “ that I as a clergyman should claim that from a
sick man which I should scarcely have insisted upon
as a soldier from a man in robust health. For his
children's sake too, who are also objects of my pity, if
anything should happen to our friend, I will not ask
anything more from them than the character of my
sacred calling allows. Write then to allay their anxiety,
and that your letters may obtain the more credit, add a
letter from me in which I will engage that whatever
be the result of this illness (which we will still hope

may turn out favourably for our brother) I will grant a
year's delay for the payment of the money, and will
forego all that moiety which has accrued by right of
interest, being satisfied with the simple repayment of
the principal."

'Hereupon I poured out my chief thanks to God,
but great thanks also to my host who showed such
care for his own conscience and good name: and I
assured my friend that whatsoever he relinquished to
you he was sending on before him into heaven, and that
by refraining from selling up your father's farms, he
was buying for himself a kingdom above.

'Now, for what remains, do you bestir yourself to
repay forthwith the principal at least of the loan, and
thus take the best means of expressing the gratitude
of those who, linked to you by the tie of brotherhood,
haply by reason of their tender years, scarcely yet
understand what a boon has been granted them. Do
not begin to say, "I have joint-heirs in the estate:
the division is not yet accomplished: all the world
knows that I have been more shabbily treated than
they: my brother and sister are still under age: she
has not yet a husband, nor he a *curator*, nor is a surety
found for the acts and defaults of that *curator*." All
these pretexts are alleged to all creditors, and to unreasonable creditors they are not alleged amiss. But
when you have to deal with a person of this kind who
foregoes the half when he might press for the whole,
if you practise any of these delays you give him a right
to re-demand as an injured man the concessions which
he made as a good-natured one. Farewell.'

From these glimpses of the social life of the Roman

Provincials in the middle of the fifth century, we turn
to consider what light of a similar kind the correspondence of Sidonius throws on the internal history of the
Barbarians with whom he was brought in contact. His
first description is kindly and appreciative : so much
so, that it has been conjectured that it was meant to
be shown to the gratified subject of the portrait. In
his other character-sketches of the Barbarians, as we
shall find, the shallow contempt of the heir of civilisation
for the untutored children of Nature is more distinctly
visible.

13. Barbarian Life. *The Visigothic King*[1].

'Sidonius wishes health to [his brother-in-law] Agricola.

'You have many times asked me to write to you
a letter describing the bodily appearance and manner
of life of Theodoric[2], king of the Goths, whose love
for our civilisation is justly reported by common fame.
I willingly accede to your request, so far as the limits
of my paper will allow, and I praise the noble and
delicate anxiety for information which you have thus
exhibited.

'Theodoric is " a noticeable man," one who would at
once attract attention even from those who casually
beheld him, so richly have the will of God and the
plan of nature endowed his person with gifts corre-

---

[1] Ep. i. 2.

[2] Theodoric II, son of the veteran who fell at the battle in the
Mauriac plains, ascended the throne in 453, having won the crown by
the murder of his brother Thorismund, and was himself slain by order
of his brother and successor Euric, 466. The letter is a difficult one,
and I have therefore translated it more literally than usual.

sponding to his completed prosperity. His character is such that not even the detraction which waits on kings can lessen the praises bestowed upon it[1]. If you enquire as to his bodily shape, he has a well-knit frame, shorter than the very tallest, but rising above men of middle stature. His head is round and dome-like, his curling hair retreats a little from the forehead towards the top. He is not bull-necked[2]. A shaggy arch of eyebrows crowns his eyes; but if he droops his eye-lids the lashes seem to fall well-nigh to the middle of his cheeks[3]. The lobes of his ears, after the fashion of his nation, are covered by wisps of over-lying hair. His nose is most beautifully curved; his lips are thin, and are not enlarged when the angles of his mouth are dilated[4]: if by chance they open and show a regular, but rather prominent set of teeth, they at once remind you of the colour of milk. He cuts every day the hairs which grow at the bottom of his nostrils. At his temples, which are somewhat hollowed out, begins a shaggy beard, which in the lower part of his face is plucked out by the roots by the assiduous care of his barber. His chin, his throat, his neck, all fleshy without obesity, are covered with a milk-white skin, which when more closely inspected, is covered with a youthful glow. For it is modesty, not anger, which so often brings this colour into his face.

---

[1] Did Sidonius not believe in Theodoric's participation in the conspiracy against Thorismund, or had he forgotten, or did he deliberately ignore it?

[2] (?) 'Cervix non sedet nervis.'

[3] 'Si vero cilia flectantur, ad malas medias palpebrarum margo prope pervenit.' (!)

[4] This is questionable sense, but what is the meaning of the Latin 'Labra subtilia, nec dilatatis oris angulis ampliata'?

'His shoulders are well-turned, his arms powerful, his fore-arms hard, his hands wide-spread : he is a well set-up man, with chest prominent and stomach drawn in. You can trace on the surface of his back the points where the ribs terminate in the deeply recessed spine. His sides are swollen out with prominent muscles. Strength reigns in his well-girded loins. His thigh is hard as horn : the leg joints have a very masculine appearance : his knee, which shows but few wrinkles, is especially comely. The legs rest upon full round calves, and two feet of very moderate size support these mighty limbs [1].

'You will ask, perhaps, what is the manner of his daily life in public. It is this. Before dawn he attends the celebration of divine service by his [Arian] priests, attended by a very small retinue. He shows great assiduity in this practice, though if you are admitted to his confidence you may perceive that it is with him rather a matter of habit than of religious feeling. The rest of the morning is devoted to the care of the administration of his kingdom. Armed nobles [2] stand round his chair : the crowd of skin-clothed guards are admitted to the palace in order to ensure their being on duty ; they are kept aloof from the royal presence that their noise may not disturb him, and so their

---

[1] Gibbon points out that this curiously minute appraisement of the bodily frame of Theodoric was composed by an author and perused by readers who had probably frequented the markets where naked slaves were exposed for sale. It is such a singular indication of the kind of flattery which a Roman provincial thought it prudent to bring to a barbarian king, that I have not thought it desirable to curtail it.

[2] 'Circumsistit sellam comes armiger.' The term 'circumsistit' seems to require the plural meaning. It is impossible to render the exact force of *comes*, not yet fully developed into the feudal ' Count,' but certainly more than 'Companion.'

growling talk goes on before the doors, shut out as
they are by the curtain, though shut in by the railings[1].
Within the enclosure are admitted the ambassadors of
foreign powers : he hears them at great length, he
answers in few words. In negotiation his tendency is
to delay, in action to promptitude.

' It is now the second hour after sunrise: he rises
from his throne and spends his leisure in inspecting
his treasury or his stables. If a hunting day is announced, he rides forth, not carrying his bow by his
side—that would be beneath his kingly dignity—but
if in the chase, or on the road, you point out to him
beast or bird within shooting distance, his hand is at
once stretched out behind him and the slave puts into it
the bow with its string floating in the air, for he deems
it a womanish thing to have your bow strung for you
by another, and a childish thing to carry it in a case.
When he has received it, sometimes he bends the two
ends towards one another in his hand, sometimes he
lets the unknotted end drop to his heel, and then with
quickly moving finger tightens the loose knot of the
wandering string[2]. Then he takes the arrows, fits
them in, sends them forth, first desiring you to tell
him what mark you wish him to aim at. You choose
what he has to hit, and he hits it. If there is a mistake
made by either party, it is more often the sight of the
chooser than the aim of the archer that is at fault.

---

[1] ' *Cancelli*,' the lattice-work partition which marked off the royal
precincts, whence ' *cancellarius*,' the door-keeper, and our Lord High
Chancellor : also the chancel of a church.

[2] ' Igitur acceptum modo insinuatis e regione capitibus intendit,
modo ad talum pendulum, nodi parte conversâ, languentem chordæ
laqueum vagantis digito superlabente prosequitur.' I cannot pretend
to translate this obscure passage quite literally.

'If you are asked to join him in the banquet, which, however, on non-festal days, is like the entertainment of a private person, you will not see there the panting servants laying on the groaning table a tasteless heap of discoloured silver. The weight then is to be found in the conversation rather than in the plate, since all the guests, if they talk of anything at all, talk of serious matters. The tapestry [1] and curtains are sometimes of purple [cloth], sometimes of cotton. The meats on the table please you, not by their high price, but by the skill with which they are cooked, the silver by its brightness, not by its weight. The cups and goblets are so seldom replenished that you are more likely to complain of thirst than to be accused of drunkenness. In short, you may see there Greek elegance, Gallic abundance, Italian quickness, the pomp of a public personage, the assiduity of a private citizen, the discipline of a king's household. Of the luxury which is displayed on high-days and holidays [2] I need not give you any account, because it cannot be unknown even to the most unknown persons. Let me return to my task.

'The noontide slumber, when the meal is ended, is never long, and is frequently omitted altogether. Often at this time he takes a fancy to play at backgammon [3] : then he collects the counters quickly, views them anxiously, decides on his moves skilfully, makes them promptly, talks to the counters jocularly, waits his turn patiently. At a good throw he says nothing, at a

---

[1] 'Toreuma ;' literally, 'work executed in relief,' 'embossed with the needle.' Perhaps it should be rendered 'cushions.'

[2] 'De luxu sabbatario,' opposed to 'diebus profestis.'

[3] 'Tabula.'

bad one he laughs ; neither good nor bad makes him lose his temper or his philosophical equanimity. He does not like a speculative game either on the part of his adversary or himself, dislikes a lucky chance offered to himself, and will not reckon on its being offered to his opponent. You get your men out of his table without unnecessary trouble, he gets his out of yours without collusion [1]. You would fancy that even in moving his counters he was planning a campaign. His sole anxiety is to conquer.

'When a game is on hand, he drops for a little time the severity of royal etiquette, and invites his companions in play, to free and social intercourse. To tell you what I think, *he fears to be feared.* At the end he is delighted to see the vexation of a conquered rival, and takes credit to himself for having really won the game, when his opponent's ill-temper shows that he has not yielded out of courtesy. And here notice a strange thing : often that very complacency of his, arising from such a trifling cause, ensures the successful carriage of serious business. Then petitions, which have well-nigh been shipwrecked by the injudiciousness of those who favoured them, suddenly find a harbour of safety. In this way, I myself, when I have had somewhat to ask of him, have been fortunate enough to be beaten, and have seen my table ruined with a light heart, because I knew that my cause would triumph.

'About the ninth hour [3 o'clock] comes back again all that weary turmoil of kingship. The suitors return, the guards return whose business it is to remove them. Everywhere you hear the hum of claimants, and this is protracted till nightfall, and only ceases when it is cut

---

[1] 'Sine motu evaditur, sine colludio evadit.'

short by the royal supper. Then the petitioners, following their various patrons, are dispersed throughout the palace, where they keep watch till bedtime arrives. At the supper sometimes, though rarely, comic actors are introduced who utter their satiric pleasantries: in such fashion, however, that none of the guests shall be wounded by their biting tongues. At these repasts no hydraulic organs blow, no band of vocalists under the guidance of a singing-master intone together their premeditated harmony. No harpist, no flute-player, no choir-master, no female player on the tambourine or the cithara, makes melody. The king is charmed only by those instruments under whose influence virtue soothes the soul as much as sweet sounds soothe the ear. When he rises from table the royal treasury receives its sentinels for the night, and armed men stand at all the entrances to the palace, by whom the hours of his first sleep will be watched over.

' But what has all this to do with my promise, which was to tell you a little about the king, not a great deal about his manner of reigning? I really must bid my pen to stop, for you did not ask to be made acquainted with anything more than the personal appearance and favourite pursuits of Theodoric: and I sat down to write a letter, not a history. Farewell.'

14. Barbarian Life. *Syagrius and his Germanic neighbours* [1].

'Sidonius wishes health to his friend Syagrius.

'As you are grandson of a Consul, and that on the

---

[1] Ep. v. 5. The Syagrius, upon whose relations to his German neighbours this strange side-light is thrown by a letter from Sidonius,

paternal side, as you are sprung (which is more to our
present purpose) from a poetic stock, descended from
men who would have earned statues by their poems if
they had not earned them by their services to the state,
all which is shown by those verses of your ancestors
which the present generation studies with unimpaired
interest,—as these are your antecedents, I cannot describe my astonishment at the ease with which you
have mastered the German tongue.   I remember that
in your boyhood you were well trained in liberal studies,
and I am informed that you often declaimed before a
professional orator with force and eloquence.   But since
this is the case, pray tell me whence your soul has
suddenly imbibed the oratory of an alien race, so that
you who had the phraseology of Virgil flogged into you
at school, you who sweated over the long and stately
sentences of Cicero, now swoop down upon us like a
young falcon from the German language as though that
were your old eyrie.

'You cannot imagine how I and all your other friends
laugh when we hear that even the barbarian is afraid
to talk his own language before you lest he should
make a slip in his grammar[1].   When you are inter-
preting their letters, the old men of Germany, bent
with age, stand in open-mouthed wonder, and in their
transactions with one another they voluntarily choose
you for arbitrator and judge.   A new Solon when you
have to discuss the laws of the Burgundians, a new

is apparently the same person as the son of Aegidius, the so-called
'Roman King of Soissons,' whose defeat in 486 was one of the first
steps in the upward career of Clovis.

[1] 'Te praesente formidet facere linguae suae barbarus barba-
rismum.'

Amphion when you have to evoke music from their three-stringed lyre, you are loved and courted, you please, you decree, you are obeyed. And though the barbarians are equally stiff and lumpish in body and mind, yet in you they learn and love the speech of their fathers, the disposition of a Roman.

' It only now remains for you, oh most brilliant of wits, to bestow any spare time which may still be yours on reading [Latin], and so to retain that elegance of style which you now possess. Thus while you preserve your Latin that we may not laugh at you, you will practise your German that you may be able to laugh at us. Farewell.'

15. BARBARIAN LIFE. *Roman Intriguers at the Burgundian Court* [1].

A young kinsman of Sidonius, also named Apollinaris, had been brought into some danger through the calumnies of informers who represented to the Burgundian prince Chilperic that he was secretly plotting for the surrender of Vaison, a border fortress, to 'the new Emperor,' Julius Nepos.

Sidonius writes concerning these informers to Thaumastus, the brother of the calumniated man, with sympathetic indignation.

' These are the men, as you have often heard me say, under whose villanies our country groans, longing for the more merciful barbarians. These are the men before whom even the great tremble. These are they whose peculiar province it appears to be to bring calumnious accusations, to carry off men from their

---

[1] Ep. v. 7.

homes, to frighten them with threats, to pillage their substance. These are the men who in idleness boast of their business, in peace of their plunder, in war of their clever escapes, in their cups of victories. These are they who procrastinate your lawsuit if you engage them, who get it postponed if you pass them by, who are annoyed if you remind them of their engagement, and forget it—after taking your fee—if you do not. . . . . These are the men who envy quiet citizens their tranquillity, soldiers their pay, post-masters their tariffs, merchants their markets, ambassadors their functions, tax-farmers their tolls, the provincials their farms, the burgesses their guild-dinners[1], the cashiers their weights, the registrars their measures, the scribes their salaries, the accountants their fees, the guards their largesse, the cities their repose, the publicans their taxes, the clergy their reverence, the nobles their birth, their betters their precedence, their equals their equality, the officials their power, the ex-officials their privileges, the learners their schools, the teachers their stipends, the taught their knowledge.

'These are the men drunken with new wealth, who by the vulgar display of their possessions show how little they are accustomed to ownership, the men who go in full armour to a banquet, in white robes to a funeral, in hides to church, in black to a wedding, in beaver-skin to the litany. No set of men suits them, no time seems to hit their humour. In the market they are very Scythians, in the bed-chamber they are vipers, at the banquet buffoons, in confiscations harpies,

---

[1] *Flaminia*, literally 'their priesthoods.' But probably these old heathen dignities were only kept up for the sake of some convivial practices connected with them.

in conversation statues, in argument brute-beasts, in business snails, in enforcing a contract usurers. They are stone if you want them to understand, fire if they have to judge, quick to wrath, slow to pardon, panthers in their friendship, bears in their fun, foxes in their deceit, bulls in their pride, Minotaurs in their rapacity.

' Their firmest hopes are founded on the uncertainties of the times; they love to fish in troubled waters; yet fearful both from natural cowardice and from an uneasy conscience, while they are lions at court they are hares in the camp, and are afraid of a truce lest they should be made to disgorge, of war lest they should have to fight.'

The good bishop's invective rolls on still through some sentences, which need not be inflicted on the reader. Though well-nigh out of breath with following Sidonius' headlong rhetoric, he may still have gathered from it the important fact that the chief instruments of such oppression as was practised by the barbarian invaders upon the provincials were men who were themselves of Roman origin.

16. Barbarian Life. *The physique of the Burgundians.*

While our poet was residing at Lyons (apparently) he was asked by one of his friends, an ex-consul named Catulinus, to compose an epithalamium, perhaps for his daughter's marriage.

In a short, humorous poem of apology Sidonius incidentally touches off some of the physical characteristics of the Burgundians, by whom he was surrounded, and who, it is important to observe, troubled him, not by their hostility, but by their too hearty and demonstrative friendship [1].

'Ah me! my friend, why bid me, e'en if I had the power,
To write the light Fescennine verse, fit for the nuptial bower?
Do you forget that I am set among the long-haired hordes,
That daily I am bound to bear the stream of German words,
That I must hear, and then must praise with sorrowful grimace
(Disgust and approbation both contending in my face),
Whate'er the gormandising sons of Burgundy may sing,
While they upon their yellow hair the rancid butter fling?

Now let me tell you what it is that makes my lyre be dumb:
It cannot sound when all around barbarian lyres do hum.
The sight of all those patrons tall (each one is seven foot high),
From my poor Muse makes every thought of six-foot metres fly.
Oh! happy are thine eyes, my friend: thine ears, how happy
    those!
And oh! thrice happy I would call thine undisgusted nose.
'Tis not round thee that every morn ten talkative machines
Exhale the smell of onions, leeks, and all their vulgar greens.
There do not seek thy house, as mine, before the dawn of day,
So many giants and so tall, so fond of trencher-play
That scarce Alcinous himself, that hospitable king,
Would find his kitchen large enough for the desires they bring.
They do not, those effusive souls, declare they look on thee
As father's friend or foster-sire—but, alas! they do on me.

But stop, my Muse! pull up! be still! or else some fool will
    say
"Sidonius writes lampoons again [2]." Don't *you* believe them,
    pray!'

The tenor of these verses reminds us of an epigram [3] of

[1] Carm. xii.   The metre of the original is hendecasyllabic.
[2] For the explanation of this allusion see Chap. 5.
[3] 'Inter *hails* Goticum, *skapjam jam matjam jad driggkam*,
    Non audet quisquam dignos educere versus.
    Calliope madido trepidat se jungere Baccho
    Ne pedibus non stet ebria Musa suis.'
This epigram is quoted from the Anthologia Latina by Massmann and other editors of Ulfilas. It is valuable as containing four Gothic

unknown authorship, but composed probably in the fifth century.

'Round me the *hails* of the Goths, their *skapjam* and *matjam*
   and *drinkam*,
Harshly resound: in such din who could fit verses indite?
Calliopé, sweet Muse, from the wine-wet embraces of Bacchus
Shrinks, lest her wavering feet bear her no longer aright.'

17. BARBARIAN LIFE. *The young Frankish
chief and his retinue* [1].

'Sidonius wishes health to his friend Domnitius.

'You are fond of inspecting armour and armed men. What a pleasure it would be for you could you see the royal youth Sigismer, decked out like a suitor or a bridegroom, in all the bravery of his tribe, visiting the palace of his father-in-law, his own horse gorgeously caparisoned, other horses, laden with blazing gems, going before or following after him; and then, with a touch of modesty which was especially suitable to his circumstances, in the midst of his outriders and rearguard, he himself walked on foot, in crimson robe with burnished golden ornaments and white silken mantle, his ruddy cheeks, his golden hair, his milk-white skin repeating in his person those three colours of his dress. Of all the petty kings and confederates who accompanied him, the appearance was terrible

---

words—*hails*, 'your health' (the drinking shout, also found in 'wassail'); *skapjan*, 'to make or frame;' *matjan*, 'to eat;' *drinkan*, 'to drink,' together with *jah*, the Gothic 'and,' which takes at the end by assimilation the letter of the following word.

[1] Ep. iv. 20. The assignment of a Frankish nationality to Sigismer is only a probable conjecture. Domnitius or Domnicius, the correspondent to whom this letter is addressed, is the enthusiastic dice-player of the first letter. (See p. 322.)

even in their peaceful garb; they had the lower part of the foot down to the heel bound about with boots of bristly ox-leather, while their knees and their calves were without covering. Above, they had garments coming high up the neck, tight-girdled, woven of various colours, scarcely approaching their bare legs; their sleeves draped only the beginning of their arms, they had green cloaks adorned with purple fringes; their swords, depending from their shoulders by baldrics, pressed in to their sides the reindeer's skins [1], which were fastened by a round clasp. As for that part of their adornments which was also a defence, their right hands held hooked lances and battle-axes for throwing, their left sides were overshadowed by round shields whose lustre, silvery at the outer circumference and golden at the central boss, declared the wealth as well as the taste of the wearers. All was so ordered that this wedding procession suggested the thought of Mars not less emphatically than of Venus.

'But why spend so many words on the subject? All that was wanting to the show was your presence. For when I remembered that you were not looking upon a sight which it would have so delighted you to behold, I translated your feelings into my own, and longed for you as impatiently as you would have longed for the spectacle. Farewell.'

It is interesting, but somewhat perplexing, to observe that some of the details of the dress of these undoubtedly Teutonic warriors would fit equally well with the Celtic Highlanders of Scotland.

[1] The 'rheno,' or reindeer's skin, seems to have answered the same purpose as the 'waterproof' of modern civilisation, and, like it, when not actually in use, would be rolled up and slung over the shoulder.

18. BARBARIAN LIFE. *The Saxon Sea-rovers* [1].

At the end of a long letter, written by Sidonius to his friend Nammatius, after dull compliments and duller banter, we suddenly find flashed upon us this life-like picture, by a contemporary hand, of the brothers and cousins of the men, if not of the very men themselves who had fought at Aylesford under Hengest and Horsa, or who were slowly winning the kingdom of the South Saxons.

'Behold, when I was on the point of concluding this epistle in which I have already chattered on too long, a messenger suddenly arrived from Saintonge with whom I have spent some hours in conversing about you and your doings, and who constantly affirms that you have just sounded your trumpet on board the fleet, and that, combining the duties of a sailor and a soldier, you are roaming along the winding shores of the Ocean, looking out for the curved pinnaces of the Saxons [2]. When you see the rowers of that nation you may at once make up your mind that every one of them is an arch-pirate; with such wonderful unanimity do all at once command, obey, teach, and learn their one chosen business of brigandage. For this reason I ought to warn you to be more than ever on your guard in this warfare. Your enemy is the most truculent of all enemies. Unexpectedly he attacks, when expected he escapes, he despises those who seek to block his path, he overthrows those who are off their guard, he

---

[1] Ep. viii. 6. In the early part of this letter Sidonius gives that description of the inaugural oration of Nicetius which has been already quoted. (See p. 306.)

[2] 'Contra Saxonum pandos myoparones.'

always succeeds in cutting off the enemy whom he follows, while he never fails when he desires to effect his own escape. Moreover, to these men a shipwreck is capital practice rather than an object of terror. The dangers of the deep are to them, not casual acquaintances, but intimate friends. For since a tempest throws the invaded off their guard, and prevents the invaders from being descried from afar, they hail with joy the crash of waves on the rocks, which gives them their best chance of escaping from other enemies than the elements.

' Then again, before they raise the deep-biting anchor from the hostile soil, and set sail from the Continent for their own country, their custom is to collect the crowd of their prisoners together, by a mockery of equity to make them cast lots which of them shall undergo the iniquitous sentence of death, and then at the moment of departure to slay every tenth man so selected by crucifixion, a practice which is the more lamentable because it arises from a superstitious notion that they will thus ensure for themselves a safe return [1]. Purifying themselves as they consider by such sacrifices, polluting themselves as we deem by such deeds of sacrilege, they think the foul murders which they thus commit are acts of worship to their gods, and they glory in extorting cries of agony instead of ransoms from these doomed victims.

' Wherefore I am on your behalf distraught with many fears and various forebodings ; though on the other hand I have immense incitements to hope, first,

[1] Compare with this statement the classical legend concerning the sacrifice of Iphigenia at Aulis to procure favourable winds for the Grecian fleet.

because you are fighting under the banner of a victorious nation ; secondly, because I hold that the power of chance is limited over wise men, among whom you are rightly reckoned ; thirdly, because it is often when our friends at a distance are the safest that our hearts are filled with the most sinister presentiments regarding them. . . . .

' I send you the Libri Logistorici [1] of Varro, and the Chronology of Eusebius, a kind of literary file with which, if you have any leisure amidst the cares of the camp, you may rub off some of the rust from your style after you have wiped the blood from your armour. Farewell.'

19. BARBARIAN LIFE. *The woman wrongfully enslaved.*

The following account of the captivity and bondage of a poor woman of Auvergne incidentally illustrates the troubled condition of Gaul, while it astonishes us by the legal doctrine contained in it. Apparently the maxim with which our own courts are familiar, that ' a *bonâ-fide* purchaser of stolen property, without notice of the theft, may justify his holding,' even applied to the most outrageous of all thefts, that of liberty ; and a woman wrongfully enslaved, but in the hands of a *bonâ-fide* purchaser, could not claim her freedom.

' Sidonius wishes health to " Pope " Lupus [2].

' After that expression of homage which is endlessly

---

[1] A lost work, satirising the manners of the time.

[2] Ep. vi. 4. This is Lupus, Bishop of Troyes, the fascinator of Attila. (See p. 122.)

due, though it be unceasingly paid, to your incomparably eminent Apostleship, I take advantage of our
old friendship to set before you the new calamities of
the humble bearers of this letter, who, after having
undertaken a long journey, and at this time of the
year, into the heart of Auvergne, have returned with
no fruit of their labour. A woman who was nearly
related to them was by chance carried off by an inroad
of the Vargi [1]—a name borne by some local banditti—
and was taken some years ago into your district and
there sold. This they ascertained on indubitable evidence, and followed tardily but surely the indications
which they had received. But in the meantime, before
they arrived upon the scene, she, having been sold in
market overt, was living as a household slave in the
family of our friend the merchant [2]. A certain Prudens
who, they say, is now living at Troyes, appeared to
vouch for the contract of her sale, which was effected
by men unknown to me, and his subscription, as
that of a fit and proper witness [3], is now shown
attached to the deed of sale. You who are present
on the spot will, from your exalted position, be easily
able to test each link in this chain of wrongful acts.
The affair is all the more criminal because, as I am
informed by the bearers of this letter, one of the
woman's fellow-travellers was actually killed when she
was carried off.

[1] Apparently these were Teutonic depredators. *Vargs* is found in
Old High German with the signification ' an outlaw,' and *vargitha* in
the Gothic translation of the Bible by Ulfilas = ' condemnation '
(Romans xiii. 2).

[2] ' Negotiatoris nostri,' apparently an allusion to some merchant
known both to Sidonius and Lupus.

[3] Or guarantor, ' adstipulator.'

'But since the relations, who brood over this criminal affair, desire that your judgment should apply the remedy, I think it will be befitting both to your office and your character to devise some compromise whereby you may at the same time assist the grief of one party and the peril of the other. By some wise and well-considered sentence you may thus make the former less distressed, the latter less guilty, and both more secure; lest otherwise, such is the disturbed state of the times and the district, the affair go on to an end as fatal as was its beginning. Condescend to remember me, my lord Pope.'

20. BARBARIAN LIFE. *The 'Levite' of Auvergne*[1].

Another illustration of the sufferings of the poorer inhabitants from the storms of barbarian conquest, is afforded by the following letter of intercession on behalf of a man of 'the Levitical order.' By this term Sidonius probably means to indicate a person who, though married, and working for his livelihood, filled (like Amantius the fortune-hunter) the office of *Lector* (reader) in the church.

'Sidonius wishes health to Pope Censorius [Bishop of Auxerre].

'The bearer of this letter is dignified by an office which raises him into the Levitical order. He with his family in avoiding the whirlpool of Gothic depredation, was swept, so to say, by the very weight of the stream of fugitives, into your territory; and there, on the possessions of the church over which your holiness presides, the hungry stranger threw into the half-

[1] Ep. vi. 10.

ploughed sods his scanty seeds, the produce of which he now begs that he may be allowed to reap without deductions. If you should be inclined to grant him as a servant of the faith this favour, namely, that he shall not be required to pay the quota which is due to the glebe, the poor man, whose notions are as bounded as his fortune, will think himself as well-off as if he was again tilling his native fields. If, therefore, you can let him off the lawful and customary rent, payable out of his very trifling harvest, he will return from your country as thankful as if he had been splendidly entertained. If you will also by his hands bestow upon me with your wonted courtesy a reply to this letter, I and my brethren living here will receive that written page as if it had come straight down from heaven. Condescend to remember me, my lord Pope.'

With this notice of the poor expatriated 'Levite' we finish our study of the social life of the falling Empire as pourtrayed from the works of Apollinaris Sidonius. But little effort is required to draw the necessary inferences from the condition of the Gallo-Romans to that of the Italians. From the shores of Como or Maggiore, as from the mountains of Auvergne, may many a needy tiller of the soil have been 'swept away by the tide of flight from the conquering Visi-goths.' Many a Neapolitan or Tarentine woman of Greek descent and Italian nationality may have been carried away like the poor Gaulish woman by wild marauders following in the track of the invading armies, sold as a slave, and not even the place of her bondage discovered for years by her friends. The habits of the Saxon freebooters may help us to under-stand the life of bold piratical adventure led by the

Vandals, though we must not attribute the harsher features of heathen savagery to the Arian followers of Gaiseric. And in the pictures of the court and retinue of Theodoric and Sigismer we have probably some strokes which will be equally applicable to every Teuton chief who led his men over the Alpine passes into Italy, from Alaric to Alboin.

It is impossible not to think with regret of the wasted opportunities of Apollinaris Sidonius. Here is a man who evidently hungered and thirsted for literary distinction even more than for consular dignity or saintly canonisation. Yet he has achieved nothing beyond a fifth-rate position as a 'post-classical' author, and with difficulty do a few historical enquirers, like Gibbon, Guizot, Thierry, keep his name from being absolutely forgotten by the world. Had he faced the new and strange nationalities which were swarming forth from Germany, in the simple, enquiring, child-like attitude of the Father of History, he might have been the Herodotus of Mediaeval and Modern Europe. From him we might have learned the songs which were sung by the actual contemporaries of Attila and Gundahar, and which formed the kernel of the Niebelungen-Lied ; from him we might have received a true and authentic picture of the laws and customs of the Goths, the Franks, and the Burgundians, a picture which would have in turn illustrated and been illustrated by the poetry of Tacitus' Germania, and the prose of the Black-letter commentators on English Common Law. He might have transmitted to us the full portraiture of the great Apostle of the Germanic races, Ulfilas, the secret causes of his and their devotion to the Arian form of Christianity, the Gothic

equivalents of the mythological tales of the Scandinavian Edda, the story of the old Runes and their
relation to the Moeso-Gothic Alphabet.   All these
details and a hundred more, full of interest to Science,
to Art, to Literature, Sidonius might have preserved
for us, had his mind been as open as was that of
Herodotus to the manifold impressions made by
picturesque and strange nationalities.   But he turned
away with disgust from the seven-foot high barbarians,
smelling of leeks and onions, and by preference told
over again for the hundredth time and worse than any
of his predecessors, the vapid and worn-out stories
of Greek mythology.   Most truly has our own Wordsworth said,

> ' We live by Admiration, Hope, and Love,
>   And even as these are well and wisely fixed
>   In dignity of being we ascend [1].'

For want of the first two qualities and others which
spring up around them, Sidonius has missed one of the
grandest opportunities ever offered in literature.

[1] Excursion, book iv.

CHAPTER IV.

AVITUS, THE CLIENT OF THE VISIGOTHS.

Authorities.

Sources :—

OUR chief authority is of course SIDONIUS, the son-in-law and flatterer of the Emperor.

The chroniclers IDATIUS, VICTOR TUNNUNENSIS, and (especially) ANONYMUS CUSPINIANI, notice this reign in their usual brief terms. MARCELLINUS is silent about it, reflecting probably the hostile feelings of the Eastern Court towards the new Emperor. A new chronicler, MARIUS, Bishop of Aventicum (Avenches in Switzerland), takes up the work of Prosper and continues it down to the year 581. He appears to have been born about 530, and to have died after a twenty years' episcopate in 594. (See Monod's *Études critiques sur les sources de l'Histoire Mérovingienne*, p. 153.) He is thus in no sense a contemporary, but he occasionally supplies some useful details, especially as to the movements of the Burgundians, who were masters of Switzerland at the period which we are now considering.

JOANNES ANTIOCHENUS, an Eastern chronicler of the seventh century, throws some additional light on the fall of Avitus.

GREGORY of Tours, born probably in 538, who began his History of the Franks about 576, and died about 595 [1], adds some little information, of a questionable kind.

---

[1] The new edition of Gregory of Tours, in the Monumenta Germaniae Historica, accepts the date of 594, which Monod assigns for the death of Gregory (op. cit. p. 38). But the arguments for the date 595, alleged by Clinton, Fasti Romani, i. 834, do not seem to me to be fully answered.

MARCIAN.

LEO.

ZENO.

BASILISCUS.

AVITUS.

MAJORIAN.

LIB. SEVERUS.

ANTHEMIUS.

OLYBRIUS.

GLYCERIUS.

JULIUS NEPOS.

ROMULUS AUGUSTULUS.

F. J. Lees Delt

For the Delegates of the Clarendon Press, Oxford.

EASTERN AND WESTERN EMPERORS.

FIFTH CENTURY. A.D. 450-476.

WHEN Gaiseric and his Vandal horde withdrew from the scene of their depredations, silence and prostration seem to have fallen upon the city of Rome. There was no attempt to raise a new Emperor to the dignity which had been held by the murdered Valentinian and the murdered Maximus : possibly no one was found courageous enough to offer himself for so perilous a preëminence. So in the heart of the once arrogant Queen of the World reigned for two months the apathy of despair. At length on the fourteenth of August, some two months after the capture of the city, the news arrived that the Gaulish provinces had raised to the vacant throne a nobleman of Auvergne, named Avitus [1], who had assumed the purple at Arles on the tenth of July. The Imperial City bowed her head and accepted her new lord without remonstrance.

455.
State of Rome after the departure of the Vandals.

Avitus had already once played a conspicuous part in Imperial politics when it had devolved upon him to cement that alliance between Rome and the Visigoths by which the power of Attila was shattered on the

Birth and childhood of Avitus.

[1] FAMILY OF AVITUS.

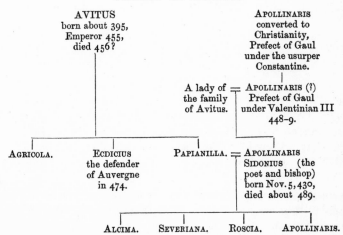

AVITUS
born about 395,
Emperor 455,
died 456 ?

APOLLINARIS
converted to
Christianity,
Prefect of Gaul
under the usurper
Constantine.

A lady of = APOLLINARIS (?)
the family   Prefect of Gaul
of Avitus.   under Valentinian III
             448–9.

AGRICOLA.   ECDICIUS   PAPIANILLA. = APOLLINARIS
              the defender   SIDONIUS (the
              of Auvergne   poet and bishop)
              in 474.   born Nov. 5, 430,
                                             died about 489.

ALCIMA.   SEVERIANA.   ROSCIA.   APOLLINARIS.

Mauriac plains. We are in possession of some other
details of his previous life, but they come to us from
the pen of a great manufacturer of indiscriminate
panegyric, and it is not easy to say what are the actual
events to which they correspond. He was descended
from a family, several members of which had held high
commands in the army and the state, and which was,
by the labours of antiquaries, connected with the old
patrician families of Rome[1]. He was born, in all
probability, about the time of the death of Theodosius,
and would therefore be close upon his sixtieth year
when he arrayed himself with the Imperial purple[2].
It was told of him that in early boyhood he came one
day upon a she-wolf, rabid with hunger, and snatching
up a fragment of rock which lay close by, hurled it at
the savage creature and broke her skull. To the studies
of Cicero and Caesar which engaged his childhood,
succeeded in youth the delights of boar-hunting and
falconry. Yet his reading had perhaps not been wholly
fruitless, for he had scarcely arrived at man's estate,
when, being chosen by his neighbours to head a deputation to Constantius, he pleaded so eloquently for

395.

---

[1] This is the explanation I would suggest of the difficult lines—

> ' Gentisque suae, te teste, Philagri,
>   Patricius resplendet apex.'
>
> Sidonius, Carm. vii. 156–157.

Philagrius was a man of letters, renowned for the magnificence of his
library (Carm. xxiv. 93). Unless the question related to the *ancient*
Patriciate of Rome and Avitus' shadowy descent therefrom, it is
difficult to see why Philagrius should be avouched as an authority.

[2] We get the approximate date of the birth of Avitus from the
fact that he was a very young man ('ephebus') when he was sent
on a deputation to Constantius, who was not yet married to Placidia,
probably therefore about 415. This points to 394 or 395 for the
year of his birth.

some remission of taxation that the admiring Governor granted all his requests.

In middle life he served with some credit under the His military exploits. greatest captain of the age, Aetius, in the wars which he waged in Belgic Gaul, and in Noricum, on the Lower Rhine, and the Middle Danube. Once at least he exposed his person to some danger in a hand-to-hand encounter. The Roman generals were at this time (about the year 439) with marvellous impolicy bringing the Hunnish hordes into Gaul to fight their battles against less barbarous barbarians. Litorius, that rash and feather-headed general, was marching a troop of these squalid auxiliaries through Auvergne, on his way from Brittany, which he had conquered, to the Gothic capital Toulouse, which he hoped to conquer. The so-called auxiliaries of Rome carried fire and sword, insolence and robbery, through the province which was conspicuous above all others by its fidelity to Rome. One of these wild mercenaries happened to quarrel with a man engaged in the service of Avitus, and struck him a mortal blow. The man in dying breathed his master's name, and coupled with it a prayer for vengeance. Avitus, when informed of his servant's death, at once donned his armour and sought the Hunnish camp. We need not believe the strained language of the Panegyrist, who solemnly informs us that in his rage for his murdered servant he slew as many of the Huns as Achilles slew Trojans after the death of Patroclus: but we seem bound to accept his story of the future Emperor's single combat with the murderer, which ended, after the third passage of arms, in Avitus breaking the Hun's breastplate, and trans-fixing his breast with his spear, which being thrust

vigorously home, stood out behind the back of the
caitiff. 'The blood and the life together ebbed away
through the double wound.'

Shortly after this event, Avitus, who had already
held three commands in the army, was raised to the
high civil office of Praetorian Prefect in Gaul, an office
which may perhaps have occupied six years of his life,
from 439 to 445. From these duties he retired to his
estate in the heart of Auvergne, to that very villa of
Avitacum overlooking the lake, and overlooked by the
mountains, of which we have already heard a description from the pen of its next possessor, Sidonius.
For the family of Avitus consisted of two sons, Ecdicius
and Agricola, and one daughter, Papianilla. This
daughter is the lady whom Sidonius married about
the year 452, and most of our information about the
career, as well as the dwelling-place of the Arvernian
Emperor, is derived from the verses or the letters of
his fluent son-in-law.

The connection which most powerfully influenced
the life of Avitus, and which alone gave him any
chance, a small one at the best, of being remembered
in history, was a friendship which, while still a boy, he
formed with the Visigothic monarch at Toulouse, and
which on the side of the barbarian was continued into
a second generation. A brother of the young Arvernian, named Theodorus, had been sent as a hostage to
the court of Theodoric I. Avitus went to Toulouse to
visit Theodorus, and by some unexplained charm of
manner, or beauty of character, so won upon the
Gothic king that he offered him large sums of money
if he would renounce his Gallo-Roman nationality, and
take up his permanent residence at the court of

Toulouse. This offer was rejected, scornfully rejected, says his panegyrist; but there is some reason to think that Avitus may have discharged for a time the duties of Governor to the young Visigothic princes[1]. His powerful intercession is said to have saved Narbonne (436) when sorely blockaded by the barbarian arms, and at the last stage of famine. And on a more eventful day (in 451), as has been already described, Avitus was the chosen intermediary between Rome and Toulouse, the man who by his personal influence with Theodoric I, did more than any other single individual to mould the great Roman-Gothic alliance against Attila, which saved Europe from becoming Tartar.

That alliance had done its work, and apparently was dissolved, when the terror from the Hun was over. But the thought probably suggested itself both to the new Visigothic king, Theodoric II, and to his Gaulish friend, that it might be revived, and might serve a useful purpose for both of them in the troubled state of Roman politics after the murder of Valentinian III. Avitus had been drawn by the Emperor Maximus from his retirement, and invested with the office of *Magister utriusque Militiae* (Captain-General of horse and foot), which gave him complete control over all military matters in Gaul. The three-months' reign of Maximus had been well employed by the new general in checking the inroads of the tribes dwelling by the lower Rhine, and his credit with the soldiers and the provincials was

[margin note: Utilised for the formation of a new Triple Alliance.]

---

[1] Sidonius makes Theodoric II say to Avitus—

> 'Mihi Romula dudum
> Per te jura placent, *parvumque ediscere jussit*
> *Ad tua verba pater*, docili quo prisca Maronis
> Carmine molliret Scythicos mihi pagina mores.'
>
> Carm. vii. 495-8.

at a high point, when tidings arrived in Gaul of the
Vandal sack of Rome and the vacancy of the Empire.

455.

Possibly the young oratorical son-in-law, Sidonius, was
employed to furbish up the old friendship with the
Visigoth, and he may have gained a point or two for
the aspirant to the purple by diplomatically losing a
few games on the backgammon-board of Theodoric.

Chief
barbarian
nations of
Western
Europe at
this time.

Four great Germanic nations were at this time
supreme in Western Europe : the Vandals, the Visigoths, the Burgundians, and the Suevi. A fifth, that
of the Franks, one day to be the mightiest of them all,
was as yet scarcely peeping over the horizon. The
Vandals, as we know, ruled Africa from Carthage, the
Visigoths South-Western France from Toulouse, the
Burgundians were settled in the valley of the Rhone,
and their chief capital was Lyons ; the Suevi held the
greater part of Southern and Western Spain, and their
capital was Astorga. The Vandals and Visigoths were
sworn foes ever since the cruel outrage practised by
Gaiseric on his Visigothic daughter-in-law. The Burgundians and Visigoths lived in a state of simmering
unfriendliness, not often passing into vindictive war.
The Suevi, who were now by the departure of the
Vandals the only barbarian power left in the Peninsula,
carried on a desultory warfare with Roman Spain, but
at this time were living at peace with their Visigothic
neighbours from whom they were divided by the
Pyrenees, and their king Rechiarius had married a
sister of the reigning Theodoric.

Such being the position of affairs, the transaction
which suggested itself, at some time in the summer of
455, to the minds of the most powerful men at Arles
and Toulouse must have been something of this nature,

'Let us join forces and form a Triple Alliance. To you, Avitus, shall fall the Imperial Purple : we Visigoths will assert your claims against any other competitor, and if need be, protect you against the hated Vandal. In return for this you shall lend us the sanction of the name and the rights of the Empire for an enterprise which we are meditating against the Suevi. Though we have been settled for the last half century chiefly on the Northern side of the Pyrenees, we have never entirely renounced the hope of including Spain in our dominion. That was the vision of the great Ataulfus, brother-in-law of Alaric, that and the welding of Roman and Visigoth into one harmonious commonwealth ; and if we can now make this compact with you, our nobler and firmer Attalus, his vision may yet become a reality. And lastly, if you, Burgundians, instead of harassing us by your aimless warfare, will join our great expedition, the territories in the valley of the Rhone, which you now hold by a friendly compact with the Empire, shall be enlarged—does not the new Augustus consent to this ?—and it may be that you shall reach even to the Mediterranean Sea.'

Such was probably the honest prose of the transaction which raised the nobleman of Auvergne to the headship of the Empire; but in diplomacy and in poetry it of course assumes a very different aspect. The Visigothic king, no doubt in collusion with Avitus, threatened an invasion of Roman Gaul. The Master of the Soldiery assembled his troops, but consented to assume once more the office of ambassador to Toulouse, in order to avert the horrors of war from the provincials. He sent before him Messianus, a high functionary of Gaul. At the appearance of this messenger,

455.

many a sturdy Visigoth, intent on the rapture of coming war, foreboded that the magical influence of Avitus would again prevail, and that they would be balked of the hoped-for struggle. Soon their fears were confirmed. The Master himself appeared on the scene erect and stately. Theodoric came forth to greet him, attended by his brother Frithareiks[1] (the king of peace). His welcome to the Roman was eager but confused ; and the three, with joined hands, entered the gates of Toulouse. It was a fortunate coincidence (if it was a mere coincidence) that just as they entered the town the news arrived of the murder of the Emperor Maximus, and the capture of Rome by Gaiseric—news which considerably improved the prospects of the new partnership.

The Visigothic Council.

On the next day a grand council of the Visigothic warriors was held. From necessity rather than choice, the veteran chiefs who assembled there did not reflect the magnificence of the sovereign. Their robes were threadbare and greasy, their scanty skin-cloaks scarcely reached down to the knee, and their boots, made of horse's hide, were hitched up around the calf by a shabbily-tied knot[2]. So were the men attired whose ' honoured poverty ' was welcomed into the councils of the nation.

The Gothic king questioned the Roman officer as to the terms of the peace which he was come to propose

---

[1] Our ' Frederick.' But it may have been Euric, or another brother.

[2]   ' Squalent vestes ac sordida macro
    Lintea pinguescunt tergo, nec tangere possunt
    Altatae suram pelles, ac poplite nudo
    Peronem pauper nodus suspendit equinum.'
                    Sidonius, Carm. vii. 454–7.

between the two nations. Avitus replied, dilating on
the old friendship which had existed between him and
the first Theodoric. ' He, I am sure, would not have
denied my request. You were a child then, and cannot
remember how he, in compliance with my advice, withdrew his blockading army from Narbonne, when that
city was already pale with famine, and was forced to
feed upon the most loathsome victuals.'

> ' E'en thou—as well these hoary chieftains know—
> In those young days beheld'st in me no foe.
> Oft have I pressed thee, weeping, to my heart,
> When thy nurse came, refusing to depart.
> Now once again I come thy faith to prove,
> And plead the rights of that ancestral love.
> If faith, affection, filial reverence die,
> Go ! hard of heart, and peace to Rome deny.'

So far Avitus : a murmur of rough voices through
the council testified their approbation of his pleadings
for peace. The next lines in the play fell to Theodoric ;
and he spoke his part with great animation and correctness. He enlarged on his old friendship for Avitus, his
reluctance to break off that friendship, his willingness
to serve ' the venerable might of Rome and the race
which, like his own, had sprung from Mars,' his desire
even to wipe out the memory of the guilt of Alaric by
the benefits which he would confer on the Eternal
City. But there was one price which must be paid for
his services. If Avitus would assume the diadem, the
Empire should have in the Visigoth the most faithful of
allies : if not, the war once proclaimed must rage on.
If the General wished to save the world, he must
govern it [1].

[1]   ' Tibi pareat orbis

Ni pereat.'   (Sidonius, Carm. vii. 517–18.)

The Master of the Soldiery heard these words, which were ratified by the solemn oath of the royal brothers, with an appearance of profound sadness. He returned to Arles, whither the tidings preceded him, that the desired peace with the Goths could only be obtained by the elevation of Avitus to the Imperial dignity. The chief officials of Gaul were hastily summoned to the Castle of Ugernum (now Beaucaire, on the Rhone, a few miles above Arles); the proposal to declare Avitus emperor was carried by acclamation, vanity perhaps concurring with policy in the scheme of giving a Gaulish ruler to Rome [1]. On the third day after the assembly at Ugernum Avitus appeared upon a high-heaped *agger* [2] surrounded by the soldiery, who put upon his head a military collar, to represent the true Imperial diadem, which was probably in safe custody at Ravenna. The new Augustus wore still the same melancholy countenance with which he had first listened to the flattering proposal of Theodoric; and it is possible that by this time the sadness may have been not all feigned, some conviction of his own inability to cope with the weight of the falling Commonwealth having already entered his soul.

The story of Avitus' elevation to the throne has seemed worth telling, because it illustrates the manner in which the great barbarian monarchies influenced the

455.
Return of
Avitus to
Arles,

and eleva-
tion to the
Imperial
dignity.

No details
as to the
reign of
Avitus.

---

[1] I have not thought it worth while to extract Sidonius' description of the Roman, as well as the Gothic, assembly, but a few words in the speech of a Gaulish noble are worth transcribing—

'Has nobis inter clades ac funera mundi
Mors vixisse fuit.'

[2] An earthen mound. In the bas-reliefs on the column of Trajan, the Emperor is generally represented as standing on such a mound when addressing his soldiers.

fortunes of the dying Empire, the degrees in which
Force and Art were still blended in order to secure
obedience to its behests, and the nature of the tie
which bound those later 'Shadow-Emperors' to their
by no means shadowy Patrons. But of the reign of this
Emperor, which lasted only sixteen months, we have
but a few faint details from the Annalists, which leave
us little more to say than that he reigned, and that he
ceased to reign.

The autumn of 455 was probably employed in an
expedition to the province of Pannonia, an expedition
which, we are asked to believe, reunited to the Empire
regions which had been lost to it for generations.   It is
possible that in the complete collapse of Attila's power,
Rome may have successfully reclaimed some portions of
her ancient dominion by the Danube ; but it is difficult
to conjecture the motives which could have sent the
new Emperor forth on so distant an expedition, while
the terrible and unsubdued Vandal was still crouching
at his gates ready to repeat his spring.

On the first day of the year 456 Rome witnessed the
usual splendid pageant which announced that the
supreme Augustus condescended to assume the historic
office of consul, and to mark the year with his name [1].

---

[1] There is an explained puzzle here. Avitus' name does *not* appear
in the Consular Fasti for the year 456, except in the Chronicles of
Idatius the Spaniard.   All other chroniclers assign the year to
'Joannes and Varanes.'   Tillemont suggests that Marcian, Emperor
of the East, refused his sanction to the elevation of Avitus; but this
does not seem a probable solution of the difficulty, especially as
Idatius says, 'Marcian and Avitus enjoyed the headship of the Roman
Empire in concord.'   Can there have been on the fall of Avitus some
judicial process like the English attainder, erasing his name from the
lists both of consuls and patricians ?   This might help to explain the

456.
Panegyric
of Sidonius.

Among the solemnities of the day, the young Sidonius recited, in the hearing of the Senate and the people [1], a panegyric 602 lines long, after the manner of Claudian, which he had composed in honour of his father-in-law [2]. This panegyric is the source—the doubtful source, it must be admitted—from which have been drawn the facts previously related concerning the private life of the Arvernian Senator and the manner of his elevation to the throne. The attempt to emulate Claudian's panegyrics on Honorius and Stilicho is evident, but the failure to reach even Claudian's standard of excellence is equally evident. The old, worn-out mythological machinery is as freely used, and with even less of dramatic fitness and truth. Jupiter convokes an assembly of the gods; all the Olympians of the first and second rank attend it. Thither also come all the great river-gods of the world [3], the Rhine, the Po, the Danube, the Nile. And thither at last, with bent head and flagging steps, without a helmet, and scarce able to drag the weight of her heavy lance, comes unhappy

difficulty as to the non-patrician rank of the family of Avitus. See note to p. 376.

[1]
    'Sistimus portu geminae potiti
        Fronde coronae
    Quam mihi indulsit populus Quirini
    Blattifer vel quam tribuit Senatus
    Quam peritorum dedit ordo consors
        Judiciorum.'   (Ep. ix. 16.)

Is it possible that the last two lines can refer to a still existing order of knights, still theoretically invested with the Judicia?

[2] This is now seventh of the 'Carmina' of Sidonius, which are not arranged in order of date.

[3] The last of these is happily enough described—
    'The Nile whom all know for his source unknown.'
    '— et ignotum plus notus Nile per ortum.'

Rome. She begins at first with some naturalness and spirit, longing for the happy days when she was still small, obscure, and safe, before greatness had brought its harassing penalty. She recurs with dread to the omen of the twelve vultures seen by the Etrurian augur on Mount Palatine at the foundation of the city. If those twelve vultures did truly mean, as some supposed, that she should have twelve centuries of greatness, her day is done, for the allotted time expired eight years ago (in A.D. 447).

456.

Soon, however, the unhappy Queen of the World wanders off into mere Roman history. She repeats to great Jove a versified compendium of Livy, and condenses the lives of the first twelve Caesars into an equal number of lines, which might have been prepared as a *Memoria Technica* by a Roman schoolboy.

The father of gods and men takes up the tale, and shows that he is not to be outdone in knowledge of Livy and Tacitus. Then, having vindicated his scholarship, he tells her that he has prepared a man for her deliverance, born in Auvergne, a land fertile in heroes. This destined deliverer is Avitus, whose respectable life and fortunes Jupiter describes in 460 lines of unbroken monologue. We listen in weariness to the long, level narrative, and think what a change has come over the Court of Olympus since, in a few majestic words, the Thunderer granted the earnest prayer of silver-footed Thetis. Then Jupiter nodded, now his hearers.

To the taste of the Romans of the fifth century, however, the fluent hexameters of the young Gaulish poet probably appeared really meritorious. At any rate they were written by the son-in-law of Augustus, and consequently every good courtier was bound to

Sidonius rewarded by the erection of a statue.

admire them.   The Senate decreed that 'an everlasting
statue' of brass should be raised in honour of Apollinaris
Sidonius, which should stand between the Greek and
Latin libraries in the Forum of Trajan [1].

While the new Emperor was thus inaugurating his
reign at Rome, his powerful patron at Toulouse was
using the new alliance for his own purposes.   Embassies
passed to and fro between the king of the Visigoths and
the king of the Suevi.   The former, whose messengers
were accompanied by the Gaulish Count Fronto, as
representative of Rome, called upon his Suevic brother-
in-law to cease from the attacks which he had been
lately making on Roman Spain, the Empire and the
Visigothic monarchy being now united in mutual
league, and the invaders of the one being the enemies
of the other.   To this embassy Rechiarius returned a
haughty answer : 'If thou complainest of what I am
doing here, I will come to Tholosa where thou dwellest ;
there, if thou art strong enough, resist me.'   This
insolent defiance hastened the warlike preparations
of Theodoric.   Early in the year 456 (apparently) he
invaded Spain with an enormous army, to which the
two kings of the Burgundians, Gundiok and Chilperic,
brought their promised contingent ; and he was able to
assert (probably thereby commanding some assistance
from wavering provincials) that he came 'with the will
and by the ordinance of Avitus the Emperor.'

Margin notes:
456.

War be-
tween Visi-
goths and
Suevi.

[1]   'Cum meis poni *statuam perennem*
Nerva Trajanus titulis videret
Inter auctores utriusque fixam
         Bibliothecae.'   (Sidonius, Ep. ix. 16.)
'Nil vatum prodest adjectum laudibus illud
    Ulpia quod rutilat porticus *aere meo.*'
                              (Sidonius, Carm. viii. 7–8.)

This campaign destroyed the greatness of the Suevic kingdom [1]. Rechiarius was defeated in a great battle at the river Urbicus, twelve miles from Astorga (5th October). Theodoric pushed on to Braga, took that place on the twenty-eighth of October, and though that day was a Sunday, and the victory had been a blood-less one as far as his host was concerned, he used his success in a manner which horrified his contemporaries; carried off vast numbers of men, women, and children into captivity, stripped the clergy naked, filled the holy places 'with horrors of horses, cattle, and camels,' and in short repeated all the judgments which the wrath of God had suffered to fall on Jerusalem. The fugitive Rechiarius was taken prisoner next year 'at a place called Portucale' (Oporto), and after some months' captivity, was put to death by his vindictive brother-in-law, who could not forget his insulting message about the visit to Toulouse.

456.

While Theodoric was thus engaged with the Suevi, news was brought to him of an important victory which his Imperial ally had gained over the Vandals. Sixty of their ships had set sail from the harbour of Carthage; they had reached Corsica and cast anchor there, seeming to threaten Italy and Gaul at once. The brave and capable Count Ricimer followed them thither, out-manoeuvred and surrounded them with his fleet, and slew of them a great multitude [2].

Ricimer's victory over the Vandals.

---

[1] It lingered on, however, in an enfeebled condition for more than a century longer, till it was in 584 finally overthrown by Leovigild, king of the Visigoths.

[2] Idatius, s. a. 456, gives us this information: 'Hisdem diebus Rechimeris Comitis circumventione magna multitudo Wandalorum, quae se de Carthagine cum LX navibus ad Gallias, vel ad Italiam

456.

So far all seemed going well with the Romano-Gothic confederation, and the moment when Hesychius, the Imperial ambassador, presented himself at the camp of Theodoric in Gallicia with these tidings, with presents from the Emperor, and with the further intelligence that his master had come to Arles, probably to meet his Visigothic ally,—this moment was probably the apogee of the new combination. But there was a worm at the root of this apparent prosperity. Ricimer was after his late victory the idol of the army and the most powerful man in the Empire, and Ricimer had determined to shatter the new alliance. Nor was such a determination wonderful, since this strange and perplexing character who, for the next sixteen years, played the part of King-maker at Rome, was himself the son of a Suevic father, though of a Visigothic mother, and was not likely to hear well-pleased the tidings of the sack of Braga and the countless horrors which had befallen his countrymen at the hand of the ally of Avitus.

Disaffection of Ricimer.

Deposition of Avitus.

He resolved that the Arvernian Senator must lay aside the purple, and he probably had the popular voice with him when he pronounced Avitus unfitted for the emergencies of the Empire. The Gaulish nobleman was a man of unspotted private character, and had once possessed some courage and capacity for war, but he was fond of ease, perhaps of luxury, and the almost childlike simplicity and openness of his nature, to say nothing of his sixty years, unfitted him to cope with the lawless intriguers, Roman and Barbarian, by whom he was surrounded. Famine broke out in Rome, and for

moverat, regi Theuderico nunciatur occisa per Avitum.' 'Per Avitum' depends, I think, on 'nunciatur,' not on 'occisa.'

this the people blamed Avitus (who had now returned into Italy) and the crowd of hungry dependents whom he had brought with him from Gaul. Under popular pressure he was compelled to dismiss his Visigothic body-guard. Having no funds in his treasury wherewith to pay them, he stripped the public buildings in Rome of their copper (completing perhaps the half-finished Vandal spoliation of the temple of Jupiter Capitolinus), and turned the copper into gold for his Gothic friends. All this of course increased his unpopularity in Rome [1]. The revolt, now openly headed by Ricimer and his young comrade Majorian, spread to Ravenna. On the 17th of September, Remistus, the Patrician (an official who is otherwise unknown to us), was killed in the palace at Classis. The Emperor fled from Rome, hoping to reach his native and friendly Gaul. But he was taken prisoner at Placentia by Ricimer, who now held the all-important office of Master of the Soldiery. On the 17th of October, the Patrician, Messianus, a Gaul, and probably the intimate friend of Avitus, the same who had acted as his *avant-courier* to the court of Theodoric the year before, was put to death. Avitus himself was spared. Even the stern Ricimer could not bring himself to take the life of the innocent old man. But he was stripped of the purple, and (strange fate for an Augustus) was consecrated Bishop at Placentia. Of the name of his See [2] and of his subsequent fate we have no certain information. It seems probable that he died by a natural

456.

His consecration as Bishop,

---

[1] These particulars are derived from Joannes Antiochenus, fragment 202.

[2] It does not seem quite clear whether the chroniclers mean to describe him as ordained Bishop *at* or *of* Placentia.

death, though possibly hastened by disappointment and alarm, within a twelvemonth after he had abdicated the Empire [1]. A tradition, recorded by Gregory of Tours (who was himself a native of Auvergne), related that the forlorn Bishop-Emperor, fearful for his life, left Italy by stealth to repair to the tomb of Julian the martyr, an Arvernian saint, whose protection he hoped to purchase by rich presents, the wreck it may be of his Imperial splendour; that he died on the road, but that his body was taken and buried at the feet of the martyr in the village of Brioude in Auvergne. Few things in the fitfully-illuminated history of the times are stranger than the fulness of information which is given us as to the rise of this unfortunate Emperor, and the barrenness of the history of his fall. And yet he was the keystone of a great and important political combination, a combination which, had it endured, would certainly have changed the face of Europe, and might have anticipated the Empire of Charles the Great in favour of a nobler nation than the Franks, and without the interposition of three centuries of barbarism.

---

[1] According to Joannes Antiochenus he was either starved to death or strangled.

NOTE F. On the Alleged Immoralities of Avitus.

The charges made by Gibbon (cap. xxxvi. note 25), and repeated by his copyists, against the moral character of this Emperor, rest on no solid basis of evidence.

1. In the contemporary chroniclers there is no hint of anything of the kind.

2. Victor Tunnunensis, who, though not a contemporary (he died 569), seems to have had access to full and trustworthy sources of information, calls Avitus 'a man of entire simplicity' ('vir totius simplicitatis'). It is true that the MSS. waver here between Anitius and Avitus, but the latter is evidently intended. Again, he says that Ricimer, 'sparing the inoffensiveness of Avitus' ('cujus innocentiae parcens'), allowed him to live after he had dethroned him. No doubt these expressions are meant to be somewhat contemptuous of the intellect of Avitus, but they would hardly be used of a man who was guilty of the wanton profligacy which Gibbon ascribes to him.

3. The very fact of his ordination as bishop, at that period of the Church, and under such a strict disciplinarian as Pope Leo I, is almost a guarantee for the correctness of his private life.

What then are the opposing testimonies?

4. Gregory of Tours (ii. 11) says—'Avitus, one of the Senators, and, as is very manifest, a citizen of Auvergne, when he had schemed for the Imperial dignity of Rome, wishing to act luxuriously (luxuriosè agere volens) was cast forth by the Senate, and ordained Bishop at the city of Placentia. But finding that the Senate, still indignant, wished to deprive him of life he sought the Basilica of St. Julian, &c.'

Gregory (who died about 595) is in no sense a contemporary, and is not a first-rate authority for what happened in Italy at this period, Gaul, under the Frankish kings in the sixth century, being the ground upon which he is really strong. In this particular instance it is almost certain that he has over-stated the share of the Roman Senate and under-estimated that of Ricimer in the deposition of Avitus. It is true that Gregory, as being himself a native of Auvergne, might have some special information as to the life of his countryman. But let his authority be taken for what it is worth; it establishes, at the worst, a charge of 'luxury' against Avitus.

5. An anonymous epitomiser of Gregory, said by some to be Fredegarius (who lived in the middle of the seventh century), but of whose name and date we really know nothing, tells a disagreeable story about the capture of Trier by the Franks, which was occasioned by the dishonour inflicted by the Emperor Avitus on the lovely wife of the Senator Lucius, a crime about which the Emperor was foolish enough to jest in the hearing of the outraged husband, who, in revenge, delivered up the city to the Franks (' Dom Bouquet, Recueil des Historiens des Gaules,' ii. 395). But it is quite clear that this story, whatever its truth may be, relates to events which occurred more than forty years before Avitus' accession to the Empire, and that the insertion of his name is a mere slip on the part of the epitomiser. Paragraph VI describes the usurpation of the Imperial title by Jovinus (about 411). Paragraph VII contains the above-mentioned story about the cause of the fall of Trier, and that event, as we know from Gregory (ii. 9), also occurred in or about the year 411. Paragraph VIII mentions a campaign of Castinus against the Franks (417). Paragraph IX gives the accession of Chlodeo, assigned to 428, and the reign of his son Meroveus. Then at last in Paragraph X we have a short notice (in the words of Gregory of Tours) of the real Avitus, his luxurious life, ordination as a bishop, and death.

It is plain therefore that Paragraph VII does not relate to Avitus the Emperor, and that his name has been substituted for that of some other Roman Emperor residing at Trier, probably Jovinus, by a clerical error of the epitomiser. Gibbon's attempt to transfer the story to Rome by the remark that 'it seems more applicable to Rome than to Trier' is quite inadmissible. The story is an account of the circumstances which led to the fall of Trier, or it is nothing.

Muratori's criticism (Annali d' Italia, iii. 174) is here sounder than that of Gibbon or even of Tillemont.

Upon a review of the whole evidence it is contended that, except for a vague and feebly-supported charge of 'luxury,' the moral character of Avitus is without a stain.

[It is satisfactory to find so careful a writer as Holder-Egger entirely concurring in the view here taken : ' Avitus as Emperor can never have been in Trier, as Fredegarius represents him to have been. If a germ of historic truth, as is probable [?], lurks in this story, some confusion of persons, due to a similarity of names, must have caused it to assume its present shape. We must not follow Gibbon in considering this tale as historic fact.' Neues Archiv, ii. 274, n. 1.]

CHAPTER V.

SUPREMACY OF RICIMER.   MAJORIAN.

Authorities.

Sources :—

IT will be seen that our chief information as to this reign is
again drawn from the Poems and still more from the Letters of
SIDONIUS.

Of the Annalists IDATIUS is perhaps the least meagre, and as
the turning-point of Majorian's career was in Spain, this Spanish
bishop may be quoted with some confidence for that event.

The ANONYMUS CUSPINIANI, as usual, supplies us with dates
and PROCOPIUS with romance.

Analogy
between
the fall of
the Roman
and that
of the
Ottoman
Empire.

THERE is danger in endeavouring to illustrate the
history of a long-past age by the vivid light of modern
politics ; danger from the incompleteness of our knowledge of the present, and danger from the heat of controversy with which every topic debated by men struggling for place and power in the world of action around
us, must necessarily be environed.

But the correspondence between the position of Old
Rome at the point of her history which we have now
reached, and that of 'New Rome,' or Constantinople, at
the present day, is in some respects so close that we
are almost compelled to notice it. The obvious differences between the conditions of the two Empires are
many, but the resemblances are more, and more striking. The Roman, like the Turk, having been the
terror of the world, had become its pity. He had lost,

like the Turk, his once pre-eminent faculty of founding
Empires; he had lost the faculty of generalship, and,
unlike the Turk, he had lost the mere animal courage
of the common soldier.   A world of new and alien
nationalities was seething round him, nationalities
which had a prophetic instinct that to them and
not to him belonged the Future of Europe; nationalities whose gentlest and most friendly touch meant
ruin to the old order of things, yet nationalities
which, strange to say, did not, with one exception, wish
to destroy his Empire if by any means the breath of
life could still be preserved in· it.   What 'the Frank'
is to the Ottoman of to-day, the Barbarian was to the
subjects of Honorius and Valentinian.

I have said that there was one exception.   The
Vandal, during the last quarter of a century of the
independent life of Rome, was her one implacable
enemy.   He had had his hour of triumph in 455;
intent on pillage rather than on conquest he had not
then sought permanently to annex Italy to his Empire,
but he remained watching her death-struggles, gloating
over her feeble misery, and perhaps speculating on the
day when she would fall without effort into his hands,
and Rome be ruled as a dependency from Carthage.

We have seen some reasons for supposing that this Barbarian
result was dreaded by the other Teutonic nations in the adventurers at
West of Europe, and that political combinations, rude the Roman
Court.
and well-nigh forgotten, were formed in order to keep
Rome for the Romans, even as they have been formed
in our own day to keep Stamboul for the Turks.   But a
more undoubted point of resemblance is the career of
the many Teutonic adventurers who brought their
knowledge of war, their energy, their courage, and

sometimes their unscrupulousness to the service of the dying Empire. Merobaudes and Bauto, Arbogast and Gainas, were the prototypes of the German and English officers who in our own day have reorganised the armies or commanded the fleets of the Sultan, and led the expeditions of the Khedive. Not more strange to us probably is the affix of Pacha to an English surname than were, in the ears of the men of that generation, the titles of Consul or Patrician when borne by a full-blooded Barbarian. And these alien administrators of the State and Army of Rome resembled those 'Frankish' admirals and generals employed by the Ottoman Porte, in the knowledge that, however great the actual power which they might possess, the appearance of sovereignty would always be denied to them. As none but a lineal descendant of Othman can sit on the throne of Soliman, so, even in the most degenerate days of Rome, public opinion, if not positive law, forbade that any one who was the son of a barbarian father and a barbarian mother should be robed in the Imperial purple.

Ricimer.   Such a Romanised Teuton was *Ricimer* [1], the man

[1] FAMILY CONNECTIONS OF RICIMER.

who for sixteen years after the deposition of Avitus was virtually head of the Roman commonwealth. It is worth while to notice how intimately he was con- 456-472. nected with two if not three of the ruling barbarian families. He was the son of a Suevic father, who His family probably enough was sprung from the royal family of his nation. His mother was daughter of Walia, king of the Visigoths, the successor and avenger of Ataulfus; and his sister was married to Gundiok, king of the Burgundians. A man thus connected, and concentrating in his hand whatever yet remained of the forces and the treasure of Rome, was well placed for repelling that storm of Vandal invasion which was the most pressing danger of the Empire.

Historians are unanimous in condemning the cha- and character. racter of Ricimer, and, as we shall see, not without reason. He raised his unhappy puppets one after another to the Imperial throne, and one by one, as he grew tired of their subservience or was irritated by their opposition, was cast aside and broken by his hand. There is not a word in the Chroniclers, not a line in the venal panegyrics of Sidonius, to suggest that he had a heart accessible to any generous or tender emotion. A cold, self-seeking player with men as with counters he appears from first to last. But let us endeavour to understand what he was and why Rome bore with him. There can be little doubt that as a general he was the greatest whom the Empire could produce. That destruction of the Vandal fleet off Corsica [1], of which the Chroniclers give us such scanty details, was probably a great achievement, and one which liberated Italy and Gaul for years from the fear of another regular inva-

[1] See p. 389.

sion.   He thus succeeded, as it were of right, to that
great position in the State which had been held before
him by Stilicho and Aetius.   But both these generals
had served the Emperors only too well for their own
safety.   The feeble Honorius had compassed the death
of Stilicho ; the dissolute Valentinian had planned
the assassination of Aetius.   Ricimer resolved that his
life should not be at the mercy of any similar palace
intrigue, and as soon as any of the retainers, whom
he permitted to use the name of Caesar, showed signs
of acquiring an independent authority in the State
which might be dangerous to *his* authority and life, he
gave the word to some trusty barbarian henchman, and the
purple robe was found to be enveloping a corpse.   There
is only one thing to be said in mitigation of our abhor-
rence for this man ; and that is that he does seem to
have been faithful to Rome.   We do not find any
trace of that disposition to make a separate bargain for
himself, which so often comes out in the lives of the
statesmen of a collapsing monarchy.   Rome seems to
have understood this, to have accepted him, with all his
odious qualities, as ' the necessary man ' for the situation, and she may have owed it to this acquiescence in
his rule that the Vandal invasion, often threatened,
never actually arrived during the sixteen years of his
domination.

Ricimer [1] was probably already a man in middle life

---

[1] The name is, perhaps, the same as that of Count Richomer who
fought in the battles of Ad Salices and Hadrianople (see vol. i.
pp. 261 and 269).   The beginning seems to be the Gothic *reiks*,
which terminates Ala*ric*, Theodo*ric*, Childe*ric*, and many other Teutonic names.   The ending syllable is that which we find in the
Ostrogothic Wala-mir, the Frankish Sigis-mer, &c., and probably

when he thus came to the helm of the Roman State.
He was simply Count Ricimer when he achieved his
Corsican victory. That exploit it was, in all likelihood,
which earned for him the office of Master General of the
Soldiery. A pause ensued upon the deposition of Avitus,
perhaps in order to allow time for communications with
Byzantium, but during this interval there can be no
doubt that the Master of the Forces wielded the whole
powers of the State. In four months' time (on the
28th February, 457) Ricimer abandoned his office of
Master of the Soldiery in favour of a young general
named Majorian, while he himself assumed the proud
title of Patrician [1]. This title carried with it the right
to be called the father of the Emperor (as soon as an
Emperor should be declared) and practically a life-tenure
of the office of Prime Minister.

The extraordinary development of the power of ' the Office of the Patrician.
Patrician' is one of the unexplained changes in the constitutional history of the last days of the Empire. The
caste of Patricians had, as every one knows, lost their
exclusive civil privileges long before the close of the
Republic. Under the Empire most of the still surviving Patrician families perished by slow decay, or fell
victims to the terrible trade of the *delator* (informer).
The Emperor Constantine revived the name, not now
as an hereditary order in the State, but as a personal
dignity, conferring high honour on the wearer but
probably no power. The words of Zosimus (the only

means 'famous' (compare the Gothic ' vaila-*merjan*,' to proclaim glad-
tidings : '*meri*-tha,' fame). Thus Ricimer = 'famous ruler.'
[1] ' Constantino et Rufo Coss. Ricimer Mag. Mil. Patricius factus
est prid. Kl. Marcias. Et factus est Majorianus Mag. Mil. ipso die '
(Anon. Cuspiniani).

457.

historian apparently who describes this innovation) are these [1] : 'The dignity of Patrician was first introduced by Constantine, who passed a law that those who were honoured by it should take precedence of the Praetorian Prefects.' This enactment is lost. Only one law in the whole Theodosian Code [2], which decrees that 'even the splendour of the Patriciate' is to be considered subordinate in rank to the Consular office, mentions the name of the new dignity, which moreover does not occur from beginning to end of the 'Notitia Dignitatum.' Evidently 'the Patrician' of the fifth century, like 'the Premier' and 'the Cabinet' of our own day, was a term more familiar to the mouths of ordinary men than to the written documents of the constitution.

For the last twenty years of his life the great Aetius wore the name of Patrician ; and we may perhaps conjecture that it was during that time that men, seeing him ever the foremost figure in the state, of which he was the real ruler, came to look upon the new designation as something more than a mere title of courtesy, and upon the holder of it as an irremovable depositary of power above the moving, changing throng of Consuls and Praetorian Prefects. The words of a contemporary chronicler, describing the deposition of Avitus, 'And

---

[1] ii. 40.

[2] Lib. vi. tit. 6. The order of precedence established by Gratian in this enactment still prevailed 150 years later, when Cassiodorus compiled his 'Formulae.' The gradation was still (i) Consul, (ii) Patriciate, (iii) Praetorian Prefect. 'The great distinction of the Patriciate' (King Theodoric is made to say) 'is that it is a rank held for life, like that of the priesthood from which it sprang. The Patrician takes precedence of Prefects and of all other dignities except the Consulship, and that is one which we ourselves sometimes assume.'

his Patrician Messianus was killed [1],' seem to imply an especial connection between the Patrician and the Emperor, just as we should say 'a Colonel and his Major,' but not 'a Colonel and his Captain.' But howsoever and whensoever the peculiar pre-eminence of the Patrician began, there can be no doubt that it existed during the period which we are now considering, and that citizens of Rome must have spoken of the Patrician with at least as much awe as the citizens of Constantinople speak of the Grand Vizier, or the subjects of Louis XIII. spoke of the Cardinal.

457.

The official 'Father of the Emperor' was not long in providing himself with a son. His young comrade, Majorian, 'was raised to the Empire on the 1st of April in the camp at Columellae, at the sixth milestone' no doubt from Ravenna [2]. The Emperor Leo, who, two months before, upon the death of the brave old Marcian, had been in a somewhat similar manner raised by *his* barbarian patron Aspar to the Eastern throne, approved the choice, and the two Emperors, between whose characters there was no little resemblance, reigned together with more harmony and more unity of purpose than had often marked the counsels of Ravenna and Constantinople.

Elevation of Majorian to the Empire. 457.

The new Emperor, *Julius Valerius Majorianus*, came of an official stock. His maternal grandfather, Majorian, was Master General of the Soldiery in 379 when Theodosius was raised to the Empire. The elevation of that

Previous history of Majorian.

---

[1] ' Et occisus est Messiam (*sic*) Patricius ejus XVI Kal. Nov.' Anon. Cuspiniani, s. a. 456.

[2] Anon. Cuspiniani. Rubeus, the historian of Ravenna, does not throw any light on the position of Columellae, though he unhesitatingly places it at six miles *from Ravenna*.

Emperor took place at Sirmium (not far from Belgrade),
and Majorian's head-quarters were then at Acincus,
well-known to us under its modern name of Buda as the
western half of the capital of Hungary.   The son-in-law
of the elder, and father of the younger, Majorian was a
faithful comrade of Aetius, and reached the 'respectable' office of Quaestor.   The future Emperor served his
apprenticeship to arms under his father's friend, and
was rising high in the service when suddenly Aetius
dismissed him from his military employments.   No
reason was assigned for this harsh step, but the young
officer and his friends maintained that it was solely due
to the envy of the Patrician's wife, who feared that the
fame of her husband and son would suffer eclipse by
Majorian's growing reputation[1].   He retired for the
time to his estate, and to the pursuits of agriculture,
but when Aetius himself fell under the dagger of the
assassin, his fortunes naturally revived, and Valentinian
III. called him forth from his seclusion to bestow upon
him one of the highest posts in the army.   In this
position he probably co-operated with Ricimer in the
overthrow of Avitus[2].   What is more certain is that,
as already related, he was raised on the last day of
February, 457, to the dignity of Master of the Soldiery,
and on the 1st of April in the same year was saluted as
Augustus.

At once a flash of something like the old defiant spirit

[1] This is probably the prosaic kernel of Sidonius' declamation.
Through 131 angry hexameters he makes the wife of Aetius rave
on, recounting the exploits of the young Majorian, and urging her
husband to slay both him and Ricimer, who are both too illustrious
not to arrive at supreme power.

[2] As we are informed by the chronicler Marius, 'Dejectus est
Avitus Imperator a Majoriano et Ricimere Placentiâ.'

of Rome shewed her enemies that she had again a
soldier for Emperor.   In the short interval between
February and April, Majorian had sent an expedition 457.
Campaign
which successfully repelled an inroad of 900 Alamanni, against the
Alamanni
who had forced their way over the Rhaetian Alps to the
northern shore of Lake Maggiore.   He was next summoned to Campania, to whose rich plains Gaiseric had
this year directed his piratical fleet.   The lordly Vandal, and the
Vandals.
fat with luxurious living, sat lazily in his galley while
the Mauretanian peasant, himself a slave, ravaged the
country, dragging off captives, cattle, spoil, everything
that could be carried away, and swept them into the
holds of the Vandal war-ships.   Such was the picture
of arrogant and indolent rapacity when the troops of
Majorian appeared on the scene.   In an instant all was
changed ; horses were landed, suits of mail were donned,
poisoned arrows were fitted to the string, and fiery
darts were brandished in the hand.   On both sides the
trumpets sounded, and the dragon ensigns floated sinu-
ously to the breeze.   Then came the clash of opposing
squadrons, soon followed by the flight of the Vandals.
Horses and men crowded into the water in an agony
of fear, and only the strongest swimmers succeeded in
reaching the ships.   When the fight was over, Majorian
roamed over the battle-field examining the bodies of the
slain.   Among them was a well-known corpse, that of
the husband of Gaiseric's sister.   All the wounds of the
Roman soldiers were in front ; all those of the Vandals
in the back.   Such is the account which Sidonius gives
of the encounter.   After making every deduction for
rhetorical amplification, we are bound to believe that
the Vandal was worsted in a skirmish, and retired from
the shores of Campania.

A campaign in Pannonia apparently followed; the obscure details of which need not be given here. But it may be observed that among the subject nations who are represented as following the standards of Majorian are mentioned the Rugian and the Ostrogoth [1]. So invariable was the course of barbarian movement into Italy. The tribes who were to be the next conquerors of Rome always first figured as her stipendiaries.

457.

The second year of Majorian's reign was signalised by his accepting the office of Consul in conjunction with his Byzantine colleague, Leo. Scarcely since the palmy days of the Republic had two men so worthy of that famous dignity ridden behind the Lictors and Fasces and given their names to the year. The address of Majorian to the Senate, written at Ravenna and preserved among his laws, makes a show of moderation and deference for that ancient body, which though it was probably understood by all concerned to be only a piece of acting, was yet gracious and dignified acting. He says that having been elected by the free choice of the Senate, and by the will of his valiant army, he consents to assume a dignity for which he has himself no desire, in order that he may not be accused of ingratitude to the Commonwealth, nor seem to wish to live only to himself. He implores the favour of Heaven, and asks

*45
Majorian
Consul.*

*His letter
to the
Senate.
Novellae
Majoriani,
Tit. III.*

---

[1] Here is the list from Sidonius, to be taken for what it is worth. Strict ethnological accuracy is not to be looked for from so declamatory a writer—

> ' Bastarna, Suevus,
> Pannonius, Neurus, Chunus, Geta, Dacus, Alanus,
> Bellonothus, *Rugus*, Burgundio, Vesus, Alites,
> Bisalta, *Ostrogothus*, Procrustes, Sarmata, Moschus,
> Post aquilas venere tuas.'

(Sidonius, Carm. v. 474–478.)

for their co-operation with the Emperor of their choice.
'Let them take heart as to their own fortunes. As a
private man he always condemned the infamy of informers, and he is not going to encourage them now
that he is Emperor. The military affairs of the State
shall receive the ceaseless attention of himself and his
father and Patrician Ricimer. They two together by
hard service in the field have freed the State of the
Roman world from foreign foes and civil broil, and with
the help of Providence they will yet preserve it.'

'Fare ye well, Conscript Fathers of the most venerable order.'

The years 458 and 459 were probably spent in war
with the Visigothic king, naturally indignant at the
overthrow of his candidate for Empire. It would
necessarily be waged in Gaul, but we know nothing
concerning it but the result, a glorious one for Majorian.
In the year 459 'Ambassadors were sent to the Galli-
cians by Nepotian, Master of the Soldiery, and Sunieric
the Count, announcing that Majorian the Augustus, and
Theodoric the King, have ratified with one another the
firmest bonds of peace, the Goths having been overcome
in a certain conflict [1].'

But though we know nothing else of these campaigns
in Gaul, they have a certain interest for us as having
been the means of bringing Majorian within the orbit
of the universal panegyrist, Sidonius. That unfortunate courtier must have seen with deep chagrin all
his hopes of official advancement blasted by the de-

Margin notes: 458. — Transactions in Gaul. — Majorian and Sidonius.

---

[1] Idatius (sub anno). Observe the interesting Gothic name
Sunieric = Sunja-reiks, the king of truth. So in Ulfilas' translation
of John xviii. 38, 'Thanuk quth imma Peilatus, "Wa ist so *sunja?*"'
'Then quoth Pilate to him, "What is the *truth?*"'

458.

thronement of his father-in-law. Apparently he did
not accept the triumph of the party of Ricimer without
a struggle. Did he actually join himself to the Visigoths, and fight under their banners against Rome?
Did he stir up revolt among the Gaulish provincials,
and strive to maintain the cause of some other claimant
to the purple? Did the city of Lyons join the revolt,
and was she only reduced to obedience by the motley
army of Majorian after a stubborn resistance? Such
are some of the conclusions drawn by commentators
from a few obscure passages [1] in the works of Sidonius, who naturally describes the conversations of the
Olympian deities with much greater minuteness than
his own exertions on behalf of an unsuccessful cause.

---

[1] Evidence that Sidonius resisted the Ricimer-Majorian party
with the sword—

> 'Sic mihi *diverso nuper sub Marte* cadenti
>   Jussisti erecto, victor, ut essem animo.'
>
>   (Carm. iv. 11–12, addressed to Majorian.)

Hint of a conspiracy (date uncertain)—

> 'Quum de capessendo diademate conjuratio Marcelliana co-
>   queretur.'   (Ep. i. 11.)

Evidence that Lyons had suffered in war, possibly civil war—

>   'Bove, fruge, colono
> Civibus exhausta est [Lugdunus]; stantis fortuna latebat;
> Dum capitur vae quanta fuit! . . . .
> Etsi concidimus, veniens tamen omnia tecum
> Restituis; fuimus vestri quia causa triumphi
> Ipsa ruina placet.'   (Carm. v. 580–6.)

These last words are generally interpreted as a piece of abject flattery,
addressed to Majorian by the leader of a revolt which he had quelled.
But they would be equally suitable and less base if Lyons had fallen
into the hands of the Burgundians or Visigoths, and had been re-
captured by Majorian after an obstinate siege. The passage

>   'Nostrae de moenibus urbis
> Visceribus miseris insertum depulit ensem.'   (Ib. 572–3.)

seems to me rather to favour the latter conjecture.

The provoking silence of the chroniclers prevents us from either affirming or denying these conclusions. One can only say that it is extraordinary that a civil war, and the reduction by force of so important a city of the empire as Lyons (if these events really occurred) should have been left altogether unnoticed by the historians.

458.

However this may have been, there is no doubt that Sidonius was in disgrace, that the triumphant Emperor was at Lyons, and that a hint was given that a panegyric would be the price of the poet's restoration to favour. The broker in this transaction was the Emperor's secretary, Petrus, himself a man of letters and a distinguished diplomatist. The panegyric was accordingly composed and recited, no doubt in the Emperor's hearing, amidst the applause of the courtiers. It was a hard task for the son-in-law of Avitus to bring his flowing rhetoric to glorify the rival, perhaps the executioner of his relative. But the instinct of reverence for success carried Sidonius safely through his perilous undertaking. In 603 lines (one more than he had given to his father-in-law) he sang the joy of Rome in the triumphs of Majorian, and the very difficulty of the enterprise invigorated his Muse. The personifications are decidedly less tedious, the imagery more imaginative, the flow of declamation more animated, in this work than in the panegyric on Avitus[1].

Sidonius atones for his treason by a panegyric.

---

[1] The poem is prefaced by two dedications, one to Petrus and one to the Emperor, in which a natural comparison is made between the author's position and that of Virgil and Horace. Majorian is obviously another Augustus, Petrus another Maecenas. There is some literary interest in these dedications, if it be true, as stated by M. Monfalcon (quoted by Grégoire), that they are our sole authority for the

This is the plan of the poem. Rome sits on her throne, and receives the homage and the appropriate presents of the nations from India to Spain. To her enters Africa, 'the third part of the world,' her black cheeks scarred, and the ears of corn which crowned her bending forehead all broken. She complains that she is made miserable by the insolent happiness of one man (Gaiseric), the robber, the maid-servant's son, who has insinuated himself into her home, and made himself master of her resources. She calls on Rome to deliver her from this hateful vassalage ; on Rome, now able to strike by the strong arm of Majorian, whose parentage and past exploits she recounts at considerable length. That Rome may not think the exploit beyond her strength, she informs her that Gaiseric is now sodden and enervated by the life of vicious luxury which he has been leading. His pale cheeks and bilious habit show that his endless banquets have at last begun to tell upon his health. What Capua was to Hannibal, the cook-shops of Carthage have been to the Vandal.

Rome, in a few dignified words, assures Africa of coming succour. Gaul, which for nearly eighty years has been left unvisited by Emperors, has now been visited by Majorian, who has corrected the disorders caused by that long absence, and who is now coming 'through these wars to thy war. Why waste we our time in speaking ? He will arrive : he will conquer.'

Here ends the allegorical part of the poem. Then, in his own person, and with some poetic fire, Sidonius recounts the later exploits of the Emperor ; the fight

universally received tradition that it was the good offices of Maecenas, that procured the pardon of Horace after the battle of Philippi.

by Maggiore, the defeat of the Vandal pirates, the passage of the Alps by his motley armament.

458.
Description of Majorian crossing the Alps.

'	'Twas Winter. Through the marble-shining Alps
	The rocks affronting Heaven, the cliffs whose brows
	Threaten incessantly the wayfarer
	With the dry deluge of the avalanche [1],
	Through these thy foot first passes: thou the first
	Dost plant thy pole upon the slippery slopes.
		And now the host has reached the midmost pass:
	Their limbs begin to stiffen with the cold;
	Blocked in the narrow windings of the way,
	To walk, or e'en to creep incapable,
	So great the glassy smoothness of the ground.

Murmurs of his barbarian followers.

		Then one, by chance, from out that straggling file,
	Whose wheel the frozen Danube once had worn,
	Exclaims, "I choose instead the gory sword
	And the chill awfulness of quiet death.
	A rigid torpor binds my stiffening limbs,
	With fire of frost my parchèd frame consumes [2].
	We follow one who labours without end,
	Our stripling leader [3]. Now the bravest brave,
	Monarch or people, safe are housed in camp,
	And, e'en in camp, lie under shaggy hides.
	But we—we change the order of the year.
	What he commands transcends e'en Nature's laws.
	He bends not ever from his ruthless schemes
	And grudges Victory to the angry sky.
	Oh, where and of what nation was he born
	Whom I, the Scythian, cannot cope with? Where,
	Under what rock Hyrcanian did he grow,
	Sucking the milk of tigers? To this pitch

[1]	'Siccamque minantes
	Per scopulos pluviam.'
[2]	'Quodam mihi corpus adustum
	Frigoris igne perit.'
So Milton—
			'The parching air
	Burns frore, and cold performs the effect of fire.'
[3] The picture of the young Napoleon crossing the Alps on his way to Marengo will suggest itself to every reader.

What drearier clime than mine has hardened him?
Lo, where he stands upon that topmost peak,
458.   Urges his shivering ranks, and laughs at cold,
Hot with his spirit's ardour.   When I heard,
Long since, the bugles of a Northern king,
They told me the Imperial arms of Rome
And Caesar's household dwelt in soft repose,
Lapped in perennial luxury.   For me
Nought boots it to have changed my former lords
If this be Roman kingship."

His proud answer.   More he had said,
But from thy cliff thou hurlest thy words of scorn,
"Whoe'er thou art whom daunts the difficult way,
Cut with thine axe the hanging water's hide[1],
And make thee steps out of the frozen wave.
Stop those unmanly murmurs.   Sloth is cold,
But work will warm you.   Soldiers! look on me!
Hath Nature given me the Centaur's limbs;
The wings of Pegasus; the plumèd heels
Of Zetes or of Calaïs?   Yet I crunch
E'en now the snowy summit of the Pass.
You groan beneath a winter in the Alps.
I promise you a soldier's recompense—
A summer 'neath the sun of Africa."
Thus with thy voice thou cheerest the fainting ranks;
Thus thine example stirs them.   Every toil
By thee ordained is first by thee endured.
The crowd with eagerness obey thy laws,
Seeing their author is their promptest slave.'

Passing on from the story of Majorian's campaigns, the poet here interweaves a little skilful panegyric on his friend Petrus, and then comes to the practical part of his effusion.   'Look upon the ruined estate of our city of Lyons, and lighten her load of taxation.'

'And since to these o'erwearied hearts of ours,
Our only Hope, thou comést, help our fall:

[1]   'Frange cutem pendentis aquae, scalptoque fluento
Sit tibi lympha gradus.'

And while thou passest turn a pitying eye
On this thy city, Lyons' Conqueror!
Broken with toil, she looks to thee for rest.
Peace hast thou given: give hope for days to come.
The ox, after short respite from the plough,
Better resumes his struggle with the soil.
Our Lyons sees herself bereft of all,
Oxen and corn, the serf, the citizen.
While still she stood she felt not all her bliss:
Captive, she knows her past prosperity.
  Oh Emperor! when Delight is ours once more,
'Tis sweet to muse on vanished Misery.
Though sack, though fire have laid our glories low,
Thy coming pays for all. Ruin herself
Shall please us if she make thy triumph more.'

458.

The word triumph suggests the thought of the Emperor's car climbing the Capitolian slope, of the mural and civic crowns encircling his forehead, of all the spoils of the defeated Vandal borne proudly before him, 'I will go before thee through the struggling crowds. I will make my feeble note heard through all their noisy shoutings. I will say that thou hast conquered seas and mountains, the Alps, the Syrtes, and the Libyan hordes; but I will say that before and beyond all these victories, thou hast conquered my heart by thy clemency.'

Who could resist such energy of praise? Not Majorian, whose frank and hearty nature accepted the flattery with all goodwill, and who appears to have not merely pardoned the poet, but received him into the circle of his friends. Emboldened by the success of his first petition, Sidonius essayed another of a more personal kind than that which he had already preferred on behalf of his fellow-citizens. He himself individually was groaning under the weight of a heavy assessment,

Sidonius, received into favour by the Emperor, petitions for a reduction of his assessment.

458.

perhaps imposed upon him as a penalty for some insurrectionary movements after the downfall of Avitus. We are not able to ascertain the precise mode of this assessment, but it is clear that it was denoted by heads (*capita*), and that a wealthy or an obnoxious citizen paid taxes upon so many more *capita* than his poorer or more loyal neighbours. Sidonius considered that he had at least three *capita* too many ; that is, probably, that his taxes were fourfold what they ought to be. In a short epigrammatic poem he reminds the Emperor of a certain fortunate hunting excursion of his, in which he had killed three animals on one day—a stag, a boar, and a serpent[1], and hints that another day's sport of the same kind would now be acceptable. Hercules killed the three-headed monster Geryon; let Majorian, the new Hercules, knock the three *capita* from the poet's taxability, and give him a chance of unharassed life. The answer to this curious petition is not stated, but it was probably favourable, since the author included the epigram in the list of his published poems.

The banquet at Arles, and the lampoons of Sidonius.

Majorian's war with the Visigoths detained him for more than a year in Gaul, which he afterwards revisited, and Sidonius had frequent access to the Imperial presence. To the end of his life but slight solicitation was needed to draw from him the story of the high doings which he witnessed ' in the times of Augustus Majorian.' One of these anecdotes, though trifling in itself, may serve to introduce us into the private life of a Roman Emperor of the last days. The scene is laid at Arles,

---

[1] This feat is also referred to in the Panegyric—

'Tribus hunc tremuere sagittis
Anguis, cervus, aper.'　　　(153-4.)

the capital of Roman Gaul ; the time is the year 461 [1].
There had suddenly appeared in the city a copy of
anonymous verses, bitterly satirising some of the chief
persons in the Imperial Court, cleverly hitting off the
favourite vices of each, and all but mentioning their
names. The nobles were furious, and none more so
than a certain Paeonius, a demagogue turned courtier,
a man who had played a little with revolutionary
intrigue and then sold himself for office, a slave to
money-getting till the time came when he saw an opportunity of bartering money for position, and purchasing a highly-placed husband for his only daughter by a
lavish and unusual dowry. This was the person who,
born in obscurity though not in poverty, had clambered
up, no one exactly knew how, during the troubles and
anarchy at Rome, to the distinguished position of Prefect of the Gauls. This was he who, having been
among the courtiers most severely lashed by the anonymous satirist, was the keenest in his endeavours to find
out and punish the author. That author, there can be
little doubt, was Sidonius himself. He affects to consider it a great injustice that the piece should have
been fathered upon him ; but in the letter [2] (written
several years later) in which he tells the story, he
nowhere expressly repeats his denial, and the impression
left on our minds is that though, as a nobleman and
a bishop, he deemed it decorous to disavow the lampoon,
as an author he was very proud of the excitement which
it had occasioned.

461.

[1] Clinton's date 461 is put beyond a doubt by the mention
of Severinus as Consul Ordinarius. The year of his Consulship
was 461.

[2] Ep. i. 11.

At the time when the satire appeared, Sidonius was still at his country-house in Auvergne ; but public opinion, guided by Paeonius, tried him for the authorship, and found him guilty, in his absence. When he appeared at Arles shortly afterwards, and, having paid his respects to the Emperor, descended into the Forum, what unaccountable change had come over his former friends ? One came up to salute him, bowed profoundly, so as almost to touch his knees, and passed on ; another, with gloomy face, stalked past him without uttering a word; the greater number skulked behind a column or a statue, so as to avoid the disagreeable necessity of either saluting or ignoring him. Sidonius professes to have been utterly bewildered by this strange conduct, till at length one of the number, deputed by the rest, approached and saluted him. ' Do you see those men?' said he. ' Yes, I see them, and view their odd conduct with wonder, but certainly not with admiration.' 'They know that you have written a lampoon, and all either detest or fear you in consequence.' 'Who? What? Where? When? Why?' Sidonius asked in well-simulated wrath. Then, with greater composure and with a smile on his face, ' Be good enough to ask those angry gentlemen whether the base informer who dares to accuse me of such an offence pretends to have seen the lampoon in my handwriting. If he does not, they will do well to retract their charge, and behave a little less offensively.' With this equivocal denial, the courtiers were, or professed themselves to be, satisfied, and they came forward promptly and in a body to clasp his hand and kiss him on the cheek.

The next day the Emperor gave a banquet in connection with the games of the amphitheatre. Among the

invited guests were the consul of the year, two ex-
consuls, two other men of high rank, and Paeonius and
Sidonius, whose black looks at one another no doubt
caused much secret amusement to their fellow-guests
and to the Emperor himself.   Host and guests, eight in
all, reclined upon the *triclinium* (triple couch) with the
table in the midst.   It is interesting to observe the
order of precedence.   The most distinguished guest,
Severinus (the consul for the year), reclined at the end
(or ' horn,' as it was called) of the left-hand couch.
Opposite to him, at the first seat of the right-hand
couch, reclined the Imperial host.   The other guests
lay according to their order of precedence, counting
from the seat of Severinus ; and so it came to pass that
Paeonius, as ex-prefect of Gaul, reclined in the fourth
place, at the middle couch, and that Sidonius, who as
yet had no official rank, was the lowest placed among
the guests, but by that very inferiority was brought
into the closest contact with the Emperor.

When the banquet was nearly ended, Majorian began
to talk.   First, in few words, to the Consul Severinus.
Then ensued a more lively dialogue on literary subjects
with the consular who lay next him.   Camillus came
next, a consular, and nephew of a consul.   ' Brother
Camillus,' said the Emperor, ' you had an uncle, for
whose sake I think I may congratulate myself on having
given you a consulship.'   ' Do not say *a* consulship,
Lord Augustus !   Call it a *first* consulship.'   This
clever hint, that further favours of the same kind
would be welcome, was received with a tumult of
applause, notwithstanding the Emperor's presence.
Then passing Paeonius by unnoticed, the Imperial host
put some question to Athenius, the fifth in order of the

461.

461.

guests.   Paeonius rudely interposed a reply.   The Emperor noticed the discourtesy, and the peculiar smile
which played upon his face (for he greatly enjoyed
a joke, and had a happy way of sharing in it without
compromising his dignity) amply avenged Athenius[1].
The latter, who was a wily old fellow, and who already
had a grudge against Paeonius for taking precedence of
him at the banquet, slily said, 'I don't wonder, Emperor, that my neighbour has stolen my place, since he
is not ashamed to take the words out of your mouth.'
'A fine opening this for satirists!' said the sixth guest,
whose turn in the conversation was now come.   Thereupon the Emperor turned his head round to his next-
door neighbour and said, 'I hear, Count Sidonius, that
you are a writer of satires.'   'I *hear* it, too,' he answered.

Majorian (laughing).   'Spare ourselves at any rate.'

Sidonius. 'In refraining from forbidden jests I spare
myself.'

Majorian. 'And what shall we do to those who
molest you?'

Sidonius. 'My lord Emperor! let my accuser accuse
me in public.   If he makes good his charge, I am ready
to pay the penalty : but if, as is probable, I succeed in
refuting it, let me have the leave of your Clemency to
write what I like against him.'

The Emperor glanced at Paeonius, to see if he consented to the conditions ; but the ex-prefect sat silent,
with a blush of anger and shame upon his face.   'I
will grant your request,' said Majorian, 'if you will this

---

[1] 'Subrisit Augustus, ut erat auctoritate servatâ, cum se com-
munioni dedisset joci plenus, per quem cachinnum non minus obtigit
Athenio vindictae, quam contigisset injuriae.'

moment put it into verse.' 'Agreed,' answered Sidonius. He turned round and looked at the servant as if
asking for water to dip his fingers in. There was an
instant's pause while the nimble slave ran round the
triclinium. Then said the Emperor, 'The verses are to
be improvised, remember :'

461.

> 'Who says I write Satires? Dread sovereign! I cry,
>   Let him prove his indictment, or pay for his lie[1];'

was the immediate repartee of Sidonius. There was
again a tumult of applause, and the Emperor, in a tone
perhaps of mock solemnity, called God and the Commonwealth to witness that the poet should henceforth
write whatever he chose, adding that he considered it
to be the duty of the wearer of the purple to repress
this kind of vague and unproven accusation, brought
by malice against innocent members of the nobility.
Sidonius bowed his head and modestly uttered his
thanks ; Paeonius turned pale, dejection succeeded to
rage, and he looked like a criminal on his way to execution. Soon after, the guests rose up. When they had
donned their cloaks (*chlamydes*) and gone a few steps
from the Imperial presence, the consul fell on the neck
of the favoured courtier, the two consulars [2] kissed his
hand, and Paeonius, with fawning and pitiable gestures,
implored pardon. On the intercession of the other
members of the party, Sidonius consented to grant it,
and to promise that he would leave Paeonius unlashed
by his satires if he would take warning by the miserable

---

[1] 'Scribere me Satyram qui culpat, maxime princeps,
    Hanc rogo decernas aut probet aut timeat.'
[2] Literally the ex-prefects, but they were consulars also, and
Paeonius was not.

success of this attempt to blacken his character and cease to molest him for the future.

The story of this banquet at Arles is no doubt trivial enough, and may seem scarcely worth the telling, but it illustrates the immense social deference which was still paid to the name of Augustus, and the glamour of the purple robe.   When we are reading the history of far-distant times, we are sometimes disposed to marvel how men could be found willing to take prominent positions in the world, when the state of affairs was so hopeless that they must inevitably become either the pity or the laughing-stock of the universe.   Perhaps the explanation is to be found in the fact that so long as Power commands the reverence of the few score of persons with whom it comes into daily contact, it will have irresistible attractions for mankind.   Further than its own immediate environment it need not and will not look : least of all will it trouble itself about the sort of figure that it will make in History.   Here was Julius Majorianus, struggling bravely it is true, but almost desperately, for the last tatters of the Roman inherit-ance that were left to him by the Rhone and the Ebro ; yet his favour still gave life, a harsh word from his lips or a frown on his brow sent the unhappy object of his displeasure out of the Imperial presence, pale, trembling, half-choked with terror ; the courtiers still contended for the smile of 'the Purple-wearer' as eagerly as when he was the master of sixty legions, and when none could escape his wrath or stay his hand, from Cheviot to Caucasus.

Social de-ference still paid to the Emperor.

Legisla-tion of Majorian.

458.

The short reign of Majorian was a time of consider-able legislative activity.   Especially was the year of his consulship (during which his head-quarters seem to have been at the palace in Ravenna) marked by his additions ('*Novellae*') to the Theodosian code. But the laws all tell one tale; all speak, in one relation or another, of the desperate misery which was engulfing the inhabitants of Italy. Population was decreasing so Laws against celibacy. fast that the Emperor, notwithstanding the strong feeling of the Church in favour of virginity, and against Novellae Majorian, Tit. VII. second marriage, found himself compelled to forbid women to take the veil under forty years of age, and to command all childless widows to marry a second husband within five years of the death of the first, or else to forfeit half their property to their relatives or to the exchequer. The cost of maintaining a family was so great, Tit. II. the rivalry for the paternal inheritance so keen, that in many instances an unpopular son or brother was forced into the ranks of the clergy and actually ordained Priest against his will. Where such an offence was proved to have been committed, the unjust parents were condemned to forfeit a third of their property to the unwillingly consecrated son, who was permitted to return into the world, a forced ordination having no binding power. The Archdeacon who might have wittingly co-operated in the offence, was liable to a fine of ten pounds of gold (£400). A curious provision that if a Bishop had been consecrated without his consent the ordination could not be impugned, is perhaps a concession to the harmless comedy of the *Nolo Episcopari*, which was so commonly played in those days. Or possibly it may have proceeded from an uneasy consciousness of the Legislator's own share in the forced consecration of his predecessor at Placentia.

Majorian's laws are remarkably outspoken as to the rapacity of the tax-collectors, especially those who were clothed with military authority, whose extortions he denounces in the strongest terms. 'Raging against the bowels of the unhappy Provincials, they are safe from punishment, for none cares to accuse them before a provincial judge, too often supine and cowardly and ready to cringe and fawn at the mere sight of an officer's belt, while the expense and vexation of an appeal to the Imperial court is so great that most men will submit to any injustice rather than resort to it.' A change in administration, bringing fiscal questions under the more immediate notice of the Governor of the Province, was meant to remedy this evil, which may have been partly relieved by another short but emphatic edict concerning the election of the *Defensor*, that singular official of whose functions some account has been already given [1] and who was perhaps the only functionary whom Power has ever avowedly created as a safeguard against its own exorbitances. The harassed citizens were daily leaving the towns, to pick up a precarious subsistence in the remote country districts, where they were at least safe from the hated presence of the *Apparitor* [2] and the *Canonicarius* [3]. In order to check this process of depletion, Majorian ordained that in accordance with ancient usage, the magistracy and people of each considerable town should assemble and choose a *Defensor*, who, when confirmed in his office by the Emperor, might avail to keep the insolence of the revenue officers in check and tempt back the scattered citizens to their homes.

The exactions of the tax-gatherers, themselves very likely (as is the custom in decaying States) often

Against rapacious Tax-collectors.
Nov. Maj. Tit. IV.

The Defensor.
Tit. V.

Laws about the Currency.

---

[1] See vol. i, pp. 626–628. [2] Magistrate's officer.

[3] Tax-collector.

defrauded of their lawful salaries, were sometimes so
extravagant as to be almost amusing.   Thus continual
objection was made to taking the Imperial *Solidus*
(twelve shilling piece), even though it was of full
weight ; and some strange tricks, the nature of which
we can but faintly conjecture, were played upon the
popular partiality for gold pieces with the head of
Faustina [1], coins which, if they represented the pure
undepreciated currency of the Antonine period before
the terrible debasements of the coinage in the third
century, were not undeserving of a high place in public
favour.   All this elaborate machinery of injustice was
destroyed, as far as mere decrees could destroy it, by
Majorian, and the officers of the Tribute were ordered
to take all coins alike which were of full weight, except those minted of Gaulish gold, which was admitted
to be of an inferior quality.

Nov. Maj.
Tit. I.

Some other unwarranted importunities of the official
hierarchy were repressed by the same series of decrees.
Servants of the Governors asking for New-Year's
Gifts [2], Presents on the first day of the month [3], or
Drink-money [4] (literally Dust-money, an indemnification for the dust which the messenger had contracted
on his journey), all these were punished by a fine of
£40 for each offence.   Governors of Provinces were not

Illegal
exactions.
Nov. Maj.
Tit. I.

---

[1] 'Illis quoque fraudibus obviandum est, quas in varietate pon-
derum exactorum calliditas facere consuevit, qui vetustis caliginibus
abutentes Faustinae aliorumque nominum nescientibus faciant men-
tionem.'   Ritter in his note understands this passage as relating to
Faustina, the third wife of Constantius II ; but surely the two
Faustinae, the wives of Antoninus Pius and Marcus Aurelius, whose
coins we possess in such abundance, are far more likely to be meant.

[2] Strenae (the lineal ancestor of the French *Étrennes*).

[3] Kalendae.   [4] Pulveraticum.

to be at liberty to half-ruin a city by taking up their quarters therein for an indefinite time, and calling upon the inhabitants to bring a constant supply of rare and costly delicacies to their table. Three days' provisions for himself and suite, on a scale of expense to be settled by the Prefect, were all that the Governor might require annually from each city.

Tit. IV.
These enactments, together with a remission of arrears of tribute of more than eleven years' standing, seemed to show a generous consideration for the poverty of the exhausted people. They were however
Tit. I.
to some extent counterbalanced by a little clause in the longest edict, which stated that now that the cultivator was relieved from so many presents to governors and other illegal exactions, he could not think it burdensome if his land-tax [1], which now stood at two per thousand on capital (equivalent perhaps to two per cent. on income [2]), was increased by one quarter so as to stand thenceforward at two-and-a-half per thousand.

Destruction of public buildings.
One more law must be noticed, since it shows the disintegrating influences which were already at work upon the buildings of old Rome, influences internal and domestic, which, far more than the transitory visits of Goth or Vandal, have brought about her present desolation.

Nov. Maj. Tit. VI.
'We, as Rulers of the Republic, are determined to remedy the detestable process which has long been going on, whereby the face of the venerable city [of Rome] is disfigured. For it is too plain that the public edifices, in which all the adornment of the city

---

[1] 'Canon.'

[2] Taking the average rate of interest at 10 per cent.

consists, are being everywhere pulled to pieces at the suggestion of the city officials, on the pretence that stones are wanted for the public works. Thus the stately piles of our old buildings are being frittered away, and great constructions are ruined in order to effect some trifling repair. Hence, too, it arises that private individuals engaged in house-building, who are in a position to curry favour with the city judges, do not hesitate to supply themselves with materials from the public buildings, although these which have so much to do with the splendour of the city ought to be regarded with civic affection, and repaired rather than destroyed.

'We therefore decree that no buildings or ancient monuments raised by our forefathers for use or beauty, shall be destroyed by any man; that the judge who orders their destruction shall pay a fine of fifty pounds of gold [£2000]; and that the clerks and other subordinates who have fulfilled his orders shall be beaten with clubs and have their hands struck off—those hands that have defiled the ancient monuments which they ought to have preserved.

'The buildings which are altogether past repair shall be transferred, to adorn some other edifice of a not less public character.'

It is interesting to observe that this decree, so purely Roman and local in its character, was like the others issued from Ravenna (10th July, 458).

But it was not for legislation, nor for administrative reform, but for war that Julius Majorianus had been robed in the mantle of the Caesars. To him all the Roman world looked with hope, to exorcise the cruel

Majorian a warrior.

and mocking fiend that had entered the corpse of Carthage. If the Vandals could be subdued, he was surely the man to do it. He had felled the forests of the Apennines, and filled the harbours of the Upper and Lower Sea with Roman triremes. His campaign in Gaul had been successful, and the haughty Visigoth was now his submissive ally. It might have been expected that he would repeat the exploit of Scipio Africanus, transport his troops to the Libyan shore, and fight another Zama within a week's march of Carthage. For some reason not clearly explained to us, possibly because he knew of disaffection among the Mauretanian and Numidian allies of Gaiseric, he adopted a different course. He determined to make Spain his base of operations, and to assemble his navy, consisting of 300 ships [1], in that magnificent bay, one of the finest natural harbours in the Mediterranean, which we call Carthagena, and which then still bore the name of 'the New Carthage.' It seemed as if history was about to repeat itself, and as if Spain might play the same part now, in the thirteenth century of Rome, which she had played in the sixth century, when the Hasdrubals and the Scipios fought there. But while all Europe was watching the movements of the Roman triremes in that spacious bay, suddenly the enterprise collapsed. Gaiseric first laid waste with fire and sword the provinces of Mauretania which Majorian meant to make his base of operations, and poisoned the wells along his expected line of march. Then by some stratagem, of which we know nothing, the Vandals, 'warned by traitors,' carried off the ships from out of the Bay of Carthagena. One chronicler [2] places the

---

[1] So Priscus, fr. 13 (ed. Bonn).   [2] Marius.

scene of this mysterious event not at Carthagena itself, but at Elice (now Elche), a sea-side town about forty miles north of Carthagena, often visited by modern travellers who wish to see the forests of palm-trees which impart to it a thoroughly Oriental aspect, and have earned for it the name of 'the Palmyra of Europe.' 'No Palm of Victory for me,' may have been the thought of Majorian as he sadly turned his face northwards—the preparations of three years wasted, and vengeance on the Vandal indefinitely postponed.

460.

This happened in May, 460. On the second of August in the following year he was dethroned and put to death near the city of Tortona (in the southeast corner of the modern Duchy of Piedmont). No cause is assigned by any of the chroniclers for his fall, except 'the jealousy of Ricimer, acted upon by the counsels of envious men;' nor is anything told us of the circumstances of his death. Probably enough, the early successes of Majorian were the real cause of his ruin, for which his final disaster furnished the pretext.

Deposition and death of Majorian.

The high estimate usually formed by historians of the character of Majorian, and of what, under happier auspices, he might have accomplished for the restoration of the fortunes of Rome, is justified by nothing so much as by the impression which he produced on his most unwearied enemies, the Vandals. The Byzantine historian, Procopius, writing a century after these events, and describing the overthrow of the Vandal Empire by Justinian, gives us the following paragraph about Majorian, which must surely have been derived from Vandal sources, and may possibly have formed part of some song or Saga about Gaiseric. Scarcely a

The Majorian-Saga of the Vandals as told by Procopius.

detail in the picture is historically true, and the chief
event recorded—the visit to Carthage—is almost certainly fictitious, but the portrait, taken as a whole,
and especially if drawn by enemies, is undoubtedly the
likeness of a hero.

De Bello
Vandalico,
I. 7.
'I ought also to make mention of Majorian[1], who
some time before [Anthemius] occupied the Western
Throne. For this Majorian, who surpassed all that
had been emperors of Rome in every virtue, could not
tamely endure the misery of Africa, but collected in
Liguria a most potent armament against the Vandals,
and determined to head the expedition himself, being a
man eager to take his full share in every hardship, and
especially in every danger.

'Now, thinking it would be expedient to ascertain
previously the forces of the Vandals, the temper of
Gaiseric, and the good or bad dispositions towards him
of the Libyans and Moors, he took this duty upon himself. He therefore sent himself as his own ambassador,
under a feigned name, to the court of Gaiseric; and,
fearing lest he might be discovered, and so ruin both
himself and his enterprise, he hit upon this plan. As
all men knew that his hair was so yellow as to be
likened to pure gold, he applied to it a wash invented
expressly for the purpose, and was able within the
appointed time to turn it into a bluish black.

'Now, when he came into the presence of Gaiseric,
among other devices of that king to strike terror into
the soul of the supposed ambassador, he was led as a
friend into the arsenal where all the weapons were
collected, which were many and extremely wonderful.
At his entrance, say they, all these arms stirred of

[1] The form of the name adopted by Procopius is 'Majorinus.'

their own accord, and made such a clash and uproar that Gaiseric thought an earthquake was happening. But when he came forth and enquired about the earthquake, and could meet with no one who knew anything about it, great fear fell upon him, though he was still far from conjecturing *who* had been the cause of this portent.

'Majorian then, having accomplished all that he intended, departed to Liguria, and leading his army by land, marched to the Pillars of Hercules, intending to cross by those straits, and so conduct his troops from thence to Carthage. Now when Gaiseric heard this, and perceived that he had been imposed upon in the matter of the embassy, great fear fell upon him, and he set everything in readiness for war. The Romans, on the other hand, relying on the proved valour of Majorian, were in good hopes that they should win back Africa for the Empire. But all these hopes were foiled by the death of Majorian, who was attacked by dysentery. He was a man in all things gentle to his subjects, but terrible to his enemies.'

CHAPTER VI.

SUPREMACY OF RICIMER (continued). SEVERUS II, THE
LUCANIAN, A.D. 461–465. ANTHEMIUS, THE CLIENT
OF BYZANTIUM, A.D. 467–472.

Authorities.

Sources :—

THE Panegyric and Epistles of SIDONIUS, as quoted in the
text.

The Chroniclers as before, with the addition of CASSIODORUS,
minister of Theodoric the Ostrogoth (480–575). Now that he
no longer has Prosper to copy from, his chronicle becomes valuable as an independent authority.

We are also compelled here, in the great dearth of contemporary information, to rely occasionally on THEOPHANES, though
a Byzantine historian of a poor type. Theophanes was born in
758 and died in 817. He was of noble birth, embraced the
monastic life, and took part in the Iconoclastic controversy as
a vehement upholder of the worship of images. His 'Chronographia' extends from the accession of Diocletian to the second
year of the Emperor Michael I. (284–813).

For the life of Marcellinus our chief authority is the Lexicon
of SUIDAS (of uncertain date, possibly not later than Theophanes).

For the quarrel between Anthemius and Ricimer the main
authority is ENNODIUS, De Vitâ Epiphanii, described in the
text. Ennodius, Bishop of Ticinum, lived from about 473
to 521.

For the close of the reign of Anthemius some valuable details
are furnished by the recently discovered fragments of the history

of JOANNES ANTIOCHENUS. The author was an orator of Antioch, probably of the seventh century, who wrote the history of the Empire from the Creation to the great earthquake and fire at Antioch in 526. Holder-Egger (Neues Archiv, I. 295) considers that Joannes had before him the history of Priscus and thence drew some valuable information. The few remains of his work which have been discovered are published in Müller's 'Fragmenta veterum Historicorum Graecorum.' PRISCUS, of Panium (described Book ii, Chap. 2), gives the diplomatic history of the times with some fulness. Unfortunately we have his work only in fragments, relating to the negotiations in which the Empire was engaged, but as far as his information goes we may trust him thoroughly, as a contemporary and a man of truthful character.

PAULUS DIACONUS (about 720 to 790) in his Historia Romana, a continuation of Eutropius, gives us some valuable fragments of information, but cannot be considered a first-rate authority for this period, though he will be invaluable for later centuries.

Guide :—

From this point onwards to the close of the Western Empire I am under constant obligation to Pallmann, Geschichte der Völkerwanderung. His second volume deals with the cycle of events which led to the elevation of Odovacar to supreme power in Italy, and with his subsequent overthrow by Theodoric the Ostrogoth.

LIBIUS SEVERUS, 'a Lucanian by nation,' was the man whom Ricimer had selected to wear the diadem snatched from the head of the murdered Majorian. He was proclaimed Emperor at Ravenna, on the nineteenth of November, 461. He died at Rome on the fifteenth of August, 465. These two dates sum up in truth the whole of our knowledge respecting this faint shadow of an Emperor. It should, perhaps, be added that one authority states that he 'lived religiously [1].'

Accession of Severus II, the Lucanian.

Anonymus Cuspiniani.

---

[1] 'Severus Romae imperavit annis quatuor: ibique religiosè vivens decessit' (Catalogus Imperatorum, ed. Roncalli).

461-465.
His meek
character

To one who is familiar with the name of the Lu-
canians, and who remembers the part which this stern
Sabellian tribe, dwelling in the extreme south of Italy,
played in three of Rome's greatest wars (the Pyrrhic,
Second Punic, and Social), it seems strangely incon-
gruous that the only contribution which Lucania furnished to the list of Roman Emperors should have
been this meek inoffensive cipher-Augustus, who ' lived
religiously,' and died quietly at Rome after four years
of sovereignty, neither by his life nor by his death
making a ripple on the downward stream of the
Empire's fortunes.

and death.
Did Rici-
mer poison
him ?

The only question which can raise a momentary
interest in connection with this Emperor is as to the
manner of his death.   Was it due to the ordinary
course of nature or to the hand of Ricimer ?   Cassiodorus, who is a good authority, and who wrote about
half a century after these events, says cautiously, ' as
some aver, by the hand of Ricimer, Severus was taken
off by poison in the palace at Rome.'   On the other
hand, all the other chroniclers, one or two of whom
are yet nearer in date than Cassiodorus, tell us simply
that ' Lord Severus died ; ' and Sidonius, in a poem
recited in the presence of Ricimer and his next succeeding puppet, says,

> ' August Severus now *by Nature's Law*
> Hath mingled with the company of gods[1].'

Though it is hazardous to determine what a poet bent
on praising Power will *not* say, it seems probable that
had the common voice of fame in the year 467 con-

---

[1]   ' Auxerat Augustus naturae lege Severus
     Divorum numerum.'   (Carm. ii. 317–318.)

nected the death of Severus with the poison-cup in
the hand of Ricimer, that subject would have been
judiciously evaded by Sidonius [1].

The four years of the nominal reign of Severus seem
to have been a time of desultory and exhausting strife.
The rule of Ricimer, if accepted as a disagreeable necessity by the inhabitants of Italy, was regarded with
aversion by their neighbours, and we may infer that
the hatefulness of the man more than counterbalanced
the undeniable capacity of the general and the statesman. To understand the course of events during this
obscure [2] time, we must look at the relations existing
between the court of Ravenna and those of the four
following cities, Constantinople, Carthage, Soissons,
and Spalato.

1. Leo, 'the Emperor of the Eastern Romans,'
beheld, evidently with deep displeasure, the downfall
and murder of Majorian, a kindred spirit to his own,
and the substitution of the puppet-Emperor Severus.
The chronicler, who most faithfully represents the
sympathies of the Byzantine Court [3], uses such expressions as these : 'Severus invaded the place of
Majorian,' 'Severus, who snatched the sovereignty of
the West,' and refuses to insert him in his proper year
in the list of Consuls. When the 'Romans of the
West' applied for ships to replace the three hundred
destroyed at Carthagena, the loss of which left them
at the mercy of Gaiseric's invasions, Constantinople

---

[1] Holder-Egger (Neues Archiv, i. 303, n. 1) pronounces without
hesitation for the natural character of the death of Severus.

[2] Obscure, but fitfully enlightened by the fragmentary information
preserved by Priscus.

[3] Marcellinus.

coldly replied that the existing treaties with the Vandals would not allow of its rendering this assistance.

461–465.
It despatched indeed during this interval one or two embassies to the court of Gaiseric, exhorting him to abstain from invading Sicily and the Italian provinces; but an embassy more or less was a matter of no concern to the Vandal monarch, and he continued his depredations unmoved by the Byzantine rhetoric.

with Gai-
seric, king
of the
Vandals;
2. Gaiseric himself had his reasons for viewing the course of events at Rome with displeasure. He had a candidate of his own for the Imperial Purple, and was deeply offended at that candidate's rejection. It will be remembered that after the sack of Rome he carried the Empress Eudoxia and her two daughters as state-prisoners to Carthage. Incessant embassies [1] from Byzantium had prayed for the surrender of these royal ladies whose captivity, like that of Placidia half a century before, was felt to be an especial insult to the majesty of an Augustus. At length, in the

462.
seventh year of their exile, Gaiseric sent the widowed Empress with one daughter to Constantinople, and this was no doubt the occasion of that treaty of alliance between Africa and the East which Leo refused to endanger when the Romans applied to him for help.

---

[1] About the year 456, Marcian, as we are informed by Priscus, sent on this errand 'an ambassador named Bledas, a Bishop of Gaiseric's own sect (for it so happens that even the Vandals adhere to the religion of the Christians). This Bledas, when he found that his embassy was not going to be successful, took a bolder tone and said, "It will not turn out to your advantage, Gaiseric! if, puffed up by your present prosperity, you challenge the Eastern Emperor to war and refuse to give up the royal ladies." But neither his former blandishments nor his present threats availed to bring Gaiseric to reason, for he sent Bledas about his business and again despatched his forces to ravage Sicily and Italy' (Priscus, p. 216, ed. Bonn).

The other daughter, Eudocia, Gaiseric had already given in marriage to his son Hunneric—an ill-assorted union, for the lady was a devout Catholic and her husband a most bitter Arian. Placidia, the sister who was allowed to retire to Constantinople, was the wife of a Roman Senator, named Olybrius, and it was this man, bound to him by a somewhat loose tie of affinity, as being his son's brother-in-law, whom Gaiseric desired to place, and as we shall see, eventually did place for a few months on the Western throne. 461–465.

Here then was one grievance of the Vandal against Ricimer. Another was the refusal to comply with his claim to have all the property of Valentinian III and Aetius given up to him. The claim to the late Emperor's wealth of course rested on the alliance between his daughter and the Vandal prince. The more preposterous demand for the property of Aetius was probably in some way connected with the fact that his son Gaudentius had been also carried captive to Carthage. But, whatever the foundation for them, these two demands were urged by the Vandal king with insolent pertinacity, and were the occasion of countless embassies. As they were not complied with, and as the friendship now established between Carthage and Constantinople forbade him to molest the coasts of Greece, Gaiseric decided that 'the nation with whom God was angry [1]' was the Italian. Every year, with the return of spring, he sailed his piratical fleet to the coasts of Campania, or Sicily, or Apulia. He avoided the large towns, fearing to find there sufficiently large bodies of troops to check his advance, and fell by preference on the villages and unwalled towns, carrying off all

[1] See p. 252.

the moveable wealth, and making slaves of the inhabitants.   This man's instincts were essentially those of
the robber rather than the conqueror.   He was, so to
speak, the representative of that brood of pirates whom
Pompey exterminated, the forerunner of those countless spoilers of the sea, Saracen, Moorish, Algerian, by
whom the Mediterranean coasts have been wasted,
almost down to our own day.

461-465.

3. The romantic and mysterious career of Aegidius,
comrade of Majorian, Master of the Roman Soldiery,
voluntarily chosen king of the Franks during the exile
of an unpopular chieftain, lies beyond our proper limits,
and some of its chief events rest on too doubtful authorities to make it desirable here to describe it at length.
But we are fully warranted in saying that he ruled as
an independent governor, possibly with the title of
king, at Soissons (in Belgic Gaul), that he bitterly
resented the death of his old companion-in-arms, Majorian, and was preparing to avenge it upon Italy—
that is, upon Ricimer—that, probably in order to further
these purposes of revenge, he sent ambassadors 'across
the Ocean to the Vandals,' and that Rome [1] remained for
a considerable time in the greatest terror and distress
in anticipation of this new Gaulish invasion.   Eventually however he was 'drawn off from war with the
Italians by a difference with the Visigoths respecting
frontiers, which led to a campaign, in which Aegidius
performed acts of the greatest heroism [2].'   In this war
Frederic, brother of the Visigothic king, was killed, and
apparently Aegidius himself died (or was treacherously

with
Aegidius,
'tyrant' of
Soissons ;

463.

464.

---

[1] Priscus (p. 156) is our authority for attributing so much importance to the hostile enterprises of Aegidius and Marcellinus.

[2] Priscus (as quoted above).

slain) soon after.   The Visigoths annexed a large part
of his territory, but the city of Soissons and his strange
ill-defined power descended to his son Syagrius, whose 461–465.
acquaintance we have already made as a correspondent
of Sidonius, and with whose overthrow by Clovis every
student of French history is familiar, as one of the
earliest incidents in the career of the young Merovingian [1].

Possibly the English reader is more familiar with
the name of Aegidius than he is aware of.   For some
unaccountable reason the French have modified that
name into Gilles.   Saint Gilles, the hermit of Languedoc, who lived about a hundred years after Count
Aegidius, attained great renown both in France and
England.   The parish of St. Giles' in London and the
name Giles, once so common, especially in the rural
districts of England, are thus linked certainly, if somewhat obscurely, with the memory of the 'Tyrannus' of
Soissons and the friend of Majorian.

4. We pass from Soissons by the Aisne to the long with Marcellinus,
arcades of Spalato, among the bays and islands of the Dynast of
Dalmatia.
Dalmatian coast.   Here [2], in the vast palace of Diocletian, lived and reigned Marcellinus [3], 'Patrician of
the East,' ' ruler of Dalmatia and of the Epirote Illy-
rians.'   The pupil of Aetius and the counsellor of
Majorian, he had in the deaths of those two men a
double reason for withdrawing from the blood-stained

---

[1] This was the event which led to the quarrel between Clovis and
one of his soldiers.   'Thus didst thou serve the vase of Soissons.'

[2] The assignment of Spalato as the scene of the Court of Marcellinus is only a conjecture, but it seems probable that a ruler of
Dalmatia would make that place his head-quarters.

[3] Not to be confounded with the chronicler of that name.

circle of Roman politics. Yet he does not seem, like
Aegidius, to have broken with Ricimer immediately
461–465. upon the death of his friend. He fought in Sicily at
the head of the Imperial troops, and achieved some
considerable successes over the Vandals. Finding however that Ricimer was endeavouring, by bribes, to steal
away the hearts of his soldiers, and knowing that
he could not hope to vie in wealth with the Suevic
Patrician, he retired to Dalmatia, and there founded
an independent and hostile principality. 'A reasonable
and noble man,' we are told [1], 'learned, courageous, and
statesmanlike, keeping his government free, not serving
the Roman Emperor, nor any prince or nation, but
ruling his own subjects in righteousness.' Apparently
one of the few men in high office who still clung to
the old Pagan religion and worshipped Jupiter Capitolinus, while all the rest of the world was ranging
itself for or against the Council of Chalcedon ; prac-
tising divination and holding long conversations with a
certain philosopher Sallust, who shared his most secret
counsels and dwelt in his palace; this relic of an earlier
world, deposited by the vicissitudes of the times upon
the shores of Dalmatia, is one of the most unique figures
of the age, and we would gladly know more of his
history. What concerns our present purpose however
is the settled hostility which he displayed for some
years to the domination of Ricimer, and the constant
fear which pervaded Italy during that time of an invasion from the opposite coast of the Adriatic. At length
(probably about 465) the good offices of Byzantium
were asked and obtained ; an ambassador was sent by

---

[1] By Suidas, himself a late writer, but almost certainly here preserving in his Dictionary some scraps of contemporary tradition.

the Eastern Emperor to entreat Marcellinus to lay aside his plans of revenge; he complied with the request, and, as we shall soon see, even co-operated once more with Rome against the Vandals. 461-465.

Neither of these two men, Aegidius and Marcellinus, founded any enduring monarchy out of the fragments of the Empire; nor did any other Roman succeed in the attempt. All the political reconstruction was the work of barbarian hands. Yet on the dissolution of Alexander's Empire, states and monarchies innumerable were established throughout Asia and Africa by Greek adventurers. When the Khalifate fell, Saracen chiefs profited by the ruin. When the Mogul Empire of Delhi lost its vitality, Mohammedan as well as Hindoo Rajahs founded sovereignties which endured for many generations. In the early part of this century the Ali Pasha of Egypt entirely succeeded, and the Ali Pasha of Albania all but succeeded, in rendering themselves virtually independent of the Ottoman Porte. Reasons might probably be easily assigned why no such success was attainable by a Roman Prefect of the Praetorium, or Master of the Soldiery, but we cannot wonder that the experiment was made, nor should we have been surprised if it had been made more frequently. No Roman adventurer succeeded in founding a kingdom for himself in the breaking up of the Empire.

Other enemies besides those whom we have enume-rated were probably making Ricimer's position at the helm of the Commonwealth a difficult one. In the year 464 Beorgor, king of the Alans, was routed and killed by the Patrician, 'at Bergamo, at the foot of the mountains [1].' We hear nothing more about this Invasion of Alans. 6 February.

[1] Cuspiniani Anon.: 'Rustico et Olybrio Coss. occisus est Beorgor Rex Alanorum Bergamo ad Pedem Montis VIII Idus Februarias.' Though Bergamo is in the district which we now call the Milanese, does not this description look like the beginning of the name Piedmont?

descent of the savage half-Tartar tribe into the plains of Lombardy. Possibly Beorgor was the successor of that Sangiban, king of the Alans, who fought, with doubtful fidelity, under Aetius on the Mauriac Plains, and he may have forced his way over the Splugen from Coire to Chiavenna, and thence to Bergamo. For one invasion of this kind, leading to a pitched battle, which has claimed a place in the meagre pages of the chroniclers, there were probably many lesser inroads and skirmishes of which no record has been preserved.

461–465.

Interregnum of twenty months after the death of Severus.

It was in August, 465, as was before said, that the unnoticeable Severus died. For a year and eight months from that time no man was saluted as Augustus in the Western half of the Roman Empire. This absolute vacancy of the Imperial office tells a far more striking tale in a pure autocracy, such as the Roman Government had become, than in a constitutional state, where the powers of the sovereign may be, so to speak, 'put in commission.' During all those twenty months, the Patrician must have been avowedly the sole source of power, legislative, military, judicial, and the question must have forced itself on many minds, 'What is the use of wasting the dwindling income of the state on the household of an Emperor, when all the work of ruling is done by the Patrician?' Thus the interregnum of 465–467 prepared the way for the abolition of the dignity of Augustus in 476. It is doubtful, however, whether Ricimer at this period entertained any thoughts of dispensing with the '*fainéant*' Emperors. It seems more probable that he was balancing in his mind the respective advantages to be derived from an alliance with Carthage or with Constantinople, the isolated position which Italy had occupied for the last six years being obviously no longer tenable. If this view be correct, there is perhaps a slightly greater probability of his innocence of the death of Severus. An inoffensive and almost useful tool would hardly have been removed by force, if his employer had not decided how he was to be replaced.

467.

However this may be, the interregnum was termi- Ricimer nated by a decision in favour of Constantinople. Not allies himself with Olybrius, the brother-in-law of the son of Gaiseric, but Constantinople and Anthemius, the son-in-law of the deceased Emperor gives the purple to Marcian, was selected by Ricimer to be the wearer of Anthemius. the purple; and great was the Vandal's rage in consequence. The equivalent which the Eastern Empire was to pay for the still-coveted honour of giving an Augustus to Rome was hearty support against the African enemy, with whom it is probable that her own relations had for some months been growing less friendly. A great combined campaign of 468 against the Vandals—a campaign in which Leo, Marcellinus, and Ricimer all joined their forces—was the fruit of this alliance, and it will be well first to describe this campaign, postponing for the moment the merely complimentary proceedings connected with the new Emperor's accession to the Western throne.

The Court of Constantinople must have been at this Factions at the time a curious study for any unprejudiced observer Byzantine court. who could keep his head cool in the whirlpool of its contending factions. Passions and ambitions as old as humanity were there, striving side by side with special theological formulae whose very names are almost forgotten among men. While the mob of Constantinople were eagerly discussing Bishop Timothy the Weasel's revolt against the Council of Chalcedon, or Bishop Peter the Fuller's addition of four words to the Trisagion, Basilicus, the brother of the Emperor's wife, and Zeno, the husband of the Emperor's daughter, were playing their stealthy, remorseless, bloody game for the succession to the throne of the Emperor, Leo.

When Ricimer's proposals for an alliance reached Constantinople, power was slipping from the hands of the general who had for forty years been the most powerful man in the Eastern Court—Aspar, the son of Ardaburius. An Alan by extraction, he, with his father, had been sent as long ago as 424 on the expedition to Italy, which overthrew the usurper Joannes and established the young Valentinian on the throne of his uncle Honorius [1]. Since then he had been a consul (434), and the father of consuls (447, 459, 465). He was called ' First of the Patricians ' [2] ; he stood on the very steps of the throne, and might have been Emperor himself, but he was an Arian. Being therefore by his theological tenets, which he had probably inherited from his barbarian ancestors, and was too proud to forego, disqualified from himself reigning over ' the orthodox Romans,' he made it his care that the purple should at least be always worn by men subservient to his interests. The brave young soldier who stretched himself to sleep in the courtyard of Gaiseric's palace, whom the hovering eagle overshadowed, and whom the Vandal dismissed with a true presage of his future greatness, was Marcian, *'domesticus'* of Aspar [3]. So long as he reigned (450–457) the influence of his patron appears to have remained unshaken. On his death there seems to have been some expectation that

467.

Aspar and
his sons.

---

[1] See vol. i. p. 846.   [2] Marcellinus, s. a. 471.   [3] See p. 261.

his son-in-law, Anthemius, would succeed him [1], but
the predominant influence of Aspar and his son Ardaburius again secured the election of a dependant, their
curator, Leo.

But, whatever might be the manner of a man's eleva- Accession of Leo.
tion to the supreme dignity of the state, even though, Servility
as in the cases of Marcian and Leo, something like Eastern
domestic service might be the ladder of his promotion, Courtiers.
when once he was hailed Augustus, the elaborate court-
ceremonial of Byzantium enveloped him in the eyes of
acclaiming crowds and literally adoring courtiers with
all 'the divinity that doth hedge a king.' We have an
apt illustration of this in one of those anecdotes with
which the chroniclers so curiously diversify their otherwise meagre pages. A few years after Leo's accession, 462.
as we are informed by Marcellinus, he fell sick of a
fever. Jacobus, a man of Greek nationality and Pagan
faith, and one in whom a great natural genius for the
healing art had been enriched by a long course of study,
was called in to prescribe for the Imperial patient.
When he entered 'the sacred bed-chamber,' he presumed to take a seat by the Emperor's bedside without
having received any sign that he was at liberty to do
so, and then proceeded to make his diagnosis of the
case. When he returned at noon to 'the sacred couch,'
he found the possibility of such impertinence averted by
the removal of the chair. He perceived the meaning of
the hint, and at once, with awful 'intrepidity,' sat down
upon the Imperial couch itself, explaining to the sick
Emperor that he did so in conformity with the rules

---

[1] Sidonius represents Anthemius as refusing the diadem and as not
choosing to be indebted to his wife for the purple (Carm. ii. 210–219),
but it is quite possible that they were never offered to him.

laid down by the old masters of his art, and not out of any disrespect to him.

To Leo the servility of the Byzantine Court was perhaps useful, as giving him courage to resist the too imperious mandates of his old master. It happened, apparently in the first year of his reign, that Aspar asked him to appoint one of his brother Arians to the post of Prefect of the City. Cowed by his long habit of deference Leo assented, but regretted his compliance the moment afterwards. That night he sent for an orthodox senator, and installed him, stealthily and with haste, in the vacant office. Great was Aspar's wrath when he heard of this act of disobedience on the part of his sovereign. He came black-browed into the purple presence-chamber, and grasping the Emperor's robe, said to him, 'Emperor! it is not fitting that he who is wrapped in this purple should tell lies!' To which Leo replied, 'Yea, rather, it is not fitting that the Emperor should be bound to do the bidding of any of his subjects, especially when by his compliance he injures the state [1].'

[1] This characteristic story rests directly upon nothing but the poor authority of Cedrenus (11th or 12th century). But it harmonises with the circumstances of the Byzantine court at this time, and it receives, I think, quite sufficient confirmation from the following passage of the contemporary historian Candidus (quoted by Photius, Bibliotheca Cod. lxxix), 'He also speaks [at the beginning of Leo's reign] concerning Tatian and Vivianus, and *how there was a dispute between Aspar and the Emperor concerning them, and what words they uttered to one another.*' One may almost venture to assign the parts to the two rivals. Tatian, a trusted and orthodox counsellor (who presided at the Council of Chalcedon), is probably the Senator who was installed in the dead of night as prefect; Vivianus the disappointed competitor for this post, is soothed by being appointed consul in the year 463. The whole of this excerpt of Photius is of great value for the history of the Emperor Leo.

For thirteen years the breach between the First of
the Patricians and his late *curator* went on widening.
Yet Aspar was still a great power in the State, and it
seemed not improbable that one of his three sons, Ardaburius, Patricius, or Hermenric, would succeed the son-
less Leo who was already passing the prime of life. To
strengthen himself against the anger of his former
patron, the Emperor began to cultivate the friendship
of some of the Isaurian adventurers who at that time
abounded in Constantinople, wild, rugged, unpopular
men from the highlands of Asia Minor, but men who
were not likely to fail him ' when hard came to hard.'
One of these men, who was known by the barbarous
appellation Tarasicodissa, son of Rusumbladeotus,
changed his name to Zeno, and received the Emperor's
daughter Ariadne in marriage.   Thenceforward it was
understood that Zeno was the head of the party opposed
to Aspar, and that he would, if possible, compass for
himself, or at least for the younger Leo, his son by
Ariadne, the succession to the Imperial throne.

On the other hand, a powerful counterpoise to the
influence of Zeno was found in Basiliscus, the brother of
the Emperor's wife Verina. This man's craving to
wear one day the Imperial diadem was so passionate and
so ill-concealed, that it made him almost the laughing-
stock of the Court ; but it was well-known that he was
the confidant of the still influential Aspar, and that in
the fierce resentment of himself and his party against
the Council of Chalcedon, they were willing to accept
help even from the Arians in order to annul its decrees.
Basiliscus, the Monophysite, practically denied the true
Manhood of Jesus Christ ; Aspar, the Arian, denied his
true Godhead ; but they were ready to co-operate in

458-471.

New
favourites.

Zeno the
Isaurian.

Basiliscus.

order to drive out of Church and State the men who, in obedience to the Council of Chalcedon, maintained the combined Manhood and Godhead of the Saviour.

468.

Great armament against the Vandals under the command of Basiliscus.

Such was the state of parties at Constantinople when in the spring of 468 Leo despatched his long prepared armament against the Vandals. It was meant to deal a crushing blow. The Western Empire contributed probably some supplies both of men and money ; Marcellinus left his Dalmatian palace and his independent principality to serve as a general under the orders of the Roman Emperors ; but the chief weight of the preparations fell, as was natural, on the comparatively unexhausted Empire of the East. Leo, who was a man of courage and capacity, was determined to spare neither trouble nor expense on this great enterprise. A thousand ships, a hundred thousand men, a hundred and thirty thousand pounds' weight of gold (£5,850,000 sterling), had been collected at Constantinople [1]. All seemed to promise well for the success of the armament, but all was ruined by the selection of its head. Basiliscus was appointed Generalissimo : and showed such miserable weakness in his command that later generations believed that Vandal gold, or the secret orders of

---

[1] Joannes Lydus, who as an official had good means of ascertaining the facts, though he wrote in the following century, puts the expenditure on this expedition at 65,000 lbs. weight of gold and 700,000 lbs. of silver, say a little over £5,000,000 sterling. He quite confirms the view taken by Procopius as to the mismanagement of the expedition, and the ruinous result of its failure. He says Καὶ μετὰ ταῦτα πάντα ναυάγιον τῆς πολιτείας. (De Magistratibus, iii. 43.) Candidus, who is an even better authority than Joannes Lydus, says that the treasure collected for this expedition amounted to 47,000 lbs. weight of gold and 700,000 lbs. of silver, and that this was partly raised from the sale of confiscated estates, partly contributed by Anthemius.

Aspar, anxious that his Arian fellow-believers should not be too hardly pressed, caused his failure. Either hypothesis may be true, but historians are too apt to forget the infinite depths of simple human stupidity.

468.

Marcellinus sailed to Sardinia, and expelled the Vandals from that island. Heraclius, another Byzantine general, made a successful descent on Tripolis, took the cities of the Vandals in that region, and marched from thence westwards to the city of Carthage. The proceedings of Basiliscus and the main body of the host shall be told in the very words of the historian Procopius, who is here our only authority. Though he wrote more than half a century after the event, yet as he was an Eastern Roman, and served in that very campaign against Carthage, in which Belisarius did what Basiliscus failed to do, we may listen to his story with some confidence in its general correctness.

533.

'Basiliscus meanwhile, with his whole force, sailed for a town about thirty-five miles from Carthage, called Mercurion, from an old temple of Hermes there ; and if he had not with evil purpose lingered at that place, but had at once commenced his march to Carthage, he would have taken the city at the first shout, annihilated the strength of the Vandals, and reduced them to slavery ; so thoroughly was Gaiseric now alarmed at the irresistible might of the Emperor Leo, who had taken from him Sardinia and Tripolis, and had sent against him such an armament under Basiliscus as all men said the Romans had never fitted out before. All this was now hindered by the general's procrastination, which was due either to cowardice or treachery. Profiting by the supineness

Success at the outset.

468.

of Basiliscus, Gaiseric armed all his subjects as well as he could, and put them on board troop-ships. Other ships, fast-sailors and carrying no soldiers, he held in reserve. Then sending ambassadors to Basiliscus he begged for a delay of five days, pretending that if this were granted him he would consider how he might best comply with the wishes of the Emperor. And some say that he sent a large sum of money to Basiliscus, unknown to his soldiers, in order to purchase this armistice. He devised this scheme in the expectation, which was justified by the event, that in the meantime a wind would spring up which would be favourable to his purposes. Basiliscus then, either in obedience to the recommendation of Aspar, or as having been bribed to grant this truce, or because he really believed that it would be better for the army, stayed quietly in his camp waiting the convenience of the enemy. But the Vandals, as soon as ever the wind arose which they had been patiently expecting, unfurled their sails, and, taking the empty ships in tow, sailed against the

Vandal Fire-ships.

enemy. As soon as they came near they set the empty ships on fire, and sent them with bellying sails full against the anchorage of the Romans. The ships of the latter, being tightly packed together in the quarter to which the fire-ships were directed, soon caught fire, and readily communicated it to one another.

'When the fire was thus kindled, great terror naturally seized the Roman host. Soon, the whistling of the wind, the roar of the fire, the shouts of the soldiers to the sailors, and of the sailors to the soldiers, the strokes of the poles with which they strove to push off the fire-ships or their own burning companions, created a wild hubbub of discordant noises. And now were the

Vandals upon them, hurling javelins, sinking ships, or stripping the fugitive soldiers of their armour. Even in this crisis there were some among the Romans who played the man, most of all Joannes, second in command to Basiliscus, and quite guiltless of all his treachery. For when a great multitude of the enemy surrounded his ship, he from the deck killed numbers of them with his furious blows right and left; and when he saw that the ship was taken, he sprang in full armour from the quarter-deck into the sea. Then did Genzo, the son of Gaiseric, earnestly importune him to surrender, offering him assistance and promising him safety, but he none the less committed his body to the sea, with this one cry, "Never will Joannes fall into the hands of dogs."

468.
Roman Defeat.

' With this the war was ended. Heraclius returned home. Basiliscus, when he arrived at Byzantium, seated himself as a suppliant in the temple which is dedicated to the great Christ and God, and which is called Sophia [Wisdom] because the Byzantines think that epithet the most appropriate to God. On the earnest entreaty of his sister, the Empress Verina, he escaped death, but his hopes of the throne, for the sake of which he had done all these things, were for the present dashed [1] ' by the soon following fall of Aspar and Ardaburius.

Basiliscus pardoned on his return to Constantinople.

Truly in reading Procopius' account of all the valour and treasure wasted in this campaign, one can heartily echo the saying of a more recent Byzantine historian [2], ' Better is an army of stags led by lions than an army of lions led by a stag.'

In some mysterious manner the close of this campaign

[1] Procopius, De Bello Vandalico, i. 6. [2] Cedrenus.

was connected with the fall of the brilliant and courageous Marcellinus.   We are told that he ' perished by the treachery of one of his colleagues [1],' that he was killed in Sicily [2],' that ' while bringing aid and succour to the Romans fighting against the Vandals near Carthage, he was guilefully struck down by the very men whom he was coming to help [4].'   We know that the Dalmatian palace was left empty, that there were no more talks by the shore of the plashing Adriatic between the general and his philosopher friend Sallust, concerning the nature of the gods and the causes of the ruin of this perplexing world.   But why or by whom Marcellinus died remains a mystery.

*468.
Death of
Marcelli-
nus.
Aug. 468 [3].*

*Entry of
Anthemius
into Rome.*

The unsuccessful campaign against Carthage occurred, as has been said, in the spring and summer of 468. We return to the events of the preceding spring in Italy.   On the 12th of April 467, the population of Rome poured forth to meet the new Emperor who was henceforth to rule over them in firm alliance with his brother Augustus of Constantinople.   At the third milestone from the city [5] Anthemius was solemnly proclaimed Emperor of Rome in the presence probably of a brilliant escort from Byzantium, including his wife Euphemia, daughter of an Emperor, and now Empress herself, of his three sons, Marcian, Romulus, and Procopius, and a daughter, Alypia [6], who was to play an important part in cementing the new alliance between

---

[1] Procopius, as quoted above.   [2] Cassiodorus, s. a. 468.

[3] Cuspiniani Anon. s. a.   [4] Marcellinus, s. a. 468.

[5] Presumably on the road to Ostia, and ' at a place called Brontotus,' says Cassiodorus.   I have not found any other passage which throws light on this name.

[6] The name of Alypia is mentioned by Joannes Antiochenus, frag. 209.

East and West. The Patrician Ricimer was there doubtless, scanning the features of the new sovereign, and endeavouring to find an answer to the question, '467.' 'To rule or to be ruled?' There too were the Senate, the copious German guards, the dwindled ranks of the legionaries, and the Roman populace, those jaded and dissipated sons of slaves who still called themselves Quirites, and talked of Father Mars and the She-Wolf's nurslings.

The new Emperor was not merely son-in-law of Mar- Pedigree and early cian, but in his own right a great Byzantine noble. On history of his father's side he was descended from that Procopius, mius. Anthemius.

FAMILY OF ANTHEMIUS.

whose revolt against Valentinian and whose short-lived sovereignty were described at the beginning of this

---

[1] Ariadne begged her husband the Emperor Anastasius to bestow on this Anthemius the office of Praetorian Prefect, but he refused, with some anger, saying that it ought to be held only by men of letters (Joannes Lydus, De Magist. iii. 50).

[2] Marcian married Leontia, daughter of the Emperor Leo. He was therefore brother-in-law of Ariadne, and through her, of the Emperors Zeno and Anastasius (Evagrius, iii. 26).

history [1].   On his mother's side he traced his descent
from Anthemius, Praetorian Prefect of the East, and
virtual Regent during the early years of the minority
of Theodosius II.   Both this Anthemius (his maternal
grandfather) and Procopius (his father) had been employed in important embassies to the Persian Court [2].
He himself, aided no doubt by his fortunate marriage to
Euphemia, had in early manhood attained the successive
dignities of Count of Illyricum, Master of the Soldiery,
Consul (455), and Patrician.   The expectation of some

457.   of the courtiers had marked him out as a probable successor of Marcian, but when the all-powerful voice of
Aspar decreed the diadem to Leo, Anthemius sensibly
took the disappointment in good part, attached himself
loyally to the fortunes of the new Emperor, and was
soon entrusted by him with an important command on
the Lower Danube.   Walamir the Ostrogoth, and Hormidac the Hun, were apparently both threatening the
Roman inhabitants of the country which we now call
Bulgaria.   The populous city of Sardica (now Sofia),
upon the northern slope of the Balkans, was in especial
danger.   Anthemius distinguished himself by the strict
discipline which he maintained among his troops—
often in those degenerate days more terrible to friend
than foe—and in a pitched battle with Hormidac, he

---

[1] See vol. i. pp. 139–160.

[2] The embassy of Anthemius, which was before 405, is mentioned
by Theodoret (de Vita Patrum, cap. 8), that of Procopius by Sidonius
(Carm. ii. 75 et seq.)—

  'Huic [Procopio] quondam juveni reparatio credita pacis
    Assyriae: stupuit primis se Parthus in annis
    Consilium non ferre senis' &c.

But I confess that I doubt whether Sidonius has not made a blunder
between the grandfather and the father of his hero.

obtained, we are told, a decisive victory, notwithstanding the treacherous conduct of a subordinate—probably a barbarian—officer, who in the very crisis of the battle drew off all his cavalry, and left the Imperial flank exposed. After the victory the Roman general imposed one indispensable condition of peace upon the conquered Huns—the surrender of his traitorous colleague, who was put to death in the sight of both armies [1].

467.

Such was the past history of the richly-clothed Byzantine official who, in the spring of 467, rode proudly in through the gate of Rome, amidst the acclamations of soldiery and populace. 'Long live Anthemius Augustus! Long live Ricimer, the Patrician! Long live the Concord of the Emperors!'

When the tidings of these Roman pageants reached the banks of the Rhone, one can imagine what envy they raised in the heart of Sidonius. 'An Emperor acclaimed, and I not there to weave his praises into hexameters!' was a bitter reflection for the Gaulish poet. He had still some unused metaphors in his head; the necessary compliments to the Eastern Empire would give a motive entirely different from those of his two previous panegyrics; there was always the possibility of turning a few chapters of Livy into sonorous verse, and, in short, he resolved to resume the 'useful toil' of a Panegyrist. A deputation of citizens of Auvergne was appointed to congratulate Anthemius on his accession, perhaps to solicit the redress of grievances, or help against the Visigoths; but it is plain from Sidonius' letters [2] that the message entrusted to the

Sidonius hears of the accession of Anthemius and meditates a new Panegyric.

---

[1] Or perhaps slain by the Huns and his corpse delivered to the Romans. 'Atque peregrino cecidit tua victima ferro' (Sidonius, Carm. ii. 298).   [2] Sidonius, Ep. i. 5 and 9.

deputation was the last thing in his thoughts ; the real
business to him was the Panegyric.

His errand having received the sanction of 'the
sacred autograph,' he was entitled to travel at the
public charge, by that admirably-organised postal
service (the *cursus*) which was probably about the last
to perish of the Imperial institutions.   In a letter to a
friend, he describes his journey with a few life-like
touches, though some sentences reveal the rhetorician.
But the friendly aspect of the well-known villas by the
Rhone, the short climb up the torrent-beds and over
the snows of the Alps, the voyage from Ticinum (*Pavia*)
down the Ticino and the Po, past cities which recalled
the honoured name of Virgil, and through woods of oak
and maple alive with the sweet song of birds, are all
vividly brought before us.   He admired the situation
of Ravenna[1], so strong for defence, so convenient for
commerce, and was in doubt whether to say that the
city and the harbour (Classis) were connected or divided
by the long 'Street of Caesar' which passed between
them.   But, though provisions of all kinds were to be
had at Ravenna in abundance, he found, as other poets
had found before him, that water fit for drinking was
an unattainable luxury in that city, and he suffered
the pangs of thirst though surrounded by streams[2].
Across the historic Rubicon and Metaurus, through the
plains of Picenum and the valleys of Umbria, the
Gaulish poet journeyed, no doubt with the lines of the
fateful Panegyric churning in his head.   But either
the Sirocco blowing over the plains, or (as was probably

---

[1] This description of Ravenna was quoted in vol. i (p. 859).

[2] 'In medio undarum sitiebamus.'   I need not quote the parallel
passage from the 'Ancient Mariner.'

the case) the imperfect drainage of Ravenna[1], had by
this time touched him with a fever. Alternately
burning and shivering, he quaffed, but in vain, the
waters of every stream and fountain near which his
journey led him; and when the towers of Rome
appeared upon the horizon, his feeling was that all the
aqueducts of the City, and all the mimic seas of the
amphitheatres[2], would be insufficient to quench his
thirst.

467.

However, before entering the city he visited the
tombs of the Apostles, and after he had prostrated
himself there, he felt that the languor of the fever
departed from his limbs. He found the whole city in
an uproar, on account of the wedding between the
Patrician Ricimer and the daughter of the Ever-August
Emperor; an union which, while it reversed the relations between 'the Father of the Emperor' and his
new father-in-law, was avowedly based on state considerations, and was looked upon as affording a new
guarantee for the public tranquillity by cementing the
alliance between Byzantine legitimacy and the rough
strength of Ricimer's barbarians. Theatres, markets,
temples, were all resounding with the Fescennine verses
in which the populace, sometimes not too decorously,
expressed their congratulations to the wedded pair.
The bridegroom, with a crown upon his head, and the
flowered robe (*palmata*) of the Consular upon his
shoulders, went to fetch the bride from the house of

Sidonius finds Rome en fête on account of the marriage of Ricimer.

---

[1] Sidonius himself speaks of the ' Cloacalis puls fossarum discursu
lintrium ventilata.'

[2] 'Inter haec patuit et Roma conspectui: cujus mihi non solum
formas, *verum etiam naumachias* videbar epotaturus' (Sidonius, Ep.
i. 5).

her father. In the universal hubbub, no one had any ears for the Gallic deputation, and the Transalpine poet, seeking the comparative quiet of his inn, drew, for the benefit of his correspondent at Lyons, an amusing picture of the 'earnest holiday[1]' of the humming city.

When he next took up the pen he was able to announce a brilliant success. The great poem had been recited on New Year's Day (468), and had earned for its author applause and a high office in the state. As soon as the wedding turmoil was over, and the riches of two empires had been sufficiently displayed to public view, the affairs of the state resumed their ordinary course. The Gallic deputies met with entertainment and a courteous reception at the house of one Paulus, a venerable man and an ex-prefect. Sidonius describes with amusing *naïveté* how he then set to work to attach himself to a patron, Paulus being presumably too old to give him efficient assistance. The choice lay between two men, both of consular rank, and confessedly the most influential persons in the state after the Emperor, 'always excepting the predominant power of the military party'—a most significant exception, which probably included Ricimer and all his immediate followers.

These two possible patrons were Gennadius Avienus and Caecina Basilius. Avienus had obtained the consulship in 450, and had been congratulated by all his friends on his early promotion. Basilius had been made consul in 463, and all the City had said, 'Why was not so good a man raised to the office before?'

467.

Sidonius chooses a patron.

Characters of Avienus and Basilius.

---

[1] 'Occupatissimam vacationem totius civitatis.'

Either nobleman saw his gate thronged with suitors, and was followed through the forum by a crowd of obsequious clients; but the composition of the two bands of retainers was very different, and so was the nature of their hopes. Avienus was most successful in pushing the fortunes of his sons, his sons-in-law, and his brothers: when all this had been accomplished, there was not much court-influence left for more distant clients, whom he accordingly charmed with his affable demeanour, but who somehow found that they were not drawing any nearer to the goal of their wishes, notwithstanding all the hours that they spent at their patron's vestibule. Basilius had far fewer of his own friends to provide for, and his manner with those whom he admitted into the circle of his dependents was much more reserved, almost haughty; but when he did accept the homage of a client, he was almost certain to obtain for him the fulfilment of his desires. Upon this estimate of their respective characters, Sidonius wisely decided to attach himself to the *clientèle* of Basilius, while not omitting to pay frequent visits of ceremony at the door of Avienus.

467.

Favoured by the efficient help of Basilius, the affairs of the Arvernian deputation were soon in good train for settlement. One day the Patron said to the Poet, 'Come, my Sollius! The Kalends of January are at hand, and the name of our Emperor is to be inscribed on the Fasti of this New Year. Though I know that you are weighed down with the responsibility of your deputation, can you not call upon your old Muse to inspire you with some lines in honour of the new consul? It is true that in so short a time they will have to be almost the result of improvisation, but I can

Basilius proposes to Sidonius the production of a panegyric on Anthemius.

promise you a hearing for your verses, and at least my
hands for their applause.'

468.
The Pane-
gyric re-
cited on
New Year's
Day.

It needs not to be said that the suggestion of
Basilius was eagerly accepted, and that upon the
morning of the first day of 468 Sidonius was ready
with an 'impromptu' of 547 lines in praise of Anthemius.   There is no need to describe this poem with
any fulness of detail, since the reader can easily imagine
its character from the two similar performances by the
same hand in praise of Avitus and Majorian.   There is
an eloquent passage in praise of Constantinople [1], and
a graphic account of the manners of the Huns [2], very
closely corresponding with the pictures drawn by
Jordanes and Ammianus.   The lineage of Anthemius
is described; the conventional prodigies which marked
his birth and infancy; the events of his military and
official career; and great stress is laid on his unwilling-
ness—real or imaginary—to accept the Western Crown,
till commanded to do so by Leo.   The real interest of
the poem for us lies in its hints as to the course of
contemporary politics, in its portraiture of Gaiseric and
Ricimer.

> ' Each Emperor that on Western soil is born
> Fails from the helm and perishes forlorn.
> Here the stern Vandal spreads his thousand sails
> And yearly for our ruin courts the gales.
> Strange fate !   Upon our shores swart Afric throws
> The nations reared amid Caucasian snows [3].

[1]
>   ' At tu circumflua ponto
> Europae atque Asiae commissam carpis utrimque
> Temperiem nam Bistonios Aquiloniş hiatus
> Proxima Chalcidici sensim tuba temperat Euri,' &c.

Carm. ii. 46–49.

[2] Carm. ii. 243–269.

[3] This is mere poetic generalisation.   Of course the Vandals had

Alone, till now, with Mars his only friend,
He on whose arm the fates of Rome depend,
Unconquered Ricimer has held at bay   468.
The Freebooter[1] who makes our fields his prey,
Who skulks from battle, yet can still contrive
To reap the victor's spoils, a fugitive.
Whose strength by such a foe would not be spent
Who gives nor Peace nor War's arbitrament?
"No peace with Ricimer," his watchword dire,
And *this* the cause that fills his veins with fire.
He knows himself the offspring of a slave,
The sire he knows not who his being gave.
Hence envy gnaws him, that his rival springs,
Great Ricimer, on either side from kings.
His sire a Sueve, a royal Gothic dame
His mother, who of Walia's lineage came;
The noble Walia, whose redoubted sword
Drove forth from Spain the motley, mongrel horde
Of Vandals, Alans, worsted in the fray,
And with their corpses covered Calpé's bay[2].'

But Ricimer alone, says the poet, can no longer ward off the perils of the Empire. There is need of an Emperor of the old type, one who can not only order wars, but wage them. Such an Emperor the East can furnish, and, on the intercession of Rome, she does furnish, in the bronzed veteran Anthemius. He and his son-in-law have prepared fleets and armies which will surely reduce Africa to its ancient obedience. In some future year, when Anthemius shall be consul for a third, or Ricimer for a second time, Sidonius promises himself the delight of again appearing before them to chant the fall of Gaiseric.

The florid Panegyric was received, its author tells us,

had nothing to do with Caucasus. For their Alan confederates the reference is less incorrect.

[1] Gaiseric.   [2] Carm. ii. 346-365.

with rapturous applause. Shouts of ' Sophos! Sophos[1]!'
(the Greek equivalent of ' bravo') resounded from the
benches where sat the senators conspicuous by their
purple *laticlaves*[2], and from the higher tiers of seats
where swarmed the common people, the representatives
of the once omnipotent Roman tribes[3]. A more striking
proof of approbation was given by the Emperor, who,
on the recommendation of Basilius, named Sidonius
Prefect of the City of Rome[4]. Thus, as he himself
piously expresses it, ' I have now, by the help of Christ
and an opportune use of my pen, arrived at the Prefecture.' In modern states (China and the great
American Republic alone excepted) it would be hard
to find an instance of honours such as this conferred
on the votaries of literature.

Sidonius was now in theory the third personage in
the Empire, on a level with the Praetorian Prefects of
Italy and Gaul, inferior only to the Emperor and the
Patrician. In practice, however, it is probable that
many a rude Herulian centurion or tribune counted for
more than the versatile thin-minded poet. Besides his
presidency over the Senate, the aqueducts, the market-
places, the fore-shores, the harbour, the statues, were
all under his care[5]. But his chief business—an in-
finitely harassing one in those dying days of the Empire

468.
Success
of the
Panegyric.

Sidonius
appointed
Prefectus
Urbis.

His
duties and
anxieties
in that
capacity.

---

[1] σοφῶς.

[2] A broad stripe on the tunic.

[3] ' Ad *Sophos* meum non modo laticlavi sed tribulium quoque
fragor concitaretur' (Sidonius, Ep. i. 9).

[4] Sidonius' words are 'egit cum consule meo ut me praefectum
faceret senatui suo.' But the Presidency of the Senate was one of
the functions of the *Praefectus Urbi.*

[5] See the 'Notitia Dignitatum in partibus Occidentis,' cap. iv, for
a sketch of the duties of the Praefectus Urbis. See also vol. i. p. 608.

—was the care of the provisioning of the City, which rested upon him and his subordinate, the Commissary General (*Praefectus Annonae*), as the Earthly Provi-dence of Rome.   It is curious to read a letter from the new Prefect to a Gaulish friend, in which he expresses his fear lest, when he next visits the amphitheatre, he should hear a harsh cry of rage from the assembled multitude[1], imputing their hunger to his incapacity. A gleam of hope shines upon him when he is informed that five ships, laden with corn and honey, have arrived at Ostia from Brindisi, and he despatches his *Praefectus Annonae* with all speed, to receive and distribute the precious cargoes.

468.

Sidonius retained his new dignity only for one year, but on laying it down he probably received the title of Patrician[2]—a title which was in his case purely hono-rary, conferring no power and imposing no responsibility. The short tenure of his office does not exactly imply disgrace, but it may probably be asserted that if the Gaulish man of letters had shown any conspicuous ability in his Prefectorate, his office would have been renewed to him at least for two or three years[3].   He

His retire-ment from office.

---

[1] Like the 'Pretium pone carnis humanae,' which was shouted by the people in the Colosseum, in 410, when Attalus was Emperor.

[2] This is inferred by his biographers from the letter to his wife, Papianilla, quoted above (p. 347), in which he speaks of himself as having achieved Patrician honours.

[3] In the list of Prefects of the City from 254 to 354, published by Mommsen (Abhandlungen der Königl. Sächs. Gesellschaft der Wissenschaften, 1850, pp. 627–630), there is one instance of the office being held for four years.   A tenure of two years is the most frequent, one of three years is not uncommon.   About forty-five Prefects in the century did not hold office for two consecutive years; but these more frequent changes generally coincide with periods of unsettlement and revolution in the Empire.

quitted Rome in the year 469, never to return to that
scene of petty intrigues and worn-out splendours—

469.

pigmies masquerading in the armour of giants—a scene
which must have filled a thoughtful man with sadness
and a cynic with a rapture of scorn.

Trial of
Arvandus,
Praetorian
Prefect
of Gaul.

But before he went he witnessed the commencement
of a process which attracted his deepest interest, and
filled him with varied emotions—the trial and condemnation of Arvandus. This man, a fellow-countryman
of Sidonius, had for five years held the office of Praetorian Prefect of Gaul. The popularity which marked
his earlier years of office had utterly deserted him
before its close. He had become involved in debt,
from which he sought to free himself by the most
unjust exactions from the provincials; he had grown
moody, suspicious, implacable ; and finally, knowing
the universal disfavour with which the Roman population regarded him, he had commenced a traitorous
correspondence with the Visigothic king. Three Gaulish
noblemen were sent as a deputation to Rome to im-
peach Arvandus before the Senate on charges of extortion and high treason ('*rerum repetundarum et
laesae majestatis*').

The arrival of this deputation, and of the accused
governor, placed Sidonius in an awkward position.
The deputies were all of them acquaintances of his,
and one (Tonantius Ferreolus) was his relative and
intimate friend [1]. On the other hand, Arvandus had
been long known, though never liked by him, and he
says that he would have thought it base and barbarous
to desert him in the day of his calamity. This difficulty
however was soon solved by the accused himself, who,

[1] See the letter, quoted on p. 324, describing the visit to his house.

when Sidonius and a fellow-noble ventured to give him
some hints as to the necessity of tact and moderation
in the conduct of his case, flamed out upon them with
the words, 'Away with you, ye degenerate sons of
Prefects! Who wants your fussy anxiety on my
behalf? Arvandus' conscience suffices for Arvandus.
I can scarcely bring myself even to hire an advocate
to defend me from the charge of extortion.'

All the rest of his conduct was of a piece with this
outburst of petulance. While the Gaulish deputies
were walking about in sad-coloured garments, with
downcast faces, as men who had a painful duty to
perform on behalf of the oppressed, Arvandus, in a
white toga, with scented hair and pumice-stoned face,
gaily promenaded the Forum, nodding to his friends
as if his salutation were still of the highest value,
frequenting the jewellers' shops, chaffering over the
price of fashionable knick-knacks, and all the while
keeping up a running fire of complaints against the
Emperor, the Senate, and the laws, for allowing a
person of his quality to be subjected to the indignity
of a trial.

The eventful day arrived. The Senate-house was
crowded. The defendant, fresh from the hair-dresser's
hands, walked boldly up to the benches of the 'prefec-
torians,' and took his seat, as if of right, in the most
honourable place among his judges. Ferreolus, on the
contrary, equally entitled to a seat among the 'prefec-
torians,' placed himself, along with his fellow-deputies,
on one of the lowest benches of the Senate-house. The
deputation set forth their case, and read the mandate
which they had received from their fellow-citizens.
Instead of lingering over the outworks of the indict-

469.

ment, the charges of peculation and extortion, they went rapidly to the heart of the matter, the accusation of treasonable intrigues with the Barbarians. A letter was produced, in the handwriting of the amanuensis of Arvandus, addressed to the Visigothic king. It tended to dissuade him from making peace with 'the Greek Emperor' (Anthemius), suggested that he should attack the Bretons[1], who were allies of the Empire, and recommended that 'the Visigoths and the Burgundians should divide Gaul between them, according to the law of nations.' There might have been some difficulty in tracing the composition of this letter to Arvandus, but the infatuated culprit aimed the weapon against himself by at once boldly proclaiming that he was the author.

Condemnation of Arvandus. 'Then you are guilty of high-treason' (*laesa majestas*), said every voice in the assembly. He then tried to retract and to qualify his previous admissions, for with incredible folly[2] he had hitherto supposed that nothing short of the actual assumption of the Imperial purple would have justified a condemnation for high-treason. But it was too late; his guilt was manifest. He was stripped of all his dignities, and the delicately-dressed and scented culprit was hurled, with every mark of disgrace, into a squalid dungeon on the Insula Tiberina, sentenced to be there killed by the executioner, to have his body dragged by an iron hook through the streets, and then to be cast into the Tiber.

---

[1]   'Britannos super Ligerim sitos impugnari oportere.'

(Sidonius, Ep. i. 7.)

[2] Possibly the dislocated relations of all the members of the Western Empire at this time might have afforded some precedents as a basis for this wild notion.

By the wise and merciful legislation of Theodosius, due to the suggestion of Ambrose[1], an interval of thirty days necessarily elapsed between the utterance and the execution of a capital sentence. This interval Sidonius employed in pleading for a mitigation of the punishment of the fallen Prefect, though, as he contemptuously remarked, ' No greater calamity can befall him than that he should wish to live, after all the ignominy that has been heaped upon him.' An entry in one of the Chroniclers[2] seems to justify the inference that the intervention of Sidonius was successful, and that the capital sentence was commuted into one of perpetual exile.

469. Sidonius pleads for a mitigation of the sentence.

It is not improbable that one cause of Sidonius' departure from Rome may have been that he saw the political horizon darkening with the impending rupture between Ricimer and Anthemius. The great enterprise against Carthage, which should have united them, had failed, as was before stated (468); and thus, both Rome and the Suevic chief had humbled themselves before Byzantium for nothing. Anthemius was hot-tempered, and probably felt himself by intellect as well as by birth fitted for something better than to be the mere puppet of a barbarian. We have no hint as to the part taken by his daughter, in soothing or in exciting the combatants, but we can imagine that she let the middle-aged Patrician, her husband, see too plainly how vast she considered her condescension in becoming the wife of a barbarian. In 470 another event added fuel to the

Anthemius and Ricimer at feud.

---

[1] See vol. i. p. 533.

[2] Cassiodorus s. a. 469, 'Marcianus et Zeno. His conss. Arabundus imperium temptans jussu Anthemii exilio deportatur.' The old reading Ardaburius is no doubt rightly rejected by Mommsen.

471.

fire. The Emperor, who found his health failing him, believed that he was the victim of magical arts, and arrested many persons upon the charge of thus compassing his death. A certain Romanus, an adherent of Ricimer, himself bearing the title of Patrician as well as that of Master of the Army, was among the persons put to death on this accusation. Thereat Ricimer, in a fury, flung out of Rome and called to his standards 6000 men who had served under him in the Vandal war [1].

Ricimer's head-quarters at Mediolanum.

In the spring of the year 471 [2] Ricimer was at Milan, surrounded, no doubt, by the Teutonic auxiliaries, and leaning perhaps somewhat on the aid of his brother-in-law, the king of the Burgundians, who held all the northern passes of the Western Alps, since he ruled in Valais and Savoy, in Dauphiné and the Lower Valley of the Rhone. Anthemius was not at Ravenna, but in Rome, relying on the favour with which he was regarded by the populace of the City [3], on the sympathies of the official class, and on the patriotism of whatsoever purely Roman and Italian elements might be left in the legions. Between these two men, all Italy perceived with horror that war was inevitable.

Such being the state of things, the nobles of Liguria

---

[1] Joannes Antiochenus, fr. 207; Cassiodorus, s. a. 470.

[2] Or 472; but as Epiphanius returned from his embassy on the 14th day before Easter, as he was for the time successful and as Olybrius was raised to the throne by Ricimer in April, 472, it seems almost certain that we must refer the first outbreak of civil war and the mediation of Epiphanius to 471. Easter fell on the 16th of April in the year 472 (see 'l'Art de vérifier les Dates'). Tillemont assigns the embassy of Epiphanius to 469, but, I think, on insufficient grounds. It *might* be 470.

[3] Joannes Antiochenus expressly says that 'on the side of Anthemius were ranged those in office and the people, and on that of Ricimer the multitude of his own barbarians.'

assembled at the palace of Ricimer, and adoring the
Suevic Patrician with self-prostration, after the manner
of the Orientals, besought him to consent to an accommodation with his father-in-law.   Ricimer was, or professed to be, mollified by their arguments.   ‘But whom
will ye send as mediator?’ said he; ‘Who can bring
this hot-headed Galatian[1] prince to reason?   If you
ask him for the smallest favour he bubbles over with
fury, and there is not a man living who can remain in
a passion so long as he.’   ‘There is a person in this
province,’ said the nobles, ‘to whom you may safely
entrust this commission; a man to whom even wild
beasts would bow their necks; a man whom a Catholic
and a Roman must venerate, and whom even the little
Greek Emperor cannot help loving if he is privileged to
behold him[2].’   And then they proceeded to sketch the
life and recount the virtues of Epiphanius, the saintly
young Bishop of Pavia, in somewhat similar words possibly to those in which they are now recorded for us by
his admiring disciple Ennodius, from whom we derive
our knowledge of this incident.

In the life of Epiphanius we meet of course with
many incidents and traits of character common to a
saint of that period of the Church.   A supernatural
light shone round his cradle when he was still busy with

*471.
The Ligu-
rian nobles
interpose.*

*Life of
Epipha-
nius the
chosen
mediator.*

---

[1] There is some sting in this word Galatian which we cannot
explain.   Possibly it is connected with the fact that the ancestral
Procopius, who assumed the purple in the year 365, was ‘ *in Ciliciâ
natus et educatus* ’ (Ammianus, xxvi. 6. 1), Cilicia and Galatia being
provinces not far distant from one another.

[2] ‘Est nobis persona nuper ad sacerdotium Ticinensis urbis adscita,
cui et belluae rabidae colla submittunt ... cui est vultus vitae similis,
quem venerari possit quicunque, si est Catholicus et Romanus;
amare certe, si videre mereatur, et Graeculus.’

471.

the rattle and the baby's-bottle [1]. On the strength of this omen he was at eight years old received into the Ministry of the Church as a Reader (*lector*), and before long distinguished himself by the rapidity and accuracy with which he practised the art of an ecclesiastical short-hand writer (*exceptor*). Ordained a Deacon at twenty, Priest at twenty-eight, and almost immediately afterwards elected Bishop of Pavia, he was already in his early manhood marked out for the veneration of his contemporaries. 'He knew not that he was a man,' says his biographer, 'except by his power of enduring toil; he forgot that he was in the flesh except when he meditated on his mortality.' No great miracles are recorded of his earlier years, but the saintly patience and dignity with which he, a young Ligurian of noble blood, endured the cudgelling administered to him by a rustic boor named Burco, who had a dispute with the Church of Pavia about boundaries, endeared him to his fellow-citizens, and enabled him to plead successfully for the life of his antagonist when the indignant populace clamoured for his execution. Altogether, though the robes of these ecclesiastical personages are beginning to fall stiffly, and though the fifth-century type of holiness lacks, to our thinking, the freshness of a true humanity, we cannot but feel that Epiphanius was one of those men to whom mere goodness gives a wonderful magnetic power over all who come in contact with them. His sweet and pure figure is a refreshing contrast to the wild passions and base treacheries with which his age is filled.

Mission of Epipha-nius.

Such was the man who, on the invitation of the Ligurians, with the assent of Ricimer, while greatly

---

[1] 'Dum esset in crepundiis lactentis infantiae.'

doubting his own sufficiency for the task, undertook the mission to Anthemius. When he reached Rome, all the officers of the household went forth to meet him without the gates. They brought him into the Imperial hall of audience, where the flash of gems and the sombre magnificence of the purple still, as in the mightiest days of the Empire, attested the presence of Augustus. But all eyes were fixed, not on the Emperor, but on the tall ecclesiastic, with brow of marble whiteness and delicately formed limbs [1], who, sparing of words in his ordinary conversation, was about to speak on behalf of Italy and Peace.

'Dread sovereign!' he began, 'we recognise the hand of God in calling to the highest place in this commonwealth you who have shewn yourself a faithful adherent to the teaching of the Catholic faith, in permitting you to eclipse the triumphs of war by the arts of peace, and to restore the interrupted harmony of the Roman world. Be this still your glory, oh Emperor! Still blend gentleness with force, and thereby make your rule a copy of the heavenly kingdom [2]. Remember how David, by sparing King Saul when he was in his power, earned more glory than would have accrued from the most righteous vengeance. This is the request of Italy, this the message which Ricimer has entrusted to the mouth of my Littleness. Earn for yourself a bloodless victory, overcome even this proud Goth by your benefits. Or,

471.

Speech of Epiphanius to the Emperor.

---

[1] See the description of the personal appearance of Epiphanius in the beginning of the life by Ennodius.

[2] 'Supernae namque dominationis instar possidet, qui imperium suum pietate sublimat.'

'And earthly power doth then show likest God's
When Mercy seasons Justice.'

if you are still in doubt, consider all the chances of war, war in which you may be defeated, and in which even victory must lessen the resources of your Empire, while by a peaceful compact with Ricimer you might have enjoyed them undiminished.'

He ended, and Anthemius, raising his eyes, saw that the hearts of all the by-standers were won by the words of peace. With a deep sigh he said, 'Holy Bishop! The causes of my anger against Ricimer are such as cannot be fully set forth in words. I have loaded him with benefits; I have not even spared my own flesh and blood, but have given my daughter to this skin-clothed Goth [1], an alliance which I cannot think upon without shame for myself, my family, and my kingship. But the more I have distinguished him with my gifts, the more bitterly has he become mine enemy. He has stirred up foreign nations to war against the Commonwealth; where he could not himself hurt, he has suggested to others schemes for hurting me. I myself believe that it is better to treat such a man as an open foe. To feel your enemy is the first step towards overcoming him, and anything is better than the machinations of secret hatred. But since you interpose your venerable office and your holy character as a pledge for his sincere desire for peace, be it so. I cannot resist anything which such a man as you pleads for. If your perceptions have been deceived, and if he still have war in his heart, on him shall rest the guilt of renewing

---

[1] 'Quis hoc namque veterum retro principum fecit unquam, ut inter munera quae *pellito Getae* dare necesse erat, pro quiete communi filia poneretur?' Of course the 'skin-clothed Goth' is a figure of speech. Probably the toga of Ricimer was as faultless as that of his father-in-law.

the combat. I commit and commend myself and the commonwealth, whose pilot I am, entirely into your hands, and I grant to you the pardon which Ricimer himself should not have obtained, no, not if he had been grovelling in the dust before my feet.'

The Bishop thanked God for having put these peaceful counsels into the heart of him whom he had chosen as the Vicar of his supreme power among men[1] ; he then took a solemn oath from Anthemius to hold fast the newly re-cemented alliance, and departed in all haste for Liguria. He travelled so rapidly, although his strength was reduced by a rigorous Lenten fast, that he returned to Pavia on the sixth day after he had quitted it, and the joyful shouts of the people surrounding his house, and learning from his own mouth the news of the ratified treaty of peace, were the first intimation to Ricimer that his messenger had quitted Rome.

Return of Epiphanius to Liguria.

However, the peace between the two rival Powers in the State was of short duration. Some expressions in the narrative would lead us to suppose that the position of Anthemius, at the time of the embassy, was slightly the stronger of the two, and that Ricimer showed his usual cunning in accepting the good offices of the Bishop. Within fourteen months (possibly within two months) after the negotiations at Milan, we find the two parties again in arms against one another. Ricimer proclaimed Olybrius Emperor, thereby conciliating the support of the Vandal king, and perhaps neutralising the opposition of the friends of Anthemius at Constantinople, for Olybrius was also a Byzantine, and also

The quarrel breaks out anew.

472.

Proclamation of Olybrius, April 472.

---

[1] 'Princeps, quem ad instar superni dominatus vicarium suae potestatis voluit esse mortalibus.'

allied to the Imperial family [1]. He marched to the
outskirts of Rome and pitched his camp near a bridge
over the Anio, probably the Ponte Salaro [2]. Within
the walls opinion was divided, some even of the citizens
ranging themselves on the side of Ricimer, though the
majority no doubt adhered to Anthemius. For five
months the siege lasted, Ricimer keeping a strict watch
upon the upper and lower waters of the Tiber, and suffering no provisions to enter the city. The pressure of
the famine was so great that (as Theophanes tells us)
' the soldiers were reduced to feed upon leather and
other unusual articles of food.' Then an unexpected
auxiliary appeared upon the scene [3]. ' Bilimer, ruler
of the Gauls' (we have no clue to the true character
of this mysterious personage), ' hearing of the conspiracy against Anthemius, came to Rome earnestly
desiring to give him assistance. He joined battle with
Ricimer by the bridge of Hadrian' (the bridge leading
to the castle of S. Angelo) ' and was immediately overcome and slain. On his death Ricimer entered the city
as conqueror, and slew Anthemius with the sword.'
Another authority (Joannes Antiochenus) tells us that
' the followers of Anthemius opened the gates to the

472.
Siege of
Rome.

Death of
Anthemius

---

[1] Paulus Diaconus (Hist. Romana, xv. 3) makes Leo himself send
Olybrius to Rome to wrest the crown from Anthemius. Perhaps the
concurring testimonies of Theophanes and the Paschal Chronicle may
be accepted as showing that this was the received version of the
story at Constantinople.

[2] There can be little doubt that the ' *Pons Anicionis*' of Paulus is
equivalent to *Pons Anienis*.

[3] Paulus, whose sources of information are here unusually good (see
Neues Archiv, i. 307), is our authority for this element in the story.
He says also that from the famine which was raging in Rome two
' regions' were exempt in which Ricimer dwelt with his followers.
Perhaps these were on the West of the Tiber.

barbarians, leaving their master defenceless, that he
mixed with the crowd of mendicants, and sought refuge
at the tomb of the martyr Chrysogonus[1], and being
there discovered was instantly beheaded by Gundobad,
the nephew[2] of Ricimer. He received a royal burial at
the hands of his enemies.' Anthemius perished on the
11th July, 472; and only five weeks afterwards his turbulent son-in-law followed him to the grave. On the
18th August, Ricimer, the Patrician, who had held
supreme power in Italy for sixteen years, died of a
sudden hemorrhage, and thus the stage was left clear
for new actors. What they will make of the defence
or extension of the Roman Empire we shall see in the
following chapter.

472.
and of
Ricimer.

[1] The Basilica of Chrysogonus (one of the martyrs under Diocletian) stands in the Trastevere, about a quarter of a mile west of
the Ponte Rotto.

[2] Joannes says ' brother,' but this is an error.

GENEALOGY OF OLYBRIUS.

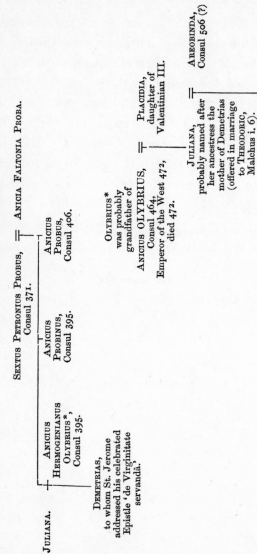

SEXTUS PETRONIUS PROBUS, Consul 371. ══ ANICIA FALTONIA PROBA.

ANICIUS HERMOGENIANUS OLYBRIUS*, Consul 395.

ANICIUS PROBINUS, Consul 395.

ANICIUS PROBUS, Consul 406.

JULIANA.

DEMETRIAS, to whom St. Jerome addressed his celebrated Epistle 'de Virginitate servandâ.'

OLYBRIUS* was probably grandfather of ANICIUS OLYBRIUS, Consul 464; Emperor of the West 472, died 472.

PLACIDIA, daughter of Valentinian III.

JULIANA, probably named after her ancestress the mother of Demetrias (offered in marriage to THEODORIC, Malchus i. 6).

AREOBINDA, Consul 506 (?)

OLYBRIUS, Consul 491.

══ IRENE, daughter of MAGNA, sister of Emperor ANASTASIUS.

CHAPTER VII.

OLYBRIUS, THE CLIENT OF THE VANDAL, A.D. 472.
GLYCERIUS, THE CLIENT OF THE BURGUNDIAN, A.D.
473–474. JULIUS NEPOS, THE CLIENT OF BYZAN-
TIUM, A.D. 474–475. ROMULUS AUGUSTULUS, SON
OF ORESTES, A.D. 475–476.

Authorities.

Sources :—

CASSIODORUS, THEOPHANES, and JOANNES ANTIOCHENUS have
been described in previous chapters. MARCELLINUS and the
ANONYMUS CUSPINIANI give the versions of the facts current at
Constantinople and Ravenna respectively.

A new and most valuable source is opened out to us by the
writer called the ANONYMUS VALESII. The two fragments which
pass under this name were published by Henricus Valesius
(Henri de Valois, 1603–1676) in his edition of Ammianus Marcellinus, and they have since been generally appended to the
history of that author, with which however they have no natural
connection. The first fragment deals with the history of Constantine the Great; the second and much longer fragment
describes, in a very peculiar style, the affairs of Italy from the
accession of Nepos in 474 to the death of Theodoric in 526.
It is tolerably certain that the two fragments which are thus
classed together are by two different authors. With the question
of the authorship of the first we need not here concern ourselves.
Waitz [1] has argued with much probability that we have in the

---

[1] Nachrichten von der k. Gesellschaft der Wissenschaften, &c., zu Göttingen,
1865, p. 112.

second an actual portion of the Chronicles of Maximian, Bishop of Ravenna, from 546 to 556 (see vol. I. p. 913–914). In favour of this conjecture is the fact of the author's evident close connection with Ravenna and his knowledge of Eastern affairs, since we know from the story of his elevation that he was for some time a resident at Constantinople. Holder-Egger (Neues Archiv, I. 324) argues, on the other hand, that the poor style and frequent barbarisms of the Anonymus Valesii do not correspond with what Agnellus tells us [1] of the learning of Bishop Maximian, and his care to secure accurate copies of the Scriptures and other ecclesiastical books. There is no doubt some force in this argument, but on the whole Waitz's theory seems to me a very probable guess : higher value than this we cannot assign to it. One feature in the Anonymus Valesii, which it is not easy fully to account for by any theory, is his strong bias in favour of the Eastern Emperor Zeno.

Guides :—

Besides Pallmann, *Binding* in his ' Geschichte des burgundisch-romanischen Königreichs ' (Leipzig, 1868) gives some useful comments on this portion of history.

THE new Emperor, Anicius Olybrius, might possibly have procured some breathing-space for the exhausted commonwealth, if he had worn the purple for any considerable length of time.

Of the great Anician family, and probably descended from one of those brother consuls, Olybrius and Probinus, whose accession to office in the year 395 Claudian celebrated with such courtly enthusiasm ; the husband of the great grand-daughter of Theodosius, and the representative, as far as there could be a representative, of the claims of that Imperial house ; on good terms with the Eastern Augustus, perhaps openly supported by him ; above all, the brother-in-law of the heir-apparent to the Vandal crown, the long proposed and

Pedigree and connections of Olybrius.

---

[1] Liber Pontificalis, 81.

at last successful candidate of Gaiseric ; Olybrius, as to whose personal qualities the page of history is a blank, possessed in these external circumstances exceptional advantages for a Roman Emperor in the year 472. But whether the care of ruling a troubled court, which had made Petronius Maximus sigh for the happier lot of Damocles, or the air of Rome, so often fatal to alien rulers, overpowered him, we know not. So it was that on the 23rd October 472, little more than three months after the death of his rival, Olybrius died at Rome of dropsy [1]. Had Ricimer been still living, this death would of course have figured in his catalogue of crimes, but the rough-handed Sueve had gone before Olybrius, as has been already stated, on the 18th of August.

472.

His death.

During his short reign Olybrius conferred the dignity of Patrician on the young Burgundian prince Gundobad, whose mother was sister to Ricimer, and who apparently had come to Italy to push his fortunes by the help of his all-powerful uncle [2]. It is conjectured with much probability that the barbarian element in the Roman army, which knew something of its strength, and was suspicious of any but a barbarian leader, transferred its fealty, or its attachment, or its obedience (it is difficult to find a word to express the nature of the tie which bound these troops to their leader) from Ricimer to his nephew, and that this transference brought with it, almost as a matter of course, his elevation to the rank of Patrician and 'Father of the Emperor.'

Gundobad Burgundian Prince and Roman Patrician.

---

[1] A recently-discovered fragment of Joannes Antiochenus gives the nature of the maladies both of Ricimer and Olybrius (' αἵματος αὐτῷ (ʽΡεκίμερι), πλείστου ἐξεμηθέντος . . . ᾽Ολύβριος δὲ μετὰ τοῦτον ιγ´ μόνας ἐπιβιοὺς ἡμέρας ὑδέρῳ συσχεθεὶς μεταλλάττει ').

[2] It was Gundobad, who, as mentioned at the close of the last chapter, dealt the actual deathstroke to the fugitive Anthemius.

For five months Gundobad allowed himself the luxury of an interregnum ; then, on the fifth of March, 473, he raised a certain Glycerius to the throne, at Ravenna. This election of Glycerius, though he had held the high office of *Comes Domesticorum* [1] (Commander of the Household Troops) was not approved of, nor apparently recognised, at Byzantium.   Our chief Eastern chronicler (Marcellinus) tells us that Glycerius was made Caesar at Ravenna 'more by presumption than by election ; ' and steps were soon taken to furnish a successor to Olybrius whom the Easterns could recognise as legitimate.

Some changes had taken place at the Court of Constantinople since the councils preceding the elevation of Anthemius, and the expedition against Carthage.   In the year 471, Aspar and his sons were murdered in the palace by the swords of the eunuchs of the Emperor's household.   'An Arian father with his Arian offspring,' is the pious comment of Marcellinus ; but all the inhabitants of Constantinople were not disposed to consider the heterodoxy of Aspar sufficient justification for the deed.   They remembered that it was by Aspar's hand that Leo himself had been lifted to the throne ; that something had been whispered of a secret compact, according to which one of the sons of Aspar was to succeed in the Imperial dignity, and that, in fact, his son Patricius, who appeared susceptible of conversion to the Catholic faith, had been formally recognised as Caesar, and thereby designated as next in succession to the throne.   It might be convenient to cancel all these liabilities by the swords of the eunuchs of the house-

Marginal notes:
473. Elevation of Glycerius.

Affairs of the East.

Murder of Aspar and his family.

----

[1] So says Joannes Antiochenus, 209, § 2.   The Comes Domesticorum was entitled to the appellation *Illustris.*

hold; it was, no doubt, a relief to know that that terrible Patrician would never again shake his sovereign's purple robe and remind him of obligations which Orthodoxy would not suffer him to discharge; but, upon the whole, the popular instinct condemned the transaction, and branded the Emperor Leo with the epithet Macellus (the butcher), a term derived from the meat-markets of Rome.

473.

When the news of the 'presumptuous' elevation of Glycerius to the throne reached Constantinople, in the summer of 473, the Emperor Leo was probably in fail-

GENEALOGIES OF EASTERN AND WESTERN EMPERORS[1].
(474–475).

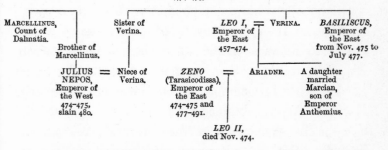

ing health. (He died in January of the following year.) The rivalry for the succession between Basiliscus, with his firm persuasion that he should one day be Emperor, and Tarasicodissa, the Isaurian, always addressed by his flatterers as Zeno, was, no doubt, becoming more intense than ever. But the threads of this and of every intrigue about the Court of Byzantium were in the hands of her who was sister of one candidate and mother-in-law of the other, Verina, the wife of the dying Augustus. Influenced, no doubt, by her, the choice of a Western Emperor fell upon Julius Nepos, by birth nephew of the

Julius Nepos, a kinsman of the Empress Verina, chosen Emperor of the West.

---

[1] Emperors of the West in roman capitals, of the East italic.

brave Marcellinus of Dalmatia, and by marriage nephew
of the Empress Verina.

The new Emperor was proclaimed in Constantinople
in August, 473 [1], but, delayed apparently by the compli-
cations connected with the illness and death of his
patron, did not land in Italy till the spring of the following year.   Meanwhile Leo died; his grandson, the
younger Leo, succeeded him, and being but a boy, associated his father, the Isaurian Zeno, with him in the
Empire.   The son-in-law had won, for the present at
least, in the race for the Eastern throne.

Ostro-
gothic
invasion
of Italy
diverted
to Gaul.

Before we start with Nepos on his quest of the
Western sovereignty, let us see how matters have fared
with the occupant whom he means to displace—with
Glycerius.   In 473, the year of his accession, a new
enemy to Rome appeared upon the northern horizon.
The Ostrogothic brother-kings, who served under Attila
at the battle in Champagne, on the overthrow of the
Hunnish Empire obtained for themselves a goodly settlement in Pannonia, on the western bank of the
Danube.   For nearly twenty years they had been engaged in desultory hostilities with their barbarian
neighbours, with Suevi and Rugians on the north and
west, with Huns and Sarmatians on the south and east.
Now, as their countryman, Jordanes, tells us [2] with admirable frankness, 'the spoils of these neighbouring
nations were dwindling, and food and clothing began to
fail the Goths.   Therefore to these men, who had long

---

[1] This hypothesis (which nearly coincides with that of Pallmann,
Völkerwanderung, ii. 280) seems best to explain the frequent abridg-
ment by the chroniclers of the reign of Glycerius from sixteen months
to five.   The 'legitimist' writers know nothing of Glycerius as
Emperor after Leo had raised Nepos to the throne.

[2] De Rebus Geticis, cap. lvi.

found their sustenance in war, peace began to be hateful.' They clustered round their kings, and clamoured to be led forth to war—whither they cared not, but war there must be. Theudemir, the elder king, took counsel with his brother Widemir, and they resolved to commence a campaign against the Roman Empire. Theudemir, as the more powerful chieftain, was to attack the stronger Empire of the East; Widemir, with his weaker forces, was to enter Italy. He did so, but, like so many of the northern conquerors, he soon found a grave in the beautiful but deathly land. His son, the younger Widemir, succeeded to his designs of conquest, but Glycerius approached him with presents and smooth words [1], and was not ashamed to suggest that he should transfer his arms to Gaul, which was still in theory, and partially in fact, a province of the Empire. The sturdy bands of Widemir's Ostrogoths descended accordingly into the valleys of the Rhone and the Loire; they speedily renewed the ancient alliance with the Visigothic members of their scattered nationality, and helped to ruin yet more utterly the already desperate cause of Gallo-Roman freedom.

It may be that this ignominious mode of dealing with an invader served to sink the insignificant Glycerius yet lower in the eyes of his people. He seems to have been keeping close under the skirts of Mont Blanc and Monte Rosa, that he might not be too far removed from the

---

[1] A curious pamphlet was published by a certain Baron von Ickstadt towards the close of last century, professing to contain the actual text, in Gothic, of the letter written on this occasion by Glycerius to Widemir. But though it was accepted as genuine by J. C. von Aretin, Librarian of Munich, who wrote about it in the Neuer Literarischer Anzeiger, 1806, it is now generally admitted to be a forgery and not a very clever one.

Burgundian countrymen of his patron, Gundobad. In
Pavia, we are told, his mother was so insultingly treated
by the populace—perhaps in order to mark their contempt for her son—that he would have inflicted severe
punishment upon them if he had not been dissuaded by
the saintly peace-maker Epiphanius [1].

474.

Nepos
triumph-
ant.

Such was the state of things when Nepos, the Byzantine candidate for empire, landed in Italy, in one of the
spring months of 474. Did the barbarian auxiliaries,
headed by the young Burgundian Gundobad, the heir
of the power of Ricimer, go forth to meet him, and did
battle follow ? The silence of the chroniclers rather
seems to indicate that the affair was settled without a
resort to arms [2]. And as we find Gundobad, shortly after
this time, peaceably reigning with his brothers over
their paternal kingdom on the banks of the Rhone, the
inference drawn by some of the most careful inquirers
into the history of the period [3] is that, the death of his
father Gundiok having occurred shortly after that of his
uncle Ricimer, he had weighed the solid advantages of
his Burgundian inheritance against the prestige of a
Roman king-maker, and found the former preponderate.
Therefore, and as he also well knew the hostile designs of
the Byzantine Court, he quietly marched back across the
Alps with the young warriors of his *comitatus,* leaving
the luckless Glycerius to fight and lose his own battles
alone. This may be accepted as the most probable explanation of Gundobad's disappearance from the scene ;

[1] ' Nam sancto viro inlatam matri a ditionis suae hominibus concessit injuriam ' (Ennodius, Vita Epiphanii, p. 219, ed. Migne).

[2] Joannes Antiochenus (fr. 209) expressly asserts that Rome was
taken without resistance.

[3] Pallmann and Binding.

but it must be pointed out that it is not the only one.
He may have stood by his client, have fought and lost
some unrecorded battle, and only then have made his
way over the unmelted April snows of the St. Bernard
or the Mont Genèvre to his Burgundian kingdom.

474.

Let the causes of the non-resistance, or unsuccessful
resistance of the barbarian Auxiliaries have been what
they may, the result is undoubted. The efforts of the
Eastern candidate were crowned with complete success,
but his triumph was not stained with cruelty. The
fortified harbour-town at the mouth of the Tiber,
opposite to the modern Ostia, which under the name
of *Portus Augusti et Trajani* commemorated the names
of two of Rome's most famous Emperors [1], witnessed in
the summer of 474 two very different spectacles. There,
on the 24th of June, Julius Nepos was solemnly raised
to the dignity of Emperor, the Senate and the People
of Rome being no doubt duly represented on the
ground, and acclaiming the new Augustus. There
also, a few days earlier or later, Glycerius, Ex-Count
of the Domestics and Ex-Emperor, received the oil of
consecration as a Bishop. The merciful conqueror,
who had spared his life, vouchsafed to him also a
sphere for the exercise of his new functions. The
Church of Salona, the capital of the dominions of
Marcellinus, was at this juncture in need of a head.
Thither Glycerius was sent, and he who had lately
held power nominally supreme in the Western world,
subsided, apparently without a murmur, into the condition of Bishop of a Dalmatian town. Even so, after
a long and costly contest for the heirship to a dukedom,
the successful litigant might solace his beaten rival by

Deposition
of Glycer-
ius, who
is conse-
crated
Bishop of
Salona.

---

[1] 'Augustus' here = Nero who dedicated the port of Claudius.

assigning to him one of the family livings. With this consecration at Portus, Glycerius but for one doubtful allusion disappears from history. There have been many worse Emperors, doubtless, than the 'not disreputable [1]' person whom Gundobad advised to become Augustus, and whom Nepos advised to become a Bishop.

474.

Affairs of Gaul.

The only memorable events in the fourteen months' reign of Julius Nepos are those which relate to the affairs of Gaul, that country which gave her first province to the Republic, and whose allegiance was the last jewel hacked from the fingers of the dying Empire.

Accession of Euric to the Visigothic throne.

466.

The Visigothic throne at Toulouse was now no longer filled by the jovial and tolerant Theodoric II, to whom Sidonius lost so many games at 'the tables.' Eight years before the period which we have now reached, that prince was slain and replaced by his equally able, but narrower and harsher, brother Euric [2]. Though it is true that he employed as his chief minister of state the polished and learned Gallo-Roman Leo, we can trace in Euric a bitterer Arianism and a more acrid and anti-Roman barbarianism than was shown by Theodoric, the inattentive listener to the ministrations of his heretical clergy, the staunch upholder of the alliance with Avitus.

Arian intolerance of Euric.

Of the religious intolerance of Euric, Sidonius, who now looked at these questions with the eyes of a

---

[1] ἀνὴρ οὐκ ἀδόκιμος is the character given of him by the chronicler Theophanes.

[2] The crime of fratricide deeply stained the annals of these early Visigothic kings. Thorismund was killed (in 453) by his brothers Theodoric and Frederic, and now again (in 466) Theodoric was killed by his brother Euric.

Churchman (having been elected Bishop of Clermont [1] in the year 472), draws a repulsive picture. 'I fear,' he says [2], 'that this Gothic king, though he is truly formidable by the resources which he wields, is plotting not so much against the walls of Roman cities as against the laws of Christian Churches. So sour, they say, to his lips, so hateful to his heart, is the very mention of the Catholic name, that you can hardly tell whether to consider him primarily as king of the Visigothic nation or as leader of the Arian sect. Moreover, he is a strenuous warrior, in the vigour of his intellect, in the prime of life; the only mistake which he makes is to attribute to the Divine blessing on his misguided zeal, those successes which are really due to his own skill and good fortune.' Sidonius then goes on to describe the melancholy condition of the Catholic Churches of Aquitaine. Bordeaux, Limoges, Perigueux, and many more, whose Bishops had died, were forbidden to elect their successors; the churchway paths were stopped up with thorns and briers, the gates wrenched from their hinges, the roofs left open to the sky, and cattle fed on the grass-grown steps of the altar.

Some of these touches recall similar passages in the Vandal persecutions—though those upon the whole were far more bloody and severe—and it is therefore not surprising to find that there was at this time a considerable drawing together of the courts of Carthage and Toulouse. There had been time for the old cruel outrage upon the daughter of Theodoric I to be forgotten, and accordingly, when Gaiseric found East and

Vandal and Visigoth draw together.

---

[1] In the language of the times *Civitas Arvernorum.*

[2] Ep. vii. 6.

West Rome uniting to invade his pirate kingdom, he appealed, and not altogether in vain, to the Visigothic monarch to join hands with him in defence of their common interests as Teutons and as Arians [1].

The weight of Euric's invasion, which apparently took place in the spring of 474, fell upon the two provinces which we now know as Berri and Auvergne, all that was still left to the Romans of the country south of the Loire. Of Berri they appear to have made an easy conquest; Auvergne, the mountain-land, defended by the stout hearts of the still undegenerate nation of the Arverni, made a much more stubborn resistance. There, in the midst of his diocese, was Bishop Sidonius, animating the people by his rhetoric and, yet more, encouraging them to hope in the miraculous efficacy of 'the Rogations,' a kind of litany or special series of prayers for times of calamity, which he adopted from the Church of Vienne. There, too, was his brother-in-law, Ecdicius, the son of the Emperor Avitus, a brave and noble-hearted man, though Sidonius trumpets forth his praises with so much bombastic exaggeration that we are in danger of not allowing to him the credit which he really deserves.

'How did we all gaze upon you,' he says [2], 'from the walls of Arverni [Clermont]. All ranks and ages, and both sexes, looked at you with wonder from our half-ruined walls, and saw you in the open plain, in the middle of the day, pierce with scarce eighteen horsemen through a troop of some thousand Goths. At the sound of your name, at the rumour of your presence, a kind

---

[1] Jordanes, cap. xlvii, vouches for this *rapprochement* between Gaiseric and Euric.

[2] Ep. iii. 3.

of stupor fell upon that highly-disciplined host, so that
the generals themselves in their blind wonderment
perceived not how many followed their standards, how 474.
few yours. They withdrew up the brow of a hill and
left all the plain to you, though you had scarcely as
many men to post in the plain as one seats guests at a
banquet.

'You came back at leisure to the city. How we all
poured forth to meet you, with greetings, with plaudits,
with laughter, and with tears! The courts of your
vast house were filled with your welcomers. They
kissed the very dust of your feet, they handled your
heavy curb-chain, clotted with blood and foam, they
lifted the saddles, steeped in sweat, from the horses of
your warriors, they unclasped the fastenings of your
hollow helmet, they vied with one another in loosening
the foldings of your greaves, they counted and measured
with trembling fingers the terrible dints in your coat of
mail.

'Need I say how, after this, you, with your own
private resources, collected a public army and chastised
the enemy for their incursions; how in several encounters you slaughtered whole squadrons of the barbarians, and when you came to number your own troops
after each battle, found but two or three missing. So
heavy was the blow struck at the enemy in these
unexpected conflicts, that they concealed the number
of their slain by an artifice more ghastly than the very
battle-field. All whom the approach of night prevented
them from burying they beheaded, that the mutilated
trunk might not by its flaxen locks reveal the nationality of the slain warrior. When day dawned they
perceived that even this brutal outrage had not availed

to hide their losses [1]; so then they set about their funeral rites in haste—haste which was as useless to

474.

conceal their trick as their trick had been to conceal the slaughter. The bodies were unwashed, unceremented; no mound of earth was heaped above them. They lay here and there about the field, carried to their respective heaps on the gory waggons, till you, pressing down afresh and unceasingly on your beaten foe, compelled them to give up the thought of burial, and to light their funeral pyres with the fragments of the waggons which had been their moving homes.'

Miseries of the Arverni relieved by Bishop Patiens.

History and romance are no doubt blended in this singular extract, in what proportions it is now impossible to determine. So much, however, seems clear, that by the brave defence of the Arverni, with Ecdicius at their head, the tide of Visigothic invasion was for that season (474) rolled back from their country. But the walls of the city were half in ruins [2], and the harvests, not only of Auvergne, but of a large part of Provence, had been swept away by the enemy. Under this imminence of famine, Patiens, the Bishop of Lyons, (the builder of the basilica commemorated in the verses of Sidonius [3]), with wise and noble munificence, collected vast stores of grain in the northern district of Gaul, transported them down the rivers Saone and Loire, and across the mountains of Auvergne, presented them as a free gift to the famishing provincials, and thus, out of his own episcopal revenues, (helped probably by the contributions of the wealthy city in which he dwelt,)

---

[1] Because of course the Romans would infer that all the headless trunks were Gothic.

[2] 'Semiruti' (Sidonius, Ep. iii. 3).

[3] See p. 329.

' like another Triptolemus or another Joseph [1],' saved a
nation from famine.

In the following year (475) there seems to have been
a change in the Gothic strategy. As determined as
ever to add Auvergne to his dominions, Euric saw that
the fight for its possession could best be waged in
Provence, or even if need were, in the valley of the Po.
He again crossed the line which had become the frontier
of the Empire, again occupied or laid waste the ' Pro-
vincia' at the mouth of the Rhone, and threatened
apparently to cross the Alps, or to march by what we
now call the Riviera, into Italy. For these aggressions
the rapid changes in the person of the Roman Emperor
suggested the occasion, and seem in some mysterious
way to have served as a justification [2]. Perhaps a
pretence was set up of vindicating against Nepos the
claims of the Burgundian *protégé* Glycerius, whom he
had dethroned. In these circumstances the ' Council
of Liguria,' an assembly of whose precise nature and
constitution we are ignorant, but which was probably
composed of the chief civil and ecclesiastical officials of
the province, again assembled, as they had assembled

---

[1] Sidonius, Ep. vi. 12.

[2] That some such argument was alleged seems clear from the
testimony of Ennodius, who distinctly connects Euric's invasion with
the accession of Nepos. ' Post quem [Glycerium] ad regnum Nepos
accessit. Tunc inter eum et Tolosae alumnos Getas, quos ferrea
Euricus rex dominatione gubernabat, orta dissensio est : dum illi
Italici fines imperii quos trans Gallicanas Alpes perrexerat, *novitatem*
spernentes non desinerent incessere : e diverso Nepos, ne in usum
praesumptio malesuada duceretur, districtius cuperet commissum sibi
a Deo regnandi terminum vindicare.' There is much which must
remain unexplained in this passage, but the coincidence of ' novitatem
imperii' with the term ' novus princeps,' applied (most probably) to
Nepos by Sidonius (Ep. v. 6), is suggestive.

four years before when civil strife seemed to be impending between Anthemius and Ricimer, to devise
means for averting the storm of war from their
country.

Again, as before, all eyes were turned upon the
saintly Epiphanius, Bishop of Pavia, the ideal peace-
maker of his age. He again undertook the office,
relying on heavenly assistance. The journey was one
of about 600 (Roman) miles, by way of Turin, Briançon,
Nîmes, and involved a climb over the steep pass of the
Mont Genevre. But the saint was determined to make
it yet more arduous by his austerities. For the mules'
sake they tarried long at the different posting-houses
(*mansiones*), and all these long halts were occupied
with vigorous psalmody or with industrious reading;
and when engaged in the latter employment he always
stood. Then at night he would choose the chilliest
nook of the forest, whither the noonday sun never
penetrated, and there, instead of in the comfortable
mansio, would he spread his couch, watering the
ground with the tears which accompanied his night-
long prayers, 'and so making fertile in spiritual blessings the soil which could never bring forth fruits of
its own.'

There is no need to transcribe from his admiring and
prolix biographer the exhortation to meekness and
charity which Epiphanius delivered to King Euric in

his Court at Toulouse. The Visigothic king's reply,
delivered by the mouth of an interpreter, contains some
characteristic expressions. 'Though the coat of mail
never leaves my breast, though my hand is ever at the
brazen hilt of my sword, and the iron guards my side,
I have found a man who, for all my armour, can

vanquish me with his words. They err who say that
the Roman's tongue is not worth a good sword and
shield, for they can turn back the words which we send
against them, while their words pierce to our very
vitals. I will do therefore, holy father, all that you
desire, though more from esteem for the messenger
than from respect for the power of him who sends him.
Promise me, therefore, that Nepos will keep unbroken
concord with me—since a promise from you is equivalent to an oath—and my warlike designs shall be laid
aside.' After giving the required pledge, the Bishop,
refusing an earnest invitation to meet the king at a
banquet, ('which would have been,' says his biographer,
'polluted by the presence of *his* priests') started at
once on his homeward journey, 'attended by so great a
crowd that Toulouse seemed to be almost deserted of
her inhabitants.'

When we read the terms of peace as they were
finally arranged between Euric and the four Bishops
of Provence[1], we doubt whether the eloquence of Epiphanius had really been so triumphant as his biographer
describes it. For it is evident that Auvergne and Berri

475.

Auvergne
abandoned
to the
Visigoths.

---

[1] Graecus of Marseilles, Leontius of Arles, Basilius of Aix and
Faustus of Riez.

The history of the negotiations between Nepos and Euric is obscure,
and it has not seemed necessary to trouble the reader with all their
details; but it seems probable that there were three embassies:
(1) that of the Quaestor Licinianus described by Sidonius (Ep. iii. 7).
It was apparently on this occasion that he brought Ecdicius his promotion to the Patriciate, upon which Sidonius congratulates his wife
Papianilla (sister to Ecdicius) in Ep. v. 16 (translated p. 340). This
embassy was probably unsuccessful. (2) The embassy of Epiphanius
of Pavia, successful in laying down the general basis of an agreement.
(3) That of the four Bishops mentioned above, who drew out the
exact terms of the accommodation.

475.

were ceded to the Goths, and the Romans seem practically to have retained of all their magnificent Gaulish possessions only the strip of territory between the Mediterranean and the River Durance, which, still under its well-known name of *Provence*, perpetuates the remembrance of the *Providentia* of the Roman Republic.

Sidonius'
anger at
this
desertion.

Bitterly does Sidonius lament this desertion by Rome of her brave Arvernian subjects. In the letter which he addressed to Bishop Graecus, after the negotiation of the treaty, his usual tone of bland deference towards a brother-prelate is replaced by something like a snort of defiance and indignation.

'Alas!' he says, 'for this unhappy corner of the land, whose lot, if fame speak truly, is to be made yet worse by peace than ever it was by war. Our slavery is to be the price paid for other people's freedom. Yes, the slavery of us the Arverni who, if the story of the past is to be retold, once dared to claim Trojan blood in our veins, and to call ourselves brothers of Latium. If you look at more recent days, we are the men who by our own private efforts have held in check the public enemy, who did not use our walls as a defence against the Goth but made him tremble in his camp, who, when our neighbours moved their army into the field, could show as many generals as we had soldiers [1]. . . . Are these the wages that are due to those who have endured hunger, fire, and pestilence, to the swords that are fat with slaughter, to the warriors who are lean with fasting? It was in prospect of this glorious peace of yours, of course, that we lived upon the herbs that grew in the chinks of our walls, and that some died,

[1] A doubtful advantage in an army.

unable to distinguish the poisonous from the harmless.
For all these daring experiments of our devotion our
reward, as I hear, is that we are to be thrown over-
board by the Empire. Oh! blush, I pray you, for this
peace which is neither expedient nor honourable.
Through you the embassies come and go. The begin-
nings and the endings of the negotiations, in the
Emperor's absence, are in your hands. Pardon the
roughness of these words of truth; the pang with
which they are uttered should take away their sting.

'You, in the Provincial Council, are not really deliberating for the benefit of the Commonwealth. You
are each of you thinking how you can mend your
private fortunes, and it is by this policy that the first
Province of Rome has become her last. . . . . The
ancestors whom we used to talk of so proudly will
soon, at this rate, have no descendants. Break off
then, break off by whatever device you can think of,
the treaty for this shameful peace. We, if needs be,
shall be delighted still to suffer siege, still to do battle
on the wall, still to famish in our homes. . . . . But if
not, if while other regions are content with slavery,
Auvergne may not have the martyrdom for which she
sighs, then I can only say, keep our seed still alive on
the earth, be ready with your ransoms for us as slaves,
open your gates to us as pilgrims. If our cities must
be open to the Goth, you must in charity open yours to
the guest [1]. Condescend to remember me, my lord
Pope!' If we compare this passionate outburst with
the similar utterances of the inhabitants of Nisibis, a

---

[1] 'Si murus noster aperitur hostibus, non sit clausus vester hos-
pitibus' (Sidonius, Ep. vii. 7). One of the paronomasiae so dear to
the heart of Sidonius.

little more than a century before, when they were abandoned by Rome to the King of Persia [1], we shall be forced to conclude that notwithstanding the frightful misery brought upon the world by the rapacity and incompetence of Roman governors, the Eternal City laid a spell, not of power only, but of love, upon the vast and various populations under her sway, such as some other races, ruling far more righteously than she ever did, have been unable to exercise.

475.

Obscurity of the history of the fall of Nepos.

Fourteen months after Julius Nepos ascended the throne, he was pushed down from it by a Roman officer named Orestes. This revolution is one of the most obscure passages in all the obscure history of this time. Jordanes tells us [2] that Ecdicius (whom he calls ' Decius ') was obliged ' to leave his country, and especially the city of Arverna [3], to the enemy and betake himself to safer quarters. Which, when the Emperor Nepos heard, he ordered Decius to leave the Gauls and come to him.' Possibly it may have been on the elevation of Ecdicius to the Patriciate that the next change occurred. ' In his room Orestes was ordained Master of the Soldiery, which Orestes, having taken the command of the army, and marching forth against the enemy, arrived at Ravenna from Rome, and there remaining made Augustulus his son Emperor. Which being ascertained Nepos fled into Dalmatia, and there, as a private man, lived devoid of royalty [4] [this is not quite accurate], where already Glycerius the former Emperor exercised the Bishopric of Salona. But Augustulus was ordained Emperor by his father Orestes at Ravenna.'

[1] See vol. i. p. 126. [2] Cap. xlv.
[3] Arverna is the form of the name used by Jordanes.
[4] 'Ibique defecit privatus regno.'

Other chroniclers [1] supply us with the dates of two of these transactions. The flight of Nepos took place on the 28th of August 475, and the proclamation of Augustulus as Emperor on the 31st of October in the same year. But what is the meaning of the transactions recorded, why we should hear of this mysterious appearance and disappearance of Ecdicius in Italy, against what enemies Orestes was leading the army (not Euric, for peace had been only just concluded with him; possibly the Burgundians or the Ostrogoths), and what was the pretext or the motive for the sudden rebellion against the authority of Nepos?—these are questions which can be but conjecturally answered, and unless further documentary evidence should be discovered, never settled.

475. Orestes heads the mutiny and proclaims his son Emperor.

A German historian [2] suggests that the barbarian auxiliaries in the army saw in the order to march 'against the enemy' a covert design to remove them from Italy, and therefore revolted. This seems a not improbable conjecture, but we must remember that nothing is said here expressly about 'barbarian auxiliaries,' or about 'leading them beyond the frontiers of Italy.' As Orestes himself was not of barbarian origin, but would be called at that time a Roman, it is open to us to suggest that dislike of a second 'Graeculus Imperator,' and indignation at the surrender of Auvergne to the Visigoths, may have had some share in the result. But the history can here be only guessed at, not related.

Of Orestes, the chief actor in the new revolution, we have, thanks to those invaluable fragments of Priscus,

Previous history of Orestes.

---

[1] Anonymus Cuspiniani and the continuer of Prosper.
[2] Pallmann, Geschichte der Völkerwanderung, ii. 287–289.

a little more certain knowledge. In the great diplomatic campaign of 448, between Byzantium and Hun-
land, he figured in a somewhat inferior position among
the envoys of Attila [1]. Himself of Roman origin, that is
to say, being an Illyrian provincial, he had taken service
under Attila, and considered himself the equal of his
fellow-envoy, Edecon, and other nobles of his Court.
But Vigilas, who knew the social code of the barbarians
well, judged differently, and pronounced that Orestes as
' a secretary, a mere squire of Attila, was greatly inferior
to Edecon, a mighty man of war and a Hun by extraction [2].' However, in the twenty-seven years which had
elapsed since he was sitting with the Byzantine ambassadors among the ruins of Sardica, Orestes (who was by
marriage, if not by birth, connected with the official
hierarchy of the Empire) had succeeded in somewhat
improving his position, and he now, without any hint
of what may have been his intervening fortune, emerges
in the full splendour of Master of the Soldiery, and,
after his successful insurrection, virtual lord of the
Western Empire.

*Why did
he not
assume the
diadem
himself?*

There can have been no reason in the nature of
things why Orestes should not have placed himself on
the vacant throne. Unlike Stilicho and Ricimer he
was a full-blooded Roman provincial, at least as eligible
for the Imperial dignity as Trajan or Diocletian. It
must therefore be taken as an indication how much the
majesty of the title of Emperor had suffered by twenty
years of revolution that he bestowed that title on his

---

[1] See p. 55.

[2] ' Αὐτὸν μὲν γὰρ ὀπάονά τε καὶ ὑπογραφέα εἶναι 'Αττήλα, 'Εδέκωνα δὲ τὰ
κατὰ πόλεμον ἄριστον, ὡς τοῦ Οὕννου γένους, ἀναβεβηκέναι τὸν 'Ορέστην πολύ'
(Priscus, p. 171, Bonn edition). See p. 63.

son, reserving for himself the rank only of Patrician, nominally inferior in dignity, but more associated in men's minds with the idea of power, perhaps also somewhat less likely to injure his popularity with the army. It is possible moreover that the remembrance of the almost menial office which he had held in the court of Attila, and the apparently higher position of his son's maternal ancestors, may have conduced to the same result.

475.

The name, and the face, and the age of the last Emperor of the West are all that is memorable in his history. Every one knows the strange turn of fate (as we call it) which gave to the last puny Emperor of Rome the same name that was borne by her first and mightiest king, the she-wolf's nursling. It is interesting to observe that the poor lad's fateful name came to him in the most natural manner possible from his maternal grandfather in his home beside the Danube. What may have been the precise origin of his epithet Augus-

Romulus Augustulus.

GENEALOGY OF AUGUSTULUS.

(Chiefly from Priscus.)

ROMULUS,
a 'comes' and
inhabitant of
Patavio in Noricum
(Passau? or Pettau?)

TATULUS.

A daughter. = ORESTES,
'a man of Roman
descent who dwelt
in Pannonia by
the River Save,'
Secretary of
Attila 448,
Patrician 475,
killed 476.

PAULUS,
killed 475.

ROMULUS
(named after his maternal grandfather),
surnamed
AUGUSTULUS,
Emperor Oct. 31, 475 to Sept. 4, 476.

tulus cannot be stated; whether given by his loyal soldiers as a term of endearment to the fair boy clothed in the purple, or by his barbarian conquerors as a term of contempt for the new kind of Imperator whom the Romans had raised over them. The latter suggestion however seems the most probable. Augustulus was a mere lad, probably about fourteen [1] years of age, and possessed great personal beauty [2]. The duration of his nominal reign was about ten months. Of course his father was the real ruler of the Empire.

In this capacity Orestes concluded a treaty with Gaiseric [3] the terms of which are not disclosed to us, but it seems probable that one of the chief conditions imposed on the Roman Emperor was the cession of Sicily. In the same year probably in which this event occurred (475), peace, a peace which lasted for two generations, was concluded between the Vandal kingdom and the Eastern Empire. The ambassador chosen by the worn and harassed Emperor, Zeno, who had only just donned his painful diadem, was a senator named Severus, a man whose justice and moderation had won him the respect of all his fellow-citizens, and whom, to give greater honour to his embassy, Zeno raised to the dignity of Patrician. A hostile raid which Gaiseric made on the Epirote city of Nicopolis seemed at first sight to promise ill for the success of the negotiations, but Gaiseric in reply to the complaints of Severus

---

[1] μειράκιον, the word used by Procopius, generally means a lad of about that age.

[2] 'Et quia pulcher erat' (Anonymus Valesii, 38).

[3] 'Annali deinceps circulo evoluto cum rege Wandalorum Geiserico foedus initum est ab Oreste patricio' (Paulus, xv. 7). The meaning of the first four words is apparently that the treaty was concluded within a year from the elevation of Augustulus.

explained that such an attack was only a way of
emphatically stating that he was still at war with the
Empire. Now that an ambassador had actually reached
his court he was quite willing to discuss with him the
conditions of peace. And in fact the pure and simple
character of Severus, his frugal manner of living, and
his absolute inaccessibility to the lavishly offered bribes
of the Vandal, so impressed Gaiseric that he not only
concluded, as has been said, a firm and durable peace
with Constantinople but consented to liberate all the
Roman captives who were in bondage to him or his
sons, having heard from the lips of Severus that such a
concession would be more gratifying to him than any
present of money or jewels. The captives who had
been allotted to the warriors of the Vandal host Gaiseric
declared that he could not liberate without the consent
of their new lords, but he would throw no obstacle in
the way of their redemption. The generous-hearted
Severus not only restored to freedom without price the
captives whom Gaiseric presented to him, but sold by
public auction the costly vessels and magnificent robes
by which he had set forth the majesty of Byzantium,
and with the proceeds purchased the liberty of as many
as he could of the slaves of the soldiers. Even the
bitter Arianism of the old king was softened by the
conversation of the friendly ambassador and a breathing-
space, though as it proved only a short breathing-space,
between the persecutions of Gaiseric and of his son, was
secured by the good offices of Severus [1].

The treaty with Gaiseric is almost the only public
act that we hear of in the short reign of Augustulus.

___

[1] Malchus, Excerpt ii. 3 (pp. 260–261, ed. Bonn), and Victor
Vitensis, i. 17.

Before witnessing the downfall of the boy-Emperor, the last act in this long series of successful rebellions, let

Nepos in
exile.

us follow the dethroned Nepos across the Adriatic to his Dalmatian capital Salona. No doubt he there possessed, *de facto*, the same petty sovereignty which his uncle Marcellinus had held before him. It seems probable also that he still claimed to be *de jure* Emperor of the Western world, still wore the diadem, the purple

The two ex-
Emperors
at Salona.

mantle, the jewelled sandals. Strange turn of fortune, which thus brought two dethroned Emperors of Rome (Nepos and Glycerius) to end their lives in the same Dalmatian city, one as its civil, the other as its religious ruler! In the modern town of Spalato, the temple which Diocletian erected to Jupiter has been converted, with as little change as the Pantheon at Rome, from a heathen fane into a Christian cathedral. If we may assume that this change took place before the end of the fifth century, we have here a subject which might be worthy of an artist's embodiment—the classic edifice reared by the great persecutor, crowded with priests and worshippers on the day of some high 'function'; two successors of Diocletian within its walls; two heads which had worn the wreath of the Imperator bowing in prayer to the Nazarene; two men who had once been engaged in what was like to have been the death-grapple for a throne, imparting and receiving 'the kiss of peace' at the celebration of the Supper of the Lord.

Assassina-
tion of
Nepos.
Was it
with the
connivance
of Glycer-
ius?

Notwithstanding a report of a different kind which once obtained general credence, it is probable that the two rivals ended their days in mutual charity. Nepos outlived the Western Empire four years, and perished by the hands of assassins on the 15th of May, 480.

'Two of his Counts, Viator and Ovida, killed him 'at
his villa' (probably a part of Diocletian's palace) 'not
far from Salona[1].' As we find Odiva (or Ovida) next
year in Dalmatia, waging war with, and conquered by
the ruler of Italy, it is reasonable to suppose that he
murdered Nepos in order to succeed to his power.
There is, however, an obscure sentence in the note-
book of Photius the Patriarch, which seems to throw
the burden of the crime upon Glycerius. He describes
his reading of the 'Byzantine History' of the Sophist
Malchus, who lived at the time of the fall of the
Western Empire. 'Malchus finishes the last book,'
says Photius, 'with the death of Nepos, who, driving
Glycerius from the kingdom, assumed to himself the
Roman power, and having cut his hair like a cleric's,
made him high-priest instead of Emperor, *by whom
also, being conspired against, he was slain*[2].' The
accusation seems distinct enough : but (1) Malchus *may*
have erred. (2) The erudite Patriarch who records in
this note-book (the Bibliotheca) his remembrances of
280 books—all read during his embassy to Assyria—
may have misunderstood or forgotten his author's
meaning. (3) The amanuensis, in his intensely concise
telegrammatic style, *may* have given a wrong idea of
what his master dictated to him. Any one of these
suppositions seems more likely than that the other
chroniclers should have omitted to notice so flagrant an
instance of ingratitude as the murder of Nepos by the

480.

---

[1] Marcellinus.

[2] This is the passage in the original : Καὶ τέλος τοῦ ἑβδόμου λόγου
ποιεῖται τὸν Νέπωτος θάνατον, ὃς ἐκβαλὼν τῆς ἀρχῆς Γλυκέριον τήν τε Ῥωμαϊκὴν
ἰσχὺν περιεβάλετο, καὶ εἰς σχῆμα κείρας κληρικοῦ ἀντὶ βασιλέως ἀρχιερέα
κατέστησεν· ὑφ' οὗ καὶ ἐπιβουλευθεὶς ἀνῄρηται. Bibliotheca Cod.
lxxviii.

rival whose life he had spared; that a Bishop, in that age of the Church, should have perpetrated so great a crime without calling forth a shout of execration from every chronicler of the period; and that Theophanes (a late writer, but not quite so late as Photius) having the proof of this terrible accusation before him, should still call Glycerius 'a not disreputable person' (οὐκ ἀδόκιμος ἀνήρ).

NOTE G.

VANDAL DOMINION OVER THE ISLANDS OF THE MEDITERRANEAN.

IT is clear that the Vandal domination (which, like that of the Athenians in the fifth century before Christ, was essentially a maritime domination) extended over several islands of the western Mediterranean, but it is not easy, from the scattered notices of the chroniclers, to draw up a precise account of the different stages of its growth.

Our chief information on this subject is derived from Victor Vitensis, who says that 'after the death of Valentinian III Genseric obtained the circuit of the whole of Africa, and moreover the largest islands—Sardinia, Sicily, Corsica, Ivica, Majorca, Minorca, and many others—and defended them with his wonted arrogance: one of which, that is Sicily, he afterwards granted to Odoacer, King of Italy, by tributary right, out of which Odoacer at certain times paid him tribute as to his lord, [Genseric] however reserving some part to himself[1].'

It seems clear, however, that, at any rate as regards Sicily, there was no *complete* conquest of it by Gaiseric so early as 455 (the date of the death of Valentinian III). In 456, and again in 465, we find him ravaging Sicily, as if it were a hostile country[2]. At the time of the great combined expedition of 468 against Gaiseric, Sicily seems to have been made a base of operations by

[1] See the original passage, quoted p. 263 (note). Victor continues, 'Quarum unam illarum id est Siciliam, Odoacro Italiae regi' (observe this title) 'postmodum tributario jure concessit; ex quâ ei Odoacer singulis quibusque temporibus, ut domino tributa dependit: aliquam tamen sibi reservans partem.' De Pers. Vand. i. 4.

[2] Priscus, Excerpts vii and x (pp. 216 and 218, ed. Bonn).

the Imperial flotilla [1]: and it was in Sicily, after the failure of the expedition, that Marcellinus was murdered by one of his colleagues [2]. All these facts seem to show that at any rate the Vandal domination was not yet securely established over the whole of Sicily, though it is probable enough that Lilybaeum, and perhaps Palermo, may have been conquered and held firmly during these years of strife by Gaiseric [3]. Apparently this is our last information as to Sicilian affairs until (as above stated) we find Gaiseric in 476 dealing with the whole island as his undoubted possession, and assigning it 'tributario jure' to Odovacar.

It is this fact which leads me to conjecture that in the treaty of 475 between Orestes and Gaiseric the island of Sicily may have been formally ceded to the Vandal king. The 'aliqua pars,' which Gaiseric reserved to himself at the time of his cession to Odovacar, was most probably the western corner of the island, including the fortress of Lilybaeum, though this does not seem to be anywhere distinctly stated.

Briefly to describe the later fortunes of Sicily, it evidently all formed part of the kingdom of Theodoric, till on the marriage of his sister Amalafrida with Thrasamund, king of the Vandals (circa 500), Theodoric ceded Lilybaeum and the adjacent territory to Thrasamund as part of the marriage-dowry [4]. To this period, doubtless, belongs the inscription recorded by Muratori (Thesaur. Inscriptt. p. 494. 4) [5] on a stone near Marsala, 'Fines inter Vandalos et Gothos. Mil. IIII.' On the fall of the Vandal kingdom Justinian claimed Lilybaeum (which had meanwhile been taken possession of by the Goths) as part of his prize of war, and the Goths' refusal to surrender it was one of the pretexts of the war, which for a time re-united not only Sicily but Italy also to the Empire.

As for the other islands mentioned by Victor—Sardinia, Cor-

---

[1] Papencordt (p. 102) infers this from the words of Priscus as to the Emperor Leo (ἐν μείζονι φροντίδι τὰ ἐν Σικελίᾳ συνενεχθέντα ποιούμενος, fr. 22), but the argument seems rather weak.

[2] Cassiodorus and Marcellinus, s. a. 468.

[3] Tillemont (vi. 224) and Baronius (s. a. 454, xxii.) infer the capture of Lilybaeum from the captivity of its bishop, Paschasinus, who wrote a plaintive letter as to his sufferings to Pope Leo. Idatius tells us that 'Gaisericus Siciliam depraedatus Panormum diu obsedit' in 440, but we do not seem to be distinctly told of his capture of the city.

[4] See vol. iii. p. 356.

[5] I take this quotation from Papencordt.

sica, and the Balearic isles—they appear to have been earlier and more firmly attached to the Vandal kingdom than Sicily. Sardinia was indeed recovered for the Empire by Marcellinus in 468[1], but it probably fell back under Vandal dominion soon after the failure of the expedition of that year, since, at the conference between Catholics and Arians at Carthage in 484, the names of several bishops from Sardinia and the Balearic isles are mentioned, and these were undoubtedly subjects of the Vandal king. After that conference forty-six Catholic bishops were sent to Corsica to hew wood for the royal navy, a proof (if proof were needed) that this island also owned the sway of the son of Gaiseric [2].

All these islands were easily won back to their allegiance to the Emperor after the fall of the Vandal monarchy in 533 [3], though at a later period Sardinia and Corsica were for a few years subject to the Ostrogothic king Totila (circa 545–552) [4].

The foregoing faint outline of the history of the Mediterranean islands seems to be all that it is possible to extract from the secular historians. Probably a careful study of ecclesiastical documents would enable us to supply much that is here missing.

---

[1] Procopius (De Bello Vandalico, i. 6).
[2] Hefele, Conciliengeschichte, ii. 611, 612.
[3] Procopius (De Bello Vandalico, ii. 5), and see vol. iii. p. 687.
[4] See vol. iv. pp. 698–9.

CHAPTER VIII.

ODOVACAR, THE SOLDIER OF FORTUNE.

Authorities.

Sources :—

THE two mysterious chroniclers, ANONYMUS CUSPINIANI and
ANONYMUS VALESII, are our best authorities for this most
meagrely furnished epoch. Cuspinian's MS. gives us all our
dates, and that of Valois nearly all our personal details as to the
dethroner of the last Roman Emperor.

It will be seen however that ENNODIUS' Life of Epiphanius
is again a valuable source of information. So is the somewhat
similar Life of Saint Severinus by EUGIPPIUS [1] (published in the
first volume of the 'Auctores Antiquissimi' in the Monumenta
Germaniae Historica, Berlin, 1877). JOANNES ANTIOCHENUS and
JORDANES also contribute some facts. The details as to revolutions and embassies at Constantinople rest chiefly on the
authority of MALCHUS and CANDIDUS, two Byzantine historians
of the end of the fifth and beginning of the sixth century.
They were read and abstracted by the all-devouring Photius.
Fragments of their works are published in the Bonn edition of
the Byzantine historians.

Guides :—

Mascou's History of the Germanic Nations is an exceedingly
valuable guide over this portion of the ground. He was perhaps
the first scholar who thoroughly apprehended the fact that the
Empire fell, not before an invasion but before a mutiny of its
own troops. Gibbon, with his wonderful historic instinct, followed Mascou's guidance.

---

[1] Head of the monastery of the Lucullanum (near Naples), who is said to have
written this book about 510.

It will at once be seen that throughout the whole of this chapter large use has been made of the labours of the industrious Pallmann (Geschichte der Völkerwanderung, vol. ii).

'WHILE Epiphanius, with this severe self-discipline, was approving himself a workman of Jesus Christ that needed not to be ashamed, the old Enemy of our race, that restless Schemer of Evil, was busy adding affliction to affliction, and devising new sufferings wherewith to torment the soul of the saint. With this view he stirred up the army against the Patrician Orestes, and sowed the seeds of discord and suspicion between him and them. He excited the minds of abandoned men with the wild hope of revolution; he breathed the desire for sovereign power into the soul of Odovacer. And then, in order that the calamity might fall upon the city of Ticinum [Pavia], he allured Orestes thither to take shelter under its strong fortifications.'

476. Ennodius' account of the Revolution of 476.

So writes the episcopal biographer of the Bishop of Pavia. We may not share his intimate acquaintance with the counsels of the Prince of Darkness, but we are bound to express our gratitude for the information which he, all but a contemporary, has given us in this paragraph concerning the immediate cause of the final catastrophe of the Western Empire. Fortified by this authority, we can unhesitatingly assert that Rome fell at last, not by an invasion of the Herulians or any other Transalpine nation, but by a mutiny of the troops who were serving under her own eagles, and were paid out of her own military chest. We are thus carried back to the remembrance of the time, a century before that which we have now reached, when the Goths on a large scale entered the Roman armies as *foederati*[1], and at

[1] See vol. i. p. 313.

the risk of a little repetition we may again consider the same subject.

Few things in the upward career of Rome are more wonderful than the skill with which she made her last-vanquished enemies the instruments of achieving yet another conquest. By the help of the Latins she subdues the Samnites; with Italian soldiers she conquers Spain; the dwellers around the Mediterranean shore carry her standards through Gaul; the Romanised Gaul beats off the German. In our own country, on the desolate moorlands between the Solway and the Tyne, were encamped Batavians from Holland, Asturians from Spain, Tungrians from the Rhine, and many another representative of far-distant lands, from which, even in these days of quickened intercourse between nations, not one in a century now sets foot beside 'the Barrier of the Lower Isthmus.' From the point of view of the subjugated and tamed provincial, this constant interchange of military service throughout that enormous Empire had much to recommend it, as bringing many widely-scattered nationalities face to face with one another, as breaking down the barriers of race and creed, and as enabling one thought to vibrate unchecked from the Euphrates to the Atlantic. But viewed from the stand-point of a nationality not yet subdued, and still fighting hard for liberty, the use which Rome made of the arms of her conquered foes may well have seemed the device of some malign deity, bent on darkening the whole heaven and on destroying the happiness of the human race. Especially must this thought have forced itself on the mind of the barbarian patriot when he heard that the people of Rome itself, the men who preëminently styled themselves Quirites, and who shouted for wars and triumphs, no longer served in the legions themselves, but passed their useless lives between the Bath and the Amphitheatre, leaving all the toil of the ceaseless campaigns with which Rome vexed the universe, to men who knew the seven hills of Rome but as some cloud-built city in a dream.

Amply would such a barbarian patriot—an Arminius, a Caractacus, or a Decebalus—have been avenged, could he have foreseen the part which these same auxiliaries were to play in completing the ruin of Rome. We have seen the young Alaric learning his first lessons in the invasion of Italy as an Irregular in the army of Theodosius. We have seen the Hunnish forerunners of the host of Attila introduced as auxiliaries into the heart of Gaul by Aetius—the same Aetius who was afterwards to behold them in their myriads arrayed against him on the Catalaunian plains. We are now to see the death-blow dealt at the doting Empire by men of Teutonic speech and origin, who had taken the *sacramentum*, the military oath of allegiance, and had been enlisted as defenders of Rome.

Part which they played in hastening the ruin of Rome.

The meagre annals of the fifth century do not enable us to state what were the relative proportions of native Italians and of barbarians in the armies of Valentinian III and his successors. We may conjecture however that the former had become a very slight ingredient in the mass, and that the Germans no longer served merely as 'auxiliaries' in the wings of the army, but were now the backbone of the Legion itself. We have a few slight indications of the progress of this change. The reader may remember that one of the vexations which made the short-lived Emperor Maximus

Proportion of barbarians in the army enormously increased.

sigh for the fate of the happier Damocles was 'the
turbulence of the *foederati*[1].' When war broke out
between Anthemius and Ricimer, the men in authority
and the mob of Rome clave to the former, but 'the
multitude of naturalised barbarians[2]' (evidently soldiers)
to the latter. And now, in the passage quoted at the
beginning of this chapter, we find 'the army' spoken
of as rising collectively against Orestes, though, as we
shall soon see, the ground of quarrel was that they as
Barbarians made a demand which he as a Roman could
not grant. As before said, therefore, it may be conjectured, if it cannot be absolutely proved, that in the
year 476 a very small number of true Roman citizens
was serving in the dwindled armies of the Western
Empire.

Recruiting
ground be-
yond the
Danube.

The chief recruiting ground for auxiliaries during
the quarter of a century after the death of Attila,
seems to have been the lands on the further side of the
middle Danube, including parts of Bohemia, Moravia,
the archduchy of Austria, and the kingdom of Hungary.
Here dwelt (in positions which are approximately indicated on the accompanying map) four nations with
the uncouth and harsh-sounding names of the Rugii,
the Scyri, the Turcilingi, and the Heruli[3]. The ante-

---

[1] See p. 202.

[2] '*τῷ δὲ Ῥεκίμερι τὸ τῶν οἰκείων βαρβάρων πλῆθος συνεμάχει*' (Joannes
Antiochenus, frag. 209).

[3] The position assigned to the Turcilingi on the map is purely
conjectural. The other tribes are in the quarters marked out for
them by Pallmann (Geschichte der Völkerwanderung, vol. ii), whose
guidance I have also chiefly followed in the few remarks made as to
the earlier history of these races. His theory of the existence of two
portions of the Heruli, an Eastern and a Western, seems to lessen
some of the difficulties in the ordinary accounts of the migrations of
that puzzling people. But Pallmann's own learned and exhaustive

cedent history of these tribes, even during the second
and third centuries of the Christian era, is not clearly
ascertained. According to some ethnologists the island
of Rugen in the Baltic still preserves the name of the
first. A more certain memorial of the second tribe is
furnished by an inscription found at Olbia (in the South
of Russia, near Odessa), which shews that as early as
the second century *before* the Christian era, the inroads
of the Scyri were formidable to the Hellenic settlers
round the shores of the Black Sea. Though a comparatively unimportant tribe, they are thus brought
into contact with the world of classical antiquity considerably earlier than the Goths themselves. Of the
Turcilingi we really know nothing. The Heruli were
the most widely extended of the four nations. In the
latter part of the third century, we are told, they
sailed with 500 ships forth from the Sea of Azof to the
shore of Pontus, and thence through Bosphorus and the
Dardanelles to the coasts of Attica, when Athens itself
suffered conflagration at their hands [1]. At the time of
the Fall of the Western Empire they appear to have
been settled on the southern slopes of the Carpathian
Mountains, the most easterly in position, and the most
powerful of the four tribes.

treatise, failing, as I think it fails, to give any clear and thoroughly
satisfactory explanation of the history of these tribes in the fourth
and fifth centuries, is an argument the more for that scientific co-
ordination of the labours of antiquarian enquirers for which he so
justly pleads. I would add another preliminary work as an indication
to antiquaries what they have to look for; an edition of Tacitus'
'Germania,' and a commentary on the 'De Rebus Geticis' of Jordanes,
at once more accurate and more exhaustive than any that we have
yet had.

[1] Georgius Syncellus (fl. about 800) i. 717 (Bonn edition), quoted
by Pallmann.

Fortunes
of the
Rugii,
Scyri,
Turcilingi,
and Heruli,
after the
death of
Attila.

Whatever may have been the previous fortunes of these races, they were probably for a time subject to the loosely-jointed dominion of the Huns; and in fact, we met with the names of some of them among the invaders of Gaul under the banner of Attila. After his death they may very likely have taken part in the great War of Independence which culminated in the battle of Nedao; at any rate, they shared in its reward, the breaking of the Hunnish yoke from off their necks. The Gepidae, whose king Ardaric had been the leader in the work of liberation, occupied the wide expanse of Dacia; the Ostrogoths took Pannonia; to the north and north-west of these two great nations stretched the domains which, as has been already said, were occupied by the four tribes with whose fortunes we are now concerned. On their southern frontier their strong Teutonic neighbours interposed an invincible obstacle to the wandering and predatory impulses which were partly instinctive, partly the result of contact with and subjection to the Huns. But on the south-western horizon no such barrier presented itself. There, at a distance of perhaps a week's march, lay Venetian Italy; the fortress of Aquileia which had once been its defence, was still the ruined heap to which Attila had reduced it; and thither stretched the still undestroyed Roman roads over the passes of the Wipbach-thal, the Predil, Pontebba, and the Sexten Thal. To reach this Land of Promise the Rugian or Herulian mercenary had but to cross the Province of Noricum (Styria, Salzburg, Carinthia); and that unhappy Province, not wholly cast off by the Empire nor regularly appropriated by the barbarians, was in the same relation to them which unpartitioned Poland occupied towards Russia in the days of the Empress Catharine, 'My door-mat upon which I tread whenever I wish to visit Europe.'

We may therefore imagine, during all the sixteen years of Ricimer's ascendancy, bands of the strongest and most restless-spirited of the warriors of the four tribes, streaming south-westwards through Noricum, under the shadow of the high rock of Juvavum [1] or over the fair plain of Virunum [2], and so on out of the last defiles of the Julian Alps into the broad valley of the Po, their final goal being Ravenna, Rome, or Milan ; any place where the great Patrician had set up his standard, and where the Tribune or the Centurion— himself perhaps a barbarian kinsman—would be in readiness to receive the young Teuton's 'Sacramentum.' It seems pretty clear that whatever differences of costume or of arms may have separated these four tribes from one another, they all bore a general resemblance to the great Gothic nation, and spoke the Gothic language, for which reason some of the Byzantine historians call their leader a Goth, and confuse the heterogeneous kingdom which they established, with the purely and truly Gothic monarchy which succeeded it.

It was not then an invasion in the strict sense of the word, this slow infiltration of the Heruli and their neighbours into the Italian peninsula. They came ostensibly to succour and to serve Rome. But so did the Swedes and the French come to help Germany in the two last decades of the Thirty Years' War ; and we may well imagine that, unwelcome as the troopers of Turenne and Wrangel were in Germany in the year

These tribes flocked into Italy as adventurers

but not strictly as invaders.

---

[1] Salzburg.
[2] Now the Zoll Feld near Klagenfurt.

The Countries on the
UPPER DANUBE
454 - 476

*Showing approximately the settlement of the
Teutonic nations after the disruption of the
Hunnish Empire, and the chief roads by which
the barbarians entered Italy*

Roman Miles

| 50 | 100 | 150 | 200 |

SCYRI

TURCILINGI

H E R U L I

Vindobona
(Vienna)

Carnuntum

Bregetio

Acincum
(Buda-Pesth)

G E P I D Æ

D A C I A)

Pelso L.
(Platten See)

(Pettau)

OSTRO-GOTHÆ

PANNONIA

Sopianæ (Funfkirchen)

Mursa (Essek)

Sirmium

Singidunum
(Belgrade)

1648, even more unwelcome to the Italian citizen
(when he could speak his mind freely without fear of
being overheard by the myrmidons of Ricimer) was the
continuous advent of these many-nationed deliverers
from beyond the Danube. It was not an invasion in
form, but in substance perhaps it was not greatly
different.

The mis-
eries of
Noricum
assuaged
by Saint
Severinus.
We return for an instant to the half-ruined Province
of Noricum, through which these swarms of Rugian and
other adventurers were yearly pouring. The long-
continued suffering of the inhabitants during thirty
years of anarchy (from about 453 to 482) was somewhat soothed by the beneficent activity of Saint Severinus, a holy man who suddenly appeared amongst
them, none knew from whence, and who, by his gentle
wisdom and by the ascendancy which the simple earnestness of his nature obtained for him over the minds of
the barbarians, was often able to interpose for the help
of the plundered provincials. In his little cell on the
banks of the Danube, round which, in the course of
time, other hermits, his disciples and imitators, built
their lowly dwellings, he practised all the regular
austerities of a monk of the fifth century, fasting till
he had reached the utmost limits of emaciation, and
walking barefoot when even the Danube was a mass of
ice. Here, in his lonely meditations, the Saint was
believed to be sometimes filled with

'The spirit of the fervent days of old
When words were things that came to pass, and thought
Flashed o'er the future, bidding men behold
Their children's children's doom already brought
Forth from the abyss of things that were to be[1].'

[1] Byron, The Vision of Dante.

and amid the visible wreck and ruin of the kingdoms
of the world, Severinus, it was thought, could foretell
something of the form and fashion of those which were
to succeed them.

A band of young soldiers of fortune from across the He pre-
dicts the
exaltation
of Odova-
car.
Danube, on their way to Italy, came one day to the cell
of this holy man to receive his blessing. They were
Christians, though of the Arian type, and the candidates
for enlistment in the Imperial army evidently did not
fear the Saint's condemnation of their enterprise.
Among them was a young man, with thick yellow
moustache [1], in sordid garb, but of commanding
height, and, it may be, with something in his mien
which marked him out as a born leader of men. As
soon as this young man stepped inside the cell, (the
lowly roof of which obliged him to bow his head in the
presence of the Saint,) Severinus, it is said, perceived
by an inward intimation that the youth was destined
to achieve high renown. The blessing was given and
the young Teuton said 'Farewell.' 'Fare forward [2],'
answered the Saint, 'fare forward into Italy; thou who
art now covered with a mean raiment of skins, but
who shalt soon bestow on many men the costliest
gifts.'

The name of the tall recruit who received and ful- Odovacar's
name.
filled this benediction was Odovacar, commonly called
Odoacer, the son of Edecon. The name has a Teutonic
ring about it, and is thought by the great German
philologist Grimm to signify 'rich in watchfulness,' or

The shape of the moustache, infrequent on purely Roman faces,
is pourtrayed on Odovacar's coins. The colour is of course the conventional 'flavus' of the Goths.

[2] '*Vade*' for '*Vale*.'

'a good watcher[1].' He suggests that it may have
been a favourite name for a watch-dog, and thence
transferred to a man-child in whom vigilance in war
was looked for by his barbarian parents. It seems
better to retain, as the German historians generally
do, the *Odovacar* of the contemporary authorities in
all its primeval ruggedness, instead of softening it
down with later historians (chiefly the Byzantine annalists) into the smooth and slippery *Odoacer*.

Odovacar's origin.   The origin and ancestry of the young soldier, who
stalked into the cave of Severinus, are among the un-
solved riddles of history. He is called by the Annalists
and by Jordanes a Goth, a Rugian, and a Scyrian[2], and
his name is also sometimes coupled both with the Turcilingi[3] and the Heruli, as if he were their especial
leader[4]. The conclusion which it seems best to draw
from all these conflicting testimonies is that he was a
Teuton (and that fact alone, according to Byzantine
usage, would entitle him to be called a Goth) ; that he
was not of royal descent (and here the story of the
mean appearance which he presented in the cave of
Severinus comes in as an additional confirmation), and
that, for this reason, after he had by an unexpected
stroke of fortune attained to one of the foremost positions in the world, each of the four tribes which formed
his motley host claimed him as of its own especial
kindred.

[1] *Audags*, Gothic for 'rich' or 'blessed;' *vakir*, Gothic for
'watcher.'

[2] Dahn (Könige der Germanen, ii. 35) pronounces in favour of the
Scyrian origin of Odovacar.

[3] Jordanes, de Rebus Geticis, 'Odovacer rex Turcilingorum.'

[4] Prosper's continuator calls him 'rex Erulorum.'

This view does not absolutely preclude the commonly received opinion that Odovacar was the son of the same Edecon who was associated with Orestes in the embassy to Constantinople, and who listened, or seemed to listen, with too favourable an ear to the scheme for the assassination of Attila. It is true that in the wrangle about precedence between the two ambassadors, the interpreter Vigilas said that the secretary Orestes was 'not to be compared in social position with Edecon, a mighty man of war and *a Hun by birth.*' But these last words need not, perhaps, be interpreted with ethnological precision. Priscus himself speaks of the discontented Roman who had *turned Hun*, and in the same way probably any of the Teutonic warriors—Gepidae, Ostrogoths, Rugians, Herulians—whose fathers or grandfathers had accepted the rule of that 'Anarch old,' the Hunnish King and Generalissimo, would, by comparison with a Roman provincial, be spoken of as 'a Hun by birth.' And if this be the true account of Odovacar's parentage, the breaking-up of the Hunnish power after Attila's death might easily cause such a change in the position of the courtier, Edecon, as to account for the humble garb in which his son presented himself before the Saint of Noricum. It must be confessed that there is a touch of dramatic completeness in the working out of the squabble for precedence between Edecon and Orestes in the persons of their sons, the first barbarian King and the last Roman Emperor in Italy, which, until the theory can be actually proved to be untrue, will always commend it to the artistic instincts of the Historian [1].

Was Edecon the father of Odovacar the same as Edecon the courtier of Attila?

[1] The point is, and Pallmann insists upon it with due emphasis, that no one author mentions the Edecon of the Embassy and the

Odovacar was born in the year 433 [1], but we are not able to fix the precise date of his first appearance in Italy and entrance into the Imperial service. It was probably, however, between 460 and 470, since by the year 472 he had risen so high that his adhesion to the party of Ricimer against Anthemius is considered worthy of special mention by the historian Joannes Antiochenus [2]. For four years from that time we hear

Edecon, father of Odovacar, and says or implies that they are the same person. Priscus gives us the first, the 'Anonymus Valesii' the second, and they may be speaking of two different persons.

There is yet a third, Edica, king of the Scyri, mentioned by Jordanes, whose history Gibbon (following Buat, Histoire Ancienne des Peuples) has combined with that of Attila's ambassador and Odovacar's father. It is very difficult to believe that this combination is the true one, though there are also great difficulties (chiefly arising from the mention of a certain *Onulf*, son of Edecon or Edeca, and brother of Odovacar) in rejecting it. At present the whole question seems so hopelessly entangled—being, moreover, one of secondary importance —that I have not thought it necessary to trouble the reader with it at length. But it is right that he should know that the smoothly-flowing narrative of Gibbon as to the early history of Odovacar rests upon *two* combinations, one unproved and the other highly improbable.

I cannot think that Pallmann has made out even a *primâ facie* case for the *Rugian* origin of Odovacar. Jordanes states it in one of his works (De Regnorum Successione), but contradicts it in the other (De Rebus Geticis). Joannes Antiochenus (fragment 209) says that he was 'of the nation of the Scyri.' The passage which Pallmann has inadvertently quoted from the same author in defence of his Rugian theory (fragment 214) says that the Emperor Zeno '*stirred up against Odovacar the nation of the Rugians*' ("Ο Ζήνων πρὸς τὸν Ὀδόακρον τὸ τῶν Ῥόγων ἐπανέστησε γένος'). It is precisely this bitter war of Odovacar with the Rugians, 486–7, which, to my mind, makes it most improbable that that should have been the tribe from which he really derived his origin.

Side notes:
Odovacar rises in the Imperial service.

De Rebus Geticis, cap. liv.

---

[1] This we know from Joannes Antiochenus (fr. 214), who tells us that he was sixty at the time of his death in 493.

[2] Fragment 209.

no more of him, but his name evidently became a word of power with his countrymen in the Imperial army.

Soon—we know not precisely how soon—after Orestes had placed the handsome boy, his son Romulus, upon the throne of the exiled Nepos, his own troubles began with the army, whose discontent he had so skilfully fomented. The *foederati* presented themselves before the Patrician at Ravenna, with a startling demand. ' Assign to us,' said they, ' one third of the land of Italy for our inheritance.' The proportion claimed was, no doubt, suggested by the Imperial system of billeting, according to which the citizen upon whom a soldier was quartered was bound to divide his house into three compartments, of which he kept one himself, his unbidden guest was then entitled to select another, and the third portion as well as the first remained in the occupation of the owner. It may be said also that the four tribes were more reasonable in their demands than some of their Teutonic kinsfolk, since the Visigoths had claimed two-thirds of the lands of Gaul ; the Vandals had not limited themselves even to that portion, and even the Burgundians, although the mildest and most civilised of the invaders of the Empire, had taken half of the moorland, orchards, and forests, and two-thirds of the arable land [1].

---

[1] This important fact, of the barbarian soldiers' demand for a division of the lands of Italy, is made known to us by Procopius (De Bello Gotthico, i. 1): ' In proportion as the barbarians increased in consideration, did the credit of the Roman soldiers decline ; and under the specious name of alliance the State fell under the tyrannical sway of the intruders. Thus many acts of unrestrained violence were perpetrated by the latter on their unresisting entertainers, and at length they demanded a settlement upon the soil of Italy. Of this

But whatever arguments may be urged to give a certain plausibility to the demand of the *foederati*, it was none the less a demand which no Roman statesman with a shadow of self-respect could possibly grant. Analogies drawn from the conduct of the Visigoths in Gaul and the Vandals in Africa, only proved what every Emperor since Honorius had tried to turn away his eyes from seeing, that the so-called Roman army was in fact a collection of aliens and enemies to Rome, trained, it might be, with some of the old legionary discipline, and armed from the Italian arsenals, but only so much the more dangerous to the country which it professed to defend.

Orestes, who ended his career with more dignity than he had displayed in any previous portion of it, utterly refused to despoil the subjects of his son in order to enrich the mercenaries. Possibly he placed some dependence on old habits of military obedience in the army and on the mutual jealousies of the foremost officers, the result of which might be that the mutineers would remain without a head. But in this calculation he was mistaken. Odovacar came forward and offered, if he were made leader, to obtain for the soldiers the land for which they hungered. The bargain was at once struck. On the 23rd of August, 476, Odovacar was raised upon the shield, as Alaric had been raised eighty-one years before, and from that day the allegiance to Augustulus of the barbarians, the backbone of the Roman army, was at an end.

Events marched rapidly. In twelve days the whole campaign—if campaign it could be called—was over.

they ordered Orestes to give them one third, and when he asserted that he would do nothing of the kind, they straightway slew him.'

Orestes took refuge within the strongly-fortified city of
Pavia (or, as it was then called, Ticinum), the city of
which the saintly Epiphanius was Bishop. The defence
must have been an extremely short one, but the biographer of Epiphanius (our sole authority here) gives us no
details concerning it. Everything, however, seems to
indicate that the army, when the barbarian adherents
of Odovacar were subtracted from it, was a miserably
feeble remnant, utterly unable to cope with the revol-
ters. The barbarians burst into the city, plundering,
ravishing, burning. Both churches and many houses
of Pavia were consumed in the conflagration. The
sister of Epiphanius, a nun, whose reputation for holiness was almost equal to his own, was dragged off by
the soldiers into captivity. The chiefs of many noble
families shared the same fate. At first there seems to
have been some disposition to treat Epiphanius himself
with harshness, on account of the insufficiency of the
sum which he offered for his ransom. The soldiery
could not understand that a Bishop of Ticinum could
be so poor as his continual almsgiving had made him.
'Oh, wickedness! that crude barbarity sought the treasures upon earth which he had sent forward to the
recesses of heaven.' Soon, however, the transparent
holiness of his character exerted its wonted influence
even upon these infuriated plunderers. 'He rescued
his venerable sister before the fatal light of that day
glided into evening;' and he also procured by his
earnest intercessions the liberation of many of the citizens, exerting himself especially to lessen the horrors of
that terrible time for the women who were about to
become mothers.

An interval of just two generations had elapsed since

476.

Pavia saw a somewhat similar scene of mutinous riot, robbery, and murder. That was in the year 408, when the intrigues of the party of Olympius against Stilicho burst forth into a flame. Then the cry was 'Down with the barbarians! Down with the Vandal, Stilicho! Slay the *foederati*!' And so the best bulwark of the Empire was sacrificed to the unworthy jealousy of the Roman party who were utterly unable to replace him by any tolerable substitute. In a certain sense it might be said that the evil deed of 408 brought about the punishment of 476, and that Odovacar avenged the blood of Stilicho.

476.
Contrast to the mutiny of Roman soldiers at Ticinum in 408.

Sack of Ticinum.

For part of two days, apparently, the work of devastation went on in Pavia, and all the time the perpetual enquiry of the enraged soldiery was, 'Where is Orestes?' At length news was brought that the Patrician, who had escaped from the city, had been discovered at Placentia, and with that the tumult subsided, and something like peace was restored to the plundered city.

Death of Orestes and his brother Paulus.

It was upon the 28th August, 476, only five days after the elevation of Odovacar, that Orestes was taken at Placentia, and being taken was at once beheaded with a sword. His brother Paulus for a few days longer defended the lost cause at Ravenna, but apparently had too few men under his command to hold even that almost impregnable fortress. On the 4th of September, Paulus, who was perhaps trying to make his escape by sea, was slain by order of Odovacar, 'at the Pineta outside Classis by Ravenna[1].' Within the walls of that city Odovacar found his helpless boy-rival

---

[1] Anonymus Valesii, 37.

Augustulus. Pitying his tender years, and touched with admiration of the beautiful face of the purple-clad suppliant, the successful Teuton, who was now strong enough to be merciful, spared the 'little Augustus,' and assigned to him a palace and a revenue for the remainder of his life. The splendid villa which, at a lavish cost, Lucius Lucullus, the conqueror of Mithridates, had erected for himself near the city of Naples, was allotted as the residence of Romulus, with the members of his family whom the war had spared ; and an annual pension of 6,000 solidi (equal to £3,600 sterling, and perhaps corresponding to about twice that amount in our own day) was granted for his maintenance. How long this pension was drawn, how many years the son of Orestes lived among the woods and fish-ponds of the 'Lucullanum,' whether he saw the downfall of his conqueror, or even, as he may very possibly have done, survived that conqueror's conqueror, Theodoric [1], on all these points History is silent [2], and her silence is an eloquent testimony to the utter insignificance of the deposed Emperor.

476. Augustulus spared and sent to Campania.

Our ignorance as to the close of his career.

The details, few and imperfect as they are, which we possess respecting the seventeen years' reign of Odovacar in Italy will be best given in connection with the history of that Ostrogothic invasion which brought it to a premature and bloody close. But a few words remain to be said as to transactions which happened at Carthage and Constantinople at the time or soon after the time when these events were occurring in Italy.

Early in the year 477, only half a year after the

477.

---

[1] Odovacar was slain in 493 by Theodoric, who died in 526.

[2] But for one doubtful allusion in the letters of Cassiodorus (Variarum, iii. 35).

dethronement of Augustulus, died the king of the
Vandals, Gaiseric.   For more than fifty years had he

Death of
Gaiseric.

been warring against Rome, and as if the energy of his
hate had sustained him under the infirmities of age,
now that the Western Empire was dead he died also.
It was soon seen how largely the might of the Vandal
name had been due to his destructive genius and
tenacity of purpose.   The strength of the kingdom
rapidly declined under his son and grandson, and little
more than half a century after his death it fell an easy
prey to the arms of the Emperor Justinian.   Gaiseric
had destroyed the fortifications of all the cities in his
dominions, in order to prevent their giving harbourage
to rebellious Africans or invading Byzantines; 'a
measure,' says Procopius, 'which was greatly praised
at the time, and which seemed in the safest way
possible to have promoted the tranquillity of the
Vandals.   Afterwards, however, when the absence of
walled towns so greatly facilitated the invasion of
Belisarius, Gaiseric was the subject of much ridicule,
and his vaunted prudence was accounted foolishness.
For men are perpetually changing their minds as to
the wisdom of any given course, according to the light
which Fortune throws upon it.'   These words of Procopius would have been fittingly spoken of some of the
fluctuations of European opinion in our own century,
veering wildly round from the extravagance of glorification to the extravagance of contempt.

Byzantine
affairs.

The years which witnessed the elevation and the fall
of Augustulus in the West saw also the climax of the
long struggle between Zeno and Basiliscus in the East.
Aided by the stratagems of the ever-intriguing Empress
Verina, his sister, Basiliscus succeeded (475) in de-

throning his rival who fled to his native Isauria, among
the mountains of Asia Minor.   Two years after, by the
treachery of the general Harmatius, who was sent to
destroy him, Zeno succeeded in turning the tables on
his antagonist, and found himself again reigning, as
undisputed Augustus, in the palace by the Bosphorus.
The promise which he had given to save the life of the
deposed Basiliscus was fulfilled by sending him, his
wife, and children, in the depth of winter, to banishment in Cappadocia, where, deprived of every comfort
and almost of necessary sustenance, they soon perished
miserably of cold and hunger.

Final
triumph of
Zeno over
Basiliscus.

Soon after the return of Zeno to his palace two
embassies waited upon him to express their congratulations on his restoration to the throne.   First of all
appeared the deputies of the Roman Senate, sent by
the command of Augustulus, which evidently was in
truth the command of Odovacar, to say ' that they did
not need a separate royalty, but that Zeno himself as
sole Emperor would suffice for both ends of the earth.
That Odovacar, however, a prudent statesman and
brave warrior, had been chosen by them to defend their
interests, and they therefore requested Zeno to bestow
on him the dignity of Patrician, and entrust to his care
the diocese of Italy.'   In confirmation of their message
and as a visible proof that the sovereignty was to be
henceforth lodged at Constantinople, these Western
deputies brought with them the Ensigns of Imperial
dignity[1].

477-8.
Embassies
to Zeno
from the
Roman
Senate

A few days after arrived from Salona the ambassadors
of the titular Emperor Nepos (these events happened

and from
Nepos.

---

[1] Ornamenta palatii (Anon. Vales. 64).

two years before his assassination), and they, while also congratulating Zeno on his restoration, besought him to sympathise with their master, like him expelled from his lawful sovereignty, and to grant him supplies of men and money to enable him to reconquer the Empire of the West.

It would seem that each embassy touched a responsive chord in the soul of the Eastern Potentate. The thought that the world needed no other Emperor but him gratified his vanity, but the fugitive's appeal to his brother fugitive excited his sympathy. He therefore, in true diplomatic style, gave an answer which was no answer, lecturing the weak, flattering the strong, and leaving the whole question in the same uncertainty in which he found it.

Ambiguous reply of Zeno.

To the messengers from the Senate he replied, 'You have received two Emperors from the East, Anthemius and Nepos, one of whom you have killed and the other you have driven into banishment. What your duty prescribes you know very well. While Nepos lives there cannot be two opinions about the matter; you ought to welcome his return.'

The precise nature of the reply to Nepos is not stated, but a message was sent to Odovacar, praising him for his judicious subservience to the wish of the Roman Emperor, exhorting him to seek the much-desired title of Patrician from Nepos, and to work for the return of that sovereign, but expressing, at the same time, the willingness of Zeno to grant him the title if Nepos should persist in withholding it. And, after giving all this admirable advice, he sent by the ambassadors a private letter with the superscription, 'To the Patrician Odovacar.' An extraordinary mystification truly, and a piece either of great vacillation or of great duplicity, but which is perhaps susceptible of explanation when we remember that Ariadne the wife, and Verina the mother-in-law of Zeno, were related to the wife of Nepos and zealous on his behalf. The admirable legitimist sentiments, and the exhortations to everybody to co-operate for the return of the Dalmatian, were probably uttered aloud in presence of those Imperial ladies. The private note with the all-important superscription, which was meant to mitigate the hostility of the terrible barbarian, was no doubt delivered to his ambassadors at some secret interview in the final moments before their departure [1].

Odovacar recognised as Patrician.

It would be a mistake to see in this curious scene at the Court of Byzantium only a solemn farce enacted by Odovacar and Zeno, to amuse the people of Italy, and soothe them with the thought that they still remained under Roman dominion. The minds of men were really unable to grasp the fact that so vast and perdurable a structure as the Roman Empire could utterly perish. If it seemed to have suffered ruin in the West it still lived in the East, and might, as in fact it did under Justinian, one day send forth its armies from the Bosphorus to reclaim the provinces which the City by the Tiber had lost. This belief in the practical indestructibility of the Empire, and the consequences which flowed from it, three centuries after the deposition of Augustulus, in the elevation of Charles the Great, have been re-established in their proper place [2],

Contemporaries did not recognise that Roman dominion in the West was at an end.

---

[1] We owe our information concerning this curious diplomatic encounter to Malchus (Byzantine Historians, pp. 235–6, Bonn edition). Candidus also makes a slight allusion to it (Ibid. p. 476).

[2] Pre-eminently by Mr. Bryce, in his ‘Holy Roman Empire.’

one might almost say, have been re-discovered, by the historical students of our own times, and the whole history of the Middle Ages has been made marvellously clearer by this one central fact.

Yet Odovacar did not rule Italy solely as Patrician appointed by Zeno.

But we must not allow ourselves to consider Odovacar, even after this Byzantine embassy, as the mere lieutenant of Zeno, ruling with an authority delegated from Byzantium. It was well pointed out by Guizot[1] that in Mediaeval Europe we scarcely ever find one theory of life or of government worked out to its logical end, and allowed to dominate uncontrolled, like the eighteenth century theories of the Rights of Man, or the nineteenth century theories of the Rights of Nationalities. In the Middle Ages, upon which, after the year 476, we may consider ourselves to be entering, fragments of political theories, which are opposed to one another, and which should be mutually destructive, subsist side by side, neither subduing nor subdued, and often in apparent unconsciousness of their irreconcilable discord. So it was with the position of Odovacar, so, in part at least, with his far greater successor, Theodoric. Among the barbarians, the warrior who had conquered Orestes and deposed his son would be known as *Thiudans*, 'the King,' simply. If any further definition were asked for he would perhaps be called the king of the Rugians, or the king of the Herulians, the king of the Turcilingi, or the king of the Scyri, according to the nationality which happened to be most largely represented in the camp of the mercenaries when the discussion was going forward. But it is more likely that all would contentedly acquiesce in an appellation

---

[1] Lectures II and III on the History of Civilisation in Europe.

which would be understood by all, though it might not be consistent with strict ethnological accuracy, '*Thiudans Gut-thiudos*,' 'The King of the Gothic people[1].' It is not certain that the title 'King of Italy' was ever assumed by him. On the other hand, among the Latin-speaking inhabitants of Italy, the vast majority of his new subjects, Odovacar probably preferred to be known as 'the Patrician,' and it would be in this capacity that he would control the organisation and wield the powers of the still undestroyed bureaucracy of Imperial Rome.

Looking back, as we now do, over an interval of fourteen centuries at Odovacar's position in history, we find it impossible to assign him a place exclusively in the old order of things, or exclusively in the new ; to say whether he was in truth the successor of Aetius and Ricimer, or the forerunner of the Kings of Italy, Pepin, Boso, and Victor Emmanuel. And if this be our doubt now, we may be sure that at least an equal doubt existed in the minds of his contemporaries, not lessened by the fact that there was always, for the space of at least one generation, a chance that the old order of things might after all be restored, and that the rule of the Teuton king might turn out to have been only an interregnum between two Emperors, such as had occurred more than once under the ascendancy of Ricimer. At the time of the embassy to Zeno there were still in the world three men who had worn the Imperial purple, and coined money as Emperors of Rome. We have reason to believe that one at least of these deposed Emperors lived through the whole reign

The de facto claim of the Barbarian and the de jure claim of the Emperor were both blended in Odovacar.

---

[1] Of the annalists, Bishop Marius and Marcellinus call Odovacar 'rex Gothorum.' The reader will remember that both are nearly contemporary authorities.

of Odovacar, perhaps to a much later period. Let us transfer now to the subjects of the new Teutonic king some of the same feelings of unsettlement and of half-acquiescence in change, with which a large part of the English nation regarded 'the Protestant Succession' during the reigns of Anne and the First George, or the feelings with which we ourselves have witnessed the establishment of a new French Republic with three hostile dynasties sitting as angry watchers by its cradle; and we shall a little understand the mental attitude, partly of perplexity, partly of listless unconcern, which contemporary statesmen assumed towards an event which seems to us so momentous as the Fall of the Western Empire.

Insignifi-
cance of
the actual
events of
476,

For, in truth, the facts of the final struggle had little in them to attract the attention of bystanders. The sack of Rome by Alaric in 410 sent a shudder through the whole civilised world, and the echo of her dirge was heard even from the caves of Bethlehem. The nations held their breath with affright when in 452 Attila wreaked his terrible revenge upon Aquileia. In comparison with these events, what was the short flurry of the citizens of Pavia, or the death of Paulus in the pine-wood by Ravenna? Indisputably we ourselves have witnessed catastrophes of far greater dramatic completeness than this, far better calculated, according to the old definition of Tragedy, 'to purify the emotions by means of Pity and Terror.' It is not a storm, or an earthquake, or a fire, this end of the Roman rule over Italy: it is more like the gentle fluttering down to earth of the last leaf from a withered tree.

and infi-
nite im-
portance

And yet the event of 476 was, in its indirect consequences, a Revolution, which affected most powerfully the life of every inhabitant of Mediaeval and even of Modern Europe. For by it the political centre of gravity was changed from the Palatine to the Lateran, _{of their results.} and the Bishop of Rome, now beyond comparison the most important personage of Roman descent left in Italy, was irresistibly invited to ascend the throne, and to wrap himself in the purple, of the vanished Augustus.

CHAPTER IX.

CAUSES OF THE FALL OF THE WESTERN EMPIRE.

WE have now followed the fortunes of Italy from the days when it was the stronghold of an apparently resistless Empire to the time when there was no longer an Imperator in Italy, and when the highest representative of law and government was the leader of the Herulian mercenaries, Odovacar.

Why did the Roman Empire fall? An adequate answer to that question would fill many volumes, and would need to spring from a deep and minute knowledge of the Roman mind, the Roman laws, and the Roman armaments, to which no pretension is here made. The answer suggested in the following pages will be confessedly imperfect and inadequate, but even the fragments of a reply to such a question can hardly be quite devoid of interest.

For the happiness of the human race it was necessary that the Roman Empire should fall. The Roman Empire of the West fell because it had completed its work, and the time had come for it to be cut down, and to cumber the ground no longer. Its rise, its extension over nearly the whole civilised world, had been a vast blessing to humanity; its prolonged existence, even had it been governed by an endless succession of Emperors like Trajan and Marcus, would have been a bane as great as the blessing. To all the

nations around the Mediterranean sea it had brought
peace, discipline, the reign of law, the preparation for
Christianity ; but it had robbed them of liberty, and as
century was added to century, the virtues of the free
man were being more and more effaced by the habit of
blind submission to authority. It was time for the
Teutonic nations to rejuvenate the world, to bring their
noisy energy into those silent and melancholy countries,
peopled only by slaves and despots. It was time to
exhibit on the arena of the world the ruder virtues and
the more vigorous vices of a people who, even in their
vices, showed that they were still young and strong ;
it was time that the sickly odour of incense offered to
imbecile Emperors and lying Prefects should be scattered before the fresh moorland-air of liberty. In short,
both as to the building up, and as to the pulling down
of the world-Empire of Rome, we have a right to say,
' It was, because the Lord God willed it so.'

Of course, this manner of stating the problem cannot
hope for acceptance from an influential school of thinkers
at the present day. ' What ! ' they will at once exclaim,
' would you bring back into historical science those
theological terms and those teleological arguments from
which we have just successfully purified it ? Are you
not aware that history, like astronomy, like physics,
like every other science, spends its infancy in the religious stage, its adolescence in the metaphysical, and
when it has reached its full maturity and become
thoroughly conscious of its powers and of its aims,
passes into the positive, or materialistic stage—that
stage from which the Will of God, the Freewill of Man,
Final Causes, and every other metaphysical or theological conception is excluded, and in which Law, fixed

On final causes in history.

and immutable, however hard to discover, must reign supreme?'

Such, it may be admitted, is the utterance of the *Zeit-Geist,*' of that convergence of many minds towards a single thought, which we call by the less forcible English equivalent, 'the Spirit of the Age.' But, looking back over many past ages, and seeing the utter death and decay of many a *Zeit-Geist,*' once deemed omnipotent and everlasting, the *Zeit-Geist* of Egyptian Hierophants, of Spanish Inquisitors, of the Schoolman, of the Alchemist, of the Jacobin, one is disposed to look the present Time-Spirit boldly in the face and ask why it, any more than its predecessors, must be infallible and eternal.

There was a time when Final Causes were the bane of all the sciences, when men attempted to deduce from their crude notions of what God ought to have done, a statement of what He has done, and thus easily evaded the toil of true scientific enquiry. Our great master, Bacon, recalled the mind of Man from these fruitless wanderings, and vindicated, for the collection of facts and the observation of law, their true place in all philosophy. But he did not share that spirit of Agnosticism, that serene indifference to the existence of an ordering mind in the Universe, which is professed by many of his followers in the present day. It could not have been said of him, as it may, perhaps, hereafter be said of some of his greatest disciples, 'Blindness in part has fallen upon the Physical Philosopher. While groping eagerly after the How of this visible universe, he has missed the clue to the vaster and more momentous questions of its Why and its By Whom.'

The belief   The present writer belongs to the old-fashioned school,

which still dares and delights to speak of God in
Nature and of God in History. To declare, as we
venture to do, with all reverence and confession of our
dim-sightedness, that we believe we can trace the finger
of the Creator and Lord of the world in events like the
Rise and Fall of the Roman Empire, is by no means to
assert that we can explain the ways of Providence in
all the occurrences either of the present or of the past;
it by no means commits us to the proposition that 'all
things have happened for the best in the best of all
possible worlds.' For one who believes in the God of
whom the Christian Revelation speaks, or even in the
God whom Socrates felt after and found, neither
optimism nor pessimism would seem to be the rational
frame of mind. We look back over our own lives; we
see faults and blunders in them past counting. Assuredly it would have been better for us and for our
little fragment of the world that these should not have
been committed—so much the pessimist truly urges.
But then, we can also see, as we think—but here each
individual of the race must speak for himself—traces
of a higher Power contending with us in our blindness,
sometimes bringing good out of our follies and mistakes,
always seeking to educate us and to raise us

> 'On stepping-stones
> Of our dead selves to higher things.'

In all this we do but ratify the statement of one who
had meditated on human nature at least as deeply as
any modern sociologist:

> 'There's a divinity that shapes our ends
> Rough-hew them as we will.'

So much the optimist may claim. Why the divinity

has not shaped the whole world's career to nought but a good end is confessedly inexplicable, and will perhaps be for ever unintelligible to us. Meantime, therefore, we hold the two unreconciled beliefs, in the Almightiness of God and in the existence of evil which is his enemy. To discard either of these beliefs, or to harmonise them, we find equally impossible, and therefore we desist from the attempt, and let both grow together till the harvest. If this be true in the Universal, of the whole ' scheme and constitution of things,' we may reasonably expect to find in the Particular—for instance, in the course of European history—some events of which we may confidently say, ' God brought them to pass in order to promote the welfare of Humanity,' and others of which we can only say, ' Why this irretrievable ruin, in which apparently there lurked no germ of benefit to the Human Race, was permitted, is a mystery.' To apply these general principles to the case before us, we assert with confidence that both the arising and the fall of the Roman Empire were blessings to the human race, and that we are justified in regarding them as the handiwork of an Unseen Power, the Maker and the Friend of Man. But that every step in the upward career of Rome was beneficial to man, or was accomplished with the smallest possible amount of human suffering, we do not believe. Nor, conversely, would we assert that the foundation of the new Teutonic kingdoms might not conceivably have come to pass at a time and in a way which would have been more beneficial to humanity. It is impossible to read the history of the Early Middle Ages without feeling that, for the first six centuries after the fall of the Western Empire, there is little or no progress. The night grows darker and darker, and we seem to get ever deeper into the mire. Not till we are quite clear of the wrecks of the Carolingian fabric, not till the days of William the Norman and Hildebrand, do we seem to be making any satisfactory progress out of Chaos into Cosmos. It is possible to imagine many circumstances which might have prevented the waste of these six centuries, and perhaps have started Europe on her new career with the faith of the thirteenth century joined to the culture of the age of the Renaissance. Had the sons of Theodosius possessed half the vigour of their father; had Stilicho and Aetius not been stabbed in the back by the monarchs whom they were labouring to defend; had the Arian controversy not made its ineffaceable rift between conquerors and conquered; had the Ostrogothic kingdom of Italy and the Visigothic kingdom of Aquitaine not been overthrown by Justinian and by Clovis; had a very slight change in the obscure politics of the Arabian tribes cut short the preaching of Mohammed son of Abdallah; it is possible that centuries of human suffering might have been mitigated, and that the freshness of heart which so many of the European nations seem to have lost in the ages since the Renaissance might still be theirs.

But our business is with the events that were, not with those that might have been. Let us, therefore, proceed to consider some of the secondary causes which in the ordering of the Providence of God, brought about the transfer of the sceptre of Rome into the hands of the Barbarians.

§ 1. *The Foundation of Constantinople.*

There is perhaps no more striking illustration of a nation's powerlessness to discern the dangers that are really most menacing to its future, than the *Persophobia* (if we may coin a word for history from politics), which, down to the very days of the Visigothic invasion, and even beyond them, seems to have haunted the minds of Roman statesmen. True, the Parthian or Persian Monarchy was the only other civilised or semi-civilised state which rose above the horizon of Roman consciousness. The defeats of Crassus and Valerian, the ignominious peace concluded by the successor of Julian in the plains beyond the Tigris, no doubt alarmed as well as humbled every Roman. Still, after making full allowance for the impressions produced by these events, it is difficult to understand why, when Hun and Vandal and Visigoth were actually streaming into the very heart of the Empire, the Persian should still have been the favourite bugbear of poets and orators. But Claudian, for example, continually speaks of ' the Mede' as Rome's most terrible foe ; and when he rises into his highest heaven of prophetic rapture over the glories of Honorius, he always predicts the conquest of Babylon or Ecbatana.

Thus, at the end of his poem on the third Consulship of Honorius, he says to the Imperial brothers,

> ' E'en now great Babylon despoiled I see,
> In fear unfeigned the Parthian horsemen flee ;
> The Bactrian cons the Roman legist's lore,
> Ganges grows pale between each subject shore,
> And Persia spreads her gems your feet before.'

And so, in many similar passages, involuntary homage

is rendered to the Sassanian monarchs of Persia, by representing them as the most formidable of the antagonists of Rome.

It was this fear of the Persian monarchy which doubtless partly induced Constantine to plant his new capital at the meeting-point of Europe and Asia. In a certain sense it may be said that the measure was justified by its consequences. Except for the disastrous retreat of Julian's army—and even his expedition was a triumph, only converted into a defeat by the overeagerness of the General—Persia won no considerable victories over Eastern Rome, and in the seventh century she was utterly overthrown by the Emperor Heraclius. Moreover, the wonderful political prescience of the founder of Constantinople was clearly shown by the tenacity with which, through the greater part of eleven stormy centuries, the Empire, which had that city for its brain, clung to life. Avars, Bulgarians, Saracens, Russians, Seljouk Turks, Latin Crusaders, foamed over the surrounding provinces and dashed themselves to pieces against its walls, but none except the Crusaders effected an entrance, and none effected a durable conquest till the terrible day when the dynasty of Palaeologus succumbed to the dynasty of Othman. And the fact that Stamboul is to this day a spell of such portentous power in the incantations of modern diplomatists, is the most powerful of all testimonies to the genius of the young prince who was hailed Imperator by the legionaries at York.

But if the question be asked, 'What was the effect of the building of Constantinople on Italy and Old Rome?' if it be considered that the true object of a statesman of the Lower Empire should have been, not to protract

The foundation of Constantinople was due to this fear of Persia and accomplished its immediate end.

the existence of a semi-Greek, semi-Asiatic dominion, a kind of bastard Rome, but to keep the true Rome, the City of the seven hills, in her high place at the forefront of humanity, or, if she must needs fall, to make her fall as honourable and her transformed spirit as mighty as possible,—then our answer will be widely different, and we shall have to rank the founder of Constantinople foremost among the destroyers of the Empire.

Jealousy between East and West one great cause of Rome's downfall.

We have seen in the course of this history the infinite mischief wrought by the rivalry between the Ministers of the Eastern and Western Empires. At the critical moment of Alaric's preparations for his invasion Stilicho alone might probably have crushed him; but the subtle Goth

'Sold his alternate oaths to either throne.'

Each Empire trusted that the blow was about to fall on the other—a blow which the sister-realm would have witnessed with Christian resignation—and thus the time for anticipating it and for destroying the destroyer passed away.

Claudian's picture of the courtiers of Constantinople.

The sort of jealousy which had sprung up between the two capitals is well illustrated by the following lines of Claudian. The passage [1] also gives us a picture of the populace of the New Rome, which, though no doubt charged with hostile feeling, connects itself sufficiently with the Athens of Alcibiades, and the Nika rioters of the days of Justinian, to justify us in accepting its main features as correct.

399

In consequence of Tribigild's revolt, Eutropius, then chief minister of Arcadius, convenes a sort of Council of War.

[1] In Eutropium, II. 325–341.

'Pert youths came there and grey beards lecherous,
Whose glory was in trencher-combats won.
A *menu* subtly changed from yesterday's
Is a most noble exploit in their eyes.
By costly fare they tickle appetite
And give to those insatiate maws of theirs
The starry birds that drew great Juno's car,
And India's emerald prattlers of the woods.
Far realms supply their dainties : their deep greed
The Aegean sea and blue Propontis' lake
And Azof's straits with all their denizens
Soothe for an hour, but fail to satisfy.
Then with what art they wear their scented robes
Silken, but heavy for those delicate limbs !
The highest praise is his whose vapid jokes
Move loudest laughter. See their ornaments,
Fitter for girls than men, their shaven cheeks,
And mark them on the days of spectacle.
The Hun, the Goth may thunder at the gates,
The dancers will not have one gazer less.
Rome's name they ever scorn, and can admire
Only the mansions which the Bosphorus laves.
Yet there are arts in which e'en these excel :
Deftly they dance and drive a chariot well.'

Of course there is spite in this description, but the fact that such a picture of the Byzantine Court was acceptable to the dwellers by the Tiber shows the estrangement which had sprung up between the Old Rome and the New.

Had the Mistress of the World, when she found herself on all sides begirt by the 'bark[1] of savage nations,' deliberately withdrawn to her own ancient citadel, put her fleets in order at Classis and Misenum, so as to command the upper and the lower seas, and sent her hardiest troops to garrison the difficult passes of the Alps, she might have lost many fair provinces, but the

Probable course of events if Rome had been the only centre.

---

[1] See Claudian's words as quoted on p. 586.

heart of the Empire could hardly have been pierced. It was the diffusion of her vital force over several nerve-centres, Carthage, Alexandria, Antioch, but above all, Constantinople, that ruined her. Some of the suckers lived on, but the old tree perished.

§ 2. *Christianity.*

Christianity and the Roman State were necessary foes.
It was not by an accidental coincidence that the great historian of the Decline and Fall of the Roman Empire was also one of the ablest opponents of the Christian Revelation to whom the last century gave birth. The sound of the vesper-song of barefooted friars in the temple of Jupiter Capitolinus, which seemed to call him to his great enterprise, suggested to him, not untruly, that an irreconcilable antagonism between the Genius of the Emperors and the Genius of Christianity had caused the ruins which were piled around him. And what seems to call for particular notice here is the fact that both the good and the evil in Christianity contributed to this result; both those great spiritual truths which made the essence of the new Religion when it came forth from the hands of its Divine Founder, and those foreign elements which it borrowed from philosophies and idolatries in the act of battling with them,—all fought against the Rome of the Caesars.

Opposition between the original ideas of the Roman and the Christian *civitas.*
First, as to the essential opposition between the uncorrupted spirit of Christianity and the continuance of the Roman State. The religious ideas of the Latin and Sabine tribes among whom the great Republic was born, were poor and homely enough, without the Hellenic grace, or the Jewish sublimity, or the Teutonic

tenderness ; but, such as they were, they absolutely
moulded the character and institutions of the Roman
people. The Church did not encroach upon the province of the State, it simply was the State. No order
of priests contended for power or privilege with the
officers of the Republic ; those officers themselves, as
they reached certain stages in their upward progress,
became ministers of the gods, and, without any question
as to spiritual fitness, only with so much pretension to
morality as an originally moral people naturally required
in its chief magistrates, they were clothed, *ex officio*,
with a certain sacred character. The word *Religio* itself,
whatever be its precise etymological significance, was
understood to express the binding, cementing force
which a constant reference to unseen supernatural
Powers exerts upon a commonwealth. Hence the same
myth-making faculty which in the brain of

> ' The lively Grecian, in a land of hills,
>   Rivers, and fertile plains, and sounding shores [1],'

created Nymphs and Naiads and Oreads, was employed
by the more prosaic Roman to invent fresh gods for
every fresh development of the social, the political, even
the financial life of Man the Citizen. Thus, according
to the curious catalogue of St. Augustine [2], ' they commended children in the act of birth to the goddess
Ops, children crying to the god Vaticanus, lying in
their cradles to Cunina, sucking to Rumina, standing
to Statilinus, arriving [3] to Adeona, departing to
Abeona. They commended them to goddess Mens
that they might have a good mind, to Volumnus and

---

[1] Wordsworth: Excursion, Book IV.
[2] De Civitate Dei, iv. 21.
[3] ' Deae Adeonae adeuntes, Abeonae abeuntes.'

Volumna, god and goddess, that they might have a good volition, to the nuptial gods that they might marry well, to the rurals, and especially to goddess Fructesca, that they might receive plenteous fruits, to Mars and Bellona that they might wage war well, to Victoria that they might conquer, to the god Honor that they might be honoured, to the goddess Pecunia that they might have plenty of money, to the god Aesculanus and his son Argentinus that that money might be both of bronze and silver. For Aesculanus was made the father because bronze money was coined before silver; and, in truth, I cannot understand why Argentinus did not beget Aurinus, since the silver coinage has been followed by one of gold.'

Such a religious system as this subjects itself easily to ridicule, as easily as the faith of a modern Italian peasant in his own particular Madonna or Bambino, in the San Cristoforo of one village, or the San Lorenzo of another. Like this latter development, too, it probably glanced lightly over the minds of the upper classes of society, and was tenaciously held in all its grotesque minuteness only by the lower. Still this was substantially the religious system under which the Great Republic had grown from youth to manhood; by its Pontiffs had been declared the days for the assembly of the people in the forum, by its augurs had the omens been taken in every one of its battle-fields. The deification of Julius and Augustus was the national expression of the feeling that the greatness of Rome was the peculiar care of the Eternal Gods, and that the spirits which had wrought conspicuously at this grand task during their earthly career, must still survive in the society of the Immortals, to watch over the work of their own hands. It was with this faith—for faith we must surely call it—in their hearts that the legions of Rome had marched on from victory to victory. Their anticipations of reward or punishment in a future life might be vague and varying, but at least they felt that the Great City with which they had linked their fortunes was eternal, and the confidence that she would survive all shocks of adverse fortune, and would treasure the names of her defenders with undying reverence, gave strength, doubtless, not only to a Decius or a Curtius, but also to many a simple Roman legionary at the moment of facing death for her sake.

The whole of this fabric of national faith, with whatsoever in it was noble, and whatsoever in it was puerile, had to fall before the Apostolic proclamation, 'To us there is but one God, the Father, of whom are all things, and we in him, and one Lord Jesus Christ, by whom are all things, and we by him.' If there was any hint in the Christian Scriptures of one nation favoured above all others, that nation was the Jewish, if any notion of a city chosen by the Eternal 'to put his name there,' that city was Jerusalem. But the latest and prevailing utterance of the new religion was, 'All nationalities are on the same level before God. He has made of one blood all nations of men, to dwell on all the face of the earth. Your citizenship, the true *civitas*, which is the highest condition that man can attain to, is in heaven. This *civitas* is within reach of all men, Barbarian, Scythian, bond or free, and makes brothers of us all.'

There was an incurable opposition between teaching such as this, and the root-idea of the Roman Commonwealth. The rulers of the State felt it, and were forced into persecution, almost against their will. Gladly

would they have consigned Christianity to the peaceful
Pantheon of the tolerated religions (*religiones licitae*),
in which already the worship of Astarte and Mithras,
of Isis and the Dea Syria, flourished happily, side by
side. But they perceived—the wisest Emperors the
most clearly—that this was a religion which would have
all or nothing, and they hunted it into the catacombs
to bar it from the throne.

Strange
jumble
which
resulted
from their
union.

The persecutions failed: they enlisted pity, generosity,
love of justice, all the nobler feelings of our nature,
on the side of the votaries of the new religion, and to
these latter they gave a drill, a discipline, we must also
in truth add a bitterness of temper, which they had
not possessed before. A time came when the Christians
found that they were the majority in the Empire, a
time when the young Emperor Constantine, with his
foot upon the ladder of fortune, was half-convinced
of the truth of Christianity, and wholly convinced of
the policy of embracing it. For three generations the
Emperors, with the exception of the short reign of
Julian, were the Christian masters of a household whose
traditions were still Pagan. Some of the anomalies
which resulted from this position of theirs have been
glanced at in previous pages. We have seen that no
Emperor till the accession of Gratian dared to refuse
the title of *Pontifex Maximus*, which marked him as
head of the State-Church of Heathenism. We have
also noticed the incongruity between the acts of Theodosius as Defender of the Catholic Faith and the conventional language of the court poet, who makes him
the favourite of Mars and Jupiter during his life, and
turns him into a star after his death.

That this strange medley of contending faiths had

no effect in enfeebling the resolution of Rome, and making her stroke uncertain, that the regiment which had fought so long under one flag would fight just as well when that flag was replaced by another, as hostile to it as the Lilies to the Tricolour, is what no one would conjecture beforehand. And that the substitution of Christianity for the worship of the deities of the Capitol had something to do with the crumbling away of the Empire in the fifth century, is a conviction which forces itself on our minds, and never so irresistibly as when we are listening to the most eloquent and the most subtle apologist for Christianity, Augustine, endeavouring to prove to us in his book on the City of God that the thing was not so. One turns over page after page of that immortal treatise—that Encyclopaedia of the whole religious thought of the age ; one feels the absurdity of the Pagan theory, the grandeur of the Christian conception of the vast unseen City of God, but, through it all, the antagonism between the true Roman ideas and the ideas of Christianity rises more and more definitely before the mind, and when we are called upon finally to adjudicate on the question 'Would the Rome of the Fabii and the Scipios, the Rome which heartily believed in and worshipped Jupiter and Quirinus, Mavors, Ops, and Saturnus, have fallen as the Christian Rome fell before the hordes of Alaric ?' we are bound in our historical conscience to answer, No.

Secondly. In the course of its three hundred years' struggle for existence the new religion had assimilated some elements, foreign as I venture to think, to its original essence ; and by these also it made war on Rome. The spirit of intolerance was one of these

Elements foreign to the original conception of Christianity which were also hostile to

extraneous elements, at any rate in so far as it relied
on the sword of the civil magistrate to carry its sentences
into effect. The words of St. Paul about heretics,
'With such an one, no, not to eat,' and of St. John,
'Receive him not into your house, neither bid him God
speed,' were aimed apparently at men whose immorality
was bringing the new society into reproach, and contemplated exclusion from that society as the heaviest
punishment to be inflicted. The general attitude
towards the heathen or the unbelieving Jew was ' What
have I to do with them that are without?'; and the
proposal to arrange the worldly affairs, even of Christians, authoritatively, was met by 'Man, who made me
a judge or a divider over you?' 'Whiles it remained
was it not thine own, and after it was sold, was it not
in thine own power?' In practice, the relation of the
professors of the new faith to 'them that were without'
during the second century seems to have been reasonable and friendly. Justin Martyr and Quadratus still
wore the philosopher's cloak after their conversion to
Christianity, and endeavoured to persuade their fellow-
countrymen by an appeal to ' the voice of the soul, who
is herself naturally Christian [1],' that the glad tidings
which they had to proclaim, though marvellous, were
not incredible, and were in harmony with the truest
presentiments of man's own moral nature. Would that
the new religion had always thus calmly addressed
herself to the consciences of mankind, that she had
never shouted nor shrieked, nor tortured, in order to
enforce the acceptance of her message! Earth would

---

[1] 'Testimonium animae naturaliter Christianae.' The phrase belongs to the following century, but the line of argument indicated by
it to this.

be by many degrees more like Heaven at this day, if she had thus remained true to her first gentle instincts.

But the persecutions came and went, and they I. Intoler-ance. changed, though they should not have changed, the temper of the Christian champions. So was rendered possible that utterance of Tertullian's (destined to an evil immortality), in which he consoled his brethren for their conscientious abstinence from the pleasures of the Hippodrome by promising them far greater spectacular pleasures in the life to come, when from the safe security of Heaven they should behold so many proud prefects, so many jeering philosophers, writhing in agony under the tortures of the never-dying fires of hell. It may be admitted that the stern, almost morose, temperament of Tertullian is answerable for some of this bitterness, but it would not be difficult to quote passages of a similar tendency from Lactantius and other fathers of the Ante-Nicene Church. In truth, it was not in human nature (though it should have been in the divine that was intermingled with it) to see parents, brothers, sisters, dragged off to an insulting and cruel death, for refusing to sacrifice to the Genius of the Emperor, without some scowl of hatred becoming fixed above the eyes which witnessed these things. And so persecution did not, as was once alleged, always and entirely fail of its end. ' The blood of the Martyrs was the seed of the Church;' but it was a Church of different habit of growth, and producing more acrid fruit than that which it replaced.

For seventy years, however, after Constantine's edicts in favour of Christianity, the new religion showed herself but little as a persecutor, at least of heathens. The tolerant spirit of Constantine had something to do with this ; the internal divisions of the Christian Church, especially the long and fierce Arian debate, still more. The Caesars of Rome, with the exception of Julian, settled down comfortably into their anomalous position, each being at once *Pontifex Maximus* of the old religion, and Moderator in the doctrinal controversies of the new. It was as if the Ottoman Sultan, still retaining his claim to the Caliphate, were to become a member of the Greek Church, and to throw himself earnestly into the discussions about the Procession of the Holy Spirit.

We have heard Theodosius, at the Council of Constantinople in the year 381, pronouncing the final triumph of the Trinitarian party within the Church, and we have seen something of the increased stringency of his determination to secure for that Church, by the power of the State, the victory over her external foes, whether Heathens or Heretics. True, these persecutions lacked the ferocity of those which were set on foot by Decius and by Galerius ; still they *were* ; and for some generations, with quiet, earnest deliberateness, the whole power of the Emperors was employed in making all Christians think alike, and in preventing non-Christians from thinking at all.

353.   Constantius had said, ' We will that all men should abstain from sacrifices, and if any shall hereafter offend against this law, let him be punished by the avenging sword[1].' But the decree seems to have remained a dead letter, and the heathen sacrifices went on nearly as before. Theodosius enacted new laws

[1] Cod. Theod. xvi. 10. 4.

against heathen worship, and by such acts as the demolition of the temple of Serapis at Alexandria, gave them
practical effect.   At the same time appeared upon the
statute book a cloud of edicts (some of which have
been already quoted) against 'the noxious Manicheans
and their execrable meetings,' against 'the heretics
of the Donatist superstition,' against 'the teachers and
leaders of the crime of the Eunomians, especially their
clergy whose madness has brought about this great
aberration,' against 'all who are tormented by the
error of divers heresies, viz., the Eunomians, the Arians,
the Macedonian deniers of the Holy Ghost, the Manicheans, the Encratites, the Apotactites, the Saccofori,
the Hydroparastatae.'   Fine, imprisonment, loss of
office, prohibition to assemble in the town or to give to
their places of meeting the appearance of churches,
restriction of their testamentary power—these are the
penalties thundered forth in many an edict against
men who had committed no crime against the State,
but whose theology was different from the Emperor's.
The ferocity and the terror of Diocletian's persecutions
have passed away, but we find ourselves breathing the
same atmosphere of petty ecclesiastical tyranny which
produced the Five Mile Act and Conventicle Act of
Charles II, the Penal Laws against the Irish Catholics
of William III and Anne.   If there were nothing more
to be said against it, this attempt to harass men into
uniformity of religious opinion was an enormous waste
of power, at a time when the energies of the State
were scarcely sufficient for its own proper work of
administration.   But what made the matter worse,
from the point of view of a Roman statesman, was that
the religion which was being maintained in domination

at the cost of all this legislative combat, was itself in no way essential to, nay, rather as has been before said, was of necessity antagonistic to, the root-idea of the Roman Commonwealth. A Mohammedan Sultan pressing heavily on the Giaour, an Israelitish monarch slaying the priests of Baal, a Most Catholic king of Spain burning Jews or expelling Moriscoes, were all acting more or less in accordance with the spirit of which their royalty was the expression. But a Roman Imperator harassing the Encratites or the Apotactites because the building in which they assembled for divine worship too closely resembled a church of the orthodox, was an utterly un-Roman Roman, an anomaly not only vexatious but ridiculous [1].

Yet it is probable that to the somewhat narrow, martinet mind of Theodosius, and still more to the dazed intellects of his sons, these measures of religious persecution appeared solemn duties; nay more, that they regarded them as peace-offerings, which would ensure the secular safety of the Empire. The increasing calamities which befell the State were taken as manifestations of the wrath of God; and no more obvious means of conjuring away that wrath suggested themselves than the enactment of a new and sharper law against the Manichean pravity or the Arian madness.

In the mist and darkness which have gathered over the history of the fifth century, a mist and a darkness through which only the bare forms of events are dis-

---

[1] The story of Generidus the heathen, and his refusal to continue in the Emperor's service unless the edict against his fellow-heathens were repealed, well illustrates the baneful effect of this persecuting legislation in the defence of the Empire (see vol. i. p. 764).

cernible, while thoughts and feelings are utterly hidden, we know little indeed of the mood of mind in which these successive Acts of Uniformity were received by the objects of them. Heathenism and Heresy, like wounded creatures, crept back to their caves and died there, but after what conflicts or with what struggles we know not. The name 'Paganus' (villager), for the worshipper of the old gods, is one among many indications that Christianity conquered first the great cities, the centres of intellectual and commercial activity, and then gradually, and we can hardly say how slowly, pushed her way into lonely glens or wide unfrequented pasture-lands, and made the dwellers there bow before the cross. Yet even in the cities and at the Imperial Courts the victory was not fully won in the reign of Theodosius. It is a noteworthy fact how many of the small band of literary men, who flourished in the latter days of the Empire, remained faithful to the old superstitions. Ammianus Marcellinus, Zosimus, Priscus, the chief historians of this period, are all Pagans, one at least of them a bitter Pagan. Nor is it by any means certain that Procopius, the great historian of the reign of Justinian, ought not to be added to the list.

Two other elements of the Christianity of the third and fourth centuries co-operated in a subordinate degree towards the decay of the Empire. These were the Priestly Hierarchy and the Monastic Self-seclusion.

The fires of Roman persecution had, doubtless, much to do with hardening and shaping, as into a point of tempered steel, that marvellous episcopal organisation which was one day to penetrate the world. As the soldiers who survive on a well-fought battle-field look towards the officers who have been with them in the

2. The Ecclesiastical Hierarchy.

thickest of the fray, so we may imagine the hearts of the believers to have glowed with fresh loyalty towards the rulers of the Church, when the rage of the Decian or the Galerian persecution was at length abated, and they had leisure to count their losses. Thus, here also to the repressive measures of the Emperors must be attributed some involuntary share in the change which came over the spirit of the Church between the first century and the fourth, and which separates the simple and scarcely differentiated Overseers and Elders of the Acts of the Apostles from the full-grown Bishops and Priests of the time of Constantine. It is not likely that such a well-disciplined and compact organisation as the Christian hierarchy can have grown up within and yet outside of the Empire without impairing somewhat of its strength. And such victories as were won by Athanasius over Constantius, or by Ambrose over Theodosius, though they command our fullest sympathy as noble triumphs of the moral over the material, had probably some effect in lessening the reverence which men felt for the Augustus as a kind of 'present[1] divinity,' and so in loosening the fabric of the Empire. Yet possibly we ought not to attribute large results to this cause. The great strifes between Bishop and Sovereign belong to a later age, to the barbarian monarchies or to the Eastern Empire. Except indirectly, in so far as it may have favoured the persecution of heathens and heretics, the Christian hierarchy need not be held responsible for a large share in the pulling down of Imperial Rome.

3. Monasticism.

Probably we may come to a similar conclusion with

---

[1] According to the often-quoted words of Horace, 'praesens divus habebitur Augustus.'

reference to that other great phenomenon of the religious life of the fourth and fifth centuries, the rise and progress of the monastic system. It is interesting to see how this was viewed by an educated, though certainly not unbiassed Pagan. Zosimus, speaking of the riots at Constantinople in connection with the exile of Chrysostom (401), says (v. 23), 'The city was filled with uproar, and the Christian church was occupied by the men who are called Monks. Now these men renounce lawful wedlock, and fill large colleges in the cities and villages with unmarried persons, profitless for war and for any other of the State's necessities. Yet have they, in the interval between that time and the present' [perhaps half a century], 'made great advances, so that they have now appropriated a large part of the land, and under pretence of distributing all their substance to the poor, have, in a manner, made all poor alike.'

The withdrawal of so many men in the prime of life from the pursuits of industry and the defence of the state, must undoubtedly have lessened the resources of the Empire, especially as these monks were not, like their successors in the Middle Ages, the restorers of the waste places, the doctors, engineers, and journalists of the community. At a time when the manliest virtue was required to stem the torrent of corruption within and barbarism without, men of noble soul and cultured intellect, like St. Jerome, retired into the caves of Bethlehem, leaving the world a prey to hypocrites and rogues, such as Olympius and Eutropius. As the latter class of men, despairing of the Roman state, sought to build up their own fortunes on the general ruin, so the former class, with the same despair of the republic in their hearts, determined at least to secure their own soul's salvation, and to live for this alone. The selfishness was of a higher kind, but it would be hard to deny that it was selfishness, and that the true Christian impulse would have been to struggle on undaunted, and persist in the endeavour to leave the world better than they found it.

But, having admitted this negative charge against monkery, we cannot assign to it, in the Western Empire at least, any great active influence for ruin. In the East, during the fifth century, the power of the monks was no doubt far more hurtful to the State. 'Armies of mad monks rushing through the streets of Alexandria [1],' and their brethren in Constantinople stirring up the people to shout for the deposition of the 'Manichean tyrant,' whenever an Emperor swerved by a hair's breadth from the razor-bridge of orthodoxy as defined in the Council of Chalcedon—these were undoubtedly disintegrating and dangerous forces ; and when they were predominant, the government of the Empire might truly be styled a government by lunatics. In the West we see no such spectacles at the time which we are now discussing, and it would be a scandalous injustice to class the calm Paulinus of Nola and the learned Claudianus Mamertus of Vienne with the turbulent Eutyches, or the blood-stained Barsumas of Constantinople.

§ 3. *Slavery.*

'It was no accidental catastrophe which patriotism and genius might have warded off : it was old social evils—at the bottom of all, the ruin of the middle class by the slave proletariat — that

[1] Kingsley, Roman and Teuton.

brought destruction on the Roman commonwealth' (Mommsen, History of Rome, book iv. chap. 11).

The men of our generation, who have read the story of General Sherman's march through Georgia, are in a better position than their ancestors for estimating the part played by slavery in bringing about the ruin of Rome. The short-lived Southern Confederacy in America had many points of resemblance to the Roman republic. It was administered by wealthy cultivators of the soil, born warriors, born orators, a proud and courageous people. All that mere fighting could do to preserve its existence was ably and, at first, successfully done; but Slavery, that rock of offence which the Planters had made the corner-stone of their new edifice, proved its ruin. The truth had been suspected for some little time before, but was fully proved when Sherman's scarcely-resisted march through three hundred miles of the enemy's country showed the hollowness of a political organisation which had been massing its armies, by hundreds of thousands at a time, on the banks of the Potomac, but which could not reckon on its own inhabitants to resist or seriously to harass an invader who had once broken through the wall of steel on the frontier. It could not reckon upon them, because the majority of them were themselves a hostile nation, made so by the institution of slavery. True, in America as in Italy, the oppressed class waited long before they dared to show on which side their sympathies lay. This is, for a time, that which turns the scale in favour of the slave-holder, that his chattels are too debased to be capable of self-organisation, too ignorant to understand the great movements in the world of politics and war, too

Effect of slavery in weakening the defence of the Empire illustrated by the American War of Secession.

servile-hearted to dare to embrace what may not prove the winning side. But if there comes at length such a time as came in Georgia lately, and in Etruria long ago, when the slave sees with his own eyes a man, mightier than his master, come to overthrow all that existing order which has weighed on him so heavily, and saying, 'Help me, and I will give you freedom,' then is seen the strange magic which lies in that word freedom for even the heaviest clods of humanity; then the comfortable persuasion of the self-deceived slave-owner, that his chattel will fight for the luxury of continuing to be a chattel, vanishes like snow in summer.

Flight of slaves to Alaric.

We have had to record one instance—many more have probably been left unrecorded—of the readiness of the Roman slaves to turn against their masters. In the interval between the first and second sieges of Rome by Alaric, the slaves, to the number of 40,000, fled to the barbarian camp. In his usual tantalising way Zosimus forgets to tell us the *dénouement* of the story, but it may be conjectured that the greater part of these slaves, if they ever returned to Rome, returned with the army of Alaric through the blazing Salarian Gate to guide their new friends to the plunder of their old oppressors [1].

No accurate account of the number of slaves in the Empire.

It would have been interesting to know what was the total number of slaves in existence at any particular period of the Empire, but a complete census of the whole population of the Roman world, free and servile, if it ever existed, has not survived to our day. Gibbon [2] guesses the number of the slaves all over the Empire at the

[1] Zosimus, v. 42. See vol. i. p. 794.
[2] Vol. i. p. 179 (ed. Smith).

time of Claudius at sixty millions ; and it seems to be
impossible either to prove or disprove his conjecture.
We are told, in round numbers, that some citizens
possessed 10,000 or 20,000 slaves apiece, and with
more apparent accuracy that a certain freedman under
Augustus, although he had been impoverished by the
civil wars, left at his death 4,116 slaves[1]. From other
sources we learn that in the days of Augustus, 200
slaves were not considered at all an exorbitantly large
establishment, and that he who had only five or ten
was looked upon as either very poor or very mean.
In view of these facts, 40,000 seems a very small
number for even the mere house-slaves in Rome at the
time of its siege by Alaric. Possibly the removal of
the Court to Ravenna, and the troublous character of
the times, had led to the withdrawal of most of the
wealthy slave-owners from Rome ; or the crowds of
freedmen and paupers supported by the public distribution of wheat may, in Rome itself, have thinned,
by a kind of competition, the number of actual bonds-
men. Or, which is perhaps the most likely supposition
of all, Zosimus, the writer from whom the story of the
fugitive slaves is extracted, is speaking in his usual
somewhat inaccurate style when he says, that 'nearly
all' the slaves in Rome deserted to the camp of
Alaric.

As mention has been made of slavery as it existed
down to our own days in the United States of North
America, and as this is that type of the 'peculiar
institution' which most readily suggests itself to our
minds, it may be well to remind the reader of a few

Compa-rison between Roman and American slavery.

---

[1] Athenaeus (vi. 104) is the authority for the first of these statements, Pliny (Hist. Naturalis, xxxiii. 10, § 47) for the second.

obvious points of dissimilarity between the two forms of servitude, the Roman and the American.

I. It seems probable that the condition of a slave under a Roman master was harder than that of the negro in the Southern States of America. Cruel men of course abused their dangerous power in both countries, while, under men of exceptional gentleness, the lot of the slave may have lost almost all that made it to differ from that of a hired labourer. But the great mass of masters, the men of average character, had in the United States a conception of duty towards their fellow-men which was, at least in some degree, influenced by the spirit of Christianity, while the Roman derived his notions of duty from such teachers as Cato the Censor, who, in a well-known passage, uttered his opinion that whenever a slave was not asleep he ought to be at work, and that a master should always sell off his aged slaves as well as his broken-down horses. Certainly this cannot have been either the theory or the practice in Virginia or Tennessee, hardly even, one would hope, in Mississippi or Alabama. It is true that the tendency of legislation under the Emperors had been towards greater mildness in the treatment of slaves. The master's absolute power of life and death was taken away; in cases where he had practised extreme cruelty he might be compelled to sell the victim of it ; and the huge gloomy *ergastula*, the prisons in which the slaves had been locked up at night after their labour in the fields (which, if not subterraneous, were always lighted by windows high up in the walls, from which there was no chance of escape), were legally abolished, and perhaps practically disused. Still, the life of the Roman's slave, especially of him who was engaged in agriculture, seems to have been hard and dismal beyond even the hardness and dismalness of ordinary negro slavery [1].

II. Yet in two aspects, more important perhaps than all beside, the condition of the Italian bondsman was better than that of the American. Love and hope were left to him. The breeding of slaves for sale was an unusual though not unknown practice; and consequently though families must sometimes have been separated, even as they are now by the ordinary economic laws of supply and demand, that great blot on the American system, the systematic tearing away of the wife from her husband and the mother from her child, did not disgrace the Roman slave-owners. Manumission also must have been a far more frequent incident of servile life among the ancients, and when it came it opened up a far happier and more unhindered career.

Family ties not so often severed. Manumission more frequent in Rome than in America.

This difference between the two systems is chiefly due to the obvious and fundamental distinction, that in Rome there did not, as in America, yawn the wide chasm of absolute diversity of race between bond and free. All nations, even the noblest of antiquity, were represented in the slave market at Rome. The Greek doctor, or pedagogue, or scribe, the lusty Cappadocian who bore the litter, the Hebrew of whose nation Titus sold 97,000 into bondage, the Syrian, the Celt, the

---

[1] Since writing this sentence, I have met with the following striking words of Mommsen (Hist. of Rome, book iv. chap. 2) : 'The abyss of misery and woe, which opens before our eyes in this most miserable of all proletariats, we leave to be fathomed by those who venture to gaze into such depths: it is very possible that, compared with the sufferings of the Roman slaves, the sum of all negro suffering is but a drop.'

Dacian, the German, were all in their various ways ministering to the luxury or providing for the wants of the Roman master. From such a motley throng combination was little to be dreaded, and on the other hand there was in them no great inferiority of race to prevent the slave, once liberated, from standing side by side with his old master. Hence, and from motives of pride and profit which made the freedman often a more desirable appendage to the family of the Roman noble than the slave himself, arose the great frequency of manumission, which was indeed slightly checked in the time of Augustus [1], on account of the number of debased citizens with whom it was flooding the Commonwealth, but which remained a sufficiently common practice sensibly to ameliorate the condition of the Roman slave by introducing into it the vast medicament of Hope.

We turn to American slavery, and we see at once a mighty contrast. There every member of the servile caste belonged to one race, and that race one separated by wide ethnological interspaces from the dominant one, and far below it in intellectual energy. It is said that a proposition once made in the Roman Senate, to order all the slaves to wear a distinctive dress, was rejected, on the ground that it would be dangerous thus to reveal to them their superiority in numbers. What the Senate had denied in that case, Nature had done ineffaceably in the case of 'persons held to bondage' under the American laws, by clothing them all with one sable livery. Hence arose, on the one hand, the pride of race which placed the meanest of 'the mean whites' above the most honest and capable man

---

[1] By the Lex Aelia Sentia.

of African descent, and which denied to the latter, however large his share of European blood, *ex parte paternâ*, any share in the duties and rewards of civil life. Hence, on the other hand, arose the fear of race, causing the State to throw the whole weight of its influence into the scale against manumission, and imposing upon every man, whose skin bore witness to the servile condition of his ancestors, the burden of proof that he was not himself a slave. This state of the law and of public feeling was of course utterly absent in old Rome.

III. And, yet again, there was a difference which probably made the position of the negro, when he began to reason and to reflect, more intolerable than that of the Dacian or the Syrian in a Roman villa or on an Italian farm. In the fifth century the conscience of the whole civilised world acquiesced in the fact of slavery; in the nineteenth it protested against it. The Roman legislator said that this abrogation of the natural rights of man was an institution of the universal law of nations [1], and his saying was confirmed by the fact that there was in all probability not one nation then existing, civilised or barbarian, wherein Slavery, in one form or another, did not exist. And so the bondsman of those days submitted to his servile condition, as men now submit to poverty or disease, grumbling indeed that they have drawn a bad number in the lottery of life, but without any intolerable feeling of injustice, without any indignant questioning,

[margin note: Slavery not felt to be so intolerably unjust in the Old World.]

---

[1] 'Libertas ... est naturalis facultas ejus quod cuique facere libet, nisi si quid vi aut jure prohibetur. Servitus autem est *constitutio juris gentium*, qua quis dominio alieno contra naturam subjicitur' (Institutes of Justinian, book i. tit. 3).

'Why was this horrible fate ever placed for me or for any one among the possible conditions of existence?'

In America we all know what far different thoughts rankled in the breast of a high-spirited and intelligent slave. Great nations were living and flourishing without this institution which made his life hateful to him. Wide sections of the Christian Church condemned it as a crime against God and man. A week perhaps, or two weeks of nightly journeying towards the North Star, would take him to a land where no slaves toiled; a few weeks more would set him beyond the possibility of recapture. Assuredly this ever present thought that Liberty was in the world, was near, but was not for him, must have made the chains of many an American slave more galling, must have raised, sometimes almost to madness, his exasperation against the social system which was his foe.

Roman Slavery therefore probably excited less bitterness of feeling than American.

IV. Upon a review therefore of the main points of likeness and unlikeness between these two conditions of society, it seems reasonable to conjecture that the men who were owned by Roman masters were less dissatisfied with their lot than those who belonged to the American planters, and that Slavery as a disruptive force was more fatal to the Southern Confederacy than to the Western Empire.

But in Rome it had been working through twelve centuries, in the United States for less than three, and therefore its evil effects were less lasting, one may venture to hope, in the latter instance than in the former. Slavery had aided in the massing together of those 'wide farms' which were the ruin of Italy[1]. Slavery had emptied the fields and villages of the hardy

[1] 'Latifundia perdidere Italiam.'

rustics who had once been the backbone of Roman power. Slavery had filled the cities with idle and profligate babblers. Slavery had indoctrinated these men, themselves often freedmen or the sons of freedmen, with the pestilent notion that manual labour was beneath the dignity of a citizen. And lastly, Slavery had surrounded the thrones of the Emperors with men like Eutropius and Chrysaphius, who, by the favour of a fatuous master, crept from the position of a menial to that of a Prime Minister, and who, when their turn came, bitterly revenged upon Society the wrongs which they had suffered at its hands.

A new and happier world was to arise out of the ruins of the old. Slavery was to be softened into Serfdom, and Serfdom was slowly to disappear, both changes being largely attributable to the benign influence of the Christian Church. The fine old mediaeval motto,

> ' By hammer and hand
> All arts do stand,'

was to drive out, at any rate from the cities, the old, irrational, scorn of handicraft ; and the *ergastulum* and the scourge were to vanish like an evil dream. And so if Slavery was a cause, the Abolition of Slavery was to be a result, though by no means an immediate result, of the Fall of the Empire.

§ 4. *' Panem et Circenses,' or the Pauperisation of the Roman Proletariat.*

The Roman State at the beginning and the end of its career pursued towards its poorer classes two opposite lines of policy, both unjust, one of which might reasonably have been expected to strangle the rising nationality in its childhood, while the other certainly hastened the ruin of its old age.

The poorer
citizens in
the earlier
ages of the
Republic
were op-
pressed by
the State,
In the first ages of the Republic the plebeian soldier was expected to leave his farm or his business to serve for a short campaign against the Aequians or Volscians, and to return to a home which had in many instances suffered from the depredations of the enemy, enriched only by a precarious portion of the booty, which, by the fortune of war or the unfairness of the dividing general, might turn out to be worth little or nothing. The real gain of the most successful wars, the public land, was farmed out often at little more than a nominal rent to the senators or a few wealthy plebeians. Thus the whole tendency of the incessant wars of the Republic was to make the rich richer and the poor poorer, a tendency aggravated by the high rates charged for interest and by the stern attitude of the Roman law towards the defaulting debtor. The well-known picture drawn in the Second Book of Livy of the brave old centurion, whose farm had been plundered during his absence with the army, and who, under the crushing load of debt and taxation, had been obliged first to part with the inheritance of his ancestors and then to surrender his person into the hands of his cruel creditor, and who at length escaped from his place of torment into the Forum, where his squalid garb, his long un-kempt hair, his old and honourable scars received in battle with the enemy, and the new and shameful scourge-marks upon his back inflicted by the slave of a Roman senator, stirred the people to fury :—this picture may not be precisely and historically true of the 259th year of the city, yet doubtless it is a type of many a

similar occurrence in those early days of the tyranny of wealth.

The characteristic of Roman Legislation at this period is its contempt for the rights of the individual, its frightfully unfair notion of the partnership between him and the State—a partnership in which he gave his time, his blood, his heroism, to promote the glory of Rome, and received in return nothing, not even permission to live on the land of his fathers.

In the later phases of the Roman Commonwealth *in the later ages, pampered.* the opposite error was committed. After the Second Punic War the State really asked nothing of the poor citizen of Rome, and gave him everything that was necessary for life, and, in so giving, deprived him of

‘ Man’s first, noblest, birthright, Toil.’

The pauperising legislation of Rome first wore the insidious form of a gentle intervention to lower the price of corn. When Spain, Sicily, and Africa were pouring in their tributes of corn or money to the exchequer of the Republic, it was not an unnatural suggestion that the wealth thus acquired might fairly be expended in easing the material condition of the Roman citizens, of the men on whom had fallen the heaviest weight of all the blows from Regillus to Cannae, by which the Roman State had been fashioned into greatness. Not an unnatural thought; and yet if the remembrance of the scourged veteran in the Forum, and of all the cruel wrongs of the early Plebeians, had anything to do with ripening it into action, we have here an instance of that strange Nemesis of Unrighteousness, which sometimes leads statesmen in the very excess of their penitence for an injustice in the past to prepare a new and greater injustice for the future. It had been a cruel wrong to send forth the Roman Plebeian to fight the Volscian or Aequian, and not even to keep his homestead free from the exactions of the creditor, who would not have been a creditor but for the military service of the bread-winner. It was not less a wrong to make the Spaniard or the Sicilian toil, in order to enable the descendants of that same Plebeian to prolong a life of idleness and dissipation in the Roman Forum.

Economic absurdity of the grain distributions.

And, indirectly, this interference with true economic laws injured Italy no less than the Provinces. How was the Etrurian or Sabine farmer to grow his corn to a profit, when the whole machinery of the administration of the Republic was being employed to sell corn from beyond the seas at far less than cost price in the Roman capital? This was not Free Trade; it was, if we may use the expression, Protection turned inside out; it was a systematic exclusion of the Italian corn-grower from his own natural market. Of course the Italian farmer, already sorely harassed by the necessity of competition with slave-labour, succumbed, and virtually disappeared from the scene. The *latifundia*, the vast domains worked by celibate slaves, took the place of the small yeomen's holdings; the horrible *ergastulum* replaced the free and happy homestead; sheep-walks, vine-yards, and olive-yards occupied the ground once employed in the growth of corn, and, more important by far than even the disappearance of her waving corn-fields, Italy ceased to produce men as she had once done, just when the need of men to bear the world-wide burden of her Empire was the greatest.

Market price of corn.

There were great fluctuations in the market price of corn under the Republic. In the Second Punic War

it rose as high as 51 shillings the quarter; in the wars
between Marius and Sulla as high as 102 shillings,
during a great famine under Augustus to 115 shillings.
But these were simply famine prices. On the other
hand, during a year of great plenty near the close of
the Second Punic War, the price was as low as two
shillings and eight pence a quarter. A little later,
according to Polybius, it was frequently sold in the
valley of the Po for two shillings and eleven pence a
quarter[1]. As between these wide fluctuations it appears
to be admitted that about 21 shillings a quarter was
the ordinary market price. Now, by the legislation of
Caius Gracchus, each citizen had the right to claim
every month a bushel and a quarter of corn from the
public stores for seventeen pence, that is to say at the
rate of nine shillings a quarter, or less than half the
average market price[2]. The rest of the legislation of
the younger Gracchus died with him, but this, its worse
feature, remained. When supreme power passed from
the Senate and the Assembly of the People to the
Caesars, these latter rulers, though in many respects
the champions of the Provincials against Rome, did not
dare to withdraw the supplies of cheap corn from the
citizens, though they did limit—eventually to 200,000
—the number of persons who were entitled thus to
purchase it. Gradually the form of sale and purchase
was done away with, and the distribution became simply

*Price fixed
by legisla-
tion of
Gracchus.*

[1] Four Obols (6½d.) for the Sicilian Medimnus. The Attic Medimnus was a bushel and a half. We cannot be quite certain that the
Sicilian Medimnus was the same quantity, and therefore this calculation is liable to some doubt.

[2] More precisely, the citizen was entitled to claim five modii at
the rate of 6⅓ asses per modius, the *modius* being equivalent to the
quarter of a bushel, and the *as* to ·53 of a penny.

gratuitous. By the middle of the second century of
our era, the monthly supplies of corn had been changed
for the far more convenient and even more pauperising
distribution of wheaten loaves, baked perhaps two or
three times a week.

When Aurelian ascended the throne, the loaf which
the Roman citizen was thus entitled to receive (we
know not for how many days' consumption), weighed
one *uncia* (that is $\frac{1}{12}$) less than two pounds [1]. As he
went forth from the gates of the city on his expedition
against the Queen of Palmyra, he announced to the
people that if he should return victorious he would
present each one of them with a crown of two pounds'
weight. The citizens expected that these crowns would
be of gold (worth more than £80 apiece), a donative which
was beyond the power and the inclination of Aurelian.
Yet were they not altogether disappointed, for when
he had been drawn in triumph up the Sacred Hill,
preceded by the weeping Zenobia, he commanded that
wheaten loaves [2], shaped like crowns and weighing each
two pounds, should be distributed to the people.
Through the remainder of his life and apparently
during the reigns of his successors, these larger loaves
were given to those who possessed the needful *tessera*
or out-door relief ticket, and this *uncia* added to the
civic rations seems to have been seriously regarded by
the patriotic but ill-advised Emperor as one of his chief
titles to greatness. In writing to Arabianus the Public
Commissary-General (*Praefectus Annonae*), he says,
'Of all the good deeds which by the favour of the

---

[1] The Roman pound weighed a little less than $\frac{3}{4}$ of our pound
avoirdupois.

[2] Called Siliginei.

Immortal Gods I have wrought for the Commonwealth
none is more splendid than this, that I have increased
the distribution of corn to every citizen by one *uncia*.
To ensure the perpetuity of this benefit I have appointed
more ship-masters for the Nile and for the river-traffic
of Rome. I have raised the banks of the Tiber and
deepened the channel of its head-strong current [1]. I
have paid my vows to Perennity and the other Gods,
I have consecrated a statue of the gracious Ceres.
Now be it thy task, my dearest Arabianus, to see that
these arrangements of mine be not unfruitful. For
there is nothing in the world more cheerful than the
Roman people when they have well eaten [2].' This same
Emperor, though fond of repressing what he considered
inordinate luxury (forbidding his wife to wear a silken
dress because silk was then worth its weight in gold,
and proscribing the use of gold threads and gilded
ceilings, whereby he considered that a metal which
ought to be as plentiful as silver was unnecessarily
wasted), nevertheless added to the rations of the Roman
people, articles which can hardly be considered as of
prime necessity. He gave them pork and oil and wine ;
at least as to the last gift he had taken measures for
planting extensive vineyards in Etruria, and cultivating
them with slave-labour for the sake of a gratuitous
distribution of wine to the citizens, but according to
one story the scheme was frustrated by the intervention
of the Praetorian Prefect who told the generous Emperor
that if he gave them wine he would have to supplement his gifts with roast ducks and chickens. He also
gave them white tunics with long sleeves imported

---

[1] 'Tiberinas exstruxi ripas : vadum alvei tumentis effodi.'

[2] Life of Aurelian, by Flavius Vopiscus, chap. xlvii.

from various provinces of the Empire, and linen garments from Africa and Egypt. A generous and popular Emperor doubtless, but Communism thus robed in the purple is an excellent destroyer of Commonwealths.

Let us now traverse an interval of a hundred years, and see what shape this system of out-door relief had assumed under the dynasty of the Valentinians. A long Title of the Theodosian code [1] is devoted to the subject. It contains fifteen laws, chiefly the handiwork of the Emperors Valentinian and Valens, partly of Theodosius I and his sons. The first point which strikes us is, that Rome no longer enjoys a monopoly of the often lauded 'Imperial Munificence.' Constantine in founding his new capital by the Bosphorus has conferred upon it also the doubtful boon of the *Annona* or free largess of corn ; and in order to meet the requirements of this largess, the corn-ships of Alexandria—as was remarked on a previous occasion—are now diverted from Rome to Byzantium. The City by the Tiber has now practically only the corn-fields of that province of which her ancient rival, Carthage, is the capital, to look to for her supplies. Antioch and Alexandria seem also to have shared in the public distributions, but the edicts relating to these cities do not appear in the code, possibly because their largesses were left to be regulated by the local authorities.

In Rome and Constantinople the Theodosian code presents us with a lively but strange picture of this organisation of pauperism. Three great classes are the recipients of that which is called by a courtly fiction 'the bounty of the Emperors.' These classes are the *Palatini*, the *Militares*, and the *Populares*, that is to

[1] Lib. xiv. tit. 17.

say, the servants of the palace, the soldiers, and the mass of the people. The last class receive their rations strictly *as householders*. The law is very decided on this point, 'Aedes sequantur annonae' (the rations must follow the houses); that is to say, if a citizen who has been receiving the ration alienates his house, he loses the right to his daily loaf. At Constantinople special stress is laid on the great Founder's desire to encourage house-building in his new city, and an attempt is made (apparently not a successful one) to limit even the soldiers' share in the *annona* to those who possess houses in the capital.

The three classes seem to have received their rations seated on some of the great public staircases in which the City of the Seven Hills abounded, and yet abounds. Some have thought that they were all collected for this purpose in the Colosseum, but it seems more probable that each of the fourteen Regions of the City had its own flight of steps on which the applicants seated themselves, as well as its own bakery, from which they were supplied. Each class of recipients is mustered apart; the *Palatini*, the *Militares*, the *Populares*, have each their own tiers of seats. The bread which is distributed to them is called 'the Step-Bread' (*Panis Gradilis*), and the separate classes are known as 'Steps.' Stringent laws forbid the transference of the *Panis Gradilis* from one 'Step' to another, and the Public Commissary-General (*Praefectus Annonae*) is warned that the severest penalties hang over him, if he suffers this regulation to be infringed. The prohibition can hardly relate to the mere physical transportation of a loaf of bread from one stone stair to another. It probably means that each class of recipients was to be

The Panis Gradilis.

considered as complete in itself, and that in case of
death or removal, the lapsed ration of a *Palatinus* was
to be transferred only to another *Palatinus*, that of a
Popularis to another *Popularis*.

Continual
evasions of
the laws
regarding
the Panis
Gradilis.
But from such an inversion of the great industrial
laws upon which Society is founded, abuse was insepar-
able.   The holders of the *Tessera*, or relief-ticket, eager
to accept the alms of the State, but anxious to escape
from the ignominy of asking for them, used to present
themselves at the great public bakeries, and there,
probably by bribery, obtain the loaves to which they
were entitled.   This practice was forbidden, and it was
ordained 'that all men should receive their step-bread
from the steps, and that none should be handed out by
the shop-keepers, lest thereby any fraud should arise
concerning the *Panis Gradilis.*'

A brazen tablet was to be affixed to the wall, near to
the steps of distribution, and on it the name of the re-
ceiver and the measure of bread due to him were to be
engraved.   'And if any one's impertinence should carry
him so far that he shall usurp for himself or his family
the right of that bread, and get his name wrongfully
inserted in the brazen tablet, he shall receive chastisement according to his condition.'

The meaning of these last words is made more clear
by a savage decree of the Emperor Valentinian (370).
It seems that some of the Senators and great men of
Rome were guilty of the meanness of sending members
of their households to receive this public bread, which
was of course intended only for the poorer class of free
citizens. Thereupon the edict runs : 'Should the steward
or slave of any Senator wrongfully obtain the *Panis
Gradilis* by direct purchase from the clerk of distribu-

tion, or by bribery, or even by his mere connivance, let such steward or slave be subjected to the torture of the *equuleus* [1]. If it appears that he was prompted to this illegality by his own impudence, without the knowledge of his master, let him serve in chains in that bakery which he has been defrauding. Should, however, complicity in the offence be traced to his master, let the house of that Senator be confiscated for the use of the treasury.

'In other ranks of life, if any one who is possessed of private resources shall confess the aforesaid crime, let him and all that he has be bound over to the service of the bakery.

'If he shall be of the very poorest classes'—a provision which shows that this demoralising largess did not even answer the purpose of a Poor-law since 'the very poorest' were not all entitled to it—'he shall be forced to labour as if he were a slave.

'As for the clerks of distribution who shall be proved to have perpetrated this forbidden wickedness, the sword which is the vindicator of the laws shall be drawn against them.'

It would weary the reader were we to trace in further detail the intricacies of the legislation concerning the *annonae*. There are arrangements for changing stale loaves (*sordidi panes*) for new, edicts granting a certain supply of oil to persons designated by the Prefect of the City 'for the refreshment of their frames,' edicts forbidding the soldiers of the Imperial Guard to transmit their right to the ration as a hereditary claim to their children, and again, other edicts repealing these [2].

A labyrinth of worse than useless legislation.

---

[1] An instrument of torture shaped like a horse.

[2] Some of this legislation has reference to Constantinople, but similar arrangements would probably be in force at Rome.

It is a labyrinth of Imperial legislation, and all leading to what end ? To the maintenance in idleness of the worthless population of four great cities, a population which every wise legislator would have sought by every means in his power to divert from the cities, to lead back into the country, to marry to the land, to raise to something of the dignity of manhood by that wrestling with Nature for her blessings, which makes up the daily life of Agriculture. But no : the old legal fiction of the sovereignty of the Roman people still survived, and therefore the so-called citizen of Rome—the descendant in all probability of a Syrian or Cappadocian slave— must be allowed to spend his days in lordly idleness, seeing the charioteers drive, and the gladiators die, and then presenting himself at the appointed time at the steps of his '*regio*' to receive his *Panis Gradilis* from the bounty of the Emperor. And, to accomplish this desirable end, the administrative energies of the declining Empire must be weighted with the duties of a vast and complicated commissariat alike in peace and in war.

§ 5. *Destruction of the Middle Class by the fiscal Oppression of the Curiales.*

Fiscal ruin of the Middle Classes in the provincial towns.

We have seen how the social and political system of Rome tended to destroy the free labourers in the country, and to degrade them in the great cities. We have now to consider that system of fiscal oppression by which the Empire crushed out the life of the middle classes in the provincial towns. A great French states-man[1], who has treated of this subject with a fulness of

[1] *Guizot* in his 'Essais sur l'histoire de France. Du régime municipal dans l'Empire Romain au ve siècle de l'ère chrétienne,'

knowledge drawn both from books and from practical politics, considers that this cause was more powerful than all others in bringing about the ruin of Rome.

The civilisation of the great Republic was essentially Origin of a municipal civilisation. An urban community herself, the Municipia. she naturally associated herself with other urban communities, and wherever her influence has profoundly and permanently modified the life of any modern people, it will be found that that people is, by choice and not from the mere force of economic laws, urban in its tastes and its habits. The towns of Italy and of the provinces possessed, during the ages of the Republic, very various privileges, and stood in very various relations to the sovereign City. Some were *coloniae*, own children of Rome, some were *municipia*, stranger towns, gathered within the circle of ' the Roman friendship or subjection.' But as the power of the Emperors grew, and as the forms of popular government by assemblies of the citizens at Rome faded into insignificance, the diversities of privilege between the various cities of the Empire faded also. Political power was now all gathered up into one centre, and lodged in the hands of one single man, the Augustus at Rome, who might delegate it to prefect or vicar, as he chose. But municipal freedom still existed—that is to say, during the first three centuries after the Christian era—and municipal power was lodged in the hands of magistrates, freely chosen by the persons who owned as much as

a fine demonstration of the morbid anatomy of a state. Guizot founds himself chiefly upon *Roth* 'de Re Municipali Romanorum,' Stuttgart, 1801. The Theodosian Code is the quarry from which both authors derive their materials. *Marquardt*, in his Römische Staatsverwaltung, i. 463–512, expands, and in some details corrects, Guizot's sketch of the earlier history of the municipalities.

fifteen acres (twenty-five *jugera*) in the borough or district round it. The affairs of the little republic were managed by an assembly modelled upon the Senate of Rome itself. It was called sometimes the Senate, sometimes the *Curia*, and its members, who obtained a seat as the Roman Senators did, by filling some office in the State, were called *Decuriones*, possibly because there were originally ten minor *Curiae* of ten members each, thus furnishing a total of one hundred members to the Senate. In the large towns, however, this number was often exceeded. Marquardt points out that at Antioch the number of *Decuriones* varied from 1200 at its best estate to sixty at its worst. The sepulchral inscriptions, which we now see in such numbers in the Italian museums, recording that the dead man was a *Decurio* of his native town, show that the title was, for several centuries, one which conferred a certain amount of social distinction on the holder, and we may perhaps say that the D E C of these Latin epigraphs corresponds to the Esq. of an English churchyard.

Local self-government existed side by side with the Imperial system.

Thus, during these early centuries of the Empire, the local government of the towns was both in name and in fact republican. We need only recur to some familiar examples in the Acts of the Apostles, to understand how these municipal liberties existed side by side with the great machine of the Imperial administration, independent in their own sphere, yet trembling lest by any unauthorised proceeding they should be brought within its far-reaching and heavy stroke. The Praetors of Philippi are afraid when their lictors bring them word that the men whom they have scourged and thrust into prison are Roman citizens. The seven *politarchs* of Thessalonica are troubled when the mob of lewd fellows of the baser sort come surging round them, accusing the inmates of Jason's house of acting contrary to the decrees of Caesar, and teaching that there is another king, one Jesus. The Recorder of Ephesus is anxious that the dispute between Paul and the silversmiths should be determined in a legal manner before the tribunal of the Proconsul of Asia, and that the authorities of the city should not have to answer difficult interrogatories as to the cause of the tumultuary assembly in the theatre. Continually we find ourselves in presence of real and living, though somewhat precarious, forms of local self-government.

The first two centuries and a half of the Empire may be perhaps considered as the golden age of the *muni-cipia*, and the large amount of prosperity and happiness thus secured to the middle classes of society was probably the chief cause of the admitted success of the Imperial administration during the greater part of that period. Numerous laws were passed in favour of the municipalities. They were permitted to receive, and probably did receive, large gifts and bequests of property from their members. Fraud practised upon them by one of their officials was made equivalent, not to simple theft, but to the heavier offence of peculation. The Decurions were exempted from capital punishment for every crime but that of parricide. Finally, the municipal treasury, devoted to the construction and maintenance of great public works, roads, bridges, temples and theatres, and to the celebration of the solemn public sacrifices, was easily kept full, and had not as yet attracted the avaricious regards of the Emperors, who 'found the treasures of Rome and the ordinary contributions of the provinces suffice for the

Golden Age of the Municipalities. B. C. 30 – A. D. 220.

needs, and even for the follies, of the central power[1].' From the brightness of this picture some abatement must doubtless be made, as regards the seventy years of anarchy and confusion which intervened between the death of Caracalla and the accession of Diocletian (217–284). It is not possible that when mutiny, rebellion, and civil war were the chronic condition of the Empire, the municipalities can have enjoyed the full measure of their former prosperity. But whatever they may have suffered in this way was probably irregular and exceptional. It could scarcely yet be said, as far as the *curiales* were concerned, that the throne of the Emperors was ' a throne of iniquity framing mischief by a law.'

Diocletian's reorganisation of the Empire fatal to local liberty. This last and fatal phase in the history of the municipalities was probably, in great measure, the result of the remodelling of the Empire by Diocletian[2]. That great statesman saw that some change was needed if

[1] Guizot, Essai, p. 10.

[2] Guizot lays the whole blame of this legislation on Constantine. No doubt the edicts on the subject in the Theodosian Code chiefly bear his name, but the cause was surely the more burdensome administration of the Empire, and it would take at least twenty years (from Diocletian's accession in 284 to Constantine's accession in 306) to bring about that great change which Guizot so well describes, by which a coveted dignity became an odious charge. And, in fact, the oppression of the municipalities by the central power had probably been going on for a much longer period. Marquardt (Römische Staatsverwaltung, i. 511) points out that as early as the time of Trajan (99–117), in what Guizot considers the golden age of the municipalities, there are already slight traces of persons ' *qui inviti fiunt decuriones*' (Trajan's Letter to Pliny in Plinii Epistolae, x. 113). And the same author seems inclined to place the beginning of the ' Verfall der Curien' as early as the beginning of the third century. But he admits that this decline did not become utter ruin till the age of Constantine.

the Empire was not to be rent asunder by the hands of its own children. The changes which he accordingly introduced have been already briefly described [1]. These changes answered their immediate purpose. The Roman Empire was held together for another century and a half, but it gained life at the cost of the means of living. According to the old fable [2], Phaethon, when entrusted with the chariot of the Sun-god, drove it too near to the earth and began rapidly to dry up all the pools and fountains of waters. Even so now, the Imperial Majesty, of which flatterers had made a kind of god upon earth, appearing in all the vigour of its new administrative powers close to every portion of the Empire, began at once to dry up many a reservoir of wealth which had escaped the rapacity of former Emperors. Especially was this true of the funds hitherto devoted to the purposes of local self-government. These, which the *Curiae* had hitherto not only raised, but administered, were now diverted to the Imperial Exchequer to provide for the pomp of the palace, the salaries of the swarms of new officials, and the donatives to the legions, while the strictly useful and reproductive expenditure on roads and bridges, and other local needs, fell day by day into abeyance [3].

In the happier days of the municipalities, plenty of citizens had generally been found ready and anxious to discharge, even at some cost to themselves, the civic

---

[1] See vol. i. pp. 14–15.

[2]   'Cum procul insanae traherent Phaethonta quadrigae,
       Saeviretque dies, terramque et stagna propinqui
       Haurirent radii.'
                          Claudian, De IV Cons. Honorii, 63–65.

[3] This must be taken as an inference from the general course of legislation rather than as an established fact.

functions of their little republics. The example of England, and still more that of America, proves that where there exists a large and flourishing middle class, endowed with local self-government, money is for the most part freely forthcoming for the wants of the community. When the State is at peace, that healthy emulation which exists between citizens, and that desire to emerge from the ranks, which is natural to men, leads one to build a bridge, another to establish a library, a third to endow a school, a fourth to spend lavishly on the duties of his mayoralty, and so on. The same disposition had, no doubt, existed in the *Curiae* throughout the Roman Empire. But now a new competitor for the generosity of the citizens appeared in the shape of the Christian Church, perpetually increasing the sumptuousness of her worship, perpetually widening the sphere of her duties as public almoner, and, for both objects, claiming and receiving large oblations from the wealthy. The parish now competed with the *Curia*, and the benevolent citizen who would have built an aqueduct in the second century, founded a church in the third.

And simultaneously with this new diversion of the funds of the charitable, the great Imperial mendicant drew nigh to the impoverished *Curia*, but speaking now with an altered tone, and saying no longer 'If you like,' but 'You must.' We see the results of the pressure which now began to be put upon the municipalities, but the exact manner of its working does not seem to be disclosed to us. An impost called the '*Aurum Coronarium*,' which had once been purely a free-will offering occasionally given by the cities to the Roman generals, was now a regular tax paid by the

Christianity diverts the stream of philanthropy from municipal to religious objects.

The Emperors begin to look upon the Curia as a mere taxing-machine.

Decurions as such, and by them only. The other taxes, which were assessed afresh every fifteen years throughout the whole Empire, were levied upon the *Curia* in its collective capacity, and if any member made default, his fellow-decurions must make good the deficiency. Under the pressure of this continually-increasing taxation, some lands went out of cultivation altogether, since there was no profit left for the proprietor after the claims of the State were satisfied. So much the more taxes must the surrounding proprietors pay, to make up for the loss to the treasury from those unsown acres[1]. It is evident that when once this process had reached a certain stage, the load of taxation on the proprietors who still endeavoured to bear it would increase, not in arithmetical, but in geometrical proportion, and life would become nothing but a cruel race between the tax-collector and his victim.

The inevitable result followed. The *Curiae*, which had once been honoured and envied communities, easily bearing the weight of their public duties, and dispensing comfort and happiness to the district round them, were now mere gaols in which the middle classes were shut up from birth till death, to toil for the Imperial Treasury. The dignity of Decurion, or *curialis* as he was now often called, was no longer bestowed on the

The office of Decurio from a coveted dignity becomes a hated charge.

[1] Possibly, as far as each particular district was concerned, this burden might be to some extent relieved at the next assessment (*indictio*) at which, theoretically at least, account was taken of the productive capacities of every province in the Empire. But as the taxes were not diminishing, but increasing, if this process of throwing lands out of cultivation on account of the rapacity of the tax-gatherer was going on extensively throughout the Empire, it is evident that the landholders who remained must have had to bear a rapidly accumulating burden.

most worthy by the suffrages of his fellow-citizens. It was a charge descending from the father to the son, which the son, however anxious to be freed from it, could not renounce[1]. The longest 'title' (as it is called) in the Theodosian Code, is that which contains the 188 laws, passed during 150 years, concerning the rights and duties of the Decurions. Of their rights perhaps eight laws speak, of their duties the remaining 180, and that in tones of inflexible severity. The perpetually recurring expression, 'the son of a Curial must be *bound* to the Curia,' formulated as it is with the word *mancipetur*, which we know so well by its opposite, emancipation, shows sufficiently how grievous a burden the service of the municipalities was considered. It is true that more than once we meet with a proviso that no one is to be condemned to enter the ranks of the Decurions as a punishment[2]. 'The splendour of the Curiae' is said to be dear to the Imperial heart, and 'a criminal should be visited with punishment, not with an accession of dignity;' but this hypocritical pretence can deceive no one who reads the laws by which this enactment is preceded and followed, and who sees therein the perpetual struggle of the middle classes to escape from their connection with the Curiae, and the ruthless determination with which Emperors and Prefects force them back into that hateful prison-house.

[1] It would seem probable that with this degradation in the rank of the Decurions, the body which they formed lost the position of a local Senate which it had previously occupied. This, however, we cannot prove from the language of the laws. Only, a new class among the Decurions, the *Principales*, seems to hold something like the same position towards the rest of the community which the Decurions held formerly.

[2] Cod. Theod. xii. 1. 66 and 108.

No provincial governor on his own authority might excuse a Decurion from his municipal obligations on the score of poverty[1]. The Emperor reserved to himself alone the exercise of this prerogative. Small, certainly, was the probability that a citizen, too poor to pay his curial dues, would be able to defray the expense of a journey to Rome in order to obtain this exemption. And yet their chronic misery may have urged many to undertake this painful pilgrimage, for we find another edict[2] whereby they were forbidden to visit the Emperor on public or private business without the leave of the Governor of the Province in which they dwelt. The prohibition went further : they were forbidden to take any kind of journey, lest they should defraud the Curia of their services, and for the same reason they were forbidden to leave the cities and take up their residence in the country[3]. That free circulation of the citizens, which makes the life of modern states, was a crime in the eyes of the Imperial legislator, because it interfered with his machinery of fiscal extortion.

Restrictions on the freedom of the Curiales.

Nothing gives us a more convincing proof of the utterly unbearable condition of the Curiales than the continual efforts which they made to divest themselves of their status, and the storm of Imperial edicts by which they were constantly met and driven back into their Curiae. In truth, the whole series of this legislation seems like an attempt to compress an incompressible fluid, or in some similar way to violate the fundamental laws of physics.

The Decurion was not to be allowed to rise into the profession of an advocate, lest he should thereby obtain

Careers closed to them.

---

[1] Cod. Theod. xii. 1. 1.   [2] Ibid. xii. 1. 9.

[3] Ibid. xii. 1. 143, 144; xii. 18.

exemption from his curial obligations; for the same reason he was not to be allowed to descend into the guild of the rag-collectors[1]; nor should he be permitted to farm the taxes of the province, lest in case of his default, the Emperor and the Curia might find themselves opposing creditors of a bankrupt estate. If a Decurion married a female slave, as the offspring of such a marriage would be incapable of representing him in the Curia, he himself was to be banished to a distant island, his slave-wife to be sent to work in the mines, and his property to pass to his next of kin, upon whom would devolve his obligations to the Curia.

Prohibition to enter the Army

It might have been thought that when every Teutonic and Scythian nationality from the Caspian to the Scheldt was pouring down upon the Empire, when the Romans were

'Ringed around with barking dogs of war[2],'

the mustering of men for the battle-field would have been an object of primary importance with their rulers, and that if an oppressive conscription were not resorted to, at least every volunteer would be eagerly welcomed. By no means: the maintenance of the Curia, as a taxing-machine in a state of efficiency, was the first consideration, for upon this depended the splendour of the Imperial household, and the rapid fortunes of Prefects and Counts.

To escape from the misery of their lot as bondslaves of a bankrupt municipality, the Decurions, who were legally bound to serve in a kind of local force, the

---

[1] *Centonarii.* The meaning of the word is doubtful.

[2] 'Septi latrantibus undique bellis.'

(Claudian, In Eutropium, ii. 486.)

militia cohortalis, thronged in multitudes into the
regular army, the *militia armata*. Law after law was
passed with tedious reiteration, forbidding the officers
to enlist any man who is under curial obligations, pre-
scribing the form in which each recruit is to declare
his freedom from such liability, and insisting on the
dragging back into the Curia of such Decurions as
might after all have crept through all this mesh-work
of opposing edicts into the army. True, if any had
already served for fifteen years in the army, he was
to be safe from further pursuit ; but then, on the other
hand, look at this provision, 'If any man of military
descent shall enlist in the *militia cohortalis*[1], and if,
with strength yet unbroken, he shall put forward the
plea of advanced age, or by reason of weakness shall be
judged unfit for the work of war, he shall be drawn
forth from the lurking-place of his cowardice, and
bound over to the duties of the Curiae.' The bondage
of the Curia—that was the Chelsea Hospital which
Rome provided for her broken-down soldiers in the
year 380 under the auspices of Theodosius.

The Church as well as the Army offered a door of
escape from Curial obligations. We are not surprised
at finding the Pagan Emperor Julian closing this door
and decreeing [2] that 'Decurions, who as Christians'
[whereby clergymen are probably intended] 'decline
the offices of their township, are to be recalled.' But
if any different strain of legislation was hoped for from
a pious Emperor like Theodosius, the Convener of the
Second Council, the glory and defence of the Catholic

or even the Church.

---

[1] 'Si quis militaris prosapiae se officio Cohortis adgregarit.' (Cod.
Theod. xii. 1. 83.)

[2] Cod. Theod. xii. 1. 50.

Church, such hopes were doomed to disappointment. 'Those Curiales,' says he [1], 'who prefer to serve the Churches rather than their Curiae, if they wish to *be* that which they simulate, let them scorn to withdraw their property from the service of their country. For we will certainly not liberate them on any other condition than this, that they renounce their patrimonies. Since it is not becoming that souls which are devoted to the contemplation of God should feel any regret at the loss of their ancestral property' (383).

It is true that some years later (390) an exemption is made on behalf of those who have already entered the ranks of the clergy. 'He who before the second Consulship of my Mildness [2]' [the mildness of him who in that very year ordered the massacre at Thessalonica] 'has reached the eminence of Presbyter, or undertaken the ministry of Deacon, or the office of Exorcist, may keep all his patrimony safe and free from curial bonds. But he who, under whatever name, shall have betaken himself to the religious ministrations of divine worship after the date of my aforesaid Consulship, let him know that he must give up the whole of his patrimony [3].'

Other laws, of an earlier as well as a later date than those which have been quoted, enacted that the curial Cleric should be withdrawn from his sacred profession and restored to the civic duties from which he had absconded. Such a provision, which shows that the ecclesiastical hierarchy, however powerful, was still far from occupying the position which she held in the days of Hildebrand, must surely have clashed against even the then existing Canons of the Church. No instances

---

[1] Cod. Theod. xii. 1. 104. [2] A.D. 388.

[3] Cod. Theod. xii. 1. 121.

however seem to be forthcoming, to show in what way
this conflict of laws was settled.

The monks, if Curiales, were handled by the State Curial Monks
even more roughly than the clergy. It should be even more roughly
stated however that the decree which is next to follow handled than the
was issued by the Emperor Valens, who, as an Arian, Curial Clergy.
had special reasons for hating the enthusiastically
Athanasian monks of Egypt at whom it is principally
aimed (365).

'Certain lovers of idleness, deserting their civic
duties, affect solitary and secret places, and under the
guise of religion are collected together with the assemblies of the Lonely-Livers (*Monazontes*). We have
therefore, on deliberation, commanded that all these,
and men like them, if taken in Egypt, shall be drawn
forth from their hiding-places by the Count of the East,
and shall be recalled to undergo the charges of their
native districts, or else, by virtue of this law, shall be
deprived of the delights of their possessions[1], which,
it is our pleasure, shall be claimed by those who have
to undertake the charge of the public functions[2].'

Besides the Church and the Army another career, if Conflict between
he only could succeed in entering it, seemed to promise the service of the
to the aspiring Curial an exemption from the crushing Palace and the
load of municipal liability. This was service in the Curia.
vast Imperial households, for the *Palatinus* of whatever rank was not only entitled, as has been already
seen, to share in the corn-largesses; he was also, as the
servant of the Emperor, free from 'mancipation' to
any other master. And in this way, no doubt, many
thousands of Decurions managed to evade the onerous

---

[1] 'Familiarium rerum carere inlecebris.'
[2] Cod. Theod. xii. 1. 63.

obligations of local self-government. There is a long
series of vacillating decrees bearing on the case of
these men. According to one edict thirty years' prescription was necessary, according to others, five years
sufficed, to prevent the dreaded sentence, ' Let him be
dragged back to his Curia.' The general impression
left on the mind by these decrees is that they soon
became waste parchment, the theory of government
requiring that the rights of the Curia should be insisted upon, while in practice the favour of the
Sovereign was powerful enough to shield from curial
pursuit the members of his household. Theodosius
(or Valentinian II), however, once breaks forth into
a strain of sublime indignation against those who
trusted to this means of deliverance (386). ' Let the
Curiales who have supposed that they could be defended by the privilege of our Household be dragged
back to their Curia, so that they may be "mancipated"
to their proper functions and may repair the public
losses. *Nevertheless if any of these shall be proved to
owe anything to our Divine household, let him pay it*[1].'
This noble sacrifice by the Emperor of everybody else
to the necessities of the country, coupled with the
sharpest attention to the interests of his own ' divine
household,' is characteristic of the legislation of that
period.

Compa-
rison with
France
before the
Revolu-
tion.

From this general survey of the laws relating to the
Decurions it will be seen that we have here a state of
things not altogether unlike that which existed in
France before the Revolution. A court and a *noblesse*
above[2], exempt from the heaviest part of the national

---

[1] Cod. Theod. xii. 1. 114.

[2] Official, it is true, rather than, as in France, hereditary.

taxation, and with their hands for ever in the national
exchequer: below, a people robbed and spoiled, *taillable
et corvéable à merci*, that is, without mercy and without foresight, and consequently some of the most fertile
countries in the world brought by the tax-gatherer to
the verge of starvation. The difference between the
two cases is that in France *taille* and *corvée* reached
down to the very lowest of the people: in the Roman
Empire, the slaves and the 'plebeians' (as the class of
freemen who lacked the curial qualification were called)
were not shut up in the taxing-pen of the Curia. It
was essentially an oppression of the middle classes that
was thus carried on; but a century and a half of this
steady, persevering tyranny had so ground down the
once prosperous and thriving Decurions, that it may be
doubted whether they were not, when the Western
Empire fell, practically lower than the lowest of the
proletariat.

M. Guizot mentions two privileges which were left
to the Curiales, and which, he thinks, may have been
some slight compensation for their many miseries.

Compensating privileges.

1. Freedom from Corporal Punishment. We find
certainly several laws which appear to concede this
privilege to the Decurions. Especially is it forbidden
to chastise them with the *Plumbatae*, the scourge with
lumps of metal knotted into its thongs, which was
ordinarily used for the chastisement of slaves. One
remarkable law, passed in the year 381, says [1], 'Let
all Judges and Governors of Provinces abstain from
usurping a power which does not belong to them, and
let them know that absolutely no Principalis nor Decurion, whatever fault or error he may have committed,

Theoretical Exemption from Corporal Punishment.

[1] Cod. Theod. xii. 1. 85.

is to be submitted to the torments of the *Plumbatae*. Should perchance any judge hereafter break forth into such pertinacity of forbidden madness as to dare to subject a Principalis and a Decurion, a man who is, so to speak, *the Senator of his Curia*, to the strokes of the *Plumbatae*, let him be condemned to pay a fine of twenty pounds of gold (£800), and branded with perpetual infamy so that not even a special rescript of our own shall suffice to remove the stigma. The officer who has administered the chastisement shall be forced to pay a fine of fifty pounds of gold (£2000) inasmuch as, the command of the judge being unlawful, we give him full liberty to disobey it.' This lawgiver seems to be in earnest, and the provision for inflicting a heavier fine on the actual wielder of the lash than on his master seems cleverly contrived to prevent the perpetration of the outrage. But one may doubt, from the frequent reappearance of similar provisions in the Code, whether the immunity from stripes—which was, after all, theoretically the privilege of every Roman citizen—was practically enjoyed by 'the Decurion, the Senator of his Curia.' For by later edicts (387 and 392) Theodosius expressly enacts that Decurions, who have been guilty of malversation in respect of the public monies[1], or 'who owe anything'[2]—a category which would of course include those whose taxes were in arrear— may be punished with the *Plumbatae*. As in Egypt at the present day[3] the bastinado, applied to the elders of the village, extracts the intolerable tax from the unfortunate *fellah*, so doubtless, many a time, in the last century of the Empire, did the cruel blows of

---

[1] Cod. Theod. xii. 1. 117.   [2] Ibid. xii. 1. 126.
[3] Written in 1879 : happily no longer true in 1892.

the *Plumbatae* wring the last denarius out of the coffers of the Decurion.

2. A more substantial privilege doubtless, though from its nature attainable by few, was the prospect of entering the Senate, and so passing from the class of the oppressed into that of the oppressors.   An inhabitant of one of the more important municipalities [1], who was possessed of large means, and had steadily climbed the ladder of official dignities in his native town, having finally attained the rank of presiding Duumvir, was to be considered free from all further curial obligations, to hold the rank of an Ex-Count, and with the title of *clarissimus,* had the right of a seat in the innermost circle at the public games, and the Governor of the Province was bound to salute him with a kiss.   Last and most important, an entrance was permitted him into the Roman Senate, 'the noblest Curia of all,' but apparently on condition of his leaving a son, or some other substitute, to represent him in the Curia from which he emerged.

Often it would occur that a wealthy and popular Curial, by official favour or by bribing his fellow-townsmen, would succeed in missing some steps of the slow ascent, and would present himself in the Senate-house at Rome before he was duly qualified.   In such a case, said the Emperor Constantius [2] (361)—

'The Decurions who shirk their own duties and betake themselves to the fellowship of our Senate shall be struck off the roll of that body, and "mancipated"

---

[1] This qualification is not expressed in the Code, but we can hardly suppose that the presiding magistrate of a mere village would be entitled to claim rank as an *ex-comes.*

[2] Cod. Theod. xii. i. 48.

to their own cities. Those, however, who have served
the office of Praetor' [which involved heavy expenses
in connection with the Praetorian games exhibited to
the people] 'may remain in the Senate, but must restore any monies which they may have abstracted from
our Imperial Exchequer, *or from the bowels of the municipalities.*' Many similar laws follow, some of which
ingeniously fasten on such premature Senators a double
pecuniary obligation, first as Curial, and, second, as
Senator. A yet harsher tone is observable in the
following law, passed in the year 398 by Arcadius,
Emperor of the East.

[1] 'All the Curiales are to abide in their original
Curies, their duties to which are of perpetual obligation. Those who by fraud or popular canvassing have
clambered up into the place of high Administrators and
Rulers of Provinces, are to be at once deprived of the
honours which they have obtained, and not only with
swift and strong hand drawn back to their own Curia,
and made to serve all its offices from the very beginning,
but shall also be mulcted in half their patrimony.' But,
by an edict which was published shortly after, these
stringent provisions were somewhat modified in the case
of a Curial who had obtained senatorial rank 'before
the Ides of November, in the fourth Consulship of Lord
Honorius Augustus, *Brother of my Eternity*, and his
colleague Eutychianus.'

'Brother of my Eternity:' such was the pompous
style in which the imbecile Arcadius spoke of the imbecile Honorius. It was time for our Teutonic kinsman,
Alaric, to tear down the purple hangings of Empire,

---

[1] Cod. Theod. xii. 1. 159, 160.

and let in the fresh air of reality upon those chambers reeking with flattery and falsehood.

One last exemption must be noticed, which points to the dwindling state of the population of the Provinces, but which rests on a basis of humanity and good sense. It was enacted by the Emperor Julian[1] (363), 'He who is the father of thirteen children not only shall not be summoned to the Curia, but even though he be a De-curion, shall be left in an honoured rest' [undisturbed by the summons to undertake any curial duty].

Exemption for the father of thirteen children.

From the sketch, necessarily brief and imperfect, which has been here given of the decline and fall of the Municipalities of the Empire, the reader can in some degree estimate for himself the share which their altered condition had in bringing about the ruin of the Empire itself. In Gaul, in Spain, in Italy, the exhaustion and impoverishment of the middle classes was, in the fifth century, so great that it had become a matter almost of indifference who ruled over them, a grandson of Theo-dosius, the Suevic Count Ricimer, the Herulian Odovacar, or Theodoric the Ostrogoth. Their condition could not be worse under the barbarian than under the crushing, organised, relentless tyranny of the Roman bureaucracy. It might be, and as far as Odovacar and Theodoric were concerned it probably was, better.

In the East no doubt the same process of exhaustion went on, but the fortunate push from without was wanting. In Egypt and in Syria the Arabs, fresh from the desert, easily overturned, amid shouts of *Lo Ellah il Allah!* the pallid resemblances of Graeco-Roman municipalities. In the other provinces of the Byzantine Empire they still cumbered the ground with the spec-

Fate of the Munici-palities in the East.

[1] Cod. Theod. xii. 1. 55.

tacle of their decay until the close of the ninth century, when Leo VI, surnamed the Philosopher, removed from the theory of the constitution both the Senate of the Empire and the Curiae of the towns. Of the latter he said, ' The ancient laws passed as to the Curiae and Decurions impose on the Decurions intolerable burdens, and confer on the Curiae the right to nominate certain magistrates, and to govern the cities by their own authority. Now that civil affairs have taken another form, and that all things depend entirely on the care and government of the Imperial Majesty, these laws wander, so to speak, vainly and without object, around the soil of legality. We therefore abolish them by the present decree [1].'

Their revival in the West.

In the West, the agony of the Municipia had been shorter, and the remembrance of the days of their prosperity and usefulness was therefore less easily effaced. It would be an interesting task, but one outside of our present field, to show how, under the barbarian kings, aided in many cases by the influence of the Church, the Curiae rose again, as it were, from the tomb, until, in the twelfth, thirteenth, and fourteenth centuries, local self-government, as set forth in the Italian *Commune*, reached, perhaps, the noblest elevation at which the world has seen, or is likely to see it. An almost equally noteworthy tribute to the memory of the old municipal organisation is paid from a different quarter. To this day the mightiest ecclesiastical organisation in the world, that which gives birth to Popes, and defies or bargains with Emperors, calls itself the Roman *Curia*.

---

[1] Novellae Leonis, 46, quoted by Guizot, Essais, &c., p. 18.

6. *Barbarous Finance.*

The Local Taxation of the Empire has been dwelt upon at considerable length, because its history can be easily traced from the Statute Book, and because in tracing that history we can clearly see a powerful degrading influence at work upon an important class of the community.

The history of the Imperial Taxation is in some respects more obscure, and to give a detailed description of it would require more space than can here be afforded. But, tried by its results, it may without hesitation be condemned as wasteful, oppressive, and, in one word, barbarous. The more one examines into the subject the more one is convinced that great as the Romans were in legislation, and great in war, in finance their genius was below mediocrity. To violently wrest the whole or a large part of the lands of a conquered people from their former owners and appropriate them to the Roman State, to destroy great seats of industry and commerce like Corinth or Carthage, and bring their gold and silver and works of art home to figure in a Roman triumph, this easy system of momentary self-enrichment the Senate and its officers were able to put in practice. But to develop, as some of the Ptolemies and some of the Tudors developed, the commercial wealth of their people, to plant wisely and water diligently the tree of manufacturing or agricultural prosperity, from which the State itself might in the time of fruit-bearing pluck a golden reward, this was a kind of enterprise for which the genius of the Roman nation was little suited, and though it cannot be said to

Roman ignorance of the principles of finance.

have been never attempted, it certainly seldom succeeded in Roman hands.

It is unfortunately quite impossible to determine with any approach to accuracy the amount of the revenue of the Empire, but the conjectures of scholars who have examined carefully into the subject point to a sum of between £20,000,000 and £30,000,000 sterling as the probable total under the Emperors. It is true that we cannot say what amount of local taxation may have existed side by side with this. But in itself the amount does not seem a crushing weight for a population of perhaps 90,000,000[1], inhabiting such countries as France, Spain, and Italy are now, as Turkey in Europe, Asia Minor, Syria, Egypt, and the northern shore of Africa were before the domination of the Mussulman had blasted them. It is difficult to resist the conclusion that a modern scientific financier, keeping a wise equipoise between direct and indirect taxation, and carefully arranging his duties so as to take only a reasonable toll from the vast commerce of the Mediterranean countries, could have easily provided for the State a revenue twice as large as she seems to have actually received, without crushing out the happiness of her subjects.

But the Roman financiers seem to have relied most on the worst kind of taxation, and to have levied it in the most wasteful and oppressive manner. Unfortunately we have no specimen of the budget of a 'Count of the Sacred Largesses' which we can submit to a modern Chancellor of the Exchequer for his criticisms.

But it is almost certain that the *portoria* or customs duties, varying from 2 to 5 per cent., and ultimately

[1] This is the result of Von Wietersheim's calculation (i. 234).

reaching as high as $12\frac{1}{2}$ per cent.[1], did not contribute
an important part of the revenues of the Empire. The
Vicesima Hereditatum, a succession duty of 5 per cent., _{Duty.}

Succession
Duty.

seems to have been enforced with some hesitation, and
to have been finally abandoned in the sixth century on
account of its unpopularity. Yet as the duty was not
paid when the property devolved upon very near
relations, few taxes, one would think, could have been
more easily justified, or should have been more in-
flexibly demanded. The *Vicesima Libertatis*, a tax of
5 per cent. on the value of every liberated slave, was
probably, in the existing state of Roman society, a
wise impost, as tending to prevent the dilution of
the ranks of Roman citizens by too large an accession
of freedmen, and it brought in a considerable revenue
to the State. It was, moreover, essentially a tax on
luxuries, for to be surrounded by a troop of obsequious
freedmen was one of the most common forms of osten-
tation among the Roman nobility. But when we read
in the pages of Juvenal, Athenaeus, and Tacitus, of the
portentous and childish expenditure of that nobility on
other luxuries, we see that here was a field from which
a modern financier would have reaped an abundant
harvest. He would not have issued sumptuary edicts
nor attempted by legislation to check the torrent of
extravagance, but he would have said in fact to these
men, the owners of half a province and the lords of an
army of slaves, 'Since it pleases you to spend such vast
sums on all sorts of ridiculous fantasies, spend them
by all means, but give the State a share of your
superfluity.' The Licenses and Assessed Taxes which
an English minister of Finance would have imposed

Duty on
Enfran-
chise-
ments.

---

[1] Marquardt's Römische Staatsverwaltung, ii. 268.

upon the Roman Senators would have fed many Legions.

Land Tax, Tithe or Tribute.

But the sheet-anchor of the Imperial Financier was evidently the share, the oppressive share, of produce which they wrested from the cultivator of the soil. In some countries this had been originally looked upon as Land-Tax properly so called, in others it had been treated as Rent for land appropriated by the Roman people but suffered to remain in the possession of the former owners as their tenants. In some it had been originally a Tithe (*Decumae*), in others it had been spoken of as Tribute (*Tributum Soli*). But it will probably be safe to say that these differences had now, in the fourth and fifth centuries, become mere matters of antiquarian interest. The various populations of the Empire, Italian and Provincial, Greek and Sicilian, Asiatic and African, were all now theoretically free and

The Indictions.

practically miserable. Every fifteen years, that great revision of taxable value, called the Indiction, took place throughout the Empire. Then the few who had prospered found themselves assessed on the higher value which their lands had acquired, while the many who were sinking down into poverty, obtained, it is to be feared, but little relief from taxation on account of the higher rate which was charged to all. They might be assessed on fewer *capita*, but each *caput* was larger on account of the increasing needs of the Imperial Exchequer. This periodical re-assessment was evidently one of the most important features of the inner life of the Empire, and was aptly expressed by the habit of dating each year from its place in the Indiction [1].

[1] The Indictions began under Constantine in the year 312. Ac-

In the breathless race between the tax-payer and the tax-gatherer which financial administration became during the decay of the Empire, the inherent vices of the Roman system of collecting the revenue grew more and more apparent. Whether because the Republic despaired of finding absolutely honest collectors among her own citizens, because she deemed it impossible for anything but the keen self-interest of a contractor to cope with the self-interest of the cultivator of the land, or because the simplicity of an auction of the taxes commended itself to the rude fiscal notions of her statesmen—whatever may have been the cause, certain it is that the Tithes and all other forms of Land-Tax seem to have been, from the beginning to the end of the Roman domination, farmed out to men who bore the well-known and hated name of *publicani*. Many familiar passages in the New Testament shew the aversion with which the subordinate ranks of this great corporation were regarded by the provincials. An often-quoted passage in Livy shews that the Senate itself, at a comparatively early period, had perceived that the vast powers for extortion wielded by the Publicans were quite incompatible with the existence of real liberty among the subject-allies of Rome [1]. Finlay, the historian of Greece, has traced in

cording to the usage then prevalent, 313 would be called the first Indiction, 314 the second Indiction, and so on. It was not till the twelfth century, according to Marquardt, that the obvious plan of numbering the periods (according to which 312–327 would be the first Indiction, 327–342 the second Indiction, and so on) was introduced (Römische Staatsverwaltung, ii. 238).

[1] 'Ubi publicanus esset, ibi aut jus publicum vanum aut libertatem sociis nullam esse' was the opinion expressed by the Senate when the organisation of the province of Macedonia was under discussion, B.C. 167 (xlv. 18. 5).

many pages of his history the disastrous effect of the
system of tithes and tithe-farming upon both Greece
and Turkey, and speaks of this system as an undoubted
legacy, and a fatal one, from the Roman Empire[1]. If
we had the materials in our possession for a complete
picture of the financial administration of Constantine

[1] Compare particularly vol. vi. p. 13. ' From the moment that the
crops began to ripen, the property of the cultivator in nine-tenths of
it was treated as a matter subsidiary to the arrangement relative to
the disposal of the remaining tenth which belonged to the sovereign.
An industrious peasant could rarely make any profit by raising an
early crop or by improving the quality of his produce. . . . No
superiority of skill or increase of labour could under such circumstances secure a higher price. . . . The effects of this system of
taxation on the condition of Greek agriculture may still be studied
in the dominions of the Turkish sultan or the Greek king, for they
rival one another in the disastrous effects of their fiscal administration [A. D. 1859].'

The wastefulness, though not the oppression, of a system of *publicani*
is further shown by the following extract from a letter to the *Times*.
It appears from this letter that the system is still the curse of Italy.

' Let me mention one more reason for Italian poverty—the oppressive and absurd fiscal laws and the pernicious system of farming the
taxes, a system which wrenches from the most necessitous classes
from 30 to 50 per cent. more taxation than is necessary. I will give
one example of this, in the ruinous system of *octroi* taxes. I know a
small town of about 2000 inhabitants, the taxes (*octroi*) of which are
let for 16,000 francs the year. The farmer annually makes a profit
of from 5000 to 6000 francs. The town is miserably poor, yet the
wretched inhabitants have to pay this heavy sum more than is needful
if the taxes were collected in a proper manner. Most of the other
taxes are farmed in a similar fashion. The drain upon the community, and especially the poor, can be easily imagined.

I am, Sir, your obedient servant,
Sept. 27, 1879. SOUTHERN ITALY.

And a letter from Angora (Sept. 28, 1879) describes in the old
familiar language the odious occupation of the publican and the
horrible wastefulness of the tithe-farming system as practised in Asia
Minor (*Times*, Oct. 18, 1879).

or Theodosius, we should no doubt find that the wasteful oppression of the *publicanus* was the main cause why so large an amount of suffering among the peasantry produced, comparatively, so small a revenue to the State.

The phenomena of commercial life in classical antiquity are not easy to understand. We are told that banking business had reached a high development both in Greece and Italy; that bills of exchange were constantly drawn and remitted from one part of the Empire to another; that the bankers (τραπεζῖται in Greece, *argentarii* at Rome) were in the habit of receiving money on deposit, and relending it on overdrawn account. And yet, on the other hand, we hear constantly of exorbitant sums being paid for interest. Twelve-and-a-half per cent. is mentioned as a frequent rate in Rome, and twenty-four per cent. as charged in Sicily. The latter rate, it is true, was exacted by the tyrannical Verres, but it is far surpassed by the righteous Brutus, who exacted forty-eight per cent. from the provincials of Cyprus. At all times of the Republic and Empire *aes alienum* (borrowed money) is spoken of as a fruitful source of danger to the State, and the debtor never seems to have a fair chance of emancipating himself from the yoke of the creditor. These are all indications of a state of things in which the usurer rather than the banker is the chief loanmonger [1], and they almost entitle us to say (whatever

---

[1] Thus distinguished. The usurer, as such, lends from his own capital; the banker, as such, from the deposits of his customers. The usurer, therefore, if he wishes to make 15 per cent. on his capital, can only do it by charging 15 per cent. to his customers. The banker may make the same percentage while only charging 3 per cent.

indications to the contrary may be afforded by scattered passages in the classics) that the true business of a banker—the acting as a broker between those classes of the community which desire to lend and those classes which desire to borrow—cannot have been understood, or if understood, cannot have been widely practised in the Roman Empire.

What effect would a Funded Debt have had on the duration of the Empire?

It would be an interesting speculation to enquire what would have been the effect of a National Debt—that distinguishing feature of modern political finance—in retarding or accelerating the ruin of the Empire. The First and Second Punic Wars seem to have been fought out to a successful issue by the Senate chiefly by means of a loan, disguised under a gigantic debasement of the currency. The *As*, which was then the unit of monetary value, and which was coined out of a pound of copper when the quarrel with Carthage commenced, consisted of only one *uncia*, (the twelfth part of a pound,) when the dispute was settled, sixty-three years later, on the field of Zama. The disastrous effect of such a sweeping alteration in the standard of value was perhaps mitigated by the partial substitution of a silver currency for one of copper. But though the State had thus made a disguised loan from

to his customers, if a sum of money equivalent to fifteen times his capital be deposited with him at 2 per cent. The usurer's best chance of profit is in being able to foreclose on oppressive terms his debtor's mortgage. The banker, who has ever before his eyes the necessity of a prompt repayment of his deposits, dreads few things more than the necessity of foreclosing a mortgage and so 'locking up' part of the funds entrusted to him. Thus, without supposing the latter to be a bit more generous or less selfish than the former, he is led by mere self-interest into a course of dealing which gives the borrower a chance of recovering himself from the burden of *aes alienum*.

its subjects, and though at times it may have borrowed inconsiderable sums of money for short periods from the *publicani,* no such institution as a permanent National Debt ever existed, or perhaps ever suggested itself as possible to the State Financiers. On some great emergencies, such as the reception of the Visigothic refugees within the limits of the Empire in 376, a loan on a large scale might have been a prudent and statesmanlike measure. The secure investment thus offered to those provincials who were shut out from the great money markets of Rome and Alexandria, might have stimulated thrift. And it is almost certain that the rulers of the Empire, had they periodically appeared before their subjects as borrowers, would have been more amenable to the legitimate influence of public opinion. Flatterers might persuade a frantic debauchee that he was pious, and unconquered, and fortunate, up to the very moment when he was ripe for assassination; but a decline in the Imperial Funds of ten per cent. would have been an unmistakable proof that he was losing the confidence of his subjects.

Arguments like these might be advanced to show that the existence of the Empire would have been prolonged by the device of national indebtedness. On the other hand, we see, by abundant evidence in the history of our own times, that the creation of Bonds and Stock-certificates is like dram-drinking to imperfectly organised States. The brief military usurpers of the third century would probably have raised loans on the national credit as furiously and as foolishly as the Presidents of any South American Republic. And even as to the great and stable States of modern times whose acknowledgments of debt command, and rightly command, for the present, as high a price as the land itself, the substratum of all national wealth, we must remember that we have as yet traced their orbit through a very small part of the World's History. We and our immediate forefathers have seen the beginning of England's borrowing, but we know not in what spirit our remote descendants may look upon its end.

7. *Causes, or Symptoms, of Decay.*

It is time to bring to a conclusion this examination of the causes of the Fall of the Roman Empire, which might range over the whole field of private and public life during the first four Christian centuries.

The Imperial power not in itself destructive

Some readers may be surprised at not finding a prominent place among those causes given to the autocratic power of the Caesars. Many instances have been noticed, even in the course of this history, in which a fatuous or vicious Emperor accelerated the ruin of Rome. But, upon a survey of the whole history of the Commonwealth before and after the consolidation of the supreme power in the hands of an Imperator, it does not seem possible to look upon that measure as anything else than preservative of the life of the State. We have to compare the Imperial System, not with some ideal Republic of Plato or More, not even with a modern European monarchy of average excellence, but with the Roman Republic during the last century and a half of its existence, at a time when the government of the fairest portion of the earth was in the hands of a combination of aristocrats the most selfish, and of democrats the most senseless, that the world has perhaps ever seen, and was being jobbed and plundered for their apparent benefit with such blind rapacity that, had Caesar not arrested the process of destruction, the provincial population must have perished in the grasp of its oppressors.

But though, upon the whole, the power of the Em- perors was exerted beneficially for the Empire, the same cannot be said of the frequent and disastrous interference of the Imperial household in State affairs. While, on the one hand, there were long intervals, notably the reigns of the Adoptive Emperors, perhaps also those of Diocletian and Constantine, during which a wise and well-organised bureaucracy (to use a modern term) gave effect to the mandates of the Supreme Power, there were other periods, especially the reigns of Claudius, of Constantius, of the sons and grandsons of Theodosius, during which the personal attendants of the Monarch, his freedmen, or even his eunuchs, succeeded in grasping the helm of the State, and their steering was uniformly disastrous [1]. The confusion between the menial servants of the Monarch and the ministers of the Empire, though obvious in a constitutionally-governed country, generally tends to efface itself under a despotism, where the Sovereign, daily fed upon such flatteries as those which Claudian offered to Honorius, comes in time to believe that the trivialities of his daily life are matters of profound interest to his subjects, and as important to the world as the welfare of provinces. Thus it was, by playing upon the weakness of a master whom in their hearts they despised, that such men as Eutropius became the chief deposi-

but the inter-ference of the Imperial household disastrous.

---

[1] An exception should be made for the great deeds of the eunuch Narses, but they lie beyond the range of the present history.

taries of power under such sovereigns as Arcadius; thus it was that they could sell the highest offices in the Empire[1], and bitterly revenge the wrongs which they themselves had suffered in their former bondage. Whatever may be the drawbacks of a constitutional system, and they are many, it at least nullifies, if it does not destroy, the baneful influence of 'the House-hold' in politics. A vigorous and hard-working Bureau-crat, who finds himself eclipsed or thwarted by a showy and pretentious speaker in a popular assembly, may reflect that even this is less humiliating than the neces-sity of courting the favour of an uneducated domestic, who has risen into power by the performance of menial offices in the bedchamber of the Sovereign.

Demorali-sation of the Army. The rapid and terrible decline in the efficiency of the Army was without doubt another potent cause of the dissolution of the Empire. When we hear the military essayist, Vegetius[2], lamenting the effeminate habits of the soldiers in his day, who were no longer able to bear the weight of helmet and coat of mail, and petitioned the Emperor, with success, that they might be allowed to lay aside these wearisome defences, we feel how vast a change has come over the spirit of the legionary since the hardy Sabine and Marsian followed Caesar to victory. This demoralisation may be partly due, as Zosimus[3] says it was, to the truckling policy of Con-stantine, who withdrew many of the legions from the arduous and unpopular duty of defending the frontiers and quartered them in the large cities of the Empire, where they spent their days at the Amphitheatre, and their nights in debauchery, a burden on the peaceful

---

[1] Compare Claudian, In Eutropium, i. 196–221.

[2] Epitoma Rei Militaris, i. 20.   [3] ii. 34.

provincials, but no longer a terror to the enemies of Rome.

But the true causes of the ruin of that wonderful machine of conquest, the Roman Army, lay deeper doubtless than in any such special mistake of military administration as this of Constantine's. Its mainspring for centuries had been the patient strength and courage, the capacity for enduring hardness, the instinctive submission to military discipline, of the populations which lined the ranges of the Apennines. Taught by their example, other races in the Empire, especially the Gauls and the friendly Germans, could do good service as *foederati* or even as actual legionaries. But after all, when the old Italian population itself was gone—and we have seen some of the economic changes which led to its disappearance before the slave-gangs of the great proprietors of Italy—there was no more reason left why the Roman army should continue to conquer. The wolves of Romulus were changed into the timid sheep of Honorius and the younger Theodosius. What had been the hammer of the nations became now their anvil.

Simple depopulation is often assigned as a cause of the fall of the Empire [1]. And with great truth, especially so far as the terrible plagues and earthquakes of the second and third centuries contributed to that depopulation. It is abundantly clear, and must have

Depopulation.

---

[1] I have nowhere seen this aspect of the question more vividly presented than in Prof. Seeley's Second Essay on Roman Imperialism (published in Macmillan's Magazine, August, 1869). 'Some principle of decay,' he says, 'must have been at work [to produce the collapse which followed the prosperity of the Antonine period], but what principle? We answer: It was a period of sterility or barrenness in human beings; *the human harvest was bad.*'

been observed by the attentive reader of this history, that there were vast solitary spaces within the border of the Empire when the barbarians streamed across it, and that their movement was one of colonisation almost as much as of conquest. Still, when one looks at the whole course of affairs after the Romans had made themselves masters of the countries bordering on the Mediterranean, depopulation seems to present itself to the mind as a symptom rather than a cause of the malady which was in time to prove fatal, and one is inclined to fix upon some of the vices of the Roman polity mentioned above, the slave-system, the *latifundia*, the extortion of the tax-gatherer, as the reasons for that terrible failure of ' the human harvest.'

Will England fall as Rome fell?

The ruin of such a mighty fabric as the world-empire of Rome can hardly be contemplated by the citizen of any State such as our own, which has extended its dominion over alien peoples and far distant lands, without stirring some foreboding fears that of our country too it may one day be said, 'How art thou fallen from Heaven, oh Lucifer, Son of the Morning!' Even so, according to the well-known story, the younger Africanus, in the very midst of the ruined city of Carthage, which he had himself destroyed, shed prophetic tears over the fate of his own country, and repeated those verses of the Iliad—

> '῎Εσσεται ἦμαρ, ὅτ' ἄν ποτ' ὀλώλῃ ῎Ιλιος ἱρή,
> Καὶ Πρίαμος καὶ λαὸς ἐϋμμελίω Πριάμοιο[1].'

But an Englishman, though his presumption may rightly be chastened by the thought of the mortality

---

[1] ' Surely a day shall come for the fall of Ilion the holy,
Priam, the stout-speared king, and all the people of Priam.'

of Rome, may derive some comfort from the reflection that she was tempted, as his country is not, by absolutely unbounded success. It was not till after the destruction of Carthage that the worst qualities of the Roman conqueror, his rapacity, his cruelty, his contempt for the rights of others began to develop themselves. The other powerful nations, both in the Old and the New World, which act as a counterpoise to our own, and sometimes administer a severe rebuke to our national pride, are in truth our best friends, preserving us from that overweening arrogance which is unendurable by God and Man.

Of the causes enumerated above, which conspired for the ruin of the Empire, some clearly affect us not. The Christian religion is with us no explosive force threatening the disruption of our most cherished institutions. On the contrary it has been said, not as a mere figure of speech, that 'Christianity is part of the common law of England.' And even the bitterest enemies of our religion will scarcely deny that, upon the whole, a nation imbued with the teaching of the New Testament is more easy to govern than one which derived its notions of divine morality from the stories of the dwellers on Olympus.

The partition of the Empire, the erection of a co-equal seat of authority in its Asiatic dependencies, can hardly be considered a danger for us in practical politics.

Slavery is not eating as a canker into the heart of the English State. Yet perhaps there may be something analogous to slavery in the condition of 'the dangerous classes' in our great cities, men leading a sunless and squalid existence from the cradle to the

grave, serfs *adscripti* to the gaol and the workhouse.
And this thought may quicken the zeal, already so
earnest, of statesmen and philanthropists to remove
from us this reproach.

To the eye of an inexperienced observer there appear
to be symptoms in the British administration of India,
especially in the preponderating importance of land-tax
as a source of revenue, and in our manner of employing
the native *foederati*, which suggest some anxious com-
parisons with the Roman imperial system. May it
prove that the resemblance is only in appearance, not
in reality!

The pulverisation of the burgher-class by the fiscal
oppressions practised upon the Decurions may possibly
contain some warnings for benevolent administrators
who, in their very zeal for the improvement of the condition of the people, may allow local taxation to attain
proportions which, were any pause to occur in the
onward march of the country, might be found well-nigh
intolerable.

But of all the forces which were at work for the
destruction of the prosperity of the Roman world none
is more deserving of the careful study of an English
statesman than the grain-largesses to the populace of
Rome. Whatever occasional ebbings there may be in
the current, there can be little doubt that the tide of
affairs, in England and in all the countries of Western
Europe, as well as in the United States of America, sets
permanently towards Democracy. Will the great
Democracies of the Twentieth Century resist the temp-
tation to use political power as a means of material
self-enrichment? With a higher ideal of public duty
than has been shown by some of the governing classes

which preceded them, will they refrain from jobbing the Commonwealth ? Warned by the experience of Rome, will they shrink from reproducing directly, or indirectly, the political heresy of Caius Gracchus, that he who votes in the Forum must be fed by the State ? If they do, perhaps the world may see Democracies as long-lived as the Dynasties of Egypt or of China. If they do not, assuredly now as in the days of our Saxon forefathers, it will be found that he who is 'giver of bread' is also lord[1]. The old weary round will recommence, democracy leading to anarchy, and anarchy to despotism, and the National Workshops of some future Gracchus will build the palaces in which British or American despots, as incapable to rule as Arcadius or Honorius, will guide mighty empires to ruin, amidst the acclamations of flatterers as eloquent and as hollow as the courtly Claudian.

[1] *Lord=Hlaford*, the Loaf-giver. The derivation is questioned by some scholars.

INDEX.

A.

Acatziri, Scythian tribe, 56 *n*; Onégesh's expedition against, 76; engagements with, 78.

Acincum or Acincus (*Alt Ofen* near Buda), head-quarters of the elder Majorian (379), 404.

Acta Sanctorum, *see* Bollandist.

Adige river (Athesis), 163.

Aegidius, 'King of Soissons,' his singular career, 436; his hostility to Ricimer, 436; his name survives in Giles, 437.

Aes Alienum, accumulating burden of, always the curse of Roman social system, 603.

Aetius, Roman general, Attila makes him present of a dwarf, 87; loads young Frankish chief with presents, 103; his wars with Theodoric I (429–439), 109; sends Avitus to form alliance with Theodoric against Attila (451), 120; raises the siege of Orleans, 121; dispositions for battle of the Mauriac Plain, 127; loses his way on the battle-field, 133; advises Thorismund to return to Toulouse, 135; reasons for mysterious conduct after the battle, 137; summarily dismisses young Majorian, 404; gives greater prominence to office of Patrician (?), 402; inactivity during Attila's Italian campaign (452), 156; murdered in the palace by Valentinian III (454), 196; his henchmen avenge his death, 198.

Africa, province of, survey of Roman Africa in the fifth century, 232–239; economical condition, 236; relations of Punic and Latin languages, 237, 238; Latin Fathers of the African Church, 238; relative position of the Proconsul and Court of, 242; conquest of, by the Vandals (428–435), 244, 248; condition of, under the Vandals, 256–264; religious struggles in, in fourth and fifth centuries, 265–268; astrologers from, in Gaul, 337.

Agintheus, general of the Roman army in Illyricum, 63; surrenders fugitives to Attila, 64.

Agricola, son of Avitus, brother-in-law of Sidonius, 352, 378.

Alamanni, repulsed by Majorian (457), 405.

Alani, described by Chinese historians under name Alanna, 30; worshipped a sabre stuck in the ground, 30; in Portugal, 222; save the Vandals from destruction at the hands of the Franks, 220; cut to pieces by the Goths (418), 223; the remnant of Spanish Alani merge their nationality in that of the Vandals, 223, 256; arranged with the Vandals into regiments, 255; those in Gaul settled in district round Valence (440), 111; join confederacy against Attila (451), 111; in battle of Mauriac Plain, 132; co-operate with Attila in 453 (?), 169; at battle of Nedao (454), 193; invade Italy (464), 439.

Alexandria, city of, shared in gratuitous distribution of corn, 572.

Alexandrian Chronicle (also called Paschal Chronicle), date of, 100 *n*; 291; 472 *n* 1.

Alps, Majorian's passage of the, 411.

Altinum, town of Venetia, destroyed by Attila (452), 153; inhabitants of, migrated to Torcello and neighbouring islands, 166.

Alypia, daughter of Anthemius and wife of Ricimer, 450; her wedding, 455.

Amantius, the fortune-hunter of Marseilles, his story told by Sidonius, 332.

Amber, traffic in, between Germany and Italy, 148.

American War of Secession illustrates effect of slavery on the defensive power of a State, 557.

American slave-system compared with the Roman, 560–564.

Ammianus Marcellinus, historian (wrote

the weight of their, 608.

Army, Roman, numbers of, in Africa in fifth century, 231; proportions of barbarians in, in fifth century, 509; Vandals in the, 217; rapid demoralisation of, 608.

Arnobius, of African birth, 238.

Arvandus, praetorian prefect of Gaul, trial and condemnation of, at Rome (469), 462–464; sentence of death commuted to banishment (?), 465.

Arverni, territory of (*Auvergne*), adopted country of Sidonius, 308; conquest of, by Euric (474), 486–488; formally ceded by Rome (475), 491.

Asdingi, royal house of the Vandals, 220, 222.

Asia, physical geography of, 6; elevation of Central, 6.

Aspar, general of Eastern Empire, son of Ardaburius, commands unsuccessful expedition against the Vandals in Africa (431), 248; Marcian his *domesticus*, 261; position at Constantinople, 442; raises Leo to the throne (457), 443; breach between him and Leo I, 444; put to death with his family by Leo I (471), 478.

Asterius, Roman governor in Spain (420), 224.

Astorga (Asturica), Spanish capital of the Sueves, 380.

Asturius, inaugurated consul at Arles (449), 306.

Athenaeus, statement as to number of slaves in a family, 559.

Athenius, present at Majorian's banquet at Arles, 417.

Atrium of Church at Lyons, 329.

Attila (Etzel) king of the Huns (433–453), his name, 16 *n* 1, cf. 166 *n* 1; accession, personal appearance, character, 41; extent of his empire, 42; receives Honoria's ring and becomes her champion, 47; treaty of Margus with Theodosius II (433), 47; lays waste the Eastern Empire (447), 52; oppressive embassies to Theodosius II, 54; his 'hunting' equivalent to modern 'mobilisation,' 64; insolence to Roman ambassadors, 64; site of his palace doubtful, 73; his triumphal entry into his capital, 74; his palace, 74; description of his banquet, 84–88; his eldest son's fear of him, 85; his simple fare and dress, 85; partiality for Ernak, his youngest son, 87; makes Vigilas confess plot against his life, 93; sends insulting message to Theodosius II, 93; legendary message to Eastern and Western emperors, 100; embassy about Honoria (450), 101; invasion of

Gaul (451), 106–142; seeks to sow dissension between Romans and Visigoths, 112; 'a subtle man and one who fought by artifice,' 112; ravages in Gaul, their extent, 114–118; forced to raise the siege of Orleans, 119–121; retreats towards the Rhine, 121; persuaded by bishop Lupus to spare Troyes, 122; auguries before battle of Mauriac Plain, 126; speech to his soldiers, 129; gives way before Visigothic assault, 132; recrosses the Rhine, winters in Hungary, 146; invades Italy (452), 147; siege and cruel destruction of Aquileia, 150–152; the picture at Milan, 154; Pope Leo turns away his wrath, 160; 'conquered by the Lion and the Wolf,' 161; alleged Gaulish campaign (453), 169; marries Ildico, 170; dies on his wedding night, 171; his funeral, 172–174; the Attila of ecclesiastical legend, 175; the Attila of the Niebelungen Lied (Etzel), 176; the Attila of Scandinavian song (Atli), 177; the Attila of Hungarian romances, 178; comparison to Napoleon, 179.

Augustine, St., Bishop of Hippo (395–430), his 'De Civitate Dei,' 547; advice to the African bishops during Vandal invasion, 245; account of his last days during siege of Hippo, 247; life of, by Possidius, 210; number of his works, 245 *n* 1; on the absurdities of the old Roman religion, 543.

Augustulus, *see* Romulus.

Aurelian, Emperor (270–275), defeats the Vandals (271), 216; increases by one *uncia* the largess-loaves, 570; his self-glorifying letter, 570; gives the citizens pork, oil, wine, and changes of raiment, 571.

Aurum Coronarium, first a free-will offering, then a tax levied on Decurions only, 582.

Auvergne, see Arverni.

Auxiliaries, *see* Foederati.

Avienus, Gennadius, consul (450), ambassador to Attila (452), 157; character sketched by Sidonius, 456.

Avitacum (*Aydat* in Auvergne), Sidonius's villa at, described by him, 308–312; identification of, with Aydat, 309, 312 *n*; Avitus at, 378.

Avitus, Emperor of the West (455–456), birth and parentage of, 375; sent on a deputation to Constantius (415?), 376 and *n* 2; serves under Aetius, slays a Hun who murdered his servant, 377; praetorian prefect of Gaul (439–445), 378; his daughter Papianilla married to Sidonius, 308; retires to Avitacum, 378; influence at the Visigothic court,

nal character of Germans, 211.

Tagliamento, river of Venetia, 163.

Tan-jou (the mighty), title of rulers of the Hiong-nu, 11; marriages of, with Chinese princesses, 12.

Tartars (or Tatars), relation of, to the Huns, 4 *n.*

Tatian, Senator, Imperial representative at Council of Chalcedon (451), made Prefect of Constantinople by Leo (?), 444 *n.*

Ta-tsin ('as great as China'), Chinese name for Roman Empire, 29.

Ta-tum-fou, or Tai-tong, south of Great Wall of China, chosen as capital by Mé-té Tanjou, 16.

Taxation, oppressive, in the Eastern Empire to raise tribute for Attila, 53; of the *curiales*, 582; Roman system of, 597–603.

Tax-gatherer (Canonicarius), Majorian's laws against extortionate, 422.

Temple of Jerusalem, sacred vessels of, taken from Rome to Carthage (455), 285; restored to Jerusalem (after 534), 286.

Tennis (pila), game of, at Lyons, described by Sidonius, 322; game of, in the country, described by Sidonius, 325.

Teou-hien, Chinese general, victorious over Hiong-nu, 26, 27.

Terence, 'Hecyra' of, Sidonius read with his pupils, 344.

Tertullian, of African birth, 238; intolerance of, 549.

Tessera = an out-door relief ticket, 570.

Testudo, formed by Roman soldiers locking their shields together, in battle of the Mauriac Plain, 130.

Thaumastus, brother of Apollinaris, letter of Sidonius to, 360.

Theodoric I, king of the Visigoths (419–451), his daughter married to Hunneric and cruelly treated by Gaiseric, 104; his friendship for Avitus, 378; receives embassy from Valentinian III, 113; joins with Romans against Attila, 114; appears under walls of Orleans, 121; takes part in battle of Mauriac Plain and falls there, 127, 132, 134; doubt as to his place of burial, 140–142.

Theodoric II, king of the Visigoths (453–466), son of the preceding, minute description of his person and habits by Sidonius, 352–358; raises Avitus to the purple, alliance against the Sueves, 379–384; victories over the Sueves (456), 389; killed by his brother Euric, 484.

Theodorus, brother of Avitus, sent as hostage to Toulouse, 378.

Theodosian Code (published 438), De Decurionibus, quoted, 584–595; scarcely mentions office of Patrician, 402; laws against celibacy, 421; against rapacious Tax-collectors, 422; about the Defensor, 422; about the Currency, 422; against illegal exactions by Governors, 423; against destruction of public buildings, 424; laws about the bread-largesse, 572–576.

Theodosius I, Emperor (379–395), legislation securing interval of thirty days between utterance and execution of capital sentence, 465; calls himself 'My Mildness,' 588; dynasty of, extinct in 455, 198.

Theodosius II, grandson of preceding, Emperor of the East (408–450), debates with Roua, king of the Huns (432), 40; character and theological position, 44; accessory to plot for assassination of Attila (448), 59; embassy to Attila, 60; insulting reply, 93, 94; thrown from his horse and dies, 97.

Theophanes, Byzantine historian (eighth century), 430; quoted, on character of Glycerius, 484, 502.

Theudemir, king of the Ostrogoths, served under Attila in Gaul, 107; attacks the Eastern Empire, 481.

Thierry, Amédée, 'Histoire d'Attila,' 38, 175; quoted, 96 *n* 2, 122 *n* 2.

Thiudans, Gothic name for king, 528.

Thorismund, son of Theodoric I, king of the Visigoths (451–453), helps to raise the siege of Orleans, 121; at battle of the Mauriac Plain, 129, 132; proclaimed king on his return to Toulouse, 135–136; reasons for not following up the victory over Attila, 136; repulse of Attila in 453 (?), 169; slain by his brother Theodoric, 352 *n* 2.

Thuringer Wald (Saltus Hercynius), trees of, felled by Attila's army (451), 108.

Thuringians (Toringi), in Attila's army, 107.

Thurocz, Hungarian romancer about Attila, 178.

Ticinum (*Pavia*), Epiphanius, Bishop of, *see* Epiphanius; people of, insult the mother of Glycerius, 482; Orestes takes refuge at, 521; siege and capture of, by the *foederati* (476), 521; intercessions of Epiphanius lessen their ravages, 521.

Timothy the Weasel, a turbulent Patriarch of Alexandria, 303.

Tingitana (*Fez*), Roman province in Africa described, 233.

Toleration, in the early Christian